THE BOOK OF THE
NEW YORK INTERNATIONAL
CHESS TOURNAMENT

1924

Containing the Authorized
Account of the 110 Games
Played March–April, 1924

With Original Annotations by
ALEXANDER ALEKHINE

Edited by
HERMANN HELMS

Dover Publications, Inc.
New York

Published in Canada by General Publishing Company, Ltd., 30 Lesmill Road, Don Mills, Toronto, Ontario.

Published in the United Kingdom by Constable and Company, Ltd., 10 Orange Street, London WC 2.

This Dover edition, first published in 1961, is an unabridged and—except for the substitution of new portraits for those in the original edition—an unaltered republication of the work originally published by the American Chess Bulletin in 1925.

Standard Book Number: 486-20752-8

Manufactured in the United States of America
Dover Publications, Inc.
180 Varick Street
New York, N.Y. 10014

PREFACE

In more than one official book of an international congress of the chess masters is to be found an assertion to the effect that the particular contest in question should be regarded as the greatest of its kind ever promoted by the followers of Caissa up to that time. The temptation to do so is strong in this case, but modesty properly places a check upon the desire to have the New York International Chess Masters' Tournament of 1924 get the fullest recognition in the eyes of the chess playing world. That inhibition upon a natural impulse comes the easier because of the absence of at least half a dozen eligibles whose participation would have added luster to even so notable a gathering as that of the eleven experts, of ten different countries, who came to the Metropolis of America to test their skill and thereby afford entertainment for devotees of the game all over the globe.

It is quite safe to allow the record of the New York Tournament to speak for itself. In no uncertain tones will a listening and appreciative, not to say grateful world be assured thereby that the congress, the history of which is to be set forth herein, if not the greatest of all time, was at least one of the best.

In one respect unquesionably it will be entitled to a unique place in the niche of fame. The Old Year went out without so much as a whisper of what the New Year had in store for lovers of good chess; and for good reason. While the idea had for some time been hatching, the impetus to act had been lacking.

To be historically accurate it should be here set down that the first meeting for organization did not take place until January 18 at the Manhattan Chess Club. This was shortly after the management of the Hotel Alamac had consented to do its share, and a little more. Once the plan had matured there was no delay and from then on the driving force of the committee which was formed was set in full motion.

It was necessary to find guarantees approximating the sum of $10,000 with which to finance the tournament on a scale to make it attractive to the most famous of the present day experts. That was done in short order and soon the cable was calling them from far-distant homes to do battle in New York for fame, for country and for gold.

Thus it came about that within three months one of the most memorable gatherings of the masters opened auspiciously on March 16, ran its scheduled course for 33 days and came to a most satisfactory conclusion on April 18. On the following day, presentation of prizes provided the final scene and America enjoyed the supreme satisfaction of having placed yet another tournament in the same category with those of New York in 1889 and Cambridge Springs in 1904.

The net result of the tournament was a brilliant triumph for Dr. Emanuel Lasker—a fitting climax to a long and honorable career. It did not really need this, his latest and, in some respects, his finest success to crown him as one of the greatest of tournament players. But it did serve the purpose of reassuring the many friends of the former world's champion that, albeit the veteran of the competition, he nevertheless had lost little, if any of the old-time prowess.

The financial report of the Treasurer will be found elsewhere, as also a list of the subscribers. Acknowledgment, however, is due for the hearty support of patrons, without whose generosity it would have been impossible to achieve success and whose numbers were not limited wholly to New York City.

The committee was very fortunate in being able to make arrangements with Mr. Alexander Alekhine for the annotation of the 110 games played in the tournament. His co-operation is a guarantee of analytical work at once intelligent and thorough.

HERMANN HELMS.

New York, January, 1925.

SCORE OF THE TOURNAMENT

PLAYERS	Dr. Lasker		Capablanca		Alekhine		Marshall		Reti		Maroczy		Bogoljubow		Dr. Tartakower		Yates		Ed. Lasker		Janowski		Total Won
Dr. E. Lasker	——		½	0	1	½	½	1	1	1	1	1	1	1	½	1	½	1	½	1	1	1	16
J. R. Capablanca	½	1	——		½	½	½	½	0	1	½	1	1	1	1	1	1	½	½	1	½	1	14½
A. Alekhine	0	½	½	½	——		½	½	1	0	1	½	½	½	½	½	1	1	½	½	1	1	12
F. J. Marshall	½	0	½	½	½	½	——		½	1	0	½	0	1	½	0	½	1	1	½	1	1	11
R. Reti	0	0	1	0	0	1	½	0	——		½	½	0	1	1	1	1	0	1	0	1	1	10½
G. Maroczy	0	0	½	0	0	½	1	½	½	½	——		0	1	½	½	1	1	½	1	1	0	10
E. D. Bogoljubow	0	0	0	0	½	½	1	0	1	0	1	0	——		0	1	1	1	½	1	0	1	9½
Dr. S. G. Tartakower	½	0	0	0	½	½	½	1	0	0	½	½	1	0	——		1	0	½	0	½	1	8
F. D. Yates	½	0	0	½	0	0	½	0	0	1	0	0	0	0	0	1	——		1	1	½	1	7
Edward Lasker	½	0	½	0	½	½	0	½	0	1	½	0	½	0	½	1	0	0	——		0	½	6½
D. Janowski	0	0	½	0	0	0	0	0	0	0	0	1	1	0	½	0	½	0	1	½	——		5
Total Lost	4		5½		8		9		9½		10		10½		12		13		13½		15		110

INDEX TO GAMES AND PLAYERS

The numbers refer to the Pages; those in the horizontal columns indicating the players having the White pieces, and those in the vertical columns the players having the Black pieces.

CONTENTS

INDEX TO OPENINGS

OFFICERS AND COMMITTEE

New York International Chess Masters' Tournament

Hotel Alamac, New York

March 16---April 18, 1924

PRESIDENT:

Herbert R. Limburg of New York.

VICE PRESIDENTS:

Arthur S. Meyer of New York.   Harry Latz of New York.

TREASURER:

Dr. Arthur A. Bryant of New York.

SECRETARY:

Norbert L. Lederer of New York.

BOARD OF TOURNAMENT DIRECTORS:

Hermann Helms of New York, chairman.   Leonard B. Meyer of New York.
Norbert L. Lederer of New York.

COMMITTEE MEMBERS:

Harold M. Phillips of New York.   Albert H. Loeb of Chicago.
Dr. Louis Cohn of New York.   Walter Penn Shipley of Philadelphia.
Felix E. Kahn of New York.   John F. Barry of Boston.
Julius Finn of New York.   William M. Vance of Princeton.
Leonard B. Meyer of New York.   Edward L. Torsch of Baltimore.
Robert Raubitschek of New York.   Carl van der Voort of Pittsburgh.
Maurice Wertheim of New York.   Stirling Kerr of Washington.
Horace R. Bigelow of New York.   Francis H. French of Davenport.

TREASURER'S REPORT

RECEIPTS.

*Subscriptions	$9,978.90
Tickets, with war tax	3,476.00
Pictures	53.68
	$13,508.58

EXPENDITURES.

Prizes: Regular, $4,050; special, $275; bonus to non-prize winners, $1,150	$5,475.00
Medals and prizes, problem-solving tourney	176.00
Passage of players	1,940.00
Expenses allowed players	3,568.00
Entertainment, including tips	573.12
Petty expenses of players at hotel, other than board	300.64
Service, ticket seller, etc.	330.00
Tournament accessories, clocks, etc.	264.84
Stationery, postage and cables	228.73
Photographs	221.25
Complimentary press tickets to banquet	85.00
News clippings	30.00
War tax on gate receipts	316.00
	$13,508.58

DR. ARTHUR A. BRYANT,

Treasurer.

*A list of the subscribers will be given in the Appendix.

THE ALAMAC HOTEL,
Broadway and 71st Street, New York.

THE COMPETITORS IN THE TOURNAMENT—Standing (left to right)—F. J. Marshall, Dr. S. G. Tartakower, G. Maroczy, A. Alekhine, R. Reti, E. D. Bogoljubow. Seated (left to right)—F. D. Yates, J. R. Capablanca, D. Janowski, Edward Lasker, Dr. Emanuel Lasker.

Dr. Emanuel Lasker, Germany
First Prize, with score of 16–4

Jose R. Capablanca, Cuba
Second Prize, with score of 14½–5½

Alexander Alekhine, Russia
Third Prize, with score of 12–8

Frank J. Marshall, United States
Fourth Prize, with score of 11–9

Richard Reti, Czechoslovakia
Fifth Prize, with score of 10½–9½

Geza Maroczy, Hungary
Sixth, with score of 10–10

E. D. Bogoljubow, Ukrainia
Seventh, with score of 9½–10½

Dr. S. G. Tartakower, Austria
Eighth, with score of 8–12

F. D. Yates, Great Britain
Ninth, with score of 7–13

Alekhine and Capablanca meet for a game prior to the International Chess Tournament in New York in 1927. Standing, left to right, Maroczy; Dr. N. Lederer, Manager of the Tournament; R. Spielmann of Austria; A. Nimzowitsch of Denmark; Dr. M. Vidmar of Yugoslavia; and Marshall.

Edward Lasker, United States
Tenth, with score of 6½–13½

David Janowski, France
Eleventh, with score of 5–15

Jose R. Capablanca and Emanuel Lasker.

Alekhine and Bogoljubow playing in Russia.

Edward Lasker and Emanuel Lasker playing in the 1924 Tournament.

Members of the Tournament Committee—Standing (left to right)—D. A. A. Bryant, W. M. Vance, N. L. Lederer, A. S. Meyer, H. R. Bigelow, J. Finn, H. Helms. Seated (left to right)—H. M. Phillips, L. B. Meyer, H. R. Limburg, Dr. L. Cohn.

The

New York International

Tournament

Acknowledgment

For their able co-operation in the work of translation and reading proofs, the Editor feels under distinct obligation to Messrs. Horace Ransom Bigelow, Maxwell Bukofzer, Hartwig Cassel, C. S. Howell, Dr. Hermann Keidanz, William M. Russel and Carlos Torre.

INTRODUCTION

By Norbert L. Lederer.

During the month of December, 1923, interest in chess was at a high level on this side of the Atlantic, largely due to the presence of Alexander Alekhine and his remarkable performances. At a social gathering on New Year's Eve the possibility of holding an international tournament in New York was discussed, the approximate cost being estimated at about $10,000. As it was realized that there would be little use in opening a subscription unless headed by a fairly large amount by some one individual to start the ball rolling, an interview was arranged with Mr. Harry Latz of the Alamac Hotel, who, previously, had expressed his interest in a proposed match between Capablanca and Alekhine for the world's championship.

At this meeting, at which Messrs. Helms, Alekhine, Latz and myself were present, I pointed out that the difficulty of raising the amount required for a title match would be very great, whereas I felt sure that amongst my colleagues at the Manhattan Chess Club I would find sufficient support for an international tournament, especially if we could be assured of the participation of Capablanca, Dr. Lasker and Alekhine. The last named assented to this new proposition and Mr. Latz, with his customary good sportsmanship, subscribed $2,500, which was the amount he had been prepared to offer for the match. In addition, he declared his readiness to extend the hospitality of his hotel to all the participants.

In order to make sure of our ground before proceeding any further, I cabled to Messrs. Richard Hirschfeld & Co. of Berlin, who very kindly offered to handle the negotiations for us on the other side. To our great satisfaction, we shortly received a reply by cable stating that all the masters we had in view, including Dr. Lasker, were willing to participate. In the meantime we had received a similar acceptance from Capablanca.

Thereupon a committee was formed under the leadership of Mr. Herbert R. Limburg, president of the Manhattan Chess Club, and a preliminary meeting took place at that club in January. Somewhat to my surprise, I was declared to be very optimistic, but not hopelessly crazy. It was decided to devote a week to intensive canvassing ("schnorring") in order to ascertain roughly the support we could count upon. At the next meeting, a week later, we found—to the surprise of everybody except myself, I believe—that we had in sight the sum of $6,500. Therefore, we decided it would be safe to go ahead with the issuance of the official invitations.

Owing to the good offices of Mr. J. Zeisler of Messrs. Richard Hirschfeld & Co. the preliminary work of obtaining passports and steamer reservations for the European masters was accomplished very quickly, and on February 26 we were able to announce that all the masters had sailed from Europe on the S. S. Cleveland.

In the meantime the members of the committee were working at top speed in collecting funds from chess lovers and others privileged to contribute without, in some cases, having ever heard of chess. Several of the members, especially Mr. Finn and the well-known Meyer brothers, not to mention others, had carried the matter to its logical conclusion, with the result that their friends refused to recognize them at casual meetings, fearing the inevitable outcome of any conversation with them.

With the hearty co-operation of Dr. Arthur A. Bryant and Mr. Helms, the preparations at this end were carried forward with the least possible delay and on March 8 we were able to welcome the masters at the docks with the satisfying knowledge that everything was ship-shape, barring, perhaps, some of the masters. Several unforeseen incidents helped to maintain the interest and contribute a bit of anxiety, chiefly the illness of Capablanca from a severe attack of la grippe, which made his participation in the tournament somewhat doubtful up to the last minute.

On March 11 a general rapid-transit tournament was held at the Manhattan Chess Club, wherein seven of the masters participated. A large number of leading local amateurs also took part. The result was a not unexpected victory for Capablanca, but the amateurs made a remarkably good showing, and among the first six prize-winners were members of the Manhattan Chess Club—Messrs. Schapiro, Tenner and L. B. Meyer.

On March 15 the opening banquet was held at the Alamac Hotel and attended by over 300 persons. It was a great success, this being due mainly to the splendid preparations made by Mr. Latz, the general manager of the hotel. The speakers were Herbert R. Limburg, Bainbridge Colby, Alrick H. Man, Dr. Emanuel Lasker, Harry Latz, Millard H. Ellison, Walter J. Rosston and Harold M. Phillips.

The number of the first round of the tournament was drawn on March 16 at 1:45 P. M. in the Japanese Room of the Alamac Hotel, which had been decorated most lavishly in the national colors of the different players. By a rule of the committee the numbers of the rounds were drawn from day to day and this made it impossible for any player to know in advance the identity of his opponent. Maintenance of interest in the competition was not a little aided thereby. The luck of the drawing gave Dr. Lasker the bye in the first round, but on the second day he was paired with Capablanca and a fitting debut was thus provided for the former world's champion.

The keen interest taken by the general public in the tournament was one of the revelations of the event, and the gate receipts footed up more than twice the amount of the most optimistic estimate. The net receipts exceeded $3,500 and would doubtless have been much more than that, but for the restricted space in the playing room. It is very encouraging to feel that at future tournaments the gate receipts can be relied upon as probably the most important contribution toward the expenses.

It is not necessary for me to dwell at length upon the progress of the tournament itself in view of the fact that this is being dealt with thoroughly elsewhere by such authorities as Messrs. Alekhine and Helms, but will content myself by saying that the competition proceeded very smoothly, without any unpleasant incident whatever, and that the conduct of all connected with it was most sportsmanlike. It is a great satisfaction to me to be able to say that the members of the board of referees were not called upon to officiate throughout the tournament, and that the few trifling incidents which arose were easily settled by the tournament directors.

Needless to say, the public interest displayed in this tournament was also reflected by the splendid report in the American newspapers. Most of this work, the importance of which cannot very well be exaggerated, was done by the two veterans, Cassel and Helms. I fear, however, that they sadly transgressed union hours.

The off-days were used by most of the masters to take in such sights as were of interest to them, and I personally spent many delightful hours with them. On those occasions I discovered, amongst other things, that even great chess masters are human at times and delightful company when out of sight of the magic squares. One of these excursions was to the Bronx Zoo and was very much enlivened by a long interview between "Suzan," prize orangoutang, and Dr. Tartakower, who dedicated his next game to the new found friend—to the utmost satisfaction of his adversary, who won it.

The final gathering for the distribution of prizes took place at the Alamac Hotel on April 19 and was honored by the presence of City Commissioner Grover Whalen, Mr. Limburg presiding. Quite a number of speeches were made, some good and some bad (I had to speak myself) and, judging from the applause, were enjoyed by the very large audience. The award of prizes was followed by an informal supper and dance, at which the younger generation of players displayed hyper-modern ideas in dancing as they had previously done in chess.

On April 1 a problem-solving contest for prizes was held. Isaac Kashdan of the College of the City of New York, first among the amateurs, made the best record of all the competitors, and Richard Reti took first prize in the master class.

In conclusion, I wish to state that the thanks of the committee are due to one and all who in any way contributed to the success of this notable meeting of the masters, and to express the hope that it may not be another twenty years before a similar high class congress is held in this country.

Review of the Tournament

In view of the very complete and painstaking analysis of the games made by Mr. Alekhine and his invaluable theoretical treatise upon the openings, to be found in the appendix, it will merely be necessary here to record the outcome of the tournament, dwell upon the outstanding features of the play and summarize the actual results. First of all then, it is in order to set down the list of entries and the countries they represented:

Jose R. Capablanca of Cuba.
Dr. Emanuel Lasker of Germany.
Alexander Alekhine of Russia.
Frank J. Marshall of America.
Edward Lasker of America.

David Janowski of France.
Geza Maroczy of Hungary.
Richard Reti of Czecho Slovakia.
Dr. Savielly G. Tartakower of Austria.
E. D. Bogoljubow of Ukrainia.

F. D. Yates of England.

A quick appraisal of what happened during the twenty-two rounds of the tournament cannot better be obtained than by a perusal of the appended table, in which the masters are placed in the order in which they finished:

Players.	Won.	Lost.	Dr.	Points. W.	L.
Dr. Lasker	13	1	6	16	4
Capablanca	10	1	9	14½	5½
Alekhine	6	2	12	12	8
Marshall	6	4	10	11	9
Reti	9	8	3	10½	9½
Maroczy	6	6	8	10	10
Bogoljubow	8	9	3	9½	10½
Dr. Tartakower	4	8	8	8	12
Yates	5	11	4	7	13
Ed. Lasker	2	9	9	6½	13½
Janowski	3	13	4	5	15

The cash prizes, none of which had to be divided, were the following: First, $1,500; second, $1,000; third, $750; fourth, $500; fifth, $250. In addition, consolation money was paid out to the non-prize winners at the rate of $25 for every win and $12.50 for each draw.

The list of special prizes included the following:

First brilliancy prize (silver cup from W. M. Vance of Princeton, N. J., and $75 in gold from Albert H. Loeb of Chicago), to Richard Reti of Czecho-Slovakia for his game against Bogoljubow.

Second brilliancy prize ($50 from Abb Landis of Nashville, Tenn.), to Frank J. Marshall of America for his game against Bogoljubow.

Third brilliancy prize ($25 from Edward L. Torsch of Baltimore, Md.), to Jose R. Capablanca of Cuba for his game against Dr. Lasker.

First special prize for the best-played game among non-prize winners ($35 from Edward L. Torsch of Baltimore, Md.), to Dr. S. G. Tartakower of Austria for his game against Yates.

Second special prize for the best-played game among non-prize winners ($25 from Albert H. Loeb of Chicago), to E. D. Bogoljubow of Ukrainia for his game against Dr. Tartakower.

Special prize for the best-defended game ($25 from J. Appleton, New York), to E. D. Bogoljubow of Ukrainia for his game against Maroczy.

Special prize for the best score by a non-prize winner against the prize-winners ($40 from the Tournament Committee, equally divided between G. Maroczy of Hungary and Edward Lasker of America, each 3½ points.

Medals were also awarded as prizes to the amateurs who made the best showing in the problem solving competition, as follows:

First prize, a gold medal, to I. Kashdan of the College of the City of New York.

Second and third prizes (a tie), silver medals, to John F. Barry of Boston and Alfred Schroeder of New York.

Owing to the fact that Dr. Lasker drew a bye in the opening round, it was not until the seventh round that he shook off those who were disputing with him the honors of first place. In the meantime, Alekhine had held the lead at the close of the second round. Dr. Tartakower enjoyed that distinction in the third and fourth rounds, but was tied by Bogoljubow in the fifth. Then, in the sixth, came a triple tie between Dr. Lasker, Dr. Tartakower and Alekhine, after which Dr. Lasker asserted himself and kept ahead until the end of the first half. In fact, barring a tie with Capablanca in the fifteenth round, in which Dr. Lasker again had a bye, he was never overtaken until premier honors were safely in his possession.

Capablanca, after playing five games without winning one, finally made his presence felt in the seventh round, when, co-equal with Alekhine and Reti at 4, he was half a point behind Dr. Lasker in wins. On the following day, Alekhine was second, with Capablanca third. The next day found Capablanca tied with Alekhine, closely followed by Reti. The situation remained unchanged in the tenth round, but in the eleventh—the half-way mark—Alekhine slipped into second place, below Dr. Lasker, with Capablanca and Reti tied at 6, half a point below. Bogoljubow, Maroczy, Marshall and Dr. Tartakower were all tied at 5 points. With slight changes, these players held their own until the close of the tournament.

With colors reversed, the eleven masters started upon the strenuous and somewhat nerve-racking second half of the tournament. First, Alekhine and Reti shared the honors of second place, with Capablanca just below. Then Reti forged ahead a bit, with Capablanca third and Alekhine fourth. In the fourteenth round the order was Capablanca, Reti and Alekhine. On the next day, when the world's champion joined Dr. Lasker temporarily, Alekhine was third and Reti fourth, while Bogoljubow, Maroczy and Marshall were bunched below.

Beginning with the sixteenth round, Capablanca and Alekhine maintained their respective positions, second and third, right to the end. Reti, after shaking off Bogoljubow, was finally joined by Marshall in the nineteenth round. From the twentieth round on, Marshall kept fourth place. Reti, on the other hand, was bracketed with Bogoljubow in the twentieth and twenty-first rounds, but pulled away safely, to secure the fifth prize, in the twenty-second and final round.

The first thing that impresses one in perusing the score table showing the cross play between the masters is the fact that the total of each stands out by itself and that there is not a single tie between any of them. In this respect the tournament is probably unique among competitions of its kind. At the end of the first half, before the players changed colors, there was a tie between Capablanca and Reti for third place, and another between Bogoljubow, Maroczy, Marshall and Dr. Tartakower, for fifth place.

In the second half, Capablanca displaced Alekhine, who was second and dropped to third, while Marshall moved up into fourth place. The American made the biggest gain and Reti suffered the severest setback by going into fifth place. Both Maroczy and Bogoljubow held their own fairly well, being placed just below the prize winners.

Dr. Tartakower, however, showed a distinct falling off in form. Yates, by gaining $4\frac{1}{2}$ points in the second half, changed places with Janowski, who added only $1\frac{1}{2}$. Edward Lasker played most consistently, scoring first 3 points and finishing with a total of $6\frac{1}{2}$. Although he did not win a game outright in the first half, he took the measure of two opponents before the end of the tournament.

Coming to the two chief winners, Dr. Lasker won outright 13 games, defeating Bogoljubow, Janowski, Maroczy, and Reti twice each. He drew games with Alekhine, Capablanca, Edward Lasker, Marshall, Dr. Tartakower and Yates. His only loss was to Capablanca in the second half.

Capablanca's only defeat was at the hands of Reti in the fifth round of the tournament, at which stage the world's champion had not won a single game outright. Reti was fifth prize winner. It was in the fifth game of the match at Havana that Capablanca first defeated Dr. Lasker. One wonders whether there is anything in numbers! The Cuban allowed nine draws, of which Alekhine and Marshall obtained two each, the rest going to Janowski, Edward Lasker, Dr. Lasker, Maroczy and Yates.

Alekhine and Marshall were the "drawing masters" of the tournament, the former topping the list with twelve and the latter coming next with ten. Alekhine, however, lost only two games to Dr. Lasker and Reti, respectively. Marshall lost four to Bogoljubow, Dr. Lasker, Maroczy and Dr. Tartakower.

Reti, the other prize winner, won more games than either Alekhine or Marshall, but also lost more. He drew but three.

The gradation from top to bottom of the list is very even, the greatest difference being between the second and third prize winners. The rest were in no case wider apart than $1\frac{1}{2}$ points.

Of the 110 games, 72 had decisive results and the other 38 were drawn. The draws, therefore, were not excessive. The prize winners scored 44 of the wins between them and the non-prize winners, 28.

Summary of the Play

FIRST ROUND—MARCH 16.

Bds. White.		Black.		Openings.	Moves.
1. Ed. Lasker........	½	Maroczy	½	Indian Defense	41
2. Marshall	½	Reti	½	Indian Defense	50
3. Yates	0	Alekhine	1	Ruy Lopez	35
4. Janowski	½	Capablanca	½	Queen's Gambit (decl'd).	20
5. Tartakower	1	Bogoljubow	0	King's Gambit	58
	2½		2½		

Dr. Lasker, a bye.

SECOND ROUND—MARCH 17.

Bds. White.		Black.		Openings.	Moves.
1. Maroczy	0	Alekhine	1	Alekhine Defense	24
2. Dr. Lasker	½	Capablanca	½	Ruy Lopez	3₿
3. Ed Lasker	½	Bogoljubow	½	Philidor's Defense	51
4. Marshall	½	Tartakower	½	Dutch Defense	37
5. Yates	½	Janowski	½	Ruy Lopez	46
	2		3		

Reti, a bye.

THIRD ROUND—MARCH 18.

Bds. White.		Black.		Openings.	Moves.
1. Tartakower	1	Yates	0	King's Gambit	45
2. Bogoljubow	1	Marshall	0	Q. P. Opening..........	56
3. Capablanca	½	Ed. Lasker	½	Queen's Gambit (decl'd).	27
4. Alekhine	0	Dr. Lasker	1	Queen's Gambit (decl'd).	36
5. Reti	½	Maroczy	½	Reti's Opening	35
	3		2		

Janowski, a bye.

FOURTH ROUND—MARCH 21.

Bds. White.		Black.		Openings.	Moves.
1. Yates	1	Ed. Lasker	0	Ruy Lopez	54
2. Janowski	0	Dr. Lasker	1	Sicilian Defense	68
3. Tartakower	½	Maroczy	½	Irregular	57
4. Bogoljubow	1	Reti	0	French Defense	45
5. Capablanca	½	Alekhine	½	French Defense	62
	3		2		

Marshall, a bye.

FIFTH ROUND—MARCH 22.

Bds. White.		Black.		Openings.	Moves.
1. Reti	1	Capablanca	0	Reti's Opening	3₿
2. Maroczy	0	Bogoljubow	1	Q. P. Opening..........	27
3. Dr. Lasker	½	Tartakower	½	Sicilian Defense	26
4. Ed. Lasker	0	Janowski	1	Irregular	62
5. Marshall	½	Yates	½	Indian Defense	40
	2		3		

Alekhine, a bye.

SIXTH ROUND—MARCH 23

Bds. White.	Black.	Openings.	Moves.
1. Capablanca 1	Tartakower 0	Dutch Defense 52
2. Alekhine 1	Janowski 0	Irregular 40
3. Reti 1	Yates 0	Reti's Opening 31
4. Maroczy 1	Marshall 0	Three Knights 81
5. Dr. Lasker .... ½	Ed. Lasker .... ½	Ruy Lopez 103

4½ ½

Bogoljubow, a bye.

SEVENTH ROUND—MARCH 25.

Bds. White.	Black.	Openings.	Moves.
1. Bogoljubow 0	Janowski 1	Queen's Gambit 44
2. Capablanca 1	Yates 0	Q. P. Opening.......... 62
3. Alekhine .... ½	Marshall .... ½	Indian Defense 61
4. Reti 1	Ed. Lasker 0	Reti's Opening 56
5. Maroczy 0	Dr. Lasker 1	Alekhine Defense 30

2½ 2½

Tartakower, a bye.

EIGHTH ROUND—MARCH 26.

Bds. White.	Black.	Openings.	Moves.
1. Janowski 0	Marshall 1	Reti's Opening (reversed) 75
2. Tartakower .... ½	Ed. Lasker .... ½	Scotch Gambit 33
3. Bogoljubow 0	Dr. Lasker 1	Ruy Lopez 71
4. Capablanca .... ½	Maroczy .... ½	Q. P. Opening.......... 30
5. Alekhine 1	Reti 0	Indian Defense 44

2 3

Yates, a bye.

NINTH ROUND—MARCH 27.

Bds. White.	Black.	Openings.	Moves.
1. Marshall .... ½	Dr. Lasker .... ½	Queen's Gambit (decl'd). 62
2. Yates 0	Maroczy 1	French Defense 69
3. Janowski 0	Reti 1	Reti's Opening (reversed) 44
4. Tartakower .... ½	Alekhine .... ½	King's Gambit 39
5. Bogoljubow 0	Capablanca 1	Q. P. Opening.......... 32

1 4

Ed. Lasker, a bye.

TENTH ROUND—MARCH 29.

Bds. White.	Black.	Openings.	Moves.
1. Dr. Lasker 1	Reti 0	French Defense 32
2. Ed. Lasker .... ½	Alekhine .... ½	Ruy Lopez 58
3. Janowski .... ½	Tartakower .... ½	Queen's Gambit (decl'd). 45
4. Marshall .... ½	Capablanca .... ½	Reti's Opening (reversed) 66
5. Yates 0	Bogoljubow 1	Ruy Lopez 33

2½ 2½

Maroczy, a bye.

ELEVENTH ROUND—MARCH 30.

Bds. White.	Black.	Openings.	Moves.
1. Alekhine .... ½	Bogoljubow .... ½	Reti's Opening 60
2. Reti 1	Tartakower 0	Sicilian Defense 74
3. Maroczy 1	Janowski 0	Two Knights' Defense.... 55
4. Dr. Lasker .... ½	Yates .... ½	Ruy Lopez 55
5. Ed. Lasker 0	Marshall 1	Three Knights 57

3 2

Capablanca, a bye.

TWELFTH ROUND—APRIL 2.

Bds.	White.		Black.		Openings.	Moves.
1.	Ed. Lasker	0	Yates	1	Indian Defense	50
2.	Dr. Lasker	1	Janowski	0	Ruy Lopez	82
3.	Maroczy	½	Tartakower	½	Alekhine Defense	29
4.	Reti	1	Bogoljubow	0	Reti's Opening	25
5.	Alekhine	½	Capablanca	½	Queen's Gambit (decl'd).	18
		3		2		

Marshall, a bye.

THIRTEENTH ROUND—APRIL 3.

Bds.	White.		Black.		Openings.	Moves.
1.	Marshall	1	Janowski	0	Queen's Gambit	54
2.	Ed. Lasker	1	Tartakower	0	Queen's Gambit (decl'd).	36
3.	Dr. Lasker	1	Bogoljubow	0	Sicilian Defense	61
4.	Maroczy	0	Capablanca	1	Ruy Lopez	57
5.	Reti	1	Alekhine	0	Reti's Opening (reversed)	31
		4		1		

Yates, a bye.

FOURTENTH ROUND—APRIL 5.

Bds.	White.		Black.		Openings.	Moves.
1.	Alekhine	½	Maroczy	½	Queen's Gambit (decl'd).	33
2.	Capablanca	1	Dr. Lasker	0	Queen's Gambit (decl'd).	50
3.	Bogoljubow	1	Ed. Lasker	0	Ruy Lopez	57
4.	Tartakower	1	Marshall	0	Reti's Opening	61
5.	Janowski	0	Yates	1	Indian Defense	81
		3½		1½		

Reti, a bye.

FIFTEENTH ROUND—APRIL 6.

Bds.	White.		Black.		Openings.	Moves.
1.	Maroczy	1	Ed. Lasker	0	Queen's Gambit (decl'd).	78
2.	Reti	0	Marshall	1	Reti's Opening	30
3.	Alekhine	1	Yates	0	Indian Defense	32
4.	Capablanca	1	Janowski	0	Reti's Opening	46
5.	Bogoljubow	1	Tartakower	0	Dutch Defense	65
		4		1		

Dr. Lasker, a bye.

SIXTEENTH ROUND—APRIL 8.

Bds.	White.		Black.		Openings.	Moves.
1.	Reti	0	Dr. Lasker	1	Reti's Opening	45
2.	Alekhine	½	Ed. Lasker	½	Indian Defense	53
3.	Capablanca	½	Marshall	½	Queen's Gambit (decl'd).	46
4.	Bogoljubow	1	Yates	0	Queen's Gambit (decl'd).	90
5.	Tartakower	1	Janowski	0	Reti's Opening	32
		3		2		

Maroczy, a bye.

SEVENTEENTH ROUND—APRL 9.

Bds.	White.		Black.		Openings.	Moves.
1.	Bogoljubow	½	Alekhine	½	French Defense	85
2.	Tartakower	0	Reti	1	Ruy Lopez	47
3.	Janowski	1	Maroczy	0	Queen's Gambit (decl'd).	29
4.	Yates	0	Dr. Lasker	1	Sicilian Defense	53
5.	Marshall	½	Ed. Lasker	½	Q. P. Opening	46
		2		3		

Capablanca, a bye.

EIGHTEENTH ROUND—APRIL 10.

Bds.	White.	Black.	Openings.	Moves.
1.	Yates 1	Tartakower 0	Sicilian Defense 50	
2.	Marshall 1	Bogoljubow 0	Queen's Gambit (decl'd). 38	
3.	Ed. Lasker 0	Capablanca 1	Irregular 60	
4.	Dr. Lasker .... ½	Alekhine .... ½	Reti's Opening (reversed) 30	
5.	Maroczy .... ½	Reti .... ½	Ruy Lopez 58	
	3	**2**		

Janowski, a bye.

NINETEENTH ROUND—APRIL 12.

Bds.	White.	Black.	Openings.	Moves.
1.	Tartakower 0	Capablanca 1	King's Gambit 30	
2.	Janowski 0	Alekhine 1	Reti's Opening (reversed) 50	
3.	Yates 1	Reti 0	Caro-Kann Defense 24	
4.	Marshall .... ½	Maroczy .... ½	Indian Defense 33	
5.	Ed. Lasker 0	Dr. Lasker 1	Queen's Gambit (decl'd). 51	
	1½	**3½**		

Bogoljubow, a bye.

TWENTIETH ROUND—APRIL 13.

Bds.	White.	Black.	Openings.	Moves.
1.	Janowski 0	Bogoljubow 1	Queen's Gambit (decl'd). 87	
2.	Yates .... ½	Capablanca .... ½	Ruy Lopez 28	
3.	Marshall .... ½	Alekhine .... ½	Queen's Gambit (decl'd). 31	
4.	Ed. Lasker 1	Reti 0	Ruy Lopez 36	
5.	Dr. Lasker 1	Maroczy 0	French Defense 50	
	3	**2**		

Tartakower, a bye.

TWENTY-FIRST ROUND—APRIL 15.

Bds.	White.	Black.	Openings.	Moves.
1.	Capablanca 1	Reti 0	French Defense 36	
2.	Bogoljubow 0	Maroczy 1	Queen's Gambit (decl'd). 48	
3.	Tartakower 0	Dr. Lasker 1	English Opening 48	
4.	Janowski .... ½	Ed. Lasker .... ½	Q. P. Opening.......... 71	
5.	Yates 0	Marshall 1	Ruy Lopez 41	
	1½	**3½**		

Alekhine, a bye.

TWENTY-SECOND ROUND—APRIL 17.

Bds.	White.	Black.	Openings.	Moves.
1.	Dr. Lasker 1	Marshall 0	Ruy Lopez 44	
2.	Maroczy 1	Yates 0	Ruy Lopez 38	
3.	Reti 1	Janowski 0	Reti's Opening 43	
4.	Alekhine .... ½	Tartakower .... ½	Three Knights 32	
5.	Capablanca 1	Bogoljubow 0	French Defense 65	
	4½	**½**		

Ed. Lasker, a bye.

The Scoring, Round by Round

The progress made by the contestants, round by round, is shown in the following tables:

	1	2	3	4	5	6	7	8	9	10	11
Dr. Lasker	...	½	1½	2½	3	3½	4½	5½	6½	7	7½
Capablanca	½	1	1½	2	2	3	4	4½	5½	6	...
Alekhine	1	2	2	2½	...	3½	4	5	5½	6	6½
Marshall	½	1	1	...	1½	1½	2	3	3½	4	5
Reti	½	...	1	1	2	3	4	4	5	5	6
Maroczy	½	½	1	1½	1½	2½	2½	3	4	...	5
Bogoljubow	0	½	1½	2½	3½	...	3½	3½	3½	4½	5
Dr. Tartakower	1	1½	2½	3	3½	3½	...	4	4½	5	5
Yates	0	½	½	1½	2	2	2	...	2	2	2½
Lasker	½	1	1½	1½	1½	2	2	2½	...	3	3
Janowski	½	1	...	1	2	2	3	3	3	3½	3½

	12	13	14	15	16	17	18	19	20	21	22
Dr. Lasker	8½	9½	9½	...	10½	11½	12	13	14	15	16
Capablanca	6½	7½	8½	9½	10	...	11	12	12½	13½	14½
Alekhine	7	7	7½	8½	9	9½	10	11	11½	...	12
Marshall	...	6	6	7	7½	8	9	9½	10	11	11
Reti	7..	8	...	8	8	9	9½	9½	9½	9½	10½
Maroczy	5½	5½	6	7	...	7	7½	8	8	9	10
Bogoljubow	5	5	6	7	8	8½	8½	...	9½	9½	9½
Dr. Tartakower	5½	5½	6½	6½	7½	7½	7½	7½	...	7½	8
Yates	3½	...	4½	4½	4½	4½	5½	6½	7	7	7
Lasker	3	4	4	4	4½	5	5	5	6	6½	6½
Janowski	3½	3½	3½	3½	3½	4½	...	4½	4½	5	5

FIRST ROUND

In accordance with a ruling of the Tournament Committee, the pairings were made in advance for the entire twenty-two rounds by a system of allotting a number to every one of the eleven contestants, but the number of each round in this schedule was not made known until drawn from a hat by one of the players fifteen minutes before the time of beginning play each day. The luck of the drawing on March 16 decreed that particular round in which Dr. Lasker had the bye. Consequently, the chief actor in this international drama remained idle for the time being and filled the role of spectator, instead of taking his place upon the stage. Alekhine and Dr. Tartakower were the two victors, the other three games being drawn.

The attendance was most gratifying and the large audience followed with close attention the moves of the masters as they were quickly reproduced by a corps of tellers on large boards hung at a convenient height upon the wall directly above where the players sat. These were surmounted by handsome shields emblematic of the various countries represented in the tournament.

After being thus recorded, the moves were relayed to the press room outside and soon the wires were busy acquainting an anxious public with the details of the play in which some of the greatest of living masters were striving to outdo one another. A special cable service, direct from the Alamac, was carrying the moves as far away as South America!

The games were timed at first by a set of clocks imported especially for the occasion, but, as they failed to give full satisfaction, they were supplanted by others of American make, which held their own well until the end of the tournament.

Coming to the actual play, Janowski sprang a new move (but not the result of midnight oil) upon the world's champion in a Queen's Gambit declined. Capablanca eventually was glad to sacrifice a Knight in order to force a draw by perpetual check, thereby relieving himself of an otherwise unsatisfactory position.

Yates was outplayed by Alekhine in a Steinitz defense to the Ruy Lopez. The British player, however, missed a continuation which might have made it exceedingly difficult for his opponent to realize upon his material advantage.

An Indian defense was played by Reti against Marshall, the former having rather the better of it throughout. The American did not allow his adversary's slight positional advantage to become consequential.

Ed Lasker started the tournament well by drawing with the master of defense—Maroczy. This was another Indian, with Lasker fighting very hard to hold his own in the ending.

Dr. Tartakower boldly essayed a King's Gambit against Bogoljubow, and his daring was rewarded with success. Nevertheless, it was a case of nip and tuck almost right to the end, when the Ukrainian, playing very hard to win, got the worst of it.

Game 1   FIRST ROUND—QUEEN'S GAMBIT DECLINED

| Janowski | Capablanca | 18 PxB | KtxKBP(g) |
| White | Black | | |

After 18 PxB

1 P—Q4	P—Q4
2 Kt—KB3	Kt—KB3
3 P—B4	P—K3
4 Kt—B3	B—K2(a)
5 B—Kt5	Castles
6 P—K3	QKt—Q2
7 R—B	P—B3
8 B—Q3	PxP
9 BxP	Kt—Q4
10 P—KR4(b)	P—B3(c)
11 B—B4	KtxB
12 PxKt	Kt—Kt3
13 B—Kt3	Kt—Q4
14 P—Kt3	Q—K(d)
15 Q—Q3	Q—R4
16 B—Q	B—Kt5(e)
17 Castles(f)	BxKt

19 PxKt	Q—Kt5ch
20 K—R(h)	Drawn

(a) Of greater promise than the antiquated method here seems to be 4...P—B3, so as to meet 5 P—K3 (better anyway, to our way of thinking, is 5 B—Kt5, P—KR3; 6 BxKt, etc.) with 5...QKt—Q2; 6 B—Q3, PxP (Rubinstein); 7 BxBP, P—QKt4; 8 B—Q3, P—QR3, followed by P—QB4.

(b) If this is not a new move (in these days one can hardly make such a claim, for, sooner or later, some person will come forward and prove black on white that he used this move decades ago in some class C tournament or perchance in a coffee house game and hence demand parental recognition) it has nevertheless been well forgotten. More promising, doubtless, is it than 10 BxB, QxB; 11 Castles, KtxKt; 12 RxKt, P—K4.

(c) The weakening of the square, K3, is not justified and causes embarrassment to Black. Instead, he might as well have held the position in abeyance while completing his development; 10...KtxKt; 11 PxKt (or 11 RxKt, P—B3; 12 BxPch, K—R, winning the exchange), P—QKt3, followed by B—Kt2, etc. It would have been difficult for White thereafter to build up a lasting King side attack.

(d) Because of his weakness in the center, Black now experiences difficulty with his QB. The text-move indicates an attempt to post the Queen upon strong squares where it may be possible to force an exchange. Such a plan White is able to frustrate most simply by means of P—R5, but his next move likewise is good enough.

(e) In order to meet 17 Kt—K5 favorably with 17...Q—B4. At the same time, a little trap is set with this move, which works out all right, too.

(f) After 17 K—B, the problem for the defense would be still far from being solved. Now the game terminates most unexpectedly.

(g) With this move the champion emerges from a somewhat precarious situation. White clearly has no alternative but to accept the sacrifice, else he would obtain no return for the lost pawn.

(h) Again forced, since 20 K—R2, QxBPch; 21 K—R, QxR; 22 B—B2, Q—R3, would have led to nothing.

Game 2   FIRST ROUND—RUY LOPEZ

Yates	Alekhine	5 Castles(b)	P—KKt3(c)
White	Black	6 P—B3(d)	B—Kt2
1 P—K4	P—K4	7 P—Q4	B—Q2
2 Kt—KB3	Kt—QB3	8 B—KKt5(e)	KKt—K2(f)
3 B—Kt5	P—QR3	9 PxP(g)	PxP
4 B—R4	P—Q3 a)	10 Q—Q3(h)	P—R3

11 B—K3	B—Kt5(i)	32 KtxP	PxB
12 Q—K2(j)	Castles	33 Q—R5	Kt—K5
13 QKt—Q2(k)	P—B4	34 Kt—Kt6ch	K—R2
14 P—KR3	B—R4	35 QxQP	Kt—Kt6ch(z)
15 B—Kt3ch(l)	K—R(m)	Resigns	
16 PxP(n)	PxP		
17 P—KKt4	PxP		

After 21 B—K6

After 21 B—K6

18 Kt—K(o)	Kt—Q4
19 PxP(p)	KtxB
20 PxKt	Q—Kt4
21 B—K6(q)	BxP(r)
22 QxB	QxPch
23 K—R	QxKt
24 R—KKt	Q—Kt4(s)
25 Q—R3(t)	Q—B3
26 B—Q5	Kt—K2(u)
27 B—K4	Kt—B4(v)
28 Kt—B3(w)	Kt—Q3(x)
29 B—Q5(y)	P—B3
30 RxB	KxR
31 R—Ktch	K—R

(a) This variation of the Steinitz defense seems to be better than P—Q3 at once, as White, after P—Q4, must reckon with either choosing an immediate drawing line (5...P—QKt4; 6 B—Kt3, KtxP; 7 KtxKt, PxKt; 8 QxP, P—QB4; 9 Q—Q5, B—K3; 10 Q—B6ch, B—Q2; 11 Q—Q5, B—K3, etc.), or being forced to embark upon a doubtful sacrificial variation beginning with 8 P—QB3.

(b) Castling makes a somewhat indifferent impression—quite possibly, wrongly so. Seriously to be considered are the following two continuations: (I) 5 BxKtch, PxB; 6 P—Q4, and Black has the unpleasant choice between a surrender of the center, which would provide splendid prospects for the White QB. For instance, 6...PxP; 7 KtxP, B—Q2 (or P—QB4; 8 Kt—KB3 and eventually P—K5); 8 P—QKt3, followed by B—Kt2, etc.; or the protection of the same through 6...P—KB3, which would bind him positionally to a further weakening of the King's side through P—KKt3 (followed by B—KKt2); and such commitments for which the opponent can take measures in advance, are for the most part fatal. (II) P—B3, if he should wish to cross Black's plan as carried out in this game. For instance, 5...P—KKt3; 6 P—Q4, B—Q2; 7 B—KKt5, etc. The further course of the game, however, shows that White has no good reason to contest this tendency on the part of Black, and precisely in this lies its theoretical value.

(c) Very enticing, inasmuch as Black holds the center and at the same time goes on with his development. The bad features of this line of play soon become apparent and thus prove the common opinion that an early fianchetto development and especially the King's fianchetto in the open game (as in the Ruy Lopez and Three Knights for Black and in the Vienna for White) shows theoretically bad position judgment.

(d) After 6 P—Q4, there could have followed 6...P—QKt4; 7 B—Kt3, B—KKt2; 8 B—Q5, B—Q2, etc.

(e) The idea underlying this seemingly unnatural move is to induce Black to adopt the less satisfactory development of the KKt at K2. In fact, after 8 B—K3, Kt—KB3; 9 QKt—Q2, Castles, Black would have completely overcome the opening difficulties.

(f) After 8...Kt—B3; 9 QKt—Q2, there would have been the threat of BxKt and PxP. Even after the move in the text, White retains the advantage of the first move.

(g) Limiting the sphere of action of the fianchettoed Bishop and opening at the right time the Queen's file as a base for future operations.

(h) This move, too, which is really the logical consequence of the last one, has been unjustly criticized. It prevents Black from castling immediately, which he might do freely after 10 Q—K2, Castles (11 R—Q, Q—K, etc.).

(i) Relatively better than 11...Castles, after which White could play with advantage B—B5, B—Kt5 (K3); 13 Q—K3, etc.

(j)   Naturally, exchanging Queens would be a flagrant repudiation of White's entire conduct of the opening until now, for it is the position of the Black Queen on the open Q file which should give him the opportunity to secure an advantage in position, however slight.

(k)   His play here is without object. By means of 13 B—B5 (somewhat better than the immediate 13 R—Q) White could have fully rounded out his selected method of play and forced his opponent into an uncomfortably cramped position, which would have led at least to the deterioration of Black's pawn structure. The actual and harmless developing move, on the contrary, leads him strangely enough to a serious disadvantage.

(l)   Or 15 B—B5, PxP; 16 QxP, R—B5; 17 Q—B2, P—K5, etc.

(m)   Not 15...K—R2, on account of 16 PxP, PxP; 17 Kt—Kt5ch, K—Kt3; 18 P—KKt4, and White is at liberty to fish in troubled waters.

(n)   In connection with the next move, this is the most effective method of getting rid of the annoying pin.

(o)   This retreat, however, fails in the light of a closely calculated counter combination which yields Black eventually a pawn. Better would have been 18 Kt—R2, whereupon Black, by means of Kt—Q4 and KtxB, could have obtained at least the advantage of two Bishops.

(p)   Or 19 BxKt, QxB; 20 PxP, B—Kt3; 21 Q—B4, QR—Q, with a far superior game.

(q)   Obviously forced.

(r)   A little surprise; if White captures with the Bishop, then Black will recapture with 22...P—KR4, with a Pawn plus and a permanent pressure. White, therefore, sacrifices a second Pawn in the hope of being able to utilize in his counter-play the white squares on which the adversary is none too strong.

(s)   Instead of this attempt to reach a winning ending through the return of a Pawn, the simple 24...B—B3 would have been all-sufficient for the purposes of defense. For instance, 25 Kt—B3, Q—B5; 26 Q—R5 or R3, P—K5, etc.

(t)   After 25 QxQ, PxQ; 26 RxP, R—B3; 27 B—Q5, R—Q, Black would have been able to realize without difficulty upon his superiority in material.

(u)   So that, after 27 BxP, QR—Kt; 28 B—K4, the carrying out of White's attack may be prevented by means of 28...Q—B5 (not RxP, because of 29 Kt—Q3 and QR—KB).

(v)   Now 27...Q—B5 would be quite futile on account of 28 BxP, followed by Kt—Q3, etc.

(w)   After this mistake, the struggle comes to an early end. 28 Kt—Q3 would have set Black a difficult problem, inasmuch as it would not have been possible to reply either with 28...Q—R5 (on account of 29 BxKt) or 28...Kt—Q3 (on account of 29 R—Kt6 and RxPch.) The best for Black, after 28 Kt—Q3, would have been 28...QR—Q (again threatening Q—R5); 29 QR—Q, P—QKt3 (thereby threatening to dislodge the Knight with P—B4—B5); 30 P—Kt4, R—Q3; 31 R—Kt4 (or 31 R—Kt2, Q—R5; 32 BxKt, QxQch; 33 BxQ, R—B6, etc.), P—KR4; 32 QxPch, Q—R3, and, after the exchange of Queens, the extra Pawn would have won eventually.

(x)   And now, in answer to 29 R—Kt6, KtxB would decide and, if 29 Kt—Q2, then Q—B5, etc.

(y)   Losing a piece. What follows is sheer desperation.

(z)   A bit of fun for a pretty ending. After 36 RxKt, Q—B8ch; 37 K—R2 (R—Kt, Q—R6 mate), R—B7ch; 38 R—Kt2, QxRch; 39 QxQ, RxQch and KxKt, Black remains with a Rook to the good.

Game 3   FIRST ROUND—INDIAN DEFENSE

Marshall	Reti		
White	Black	9 B—K3	P—QB4(d)
1 P—Q4	Kt—KB3	10 P—Q5	Kt—K4
2 Kt—KB3	P—KKt3	11 Q—K2	KtxBch
3 P—B4	B—Kt2	12 QxKt	Kt—Q2
4 Kt—B3	Castles	13 Castles	Q—R4(e)
5 P—K4	P—Q3(a)	14 B—Q2(f)	P—QR3
6 B—Q3(b)	B—Kt5	15 Kt—Q	Q—B2
7 P—KR3(c)	BxKt	16 B—B3	Kt—K4(g)
8 QxB	KKt—Q2	17 Q—K2	P—QKt4(h)

After 17 Q—K2

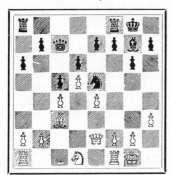

18 PxP	PxP
19 P—B4	Kt—B5
20 BxB	KxB
21 Kt—B3	Q—R4
22 P—QR4(i)	Q—Kt5
23 KtxP(j)	RxP
24 RxR	QxR
25 R—B	QxKt(k)
26 RxKt	R—QKt

27 R—B2	QxQ
28 RxQ(l)	R—Kt5
29 K—B2	K—B
30 K—B3	R—Q5(m)
31 P—KKt4	K—K(n)
32 R—K3	R—Kt5(o)
33 R—R3(p)	RxKtP
34 R—R8ch	K—Q2
35 R—R7ch	K—Q
36 P—K5	PxP
37 PxP	P—B5
38 K—K3	P—B6
39 R—R8ch	K—B2
40 R—R7ch	K—Q
41 R—R8ch	K—B2
42 R—R7ch	R—Kt2
43 R—R3(q)	P—B7
44 R—B3ch	K—Q2
45 RxP	R—Kt6ch
46 K—Q4	RxP
47 R—QR2	R—KKt6(r)
48 R—R7ch	K—Q
49 R—R8ch	K—B2
50 R—R7ch	Drawn

(a) The method of development employed here by White against the Indian defense is considered the best by several modern masters, among them Gruenfeld, Johner and others. To our way of thinking, it is apt to be favorable to the player having the move, much as in the four-pawn game in the Indian. In the latter, however, the problem is shown in a more succinct and clear form.

(b) This move, however, does not fit into the system, inasmuch as, after the exchange on KB3 the square, Q4, becomes weak. Likewise 6 P—KR3 does not seem to be the best on general principles. White has no reason to keep his adversary from moving B—KKt5, whereby he commits himself to an exchange of the Bishop sooner or later. An obligation of that kind on the part of an opponent, upon which one may reckon in advance, is per se an advantage. Besides, after 6 P—KR3, Black has at his disposal the interesting reply of 6...P—QB4; 7 PxP (7 P—Q5, which is probably better, affords an outlook for the fianchettoed Bishop), Q—R4; 8 PxP, KtxP; 9 PxP, R—K, etc. Therefore, it appears that 6 B—K2 and, if 6...B—Kt5, then 7 B—K3 (Gruenfeld vs Takacz, Meran, 1924), is the most suitable in order to retain the opening advantage.

(c) The development of the Bishop at Q3 is so contrary to position play that it would be perhaps best to withdraw that piece to K2, notwithstanding the loss of a "tempo."

(d) The continuation of 9...Kt—QB3; 10 P—Q5 (not Kt—K2, P—K4; 11 P—Q5, Kt—Q5), QKt—K4 would have led to similar positions as the text-move.

(e) Threatening to win a pawn with 14 BxKt, followed by Kt—K4, etc.

(f) Parrying that threat and at the same time preparing for the exchange of the sinister black Bishop.

(g) Preparing for the subsequent over-daring sacrifice of the pawn with the intention of avoiding a forced draw. He could have held a good game with 16...BxB; 17 KtxB, Q—R4, eventually followed by Q—Kt5. Of course, the danger of a draw would have been just as great.

(h) White could safely have captured this pawn, as Black would have difficulty in obtaining positional compensation, for instance: 18 PxP, PxP; 19 QxP, P—B5 (clearly the reason for the pawn sacrifice); 20 BxKt, BxB (or KR—Kt; 21 Q—B6, QxQ; 22 PxQ, BxB; 23 QR—B, BxP; 24 RxP, with advantage, as Black dare not capture the QR pawn, on account of 25 R—B2); 21 Kt—K3, P—B6; 22 PxP, QxP; 23 QR—B, and White would have had at least a very easy draw. After the refusal of the sacrifice, on the other hand, he can now reach that goal only after hard fighting.

(i) Comparatively better would have been to keep the Queen's side intact and to initiate play in the center with 22 P—K5. The advance of the RP turns out to be aimless.

(j) Likewise after 23 PxP, RxR; 24 RxR, KtxP; 25 R—Kt, QxKt; 26 QxKt, QxQ; 27 RxQ, R—Kt, etc., the Rook ending because of the protected passed pawn would be in Black's favor, for instance: 28 K—B2, K—B; 29 K—K3, K—K2; 30 K—Q3, K—Q2; 31 K—B4, K—B2; 32 R—QR, K—Kt2; 33 R—R6, R—QR; 34 RxR, KxR, and now Black, moving his King from R8 to Kt8 and back again, merely waits until White's pawn moves in the center and on the King's side have been exhausted, whereupon White faces the alternative of moving either the KtP or the King. In the first case would follow P—Kt6, K—R (or vice versa) and only after K—Kt5, K—Kt2, winning; in the second place, at once K—Kt2, followed by K—Kt3, with the same result.

(k) 25...Kt—Kt3 would not have altered the situation after 26 Kt—R3, followed by Kt—B4.

(l) The ending is by no means easily playable for White, on account of his weak KtP. In the subsequent play this problem is solved by Marshall in exemplary fashion.

(m) With the intention of P—KB4, etc.

(n) Now, however, he suddenly drops this plan and thereby lightens his opponent's task. To be sure, after 31...P—KB4; 32 KtPxP, PxP; 33 PxP, RxP; 34 K—Kt4, R—Q8; 35 R—K6, the draw is not out of the question, nevertheless this continuation would have offered Black better chances than the futile attempt to cross with his King to the Queen's side.

(o) Now 32...P—KB4 would certainly not do, on account of 33 KPxP, PxP; 34 PxP, RxP; 35 P—B6, etc.

(p) The saving counter attack.

(q) After the capture of this passed pawn, every shadow of danger disappears.

(r) Now the exchange of Rooks, on the contrary, would have led to loss for Black, for instance: 47...R—QKt6; 48 R—R7ch, K—Q; 49 R—R8ch, K—B2; 50 R—R7ch, R—Kt2; 51 P—Q6ch, PxP; 52 PxPch, K—B3; 53 RxR, KxR; 54 P—Kt5, K—B3; 55 K—K5, K—Q2; 56 K—Q5, and wins.

Game 4   FIRST ROUND—INDIAN DEFENSE

Ed. Lasker	Maroczy
White	Black
1 P—Q4	Kt—KB3
2 Kt—KB3	P—KKt3
3 Kt—B3(a)	B—Kt2(b)
4 P—K4	P—Q3
5 P—KR3(c)	Castles
6 QB—B4	QKt—Q2
7 Q—Q2(d)	P—B4(e)
8 P—Q5	P—QR3(f)
9 B—R6(g)	P—QKt4
10 BxB	KxB
11 Q—K3(h)	Q—R4(i)
12 Kt—Q2	P—K4(j)
13 B—K2	P—R3(k)
14 Castles	Q—Q
15 P—QR4	P—Kt5
16 QKt—Kt	P—QR4
17 Kt—B4	Kt—Kt3
18 KtxKt	QxKt
19 P—KB4(l)	PxP
20 RxP(m)	Q—Q
21 Kt—Q2	Q—K2(n)
22 Kt—B4	B—R3

23 Kt—Kt6(o)	QR—Kt
24 QR—KB	Kt—R4(p)
25 R(B4)—B3	BxB
26 QxB	RxKt
27 P—Kt4(q)	QR—Kt(r)

After 27 P—Kt4

| 28 Q—B2 | P—B4(s) |
| 29 PxKt | PxKP(t) |

30	RxR	RxR	36 P—Kt3(w)	K—K2
31	QxRch	QxQ	37 K—Q3	K—B3
32	RxQ	KxR	38 K—K4(x)	K—K2
33	K—B2(u)	K—Kt2	39 K—Q3	K—B3
34	K—K3	P—Kt4(v)	40 K—K4	K—K2
35	KxP	K—B3	41 K—Q3	Drawn

(a) This move is not to be recommended, inasmuch as White, through the premature blocking of his QBP, prescribes for himself without reason a very limited scope for development. More elastic (that is, offering more possibilities to prepare himself in the subsequent moves for the system adopted by his opponent) would be, in our judgment, 3 B—B4 at once.

(b) Concerning 3...P—Q4, which, by the way, is in no way in harmony with the flank development of the KB, see the games between Capablanca and Yates (7th round) and Marshall and Ed Lasker (17th round).

(c) The necessity of this move is not apparent here, for it was not at all required of him to prevent B—Kt5. B—B4 at once, followed by Q—Q2, seems to be, therefore, more in order.

(d) If 7 P—K5, then 7...Kt—K, threatening P—B4, etc., with advantage for Black.

(e) An advance, strategically correct in similar positions, and which increases considerably the effectiveness of the fianchettoed Bishop.

(f) But here the most effective would have been 8...R—K, in order, after 9 B—R6, to be able to retain the Bishop by means of a retreat to R square and, in addition, to prepare for an eventual P—K3.

(g) White immediately seizes this opportunity to ease his game somewhat by this exchange.

(h) The KP obviously was in need of protection.

(i) This attack was not to be criticised except in the event that Black resorted to it as a preparation for action in the center. Otherwise, the immediate 11 ...P—K3 deserved serious consideration.

(j) An astonishing strategical error, for a player like Maroczy, which suddenly gives the opponent the better game. As a matter of course, he should have played 12 ...P—K3! in order to open new lines for the black pieces, for instance: 13 PxP, PxP; 14 Kt—Kt3, Q—B2, followed by P—Q4, etc. After the text-move, blocking the position, White obtains the time he needs to complete his development and thereupon to seize the initiative for himself through the counter-stroke of P—B4.

(k) This move, as well as the next, indicates quite clearly that Black for the moment has lost his cue.

(l) White has properly utilized his opponent's error on the twelfth move and should now obtain the advantage if he had perceived in time at his next move a finesse in the defense of Black.

(m) Correct would have been 20 QxP and, if 20...Q—Q, then 21 Kt—Q2, Q—K2; 22 B—Kt5, followed by QR—K and Kt—B4. The difference between this line of play and the one actually adopted will at once be apparent.

(n) Threatening 22...KtxQP and preventing in this way B—Kt5, followed by Kt—B4.

(o) The interesting complication thus introduced should have led eventually to the loss of a pawn. But even after 23 R—K, for instance, Black would have assured himself of the far superior game through the exchange on B5, followed by bringing the Knight over to K4.

(p) Seemingly winning the exchange. White however, has in readiness an ingenious reply.

(q) Black, to be sure, loses a piece in return, but receives for it a pawn in quite simple fashion. It is hardly to be expected, therefore, that White can escape from this position with a whole skin.

(r) Black believes he has still time as 28 PxKt can be met by Q—Kt4ch. The continuation, however, shows that he should have proceeded more energetically in order to make sure of superiority in material. To that end 27...O—K4 would have been the most forceful, for instance: 28 PxKt, QxP or 28 Q—B2, R—Kt2, after which White could not save the pawn.

(s) This advance, clearly planned at his previous move, leads strangely enough only to a draw. But neither could the game have been won with 28...R—Kt2; 29 PxKt, Q—Kt4ch; 30 Q—Kt3, etc.

(t) Or 29 ...QxP; 30 Q—Kt3!, R—KB3; 31 RxP, etc.
(u) Of course not 33 PxP, K—Kt2; 34 K—B2, KxP; 35 K—K3, K—B4, and wins.
(v) Or 34 ...PxP; 35 P—R4!, K—B3; 36 KxP, etc., and draws.
(w) Had this move perchance occurred in the middle game, then the game could be resigned forthwith.
(x) White is forced to repeat the moves, as 38 K—B4 loses, for instance: 38 ... K—K4; 39 K—Kt5, KxP; 40 KxP, K—B3!; 41 K—R6, P—Q4; 42 K—R5, P—Q5; 43 K—R6, P—B5!, etc.

Game 5   FIRST ROUND—KING'S GAMBIT

| | Tartakower | Bogoljubow |
	White	Black
1	P—K4	P—K4
2	P—KB4	PxP
3	B—K2(a)	P—Q4(b)
4	PxP	Kt—KB3
5	P—QB4	P—QB3
6	P—Q4	PxP(c)
7	BxP	PxP(d)
8	BxP	B—Kt5ch
9	Kt—B3	Castles
10	Kt—K2	B—Kt5
11	Castles	QKt—Q2
12	Q—Kt3	BxQKt(e)
13	PxB	Kt—Kt3
14	B—Q3	KKt—Q4
15	B—Q2	BxKt(f)
16	BxB	R—B
17	R—B3(g)	Q—B2(h)
18	QR—KB	P—B3(i)
19	B—Q3	Kt—QB5
20	R—R3(j)	P—KKt3
21	R—K(k)	KtxB
22	QxKtch	Q—B2(l)
23	QxQch	RxQ
24	R—K2	Kt—B5
25	R—K8ch(m)	RxR
26	BxKt	P—KR4
27	K—B2	R—QB
28	BxRch	KxB
29	R—K3	P—QKt4(n)
30	K—K2	R—B3
31	K—Q3	P—R5(o)
32	R—K2(p)	P—Kt4
33	R—Kt2(q)	R—Kt3
34	P—Q5(r)	K—K2
35	K—Q4	P—KKt5
36	K—B5(s)	R—Kt
37	K—Q4(t)	R—Kt3
38	P—KR3(u)	P—Kt6
39	P—R3	K—Q2
40	K—B5(v)	R—Kt
41	R—Kt4(w)	P—B4(x)
42	P—QR4(y)	P—QR3
43	K—Q4(z)	R—K

44	K—Q3(aa)	PxP(bb)
45	RxQRP	R—K8
46	RxQRP	R—KKt8(cc)
47	R—R2	K—Q3
48	P—B4	K—K4
49	R—K2ch	K—Q3

After 31 K—Q3

50	R—QB2	K—B4
51	R—Q2	R—KB8(dd)
52	K—K2	R—KKt8
53	K—K3	K—Q3
54	P—B5ch	KxP
55	P—Q6	R—K8ch
56	K—B4	R—K
57	P—Q7	R—Q
58	KxP	Resigns

After 41 R—Kt4

(a) This unusual move is based upon two ideas: First, the White Bishop, in case Black defends the gambit pawn with P—KKt4, can be played to KB3, which makes possible the development of Kt—K2, thereby preventing the eventual attack of P—Kt5; secondly, the counter move of P—Q4, if not made at once, is less forceful than in the ordinary Bishop's gambit, inasmuch as in this case the Bishop is not directly attacked. One consequence, among others, is the circumstance that Black, in answer to B—K2, cannot well play Kt—KB3, on account of P—K5, which, where the Bishop stands on QB4, would be met by P—Q4. But, for all that, this backward maneuver of the Bishop is not to be recommended, for the reason that it carries with it not the shadow of a threat, and it allows Black, in addition to the temporary pawn plus, the choice between several worth-while developing plans.

(b) The simplest reply and perhaps also the best. Black, to be sure, is not altogether successful in demonstrating these advantages, but the improvement introduced by Capablanca in the 19th round makes this method of play worthy of consideration. Fairly good also, although not quite sufficient to work out a distinct advantage for Black, is 3...Kt—K2 (Dr. Tartakower vs. Alekhine, 9th round). The most forceful reaction to the Bishop move which blocked his own Queen, however, seems to be 3... P—KB4, for instance: 4 PxP (4 P—K5, played in a sample game to be found in the Handbuch, cannot very well be considered on account of 4...P—Q3, etc.), Q—R5ch; 5 K—B, P—Q4, and if 6 B—R5ch, then K—Q, whereupon Black would stand decidedly better, inasmuch as it would be much easier for him than his adversary to dominate the KBP, in addition to which the open KB file would afford him a welcome avenue for a direct attack upon the King. Unfortunately, however, one must apparently wait a long time before this interesting defense will be played, inasmuch as the position arrived at by White, precisely through the methods adopted in New York, would scarcely induce anyone to risk in a serious contest this variation resurrected by Dr. Tartakower.

(c) After this move, White experiences no difficulty in completing his development satisfactorily, whereupon, because of the several open lines, he obtains a slightly preferable position. Correct is Capablanca's 6...B—Kt5ch, in order first of all to prevent White from castling.

(d) Otherwise White could attempt, through an eventual P—B5, to establish a Pawn superiority on the Queen's side.

(e) Now Black makes the best of a position which is not particularly favorable, in that he allows his opponent the two Bishops, obtaining in return strong points of support for his Knights, which will permit him to bring pressure to bear upon the center pawns. Notwithstanding that appearances are favorable to White, the positions in fact are almost even.

(f) Only logical. With the support of the Knight, the white QBP could have been advanced much more easily.

(g) Also after 17 P—B4, Kt—B3; 18 P—Q5, Kt—K5; 19 B—Kt4, KR—K, Black could have defended himself successfully.

(h) By this means the BP becomes paralyzed for a long time.

(i) The weakening of the diagonal, QR2 to KKt8, was not to be easily prevented, as the important move of Kt—B5, which could not be made at once on account of 19 BxKt, QxB; 20 QxP, could not be prepared in any other way.

(j) Provoking a further weakening of the black King's position, which however, can here be endured.

(k) Black really had no good reason to avoid the following drawing combination of the opponent, for, after B—QB, Black, through 21...Q—B3; 22 P—R4, P—QR3; 23 Q—B2, P—B4, followed eventually by R—KB2 and P—QKt4, would have fortified himself on white squares and, at the least, would have no inferiority.

(l) Better than 22...R—B2, whereupon White could have continued the attack with R—K3, etc.

(m) With this additional exchange of Rooks, White obtains a microscopic positional advantage in the Rook ending, as Black must lose a "tempo" for the protection of his KRP.

(n) The simplest way to draw. The counter-attack of 29...R—B5 would have been questionable because of the immediate advance of White's passed pawns, for instance: 30 P—Q5, R—R5; 31 R—K2, R—B5; 32 P—Q6, RxP; 33 R—K7ch, K—B; 34 RxP, R—Q6; 35 RxP, RxP; 36 P—QR4, R—Q7ch; 37 K—B3, R—R7; 38 P—R5, R—R6ch; 39 K—K4, R—R7; 40 P—R6, and the white pawns on the King's side are immune. Moreover, Black did not need as yet to calculate the outcome of the pawn ending, after 29...R—K; 30 RxR, KxR; 31 P—QR4, inasmuch as he could soon practically force it under much more favorable circumstances.

(o) Did Black indeed wish still to play for a win? A draw was assured to him by 31...R—K3, for instance: 32 RxR (if the Rook should leave the K file, then would follow simply R—K8, with strong counter-play), KxR; 33 K—K4, K—Q3, followed by K—B3—Q3, and White clearly cannot penetrate anywhere. The text-move, on the other hand, initiating a strong advance on the King's wing, leads to quite interesting complications, to be sure, but of rather doubtful issue for Black.

(p) In order to answer 32 R—K3 with 33 R—Kt2.

(q) The sacrifice of a pawn by 33 P—QR4, in order to obtain two connected passed pawns in the center, would have turned out unsatisfactory, for instance: 33...PxP; 34 P—B4, P—R6; 35 P—Q5, R—QR3; 36 R—R2, P—B4; 37 P—B5, R—R5; 38 K—B3, P—B5; 39 K—Kt3, R—R3; 40 K—Kt4, P—R6; 41 PxP, P—B6; 42 K—Kt5; (or P—B6, K—K2, etc.), R—KB3, and wins.

(r) The passed pawn, in connection with the penetrating march of the King, does not make at first a reassuring impression, but Black nevertheless is able barely to save himself.

(s) A cast into the water which, however, does no harm, inasmuch as White is able to bring about the identical position.

(t) The pawn ending, after 37 RxP, RxR; 38 KxR, would only lead to a draw, for instance: 38...P—B4; 39 K—B4, P—B5; 40 K—Q3, P—B6 (or P—Kt6; 41 PxP, P—B6; 42 K—K3, etc.); 41 K—K3, PxP; 42 K—B2, P—R6, etc. With the text-move, however, he threatens 38 P—B4.

(u) Hereupon Black's chance on the King's side becomes much more serious and the hoped for capture of the RP cannot be carried out. Much more promising, therefore, would have been 38 R—K2ch, K—Q2; 39 R—KB2! (R—R3; 40 K—B5), with the threat, by R—B4, of attacking the King's side pawns. This continuation would have refuted the insufficient defense initiated by Black with 31...P—R5.

(v) Neither should this attempt to win be any more successful. In reply to 40 R—Kt4, Black could have answered 40...R—R3, etc.

(w) Now 41 RxP would lead to a lost game after 41...RxR; 42 KxR, P—B4; 43 K—B4, P—B5; 44 K—Q3, P—B6, etc.

(x) An ingenious defense, which clearly shows the inadequacy of his opponent's plan to win. After 42 RxRP, Black would have had an easy draw with 42...R—Bch; 43 KxP, (if 43 K—Kt4, R—B5ch; 44 RxR, PxR; 45 KxP, P—B5, and wins), RxP, inasmuch as the white King is now separated from the QP.

(y) Thereby White at last wins a Pawn, permitting, however, the entrance of the hostile Rook into his camp; but he had nothing better.

(z) Threatening 44 P—B4.

(aa) Again the ending would have been lost for White after 44 PxP, R—K5ch; 45 K—Q3, RxR; 46 PxR, PxP, etc.

(bb) Of course not 44...R—K5, for, after 45 RxR, PxR; 46 KxP, PxP; 47 K—Q3, the King would be found to be within the zone of the passed Pawn.

(cc) A deplorable mistake, which deprives Black of the fruits of his excellent defense. With the simple 46...R—Q8ch, the game would have been drawn, for instance: I 47 K—B4, R—Q7; 48 K—B5, RxP; 49 R—R7ch, K—K; 50 K—Q6, R—K7, etc.; II 47 K—K3, RxQP; 48 R—KR6, R—K4ch; 49 K—B3, R—K5; 50 R—KB6, R—QB5. After the text-move, White connects his passed Pawns and then wins without difficulty.

(dd) If 51...R—QB8, White wins by means of 52 K—K3, K—Q3; 53 R—Q4, R—B7; 54 RxRP, RxP; 55 K—B3, R—Kt8; 56 R—Q4, etc.

SECOND ROUND

Four of the five games in this round were drawn. The only decisive result was that between Maroczy and Alekhine. The latter, employing the defense which has been named after him, scored his second victory in succession. Maroczy did not attempt to refute the Knight's early entrance, and, a few moves later, went astray.

Dr. Lasker and Capablanca discussed a very carefully conducted Ruy Lopez, a drawing position being reached in 30 moves.

Ed. Lasker was outplayed by Bogoljubow in a Philidor's defense. Bogoljubow gradually obtained a winning advantage, but, lacking precision on his fortieth move, gave Lasker the opportunity to evolve a clever combination which forced the draw.

Marshall gained the upper hand against Dr. Tartakower's Dutch defense, winning a Pawn. The Doctor, however, fought back valiantly to the end that Marshall, to escape worse consequences, felt constrained to yield a Pawn in turn. An even Rook and Pawn ending was the outcome.

Yates vs. Janowski was a Steinitz defense to the Ruy Lopez, in which Janowski had the better of it all along. By plucky play Yates managed to hold his own. Reti had the bye.

The score as between the White and Black pieces was 4½ to 5½ in favor of Black.

Game 6   SECOND ROUND—RUY LOPEZ

Dr. Lasker	Capablanca	23 R—K2	Kt—B3
White	Black	24 K—B2	R—K2
1 P—K4	P—K4	25 B—B3	P—QR4
2 Kt—KB3	Kt—QB3	26 R—Q5	P—QKt3
3 B—Kt5	P—Q3	27 P—QR4	R—K3
4 P—Q4	B—Q2	28 R—Q	QR—K
5 Kt—B3	Kt—B3	29 KR—Q2	K—K2
6 Castles(a)	PxP(b)	30 K—K3	K—Q2
7 KtxP	B—K2	Drawn	
8 P—QKt3(c)	KtxKt(d)		
9 QxKt	BxB	After 10...Kt—Q2	
10 KtxB	Kt—Q2(e)		
11 B—R3(f)	P—QR3		
12 Kt—B3	B—B3		
13 Q—K3	Castles		
14 QR—Q	BxKt(g)		
15 QxB	R—K		
16 KR—K(h)	R—QB		
17 Q—R3	Kt—K4		
18 B—Kt2	Q—Kt4		
19 O—Kt3(i)	QxQ		
20 RPxQ	P—KB3		
21 P—KB3	K—B2		
22 P—KKt4	P—KR3		

After 10...Kt—Q2

(a) 6 BxKt, BxB; 7 Q—Q3 can also be considered in order to keep in reserve the possibility of castling on the Queen's side after the practically forced 7...PxP (7... Kt—Q2; 8 B—Kt5!).

(b) Even now this same continuation (instead of the former popular 7 R—K) would give White a very promising attack. Therefore, Capablanca makes a successful attempt to revive the system of defense by Wolf against Maroczy at Monte Carlo in 1903.

(c) At this point, where White has not lost a tempo by R—K to force PxP (this position of the Rook also diminishes his chances of a direct K side attack), the fianchetto development of the QB seems very strong.

(d) Wolf's method of simplification, the point of which is disclosed by Black two moves later.

(e) By this move the intended B—Kt2 has not been completely hindered, yet has been made very difficult. The crisis of the opening has begun.

(f) Black can easily equalize matters after this move, which Maroczy also made in the game referred to. Even the alternative, 11 Q—B4, would be without danger for him, provided he did not play 11...Kt—B4; 12 P—K5, PxP (P—QR3; 13 PxP!); 13 B—R3, Kt—K3; 14 QR—Q, etc., but simply 11...P—QB3, with the continuation of 12 Kt—Q4 (Kt—B3), Castles, and White has no time to utilize the temporary weakness at Q6, in view of the threat to equalize matters with 13...P—Q4; 14 PxP, Kt—Kt3 (or also B—B3). The game is not without theoretical interest.

(g) In the quoted game, Maroczy vs. Wolf, 14...Kt—Kt3 occurred here, whereupon White obtained a very superior game through 15 P—KB4. After this move, he has no more serious chances of attack.

(h) If here, or on the next move, B—Kt2, then Q—Kt4!, etc.

(i) The exchange of Queens, which assures the draw for Black, is hard to prevent. 19 R—K3 would be followed by 19...Q—Kt5, etc.

Game 7   SECOND ROUND—ALEKHINE'S DEFENSE

Maroczy	Alekhine
White	Black
1 P—K4	Kt—KB3
2 P—Q3(a)	P—K4
3 P—KB4(b)	Kt—B3
4 Kt—KB3(c)	P—Q4(d)
5 PxQP	KtxP
6 PxP	QB—Kt5
7 B—K2(e)	BxKt
8 BxB	Q—R5ch
9 K—B(f)	Castles
10 Kt—B3	B—B4(g)
11 Kt—K4	Kt—K6ch
12 BxKt	BxB
13 Q—K	Q—R3
14 Kt—Kt3(h)	Kt—Q5(i)
15 Q—Kt4	P—QB3
16 Q—R4	K—Kt
17 R—Q	KR—K
18 P—R4(j)	Q—B5
19 R—R3	P—QKt4(k)
20 Kt—R5	PxQ
21 KtxQ	BxKt
22 P—B3	KtxB
23 RxKt	BxP
24 RxP	R—KB
Resigns	

After 14 Kt—Kt3

(a) Herewith without more ado White foregoes the attempt to refute the move of the Knight, for, aside from 2...P—K4, which yields a satisfactory game, Black, by means of 2...P—QB4 might bring about a species of Sicilian defense, with the harmless restrictive move of P—Q3 on the part of White.

(b) This and not 3 Kt—KB3, whereupon, after 3...Kt—B3, there is not even a semblance of an advantage for White, appears to us as the only logical continuation in the spirit of old Philidor. Thereafter it behooves Black to fight very strenuously in order not to get the worst of it, and for that reason this game is of theoretical interest.

(c) White evidently gets nothing from 4 PxP, KtxP; 5 P—Q4, Kt—Kt3; 6 P—K5, Kt—K5, followed by P—Q4, etc. Of interest is the suggestion of Dr. Lasker; 4 PxP, KtxP; 5 Kt—KB3, KtxKtch; 6 PxKt, but it appears that Black in this case also has the power of fighting off successfully his adversary's mobile Pawn force in the center with

6...Kt—R4; 7 B—K3, B—Q3, etc. With his text-move White hopes to force the cramping of Black's KB through P—Q3.

(d) This bold Pawn sacrifice assures Black at least an even game. White can do no better than to accept it, because the continuation of 5 PxKP, QPxKP; 6 PxKt, PxKt; 7 QxP, Kt—Q5!; 8 Q—K4ch, B—K3 would be clearly unfavorable for him.

(e) Or 7 P—QB3, KtxP; 8 Q—K2, B—Q3; 9 P—Q4, BxKt; 10 PxB, Q—R5ch; 11 K—Q, Castles QR; 12 PxKt, KR—K, with a penetrating attack.

(f) Neglecting to castle is a blunder with serious consequences, all the more so as White presents his opponent with an additional tempo. In order would have been 9 P—Kt3, Q—Q5; 10 Q—K2, Castles QR; 11 P—B3, QxKP; 12 Castles, QxQ; 13 BxQ, B—K2! and B—B3, etc., with practically an even game.

(g) Forcing the exchange of the QB, whereupon the black squares in the white camp become lamentably weak.

(h) Likewise, after 14 Kt—B2, KtxKP; 15 Kt—Kt4, KtxKt; 16 BxKtch, K—Kt, etc., White could scarcely have maintained a valid game for long, on account of the overpowering Bishop on K6.

(i) Decisive. White's subsequent attack with the Queen, which merely hastens his downfall, is dictated by despair, since pacifity on his part would likewise have left him without hope. For instance, 15 Q—Q, KR—K; 16 P—B3, KtxB; 17 QxKt, RxQP; 18 Q—B5ch, R—Q2; 19 R—Q, Q—R3ch; 20 Kt—K2, Q—K3; 21 QxQ, RxQ, with a winning ending.

(j) Or 18 P—B3, KtxB; 19 PxKt, RxKP, etc., winning easily.

(k) Winning a piece (20 Q—Kt4, P—QR4, followed by KtxB, etc.).

Game 8   SECOND ROUND—DUTCH DEFENSE

Marshall	Tartakower		
White	Black	15 R—R3	Q—K2
		16 Q—R5	P—Kt3(j)
1 P—Q4	P—K3	17 Q—K2(k)	R—B2
2 P—QB4(a)	P—KB4	18 Kt—Kt5(l)	R—Kt2
3 Kt—QB3	Kt—KB3	19 QKt—B3(m)	Q—Kt5
4 B—Kt5(b)	B—K2	20 R—Kt(n)	P—B4
5 P—K3	Castles	21 Q—Q3	PxP
6 B—Q3	P—QKt3	22 KtxQP(o)	R—QB
7 Kt—B3	B—Kt2	23 P—K4(p)	KtxKt
8 Castles	Kt—K5(c)	24 QxKt	P—Q4(q)
9 BxB	QxB(d)		
10 BxKt	PxB	After 24 QxKt	
11 Kt—Q2	Q—R5(e)		

After 11...Q—R5

12 QKtxP(f)	Kt—B3(g)
13 P—B4(h)	Kt—K2
14 R—B3(i)	Kt—B4

25 P—R3	Q—B
26 KPxP	PxP
27 PxP	R—Q
28 Kt—K4	R—KB2(r)
29 P—Q6	RxBP

30	Q—B4ch	Q—B2		34	R—K2	R—Q6
31	QxQch(s)	RxQ		35	R—KB	K—Kt2
32	R—-K3(t)	BxKt		36	R—QB2	KR—Q2
33	RxB	RxP		37	P—R3	Drawn

(a) After this move, switching into the Dutch defense is less risky for Black than after 2 Kt—KB3, because he gets the chance sooner to develop and exchange his KB (on Kt5), which in many variations of this opening remains inactive. Likewise White's next moves are not likely to profit him much.

(b) This pinning, for instance, lacks virility and could be parried best by Black with 4...B—Kt5. Strange to relate, Dr. Tartakower does not avail himself of this natural move either here or in his game against Capablanca in the sixth round.

(c) A mistake which will soon cost a Pawn. Correct would have been 8...Q—K, as played by Dr. Tartakower against Capablanca.

(d) After 9...KtxKt; 10 BxQ, KtxQ; 11 BxBP, KtxKtP; 12 B—K2, the black Knight would be in trouble.

(e) 11...P—Q4; 12 PxP, PxP; 13 Q—Kt3, Q—B2; 14 P—B3 would have involved Black in even worse consequences.

(f) It is important for White to win the Pawn without being compelled to resort to the weakening P—KKt3. After 12 P—KKt3, Q—R6; 13 QKtxP, Kt—B3—K2—B4, Black would have obtained some compensation on account of the weakness of the adversary's white squares, which, after the continuation in the text, cannot be noticed.

(g) After 12...BxKt; 13 P—KKt3 (now no longer risky, because Black's Bishop will disappear), R—B3; 14 P—B4, etc., Black's position would be still more hopeless than in the actual game.

(h) In order to transform the defensive position on the KB file into one of attack. The weakness of White's Pawn structure in the center is, of course, easily balanced by his surplus of material.

(i) This expedition with the Rook, which has been criticized by most of the commentators, is not exactly necessary to be sure (simpler would have been 14 Kt—KB3, Q—R4; 15 Kt—QB3, followed eventually by Kt—K5 or Q—Q2, P—K4, etc.), but fulfills the definite purpose of provoking the weakening P—KKt3—a luxury White could well afford. The real blunders, through which the victory is eventually trifled away, follow presently.

(j) 16...P—R3 would have invited an attack through P—Kt4—Kt5.

(k) Threatening to force a further deterioration of Black's Pawn structure through 18 Kt—Kt5.

(l) An unfortunate maneuver of which Black energetically takes advantage. With 18 Kt—QB3 (P—KKt4; 19 PxP, QxP; 20 Kt—KB3 and P—K4, or 18...Q—QKt5; 19 R—Kt and P—QR3), followed by Kt—B3 and later on by P—K4, White could have turned his advantage to account without much difficulty.

(m) Here 19 Q—Q3, threatening P—K4, was imperative. Even 19 P—QR3, to prevent the coming troublesome sortie of the Queen, would have been preferable to the text-move.

(n) If 20 P—K4, QxKtP! (21 R—Kt, KtxQP).

(o) More obvious and likewise better would have been 22 PxP, followed by P—QKt3 and Kt—K4, still holding out excellent chances of winning.

(p) Only after this new blunder, permitting complete liquidation of the respective Pawn formations in the center, may the strength of the black Bishop as opposed to the Knight be manifested at last. The last chance was 23 P—QKt3, followed perhaps by Kt—K4.

(q) The sacrifice of the second Pawn is quite correct. It will not take long before White, having all of his forces decentralized, will be forced to relinquish his preponderance and, moreover, will be glad to escape with a whole skin. The second part of this game has been handled by Dr. Tartakower very judiciously.

(r) Parrying the only threat of his opponent and attacking at the same time.

(s) White clearly has no choice.

(t) 32 Kt—Kt5, R—B4!; 33 KtxP, RxQP, etc., might even have ended disastrously for White.

Game 9   SECOND ROUND—PHILIDOR'S DEFENSE

	Ed. Lasker	Bogoljubow
	White	Black
1	P—K4	P—K4
2	Kt—KB3	P—Q3
3	P—Q4	Kt—KB3
4	Kt—B3	QKt—Q2
5	B—QB4	B—K2
6	Castles(a)	Castles
7	B—KKt5(b)	P—B3
8	B—Kt3(c)	P—KR3
9	B—KR4	R—K
10	Q—Q3(d)	Kt—R4
11	Q—B4(e)	R—B
12	BxB(f)	QxB
13	Kt—K2(g)	P—R4(h)
14	Q—B3(i)	P—R5(j)
15	B—B4	P—QKt4
16	B—Q3	B—Kt2(k)
17	PxP	PxP
18	QR—Q	KR—K(l)
19	Kt—Kt3	KtxKt(m)
20	RPxKt(n)	Kt—B3
21	Kt—R4(o)	P—Kt3
22	Q—Q2	K—Kt2
23	Q—K3(p)	Kt—Kt5
24	Q—Q2(q)	Q—B4
25	B—K2	Kt—B3
26	B—Q3	QR—Q
27	Q—K2	B—B
28	K—R	B—Kt5
29	P—KB3(r)	B—K3
30	P—R3	R—K2
31	QR—K(s)	Q—Q5(t)
32	Q—B2	QxKtP
33	Q—B5	R—B2
34	R—QKt	Q—Q5
35	RxP(u)	P—Kt4
36	Kt—B5ch	BxKt
37	PxB	Kt—R4(v)
38	R—K	KtxPch
39	K—R2	Q—R5ch
40	K—Kt	P—B3(w)

After 31 QR—K

41	RxP(x)	PxR(y)
42	QxPch	K—Kt
43	R—Kt4(z)	Q—R8ch
44	K—B2	R—KB2(aa)
45	R—Kt8(bb)	RxR
46	QxRch	K—Kt2(cc)
47	Q—K5ch	K—B
48	Q—Kt8ch(dd)	K—Kt2
49	Q—K5ch	K—B
50	Q—Kt8ch	K—Kt2
51	Q—K5ch	Drawn

After 40...P—B3

(a) As is well known, the sacrifice of the Bishop by 6 BxPch is incorrect on account of 6...KxB; 7 Kt—Kt5ch, K—Kt; 8 Kt—K6, Q—K; 9 KtxBP, Q—Kt3; 10 KtxR, QxKtP; 11 KR—B, KPxP; 12 QxP, Kt—K4, etc. If, however, 6 PxP (in order to bring about the foregoing sacrifice, after 6...PxP?), Black obtains a wholly satisfactory game through 6...KtxKP, etc.

(b) This development of the Bishop for the most part facilitates an exchange for Black. The most telling line of play here would be 7 Q—K2, P—QB3; 8 P—QR4 (Alekhine vs. Marco, Stockholm, 1912, and Bogoljubow vs. Niemzowitsch, Stockholm, 1920).

(c) Likewise here 8 P—QR4 was to have been preferred in order to prevent P—QKt4 once for all.

(d) White plays the opening incorrectly. In order would have been 10 B—Kt3 for the purpose of forcing Black to clear the center, inasmuch as neither 10...Kt—R4 (on account of 11 KtxP, KtxB; 12 KtxBP) nor 10 ...B—B (on account of 11 PxP, PxP; 12 KtxP) would be of any avail. If 10...PxP; 11 KtxP, Kt—B4, White could have responded with 12 B—B4 with quite a good game. After the text-move, Black at once seizes the initiative.

(e) Forcing the following protective move, for if 11...P—Q4; 12 PxP, Kt—Kt3 (or BxB; 13 PxBP); 13 BxB, RxB; 14 Q—B5, etc., would follow with advantage. On the other hand, the advantages, which Black gains from the subsequently forced exchange, are much more important than this temporary success.

(f) If 12 B—Kt3, Black need not have been in a hurry with KtxB, but might have continued with B—B3 and exchanged the Bishop when it suited him best.

(g) Otherwise the entrance of the Knight at B5 would have become really unpleasant. Already the White pieces are beginning to stand around a bit awkwardly.

(h) A good move, the success of which probably surpasses the hopes of Black. The intention most likely, after the obvious reply of 14 P—QB3, was to lead into the variation, 14...PxP; 15 QxP, Kt—K4, which, on acount of the weakening of the square, Q6, and the threat to drive away the Bishop from the important diagonal with P—R5, would have gained still more ground. But that an advance along the whole line would be granted him could hardly have been expected by him.

(i) Quite a peculiar idea. The Bishop is being conducted with the loss of a tempo to Q3, where for a long time it will stand practically stalemated, and thereby blocks the Queen's file, the eventual opening of which clearly cannot be avoided. Likewise 14 P—QR4 was not to have been recommended, on account of 14...PxP; 15 QxP, Kt—B4, etc.; but 14 P—QB3 was certainly playable.

(j) Black, of course, declines to enter the transparent pitfall of 14...PxP; 15 QKtxP, QxP; 16 KR—K, Q—B5 (or Kt5 or Kt3); 17 Kt—K6, etc.

(k) Threatening eventually P—QB4 (PxP, KtxP, or PxKP, P—B5, etc.) and thereby causes the opponent to dissolve the unpleasant situation in the center.

(l) With the idea of planting the Knight on KB5 by way of B square and Kt3.

(m) The White Knight had to be kept from B5. Black must forego now the expectations with regard to the square, B5, but obtains full compensation as the strategetical consequence of the doubling of White's Pawns on the strong square, Kt5, the possession of which could be challenged only at the expense of additional weakness in the King's position.

(n) 20 BPxP would only have led to the isolation of the KP, without promise of any advantage.

(o) The Knight will have to remain inactive on this square for a long time. However, it would have had little future elsewhere.

(p) White has now reached a deadlock and moves hither and thither without any definite plan. Meanwhile Black strengthens his position at every move and it does not take very long before he has a positive win.

(q) If 25 Q—Kt6, R—R3, etc.

(r) If 29 Kt—B2, Black could have obtained a decisive advantage either by increasing the pressure in the center (doubling the Rooks on the Queen's file, followed by Kt—Q2, B—K3, etc.) or by means of a direct attack against the King with P—KR4 and R—KR, followed eventually by P—KR5, etc.

(s) In order to be able to play Q—B2, which at this stage would have been answered with 31...QxQ; 32 RxQ, P—B4, etc. But from now on the game takes a decisive turn.

(t) This move, so near at hand, and which at first blush promised the win of a Pawn (R—QKt, B—R7), had in fact to be calculated very closely, inasmuch as White gets some counter play through the subsequent sortie of the Queen.

(u) Seemingly White has managed fairly well to emerge from the affair, since the simple continuation of 35...PxR; 36 QxR, P—Kt5; 37 PxP, P—R6 (or R (Q)—Q2; 38 Q—B5); 38 Q—QR5, P—R7; 39 P—Kt5, would not have been quite convincing. The peculiar position of the White Rook, however, affords Bogoljubow an opportunity for a surprising diversion on the King's wing, which should yield him a material advantage.

(v) This is the point. White clearly has still no time to exchange Queens and 38 K—R2 would be useless on account of 38...KtxP, etc.

(w) Here, however, he falters when almost near the goal and in so doing exposes himself to the danger of losing. With 40...R—Q4; 41 Q—Kt6, PxR; 42 QxR,* Q—Q5ch (not KtxBP at once, on account of 43 R—K4); 43 K—R2, KtxBP; 44 R—K4 (if 44 BxKt mate follows in four moves), Q—B4, the game, thanks to two extra Pawns, would have been easily won for Black.

* [Alekhine missed 42 P—B6ch and Q mates.—Note by Ed. Lasker, 1961.]

(x) A pretty sacrifice, which suddenly gives White the advantage. The seemingly stronger move of 41 R—Kt4 (R—Q5; 42 RxKP) would have allowed Black an immediate draw through 41 P—K5, for instance, I.—42 BxP, Kt—K7ch; 43 K—B. Kt—Kt6ch, with perpetual check; II.—42 PxKP. Q—R8ch; 43 K—B2, Q—R5, and White has nothing better than to play again 44 K—Kt, etc.

(y) The acceptance of the sacrifice should have led to loss. The lesser evil would have been 41...Q—Q5ch; 42 QxQ, RxQ; 43 R—QB5, Kt—R4; 44 R—Kt6, Kt—B5, with a playable ending. Black probably still had visions of victory.

(z) Of course not 43 QxR, on account of 43...Q—Q5ch, etc.

(aa) Neither could 44 R(B2)—Q2 have altered the situation to any extent.

(bb) The exchange of Rooks leads to a draw. White, on the other hand, could have obtained a winning position with the simple 45 KxKt (threatening RxP or even K—B2, followed by B—B4), as the black Rooks would have been found to be inadequate for the protection of the exposed position of the King. The finish of the game was very exciting.

(cc) Not 46...R—B, on account of 47 B—B4ch, K—Kt2; 48 P—B6ch and wins.

(dd) After 48 P—B6, R—Q2; 49 Q—K6 (if Q—Kt8ch, the King approaches the KBP, captures it and then obtains freedom), Black forces the draw through 49...Q—QB8.

Game 10   SECOND ROUND—RUY LOPEZ

Yates	Janowski
White	Black

	Yates (White)	Janowski (Black)
1	P—K4	P—K4
2	Kt—KB3	Kt—QB3
3	B—Kt5	P—QR3
4	B—R4	Kt—B3
5	Castles	P—Q3(a)
6	R—K(b)	P—QKt4
7	B—Kt3	QKt—R4(c)
8	P—Q4	KtxB
9	RPxKt	B—Kt2(d)
10	PxP(e)	KtxP
11	Kt—B3(f)	P—Q4(g)
12	Kt—Q4(h)	Q—Q2
13	P—K6(i)	PxP
14	Q—Kt4	Castles(j)
15	QxKP	B—Kt5(k)

16	KtxKt	PxKt(l)
17	P—QB3	B—B4
18	B—K3	KR—K
19	QxQch	RxQ
20	P—QKt4	B—B
21	Kt—Kt3(m)	R—Q6
22	B—B5(n)	BxB
23	KtxB(o)	R—Q7(p)
24	R—K3(q)	R—B
25	R—KB	RxKtP
26	KtxKP	BxKt
27	RxB(r)	R—B7
28	R—K3	R—B3
29	P—R4(s)	K—Q2
30	P—R5	R—Q7(t)
31	P—KB4(u)	P—Kt3
32	P—R6(v)	R—K3
33	R(B)—K	RxR
34	RxR	P—B4(w)
35	R—K(x)	PxP(y)
36	PxP	R—Q5
37	R—R	RxKtP
38	RxP	RxP
39	R—R7ch	K—B3
40	RxP	R—KR5
41	K—B2	P—Kt5
42	R—R8	P—Kt6
43	R—QKt8	RxP
44	RxP	K—Q3
45	R—K3	R—R4
46	K—Kt3	Drawn

After 15...B—Kt5

(a) This defense has been preferred of late, and especially by Rubinstein, and Janowski is also of the opinion that it gives Black an even game. At any rate, the variation adopted in this game is quite satisfactory to Black.

(b) Permitting the exchange of the important KB. The following moves ought to come into consideration here. I.—6 BxKtch, PxB; 7 P—Q4, with which Black, with

7...Kt—Q2, could lead up to a variation of the Tschigorin defense. II.—6 P—Q4,
P—QKt4, whereupon, if he does not wish to bring about a position not unfavorable for
Black with 7 PxP, PxP; 8 QxQch, KxQ; 9...B—Q3, to be followed by Kt—Q2, he could
select the hitherto insufficiently examined gambit variation of 7 B—Kt3, KtxQP; 8 KtxKt,
PxKt; 9 P—QB3, PxP; 10 KtxBP, etc., in which case, in view of his better development
and the weakness of Black's Queen's wing which cannot readily be dissolved, White would
have sufficient compensation for the pawn sacrificed. At any rate, Yates obtained an
advantage, thanks to this treatment, in two games against Rubinstein (London, 1922, and
Carlsbad, 1923).

(c) This, to our mind, is more consistent, than 7...B—Kt5, as attempted by
Janowski against Dr. Lasker. In any event, this continuation allows White a forced draw,
but more than that he could not achieve.

(d) In reply to the immediate 9...Kt—Q2, White, through 10 PxP, KtxP (or
PxP; 11 Q—Q5); 11 Kt—Q4, etc., obtains the advantage.

(e) If 10 Kt—B3 Black defends his center with 10...Kt—Q2, thereby surmounting
the worst. Likewise 10 B—Kt5 (Dr. Lasker vs. Rubinstein, Maehrisch-Ostrau, 1923) is
entirely without danger for Black, on account of the simple rejoinder, 10...P—R3.

(f) Now White will still experience some difficulties in establishing equality. A
forced draw would result from 11 PxP, BxP; 12 Q—Q4, for instance: 12...Q—K2;
13 Kt—B3, P—KB4; 14 B—Kt5, Q—Q2; 15 KtxKt, PxKt; 16 RxKPch, BxR; 17 QxBch,
K-B2; 18 R—K, QR—K; 19 Q—Q5ch, K—B; 20 R—K5, RxR; 21 KtxR, Q—K;
22 Q—B3ch, K—Kt; 23 Q—Q5, with perpetual check. (Aurbach vs. Alekhine, Paris,
Oct. 1922).

(g) Now Black has a strongly posted Knight and two Bishops so that, in case
he should be enabled to find safety for his King by castling on the King's side, he would
have a clear advantage.

(h) Making difficult the development of Black's KB, on account of the threats of
Kt—B5 or Q—Kt4. Hence, the next move of Black's Queen, which challenges the
adversary for the possession of those squares.

(i) The only possibility of parrying the threats of 13...P—QB4 or 13...B—B4,
followed by Castling. The sacrifice of the Pawn is only temporary.

(j) Insufficient would have been 14...K—B2; 15 Kt—B3, Kt—B3; 16 Kt—Kt5ch,
K—Kt; 17 QxPch, QxQ; 18 KtxQ, followed by B—B4.

(k) Black underrates the ingenious evasion at the disposal of White. Otherwise
very likely he would have chosen the more promising 15...P—B4. For instance, 16
QxQch, RxQ; 17 KtxKt, QPxKt; 18 Kt—B5, P—Kt3; 19 Kt—Kt3 (K3), B—Kt2, and the
two Bishops become a mighty power.

(l) Or 16...BxR; 17 Kt—B5, QxQ; 18 KKtxQ, B—Kt5 (otherwise 19 P—QB3);
19 KtxR (not 19 KtxB, on account of 19...QR—K, etc.), BxKt; 20 Kt—K6 (better than
20 KtxB), B—Kt3; 21 B—K3, etc., with ready equalization.

(m) Now White has become too strong on the black squares so that Black can no
longer prevent the exchange of one of his Bishops.

(n) In the unjustified hope of being able still to play for a win. Otherwise 22
Kt—B5 would at once have forced the draw with Bishops commanding squares of opposite colors.

(o) Likewise the continuation of 23 PxB, P—K6; 24 P—B3, R—K4 would have
been favorable for Black.

(p) This posting of the Rook on the seventh rank will make matters very uncomfortable for White for a while. First of all, 24...P—K6 is threatened.

(q) In order to be able to meet 24...RxKtP with 25 P—B3.

(r) The Rook ending is somewhat more favorable for Black, but nevertheless
should yield a draw for White.

(s) This advance of the Pawn on the flank obtains for White good prospects on
the King's side. The threat of 29...R—B3, for instance, could now be adequately parried
only with 30 P—R5, QRxQBP; 31 R—K7, etc.

(t) Or 30...R—B3; 31 R—Qch, followed by R—K7, etc.

(u) Threatening, by means of 32 P—B5, to fix the Pawn on Kt2 and thereby force
Black's pieces into a defensive position.

(v) Through the establishment of this advance post, the threats of danger on the
Queen's side are as good as neutralized.

(w) A good move, which, however, looks more dangerous than it actually is, for
Black, because of the weakness of QR3 and KR2, is not in position to obtain two connected passed Pawns. After White's next move, this becomes clear at once.

(x) Of course not 35 PxP, on account of 35...P—R4, etc.

(y) Likewise 35...P—B5; 36 R—K3, followed by K—R2—Kt3, would have been
futile, so far as winning was concerned.

THIRD ROUND

Somewhat more decisive play marked this round, only two of the games being drawn. Dr. Lasker, after meeting his chief rival in his first game, was called upon to face the eventual third prize winner in his second. The opening was a Queen's Gambit declined, in which Dr. Lasker, playing black, made admirable use of his two Bishops. Timing his moves perfectly, he completely demolished the weakened position of the white King.

Capablanca vs. Ed. Lasker was another Queen's Gambit declined. Presently it seemed to the spectators that Lasker's Queen was getting into hot water, but careful examination fails to reveal that there was any way in which a tangible advantage could have been extracted from the situation. After an exchange of pieces, a symmetrical position was reached and a draw agreed upon.

Bogoljubow outplayed Marshall in a Queen's Gambit declined, winning a Pawn and getting the better position. By means of pretty and energetic simplification he forced the American to the wall.

Maroczy had the worst of it in his game with Reti, who adopted his own opening. A hasty move of his, however, enabled the Hungarian to turn the tables on the King's side. Reti found the only defense, but could not prevent a perpetual check.

Dr. Tartakower, with the move, again pinned his faith to the King's Gambit and won a Pawn right after the opening. Nevertheless, it was problematical even up to the end whether or not he could turn his advantage to account. This he accomplished in a manner that made it a good end-game study. Dr. Tartakower assumed the lead with 2½ points out of 3. The honors between White and Black were even—each 7½.

Game 11   THIRD ROUND—QUEEN'S GAMBIT DECLINED

	Alekhine White	Dr. Lasker Black			
			23	Kt—Kt2	B—B2
			24	KR—K	P—KR4
			25	P—KR3(l)	Kt—R2
1	P—Q4	P—Q4	26	RxRch	RxR
2	P—QB4	P—K3	27	R—K	R—Kt
3	Kt—KB3	Kt—KB3	28	Q—B	Kt—Kt4
4	Kt—B3	QKt—Q2	29	Kt—K5(m)	PxKt
5	PxP(a)	PxP	30	QxKt	P—K5
6	B—B4(b)	P—B3	31	P—B6	P—Kt3(n)
7	P—K3(c)	Kt—R4			
8	B—Q3(d)	KtxB			
9	PxKt	B—Q3			
10	P—KKt3(e)	Castles			
11	Castles	R—K			
12	Q—B2	Kt—B			
13	Kt—Q(f)	P—B3			
14	Kt—K3	B—K3			
15	Kt—R4(g)	B—QB2(h)			
16	P—QKt4	B—Kt3			
17	Kt—B3	B—KB2			
18	P—Kt5(i)	B—KR4			
19	P—Kt4	B—KB2			
20	PxP	R—B			
21	Q—Kt2	PxP			
22	P—B5(j)	Q—Q3(k)			

After 17...B—KB2

32 P—B4	RPxP(o)	35 Kt—R4	QxBF
33 B—K2(p)	PxP	36 QxQ	BxQ
34 B—R5	R—Kt7	Resigns	

(a) The best move here is 5 B—Kt5, for White has the option of exchanging during the latter phase of the game when the conditions are more favorable.

(b) Here, too, the pinning move of 6 B—Kt5 is more commendable. Now Black can obtain equalization in several ways.

(c) Should White play 7 P—KR3 in order to keep his Bishop, then the move introduced by H. Wolf (Toeplitz-Schoenau, 1922). namely 7...B—K2; 8 P—K3, Kt—K5, followed by P.—KB4, can be made good use of. Now Black compels an exchange favorable to him, even though at the expense of his development.

(d) Of three possibilities undoubtedly the least favorable. Simpler would have been 8 B—Kt3, which, however, might have been modified still more by means of 8 B—K5 and, if then 8...P—B3, then 9 B—Kt3, etc. The first player conducts this game in a vacillating and inconsistent manner.

(e) Here, for example, he ignores his original intention of playing 10 Kt—K5, on account of the hostile reply of 10...Q—R5, which would have forced 11 P—KKt3. Nevertheless, after 11...Q—R6; 12 Q—B2, etc. the strong position of his Knight would in any event have given some compensation for the weakness of his white squares.

(f) Likewise the move of 13 Kt—Kt5, suggested by several, would have yielded nothing, for instance: 13...P—KKt3; 14 KR—K, P—B3; 15 Kt—B3, B—KKt5; 16 RxR, QxR; 17 R—K, Q—Q2, etc. Better would have been the simple 13 KR—K.

(g) Loss of time! From now on White loses quickly because at any cost he strives for an attack in utter disregard of his inferior development. Had he been content to remain more passive (for instance: KR—Q and, if 15...B—KB2, then 16 B—B5, etc.), Black would have found it by no means easy to formulate an attack.

(h) Even more precise would have been perhaps 15...P—QR4.

(i) The decisive mistake. Doubtless Black had the better game, but, with 18 B—B5, in order to be able to parry B—R4 with B—Kt4, the game would still have been held. After the text-move, Black forces an additional breach in the King's wing and thereafter wins quite easily.

(j) Otherwise the invasion of the Knight via K3 becomes decisive.

(k) Threatening 23...Q—B5.

(l) Through a double Pawn sacrifice: 25 P—Kt5, PxP; 26 Kt—K5, Kt—Q2; 27 P—B4, PxP; 28 Kt—B3, the ensuing attack with its mating objective could have been staved off temporarily. That, of course, would have been but a poor consolation.

(m) Or 29 KtxKt, Q—R7ch; 30 K—B, PxKt; 31 Kt—K3, QxRPch; 32 K—K2, PxP, etc.

(n) Likewise after 31...QxP, White would have had to give in very soon. Only 31...Q—R7ch could not have been played by Black, for instance: 32 K—B, Q—R8ch; 33 K—K2, PxBch; 34 KxP, QxPch; 35 Kt—K3, K—B; 36 QxPch, K—K; 37 K—B2, etc.

(o) Dr. Lasker selects the shortest road to victory. The move 32...PxP, e. p.; 33 R—K5, or 32...PxB; 33 PxP, etc., would not have been immediately decisive.

(p) Or 33 PxP, PxB, etc.

Game 12   THIRD ROUND—QUEEN'S PAWN OPENING

Bogoljubow	Marshall		
White	Black	13 QKt—B3(e)	P—KR3(f)
1 Kt—KB3	P—Q4	14 P—KKt4(g)	KtxKt
2 P—Q4	P—K3(a)	15 KtxKt	B—B3
3 B—B4(b)	B—Q3	16 Q—K2	Kt—K5
4 P—K3	BxB	17 QR—Q(h)	QR—B
5 PxB	P—QB4(c)	18 K—Kt2(i)	B—R5
6 PxP	Q—R4ch	19 QR—QB(j)	P--KB3(k)
7 P—QB3	QxBP	20 KKt—B3	B—B3
8 B—Q3	KKt—B3	21 Kt—Q4	Q—Q3
9 Castles	Castles	22 P—B3	Kt—B4
10 QKt—Q2	Kt—-B3	23 B—Kt(l)	B—Q2
11 Kt—K5(d)	R—Q	24 Q—QB2	P—B4(m)
12 R—K	B—Q2		

After 22...Kt—B4

25	PxP	PxP
26	KtxP	Q—Kt3ch
27	Kt—Kt3(n)	QxQ
28	BxQ	Kt—K3
29	Kt—K2	R—B
30	P—B5	Kt—Q
31	Kt—Q4	Kt—B3
32	B—Kt3	BxP(o)
33	BxPch	K—R
34	BxKt	PxB
35	R—K5	B—Q2
36	P—Kt4(p)	R—B3
37	QR—K	K—R2
38	R—QR5	R—QB2
39	R—QB5(q)	P—R3
40	P—QR4	R—QB

41	P—R4	R—Kt3ch
42	K—R2(r)	R—KB(s)
43	P—KR5	R—Q3
44	R—K7	K—Kt
45	R—R5	R—R
46	R—K4	K—B2
47	R—K2(t)	P—Kt3
48	PxPch	RxP
49	R(R5)—K5	R—Q
50	R—K7ch	K—B(u)

After 50...K—B

51	R(K7)—K6(v)	K—B2(w)
52	KtxP	BxKt
53	RxR	KxR
54	R—K6ch	K—Kt4
55	RxB	P—QR4
56	K—Kt3	Resigns

(a) There is no need here to block the Bishop. Preferable, therefore, is 2...P—QB4 or Kt—KB3.

(b) This interesting and not easily handled variation leads to complicated play in the center with the chances rather favorable to White, chiefly on account of the strength of his black squares. Otherwise, turning it into the regular Queen's Gambit declined is also to be considered.

(c) Not logical. 5...Q—Q3 would have necessitated first the guarding of KB4 (6 Q—Q2 or P—KKt3) and, upon 6...P—QB4, White, sooner or later, would have had to play the move of P—B3, which is part and parcel of this system. Such inaccuracies in any opening, which in themselves are unfavorable, are usually sufficient to compromise the game seriously.

(d) White fortunately has avoided the necessity of playing P—KKt3 and in that way has gained an important "tempo" in development. The manner in which Bogoljubow now proceeds to make the most of his advantage is very instructive.

(e) Black's position is already somewhat uncomfortable. White now threatens 14 Kt—Kt5, B—K; 15 P—B5, with the isolation of the QP.

(f) 13...P—KKt3 also had its drawbacks, for instance: 14 Kt—Kt5, R—KB; 15 Q—B3, threatening Q—R3, etc.

(g) Played very energetically. Against this attack Marshall seeks his salvation at the sixteenth move through an atoning sacrifice, the acceptance of which would actually have saved him.

(h) If, by any chance, 17 KtxB, QxKt; 18 BxKt, PxB; 19 QxP, R—Q7 (not 19...QxQ; 20 RxQ, R—Q7; 21 R—QKt4), with adequate compensation.

(i) And now the Rook ending could not have been won after 18 KtxB, QxKt; 19 BxKt, PxB; 20 RxRch, RxR; 21 QxP, R—Q7, etc. With the text-move, White prepares to expel the Knight from K4, thereafter to continue with his attack.

(j) 19 Threatening also 20 P—B4.

(k) Weakening thereby the square, K3, and the diagonal from Kt to R7, which, however, could hardly be longer avoided.

(l) The simple retreat is decisive owing to its two-fold threat of 24 P—Kt4, followed by KtxP, and 24 Q—B2. The following Pawn sacrifice on the part of Black enables him merely to enter upon an almost hopeless ending, which, nevertheless, he defends for fully 30 moves with praiseworthy pertinacity.

(m) Clearly, the Queen must not be admitted to R7.

(n) 27 K—B2 was also strong enough; but the perpetual ("ewige") square, Q4, for this Knight is beckoning to White.

(o) Otherwise still another Pawn would be lost.

(p) Quite apart from the advantage in material, White's position remains far superior. The rest of the end-game is readily intelligible, but gains additional interest through a neat finale on the part of White.

(q) Threatening 40 P—Kt5.

(r) Simpler would have been 42 K—B2, B—R6; 43 R—K7, etc.

(s) Threatening 43...R—B5, which, however, is easily parried.

(t) White indulges, nautically speaking, in a bit of tacking. Had his opponent remained passive, White would have resorted to an advance by P—KB4—B5, followed by K—Kt3—B4, etc.

(u) In case of 50...K—Kt, the exchange of Rooks through 51 R—Kt2 would have sufficed to win.

(v) An elegant simplification, winning a second Pawn and curtailing further resistance.

(w) Or 51...BxR (RxR; 52 RxR); 52 KtxRch, K—K2; 53 Kt—B4ch, K—B2; 54 KtxR, KxKt; 55 R—K6ch, etc.

Game 13   THIRD ROUND—QUEEN'S GAMBIT DECLINED

	Capablanca	Ed. Lasker		
	White	Black	21	PxP(g)	PxP

	Capablanca	Ed. Lasker
	White	Black
1	P—Q4	P—Q4
2	P—QB4	P—K3
3	Kt—QB3	Kt—KB3
4	B—Kt5	QKt—Q2
5	Kt—B3	P—B3
6	P—K3	Q—R4(a)
7	BxKt(b)	KtxB
8	B—Q3	B—Kt5
9	Q—Kt3	PxP(c)
10	BxP	Castles
11	Castles	BxKt
12	PxB	P—QKt3
13	Kt—K5	B—Kt2
14	B—K2(d)	P—B4(e)
15	Kt—B4	Q—R3
16	Q—Kt2	B—Q4
17	Kt—K5(f)	Q—B
18	P—QR4	Kt—Q2
19	P—QB4	B—K5
20	KtxKt	QxKt

21	PxP(g)	PxP
22	Q—K5	Q—B3
23	P—B3	B—Kt3
24	KR—Q	KR—Q
25	RxRch	RxR
26	R—Q	RxRch
27	BxR(h)	Drawn

After 14 B—K2

(a) The much disputed Cambridge Springs variation which, thanks largely to the researches of Bogoljubow, has again become somewhat fashionable of late.

(b) As is subsequently shown, this exchange permits Black to perform his main task, namely the development of his QB without having to overcome special difficulties. The move of Kt—Q2, formerly much favored, seems to give Black a good game, because of

Bogoljubow's improvement (see the game, Ed Lasker vs. Dr. Lasker). Hence, the strongest is 7 PxP! (compare games: Janowski vs. Bogoljubow and, with moves transposed, Marshall vs. Bogoljubow).

(c) A businesslike preparation for the posting of the Bishop on the diagonal from R to R8.

(d) And neither will any other method avail to prevent the liberating move that follows.

(e) Properly recognizing that the subsequent crowding of the Queen need not necessarily have any unt oward consequences. The game demonstrates distinctly the insufficiency of 7 BxKt.

(f) Likewise 17 Kt—Q6, Q—R4 (better than 17...P—B5; 18 P—QR4, etc.) would have led eventually to nothing.

(g) Through the formation of this symmetrical pawn structure White makes it known that he is satisfied with a draw. As a matter of fact, after 21 KR—Q, Q—B3; 22 P—B3, B—Kt3, etc., he would have no advantage whatsoever.

(h) 27...Q—Kt3; 28 P—K4; P—B3; 29 Q—B3, Q—Kt8; 30 Q—Q2, might still have been played.

Game 14   THIRD ROUND—RETI'S OPENING

| | Reti | Maroczy |
	White	Black
1	Kt—KB3	P—QB4
2	P—KKt3(a)	Kt—QB3
3	B—Kt2	P—KKt3
4	P—B4(b)	B—Kt2
5	Kt—B3	P—Q3
6	P—Q3	B—Q2(c)
7	Castles	R—Kt(d)
8	B—K3	Kt—Q5
9	Q—Q2	P—KR4(e)
10	QR—Kt	B—QB3(f)
11	P—QKt4	KtxKtch(g)
12	PxKt	P—Kt3
13	P—Q4(h)	PxQP
14	BxP	Kt—B3
15	Kt—Q5	Castles(i)
16	KtxKtch	PxKt
17	B—K3(j)	Q—Q2
18	KR—Q	QR—Q
19	P—Kt5(k)	B—QR
20	P—B5	KtPxP
21	BxP	KR—K(l)
22	Q—R5(m)	Q—B4
23	BxRP	BxP
24	BxB	QxB

After 24...QxB

25	P—Kt6(n)	P—R5(o)
26	R—Q4	R—K4(p)
27	Q—R6	PxP
28	RPxP	R—KR4
29	R—KR4(q)	RxR
30	PxR	Q—Kt5ch
31	K—B	Q—R6ch(r)
32	K—Kt	Q—Kt5ch
33	K—B	Q—R6ch
34	K—Kt	Q—Kt5ch
35	K—B	Drawn

(a) It strikes one as strange that Reti should here delay his favorite move of 2 P—B4, which is so indispensable to his system without any apparent reason. The text-move could be answered by Black profitably with 2...P—Q4.

(b) With this symmetrical disposition of his pieces, White, thanks to his "tempo" plus, still has hopes of presently advancing his QP and to obtain thereby greater scope in the center.

(c) In his endeavor to make more difficult the move, P—Q4, Black hesitates in developing his King's Knight. The idea is perhaps not a bad one, but is not carried out here with sufficient consistency.

(d) Preparatory to the advance eventually of the Knight pawn. Although Black, as a matter of fact, is not likely to have time to realize his intention, the text-move is not to be criticized because it removes the Rook once for all out of the range of the White KB.

(e) In order to develop the Bishop at R3—so far everything logical and comprehensible.

(f) Now, however, he should have played in proper sequence 10...Kt—R3 and, if 11 P—QKt4, then KKt—B4 (or else first P—QKt3). The Bishop is not happily placed on B3 and his removal was in any event not worth a "tempo."

(g) Black abandons the square, Q5, obviously in order to avoid a deterioration of his pawn position in the variation: 11...P—Qkt3; 12 KtxKt, BxB; 13 Kt—K6, PxKt; 14 KxB, etc. But after 14...Kt—B3, he would have had a better outlook in this line of play than through the move in the text, which Reti utilizes with great precision.

(h) Herewith White has carried out the fundamental idea of the variation under very favorable conditions and now has decidedly the better of it.

(i) The lesser evil would have been 15...BxKt; 16 PxB, Castles, inasmuch as his QP now becomes hopelessly weak.

(j) Preventing 17...P—Q4, on account of the reply of 18 P—B4, winning a pawn.

(k) With this advance White obtains no material advantage, to be sure, but establishes for himself a decisive superiority on the Queen's wing.

(l) Saving the QP, for if now 22 QxP, then 22...Q—B! and wins; and if 22 BxQP, then 22...B—B; 23 B—B4, QxQ; 24 RxQ, RxR; 25 BxR, R—K7, and White cannot save the QRP, on account of the threat of 26...B—B4.

(m) With this, however, the fate of the RP and consequently, one would imagine, of the game as well is sealed. Black attempts one more desperate counter attack.

(n) With this move White lets slip an easy win. Black's next move could have been prevented most simply by 25 Q—Kt4 or R4, in which case White, if necessary, could have offered his Queen for exchange on Kt3 or KB4, whereupon the passed pawns would have decided the issue quickly. After the mistake in the text, White, on the contrary, will have trouble to stave off a sudden calamity.

(o) Threatening mate through 26...P—R6, which could not have been parried either through 26 Q—Q5, because of 26...R—K8ch, nor through 26 Q—R6 or Kt5, because of 26...R—K7, etc. Reti discovers the only salvation.

(p) Better than 26...R—K5; 27 Q—Q5!; or 26...R—K7; 27 R—KB4, etc.

(q) Now everything just seems to fit together again.

(r) Black clearly has no time to bring over his Rook, on account of the KtP.

Game 15   THIRD ROUND—KING'S GAMBIT

Tartakower	Yates
White	Black
1 P—K4	P—K4
2 P—KB4	PxP
3 B—K2	Kt—QB3(a)
4 P—Q4	P—Q4
5 PxP	QxP
6 Kt—KB3	B—KKt5(b)
7 Kt—B3	B—Kt5(c)
8 Castles	BxQKt
9 PxB	KKt—K2(d)
10 BxP	Q—K5(e)
11 BxP	Castles(f)
12 Q—Q2	Kt—Q4
13 B—Kt3	Q—K6ch(g)
14 QxQ	KtxQ
15 KR—QB	KR—K(h)
16 B—Q3	Kt—Q4(i)
17 P—QB4	BxKt
18 PxB	Kt—B6
19 P—Q5	Kt—Q5
20 K—Kt2(j)	QKt—K7
21 R—K	KtxB
22 RxRch	RxR

23 PxKt(k)	Kt—R5(l)
24 K—B2	P—KKt3(m)
25 R—QKt	P—Kt3
26 R—Kt4(n)	Kt—B4
27 P—R4	K—B(o)

After 27 P—R4

28 P—R5	R—Kt
29 K—K3	K—K2
30 K—Q4	K—Q3

31	R—Kt	R—Kt2
32	PxP	PxP(p)
33	R—QR	R—K2
34	P—Kt4(q)	P—B3
35	R—QKt	R—QKt2
36	P—B4	R—Kt
37	P—Kt5	P—B4(r)
38	R—KR	R—Kt2(s)
39	BxP(t)	R—KB2(u)
40	R—QKt	K—B2(v)
41	P—Q6ch(w)	K—Q
42	B—R3	RxPch
43	K—Q5	Kt—Q2
44	R—QR	K—B
45	R—R7	Resigns

After 38...R—Kt2

(a) A move wholly without purpose, after which White at once obtains the superior game. 3...P—KB4 or P—Q4 or Kt—K2 are much more apt to assure Black a substantial game.

(b) This harmless attack upon the QP is parried by means of simple developing moves, but Black from the start was on the wrong track.

(c) Merely leading to the exchange of the Bishop with improvement of White's position. More in harmony with the foregoing moves would have been the more energetic continuation of 7...Q—KR4; 8 BxP, Castles, etc., which perhaps would have permitted Black still to fish in troubled waters.

(d) The KBP can no longer be defended (9...P—KKt4; 10 KtxP, or 9...Q—Q3; 10 Kt—K5, etc.).

(e) The sacrifice of the BP is risky, to be sure, but not wholly without prospects, inasmuch as Black, by correct play, could obtain pressure later on upon the QB file. The bold move is explained possibly by the realization of Black that a tamer continuation (such as Q—Q2 or Castles QR) would leave him at a lasting disadvantage, on account of the two opposing Bishops and the open file.

(f) After 11...Kt—Q4 would follow 12 B—Q3, Q—K6ch; 13 K—R, KtxQBP; 14 Q—K, QxQ; 15 QRxQ, B—K3 (K—Q2; 16 Kt—Kt5, etc.); 16 Kt—K5, K—Q2; 17 KtxB, PxKt; 18 R—B7ch, QKt—K2; 19 B—R5, etc.

(g) Of course not 13...KtxP, on account of 15 B—Q3, etc. His best chance rests in the exchange of Queens.

(h) Here, however, he relaxes sadly. There was no future for the Rook on the King's file and it was fairly obvious that the QB file should be occupied at once. After 15...QR—B (not Kt—Q4; 16 B—K, etc); 16 B—Q3, BxKt; 17 PxB, Kt—QR4; 18 QR—Kt, P—QKt3; 19 R—Kt5, KR—Q, White still would have had difficulties in maintaining and turning to account his material superiority. With the text-move, however, a clear "tempo" is presented to him.

(i) 16...QR—QB would still have been more promising than this Knight maneuver, which almost forces a surely won, albeit difficult ending for White.

(j) Not 20 K—B2, because he wanted to provide for the possibility of an eventual retreat of the QB to B2 or K.

(k) Now there begins an instructive ending which is turned into a win by Dr. Tartakower in a manner quite as methodical as it is pretty.

(l) The Knight must move perforce, as 24 P—R4, etc., threatened.

(m) Now it becomes apparent that the placing of the Pawns on white squares makes possible White's winning combination and that for this reason 24...P—KR3 was to have been preferred. But at that moment it was not to be easily foreseen.

(n) With this move, in connection with the following, White forces an additional weakness at QKt3.

(o)   An interesting moment. Black cannot in anyway prevent 28 P—R5, for, after 27...Kt—Kt2, would follow 28 P—R5, KtxP; 29 P—B5, PxP; 30 R—Kt5, P—B5; 31 B—K2, and the Knight is lost!

(p)   32...RxP cannot be played, on account of R—R, R5, etc., with an easy win.

(q)   Herewith commences the binding of the weak points on the King's wing. First of all, 34 P—Kt5 is threatened.

(r)   After 37...PxP; 38 PxP, White would have penetrated via the KB file. Now everything seems to be blocked and at first it is not apparent just what White has gained by his whole maneuver. The more surprising, therefore, is the subsequent winning process.

(s)   In order to meet 39 R—R6 with 39...R—B2.

(t)   The beauty of this conception lies not so much in the main variation as chiefly in the circumstance that the actual reply by Black seemingly refutes the sacrifice and only by White's next move the real point becomes clear.

(u)   If 39...PxB. then 40 R—R6ch, K—B2; 41 RxPch, K—B; 42 P—Kt6, and wins.

(v)   After 40...Kt—R5, the simplest way to win would be 41 B—Q3, RxPch; 42 K—K3, followed by R—Kt4, etc.

(w)   All this is forced. After 41...KxP would follow 42 RxPch, K—B2; 43 R—KB6, etc.; and, after 41...K—B3; 42 B—K4ch, etc.

FOURTH ROUND

In a measure, this round was a repetition of the third in that White won two of the games, lost one and drew two. Dr. Lasker won a most instructive Sicilian Defense from Janowski, who was induced to weaken his King's side and was outplayed in the ensuing complications. Dr. Lasker won the exchange, but, astonishing to relate, he was guilty of a slight omission which might have made victory very uncertain. Janowski obligingly failed to take advantage and thereafter Dr. Lasker experienced little difficulty in working out a win.

Capablanca, playing white against Alekhine's French Defense, had all the better of the opening, his play culminating in the gain of a clear Pawn. Undaunted, Alekhine fought back and barely managed to save the game.

Bogoljubow vs. Reti was another French Defense and a fine example of Bogoljubow's seemingly simple style. At his twentieth turn he deliberately went in for an ending, with Bishops commanding squares of opposite colors! After a few moves, however, there came the realization that Reti's game, regardless of what he might play, was no longer tenable.

Dr. Tartakower and Maroczy played irregularly and the game was somewhat erratic throughout. Neither the opening nor the middle game was managed any too well. The ending (non-conflicting Bishops) was very interesting, although this, too, was spoiled.

Quite a complicated Ruy Lopez was played between Yates and Ed Lasker. The former's illogical advance of the center Pawns gravely compromised his position and thereafter it was necessary for him to play with the greatest precision in order to hold the game intact. Lasker weakened in the ending and Yates, declining to overlook his shortcomings, gained a full point.

Dr. Tartakower was still leading after four rounds, but Dr. Lasker, 2½—½, had the better percentage. The White pieces took a slight lead, with totals of 10½—9½.

Game 16 FOURTH ROUND—SICILIAN DEFENSE

Janowski	Dr. Lasker		
White	Black	13 Q—K(e)	Kt—K4
1 P—K4	P—QB4	14 Q—B2	R—Kt
2 Kt—KB3	Kt—QB3(a)	15 B—Q3	Kt—B5
3 P—Q4	PxP	16 B—B	B—Kt2
4 KtxP	Kt—B3	17 Q—Kt3	QR—B
5 Kt—B3	P—Q3	18 KR—K(f)	Kt—Q2
6 B—K2	P—K3(b)	19 P—B4	B—KB3(g)
7 Castles	B—K2	29 BxKt	PxB
8 B—K3	Castles	21 Kt—Q2	Q—Kt5
9 Q—Q2	P—QR3	22 Kt(Q2)—Kt	Kt—B(h)
10 QR—Q(c)	Q—B2	23 B—K3(i)	Q—Kt5
11 Kt—Kt3	P—QKt4(d	24 B—B	Kt—Kt3
12 P—B3	R—Q	25 Q—B2	B—R5
		26 P—KKt3	B—KB3

27	P—QR3	Q—R4
28	B—K3(j)	Q—R4
29	B—Kt6	R—Q2
30	R—Q2(k)	B—B3
31	KR—Q	B—K2

After 48...Q—B4

After 31...B—K2

32	P—QR4(l)	R—Kt2
33	P—R5	P—B4
34	Q—K3	P—K4(m)
35	R—KB	KPxP
36	KtPxP	B—B(n)
37	Kt—Q5	R—KB2
38	Kt(Kt)—B3	R—K
39	Q—Q4(o)	PxP
40	QxBP	B—Q2
41	B—K3	Kt—R5
42	R(Q2)—B2	B—R6
43	KtxP(p)	Q—Kt5ch
44	Kt—Kt3	Kt—B4
45	R—B3	BxR
46	QxB	KtxB
47	KtxKt	Q—B(q)
48	Q—Q3	Q—B4(r)

49	Q—Q2(s)	P—Q4(t)
50	K—Kt2	P—Q5
51	Kt—Kt4	B—Q3
52	Kt—B2	Q—Q4
53	P—B4(u)	QxBP
54	Kt(Kt3)—K4	Q—Q4
55	KtxB	QxKt
56	Kt—Q3	Q—Q4
57	K—Kt3	R—B3
58	K—B2	R—R3
59	P—R3	R—KB3
60	K—Kt3	R—Kt3ch
61	K—B2	R—K6
62	Kt—K5	Q—K5
63	P—QKt4	P—KR4
64	Q—Q	R—KB3
65	Kt—Q3	P—KKt4
66	Kt—B5	Q—Q4
67	Kt—Q3	PxP
68	KtxP	Q—K5
	Resigns	

(a) According to our judgment, this is better than 2...P—K3, because Black, after 3 B—K2, can accomplish the blocking of White's QBP (Kt—QB3) by means of 3... Kt—KB3 (4 P—K5?, Kt—KKt5; 5 P—Q4, PxP; 6 B—KB4, Q—B2, etc.)

(b) An interesting deviation from the usual method of development through P—KKt3, followed by B—Kt2, which is by no means disadvantageous for Black. Black thereby weakens his QP, which, to be sure, White cannot attack very well, in order to dispute the square, Q4, with his opponent and to strengthen indirectly the action of the open QB file.

(c) White permits the adversary to complete his plan of development without hindrance and thereby, almost unnoticeably, is placed at a disadvantage. Here, for instance, 10 P—B3 was to have been preferred in order to be able to continue, after 10 Q—B2, with 11 Kt—R4!, followed by KtxKt and Kt—Kt6 or P—QB4; or 10...P—Q4; 11 PxP, KtxP; 12 KtxKKt, QxKt; 13 P—QB4, and in this instance, thanks to White's superior development, the preponderance of pawns on the Queen's side would not be merely an empty notion, as is so frequently the case.

(d) Threatening 12...P—Kt5.

(e) All the White pieces are practically ineffective (beissen auf Granit) and are hampered in their mobility. The demonstration, initiated with the text-move against Kt6, is of course, perfectly harmless.

(f) All this in order eventually to be able to play P—B4, which perhaps may make possible shadowy threats. On the other hand, how harmoniously is the ensemble of the black pieces developed!

(g) Threatening 20...KtxKtP (21 P—K5, PxKP; 22 BxKt, PxBP; 23 Q—R3, BxKt; 24 QxPch, K—B, etc.). White, therefore, is forced to yield the advantage of two B.shops to his opponent without compensation.

(h) The maneuver with the Knight aims above all to induce a weakening of the King's wing through P—KKt3. All White can obta.n in return is the command of the square, QKt6, which, however, is not important, inasmuch as the final struggle will take place on the other side of the board.

(i) Not the loss of a "tempo" to be sure, inasmuch as the black Queen is also forced back, but, by means of 23 P—QR3, Kt—Kt3; 24 Q—B2 followed by B—K3, White could have attained the desired position two moves sooner than in the actual game.

(j) Threatening not alone to win the exchange, but the capture of the Queen as well through 29 P—K5, PxKP; 30 B—Kt6, etc.

(k) Threatening 31 P—K5, B—K2; 22 Kt—K4, etc., which could not be played right at this moment because of the unprotected Rook on Q square. Black has exactly the time necessary to parry all tactical threats.

(1) Janowski has extracted from his inferior position about all there was in it, and for the time being keeps back the Black pieces. However, the organic inferiority of his game, that is, the weakness of the Wh.te squares caused by the disappearance of the KB, cannot be removed and because of it the game eventually goes to pieces. The drastic move of 32 P—K5, in order to force P—Q4, thereby cramping the Bishop, would lead to a hopeless catastrophe; for instance: 32...Kt—R5!; 33 PxKt, BxRP; 34 Q—K3 (Q—K2, B—B6 or Q—B, PxKP!, etc.) Q—Kt5ch; 35 K—B, B—B6 and wins. By the more passive move selected Black forces a decisive advantage through the pawn advance in the center.

(m) Yielding the square, Q4, to be sure, but in return exposes the White King, who cannot any more be protected in time by the pieces engaged on the Queen's side. Dr. Lasker's entire winning play is very impressive and espec.ally considering the able defense of his opponent.

(n) Making possible with one stroke the co-operation of both Rooks at the critical turning point.

(o) The QBP, now unimportant, is poor compensation for the KP, but after the seemingly promis.ng 39...Kt—B7, Black, by sacrificing the exchange with 39...RxKP; 40 KtxR, PxKt, would have obtained an attack equivalent to victory, for instance: 41 R—Kt2 (KtxBP was threatened), B—K2!, and now it would not do to play either 42 KtxRP, on account of 42...P—B6, followed by B—QKt4, or 42 Q—K2, on account of 42...QxQ; 43 RxQ, KtxBP; 44 R—K3, B—Kt2, etc. Black, on the other hand, had threatened 42...Kt—R5, winning back the exchange with a commanding position. The text-move, however, is of help for a short time only.

(p) The loss of the exchange clearly cannot be avoided. Before availing himself of it Black forces an advantageous simplification.

(q) After the establishment of a material advantage, the matter of winning should become simply a question of technique.

(r) With this Black almost deprived himself of the fruits of his deep strategy. Correct would have been 48...P—Q4; 49 KtxP, Q—B4ch, followed by QxRP, etc.; or 49 QxQP,RxKt!; 50 RxR, B—B4; 51 Kt(Kt3)—B, Q—Kt5ch, followed by BxR and QxP.

(s) White also overlooks the move at hand, 49 Kt—K4, whereby he would have obtained a defensible position. Black, in view of the threat of Kt—Kt5, would only have had the choice between surrendering the exchange (49...RxKt; 50 QxR) and the sacrifice of the Oueen for two Rooks (49...QxRP; 50 Kt—Kt5; QxKt; 51 PxQ, RxR; 52 Q—Q5ch, R—B2). In both cases, on account of the unsafe position of the White King, Black would still have an advantage, but the win, if at all possible, would in any event not have been easy.

(t) Now, on the contrary, it is very simple, inasmuch as Black in this forward pressing Pawn has a strong weapon for attack. White's position becomes quite hopeless in a few moves.

(u) Desperation!

Game 17   FOURTH ROUND—FRENCH DEFENSE

Capablanca	Alekhine
White	Black
1 P—Q4	P—K3
2 P—K4	P—Q4
3 Kt—QB3	Kt—KB3
4 B—Kt5	B—Kt5
5 PxP	QxP
6 BxKt	BxKtch(a)
7 PxB	PxB
8 Q—Q2(b)	Kt—Q2(c)
9 P—QB4(d)	Q—K5ch
10 Kt—K2	Kt—Kt3(e)
11 P—KB3	Q—B3(f)
12 P—B5	Kt—Q4(g)
13 P—QB4	Kt—K2
14 Kt—QB3(h)	P—KB4
15 B—K2	R—KKt(i)
16 Castles	B—Q2(j)
17 Q—K3(k)	P—Kt3
18 KR—Q	PxP(l)

After 31...RPxKt

35 KxR	BxB
36 PxB	K—K2
37 R—Q2	K—K3
38 K—K3	P—QB3(w)
39 P—KR4(x)	R—KR
40 P—Kt3	R—R4(y)
41 R—R2	R—R4(z)
42 K—B4	P—B3(aa)
43 R—QB2	R—K4(bb)
44 P—B5(cc)	R—R4
45 R—B3(dd)	P—R4
46 R—B2	R—K4
47 R—B3	R—R4
48 K—B3	K—K2
49 K—Kt4	K—B2(ee)
50 R—B4	K—Kt2

After 18...PxP

19 P—Q5(m)	Q—Q3(n)
20 PxP	QxP
21 QxP	Q—QKt3
22 Q—B2	P—B5(o)
23 QR—Kt(p)	QxQch(q)
24 KxQ	B—B3
25 R—Q4(r)	Kt—Kt3
26 B—Q3	Kt—R5
27 B—B	Kt—Kt3
28 Kt—K2	K—K2
29 R—K	KR—QKt(s)
30 KtxPch	K—B
31 KtxKtch(t)	RPxKt
32 B—Q3(u)	R—Kt7ch
33 R—K2	QR—Kt
34 B—K4(v)	RxRch

After 50...K—Kt2

51 R—Q4(ff)	RxP
52 R—Q7ch	K—B(gg)
53 K—B4	K—Kt
54 R—QR7	K—B
55 P—QR4	K—Kt

56 P—Kt4(hh)	P—Kt4ch	60 K—Q4	R—KKt4
57 PxP	RxP	61 RxBP	RxP
58 R—R6	R—QB4	62 R—B5	R—Kt4(ii)
59 K—K3	K—B2	Drawn	

(a) A questionable move to which the second player committed himself without further investigation in consequence of his experience in his game with Dr. Tarrasch (St. Petersburg, 1914,) and a somewhat stronger sub-variation later found by enthusiasts of that city. It requires no specially deep examination of the position in order to ascertain that this exchange is quite untimely, inasmuch as White, after the simple 6...PxB (7 Q—Q2, Q—QR4, etc., see Capablanca vs. Bogoljubow in the 22nd round), must exert himself in order to force it. Through the move after the next on the part of Capablanca, this game takes on a theoretical significance.

(b) Until now, 8 Kt—B3 has been almost invariably played, followed by 8...P—Kt3; 9 P—Kt3, B—Kt2 (still stronger is the St. Petersburg innovation referred to: 9...Kt—Q2; 10 B—Kt2, B—R3!, and, if Kt—R4, then 11...Q—QR4, etc.); 10 B—Kt2, Q—K5ch, and White has nothing better than to play for equalization with Q—K2, inasmuch as 11 K—Q2 (Dr. Tarrasch vs. Alekhine, St. Petersburg, 1914), as well as K—B (Reti vs. Bogoljubow, Berlin, 1919) would yield an advantage to the second player. The value of the Queen's move consists chiefly in the fact that Black cannot now very well play 8...P—Kt3, on account of 9 B—K2 (threatening B—B3).

(c) The alternative would have been 8...P—QB4; 9 Q—K3!, Kt—Q2 (or 9...PxP; 10 PxP, Kt—B3: 11 Q—QB3): 10 Kt—K2, followed by Kt—B4, whereby the Queen is driven from her dominating post in the center. With the move in the text Black combined his intention to complete the flank-development of his Bishop, but, later on, to his undoing, permitted his idea to be sidetracked.

(d) This prevents in good time the eventual occupation of QB4 (through Kt—Kt3, followed by B—Q2, P—QR3 and B—Kt4). The check which follows means nothing to White, for the Queen is immediately forced away with loss of time.

(e) An unfortunate notion, through adherence to which Black soon gets into trouble. Proper would have been 10...P—Kt3; 11 P—KB3, O—Kt3; 12 Kt—Kt3 (Kt—B4, Q—R3), B—Kt2; 13 B—Q3, Q—Kt4, etc., with a thoroughly sound game, although White even in this case would still have had the better chances after 14 P—B4 (not 14 QxQ, PxQ; 15 P—KR4. P—Kt5, etc.), Q—R3; 15 P—QR4!, etc.).

(f) Likewise unsatisfactory would have been 11 Q—R5ch, on account of 12 P—Kt3, Q—R4; 13 Kt—B3! (better than 13 Kt—B4, QxBP; 14 B—Kt2, Q—R6, etc.), QxP; 14 B—Kt2, Q—R4: 15 P—B5, Kt—Q2; 16 Kt—Kt5, Castles; 17 KtxBP, R—Kt; 18 Castles, P—QR3; 19 QR—Kt, with a better game.

(g) 12...Kt—B5 will not do, on account of 13 Q—B3, P—Kt4; 14 P—QR4, etc.

(h) Threatening very strongly 15 Kt—K4, etc. Consequently, Black is forced to submit to a further weakening of his center, after which the eventual threat of P—Q5 becomes still more unpleasant.

(i) After 15...B—Q2; 16 Castles, Black would be compelled to play 16...R—KKt, because 16...P—Kt3 would be still impossible, on account of 17 P—B4.

(j) And now it is not possible to play 16 P—Kt3, on account of 17 B—Q! Black's position, due to his mistake on the tenth move, was really no longer tenable.

(k) Threatening 18 P—Q5.

(l) Black must strike out and prepare himself for a sad ending, inasmuch as no other moves offer themselves for the improvement of his position, and another freely given "tempo" (K—B for instance) would enable White to decide the encounter in his own favor during the middle game.

(m) The files hereby opened offer to the first player a winning position full of promise, due to the fact that it is impossible for Black to reunite his Rooks in time.

(n) The only move, for, after 19 PxP; 20 KtxP, Q—Q3; 21 QR—Kt, threatening Kt—Kt5, etc., deciding matters quickly.

(o) A sacrifice, for it is clear that the Pawn cannot long survive on this square. Black selected this desperate continuation in the full understanding that, after 22...QxQch; 23 KxQ, B—B3, White could have materially increased his advantage through quite simple moves, for instance: 24 Kt—Kt5, BxKt; 25 PxB, R—Kt3 (or R—Q; 26 RxRch, KxR; 27 B—B4, etc.); 26 QR—B, R—B; 27 R—B5, etc., and in the hope, through the immediate surrender of the weakling, possibly to distract the attention of the opponent.

(p) Not 23 R—Q4, on account of 23...Q—Kt7; 24 Q—K, B—R6, etc.

(q) After 23...Q—K3 or Kt3, there would follow 24 R—Kt7.

(r)   Even now 25 Kt—Kt5 would have been very strong. The winning of tne Pawn, to which White gives his attention, at least permits the second player finally to connect his Rooks.

(s)   Because of this open file Black gets a chance for some counter play. The Pawn loss, to be sure, could not be quite compensated for.

(t)   Perhaps the simplest, because the establishment of a passed Pawn on the far King's wing is made possible thereby. The plausible 31 Kt—Q3 would have invited greater technical difficulties after 31...R—Q; 32 RxRch, etc.

(u)   White overvalues his chances in the subsequent Rook play. He should have striven not to exchange the Bishops, but a pair of Rooks, because the adversary's only counter stroke, consisting in the advance of his QR Pawn, would have been as good as nullified, for instance: 32 R—Q2, P—R4; 33 B—Q3, P—R5; 34 R—QKt, RxR; 35 BxR, R—Kt; 36 B—Q3, P—R6; 37 B—K2!, threatening, by means of 38 R—Q3, to limit the Black Rook to the defense of his Pawns, whereupon the conversion of his superiority on the King's side would present no further difficulty. The selected continuation is quite to the point, but does not seem sufficiently forceful on account of the change in the Pawn "constellation." As a matter of fact, the second player, through a careful defense, is enabled to escape with a draw.

(v)   Otherwise the QRP can no longer be protected.

(w)   A necessary preparation for the eventual posting of the Rook on the fourth rank.

(x)   In this end game Capablanca's famous thoroughness fails him (compare also his 56th move). Premature would have been 39 P—B5, on account of 39...R—Kt4; 40 R—Q6ch, K—K4; 41 RxBP, R—R4, but 39 P—KR3!, in order to be able to meet 39...R—KR with 40 P—B5 and threaten K—Q4—B3, followed by P—B5, would have set Black a much more difficult problem than the move in the text.

(y)   The placing of the Rook on the fourth rank is equally effective for defense and attack, and White's plan to force a passed Pawn on the KR file is now shown to be impracticable.

(z)   With the dangerous threat of 42...K—K4, etc.

(aa)   Again preventing 43 P—Kt4, because 43...P—Kt4ch would halt the KR Pawn.

(bb)   Necessary, because 44 P—B5, followed by P—Kt4, was threatening.

(cc)   Through this move, which confines somewhat the free movements of Black's Rook, his own Rook is committed to the defense of the QB Pawn, and henceforth it is necessary for Black merely to keep an eye on the threat of K—Kt4—R3, followed by P—Kt4.

(dd)   Threatening 46 R—R3, etc.

(ee)   Necessary, for Black must be prepared to be in a position always to reply to K—R3 with P—Kt4 and, in case White thereupon should attack the Rook with K—Kt4, to defend him with K—Kt3. Next he would exchange on R5 and play his Rook from K4 to R4 and back, whereupon White could make no further advance. Capablanca endeavors as a last resort to utilize the circumstance that the Black King dare not abandon Kt3.

(ff)   Through the return of the extra Pawn the Rook forces its way to the seventh rank and the hostile King, of course, is forced back. More than this could not be expected from the position after the 39th move, but such as it is there seems to be no real danger for the second player.

(gg)   Not 52...K—R3; 53 R—KB7, etc.

(hh)   After 56 K—K3, R—B6ch; 57 K—Q4, RxP; 58 RxP, K—B2; 59 R—R8, etc.

(ii)   If 63 RxR, PxR; 64 K—K5, K—Kt3; 65 K—Q6, K—B2, etc.

Game 18	FOURTH ROUND—FRENCH DEFENSE		
Bogoljubow	Reti	8 KtxP	B—Q2(e)
White	Black	9 Q—Q3	B—B3
1 P—K4	P—K3	10 Castles	BxKt
2 P—Q4	P—Q4	11 QxB	Q—Q4
3 Kt—QB3	Kt—KB3	12 Q—K3(f)	Castles
4 B—Kt5	B—Kt5	13 Kt—B3	Q—QR4
5 Kt—K2(a)	PxP(b)	14 Kt—K4	Kt—Q2
6 P—QR3	B—K2(c)	15 P—KR4(g)	B—K2
7 BxKt	BxB(d)	16 P—KKt4	P—QKt4(h)

17	P—Kt4(i)	Q—Kt3	
18	Kt—B5	KtxKt(j)	
19	QPxKt	Q—Kt2	
20	B—Q3	P—QR4(k)	

After 20...P—QR4

21	Q—K4(l)	QxQ
22	BxQ	QR—Q
23	P—QB3	PxP
24	RPxP	P—B4(m)
25	PxP	P—K4
26	P—R5(n)	B—Kt4ch
27	K—B2	K—B2
28	B—B6	K—B3
29	BxP	KxP
30	B—B6	K—K3
31	P—B3	B—K2

32	R—QR(o)	B—Kt4
33	R—R7	R—B2
34	B—K4	P—R3
35	KR—R(p)	R—Q7ch
36	K—Kt3	B—Q
37	P—Kt5	KR—Q2
38	KR—R6ch	K—B2
39	B—B5	R—K2
40	B—Kt6ch	K—B
41	R—R8	KR—Q2
42	R—K6	R—K2

After 42...R—K2

43	R—B6(q)	KR—Q2
44	RxBch	RxR
45	RxP(r)	Resigns

(a)   This move, introduced by H. Wolf and elaborated by Bogoljubow, deserves more attention than has been given to it hitherto. Its main idea is to take up, after the partly forced PxP, a commanding post in the center with one of his Knights on K4, from which the opponent cannot dislodge it without considerable effort or weakening of position. Whether or not Black can fight successfully against this method of play is a question for the future to decide. Up to now, really convincing counter-play has not been found.

(b)   Aside from this rejoinder, which seems the most natural, the classical counter of 5...P—B4 comes into consideration before everything else. White, however, can thereupon obtain a clear advantage in development through the simple 6 P—QR3, BxKtch; 7 KtxB, PxQP; 8 QxP, Kt—B3; 9 B—Kt5, etc. It would also be interesting to try out thoroughly the pawn sacrifice, decidedly not without prospects, by means of 5...P—KR3; 6 BxKt, QxB; 7 PxP, Castles, etc. In any event, by this line of play, White would be left very much behind in development.

(c)   7...B—R4; 8 P—QKt4, B—Kt3; 9 KtxP, etc., would have resulted only in the exclusion of his own Bishop.

(d)   In two other games in this tournament 7...PxB was essayed, this having the advantage of challenging the posting of the white Knight on K4 through the threat of driving him off with P—B4 (and not so much through the act of driving itself, which in an earlier stage of the game would have considerably weakened Black's center). The recapture with the Bishop can only have the purpose of continuing as soon as possible either with P—K4 or P—QB4. Inasmuch as these moves, however, do not seem to lead to complete equalization, 6...PxB must be regarded as the more promising.

(e)   From now on the game loses all theoretical interest, for the Bishop maneuver, carried out in three moves, in order eventually to exchange it for a Knight under stress of the hostile development, should never have been taken earnestly into consideration. Nevertheless, it must be conceded that a desirable mode of development for Black is by no means easily to be found. Upon the plausible 8...P—K4, White would do well to beware against breaking up the pawn position with 9 P—Q5, for in that case Black would obtain superiority through 9...B—K2, followed by castling and P—KB4, etc. He would rather try with 9 Q—Q3! (eventually followed by Castles QR), to maintain the balance in the center in the knowledge that, after 9...PxP; 10 KtxBch, QxKt; 11 QxP, QxQ; 12 KtxQ, followed by castling QR, he would keep, at any rate, a small advantage in development. Just this very impossibility on the part of Black to remove the QP without suffering in position is a fine argument, in our judgment, in favor of the vitality of Bogoljubow's adopted child—5 KKt—K2.

(f) Naturally, White does not oblige his opponent with an exchange of Queens. the more so as 12...Q—R7 would lead to the loss of his Queen; 13 Kt—B3, Q—R8ch; 14 K—Q2, QxKtP; 15 B—Kt5ch, followed by 16 QR—R and 17 KR—QKt, etc.

(g) Inasmuch as White is not threatened, he prepares a King's attack through P moves that are not weakening.

(h) Black becomes uneasy in face of the hostile advance and, therefore, decides upon this counter movement, which compromises entirely his position on the Queen's wing. With 16...QR—Q, followed eventually by P—QB4, he would still have had some chance of holding the game. The subsequent winning continuation by Bogoljubow is most instructive in its simplicity and stamps the game as one of the best in the tournament.

(i) Bringing to a stop the hostile feint-attack and, at the same time, assuring himself of the control of the important square, QB5.

(j) If 18...Kt—B3, there could have followed with advantage 19 B—Kt2!, followed by P—Kt5.

(k) Thereupon White forces a winning ending. But after 20...Q—R3; 21 K—Kt2 (the simplest), followed by P—QB3, P—Kt5 and Q—K4, he would finally have pressed through with a direct attack upon the King.

(l) The egg of Columbus. After the exchange of Queens, Black would be fettered through the defense of the open Q file and would not be in a position for that reason to save the QKtP. After its loss, the superiority of pawns on the Queen's side must be decisive, notwithstanding Bishops commanding squares of opposite colors. Black's subsequent deperate struggle, in order to obtain counter-play at any cost, merely accelerates his defeat.

(m) Against 25 B—B6, nothing can be done (ist kein Kraut gewachsen).

(n) White, in the knowledge that his prey (QKtP) cannot escape him, plays economically and allows his opponent not the slightest chance in the subsequent moves.

(c) Preparing for the siege of the QBP.

(p) Threatening 36 KR—R6ch, K—Q2; 37 RxPch, etc.

(q) Or still simpler 43 R—Q6!, R—Q2 (R(Q7)xR; 44 PxR, followed by PxP and wins); 44 RxR (Q2), RxR; 45 P—Kt6, PxP; 46 PxP, R(Q7)—Q2; 47 B—B5, R—Q3; 48 K—B4 and wins. Of course, the intended sacrifice of the exchange is very quickly decisive.

(r) Now the passed pawns march right on to queen.

Game 19 FOURTH ROUND—IRREGULAR OPENING

Tartakower	Maroczy		
White	Black		
1 P—QKt4(a)	P—K3(b)	12 B—K2(g)	Kt—Q3
2 B—Kt2	Kt—KB3	13 Q—B	B—B3
3 P—Kt5	P—Q4	14 Kt—R3(h)	P—B3
4 P—K3	B—K2	15 PxP	PxP
5 P—KB4(c)	Castles	16 Kt—K5(i)	BxKt
6 B—Q3(d)	P—QR3(e)	17 PxB	Kt—B2
7 P—QR4	PxP	18 P—Q4	Kt—Kt4
8 PxP	RxR	19 P—B4	B—R3
9 BxR	QKt—Q2(f)	20 R—K	Q—R
10 Kt—KB3	Kt—K5	21 B—QB3(j)	R—Kt
11 Castles	P—KB4	22 Q—B2	Kt—K5
		23 B—Q3	R—Kt2(k)
		24 R—QB	Kt—Kt3
		25 B—K(l)	P—R3

After 25...P—R3

26	BxKt(m)	QPxB(n)
27	Q—B3	Kt—Q2
28	R—Kt	RxR
29	KtxR	Q—Kt2
30	Kt—R3	Q—Kt3(o)
31	B—Q2	K—B2
32	P—KKt3	Kt—B(p)
33	Q—Kt4	QxQ
34	BxQ	Kt—Q2
35	B—R5	P—Kt4
36	K—B2	K—K(q)
37	K—K2	P—B4(r)
38	Kt—Kt5(s)	K—B2
39	K—Q2	PxP
40	PxP	P—B5
41	Kt—Q6ch	K—Kt3

42	K—B3	P—K6
43	K—Q3(t)	Kt—Kt
44	K—K4	Kt—B3
45	B—B3	P—K7(u)
46	PxP	PxP

After 46...PxBP

47	B—Q2(v)	P—B6
48	KxP(w)	KtxPch
49	K—K3	Kt—B4ch
50	KxP	KtxKt
51	PxKt	BxPch
52	K—K3	B—Kt4
53	K—Q4	P—R4
54	K—B5	B—R5
55	K—Kt6	K—B2
56	K—B7	K—K
57	B—B4	Drawn

(a) An old move, the chief drawback of which is the fact that White discloses his intentions before knowing those of his opponent. He need not necessarily be at a disadvantage thereby, but is not that altogether too small a satisfaction for the first player?

(b) It is not clear why Black at the very start should close the diagonal to his QB. More logical at all events seems to be 2...P—Q4 at once.

(c) White has a definite opening purpose—the command of the black squares. To neglect development on that account, however, is surely unsound strategy, which, too, with more energetic counter-play, woud have met with its punishment.

(d) Why post the Bishop on a bad spot when first of all the Knight may be developed to a good one, (6 Kt—KB3)?

(e) More energetic utilization of the adversary's eccentricities here would have been 6...P—B4, for then (apart from 7 PxP, e. p., PxP, which clearly would have been equivalent to an avowal of bad play) White would have had only a choice between 7 P—B4 and a further development by means of 7 Kt—KB3. In the first case, after 7...PxP; 8 BxP, QKt—Q2, etc., White's backward QP would be a clear positional disadvantage; in the second, however, after 7...P—QR3; 8 P—QR4, P—B5; 9 B—K2, PxP; 10 PxP, RxR; 11 BxR, Q—R4; 12 Kt—B3, B—Kt5; 13 Q—Kt, QKt—Q2; 14 Castles, Kt—B4, etc., the opening of the QR file would in any case have given promise of greater initiative than before the move of P—B4.

(f) 9...P—B4 was still strong, even though in the variation 10 PxP, e. p., PxP, etc., the disappearance of the QR Pawns and the Rooks would have been rather a relief for White. The leap of the Knight to K5, prepared by the text-move, leads to nothing, as the Knight may easily be dislodged.

(g) Now Black as a matter of fact has no adequate compensation for the weakness of his black squares.

(h) The Knight will remain here for a long time inactive and exposed. After the immediate 14 Kt—K5, however, Black would have been able to reply with 14...BxKt; 15 PxB, Kt—B5 (!); 16 BxKt, PxB; 17 Kt—R3, Kt—Kt3, followed by Q—Q4, etc.

(i) After 16 Kt—Q4, there could have followed 16...Kt—Kt, and after 16 P—B4, then B—R3, etc. After the text-move, through the forced sequel of which the square, K5, is yielded to Black, the game takes on a drawish character.

(j) White wrongly hesitates to strike out and in consequence is placed slightly at a disadvantage. 21 PxP, BPxP (BxB; 22 PxKP); 22 Kt—Kt5, BxKt; 23 BxB, R—B, followed by Kt—Kt3, etc., would have made the peace pact easier for him.

(k) If 23...Kt—Kt3 at once, then 24 R—R, and if 24...KtxB; 25 QxKt, Kt—R5; 26 Q—R5, etc.

(l) Now 25 R—R could have been answered with 25...R—R2.

(m) He should have prepared for this exchange, which could not have been avoided in the long run, with 26 P—R3, for now Black can obtain a decisive advantage.

(n) Correct would have been 26...BPxP; 27 PxP (if 27 P—B5, B—Q6, etc., and the black pieces would force an entrance), Q—KB!; 28 B—B2, QxKt; whereupon neither 29 QxP, PxP, nor 29 PxKP, B—Kt4, nor 29 PxBP, R—B2 need have been feared by Black. The text-move not alone permits the victory to slip out of hand, but even affords the opponent a chance in the center, which, with a little care, however, attains no decisive significance.

(o) Inasmuch as Black cannot avoid an exchange of Queens, he would have done best to prepare for counter-play on the King's side (K—B2, followed by P—Kt4, etc.).

(p) Loss of time! 32...P—Kt4 could have been played without hesitation. Thereupon White would have been obliged to exchange Queens, as the complications associated with 33 P—Kt4 would have resulted in favor of Black, for instance: 33...PxP; 34 Q—B2, Kt—B; 35 QxP, Q—Kt6, etc.

(q) Here there is nothing for the King to do. With 36...K—Kt3 the game could have been easily drawn, as the white King, on account of the possible P—B5, could not then wander off to the Queen's side of the board.

(r) Hereupon Black actually gets a lost position, because the white King will at last come into play. After 37...K—B2, the game would still not have been lost.

(s) Black dare not take this intruder, for, after 39 PxB and B—B7, his Knight would be captured through the advance of the QKtP. Consequently, there remains nothing for him to seek safety on the King's side.

(t) Threatening to win a Pawn with 44 K—K4, which is first of all prevented by the next move of Black's Knight.

(u) As is easily to be seen, Black's line of play is dictated.

(v) White, who until now has conducted the interesting ending faultlessly, permits victory to slip from him here. Correct would have been 47 B—K!, whereupon the advance of the center Pawns would have been decisive: 47...P—B6; 48 P—Q5, PxPch; 49 PxP, Kt—K2; 50 P—K6, K—B3; 51 B—R4ch, K—Kt3; 52 K—K5, K—R4; 53 B—K, K—Kt3; 54 Kt—B7, etc. With the text-move the opponent is presented with the tempo he needed for a draw.

(w) Likewise 48 B—K no longer leads to the goal after 48...Kt—Kt5!; 49 KxP, Kt—Q6!; 50 KxP, Kt—Kt7, followed by KtxP, and White's remaining extra Pawn would not suffice for a win.

Game 20	FOURTH ROUND—RUY LOPEZ		
Yates	Ed. Lasker	9 P—Q4(b)	B—Kt5(c)
White	Black	10 B—K3(d)	Kt—QR4(e)
		11 B—B2	Kt—B5
1 P—K4	P—K4	12 B—B	PxP
2 Kt—KB3	Kt—QB3	13 PxP	P—B4
3 B—Kt5	P—QR3	14 P—QKt3	Kt—Kt3(f)
4 B—R4	Kt—B3	15 B—Kt2	R—B
5 Castles	B—K2	16 QKt—Q2	KKt—Q2(g)
6 R—K	P—QKt4	17 P—KR3(h)	B—R4
7 B—Kt3	P—Q3	18 P—K5(i)	PxQP
8 P—QB3	Castles(a)	19 PxP(j)	BxP

20 BxP	B—QKt5(k)	30 BxB	RPxB
21 R—K2	Kt—Q4(l)	31 R—B6	QxQ(q)
22 B—B5(m)	Kt—B6(n)	32 KtxQ	R—R
		33 P—QR4(r)	PxP(s)
		34 PxP	K—B
		35 Kt—B4	K—K2(t)
		36 Kt—Kt6	R—Q(u)
		37 R—B7ch	K—K3
		39 R—R7	K—K4(v)
		39 RxBP	Kt—Q4
		40 KtxKt	RxKt
		41 RxP	K—B3
		42 R—Kt7	K—Kt4
		43 R—Kt4	K—R5
		44 K—Kt2	P—R4(w)
		45 R—Kt6	R—Q5
		46 RxP	RxRP
23 QBxKt	RxB	47 R—R6ch	K—Kt4
24 R—B(o)	R—B2	48 R—R5ch	K—B5
25 R—K3	KBxKt	49 R—B5ch	K—K5
26 RxR	QxR	50 P—R4	K—Q6
27 QxB	Kt—B3	51 K—Kt3	R—R8
28 R—B3(p)	Q—R4	52 P—R5	P—R5
29 P—KKt4	B—Kt3	53 P—R6	R—R8
		54 R—R5	Resigns

After 22...B—B5

(a) This is the best. It is not necessary for Black to continue at once along the lines of Tschigorin's system of defense (Kt—QR4, followed by P—B4), inasmuch as White—as the games of this tournament especially demonstrate—must lose a "tempo" with P—KR3 in order to force him to do so.

(b) Because of the improvement introduced by Bogoljubow in 1922 in the variation beginning with 8...B—Kt5, the move of 9 P—KR3 must be regarded as essential to the retention of the slight opening advantage.

(c) Bogoljubow, to be sure, played first (against Capablanca in London, 1922, and against Dr. Lasker in Maehrisch-Ostrau, 1923): 9...PxP; 10 PxP and then B—Kt5, which is not so good by far, inasmuch as it permits White (as actually done by Dr. Lasker in the game referred to) to play, instead of 11 B—K3, much better 11 Kt—B3, and, after 11...Kt—QR4; 12 B—B2, P—B4, to force a very favorable ending, following an exchange of Queens, by means of 13 PxP, PxP; 14 P—K5!, etc. Bogoljubow's idea in itself, however, is quite correct, but must be carried out in the exact sequence 9... B—Kt5; 10 B—K3, PxP!), as happened in the games between Yates and Bogoljubow and Yates and Capablanca in this tournament.

(d) White has no choice, as, after 9 P—Q5, Kt—QR4, followed by the opening of the QB file by means of P—B3, Black obtains a promising game on the Queen's side—as Rubinstein, among others, has demonstrated in several excellent games in recent years.

(e) This, however, is not consistent, inasmuch as White, after 11 PxP, BxKt (11... PxP; 12 QxQ, QRxQ; 13 KtxP, B—Q3; 14 KtxB, KtxKt; 15 P—KR3, KtxB; 16 RxKt, etc., losing a pawn without sufficient compensation); 12 QxB, PxP; 13 B—B2, Kt—B5; 14 B—B, can assure himself of the possession of two Bishops with a good game. As he plays it, however, it amounts to a mere matter of transposition of moves.

(f) A deviation from Bogoljubow's method of play in the aforementioned games (Kt—R4—B3, in order to renew his pressure upon Q4 and eventually to exchange White's KB by means of Kt—Kt5). Although it seems to be somewhat less consistent, the departure is not to be criticized, inasmuch as the Knight on Kt3 guards the square, Q4, and can also assist eventually in an enterprise on the Queen's wing, beginning with P—B5.

(g) In order to recapture with the Knight after 17 PxP (not so good would be 17... PxP, after which White, by means of 18 P—K5, followed by Kt—K4, would obtain a playable game), and, moreover, to force the opponent with B—B3 to a clearance in the center. Black has now obtained a most promising game.

(h)   A move due to embarrassment and which merely forces the Bishop to better squares.

(i)   Considering the weakness of the square, QB3, in connection with the unpleasant pinning of the King's Knight, this forcible break in the center is, at any rate, of doubtful merit.   Aside from 18 PxP, there came under serious consideration also 18 P—QR4!

(j)   Of course not 19 BxP, on account of 19...PxP; 20 BxP, KtxB; 21 RxKt, BxKt, followed by B—B3, etc.

(k)   Very good.   Now White suffers from a double pinning and, in order to avoid the destruction of his King's position, has nothing better than his next move.

(l)   Bringing about a most dangerous situation for his opponent.

(m)   Unfavorable also would have been 22 P—Kt4, B—Kt3; 23 BxB, BPxB; and if 22 QR—B, B—B6!, etc.   The very ingenious text-move is the only one to hold the game intact.

(n)   This merely leads to a series of exchanges.   Black, however, selected this variation doubtless only after examining and correctly estimating the result of the very misleading 22...B—B6, for instance: 23 Kt—K4 (not 23 R—K4, BxR; 24 QxB, P—B3), BxKt; 24 PxB, BxR; 25 BxB, Kt—B5; 26 R—Q2, Kt—QKt3 (pretty, but unfortunate!); 27 BxKKtP! (and not 27 RxQ, KRxR, with eventual gain of the exchange), KxB; 28 RxQ, QRxR; 29 Q—Rch, P—B3; 30 K—R2, with advantage for White.   The fact that White adopted this complicated continuation and Black avoided it is creditable to both.

(o)   Now White clearly has nothing more to fear and the game takes on the character of a likely draw.   ,

(p)   A rather harmless effort to turn the temporary absence of the black Rook from the seat of war to an advantage in the ending.

(q)   The exchange of Queens was neither necessary nor pleasant.   After 31... P—Kt5 (Q—R6 would also do); 32 Q—K2, R—Q, or 32 R—B4, R—Q, etc., Black would have been by no means at a disadvantage.   Even so it should have sufficed for a difficult draw.

(r)   Gaining control of the square, QB4, for the Knight, and eliminating all unimportant elements on the Queen's side in order the better to utilize the weakness of Black's QR3.

(s)   Of course 34 PxP, PxP; 35 R—Kt6, etc., was threatened.

(t)   This is the deciding error.   With 35...Kt—Q4! the game could still have been held, for after 36 Kt—Kt6, KtxKt; 37 RxKt, Black plays 37...R—R2 and brings his King to B2 and then R—R, in order, should the white King abandon his base, to find there convenient objectives for attack (KR6).   If, however, White does not exchange Knights, then Black can play 35...K—K2, followed by Kt—Kt5, etc.   After the text-move, the objective disappears and with it the game is lost.

(u)   Likewise 36...R—QKt; 37 P—R5, etc., would have been in vain.

(v)   Desperation.

(w)   Still another trap: 45 R—Kt5, RxR; 46 PxR, P—R5; 47 P—Kt6, P—R6; 48 P—Kt7, P—R7; 49 P—Kt8 (Q), P—R8 (Q); 50 Q—Q8ch (?), P—Kt4; 51 Q—QKt8, Q—Rch, etc., but nowadays one does not tumble for the like of this.

FIFTH ROUND

This round provided a genuine sensation, with Richard Reti as the hero of the day. Capablanca had drawn four games in succession and his friends, no less than he, were looking forward to his first victory. Instead there came an astounding defeat, which, while highly creditable to Reti, gave the world's champion, after finishing one-quarter of his full schedule, a rating of less than 50 per cent! The manner in which he pulled up from then on, without losing another game outright or even being seriously endangered, until finally he landed in second place, demonstrated as little else could have done the sheer greatness of Cuba's chosen son.

"Reti wins from Capablanca!" This was on everybody's lips, and soon the tidings traveled to the far corners of the earth. Next to the actual victory of Dr. Lasker, this was the best news item of the tournament. Reti took his hard-earned honors with becoming modesty, but he was the lion of the hour. Such moments are to chess players what the flush of victory is to generals in the field.

Of course, it was a Reti opening. But what about the play of the champion? What was the underlying reason for this, his only defeat? The opening, it seems, he treated soundly enough. If anything, he even had a slight shade the better of it. Then he made his eighteenth move, evidently under the impression that he would win a Pawn. The outcome, however, was an inferior position. Reti timed his moves with the greatest nicety and presently was rewarded by capitulation of the one man who most seldom turns down his King in token of surrender.

Dr. Lasker's game with Dr. Tartakower was a Sicilian Defense adopted by the latter and conducted by both carefully and conservatively. Neither side was able to make any impression.

Marshall vs. Yates was an Indian, the earlier part of which was indifferently played by the American, who lost a clear Pawn. After his good opening, however, Yates failed to make further headway and played the ending rather poorly. With more effort, perhaps, the game might have been won, but Marshall came away with a draw.

Maroczy and Bogoljubow discussed a Queen's Pawn Opening, in which Maroczy endeavored to build up a winning King's side attack. Bogoljubow's defense was invincible, so much so that the admission of unsoundness was forced home to his opponent. Maroczy missed a chance to draw and lost.

Ed Lasker and Janowski followed the lines of an irregular defense to the Queen's Pawn Opening. Janowski was outplayed right from the start, but Lasker weakened after gaining the upper hand. Janowski seized a chance to initiate a pretty combination, after which he remained with Queen against Rook and Knight. This was an unfortunate loss for Lasker to incur.

At this stage, Dr. Tartakower and Bogoljubow both had scores of 3½—1½ and Dr. Lasker, 3—1. As between White and Black the score was again even, 12½—12½.

Game 21   FIFTH ROUND—SICILIAN DEFENSE

Dr. Lasker	Dr. Tartakower		
White	Black	21 P—KKt3	Q—B
		22 Q—Kt3	B—K2
1 P—K4	P—QB4	23 K—R2	R—R5
2 Kt—KB3	P—K3	24 Q—Q3	Q—K3
3 Kt—B3(a)	P—QR3	25 P—Kt3	R—R
4 P—Q4	PxP	26 B—Kt2	R—Q
5 KtxP	Q—B2(b)	Drawn	
6 B—K2(c)	Kt—KB3(d)		
7 Castles	B—Kt5(e)	After 8 B—B3	
8 B—B3	Kt—B3(f)		
9 KtxKt	QPxKt(g)		
10 B—K3	Castles		
11 P—KR3(h)	P—K4(i)		
12 Kt—R4	P—QKt4		
13 Kt—Kt6	R—Kt		
14 KtxB	KRxKt		
15 P—QR4(j)	Q—K2(k)		
16 PxP	RPxP		
17 R—R7	R—Kt2		
18 RxR	QxR		
19 Q—Q3	P—KR3		
20 R—Q	R—QR		

(a) More to be recommended here is 3 B—K2 so that, according to whatever defense Black might adopt for the next moves, he could play Kt—QB3 or else first P—QB4, for instance: 3...P—QR3; 4 Castles, QB2; 5 P—QB4, Kt—KB3; 6 Kt—B3, followed by P—Q4, etc., or 3...Kt—KB3; 4 Kt—QB3, threatening P—K5, Kt—Q4; KtxKt, followed by P—Q4.

(b) In this formation the Paulson defense is quite playable, although Black must guard himself very carefully against the attack successfully carried out by Bogoljubow against Rubinstein (London, 1922); B—Q3, Castles and K—R, followed by P—B4.

(c) After this move, on the other hand, he should experience no further serious difficulty, inasmuch as White must soon lose a "tempo" for the purpose of defending his KP.

(d) Neither is Black's play exactly precise. First should come 6...B—Kt5 and only after 7 Castles would Kt—KB3 have been in order; for, after the text-move, the reply of P—QR3 had to be seriously considered by White.

(e) Against this White had nothing better than the following offer of a sacrifice, which Black, however, rightly declines.

(f) After 8...BxKt; 9 PxB, QxP, there could have followed 10 B—B4 and P—K5, with a strong attack. After 8...Kt—B3, Black threatens to force the favorable exchange of the White KB by means of Kt—K4. White, therefore, makes up his mind to equalize the position by establishing an approximately even pawn formation.

(g) A more substantial game would have ensued from capture with the KtP. The move selected likewise assures Black fair equalization.

(h) A precautionary move in readiness for the possible B—Q3. For that matter 11 Kt—R4 might also be played at once, for instance: 11...B—Q3; 12 Kt—Kt6; BxPch; 13 K—R, R—Kt; 14 P—KKt3, and Black would get no compensation for the sacrifice of the Bishop on Kt6.

(i) Making possible a further simplification of the game. Under consideration also came 11. .B—Q3, in order to meet 12 Kt—R4 with 12...P—B4.

(j) The two Bishops hold out no prospect of a win, inasmuch as the KB is tied up because of the protection of the KP and has, moreover, no outlook on account of the respective pawn formations.

(k) 15...P—KR3 would have saved a "tempo."

Game 22   FIFTH ROUND—RETI'S OPENING

	Reti	Capablanca
	White	Black
1	Kt—KB3	Kt—KB3
2	P—B4	P—KKt3
3	P—QKt4(a)	B—Kt2
4	B—Kt2	Castles
5	P—Kt3	P—Kt3(b)
6	B—Kt2	B—Kt2
7	Castles	P—Q3
8	P—Q3	QKt—Q2
9	QKt—Q2	P—K4(c)
10	Q—B2	R—K
11	KR—Q	P—QR4(d)
12	P—QR3	P—R3(e)
13	Kt—B(f)	P—B4(g)

After 13...P—B4

| 14 | P—Kt5(h) | Kt—B(i) |
| 15 | P—K3(j) | Q—B2 |

16	P—Q4	B—K5(k)
17	Q—B3(l)	KPxP
18	PxP	KKt—Q2(m)
19	Q—Q2(n)	PxP(o)
20	BxP	QxP
21	BxB	KxB
22	Q—Kt2ch	K—Kt
23	RxP(p)	Q—B4(q)
24	QR—Q	R—R2
25	Kt—K3(r)	Q—R4

After 25...Q—R4

26	Kt—Q4(s)	BxB
27	KxB	Q—K4(t)
28	Kt—B4(u)	Q—QB4
29	Kt—B6	R—B2
30	Kt—K3	Kt—K4
31	QR—Q5(v)	Resigns

(a) This move by Niemzowitsch (Carlsbad, 1923) surely can be played without disadvantage. It seems to us, however, that in this way Black can find counter-play more easily than with the symmetrical development of 3 P—KKt3; 4 B—Kt2, etc., which, at any rate, promises to White a chance of retaining his "tempo," which is not by any means without importance as the fight to control the center begins. Moreover, it is hardly to be recommended that a player, during the first few moves, should commit himself to an exposed Pawn position on either wing merely because of the slight hope of establishing a sentinel (in this case QKt5). The opponent can prepare himself immediately for that.

(b) Capablanca treats the opening simply as well as soundly and, after a few moves, obtains a perfectly even position.

(c) After this move, which makes futile the possible advance of P—Q4, on account of the subsequent Pawn exchange and likewise prevents an eventual KKt—Q4, Black for a time has to consider the variation KtxP, BxB; KtxKt. With his next move White could not very well do this because, after BxR, he would lose at least the exchange.

(d) After 11...P—K5; 12 PxP, KtxP; 13 BxB, KxB; 14 Kt—Q4, etc., White would have some advantage. The text-move leads to an isolating maneuver with a prospective peaceful conclusion.

(e) This move, which is difficult to understand, is the best proof that Capablanca was poorly disposed that day. Could it have been his idea to render feasible the Knight maneuver of Kt—R2—B or Kt4? Be this as it may, all he succeeds in doing in this game is to weaken his King's side.

(f) Protecting the KP in preparing the combination of KtxP and seemingly threatening to win a Pawn. Black, however, accepts the offer.

(g) A clever positional trap, quite in the champion's style. Its only disadvantage lies in the fact that White need not meddle with it at all.

(h) Reti rightly declines the Grecian gift. After 14 PxRP, RxP; 15 KtxP, BxB; 16 KtxKt, B—B3; 17 KtxKtch, BxKt; 18 BxB, QxB; 19 Q—Q2, P—R4, etc., Black, on account of his excellently posted Bishop, which in connection with the open QR file held out good prospects for an attack, and because of the weakness at QR6, would have had more than sufficient compensation for the Pawn sacrificed. After the text-move, of course, White has nothing to be afraid of, but his chances of winning (Kt6 in the ending!) are also extremely slight, because of the blocked position.

(i) 14...P—Q4 would yield the square QB5 to the opponent after 15 PxP, KtxP; 16 KKt—Q2, etc.

(j) In view of the weakness of QB4 after the intended P—Q4, this is a bold strategem which leads to complications. With 15 P—K4, followed by the establishment of the Knight at Q5, White could have easily drawn the game.

(k) It was essential at this very moment to force the removal of the Queen.

(l) Not a happily chosen spot, since Black can open the diagonal of the Bishop at Kt2. Better would have been 17 Q—B, although Black even then, by means of KPxP and Kt—K3, could have retained a satisfactory game.

(m) A miscalculation. Capablanca probably overlooked the check of the Queen on the 22nd move, by means of which White protects his QKtP; otherwise he would undoubtedly have selected the simple move of 18...Kt—K3, the strength of which was patent. After 19 PxP, (there is hardly anything better) QPxP; 20 Q—B, Black's position, because of the effective distribution of his pieces, would have been somewhat preferable. After the move in the text, Reti suddenly gets the better of it and from now on plays the game to perfection.

(n) By means of his last move, Black has considerably weakened the Q file and, moreover, the exchange of his KB, so essential to the protection of his King, is next to inevitable. The lesser evil for him now would have been 19...QR—Q, followed by 20 PxP, QPxP; 21 BxB, KxB; 22 Q—Kt2ch, K—Kt; 23 Kt—K3, and White's advantage might, perhaps, still be overcome.

(o) Still hoping to win a Pawn.

(p) Not quite sufficient would have been 23 KKt—Q2, Q—B7, etc., but now it does threaten.

(q) Likewise 23...Q—B2; 24 QR—Q, Kt—B4; 25 Kt—K3, etc., was unsatisfactory. With the text-move Black endeavors to obtain a counter attack.

(r) Threatening 26 Kt—Kt4.

(s) The most compelling move. White, to be sure, by means of the surprising continuation of 26 QR—Q5, BxR; 27 P—Kt4, BxKt; 28 PxQ, BxP; 29 B—B6, etc., would have won the Queen for a Rook, Knight and Pawn, but the final tussle in that case would have been much more difficult and tedious than after the best defense possible against the move in the text.

(t) Of course, he could not play 27...RxKt, on account of 28 PxR, QxR; 29 Kt—K6 (B5), etc.; but it would have been possible to make a stouter resistance by means of 27...Kt—K4, inasmuch as White could not then capture the KtP on account of 28... Kt—-B5, etc. Thereupon he would have had to be satisfied with an ending holding forth promise of victory, after 28 Q—K2, QxQ; 29 KtxQ, etc., or else increase his pressure by means of 28 Q—Kt3 (threatening both Kt—Q5 and RxP). In either case, by correct play, the result could not have been doubtful.

(u) The unfortunate Queen will presently be unable to find another square.

(v) If now 31...Kt—B5; 32 RxQ, KtxQ; 33 R—B2, Kt—R5; 34 Kt—Q5, and wins.

Game 23 FIFTH ROUND—QUEEN'S PAWN OPENING (INDIAN)

Marshall. White.	Yates. Black.		
1 P—Q4	Kt—KB3	7 Castles	P—K4
2 Kt—KB3	P—KKt3	8 Kt—B4(d)	PxP
3 QKt—Q2(a)	B—Kt2	9 PxP	B—Kt5(c)
4 P—K4	P—Q3	10 B—K3	P—Q4
5 B—Q3(b)	Kt—B3(c)	11 PxP	QxP
6 P—B3	Castles	12 QKt—Q2	QR—Q
		13 R—B(f)	KtxP(g)
		14 BxKt	QxB

15	KtxQ	BxQ	36 Kt—Kt5	PxKt
16	KRxB	RxKt	37 RxKt	RxR
17	Kt—Kt3	R—Q3(h)	38 RxR	BxP
18	B—K2	R—K3(i)	39 B—Q5	R—KB
19	B—B3	P—B3	40 RxKtP	BxRP
20	Kt—R5	R—K2	Drawn	

21	R—B4	Kt—Q4
22	P—KKt3	KR—K
23	P—Kt3	Kt—B6
24	R—Q2	B—R3(j)
25	R—Kt2	Kt—Q4
26	P—QKt4	B—Kt2(k)
27	R—Kt3	P—QR3
28	R—B2(l)	Kt—Kt3
29	R—Q3	Kt—Q2
30	Kt—B4	B—B(m)
31	K—Kt2	R—Kt
32	P—QR3	P—QB4(n)
33	R(B2)—Q2	Kt—B3
34	PxP	R—B2
35	Kt—Q6	Kt—Q2

After 13 R—B

(a) This move, instead of the development of the QB, should, to our way of thinking, be avoided on general principles, because White obligates himself unnecessarily without influencing the development of his adversary. The consequences of such strategy become apparent very soon.

(b) Likewise this posting of the Bishop is here without effect.

(c) For an exception this Knight move, otherwise not suitable to the "Indian," is here opportune, a circumstance which very clearly shows how colorless were the first moves of White.

(d) An evident mistake which affords Black an immediate advantage. With 8 PxP (after 8 P—Q5, Kt—K2 and, later, Kt—K and P—KB4, Black, as experience teaches, could have broken through on the King's side before White could counter on the Queen's) PxP; 9 Kt—B4, White might have equalized the position.

(e) Now White has no compensation at all for his loose center pawns.

(f) Even after 13 B—K2, which was somewhat better anyway, Kt—K5 (14 B—QB4, Q—KB4, etc.) the weakling could not have been held much longer.

(g) After this simple gain of a pawn (and not 13 QxRP; 14 Kt—B4, etc., which White probably had hoped for) Black's victory, despite Marshall's tenacious defense, should have become merely a question of time.

(h) Not 17...R—Q2, because of 18 Kt—B5, etc. After the text move, White does not dare to capture the pawn on B7. For instance, 18 RxP, KR—Q; 19 Kt—B, B—R3; and wins.

(i) This allows a more convenient defense of the Queen's side than 18...RxR; 19 BxR, P—B3; 20 Kt—R5, R—Kt.

(j) From now on Black begins to elaborate and in that way gradually spoils his position. He was not being threatened so that he could have played B—B3 and K—Kt2, and then made an attempt to exchange a Rook.

(k) Here 26...P—QR3 at once would have been better.

(l) In preparation for P—QR4, which, on account of Kt—Kt3, would not do right away.

(m) In such fashion, of course, no game can be won!

(n) Under the circumstances, this simplifying process is the most sensible; otherwise (perish the thought!) White soon could start playing for a win.

Game 24   FIFTH ROUND—QUEEN'S PAWN OPENING

Maroczy	Bogoljubow
White	Black
1 P—Q4	Kt—KB3
2 Kt—KB3	P—K3
3 P—K3(a)	P—B4
4 B—Q3	P—Q4
5 P—QKt3	Kt—B3(b)
6 Castles	B—Q3
7 B—Kt2	Castles
8 Kt—K5(c)	Kt—K2(d)
9 Kt—Q2	P—QKt3
10 P—KB4	B—Kt2
11 Q—B3(e)	R—B
12 Kt—Kt4(f)	KtxKt
13 QxKt	Kt—Kt3(g)
14 Kt—B3(h)	P—KB4
15 Q—R5	B—K2(i)

16 P—KKt4(j)	P—B5
17 PxKBP(k)	KtxP(l)
18 PxKt	PxB
19 Kt—Kt5(m)	BxKt
20 PxB	RxQBP(n)
21 P—Kt6	P—KR3
22 B—R3	RxBP
23 RxR	PxR
24 QxBP	Q—B3(o)

After 15...B—K2

After 24...Q—B3

25 R—K(p)	R—K7(q)
26 R—KB(r)	QxPch
27 K—R	Q—B3
Resigns	

(a)   In view of the present theory of the Queen's gambit, there is no good reason why White should evade the variations resulting from 3 P—B4.

(b)   Black desires to hold the center in abeyance for a while in order later on to be able to operate through the threat of P—QB5.   Likewise worthy of consideration would have been 5...PxP; 6 PxP, B—Kt5ch, which, to our way of thinking, could have been best answered by White with 7 K—B.   The forfeiture of castling would there be fully compensated for by control of the center and the more mobile Pawn formation (eventually P—QB4).

(c)   As little effective as 8 QKt—Q2, with which Bogoljubow came to grief against Capablanca.

(d)   This clever maneuver of the Knight, with the idea of increasing the action of the Rook on the QB file later on and at the same time guarding the King's side, had already been employed successfully by Bogoljubow in his match with Rubinstein (Stockholm-Goteborg, 1920).   Black indeed seems to obtain a satisfactory defensive position thereby.   Still better, however, is 8...Q—K2, 9 P—KB4, PxP, after which the exchange of the adverse Bishop is forced.

(e)   White can retain attacking prospects only if he contends for the possession of K4 with the hostile Knight.

(f)   The consequences of 12 P—KKt4, P—B5; 13 PxP, PxP; 14 QxB, PxB; 15 PxP, QKt—Q4, would not be healthy for White.   With the text-move he dismisses his anxiety concerning the square, K4.

(g)   Simpler would have been 13...P—B4 at once, which would probably have led to the actual variation.

(h) Inadequate, for the purpose of obtaining an advantage, would have been 14 BxKt, RPxB; 15 Kt—B3, PxP; 16 Kt—Kt5, B—K2; 17 BxP, BxKt (but not R—B7; 18 KtxKP, PxKt; 19 QxKtP, etc.); 18 PxB, R—B7, and White cannot bring about the attacking formation with Q on R4 and R on R3 on account of the disturbing counter stroke of P—K4; for instance, 19 R—B3, P—K4; 20 BxKP, P—Q5; 21 P—K4, Q—K2; 22 BxQP, QxKP.

(i) Necessary, on account of the threat of 16 Kt—Kt5. But now it was essential for White to consider the move 16...P—QB5.

(j) A faulty combination which leads to a downright lost position. After 16 P—B3 (with the object of retaining the KB on the offensive diagonal), P—B5; 17 B—B2, White would still have kept the chance of holding the initiative through the opening of the Knight file, after which the outcome of the game could not have been predicted.

(k) Or 17 B—K2, PxQKtP, followed by R—B7, etc.

(l) This strong rejoinder was probably overlooked when White made his sixteenth move.

(m) Likewise 19 PxQP would have been fruitless in the long run, for instance, 19...RxP; 20 Q—Kt4; R—B7; 21 R—B2, RxR; 22 KxR, B—Q3; 23 Kt—K5, Q—B3, etc.

(n) Now White establishes a sentinel at Kt6, and, because of the mating threats entailed, is enabled to bring about a playable ending. Decisive would have been 20...RxKBP; 21 RxR, PxR; 22 PxP, Q—K2; 23 Q—B3, R—B7; 24 R—Kt (24 B—B, RxBch, etc.), QxPch; 25 Q—Kt3, Q—Q7; 26 B—R3, P—B5; 27 Q—R3, B—B, and wins.

(o) Since his omission on the 20th move, all of Black's moves have been forced.

(p) This should lead to a less unfavorable ending than 25 R—KB, QxQ (but not 25...QxQPch; 26 K—R, Q—B3; 27 Q—K6ch, etc.); 26 RxQ, R—B; 27 K—B2, R—K; 28 R—K5, RxR; 29 PxR, B—B, and Black would have won the KtP also.

(q) Clearly forced.

(r) Inconsequent and immediately disastrous. After 26 RxR, PxR; 27 QxQ, PxQ; 28 K—B2, B—R3; 29 B—Q6, B—Q6; 30 B—Kt8, Black would have been compelled either to part with the KP or the two Pawns on the Queen's side. After this the ending, after 30...P—QR3; 31 B—B7, P—Kt4; 32 B—R5, K—Kt2; 33 K—K3, B—Kt8; 34 KxP, BxP (P—Kt5; 35 K—Q2, etc.); 35 P—Kt4, KxP 36 K—K3, would very likely have led to a draw, notwithstanding the unequal material.

Game 25   FIFTH ROUND—QUEEN'S PAWN OPENING

Ed. Lasker	Janowski
White	Black
1 P—Q4	Kt—KB3
2 Kt—KB3	P—QKt3
3 P—B4	B—Kt2
4 Kt—B3	P—Q3(a)
5 B—Kt5	QKt—Q2
6 Q—B2	P—K4(b)
7 P—K3	P—KR3(c)
8 B—R4	P—KKt4
9 B—Kt3	Kt—R4
10 Castles	KtxB
11 RPxKt	B—Kt2
12 B—Q3	P—Kt5(d)
13 Kt—KR4	PxP
14 PxP	Q—Kt4ch
15 K—Kt	CastlesQR(e)
16 B—K4	KR—K(f)
17 BxBch	KxB
18 Kt—K4	Q—QR4
19 Kt—KB5(g)	B—B
20 R—R5	Q—R3
21 Kt—K3(h)	P—QB4(i)
22 KtxKtP	PxP

23 RxQP	Kt—B4
24 KtxKt(j)	KtPxKt
25 R—K4	Q—B3
26 Kt—B6	R—K3
27 R—B5(k)	K—Kt
28 P—B3	B—Kt2
29 Kt—Q5	R—Q2
30 P—Kt3(l)	P—QR4

After 18...Q—QR4

31	P—R4(m)	R—R2(n)
32	Q—K2	Q—K
33	Kt—B6	Q—QB
34	Kt—R5	B—Q5
35	Kt—B4	R—K4
36	P—KKt4(o)	RxR(B5)
37	PxR	QxP
38	P—KKt4	Q—R2
39	K—B	B—K4
40	Kt—Q5(p)	P—B4
41	PxP	R—KKt2
42	P—B4	R—Kt8ch
43	K—Q2	R—QKt8
44	Q—R5	Q—KKt2(r)
45	Q—K8ch(s)	K—R2
46	Q—Kt6(t)	BxPch(u)
47	RxB	Q—Kt7ch
48	K—K3	QxPch
49	K—B2	Q—B7ch
50	K—Kt3(v)	R—KKt8ch
51	K—R3	R—R8ch
52	K—Kt3	R—Kt8ch
53	K—R3	RxQ
54	PxR	QxKtP(w)

55	K—R4	K—Kt2
56	K—R3	Q—K
57	K—R4	K—B3
58	R—Kt4	Q—K7
59	K—Kt3	Q—Q6ch
60	K—R4	Q—QB7
61	Kt—K7ch	K—Q2
62	Kt—Q5	Q—R7mate

After 46 Q—Kt6

(a) This deployment of the Pawns on black squares promises no positional advantage for Black, but certainly has a bad feature in that it weakens the white squares in his own camp. The supplementary move to P—QKt3 is P—K3, exactly as in the Indian defense P—KKt3 is supplemented by P—Q3.

(b) The lesser evil would have been 6...P—QB4 in order, after 7 P—Q5, to fianchetto the second Bishop. After the text-move, a line clearance favorable only to the better developed opponent becomes inevitable.

(c) Leading, in connection with the next move, to a decisive dissolution of the King's position, the utilization of which is made easier for White by the opening of the KR file. Therefore, White's position after the eleventh move may already be regarded in the light of a strategical victory.

(d) A further injury to the position. However, Black by this time stands so poorly that it seems next to impossible to find a satisfactory plan of defense. Of course, 12...BxKt; 13 PxB, PxP; 14 PxP, BxP would not do on account of 15 B—K4, etc.

(e) Black after all succeeded in landing his King in safe quarters. For that, however, he is obliged to permit the exchange of his proud Queen's Bishop.

(f) If 16...P—QB3, then 17 Q—R4, K—B2; 18 Kt—B5, KB—B; 19 QxP, R—QR; 20 Kt—Kt5ch! and wins.

(g) Decisive. The Pawns on the Black King's side can clearly not be defended and may be picked off by the opponent in any order he may prefer.

(h) Still better than 21 KtxP, for this Pawn in any case does not run away.

(i) In order to open up some prospects at least for the Bishop.

(j) Herewith White unnecessarily complicates his chances of winning. Much simpler would have been to take along another Pawn with 24 KtxP, the more so as a third one would have been attacked thereby. From now on Janowski defends himself with great tenacity.

(k) Threatening the win of a pawn through 27 Kt—Q5, R—Q2; 28 RxP, etc., which Black prevents with his next move.

(l) In order to able to reply to 30...R—Kt2 with 31 RxP.

(m) Here, however, Q—K2 at once was simpler, inasmuch as the continuation, 31 ...P—R5; 32 RxR, PxR; 33 QxP, PxP; 34 PxP, was not to be feared (34...Q—R3; 35 Q—K8ch, or 34...R—R2; 35 Q—Kt8ch, and wins).

(n) A clearance move for the Queen which makes White's winning line somewhat more difficult.

(o) A well calculated pawn sacrifice which Black would do better to decline with 36...R(R2)—K2, for, after the acceptance, the game must be lost for him in a few moves.

(p) Now the position has been clarified. Against P—KB4 and the subsequent entrance of the White pieces Black no longer has a defense.

(q) It is not necessary for White to bother himself about the consequences of the loss of the exchange on K5, inasmuch as the plan he thought out on playing 36 P—KKt4 is fully adequate.

(r) A final trap, for the success of which two miracles are required.

(s) The first miracle: the simple 45 PxB would have won at once, for instance: 45 ...Q—Kt7ch (or 45...R—Kt7ch; 46 K—B3, etc.); 46 R—K2! R—Kt7ch; 47 K—B3 and, if 47 Q or RxR, then mate in five moves beginning with 48 Q—K8ch, etc.

(t) And here's the second; not to mention that 46 PxB would even now have won similarly as on the previous move, he could have brought about in addition a victory-yielding ending by means of 46 Q—K7ch, QxQ; 47 KtxQ, etc.

(u) This obvious check, which makes possible the decisive entrance of the black Queen, was evidently completely overlooked by White.

(v) After 50 K—B3, R—B8ch, the King would have been forced to the Knight file anyway.   . . .

(w) After the capture of the Queen, the game of course is quite easily won.

SIXTH ROUND

This round at last brought victory to Capablanca and, at precisely the same time, the first defeat for Dr. Tartakower. The only draw was between Dr. Lasker and Ed Lasker, which required three sessions and went to 103 moves! But for this the White pieces would have made a clean sweep on all the boards. As it was, Black suffered to the extent of 4½—½.

The game between the two Laskers has been characterized as the greatest fighting game of the tournament, and rightly so. The different phases cannot very well be dealt with here, but have received the most painstaking scrutiny from Mr. Alekhine. Suffice it to say that Dr. Lasker failed to exact the maximum penalty when tribute was coming his way. Thereafter Ed Lasker's defense was superb and, toward the last, he was actually in the ascendancy. Dr. Lasker, with a lonely Knight, drew against Rook and Pawn in a classical ending.

A Dutch Defense by Dr. Tartakower against Capablanca was the first really pleasurable game on the part of the champion, and a fine example of his machine-like precision and superior technique. The ending came to a classical position, with K on KB6, P on KKt6 and R at KR7. Although Dr. Tartakower was two Pawns ahead, he could not stem the tide.

Alekhine vs. Janowski was another irregular defense to the Queen's Pawn Opening and mismanaged strategically by Janowski, who castled on the Queen's side in the face of a grilling attack promptly worked up by Alekhine. The Black QB remained out of the game after six moves.

A second setback came to Marshall at the hands of Maroczy in a Three Knights Opening. The Hungarian cunningly induced the American to sacrifice a Pawn for an attack which was not sufficiently compensating. The manner in which Maroczy improved his position thereafter was most instructive. He forced the exchange of Queens and, timing his moves with precision, won the Rook ending, despite Marshall's stubborn resistance.

Reti played another fine game against Yates, the development of the opening being peculiarly his own. He placed his pieces as follows: Q on QR; B on QKt2 and KKt2; R on QB and QB2. When the break came Yates could not hold the position in the center.

Thanks to the great drawing effort against his namesake and Capablanca's victory, Dr. Lasker, after completion of all the games of this round, was tied with Alekhine and Bogoljubow at 3½—1½, followed by Dr. Tartakower, with 3½—2½. White went went ahead in the race between the colors, the score reading: White, 17; Black, 13.

Game 26

SIXTH ROUND—RUY LOPEZ

Dr. Lasker	Ed. Lasker
White	Black
1 P—K4	P—K4
2 Kt—KB3	Kt—QB3
3 B—Kt5	P—QR3
4 B—R4	Kt—B3
5 Castles	B—K2
6 R—K	P—QKt4
7 B—Kt3	Castles(a)
8 P—B3	P—Q3(b)
9 P—KR3(c)	Kt—QR4
10 B—B2	P.—B4
11 P—Q4	Q—B2
12 QKt—Q2	BPxP(d)
13 PxP	B—Q2
14 Kt—B	KR—B(e)
15 R—K2(f)	Kt—R4(g)
16 PxP	PxP
17 KtxP(h)	BxP
18 KtxP(i)	B—K3

35 K—R2(t)	RxR(u)
36 KtxR(v)	Q—K2

After 36...Q—K2

37 RxB(w)	QxR
38 QxKt	Q—B5(x)
39 Q—K7(y)	Q—B
40 Kt(Q)—B2(z)	P—R3
41 Q—R7(aa)	Q—K3
42 Q—Kt7	Q—Q4
43 Q—Kt6(bb)	R—Q3
44 Q—K3	R—K3
45 Q—QB3	Q—B5(cc)
46 Q—KB3	Q—B3
47 Q—Q3	R—Q3
48 Q—Kt3ch	Q—Q4
49 Q—Kt	R—K3(dd)
50 Kt—Kt4	R—K7(ee)

After 16 ...PxP

19 Kt—Kt5	B—B5
20 B—Q3	R—Q
21 R—B2(j)	Kt—B5
22 BxKt	QxB
23 Kt—R3	Q—K4
24 BxBch	KtxB
25 Q—K2(k)	R—Q5
26 P—B3	QR—Q
27 QR—B	B—B4
28 K—R	B—Kt5(l)
29 P—QKt3	Kt—Q7(m)
30 Kt—K3(n)	B—R6
31 R—Q	B—Kt5(o)
32 P—R3(p)	B—R4
33 P—QKt4	B—B2(q)
34 P—B4(r)	KtxP(s)

After 50...R—K7

51 KtxPch(ff)	PxKt
52 Q—Kt6ch	K—B
53 QxPch	K—K
54 Q—Kt6ch	K—Q

55	Q—Kt3(gg)	R—K(hh)	
56	Q—B2	R—Kt	
57	Q—Kt2(ii)	Q—Q3(jj)	
58	Q—B3	K—Q2	
59	Q—B3	K—B2	
60	Q—K4	R—Kt2	
61	Q—B5(kk)	R—K2	
62	Kt—Kt5(ll)	R—K6	
63	Kt—K4	Q—K2(mm)	
64	Kt—B6	K—Kt(nn)	
65	P—Kt3(oo)	RxP	
66	K—R3	R—R8(pp)	
67	Kt—Q5	R—R8ch(qq)	
68	K—Kt2(rr)	Q—KR2	
69	QxQ(ss)	RxQ	
70	K—B3	K—Kt2	
71	P—Kt4	K—B3	
72	K—K4	R—R(tt)	

After 72 K—K4

73	Kt—K3(uu)	R—Kch
74	K—Q4	R—Qch
75	K—K4(vv)	P—R4
76	PxP	P—Kt5
77	P—R6(ww)	K—B4(xx)
78	P—R7	P—Kt6
79	Kt—Q	R—QR(yy)

80	P—Kt5	RxP
81	P—Kt6	R—Q2
82	Kt—Kt2	R—Q7
83	K—B3(zz)	R—Q
84	K—K4	R—Q7
85	K—B3	R—Q
86	K—K4	K—Q3(aaa)
87	K—Q3	R—QB
88	P—Kt7	K—K3
89	P—Kt8(Q)	RxQ
90	K—B4	R—Kt6
91	Kt—R4	K—B4
92	K—Kt4	KxP

After 92..KxP

93	Kt—Kt2	K—K5
94	Kt—R4	K—Q5
95	Kt—Kt2	R—KB6(bbb)
96	Kt—R4	R—K6
97	Kt—Kt2	K—K5
98	Kt—R4	K—B6
99	K—R3	K—K5
100	K—Kt4	K—Q5
101	Kt—Kt2	R—R6
102	Kt—R4	K—Q6
103	KxP	K—Q5ch
	Drawn	

(a) This move may also be made in advance of P—Q3; if properly answered, however, it amounts merely to a transposition of moves.

(b) Simply because the pawn sacrifice, by 8...P—Q4, attempted by Marshall against Capablanca (New York, 1918), was refuted by the latter in the following manner: 9 PxP, KtxP; 10 KtxP, KtxKt; 11 RxKt, Kt—B3; 12 R—K, B—Q3; 13 P—KR3, Kt—Kt5; 14 P—Q4, Q—B3; 15 Q—R5, KtxP; 16 R—K2, and Black was unable to obtain proper compensation for the following sacrifice of 16...B—KKt5.

(c) This preparatory move is necessary here in order to prevent the very unpleasant pinning by means of B—KKt5. Aside from this, it prepares the way for an eventual demonstration against the King's wing.

(d) In the hope of being able to make use of the QB file as a base of operations. As, however, is shown by this game, and especially so by the one between Maroczy and Reti (18th round), White can easily dispute this file with the opponent and thereafter.

by cramping the hostile forces with the eventual P—Q5, gain an advantage. In consequence of this, the older method of 12...Kt—QB3 whereby Black foregoes an immediate counter-sally, appears nevertheless to be somewhat more enduring.

(e) The other Rook is to be utilized either on the QR or QKt files. Black, however, does not get so far.

(f) This move, to be sure, is quite good enough, but appears somewhat strange and, therefore, furnishes the opponent something new to think about. Somewhat more natural and at least qu.te as good would have been 15 B—Q3, as played by Maroczy against Reti.

(g) The pawn sacrifice involved is quite ingenious and interesting, but in the end turns out to be incorrect. The proper continuation would have been 15...P—Kt5; 16 B—Q3, Q—Kt, in order to ease the defense through an exchange by means of B—Kt4, etc. White's superiority, however, would have been evident even after that line of play.

(h) Dr. Lasker does not allow himself to be frightened by the approaching complications and quietly accepts the proffered gift. The following intricate combinations are splendidly handled by him until a winning position is reached.

(i) With the terrible threat of 19 Q—Q5.

(j) This leads to a more favorable defensive position than the immediate exchange, for instance: 21 BxBch, KtxB (if 21...QxB; 22 Q—B2, QxQ; 23 RxQ, KR—Q; 24 Kt—B3, etc.); 22 Q—Kt3, Kt—B5; 23 BxKt, QxB; 24 Kt—R3 (if 24 Kt—K6, Q—Kt5, etc.), Q—K4, with drawing chances as in the actual game.

(k) Now White has a substantial pawn to the good and it is merely necessary to drive away the black Knight from his commanding post which in the long run cannot be prevented. The temporary control of the black squares does not compensate Black for the pawn.

(l) The exertions of Black have resulted merely in emphasizing the threat of P—QKt3. The invasion of Q7 by the Knight, contemplated with the text-move, is an act of desperation which should not alter the fate of the game.

(m) After 29...Kt—Kt3 (if 29...Kt—Q3, Kt—K3), White, by means of 30 R—B6, B—R6; 31 QR—B2, could next force the exchange of a Rook, thereby lessening the pressure upon the Q file. The text-move leaves the Knight in a sort of blind-alley.

(n) Now the threat is QR—Q, followed by driving the Bishop off the diagonal, K sq to QR5, with the gain of a piece, while the counter-combination of 30...KtxKP; 31. PxKt, RxP would be neutralized by means of 32 R—B8, etc. Being of the opinion that he has discovered a hidden defense, Black surprises the adversary by forcing him to execute his threat at once. In the end, however, he is doomed to disappointment.*

(o) Clearly insufficient would have been 31...B—Q3, on account of 32 Kt—Kt4, etc.

(p) It was necessary to calculate this winning maneuver with great exactness.

(q) The threatened mate cannot now be properly met with 34 Kt—Kt4, on account of the reply 34...KtxKP, etc. White, however, has prepared a much more effective reply.

(r) Leaving Black with but one answer.

(s) Not 35 PxQ, Kt—Kt6ch; 36 K—R2, KtxQ; 37 RxB, RxR; 38 KtxR, RxKt; 29. Kt—Kt5, R—Q; 40 R—R7, etc., which to be sure, gives promise of fair winning chances, but White's continuation is far more forceful.

(t) The next move is forced.

(u) Or 35...Q—K2; 36 Kt—B5, etc.

(v) Of course not 36 PxQ, BxPch; 37 P—Kt3, QR—Q7, etc.

(w) Here, however, he loses the fruits of his solid position play. The simple 37 QKt—B2, R—Q5; 38 Q—K3 would have won a piece, for 38...B—Kt3 would be met by 39 R—B8ch, K—B2; 40 KtxKt, RxKt; 41 QxR, followed by 42 Kt—Kt5ch. After that, of course, the game would be over. The text-move, on the other hand, makes it at least very difficult to win the game.

(x) If 38...RxKt; 39 Q—K8 mate.

(y) Neither here nor later can White win if he exchanges the Queens, because Black would spread himself in the end-game over the Queen's side of the board by capturing the QRP, in addition to exchanging the Pawn on QKt4, whereupon the remaining pawns on the King's side would not suffice to bring about a win. Through the avoidance of the exchange, however, he presently reaches a defensive position in which he is not entitled to expect a legitimate win. Nevertheless, he persists in trying to win—and in that lies the explanation of the sacrifice on the 51st move.

(z) The Queen ending, after 40 Kt—Kt5, RxKt; 41 Q—B7ch, K—R; 42 Q—R5, P—R3; 43 QxR, PxKt; 44 Q—R5ch, K—Kt; 45 QxP, Q—B8, etc., promised only slight winning chances, and 40 Kt—K3 would not do on account of 40...R—K.

*[Alekhine overlooked that R—B8 fails against R—Q. The flag on Ed. Lasker's clock was about to fall and, forced to move immediately, he did not risk the sacrifice. It would have won the game.—Note by Ed. Lasker, 1961.]

(aa)   41 Kt—K4 offered better chances, for, after 41 R—K; 42 Q—B5, QxQ; 43 KtxQ, R—K6; 44 KtxP, RxP; 45 Kt—B5, the White QKtP can be held. Consequently, Black would have to answer 42 Q—B5 with Q—K3—at any rate with a more difficult defense than in the actual game.

(bb)   Exchange of Queens, as well as 43 QxRP, R—R, followed by RxP, etc., could not, of course, be considered as part of a winning plan.

(cc)   Black's position has been improved quite considerably during the last eight moves.

(dd)   Now the Rook threatens a counter attack (particularly upon the QRP) and White, should he not be satisfied with a draw through repetition of moves, must now positively "discover" something.

(ee)   Black has correctly weighed the futility of the sacrifice contemplated by the opponent and quietly allows it, the more so as, by some other continuation, the posting of the Kt on K5 might have brought White slight winning chances.

(ff)   The hopes of victory bound up with this combination are shattered by the circumstance that the Knight, because of the unsafe position of the King, cannot co-operate at the right time.   Moreover, through persistent avoidance of drawing possibilities, White, in consequence of his weak QRP, actually drifts into the shallows of defeat.

(gg)   A simple draw could have been reached here through 55 Q—Kt6ch, K—K; 56 Q—Kt8ch, K—K2; 57 Q—R7ch, K—B; 58 Q—Kt8ch, R—K; 59 Q—R7, after which Black would have had nothing better than to resort to 58...R—K7.   Similar opportunities also will offer themselves to White during the next few moves.

(hh)   After 55...R—Q7, threatening R—Q6, White, by means of a series of checks beginning with 56 Q—R4ch, could always have forced a cessation of the threatened mate at Kt2.

(ii)   Here likewise Q—Kt6ch, etc., would have compelled the draw.

(jj)   Safeguarding the King against further checks and preventing attack by the Knight.

(kk)   White has carried through his plan fully and, by means of fine Queen maneuvering, assured the co-operation of the Knight.   It seems, however, that this last is at this stage of minor importance and does not in any way prevent the fall of the QRP.

(ll)   There was still time to make the Queen's side safe by means of 62 Q—B2ch, K—Q; 63 Q—B3, etc.   The tempting move of the Knight, on the contrary, should cost the game.

(mm)   Threatening to win the Queen by 64...Q—R5ch, etc.

(nn)   Whereby the fate of the QRP is sealed.   Black, since his 38th move, has defended himself quite faultlessly and has now attained a winning position.

(oo)   Aimless would have been 65 Kt—Q7ch, on account of K—B2, etc.

(pp)   66...QxP would have permitted White a draw by perpetual check (67 Q—K5ch, K—Kt2; 65 Q—Q5ch, etc.).

(qq)   By means of this move and the following Black forces the exchange of Queens and a winning, albeit difficult ending.   More compelling, however, would have been 67...Q—Q3, thereafter driving the Knight from Q5 by means of R—Q8, and to play for the capture of the QKtP in conjunction with a direct attack upon the King.

(rr)   Of course not 68 K—Kt4, on account of 68...Q—K7ch, etc.

(ss)   White cannot avoid exchange of Queens, because, after 69 Q—K5ch or Q—KB8ch, he would have had no more checks and his King would have been obliged to succumb eventually to the combined attack of the two Black pieces.

(tt)   This plausible move grants White a hidden possibility for a draw.   Correct would have been 72...R—Q2, which would have forced the retreat of the Knight without taking the Rook from the seventh row; for instance: 72...R—Q2; 73 Kt—K3 (if 73 Kt—B6, R—Q; 74 P—Kt5, P—R4; 75 PxP, P—Kt5; 76 P—Kt6, P—Kt6, and wins), P—R4; 74 PxP, P—Kt5; 75 P—Kt5 (P—R6), K—B4; 76 Kt—B2, P—Kt6; 77 Kt—R3, P—Kt7; 78 P—Kt6, K—Kt5; 79 Kt—Kt (or 79 Kt—B2ch, K—Kt6), R—Q8; 80 P—Kt7, R—Kt8, followed by RxP, and wins.

(uu)   After 73 Kt—B6, 73...R—Q, followed by P—R4, would have been decisive.

(vv)   White will not permit his King to be separated from his passed Pawn and eventually he is seen to be right.   After 75 K—B3, Black most likely would have continued with 75...R—Q3, so that, after a move of the Knight, he might have occupied Q8 with his Rook, but, after a Pawn move, to cross over with his King to the defense. A direct loss for White does not appear in this variation; the text-move, however, which leads to a clear drawing position after a short and sharp struggle, is more convincing.

(ww)   The only move.   Obviously insufficient, for instance, would have been 77 P—Kt5, P—Kt6; 78 Kt—B4, K—B4; 79 Kt—Kt2, R—Q7; 80 Kt—Q3ch, K—B5; 81 Kt—K5ch, K—B6, and wins.

(xx) Richer in possibilities than 77...P—Kt6; 78 Kt—B4, K—Kt4; 79 Kt—Kt2, KxP (79...R—Q7; 80 P—R7 comes to naught); 80 K—K3, K—Kt4; 81 P—Kt5, K—Kt5; 82 P—Kt6, K—B6 (or R6); 83 Kt—R4ch (or Kt—B4ch), and Black dare not venture upon K—B2 or R2, on account of P—B5, followed by P—Kt7, etc.

(yy) 79...K—Kt3; 80 K—K3, KxP; 81 Kt—Kt2, etc., would lead into the variation outlined above.

(zz) The point of the whole defense; the Knight, of course, cannot be captured on account of 84 P—Kt7, and Black, therefore, in case he desires to continue playing for a win, must permit the approach of the hostile King to his passed Pawn.

(aaa) With this move, to be sure, White's two passed Pawns are forcibly captured, nevertheless the ending, despite the great advantage in material, strangely enough cannot be won.

(bbb) An attempt to bring over the King to Q7 in the rear of the Rook. Meanwhile, however, White had time to post his King on Kt2 so that further attempts to approach must remain futile. An unusual game rich in vicissitudes.

Game 27

SIXTH ROUND—DUTCH DEFENSE

	Capablanca White	Tartakower Black
1	P—Q4	P—KB4
2	Kt—KB3	P—K3
3	P—B4	Kt—KB3
4	B—Kt5	B—K2(a)
5	Kt—B3	Castles
6	P—K3	P—QKt3
7	B—Q3	B—Kt2
8	Castles	Q—K(b)
9	Q—K2(c)	Kt—K5
10	BxB	KtxKt
11	PxKt	QxB
12	P—QR4(d)	BxKt(e)
13	QxB	Kt—B3
14	KR—Kt	QR—K(f)
15	Q—R3(g)	R—B3(h)
16	P—B4	Kt—R4
17	Q—B3	P—Q3(i)
18	R—K	Q—Q2(j)
19	P—K4	PxP
20	QxP	P—Kt3

21	P—Kt3(k)	K—B
22	K—Kt2	R—B2(l)
23	P—R4	P—Q4(m)
24	PxP	PxP
25	QxRch	QxQ
26	RxQch	KxR
27	P—R5(n)	R—B3
28	PxP	PxP
29	R—R	K—B
30	R—R7	R—B3
31	P—Kt4	Kt—B5
32	P—Kt5(o)	Kt—K6ch
33	K—B3	Kt—B4(p)
34	BxKt(q)	PxB

After 34...PxB

35	K—Kt3(r)	RxPch
36	K—R4	R—B6
37	P—Kt6	RxPch
38	K—Kt5	R—K5
39	K—B6	K—Kt
40	R—Kt7ch	K—R
41	RxP	R—K

After 23 P—R4

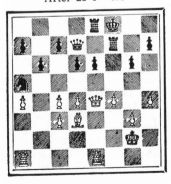

42	KxP(s)	R—K5
43	K—B6	R—B5ch
44	K—K5	R—Kt5
45	P—Kt7ch	K—Kt
46	RxP	R—Kt8
47	KxP	R—QB8

48	K—Q6	R—B7
49	P—Q5	R—B8
50	R—QB7	R—QR8
51	K—B6	RxP
52	P—Q6	Resigns

(a) With this and the following moves, Black's main disadvantage in this opening, that is, the difficulty of developing his Queen's Knight at the proper time, without weakening his basically unsound pawn formation still more, is by no means eliminated. More suitable for this purpose would have been 4...B—Kt5ch; 5 QKt—Q2 (5 Kt—B3, P—QB4), Kt—B3; 6 P—K3, Castles, followed eventually by P—Q3 and P—K4.

(b) At all events better than 8...Kt—K5, which occurred in the game between Marshall and Dr. Tartakower. Black now even threatens a lighthorse attack through Q—R4, followed by Kt—Kt5, etc.

(c) Discounting this intention in the most simple manner, since, after 9...Q—R4, 10 P—K4 would follow with advantage for White. Black, therefore, applies himself to the task of simplification.

(d) In order to answer 12...Kt—B3 with 13 KR—QKt (threatening P—R5), Kt—R4; 14 P—B5, followed by K—Kt5.

(e) This exchange is made clearly in order to avoid the aforementioned variation. Now, however, it happens—as usual in mobile pawn formations—that the Bishop is superior to the Knight. The rest of the game is a very fine example of the utilization of such an advantage.

(f) Not yet necessary. 14...Kt—R4 (15 P—B5, PxP; 16 R—Kt5, P—QB5), as well as 14...P—KKt4, could safely have been played.

(g) Gaining time for P—KB4, whereby Black's P—K4 is retarded for a long while.

(h) This move also might well have been replaced with 13...P—KKt4, which after all was inevitable.

(i) After 17...P—B4, White could have launched an attack beginning with 18 P—KKt4. After the text-move, however, he obtains even better objects for attack in the center.

(j) After 18...P—K4, there follows 19 P—K4, and the opening of the file would only benefit White.

(k) The plan of attack is clear; after proper preparation, the KR pawn must advance.

(l) Or 22...Q—QB3, 23 QxQ, KtxQ; 24 P—B5, threatening B—Kt5, etc.

(m) In face of the threatening attack Black decides upon this simplification, but the weaknesses of his position grow even more acute in the ending. A few chances of salvation might be offered by the likewise uninviting Rook ending after 23...KtxP; 24 BxKt, P—Q4; 25 BxP (Q—K5 leads to nothing, as likewise Q—Q3, PxB, followed by Q—Q4ch, etc.), QxB; 26 P—QR5!

(n) That is the calamity—the Rook now enters the hostile camp by way of the KR file.

(o) Threatening R—R6, followed by P—B5, and against it there is nothing to be done.

(p) Or 33...Kt—Q8; 34 R—R6, K—B2; 35 P—B5, RxP; 36 PxPch, K—Kt; 37 K—K2, Kt—Kt7; 38 B—B5, with an easy win.

(q) Simple and compelling.

(r) Decisive! White sacrifices material in order to obtain the classical position with K on KB6, P on KKt6 and R on KR7, whereupon the black pawns tumble like ripe apples.

(s) Again the simplest. 42 K—B7 would not yet have been disastrous, because of 42...R—Q, etc.

Game 28   SIXTH ROUND—IRREGULAR DEFENSE

Alekhine	Janowski		5	B—Kt2	QKt—Q2
White	Black		6	P—K4	B—Kt3
1 P—Q4	Kt—KB3		7	KKt—K2	P—K4(c)
2 P—QB4	P—Q3		8	P—KR3(d)	Q—Kt3
3 Kt—QB3	B—KB4(a)		9	Castles	Castles(e)
4 P—KKt3(b)	P—QB3		10	P—Q5(f)	Kt—B4

11	B—K3	PxP	34	KxQ	B—Q
12	BPxP	Q—R3(g)	35	R—Kt2	K—B
13	P—B3(h)	K—Kt(i)	36	BxKt	PxB
14	P—QKt4	QKt—Q2	37	B—Kt6	B—Kt4
15	P—QR4(j)	Q—B5	38	R—B2ch	K—Kt2
16	Q—Q2(k)	QxKtP	39	P—Q6	P—B4
17	BxPch	K—R	40	P—Q7	Resigns
18	KR—Kt	Q—R4			
19	B—K3	Kt—B4			
20	R—Kt5	Q—B2			
21	P—R5	KKt—Q2(l)			
22	Kt—B	R—B			
23	Kt—Kt3	Kt—R3(m)			
24	Kt—R4	B—K2(n)			
25	Kt—Kt6ch(o)	K—Kt			
26	R—B	KKt—B4			
27	KtxKt	PxKt			
28	KtxR	RxKt			
29	B—B	Q—Q2			
30	R—Kt6	P—B5(p)			
31	RxP	RxR			
32	BxR	QxP			
33	Q—KKt2(q)	QxQch			

After 24...B—K2

(a) The course of this game demonstrates in the most convincing manner that the development of the Bishop at B4 is not desirable here. The most effective play is 3... P—KKt3, followed by B—Kt2, because for the time being it obligates Black the least.

(b) The correct reply which obtains for White the formation of a powerful center.

(c) In order, among other things, to reserve the opportunity still to develop the KB. On the other hand, Q3 is marked as a potential weakness, while the Black pieces, as before, are without a future.

(d) A necessary positional move to safeguard permanently the square, KKt4, and thereby make possible the development of the QB at K3.

(e) This supplies the opponent with an objective for a direct attack which, owing to the unfortunate disposition of Black's pieces, will have catastrophic consequences. After 9...B—K2; 10 B—K3, Q—B2, it would not have been so easy for White to transform his positional advantage into victory.

(f) Demolishing all of Black's hopes for an eventual delivery by means of P—Q4. The temporary release of QB5 is, in comparison with this main motive, altogether immaterial.

(g) Acceptance of the pawn sacrifice would have led to a clearly losing position. For instance, 12...QxP; 13 BxKt, PxB; 14 Q—QR4, Q—Kt3; 15 P—B4, PxP; 16 PxP, etc., but the continuation in the text is likewise without prospects.

(h) Simple and decisive. Black has no longer a defense against P—QKt4.

(i) If 13...Q—Q6, then 14 Q—QB, etc.

(j) But this is lack of precision, which permits the opponent to regain control of QB5, and in that way to resist a while longer. 15 Q—Q2, Q—B5; 16 QR—Kt, followed by KR—B, would have deprived him even of this last chance.

(k) Even now 16 QR—Kt would have been very strong.

(l) Black has weathered the first onset successfully; but, inasmuch as White can attack the hostile King with all of his seven pieces, while Black's King's side is wholly undeveloped and his QB has long since forgotten that he is able to move, it is only a question of time when White must win.

(m) After 23...KtxKt, would follow 24 P—R6, forcing P—Kt3, for, after 24... KtxR (or KtxQ); 25 PxPch, followed by mate in a few moves.

(n) Black makes up his mind to give up the exchange, knowing that, if 24... K—Kt, White, with 25 R—QB, Q—Q; 26 R—B6, would have proceeded to institute a decisive attack.

(o) The crisis. After 25...KtxKt, would follow 26 PxKt, Q moves; 27 RxKt and wins.

(p) Desperation, for, after 30...B—Q; 31 R—Kt2, this pawn could not be defended.

(q) The conductor of the White pieces perceived quite well that 33 BxKt was also possible, with the following variation: 33...QxPch; 34 Q—Kt2, Q—K8ch; 35 K—R2, QxB; 36 RxPch, K—R; 37 Q—Kt2, Q—B5ch; 38 K—Kt2, Q—Kt4ch; 39 K—B, winning. This, however, would have been a seven-move combination and White was justified in assuming that Black, after the text-move compelling the exchange of Queens, would resign forthwith.

Note—We designate as "irregular" only such openings which represent sporadic attempts, easily refuted as to position and possessing merely a superficial similarity to the systems of development scientifically evolved during later years.

Game 29   SIXTH ROUND—THREE KNIGHTS OPENING

Maroczy	Marshall
White	Black
1 P—K4	P—K4
2 Kt—KB3	Kt—KB3
3 Kt—B3	B—Kt5(a)
4 P—Q3(b)	P—Q4
5 PxP	KtxP
6 B—Q2	Castles
7 B—K2	QKt—B3
8 Castles	B—K3(c)
9 R—K	P—KR3
10 KtxKt	BxB
11 KtxB	BxKt
12 B—B3	Q—Q3
13 Kt—K4	BxKt
14 BxB	QR—K
15 BxKt	QxB(d)
16 Q—Q2	R—K3
17 R—K3	R—Kt3
18 P—KKt3(e)	P—B4(f)

After 18 P—KKt3

19 RxP	P—B5
20 P—Q4	Q—Q2
21 Q—Q3	R(Kt3)—KB3
22 QR—K	PxP
23 BPxP	R—B6

24 KR—K3	R(B6)—B2(i)
25 P—B3	Q—Q4(j)
26 P—B4	Q—Q2
27 P—Q5	Q—Q3
28 Q—Q4	Q—KKt3
29 R—K6	Q—B7
30 R(K6)—K2	Q—B4
31 R—K8	P—QKt3
32 Q—K3	K—R
33 RxRch	RxR
34 P—Kt3	Q—B7
35 Q—K2	Q—Kt3
36 Q—K4	Q—KB3
37 Q—B4(k)	Q—Q
38 Q—K5	Q—QB
39 Q—K6	Q—R3
40 Q—K7	K—Kt
41 R—K2	Q—R4(l)
42 QxP	Q—B7
43 Q—K5	Q—B6
44 P—KR4(m)	Q—B8ch
45 K—R2	P—KR4
46 R—KKt2(n)	Q—Kt8(o)
47 P—Q6(p)	Q—Q8
48 Q—K6ch	K—R2
49 Q—K2(q)	R—B8
50 QxQ	RxQ
51 P—QKt4	RxP
52 R—QB2	K—Kt3
53 K—Kt2	K—B4
54 P—B5	R—QB3
55 K—B3	K—K4
56 P—KKt4(r)	PxPch
57 KxP	K—K5(s)
58 R—QB(t)	K—K6
59 R—Kch	K—Q5(u)
60 R—Qch	K—K4(v)
61 R—B	K—K5(w)
62 P—R4	K—K6
63 P—Kt5(x)	R—Kt3ch(y)
64 K—R3	PxP

65	RxP	R—KB3	80	R—R7ch	K—Kt6
66	R—B3ch	K—B7	81	P—R6	Resigns

65	RxP	R—KB3
66	R—B3ch	K—B7
67	R—B7	P—R3
68	R—B2ch	K—B6
69	R—B6	R—B5
70	RxP	R—Kt5
71	R—R7	R—Kt6ch
72	K—R2	R—Kt7ch
73	K—R	R—Kt5
74	P—Kt6	RxPch
75	K—Kt	P—Kt4
76	R—B7ch	K—Kt6
77	P—Kt7	R—QKt5
78	K—B	P—Kt5
79	P—R5	K—R6

80	R—R7ch	K—Kt6
81	P—R6	Resigns

After 57...K—K5

(a) In this variation, a "Ruy Lopez" for Black, frequently made use of by Pillsbury, White is able in simple fashion to obtain the advantage of two Bishops: 4 KtxP, Castles; 5 B—K2, R—K; 6 Kt—Q3, BxKt; 7 QPxB, KtxP; 8 Castles, etc.

(b) This defensive move, on the contrary, is in no way intended to retain the advantage of the opening. White is now playing the Steinitz defense with a tempo plus, which, however, merely suffices for equalization.

(c) But this move does not fit into the system, inasmuch as he makes additional exchanges possible for the opponent, thereby easing up on the position. More promising and analogous to the Ruy Lopez would have been either 8...KtxKt; 9 PxKt, B—R4; or 8...BxKt; 9 PxB, Q—Q3, etc.

(d) Even at this stage a draw might properly have been agreed upon, for, with ordinarily careful play, it should not be lost by either side.

(e) Of course, 18 R—Kt3 could have been played; the text-move, however, is somewhat cunning, for by creating a weakness that is not dangerous, he induces the opponent to undertake a direct offensive.

(f) After 18...R—K3; 19 QR—K, KR—K, etc., the game, of course, would become a positive draw. The sacrifice of the Pawn, on the other hand, which seemingly rests upon the underestimating of the defensive strength of the move, 20 P—Q4, yields only a short-lived attack, which Maroczy defends with accustomed care in order thereafter to make effective, slowly but surely, his material superiority.

(g) Among other things, Black threatens, by means of 20...PxP; 21 RPxP, Q—Kt3! (attacking simultaneously the QKt and KKt Pawns) to recover his Pawn with the better game.

(h) This counter-threat destroys Black's entire attacking formation.

(i) After 24...R—B7, there would follow 25 R—K8!, etc.

(j) It was certainly not necessary to challenge the advance of the white Pawns, but Black clearly had no real chances and could only hope for an error on the part of his opponent.

(k) With this move the hostile Queen is at last driven back, as 37...QxQ; 38 PxQ; 38 PxQ, RxP; 39 R—K7, etc., clearly would have held out nothing for Black.

(l) The only remaining possibility to continue the game, as 41...R—B; 42 Q—Q7!, followed by R—K7, etc., would have been quite without prospect.

(m) Forced, but quite sufficient, for, after 44...Q—B8ch; 45 K—R2, R—B7ch; 46 RxR, QxRch; 47 K—R3, Q—B8ch; 48 K—Kt4, Q—Q8ch; 49 K—B5, etc., Black might as well have resigned.

(n) Of course not 46 QxP, on account of 46...R—B7ch; 47 RxR, QxRch; 48K—R3, Q—B8ch; 49 K—Kt4, Q—K7ch; 50 K—Kt5, Q—K4ch, with perpetual check.

(o) Threatening 47...R—B8.

(p) Which could now be defended with 48 Q—K8ch, K—R2; 49 QxPch, K—Kt; 50 Q—Q5ch, K any; 51 R—K2, etc.

(q) White sacrifices a Pawn for the sake of simplification in order to force exchange of Queens. In the subsequent Rook ending, however, Marshall understands, by interposing technical difficulties, how to prolong the game considerably.

(r) If now or on the next move PxKtP, then, of course, not RxR, PxKtP, but simply RxKtP, with excellent chances for a draw.

(s)   White in splendid fashion gains a decisive tempo.

(t)   Not at once 58 P—R4, on account of 58...K—Q6; 59 R—B, K—Q7, etc. Now, however, 58...K—Q6 can be successfully met by R—Qch and Q6, etc.

(u)   After 59...K—Q6, would follow 60 R—K7, PxP; 61 PxP, P—R4; 62 RxP, RxP; 63 P—R5, winning.

(v)   Otherwise would follow 61 R—Q6.

(w)   And now we again have the position after White's 58th move, with the difference that it is his turn to move.

(x)   Decisive.

(y)   Or 63...RxP; 64 RxR, PxR; 65 P—R5, P—B5; 66 P—Kt6, PxP; 67 PxP, P—B6; 68 P—Kt7, P—B7; 69 P—Kt8 (Q), P—B8 (Q); 70 Q—B4ch, winning the Queen.

Game 30   S'XTH ROUND—RETI'S OPENING

Reti	Yates
White	Black

1	Kt—KB3	P—Q4
2	P—QB4	P—K3(a)
3	P—KKt3	Kt—KB3
4	B—Kt2	B—Q3
5	P—QKt3	Castles
6	Castles	R—K
7	B—Kt2	QKt—Q2
8	P—Q3(b)	P—QB3
9	QKt—Q2	P—K4(c)
10	PxP	PxP
11	R—B(d)	Kt—B
12	R—B2	B—Q2(e)
13	Q—R	Kt—Kt3
14	KR—QB	B—QB3(f)
15	Kt—B	Q—Q2(g)
16	Kt—K3(h)	P—KR3(i)
17	P—Q4(j)	P—K5(k)
18	Kt—K5	BxKt (l)
19	PxB	Kt—R2
20	P—B4(m)	PxPe.p.
21	PxP	Kt—Kt4
22	P—B4	Kt—R6ch

23	K—R	P—Q5(n)
24	BxP	QR—Q
25	RxB(o)	PxR
26	BxBP	Kt—B7ch
27	K—Kt2	QxB
28	QxQ	RxQ
29	BxR	Kt—K5
30	P—K6	R—Q7ch(p)
31	K—B3	Resigns

After 16...P—KR3

(a) This defense to the new opening (also employed in the game, Reti vs. Ed. Lasker, Reti vs. Bogoljubow, Alekhine vs. Bogoljubow and, with colors transposed, Marshall vs. Capablanca) failed to stand the test, which is not to be wondered at, inasmuch as the QB is thereby imprisoned from the start. On the other hand, the London system (Alekhine vs. Euwe and Capablanca vs. Reti, London, 1922) essayed by Dr. Lasker against Reti seems to insure equality for Black.

(b) Thereby White unnecessarily allows the move, P—K4, with the subsequent development of the QB, thus removing the main disadvantage of Black's position. 8 P—Q4 instead (see Marshall vs. Capablanca and Reti vs. Bogoljubow) would have retained the opening advantage.

(c) This had to be done at once, otherwise White (as in the game Alekhine vs. Bogoljubow) might have hit upon the idea of getting on the right track by means of 10 P—Q4.

(d) The beginning of a ponderous maneuver, purposing chiefly the preparation for the eventual entrance of the Knight at K5 in the variation P—Q4, P—K5. For that reason the Queen had to be posted on QR square. But Black managed to prevent this easily as will be seen.

(e) A good alternative here would have been 12...B—KB4, in order, after 13 Q—R, to ret.re the Knight to Q2, where that piece would have been posted to better advantage than at KKt3, as in the game.

(f) A double error of judgment. First, the square, KB4, is left unguarded, and secondly, nothing is done to counteract the opponent's plan as outlined. In order would have been 14...Q—K2 so as to connect the Rooks and, at the same time, to provide ample protection for the square, K4. Thereupon, for instance, could have followed 15 Kt—B, QR—B; 16 RxR, RxR; 17 RxR, BxR; 18 P—Q4, P—K5; 19 Kt—K5, Q—B2, with speedy equalization. After the text-move, White at last obtains free play.

(g) Somewhat better would have been 15...Q—K2 in order to reply to 16 Kt—K3 with 16 B—Q2; 17 Kt—Q2, B—K3, etc. Black does not seem to have noticed the intention of his opponent.

(h) P—Q4 at once should have been played. After the text-move, Black had a safe position.

(i) The decisive blunder. After 16...P—Q5!; 17 Kt—B4, B—B2, Black would still have had a tenable position. Hereafter Reti utilizes his chances splendidly.

(j) Clarifying the pawn position in the center at the right moment and thereby gaining either Q4 or K5 for his Knight. From now on Black's game deteriorates rapidly.

(k) Also after 17...PxP; 18 KtxQP, followed by the doubling of the White Rooks on the Q file, the game could not have been saved for any length of time.

(l) Clearly forced.

(m) The control of the black squares and the weakness of the hostile QP are now decisive factors in favor of White. By the subsequent exchange, in conjunction with the tour of the Knight to R6, the opponent, of course, makes victory easy.

(n) Desperation.

(o) By means of this energetic maneuver White brings about an absolutely winning ending.

(p) The familiar spite-check.

SEVENTH ROUND

On the whole, this was a field day for the "favorites." Dr. Lasker, Capablanca, Reti and Janowski were the winners, with a hard-fought draw between Alekhine and Marshall.

Dr. Lasker in his game with Maroczy started out with Alekhine's Defense, which was transposed into a French Defense. Maroczy sadly mismanaged his side of it and indulged in an ill-fated advance on the King's side. Dr. Lasker's play was beautifully timed. He made the best possible use of his pieces on the strong lines opened up and completely repulsed the attack. Without moving his Queen once, he rendered White's game quite hopeless!

A highly interesting Queen's Pawn Opening was developed between Capablanca and Yates, the Cuban displaying genuine artistry in his treatment. In the ending Capablanca had three Pawns and two Knights, and Yates, one Pawn, Bishop and Knight. Had the latter been able to exchange his pieces for the other's Pawns he still would not have been able to avert defeat, because of the inconvenient Pawn at K3! That this possibility came within an ace of actuality in a masters' tournament was most refreshing.

Alekhine obtained slightly the better of it against the Indian Defense adopted by Marshall and increased this advantage with a fine combination in the middle game. After that the Russian relaxed twice, thereby reversing matters, and it required all his skill to hold the game intact. Altogether it was a very pleasing game throughout.

Reti's Own again made its appearance on the board between him and Ed Lasker, the latter being outmaneuvered. The Black QKt was practically stalemated at QR3 when Reti posted his Bishop at Q6. Next came the advance of the QKt Pawn. All this with Queens on the board and an exposed King! The game was a little beauty.

Janowski played his best game of the tournament against Bogoljubow in this round. In order to win a Pawn the latter permitted his opponent the use of two Bishops—deadly weapons in the hands of Janowski at his best. So well did the representative of France maneuver them that he gradually gained control of the board, holding the White King in a vise-like grip from which he never escaped.

With six completed rounds Dr. Lasker, 4½—1½, held the lead, trailed by Alekhine and Reti, each 4—2. White and Black divided the points, the total record being 19½—15½ in White's favor.

Game 31   SEVENTH ROUND—ALEKHINE DEFENSE

	Maroczy	Dr. Lasker			
	White	Black	23	Kt—B4(k)	R—K5(l)
			24	Q—Kt3ch(m)	K—R
1	P—K4	Kt—KB3	25	Kt—R4	KtxP
2	Kt—QB3	P—Q4(a)	26	Q—KR3	R—B7
3	P—K5	KKt—Q2	27	P—Kt6	B—B3
4	P—Q4	P—K3(b)	28	Kt—B3	P—R3
5	QKt—K2(c)	P—QB4	29	Kt—K6	KtxKt
6	P—QB3	Kt—QB3	30	BxP	R—R5
7	P—KB4	B—K2(d)		Resigns	
8	Kt—B3	Castles			
9	P—KKt3	PxP			
10	PxP(e)	Kt—Kt3			
11	B—R3(f)	B—Q2			
12	Castles	R—B(g)			
13	P—KKt4	P—B3			
14	PxP	BxP			
15	P—Kt5	B—K2			
16	K—R(h)	Kt—B5			
17	Kt—B3	B—Kt5			
18	Q—K2	R—K			
19	Q—Q3	Kt—Q3			
20	P—B5(i)	KtxBP			
21	KtxP	B—Q3			
22	BxKt(j)	PxB			

After 19...Kt—Q3

(a) The best reply, in our judgment, is 2...P—K4, switching into the Vienna game, because White, after the text-move, has the option of bringing about, by means of 3 PxP, KtxP; 4 B—B4, etc., a favorable variation of the Scandinavian opening.

(b) Here 4...P—QB4! is more energetic. In the game between Bogoljubow and Alekhine (Karlsbad, 1923) there followed 5 B—Kt5, Kt—B3!; 6 Kt—B3, after which Black, instead of the impetuous 6...P—QR3 (7 BxKt, PxB; 8 P—K6!, etc.) was able to obtain a favorable position with the simple 6...P—K3. However, Black also obtains excellent prospects by means of the text-move which turns into Steinitz's attack.

(c) It is truly a psychological riddle why Maroczy should select a variation he himself refuted years ago! More consistent at least would have been the double-edged offensive by means of 5 P—KB4, P—QB4; 6 PxP, Kt—B3; 7 P—QR3, BxBP; 8 Q—Kt4, Castles; 9 B—Q3, etc., for then White, because of his futile endeavor to sustain his Pawn formation in the center, should experience dire embarrassment.

(d) This, however, grants the opponent too much time. In the game between Alapin and Maroczy (Vienna, 1908) there occurred the much stronger 8...Q—Kt3; 9 Kt—B3, P—B3; 10 P—KKt3 (otherwise the King's side can hardly be developed), BPxQP; 10 PxP, BPxKP; 11 PxP, B—Kt5ch; 12 Kt—B3, Castles; 13 B—B4, B—K2!; 14 Q—Q2, P—KKt4, winning a pawn.

(e) White should make use of his opportunity to bring his Knight into action by way of 10 Kt(K2)xP, and then, instead of an illusory King's side attack, to play for the maintenance of the balance in the center. After the text-move, Black gets his cue for attacking the Queen's side on the strength of the open B file, all the more so since White's pieces are deployed somewhat clumsily for an assault upon the hostile King.

(f) Undeniably, the Bishop here acquires a certain range of action, yet that neither solves the problem of the misplaced Knight on K2 nor initiates precautionary action for the defense of the Queen's side. A better method of overcoming these disadvantages would have been 11 Kt—QB3, followed by B—Q3, Castles, Q—K2, B—K3, in order to divide his forces as much as possible between the two wings and hence prepare for any emergency.

(g) Black's position on the Queen's side grows steadily more menacing, while White still has difficulty (on account of Kt—B5) in getting his QB into the game. For that reason he plays his trump card on the King's side, thereby merely effecting, however, the opening of another file, which works out in favor of the better developed opponent.

(h) Clear loss of time. Immediately 16 Kt—B3, followed by Q—K2, would have been in order. Of course, White's position was already so poor that a tempo, more or less, hardly made any difference.

(i) A somewhat premature act of despair. To be sure, 20 B—Q2, Kt—R4! (threatening BxKt and B—Kt4), followed by Kt—B5, etc., was not very cheering, still some sort of resistance would have been poss.ble thereby. What follows now is plain butchery.

(j) After 22 B—B4, would follow not 22...PxKt; 23 BxKt, BxB; 24 BxRPch, K—-R; 25 Kt—R4, etc., but 22...Kt—Kt5; 23 KtxKt, BxKt, with a winning position.

(k) And if now 23 B—B4, then 23...B—K3!, etc.

(l) The signal for the counter-attack.

(m) Upon a move of the Knight would follow 24...Kt—Kt5, with deadly effect.

Game 32   SEVENTH ROUND—INDIAN DEFENSE

	Capablanca	Yates			
	White	Black	21	KtxQ	P—Kt3
1	P—Q4	Kt—KB3	22	Kt(B5)—R4	R—Kt
2	Kt—KB3	P—KKt3	23	Castles QR	P—QKt4(n)
3	Kt—B3	P—Q4(a)	24	Kt—B5	R—Kt3
4	B—B4	B—Kt2	25	P—R4(o)	Kt—R4
5	P—K3	Castles	26	P—QKt3	BPxP
6	P—KR3(b)	P—B4	27	BPxP	PxP
7	PxP(c)	Q—R4	28	Kt(B3)xP	R—QB3
8	Kt—Q2(e)	QxBP(e)	29	K—Kt2	Kt—B3
9	Kt—Kt3	Q—Kt3	30	R—Q2	P—QR4(p)
10	B—K5(f)	P—K3(g)	31	KR—Q	Kt—Q4
11	Kt—Kt5(h)	Kt—K	32	P—Kt3	R—KB2
12	BxB	KtxB	33	Kt—Q3(q)	R—QKt2
			34	Kt—K5	R(B3)—B2
			35	R—Q4	K—Kt2
			36	P—K4(r)	PxP
			37	RxP	R—Kt4
			38	R—QB4	RxR
			39	KtxR	B—Q2

After 12...KtxB

After 39...B—Q2

13	P—KR4(i)	P—QR3
14	Kt—B3	Kt—B3
15	B—Q3	P—B4(j)
16	Q—Q2(k)	Kt—K4
17	B—K2	Kt—B5(l)
18	BxKt	PxB
19	Q—Q4	Q—B2
20	Q—B5(m)	QxQ

40	Kt—B3(s)	R—B4
41	Kt—K4	R—Kt4
42	KtK4—Q6	R—QB4

43 Kt—Kt7	R—B2	61 Kt—Q6	B—Kt4
44 Kt(Kt7)xP	B—QKt4	62 R—R5	B—B8(t)
45 Kt—Q6	B—Q2	63 R—R8(u)	P—Kt4
46 Kt(R5)—B4	R—R2	64 BPxP	PxP
47 Kt—K4	P—R3	65 PxP	B—Kt7
48 P—B4	B—K	66 R—K8	R—QB2(v)
49 Kt—K5	R—R	67 R—Q8	Kt—B3
50 R—QB	B—B2	68 Kt—K8ch	K—B
51 R—B6	B—Kt	69 KtxR	KtxR
52 Kt—B5	R—K	70 K—B3	B—Kt2
53 R—R6	R—K2	71 K—Q4	B—B
54 K—R3	B—B2	72 P—Kt6	Kt—Kt2
55 P—QKt4	Kt—B2	73 Kt—K8	Kt—Q
56 R—B6	Kt—Kt4ch	74 P—QKt5	K—Kt
57 K—Kt2	Kt—Q5	75 P—Kt5	K—B
58 R—R6	B—K	76 P—Kt7ch	K—Kt
59 P—Kt4	K—B3	77 P—KKt6(w)	Resigns
60 Kt—K4ch	K—Kt2		

(a) This reaction against 3 Kt—B3 does not seem positionally opportune, because the King's Bishop thereafter may be given an outlet only by means of time-robb ng efforts. More in the spirit of the fianchetto is the move, 3...P—Q3, employed by Maroczy in twc games in this tournament with the object of attacking as soon as possible White's center with P—B4 and thereby obtaining scope for the Bishop. In fact, Maroczy gained an advantage by means of this meneuver.

(b) Not exactly necessary, as neither 5...B—Kt5 (6 P—R3), nor 5...Kt—R4 (6 B—KKt5) was to be feared. For that reason 6 B—Q3 would probably have been the most suitable. After the text-move, Black obtains some counter-play the defense of which will demand all of the world's champion's care.

(c) At first blush this makes a strange impression, but it is based upon a profound conception of the position. White may permit h s only pawn to disappear from the center, inasmuch as he commands it sufficiently with his p eces.

(d) This unpleasant maneuver, which is now forced by the threat of Kt—K5, would not have been necessary for White had he played 6 B—Q3 and been able to castle here.

(e) Unsatisfactory would have been 8...Kt—K5, on account of 9 KtxKt, PxKt; 10 P—QB3, etc.

(f) Lead ng up to an exchange of pieces by which the black squares in the opposing position are considerably weakened, a circumstance which will turn out to be determining factor in the approaching ending. This is Capablanca!

(g) Clearly forced on account of the threat of 11 BxKt, followed by KtxP, etc.

(h) Threatening not alone 12 Kt—B7, but also 12 B—Q4, followed by KtxP, therefore forcing the reply.

(i) And yet some will say that Capablanca's play is altogether too dry! His planning of the game under cons deration (apart from the not wholly exact sixth move) is so full of that freshness of his genius for position play that every "hyper-modern" player can only envy him. Of course, he did not for a moment hope by means of this unexpected move to checkmate his opponent without more ado, but through the threat of open ng the KR file to mislead Black into creating a new weakness (15th move), whereupon White will bring about an ending which is partly won from the very start.

(j) It is becoming uncomfortable for Black. After 15...Kt—K4, there might follow, for instance, 16 P—R5, KtxBch; 17 PxB, KtxP; 18 P—Kt4, followed by Q—B3, etc., with a very promising position for attack.

(k) In order to be able to bring the Knight eventually to B5 by way of R4, without being disturbed by check of the Queen on Kt5.

(l) If 17...B—Q2, then 18 Q—Q4, Q—Q3 or B2 (QxQ; 19 PxQ, etc.); 19 Q—KB4! However, the text move equally meets White's plans, inasmuch as it not only permits exchange of Queens, but at the same time opens the important Q file for him.

(m) Played under the conviction that the Knight, following the exhange, can be kept out of play for only a very short time.

(n) Forced, on account of the threat of 24 R—Q6, etc.

(o) Very convincing. The sol.d chain of black pawns on the Queen's side must disappear in order that the Knight may thereafter pounce upon the remaining weaklings.

(p) The pawn might better have remained on R3, where he was protected by the Bishop. Altogether it was not easily to be foreseen at this point in just what manner White could capture it.

(q) In order shortly to force a simplifying exchange of Rooks and, in addition, to bring over the Knight to B4 for an attack on the RP.

(r) Incidentally, a further weakness is created at K3 through the opening of the King's file.

(s) A remarkable winning maneuver! This Knight makes five moves one after the other in order by main force to travel from R4 to R5, and there to dispose of a pawn. The remaining not difficult, but protracted end-game is managed by Capablanca with his usual precision.

(t) Thereby the Bishop is at last dislodged from the King's side and the ending enters upon a decisive stage.

(u) Threatening 64 Kt—K8ch, K—R2; 65 Kt—B6ch, K—Kt2; 66 P—Kt5, followed by mate.

(v) Or 66...RxR; 67 KtxRch, K—B; 68 P—Kt6, etc.

(w) After which mate in 3 or 4 moves is not to be prevented.

Game 33   SEVENTH ROUND—INDIAN DEFENSE

	Alekhine	Marshall			
	White	Black			
1	P—Q4	Kt—KB3	18	Q—Q2(n)	QKt—B3
2	P—QB4	P—Q3(a)	19	PxP(o)	P—KKt4
3	Kt—QB3	P—KKt3	20	B—Kt3	Q—K2(p)
4	P—K4	B—Kt2	21	K—R(q)	K—Kt
5	P—B4(b)	Castles	22	KR—K(r)	Q—B4
6	Kt—B3	B—Kt5(c)	23	R—K6	QR—Q
7	B—K2	Kt—B3(d)	24	Q—K2	K—R(s)
8	P—Q5(e)	Kt—Kt	25	P—KR3	RxR
9	Castles	QKt—Q2(f)	26	PxR	Kt—KR4
10	Kt—KKt5(g)	BxB	27	Kt—K4	Q—B3(t)
11	QxB	P—KR3(h)			
12	Kt—B3	P—K3(i)			
13	P—K5(j)	PxKP			
14	BPxP	Kt—Kt5			
15	B—B4(k)	PxP(l)			

After 27...Q—B3

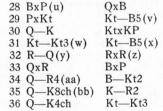

After 15...PxP

16	P—K6(m)	R—K
17	PxPch	KxP

28	BxP(u)	QxB
29	PxKt	Kt—B5(v)
30	Q—K	KtxKP
31	Kt—Kt3(w)	Kt—B5(x)
32	R—Q(y)	RxR(z)
33	QxR	BxP
34	Q—R4(aa)	B—Kt2
35	Q—K8ch(bb)	K—R2
36	Q—K4ch	Kt—Kt3

37	Kt—R5(cc)		Q—B8ch
38	K—R2		Q—B3
39	Q—Q3		QB2ch
40	K—R		B—R(dd)
41	Q—K4		Q—B8ch
42	K—R2		Q—B2ch
43	K—R		Q—B2
44	Q—B2		P—Kt4(ee)
45	Q—B6		P—Kt5
46	Kt—Kt3(ff)		QxP
47	Q—Kt7ch		B—Kt2
48	Kt—B5(g)		Q—R8ch
49	K—R2		Q—B3(hh)
50	QxRP(ii)		P—Kt6
51	Q—Kt7		P—Kt7
52	Kt(B3)—Q4		Kt—K4(jj)
53	QxP(kk)		KtxPch
54	K—R3(ll)		Q—K4(mm)
55	P—Kt3(nn)		Q—K5(oo)
56	Q—B2(pp)		QxQ
57	KtxQ		P—R4

58	Kt—K3		KtxKt
59	KtxKt		B—Q5
60	Kt—B5		B—B4
61	P—Kt4		K—Kt3
62	Kt—R4ch		Drawn

After 54...Q—K4

(a) This permits the opponent to select a method of attack known for years Schwartz vs. L. Paulsen, match of 1884, and Englisch vs. Dr. Tarrasch, Hamburg, 1885), the characteristic theme of which is the immediate advance of the four center pawns. The result of the games played with this opening in the last few years was generally in favor of White, albeit that the defense in most cases was not always of the best. This method of play has only a relatively theoretical value, as Black can readily evade it by first of all playing 2...P—KKt3 in order, after 3 Kt—QB3, to hold in reserve the possibility of 3...P—Q4! (Gruenfeld).

(b) Anent 5 Kt—KB3, see the game, Marshall vs. Reti (first round).

(c) In addition to this move, which, as will be seen, does not yield a satisfactory result, there have been tried here without particular success, 6...QKt—Q2 (Dr. Tarrasch, Hambuurg, 1885); 6...KKt—Q2 (Sir George Thomas, Karlsbad, 1923); and 6...Kt—B3 (Yates, Hastings, 1923); and not until the game, Alekhine vs. Ed. Lasker, in the 16th round of this tournament, was the interesting novely, 6...P—K4!, introduced, which affords Black outlook for a playable game.

(d) This move, so well thought of in England, should be replaced, however, with the more logical 4...QKt—Q2 (Price vs. Yates, Hastings, 1923), whereupon White, as in the game under consideration, should take seriously into account the reply of 8 Kt—KKt5, in order to exchange the inactive KB.

(e) This must be done at once, inasmuch as Black, after 8 B—K3, would obtain counter-play by means of 8...BxKt; 9 BxB, P—K4; 10 PxP, PxP; 11 P—Q5, Kt—Q5! (12 BxKt, PxB; 13 QxQP, KtxKP), etc.

(f) Somewhat better here would have been 9...BxKt, although he would have yielded to the opponent a pair of Bishops for weapons.

(g) Much stronger than the common 10 P—KR3, for, after the enforced exchange of Bishops, the threat of P—K5 again becomes acute, added to which the disturbing position of the Knight on Kt5 sooner or later forces an appreciable weakness of Black's King's side.

(h) After 11...Kt—K, in order to prevent P—K5, the sacrifice of a pawn by 12 P—K5, PxP; 13 P—B5, etc., would have been full of prospects.

(i) If 12...P—K4, White would have been satisfied with the variation, 13 PxP e. p., PxP; 14 Kt—KR4, K—R2 (Q—K; 15 QKt—Kt5), 15 R—B3, etc. After the text move, however, he has still more forceful continuation at his disposal.

(j) At first this appears somewhat dangerous, but in reality is the introduction to a decisive attacking maneuver.

(k) Threatening, of course, 16 P—KR3, etc.

(1) In order to reply to 16 PxP (or also 16 P—KR3) with 16...KKtxKP; 17 KtxKt, KtxKt; 18 BxKt, R—K; 19 Q—B3, RxB; 20 QxPch, K—R2, etc. It happens differently, however.

(m) Concern.ng this advance, which constitutes the point of the maneuver initiated by White on the 13th move, Black has not much choice, inasmuch as he cannot play 16...PxP, because of QxPch and QxKt; not 16...Kt—B4, because of 17 P—K7, and, after 16...Q—B3, then simply 17 PxKt, QxB; 18 KtxQP, Q—Q3; 19 QR—Q, etc., with a clear advantage.

(n) Now, however, when the time seemed to be ripe to gather the fruits of his strategy up to this point, White stumbles and thereby surrenders almost h.s entire advantage. The correct move would have been 17 Q—QB2!, which above all would have confined Black's exposed King to the defense of the square, Kt3. Thereupon Black would have been left without a fully satisfactory reply, for instance: 18...PxP (or P—Q5); 19 Kt—Q5; or 18...QKt—B3; 19 KtxQP, KtxKt; 20 PxKt, QxQP; 21 QR—Q, with a winning attack. The text move leads to a game full of difficulties for both sides.

(o) Or 1 19 KtxP, KtxKt; 20 PxKt, K—Kt!; 21 P—KR3, Kt—B3; 22 BxRP, QxP; II. 19 P—KR3, P—Q5!; 20 KtxQP, Kt—K4, etc., both without any danger for Black.

(p) The best. Black threatens exchange of Queens and, after 21 QR—K, there would follow 21...Q—B4ch; 22 K—R, Kt—K6., etc., with advantage.

(q) Threatening 22 P—KR3.

(r) White still hopes to profit from the position of his Knight at Kt5. The move nearest at hand, 22 Kt--Q4, would have led only to a draw afer 22...Kt—K6; 23 Kt—B5, KtxKt; 24 RxKt, Kt—K5; 25 KtxKt, QxKt; 26 QR—KB, K—K2, etc.

(s) Better would have been 24...RxR; 25 QxR (25 PxR is likewise good enough) K—R; 26 Kt—K5, Kt (Kt5)xKt; 27 BxKt, R—K; 28 Q—B5, etc. But even in this case Black would have been at a slight disadvantage.

(t) Likewise after 27...KtxBch; 28 KtxKt, Kt—B3; 29 R—K, etc., the White passed pawn would have eventually decided the issue.

(u) Herewith White again lets the w.n slip through his fingers and this time actually gets a disadvantage. With 28 Kt (B3)xKtP! he could have won a pawn and by that means doubtless the game, for, after 28...KtxBch; 29 KtxKt, PxKt; 30 QxKt, he would have obtained in addition to material superiority, a d.rect attack against the exposed position of Black's King as well.

(v) Capturing the fine passed pawn and thereby, in consequence of the strong pos:-tion of the Bishop and White's weakened King's side, obtaining good winning chances.

(w) The beginning of the plan by means of which the game is eventually saved. White relinquishes the attempt to salvage the threatened QKtP in order, on the other hand, to force an exchange of Rooks, wh.ch will permit him, with the aid of the Queen and Knights, to institute a lasting counter-attack. The final phase of the contest is quite as exciting as the middle game.

(x) Threatening to win a piece by means of 32...Kt—Q6.

(y) Purposeless would have been 32 R—B, Q—Q2, etc.

(z) Of course not 32...Kt—Q6; 33 RxKt, RxR; 34 Q—K8ch, followed by 35 Q—K4ch, etc.

(aa) The only way possible in which to force an entrance with the Queen into the enemy camp.

(bb) Not the only way possible in which to force an entrance with the Queen into the enemy camp.

(bb) Not 35 QxRP, on account of 35...Q—B7; 36 Q—Kt, QxRP, etc.

(cc) After 37 Kt—B5, Q—B8ch; 38 Kt—Kt (38 K—R2, Q—B5ch), Q—B3; 39 Q—K (Q—Q3, QxKtPch), K—R; 40 Kt—B3, Kt—B5, etc. Black would have had better chances of realizing upon his material advantage than after the text move.

(dd) Otherwise White would play 41 KtxB, followed by 42 Kt—Q4, etc.

(ee) After Black has been convinced that he can accomplish nothing through maneuvering with the Queen, he attempts to bring about a decision through immediate realization of his pawn superiority. White, however, in consequence of this error, obtains new squares for his Queen on the Queen side of the board and, after a short and sharp conflict, brings about a clearly drawing position.

(ff) In order to occupy the more effective square, KB5.

(gg) Of course, much more vigorous than 48 QxKtP.

(hh) Necessary, on account of the threat of 50 Kt(B3)—Q4, etc.

(ii) It will soon become apparent that Black, in consequence of his fettered condi-ticn, is not so situated as to be able to defend the QKtP. A few pretty variations are yet to come.

(jj) If 52...Q—K4ch; 53 P—Kt3, Kt—R5, White would not answer, 54 KtxB, QxKt; 55 Q—K4ch, Kt—Kt3, but 53 K—R3!, KtxKt; 54 KtxKt and, after the inevitable exchange of the remaining minor pieces, the Queen ending would be drawn.

(kk) And not 53 K—R3, on account of 53...P—R4!; 54 PxP, Q—B2!, etc.

(ll) As will be shown in the next comment, 54 K—Kt3 could have been played, inasmuch as 54...Q—K4ch was not to be feared seriously. The text-move, however, is simpler.

(mm) After 54...P—R4, White's best answer would have been 55 Q—QB2, etc.

(nn) Again the simplest. It is interesting, however, that Black would not have had a win even after 55 KxKt, for instance: I. 55...Q—B5ch; 56 K—R5, P—Kt5; 57 KtxRP!, BxKt; 58 Q—B2 or Kt7ch, etc. II. 55...Q—K5ch; 56 K—R3 (not 56 K—R5, BxKt; 57 QxB, Q—K7ch; followed by 58...Q—K mate), BxKt; 57 QxB, QxKtch; 58 K—Kt3, and with correct defense the Queen ending should remain a draw.

(oo) Still another and a last trap. After 56 KtxB Black obviously would have attempted to try his luck further in troubled waters with 56...Kt—K6!, 57 K—R2, Kt—B8ch; 58 K—Kt (58 K—R3, Q—R8ch; 59 K—Kt4, Kt—K6 mate) KtxP. White's reply puts an end to these hopes.

(pp) Forced.

Game 34   SEVENTH ROUND—RETI'S OPENING

Reti White	Ed. Lasker Black	After 35...BPxP

After 35...BPxP

	Reti White	Ed. Lasker Black
1	Kt—B3	P—Q4
2	P—QB4	P—K3(a)
3	P—KKt3	P—QB3(b)
4	P—Kt3	Kt—KB3
5	B—KKt2	Kt—K5(c)
6	Q—B2(d)	B—K2
7	B—Kt2	Castles
8	Castles	Kt—Q2
9	P—Q3	Kt—Kt4(e)
10	QKt—Q2	KtxKtch
11	KtxKt	B—B3
12	P—Q4(f)	R—K
13	P—K4(g)	Kt—Kt3
14	Kt—K5	B—Q2
15	Kt—Kt4(h)	R—QB
16	KtxB	QxKt(i)
17	P—QR4	KR—Q
18	P—R5	Kt—R
19	P—K5	Q—Kt3
20	Q—K2(j)	Kt—B2
21	B—QR3(k)	Kt—R3
22	KR—Q	B—K
23	B—Q6	P—KB4(l)
24	P—B4	Q—R3
25	B—B3	P—KKt4
26	R—R2(m)	PxP
27	PxP	R—Q2(n)
28	Q—K3	R—Kt2ch
29	R—Kt2	RxRch
30	KxR(o)	B—R4
31	BxB	QxB
32	R—KKt	K—B2
33	K—R	R—KKt(p)
34	RxR	KxR
35	PxP	BPxP

36	P—Kt4(q)	K—B2
37	Q—Q3(r)	Q—R5(s)
38	Q—B(t)	Q—Q
39	Q—R3	K—Kt3(u)
40	Q—Kt3ch	K—B2
41	Q—Kt5	Q—QB(v)
42	P—Kt5	Q—B8ch
43	K—Kt2	Q—Q7ch(w)
44	K—R3	Q—K6ch
45	K—R4	Q—K8ch
46	K—R5	Q—K7ch
47	K—R6	QxPch
48	Q—R5ch	QxQch
49	KxQ(x)	K—Kt2
50	PxKt	PxP
51	B—B5	K—B2
52	K—R6	K—Kt
53	BxP	K—R
54	B—Kt6	K—Kt
55	B—Q8	K—R
56	B—R4	Resigns

(a) There is no urgent reason to lock in the Bishop in this fashion. We consider 2...P—QB3 to be the best answer.

(b) 3...P—QB4, after 4 PxP, PxP; 5 P—Q4, etc., would have led into the Rubinstein variation of the Queen's gambit. Better than the text-move, however, would have been first to develop the King's side by means of Kt—B3, B—Q3 or K2, followed by Castles, and only then, after the opponent's plan of mobilization had become clearer, to build up the other side.

(c) Original, but costing time and hence unprofitable. The idea manifestly is to prevent 6 B—Kt2 for the moment, because Black would thereupon have won a pawn through 6...Q—Kt3; 7 Castles, PxP, etc. However, even in this line of play White would have obtained excellent chances for an attack which would have made up fully for the loss of the pawn, for instance: 8 Q—B2, Kt—Q3; 9 PxP, KtxP; 10 B—Q4, Q—R3; 11 Q—B3!, P—B3; 12 BxP, PxB; 13 QxP, R—Kt; 14 Kt—Kt5, etc.

(d) But this simple reply, which makes possible the contemplated plan of development, is still more logical.

(e) This roving about with the same piece, only to exchange it in the end with the loss of a tempo, is by itself enough to lose the game. It is instructive, however, to observe how Reti with seemingly matter of fact moves gets the best of it. Comparatively better would have been 9...Kt—Q3, with th idea perhaps of undertaking some counteraction on the Queen's side by means of P—Kt4.

(f) In accordance with the principle that exchanges should be avoided where possible in positions where the opponent is cramped. Aside from this the move tends to control the square, K5.

(g) In order to answer 13 QPxKP with Kt—K5! Black's best chance would then have been 13...PxBP; 14 PxP (14 P—K5?, PxP), P—K4, etc., in order in this way finally to set free his QB. Having neglected this opportunity also, he will now be smothered completely.

(h) Very good! Black now has the choice between 15 B—K2, with next 16 P—B5, Kt—B; 17 P—K5, followed by Kt—K3, P—KB4, and eventual break by means of P—KB5, or permitting the exchange of his KB, as in the actual game, whereupon the Black squares in his position become hopelessly weak.

(i) White now commands the entire board and, after straightening out the center, sooner or later will break through successfully on one of the wings. From this point on there are several ways that "lead to Rome."

(j) It is clear that for the execution of his plans of attack White's Queen has to play an important role.

(k) Preventing among other things Kt—K, on account of the reply of B—K7, etc.

(l) The only possibility to bring about the co-operation of the Bishop. Thereby, however, the opponent is supplied with a welcome object for attack and, if Black on the move after the next had not decided upon the desperate advance of P—KKt4, then, after proper preparation, would have followed the break by White with P—KKt4 with decisive result.

(m) A complicated, typical Reti move. Instead of compelling the further advance of the KKtP w th 26 B—K7 and thereafter preparing for the opening of the KR file with P—KR3, Reti, by means of the text-move which threatens nothing at all, inveigles the opponent into opening the KKt file, a maneuver which will shorly turn out disastrous to Black on account of his lack of mobility.

(n) After 27...QxP; 28 Q—Kt2ch, K—R, White would win by 29 B—K7, B—Kt3; 30 P—R4!, QxPch; 31 R—B2, etc.

(o) White, with correct positional insight, apprehends that he no longer needs to retain the two bishops here, inasmuch as his QB alone suffices for the purpose of disposing of the hostile Knight.

(p) The exchange of this Rook is utilized very cleverly by White for the capture of the Knight. But 33...Kt—B2 would not do on account of 34 Q—Kt3, Q—R3; 35 BxKt; and, also after 33 Kt—Kt, White, by means of 34 R—QB! (threaten ng PxP), PxP; 35 PxP, etc., would have obtained a decisive advantage in position.

(q) White's last moves were played to obtain just this position. The threat of P—Kt5 can be defended by Black only through the eventual removal of his Queen from the King's side, but then would follow a direct attack which would compel the surrender of the Knight. The finish is quie simple yet attractive because of its unremitting log'c.

(r) Not at once 37 P—Kt5, because of 37...Kt—B2; 38 BxKt, Q—Q8ch; 39 K—Kt2 (39 Q—Kt, Q—B6ch, drawing), Q—B7ch and QxB.

(s) Threatening Q—K8ch, followed by KtxP.

(t) The completion of the maneuver. Now there remains for Black only the withdrawal of the Queen in anticipation of 39 P—Kt5.

(u) Manifestly forced.

(v) Exchange of Queens, of course, would be equivalent to resigning. With the text-move he threatens a few checks, but White calculates exactly that his King will soon be in safety.

(w) Q—Kt7ch and QxKtP would not do on account of the subsequent mate in two moves.

(x) And now at last the game is at an end.

Game 35 SEVENTH ROUND—QUEEN'S GAMBIT

Bogoljubow	Janowski
White	Black
1 P—Q4	P—Q4
2 Kt—KB3	Kt—KB3
3 P—QB4	PxP
4 P—K3	P—K3
5 BxP	P—QB4
6 Kt—B3	Kt—B3
7 Castles	B—K2
8 Q—K2	Castles (a)
9 R—Q	Q—B2
10 P—QR3	P—QR3 (b)
11 PxP	BxP
12 P—QKt4	B—K2 (c)
13 B—Kt2	B—Q2 (d)
14 QR—B	QR—B
15 B—Q3	KR—Q
16 Kt—K4 (e)	KtxKt
17 BxKt	B—K (f)
18 Kt—Q4	Q—Kt3
19 Q—B3 (g)	Kt—K4 (h)

23 Q—KR5	B—QR5
24 R—K	Q—Q3
25 P—KR3	B—B7 (j)
26 Q—B3 (k)	P—QKt4
27 Q—K2 (l)	B—QR5
28 Q—B3 (m)	R—B5 (n)
29 B—R (o)	KR—QB
30 R—Kt	P—K4
31 Kt—K2 (p)	B—QB7
32 QR—B	B—K5
33 Q—Kt4	B—Kt2 (q)
34 RxR	RxR
35 P—B4 (r)	Q—Q7
36 Q—Kt3 (s)	R—K5 (t)
37 B—B3	Q—Q4
38 BxP	RxKP (u)

After 38 BxP

After 19 Q—B3

20 BxPch (i)	KxB
21 Q—R5ch	K—Kt
22 QxKt	B—KB3

39 Q—Kt4	BxB
40 PxB	RxKP
41 K—R2 (v)	Q—Q7
42 Q—Kt3	P—B3
43 P—KR4	B—Q4
44 Q—B2	B—B5
Resigns (w)	

(a)   As is well known, the pawn cannot be maintained after 8...PxP; 9 R—Q, etc., and White, after its recapture, obtains freer scope for his pieces.

(b)   In a consultation game, Alekhine and A. Schroeder against Janowski and L. B. Meyer (New York, January 18, 1924) there occurred here 10...P—K4, which was refuted by 11 PxKP, KtxP; 12 KtxKt, QxKt; 13 P—K4. Although White thereby is able to keep a small advantage, the text-move is the correct reply.

(c)   After 12...B—Q3; 13 B—Kt2, Black could not very well have played either 13 P—QKt4 (on account of 14 BxKtP), nor 13...Kt—K4. For instance, 14 KtxKt, BxKt; 15 P—B4, BxKt; 16 BxB, P—QKt4; 17 BxKt, QxB; 18 Q—Kt4, P—Kt3; 19 Q—Kt5 winning.

(d)   More suitable for defense than 13...P—QKt4; 14 B—Q3, B—Kt2; 15 QR—B, followed by Kt—K4, etc.

(e)   Up to here White has played correctly. However, by this exchange, which frees the opponent, he allows his opening advantage to slip from him. He really had two good continuations to make the most of Black's somewhat cramped position: (I) 16 Kt—QR4, in order to post this Knight on QB5 and so, sooner or later, force the exchange of one of the adverse Bishops; (II) 16 Kt—KKt5, followed by KKt—K4, to open a free passage for the Queen to the King's side, and, with her help, to institute a direct attack.

(f)   The threat was 18 Kt—K5, to be followed by an exchange on QB6 and the winning of a pawn.

(g)   19 Q—Kt4 could also have been answered by Black in the same vigorous manner. The simplest way out was the exchange on B6 and Q8, with a drawn game.

(h)   A correct pawn sacrifice, which promises Black a game with powerful pressure on the unguarded White squares of his opponent. To be sure, it should not suffice for victory. White indeed only loses because in the course of the game he strives to maintain and capitalize at any cost his material preponderance.

(i)   Clearly, White could accomplish nothing with 20 Q—R3, Kt—Kt3! etc.

(j)   Premature would be 25...P—QKt4, on account of 26 R—B5, etc.

(k)   White would have done best to assure himself if, after 26 Q—K2, B—R5 (B—K5; 27 KR—Q, etc.); 27 Q—R5, his opponent was satisfied with a draw. His text-move merely induced a strengthening of Black's game.

(l)   And here 27 B—R would have been in order. Only after the loss of the "tempos" does White's position become precarious.

(m)   The move probably intended by White, 28 Kt—B3, will not do on account of 28...RxR; 29 RxR, B—Q8; and 28 Q—R5 would draw the same reply as in the text.

(n)   Forcing control of the open file or a passed pawn. Again White chooses the major evil.

(o)   At all events, more passable would have been 29 RxR, PxR; 30 B—B3 etc.

(p)   Likewise, after 31 Q—Kt3, Q—Q4; 32 Kt—B3, R—K, the situation would not have been pleasant because of the "stalemate" position of the white Queen; yet this continuation could hardly have led to such a speedy debacle as the retreat selected, through which the Knight is completely misplaced and serves as a welcome object of attack.

(q)   On this diagonal the Bishop is invested with deadly range.

(r)   Forced, for if 35 Q—Kt3, Black wins through 35...R—B7; 36 K—B, B—K5 (threatening RxKt), etc. Now, however, the squares K3 and Kt2 are decisively weakened.

(s)   Or 36 K—B2, PxP, threatening to win the Queen.

(t)   A convincing continuation. Still simpler, however, would have been 36... PxP; 37 KtxP, R—B8; 38 BxB, QxRch; 39 QxQ, RxQch; 40 K—B2, R—B8, with an easily won end-game.

(u)   The deciding turn. Now White perishes on account of his pinned Knight.

(v)   In order to be able to answer 41...R—Kt4 with 42 Kt—B4.

(w)   This was the Janowski of former days!

EIGHTH ROUND

Dr. Lasker, Alekhine and Marshall were the winners in this round, Capablanca being held to a draw by Maroczy. Thus the first-named maintained a half-point lead.

Bojoljubow played the Ruy Lopez against Dr. Lasker and the game went to 71 moves before the former resigned. Taking advantage of the opportunity offered by his opponent on the 13th move, Dr. Lasker gradually began to get a grip on the game and then steered for the ending—one of the most interesting in the tournament—in which he had a Rook and Knight against a Rook and Bishop. The superior position, coupled with subtle play of a high order, enabled Dr. Lasker eventually to reach his goal.

A Queen's Pawn Opening, the black side of which was handled very well by Maroczy, served to hold Capablanca in check. At no time did the Hungarian permit the champion to make the semblance of an impression.

Reti resorted to the Indian Defense against Alekhine and the game which resulted was of great theoretical interest. Reti's play can hardly be censured, but, through a weak QP, the defense got the worst of it nevertheless. The final storming of the King's side with only three minor pieces is very instructive and once more the great power of two Bishops was illustrated.

Marshall, in a very lively Reti Opening (reversed), defeated Janowski in 75 moves. The American outplayed his adversary at the start, but, once he had obtained a winning position, he relaxed. Thereupon, Janowski immediately seized the chance to escape from his major troubles, although he was still left with a very difficult game. Thanks to forceful tactics, Marshall again obtained the upper hand, but, missing the right continuation, he emerged with a Queen against three minor pieces. Janowski hesitated and Marshall, with a pretty surprise, won a piece and the game.

Dr. Tartakower, with the move, essayed a Scotch Gambit against Ed. Lasker, treating it in his own individual style. Lasker was forced to play with the greatest care in the ending to avoid drifting into a bad game.

The scores: Dr. Lasker, 5½—1½; Alekhine, 5—2; Capablanca, 4½—3½; Reti and Dr. Tartakower, each 4—3. The black pieces had the better of it by 3—2 this day.

Game 36　　　EIGHTH ROUND—RUY LOPEZ.

Bogoljubow.	Dr. Lasker.
White.	Black.
1 P—K4	P—K4
2 Kt—KB3	Kt—QB3
3 B—Kt5	Kt—B3
4 P—Q4(a)	PxP
5 KtxP(b)	B—K2
6 Castles	P—QR3(c)
7 KtxKt(d)	KtPxKt
8 B—Q3	P—Q3(e)
9 Kt—B3	Castles
10 P—KB4	R—K
11 K—R(f)	Kt—Q2
12 B—K3	B—B3
13 Q—B3(g)	R—Kt
14 QR—Kt(h)	BxKt(i)
15 PxB	RxR
16 RxR	P—QB4
17 P—B4(j)	Q—K2
18 P—KR3(k)	Kt—B3(l)
19 B—B2	B—Q2(m)
20 P—K5	PxP
21 PxP	QxP
22 B—Kt3	Q—K3
23 BxP	B—B3
24 Q—B5(n)	QxQ(o)

After 24 Q—B5.

25 BxQ	B—K5
26 BxB	KtxB
27 R—Kt6(p)	R—R
28 R—QB6	P—KR4(q)
29 B—Kt6	P—R5(r)
30 K—Kt(s)	R—K
31 BxP(t)	R—Q
32 K—B(u)	R—Q7

33 P—R4(v)	RxBP
34 B—Kt4(w)	R—B7ch(x)
35 K—Kt(y)	R—R7(z)
36 B—K	RxP
37 BxP	Kt—Q7(aa)

After 37 BxP.

38 B—Q8	KtxP
39 P—Kt4(bb)	Kt—Q7
40 R—B8	K—R2
41 R—R8	R—R7
42 K—Kt2	Kt—Kt6ch
43 K—Kt3	Kt—Q5(cc)
44 P—KR4(dd)	R—R6ch
45 K—B2	Kt—B3
46 B—B7	Kt—K2
47 B—Q6	R—R7ch
48 K—B3(ee)	Kt—B3
49 B—B7	Kt—Q5ch
50 K—Kt3	R—R6ch
51 K—B2	R—R5
52 K—Kt3	Kt—K3
53 B—Kt6(ff)	R—R6ch
54 K—Kt2(gg)	Kt—B5ch
55 K—B2	Kt—Q6ch
56 K—Kt2	Kt—K4
57 P—Kt5	Kt—Kt3
58 B—B2	Kt—B5ch
59 K—R2	K—Kt3
60 R—R7	P—R4
61 B—Kt3	R—R7ch
62 K—R	Kt—R4
63 B—K5(hh)	R—R5
64 K—Kt2	RxP
65 R—R6ch	KxP
66 RxP	K—Kt3

67 K—B3	P—B5	70 B—Q6	R—B3
68 B—Q6	R—Q5	71 B—Kt8	K—R3
69 B—B7	R—QB5	Resigns	

(a) This move, before castling and the advance of Black's QP, permits, as is well-known, Black's easy equalization. Much better would be 4 Castles.

(b) Or 5 P—K5, Kt—K5; 6 Castles, B—K2; 7 R—K, Kt—B4; 8 KtxP, KtxKt; 9 QxKt, Castles, etc. Mere transposition of moves would have been 5 Castles, B—K2; 6 P—K5 or, as in the actual game, 6 KtxP, etc.

(c) 6...Castles could have been played here without hes:tation, to be followed by 7 Kt—QB3, KtxKt; 8 QxKt, P—B3, and Black could continue with P—Q4 (9 B—QB4, P—QKt4, etc.). The text-move, however, is stronger and entirely in order at this stage.

(d) White hardly has anyth.ng better: A. 7 B—R4 would not do, on account of 7...KtxKt; 8 QxKt, P—B4, followed by P—QKt4 and P—B5. B. After 7 B—QB4, then 7...P—Q4 could be played, for instance: 8 PxP, KtxQP; 9 KtxKt, PxKt, and the position of the Knight on Q4 is a full equivalent for the deterioration of Black's pawn position. C. 7 B—K2 will also not do on account of the unprotected KP. D. F.nally, after 7 BxKt, Black can best recapture with the QP, after which with his two Bishops he would have a splendid game. After the text-move, the position assumes a distinct s.milarity to a much played variation in the Scotch game.

(e) If, in the variation of the Scotch just referred to (that is, after the moves 1 P—K4, P—K4; 2 Kt—KB3, Kt—QB3; 3 P—Q4, PxP; 4 KtxP, Kt—KB3; 5 KtxKt, KtPxKt; 6 B—Q3) the move, P—Q4, is accepted as the best, then it would be even much more in order now where the difference in the position is distinctly in favor of Black: 1. Should White select the exchange variation then, after 9 PxP, PxP, he can no longer resort, because of P—QR3, (which Black has made to no purpose) to Maroczy's maneuver of B—Kt5ch and BxBch (Maroczy vs. Janowski, London, 1899), which creates a weakness in Black's center and makes White's game to a certain extent playable. II. On the other hand, should he attempt, in imitation of a variation frequently played of late by Mieses, 9 P—K5, then Black, after 9...Kt—KKt5; 10 B—KB4 (as meanwhile B—K2 and castling by White have been played), can play much better in that case 10...P—KB3 and thereby obtain the superior game, for instance: 11 P—K6, BxKP; 12 R—K, Kt—K4: 13 BxKt, PxB; 14 RxP, Q—Q3; 15 Q—K2, K—Q2, and White's bluster is at an end. The move selected, to be sure, is harmless, but above all yields to White a comfortable initiative.

(f) A somewhat old-fashioned move. Formerly it was the custom to tuck away the King quickly in the corner when the KBP has been advanced, so that, perish the thought, he might not be checked on the diagonal. Nowadays greater care is exercised in making such moves with the King, because, as in th:s instance, they signify for the most part not alone an immed:ate loss of a tempo, but besides may become more often a deciding factor in a possible ending due to the further removal of the King from the center; and as a matter of fact, it soon becomes apparent that the move, P—KR3, which quite as much as the text-move had prepared for B—K3, could not have been avoided. After 11 P—KR3, Kt—Q2; 12 B—K3, B—B3; 13 Q—Q2, to be followed by QR—K (if QR—QKt, then P—Kt3), and the transfer of the Knight to the King's side, White would have obtained a very promising position for attack.

(g) This insufficintly considered move is immed:ately utilized by Dr. Lasker in energetic fashion. 13 Q—Q2, QR—Kt; 14 P—QKt3, followed eventually by QR—K and Kt—K2, etc., would still have offered better chances.

(h) The alternative of 14 Kt—Q appeared still less inviting because of 14...P—QB4.

(i) By means of this and especially the subsequent exchange, Wh:te's prospects for attack are reduced well-nigh to zero and, moreover, his pawns on the Queen's side are split up and the square, K4, additionally weakened. The open QKt file which White obtains holds out but a slight compensation, inasmuch as the entrance of the Rook can be easily prevented.

(j) Sooner or later this was unavoidable because of the eventual threat of P—B5. The White KB, however, is thereby practically degraded for the time being to the rank of a pawn.

(k) Compare with the comment on White's eleventh move.

(l) Hereby Black permits dissolution of the center through P—K5, which opens up new lines for the White Bishops, thereby allowing White drawing chances. More in order would have been to halt the KP by means of 18 P—KB3 in order thereafter to proceed with Kt—B. followed by B—Q2—QB3. In that case, to be sure, White, after Kt—B, could have weakened the attack on the KP by means of R—Kt8, B—Q2; RxR, QxR; but in that case an eventual sort.e of the Queen to QR5 was to have been dreaded and in any case this line of play by White would have set a more difficult problem than Kt—B3.

(m) Of course not 19...KtxKP?; 20 BxKt, QxB, on account of 21 QR—K, etc. Now, however, a quadruple attack on the KP is threatened with 20...B—B3 and White, therefore, is forced to the subsequent dissolution.

(n) Black, bcause of the super.or position of his pieces and pawns, unquestionably has the advantage, but there surely was no sufficient reason for this pawn sacrifice. After 24 Q—Kt3 (Kt—R4; 25 Q—R4 or 24...Kt—K5; 25 Q—K3), there would have been no immediate danger in store for White. The text-move, on the other hand, should have led to direct loss.

(o) The ending initiated hereby is favorable to Black, to be sure, principally because of the dominating position of his Knight, but st.ll offers White good drawing chances. Much more convincing, therefore, would have been the simple pawn capture by 24...BxPch; 25 KxB (or 25 K—R2, QxQ; 26 BxQ, B—K5, etc.),Q—B3ch; 27 Q—B3, QxB, whereupon White's game could not have been maintained for long.

(p) Th.s attack upon the Queen's side pawns, which, as a matter of fact, is possible only because the Black King has no exit yet, is here White's only chance but by no means one to be underestimated.

(q) Not 28...R—QB, on account of 29 RxP, etc. Now, however, there looms up a threat.

(r) Herewith the isolated corner position of the hostile King is utilized for the purposes of a direct attack. White finds the best defense.

(s) Because the capture of the QBP would have brought him into difficulties, for instance: 30 BxP, R—Q; 31 B—Kt, R—Q7; 32 RxP, P—B4! 33 P—B5 (not 33 P—R4, on account of 33...P—B5, with the threat of P—B6, which White could parry with R—R3), RxBP; 34 P—B6, P—Kt4, and White could not long hold the OBP, for instance: 35 R—R8ch, K—B2; 36 R—R7ch, K—K3; 37 P—B7, P—B5!, etc. The possibil.ties for attack by Black on the King's side are quite remarkable in view of the reduced forces.

(t) Now, however, White plays inconsistently. The apparent purpose of the last move was to withdraw the King from his cramped position in the corner and this plan could have been carried out successfully with 31 K—B. The fact that Black then could have protected his QBP was of no importance, inasmuch as White in that case would have obtained an attack against the more important QRP through B—B7. 1. If 31...R—K4, there would follow K—K2 (not 32 B—B7, on account of 32... R—B4ch; 33 K—Kt, R—B7; 34 RxP, RxBP, etc., with good winning chances). And now 32...R—B4; 33 K—K3, as well as 32...R—KKt4; 33 K—B3, P—B4; 34 B—B7, etc., remain without effect. The checks on Q7 and KKt6 are likewise ineffectual, as only the position of the Knight on K5 is at all dangerous for Wh.te, for instance: II. 31...Kt—Kt6ch; 32 K—B2, R—K7ch; 33 K—B3, RxP; 34 RxP, RxRP(if R—B6ch; 35 K—Kt4); 35 R—B8ch, K—R2; 36 P—B5, and White's passed pawn becomes a power. III. 31...Kt—Q7ch; 32 K—B2, R—K4; 33 B—B7, R—K2; 34 B—Q8, etc. White therefore, would have had excellent drawing chances with 31 K—B!. The text-move, on the other hand, increases the difficulties of his defense considerably.

(u) After 32 B—K3 (or even 32 K—R or R2), R—Q8; 33 K—R2, P—B4; 34 RxP, Kt—Kt6 (not P—KKt4, on account of 35 BxKKtP); 35 B—Kt, P—B5; 36 R—R3, R—QB8; 37 P—B5, RxBP, etc., White arrives at a similar situation as the one outlined in the comment upon his 30th move. Now, however, the entrance of the Black Rook on the seventh row becomes quite uncomfortable.

(v) Somewhat better here would have been 33 P—R3. Even in this case, however, Black would have had a very promising continuation. (Compare the comments upon his 37th move). Moreover, 33 B—K3 would not do here or on the next move, on account of 33...Kt—Kt6ch; 34 K—K (or 34 K—Kt, R—Q8ch, followed by mate on the next move), R—K7ch, winning the B:shop.

(w) Still the only defense. If 34 B—R7, the simplest continuation would have been P—B4—B5, etc.

(x) Hereupon White is obliged either to yield up the KKtP or to expose himself to the same old mat.ng position. Consequently he has only the choice between two evils equally grave.

(y) Now Black can either win a pawn or, which may perhaps be still stronger, to continue with an attack full of promise of success without stopping to gain material. But likew.se 35 K—K, which would have tended toward more complicated positions, would not have sufficed with correct play. The following continuations could then have oc-

curred: I. 35...RxP; 36 R—B8ch (if RxRP, Black would have an easy win in 36...
P—KKt4, etc.), K—R2; 37 P—B5, P—Kt4 (or A and B); 38 P—B6, P—Kt5; 39 P—B7,
R—QB7; 40 K—Q! (not at once R—K8, on account of R—QB8ch, followed by Kt—Kt6ch,
etc.), R—B5; 41 R—K8, etc. (A) 37...P—KB4; 38 P—B6, R—QB7; 39 P—B7, P—B5
(or R—B5); 40 R—K8, etc. (B) 37...R—QKt7!; 38 B—R5, R—QB7; 39 P—B6 (or
39 B—Kt6, P—KKt4, etc.), Kt—Q3; 40 P—B7, R—B5! (against the threat of B—Kt4),
and now the passed pawn is stopped thereby permitting Black, through the approach of
his King, to atta.n victory with the subsequent advance of the pawns on the King's side.

(z) Also threatening 36...R—R8ch; 37 K—R2, Kt—Kt6, followed by mate.

(aa) Black contents himself with the winning of a pawn and in consequence must
yet overcome great technical difficulties before he wins the ending. Had White, however, played P—R3 on his 33rd move, and as a result the pawn been captured on that
square, then Black would have been obliged to adopt the following method of play: 37...
R—R8ch; 38 K—R2, P—KKt4; 39 B—Kt3, P—KB4; 40 B—K5, R—R4; 41 B—Q4
(or B—B7, R—R7), K—B2! (threatening P—B5 or R—R7, neither of which was so good
for the moment on account of the reply R—K6). Then White would have had an extraordinarily difficult game, w.th his King in the corner without any prospect of emerging and continually threatened with mating attacks; his Bishop w.thout a permanent
support and exposed to the tempo-attack of the Black pieces; his passed pawn practically valueless through the approach of the Black King; and, finally, the passed QRP—
all these factors in the hands of the great end-game artist should have attained victory.
After the text-move, the dramatic part of the ending is past and a labored realization
of the slight material advantage begins.

(bb) In order to prevent the Black KBP from being eventually used to advantage
at the moment of attack and also at last to afford the King greater freedom of movement.
The move, to be sure, is not altogether an agreeable one, as he weakens the pawn position, but it is after all necessary.

(cc) The advance of the RP at present would be premature, for instance: 43...
P—R4; 44 R—R7, K—Kt3; 45 P—KR4, P—KB3; 46 P—R5ch, K—R3; 47 B—Kt6!,
threatening B—K3, followed by P—R6, etc. Black must now tack about in order further
to weaken the White Pawns where possible, for victory lies only on the King's side.

(dd) This move was not to be avoided even after 44 B—Kt6, Kt—K3. Now Black
will attempt, through an attack with the Knight, to force the further advance of the
KKtP which will make possible the active participation of his King.

(ee) More to the point at any rate would have been 48 K—Kt3 in order not to
expose the King, after Kt—B3, to an eventual check on Q5.

(ff) If 53 B—Q6, Black would have been able to play 53..P—R4; 54 R—R7,
P—B3, etc.

(gg) Permitting the Knight to go to K4, after which he goes downhill quickly.
With 54 K—B2 and, if Kt—B5, then 55 B—B7, Kt—Q4; 56 B—Q8, etc., White could
have offered a much longer resistance. Black doubtless, after 54 K—B2, must have
dec:ded upon the march of the King to Kt3 and B3, but in any event the proposition
would still have been very difficult.

(hh) If 63 B—K, then 63...R—R8 (or simply 53...P—R5); 64 R—K7, K—B4; 65
K—Kt2 (RxBPch, K—K3; 66 R—B, Kt—Kt6ch, etc.), K—Kt5, etc., with an easy win.
After the text-move both pawns perish.

(Phew! and good riddance to them!—Ed.)

Game 37   EIGHTH ROUND—QUEEN'S PAWN OPENING

Capablanca White	Maroczy Black
1 P—Q4	Kt—KB3
2 Kt—KB3	P—Q4
3 B—B4(a)	P—QB4
4 P—K3	Q—Kt3(b)
5 Q—B(c)	Kt—QB3
6 P—QB3	B—B4
7 PxP(d)	QxP(e)
8 QKt—Q2	R—B
9 Kt—Kt3	Q—Kt3
10 Q—Q2	P—K3
11 B—Q3	B—K5(f)
12 Q—K2	B—K2
13 Castles	Castles
14 B—KKt5(g)	BxB
15 QxB	KR—K
16 BxKt	BxB
17 KR—Q(h)	KR—Q
18 Q—K2	Kt—K4
19 KtxKt	BxKt
20 R—Q2(i)	B—B3
21 QR—Q	R—B5
22 Kt—B	KR—QB

After 11 B—Q3

23 Kt—Q3	P—QR4
24 P—QR3	Q—B2
25 P—KKt3	P—QKt4
26 K—Kt2	B—K2
27 K—Kt	B—Q3(j)
28 R—QR	Q—B3(k)
29 R(Q2)—Q	Q—B2
30 Q—R5	Drawn

(a) This deployment of the Bishop offers prospects only after Black has locked up his QB by means of P—K3 (as, for instance, in the game, Bogoljubow-Marshall).

(b) From here the Queen exerts a lasting pressure on the Queen's side of the adversary. Right from the first move Black assumes to play first fiddle and retains his initiative until the end, which, after all, is quite peaceful.

(c) Even less desirable would have been 5 Kt—B3, P—B5; 6 R—QKt, B—B4, etc.

(d) So as to develop at least his QKt with the gain of a "tempo." After 7 B—K2, P—K3, followed by R—B, White likewise would have had no prospects for a counter attack and even fewer chances, as in the actual game, to bring about simplifying exchanges.

(e) From now on White must reckon for some time with the threat of Kt—QKt5.

(f) Better than 11...Kt—K5, which would have caused a half-pinning rather favorable to White. As it is, White must lose another full "tempo" with his Queen, because 12 Castles, BxKt; 13 PxB, P—Kt4; 14 B—Kt3, P—KR4, would certainly not be without disadvantage.

(g) White strives for simplification before the opponent's pressure becomes altogether too unpleasant. Less suitable to that end would have been 14 Kt—K5, because the then possible exchange on QB6 would re-enforce still more Black's Pawn formation, while White would expose unnecessarily two pieces—his KKt and QB.

(h) P—K4 would be contrary to all position judgment here or on the next move, since every attempt to open the position would increase the potential power of the opponent's Bishop.

(i) White is content to limit himself to defense, knowing that his position is hardly assailable. Maroczy undertakes to break through in the only plausible way, but soon convinces himself that, even if successful, there is nothing to be gained by it. All in all, this is a game quite readily comprehended.

(j) if 27...P—Kt5; 28 BPxP, PxP; 29 PxP, BxP; 30 KtxB, RxKt, White would play 31 R—Q4, and, if Black should avoid the exchange of Rooks, open a file for himself with P—K4, whereupon a draw would be certain.

(k) And now 28 P—Kt5 would be parried by 29 RPxP, PxP; 30 PxP, BxP; 31 KtxB, RxKt; 32 R—B2, etc. Further exertions, therefore, seem to be quite useless.

Game 38 EIGHTH ROUND—INDIAN DEFENSE

Alekhine	Reti		
White	Black		
1 P—Q4	Kt—KB3	22 PxQ	R—Q2
2 P—QB4	P—KKt3	23 Kt—Kt5	RxP(r)
3 P—KKt3(a)	B—Kt2	24 Kt—B3	R—R3
4 B—Kt2	Castles	25 R—Kt	R—Kt2
5 Kt—QB3	P—Q3(b)	26 B—B5	RxRch
6 Kt—B3	Kt—B3(c)	27 KtxR	Kt—B3(s)
7 P—Q5	Kt—Kt	28 Kt—B3(t)	R—R4
8 Castles	B—Kt5(d)	29 B—Kt6(u)	R—R6
9 P—KR3(e)	BxKt	30 B—B5	R—R4
10 PxB(f)	P—K3(g)	31 B—K3	Kt—QKt5(v)
11 P—B4(h)	PxP	32 R—Q2	P—R3(w)
12 PxP(i)	P—B4	33 P—QR4(x)	Kt—K5
13 PxP,e.p.	KtxP	34 KtxKt	PxKt
14 B—K3	Q—Q2	35 R—Q8ch	K—R2
15 Q—R4(j)	QR—B	36 BxP	RxP(y)
16 QR—Q(k)	P—Kt3		
17 P—Kt3(l)	KR—Q		
18 R—Q3(m)	Kt—K2(n)		

After 18...Kt—K2

After 36...RxP

19 Kt—Kt5	P—Q4(o)	37 P—B5(z)	R—R3
20 KtxP(p)	R—R	38 P—R4	P—R4(aa)
21 BxKtP	QxQ(q)	39 P—Kt4	R—R4(bb)
		40 BPxPch	PxP
		41 PxP	RxP
		42 B—Kt5(cc)	B—B6
		43 R—Q7ch	K—Kt
		44 BxP(dd)	Resigns

(a) In order to avoid the main variation of the Gruenfeld defense (3 Kt—QB3, P—Q4!, etc.). The best reply thereto seems to be 3...P—B3, although White even in that case, after 4 B—Kt2, P—Q4; 5 PxP, PxP; 6 Kt—KB3, B—Kt2; 7 Castles, will for sometime retain the advantage of the move (in a narrower sense—the tempo).

(b) With this Black changes into the Indian defense, in connection with which, however, the fianchettoing of the White KB is very much in order.

(c) If Black has nothing better—and this seems to be the case—than to induce the advance of the White Pawn to Q5 by means of such efforts (where, to be sure, he shortens for the time being the diagonal of the Bishop, but on the other hand, brings considerable pressure upon Black's position), then his plan of development surely is not to be recommended.

(d) The exchange of this Bishop contemplated herewith is not reasonable and merely lessens the power of resistance in Black's position. Likewise unsatisfactory would be 8...P—K4, on account of 9 PxP, e. p., PxP; 10 B—Kt5, etc. (Alekhine vs. Sir G. Thomas, Karlsbad, 1923). On the other hand, there comes under consideration 8

...P—QR4 in order to secure the square, B4, to the Knight for awhile; but in this case also White would maintain his superior position by means of P—KR3, B—K3, Q—B2, P—Kt3, P—QR3 and, finally, P—QKt4.

(e)   It was important to clear up the situation before the opponent concluded his development.

(f)   Much better than to recapture with the Bishop, by which process either the KP would have remained inactive a long time or, if advanced, would have restricted the action of his own pieces.   After the text-move, however, he takes over the guarding of the important square, K4, and, aside from this, Black must reckon with an eventual hostile action on the K file opened hereby.

(g)   The KP had to be exchanged, but it would have been relatively better for him to have done so through 10...P—K4.   White thereupon would have had only one good reply (11 PxP e. p.), inasmuch as 11 P—B4, PxP; 12 BxP, QKt—Q2, etc., clearly would have been quite tolerable for Black.   After the actual move, on the other hand, White has the pleasant choice between two good continuations.

(h)   Even more favorable than 11 PxP, PxP; 12 R—K, Q—Q2, etc., whereupon it would have been by no means easy to profit from the weaknesses in Black's center.

(i)   Now, however, Black has to make his choice between three distinct evils: I. Weakness on QB2, in case he should allow the Pawn position to remain intact.   II. Weakness on QB3 in case, after P—B4, PxP, e. p., he should recapture with the Pawn and later on to be forced to play P—Q4.   III.   And, finally, the line actually selected by him, through which he obtains an isolated QP, the protection of which, made difficult through the powerful co-operation of the hostile Bishops, will soon lead to a decisive weakening of his Queen's side.

(j)   A most effective square for the Queen from which that piece will exert a troublesome pressure upon the Black Queen's wing.

(k)   Both players follow out the same idea, that is, the QKt Pawns must be removed beyond the reach of the hostile Bishops.   Incidentally, 16 BxP would not do here, of course, on account of 16...R—R, etc.

(l)   This move has the additional purpose of further protecting the Queen in anticipation of the subsequent complications.   How important this is will very soon become apparent.

(m)   It would have been premature to play 18 Kt—Kt5 at once, on account of 18 ...P—Q4, etc.   Now, however, White threatened to make this move after doubling the Rooks and, therefore, Black endeavors, through an exchange, to relieve the pressure exerted by the White Queen.

(n)   In this way indeed it cannot be done and Black right away is at a material disadvantage.   Somewhat better would have been 18...Kt—R4; 19 Q—R3, B—B; 20 KR—Q, etc., with a difficult game for Black, to be sure, but yet making defense possible.

(o)   Clearly forced.

(p)   This line was also made possible by White's 17th move.

(q)   Black had nothing better, because, after 21...R(Q)—Kt, White would have continued simply with 22 QxQ, KtxQ; 23 B—K3, R—Kt2; 24 BxP, KtxB; 25 RxKt, R(R)xKt; 26 BxR, RxB; 27 R(B)—Q, etc., with decisive superiority.

(r)   Threatening also 24...R—Kt5; 25 R—Kt3, RxR; 26 PxR, R—Kt2, etc.

(s)   The position is now cleared up, White having maintained his passed Pawn, while Black's QP still remains weak.

(t)   The quickest method of winning.   While he relinquishes the QRP, White for its return is enabled to force an entrance for his Rook into the enemy camp, whereby the decisive Pawn attack is made possible.   The tame 28 P—R3 would have permitted the opponent a more stubborn resistance after 28...R—R4; 29 B—K3, R—Kt4, etc.

(u)   Gaining time.

(v)   After 31...P—Q5, then would follow not 32 BxP, KtxB; 33 RxKt, Kt—Q4!, etc., with drawing chances, but 32 BxKt!, PxKt; 33 P—QR4, winning.

(w)   If at once 32...Kt—K5, then 33 KtxKt, PxKt; 34 R—Q8ch, B—B; 35 P—B5! and wins.

(x)   Threatening 34 B—Kt6, etc., and thereby forcing Black's next move.

(y)   If 36...P—B4, then 37 R—Q7!, K—R (or PxB; 38 B—Q4, R—Q4; 39 RxBch, K—R: 40 R—O7ch, followed by exchange of Rooks and w.nning) ; 38 B—Q4, BxB; 39 RxB, PxB; 40 RxKt and wins.

(z)   The initiation of the deciding pawn charge.   For the present 38 PxPch, PxP; 39 R—Q6 is threatening.

(aa)   Forced on account of the threat of 39 P—R5.

(bb)   Or 39...P(R4)xP; 40 P—R5, etc.

(cc)   Winning at least the exchange.

(dd)   Now, after 44...R—R, White wins quite easily by the advance of the RP.

Game 39 EIGHTH ROUND—RETI'S OPENING (FOR BLACK)

Janowski	Marshall
White	Black
1 P—Q4	Kt—KB3
2 Kt—KB3	P—Q3
3 P—KR3	P—KKt3
4 B—B4	B—Kt2
5 QKt—Q2(a)	P—B4
6 P—K3	PxP(b)
7 PxP	Kt—B3
8 P—B3	Castles(c)
9 B—K2	R—K
10 Kt—B4	B—K3(d)
11 Castles	Kt—Q4
12 B—Q2(l)	QR—B
13 Kt—Kt5(f)	B—Q2

After 32 R—B3

33 RxP	BxR
34 BxB	QxB
35 P—Kt3	Q—R3
36 PxR	QxP(t)
37 B—K4(u)	R—B5(v)
38 BxP(w)	R—B5
39 Q—Q2	PxRP
40 R—K	Q—Kt4ch
41 Kt—Kt3	Kt—K4
42 R—K3(x)	Q—B3(y)

After 13...B—Q2

14 Q—Kt3(g)	P—KR3(h)
15 B—B3(i)	PxKt
16 BxKt	P—K3
17 B—B3	Q—B2
18 Kt—K3(j)	Kt—R4
19 Q—Q	P—Kt4
20 R—K	P—B4
21 Kt—B	KB—B3
22 Kt—Kt3(k)	Kt—B5
23 B—B	P—Q4(l)
24 Kt—B(m)	K—Kt2
25 B—K2	Kt—Q3
26 B—Q3	R—KR
27 R—K3	R—R5(n)
28 R—Kt3(o)	Kt—B2
29 Kt—Q2	P—K4(p)
30 PxP	BxP
31 Kt—B(q)	P—B5(r)
32 R—B3	P—Kt5(s)

After 42...R—K3

43 Q—K	P—R7ch
44 K—R	Kt—Kt5(z)
45 R—K7ch	K—R3
46 RxB	KtxPch
47 K—Kt2	Q—R5(aa)
48 QxKt(bb)	RxQch
49 KxR	Q—Kt5(cc)
50 R—KB7	Q—Q8
51 B—Kt2	Q—Kt8ch

52	K—B3	Q—Q8ch
53	K—B2	Q—Kt8ch
54	K—B3	Q—Q8ch
55	K—B2(dd)	Q—B7ch
56	K—B3	QxP
57	R—B4(ee)	QxPch
58	K—Kt4	Q—Q7
59	B—K4	Q—Q2ch(ff)
60	K—B3	K—Kt4
61	R—KB8(gg)	Q—Q8ch(hh)
62	K—Kt2	Q—Kt8ch
63	K—R3	P—R4
64	B—Q5(ii)	Q—Q5
65	B—K4(jj)	Q—Q2ch
66	K—Kt2(kk)	P—R8(Q)(ll)
67	KtxQ(mm)	Q—K2(nn)
68	R—B3	QxB
69	Kt—B2	Q—Q4
70	P—R3	P—Kt5
71	PxP	PxP

After 63...P—R4

72	Kt—R3ch	K—Kt5
73	Kt—B2ch	K—R5
74	Kt—Q3	P—Kt6
75	K—B2	P—Kt7
76	Resigns	

(a) Herewith White enables the opponent to switch at once into a variation of the Reti system. With 5 P—B3! this could have been avoided.

(b) Marshall has an outspoken predilection for clarified pawn configurations (compare his treatment of the Queen's gambit) and eschews hanging positions whenever possible. In the present state, however, it was a direct advantage for him to keep his opponent in the dark for a little while longer about his intentions and to castle first. Now his plan to play P—K4 is adroitly prevented by Janowski and, because of limited scope for development, he gets a little the worst of it.

(c) Threatening now 9...P—K4.

(d) Recognizing that his original idea cannot very well be realized (10...Kt—Q4; 11 B—Kt3, P—K4; 12 Castles), Black changes his plan. His pieces, however, are now sent to unsafe posts from which the adversary soon drives them with loss of time. The whole arrangement of his game shows insufficient reflection.

(e) Inasmuch as White need worry no longer over the possibility of P—K4, he is quite justified in keeping his Bishop on the diagonal, QB to R6.

(f) Quite good, and sufficient for the retention of the advantage. More in the style of Janowski, however, would have been to make preparation for this sortie with 13 R—K, whereby all subsequent threats would have been strengthened.

(g) Herewith White enters upon a complicated sacrificial combination and only at the last moment assures himself that it is not sound. With 14 B—B3!, Kt—Kt3; 15 KtxKt, QxKt; 16 Q—Kt3!, R—B2, 17 KR—K, etc., he might have retained some minor positional advantage. The inadequate text-move is made the most of by Marshall in very energetic fashion.

(h) This simple move required long and exact calculation.

(i) The alluring sacrifice of the Knight is thwarted only by the following line of play: 16 KtxBP, KxKt; 17 B—B3, B—K3! (After 17...P—K3; 18 KtxPch, K—Kt; 19 KR—K!, etc., White would have had splendid chances); 18 KR—K!, Kt—B2! (18 ...Q—Q2 as well as 18...Kt—R4 are insufficient on account of the possibility of RxB, or first KtxKt); 19 RxB, KtxR; 20 B—Q5 (20 P—Q5, Kt—B4), Q—Q2; 21 BxKtch, QxB; 22 P—Q5 (or 22 R—K, Kt—R4!), Q—K7!; 23 PxKt (or 23 R—K, Kt—Q5!, etc.), P—Q4!; 24 PxP, RxKt, etc. But comparatively better than the text-move, which allows an exchange that strengthens Black's pawn group, would have been the simple retreat of 15 Kt—B3 and, if 15...Q—B2, then 16 P—QR4, with a satisfactory game.

(j) Likewise 18 BxP, KtxP; 19 PxKt, QxKt; 20 OxP, R—B2, followed by QxQP, etc., would have been advantageous for Black. Now White is forced into a general retreat.

(k) White suffers from a lack of anchorage for his pieces, with no prospects of a dynamic treatment of the position and this circumstance is the more painful as the procedure of Black—utilization of the KR file for a direct attack—is plainly indicated. White, with his Knight move, seems bent on a new sacrificing continuation.

(l) Safer would have been first 23...K—Kt2.

(m) In place of this retreat, with which White condemns himself to unresisting annihilation, he could have attempted by means of 24 B—R5! (?), PxB (K—Kt2; 25 KBxP, etc.); 25 QxP, B—B3 (or R—K2); 26 BxP, BxB; 27 QxBch, Q—Kt2; 28 Q—R4, threatening Kt—R5, etc., to continue fishing in troubled waters with two Pawns in return for a piece. Certainly a desperate resort—but the position was ripe for despair!

(n) Black's attack plays itself.

(o) The Rook ventures into a blind alley. But otherwise the doubling of the Rooks on the KR file, followed by P—KKt5, would be decisive.

(p) This should compel the gain of material. If now 30 Kt—B3, then of course 30...P—K5; 31 KtxR, PxKt, etc.

(q) If 31 Kt—B3, then would follow 31...BxR; 32 PxB, RxP!; 33 PxR, QxPch, followed by QxRPch and P—KKt5, with a winning attack.

(r) After 31...BxR; 32 PxB, followed by B—K3—Q4ch, White could still have maintained some resistance. The text-move is more forcible.

(s) From this point on Black begins to dawdle. It is quite true that the exchange for which this move prepares yields winning chances because of White's disorganized King's side position, but simpler would have been 32...B—KB3 (33 P—KKt3?, RxP; 34 PxP, B—Kt5, etc., followed by Kt—K4, whereby he would have won the exchange without diminishing the pressure noticeably.

(t) After 36...PxP, White would have had a sufficient defense in 37 B—K2. Now, however, there is a very strong threat in 37...QxP, followed by R—KR.

(u) A splendid move, which, with the gain of a tempo, places the Bishop on the right diagonal. It becomes apparent now how Black aggravated the difficulty of his work by his 32nd move.

(v) As 37...PxB; 38 QxB and QxKtP leads to nothing, he at least utilizes the opportunity to get his Rook effectively into the game. His own King's position, however, has meanwhile become somewhat unsafe.

(w) If 38 QxP (?), then B—B3, etc.

(x) Despite his ingenious defense, White's situation has grown worse. The text-move constitutes a last attempt to parry the terrible threat of 42...P—R7ch or Kt—Kt5.

(y) The sacrifice of a piece which he now plans turnsout not to be decisive. On the other hand, a win would have been led up to by 42...P—R7ch!; 43 K—R (43 KxP, RxPch, winning, or 43 K—Kt2, R—R5; 44 K—R, Kt—B5; 45 BxKt, B—B3ch, etc.), Kt—Kt5; 44 R—B3, KtxPch!; 45 RxKt (45 QxKt, QxB or 45 KxP, R—R4ch, winning), QxKt with the threat of mate on Kt8.

(z) Note the only continuation for the attack.

(aa) And not 47...Q—Kt4 (threatening P—R8, queening), on account of 48 B—Kt8!!, etc.

(bb) The Queen sacrifice is forced, for, 48 B—K6, Kt—K5!; 49 B—Kt8, Kt—B3, etc., would follow with advantage.

(cc) In spite of his material inferiority, Black attempts to profit from the circumstance that the White pieces for the time being are tied up by his passed Pawn and accordingly avoids a draw. He could, however, have fared badly because of it.

(dd) Herewith the same position is brought about for the third time with the same player to move and White, therefore, might have claimed a draw. However, he does not avail himself of this right—clearly in the hope of gaining an advantage himself through further attempts to win on the part of his opponent. Both are playing with fire.

(ee) Threatening 58 R—R4ch, etc.

(ff) If there is anything to be gained, it could only be through 59...QxP; 60 R—B6, K—Kt2; 61 RxPch, K—B2, etc. After the text-move, White retains his QRP.

(gg) The only move, but it suffices.

(hh) Or 61...Q—Q7; 62 R—KKt8, etc.

(ii) Janowski had so far accomplished a great deal. After the matter-of-course 64 R—KKt8(threatening 65 RxPch, K—B5; 66 Kt—K2ch), K—B5; 65 RxP, K—K6; 66 R—Kt5, etc., it would have been Black's turn to fight for a draw. Instead, his Bishop move once more exposes him to the danger of loss.

(jj) There is no longer a wholly satisfactory move. After 65 R—Q8, then 65... Q—R5ch; 66 K—Kt2, K—B5, etc., would have been unpleasant, and after 65 B—B3, Q—Q2ch, the QRP likewise would have been lost.

(kk) Losing a piece, but even after 66 KxP, Q—Q7ch and QxP, the three pawns would finally have decided.

(ll) A painful surprise.

(mm) Or 67 KxQ, Q—R6ch, etc.

(nn) This at last decides the issue of the day. A game rich in vicissitudes.

Game 40   EIGHTH ROUND—SCOTCH OPENING

Tartakower   Ed. Lasker   After 12 Castles
  White   Black

1	P—K4	P—K4
2	Kt—KB3	Kt—QB3
3	P—Q4	PxP
4	KtxP	Kt—B3
5	KtxKt	KtPxKt
6	Kt—Q2(a)	B—B4
7	P—K5	Q—K2
8	Q—K2	Kt—Q4
9	Kt—Kt3	B—Kt3(b)
10	B—Q2	P—QR4
11	P—QR4(c)	Castles
12	Castles(d)	P—Q3(e)
13	PxP	PxP
14	QxQ	KtxQ
15	B—KB4	P—Q4
16	B—Q6	R—K
17	B—B5(f)	BxB
18	KtxB	Kt—Kt3(g)
19	B—Q3	Kt—B5
20	P—Kt3	Kt—K3
21	KR—K	K—B
22	KtxKtch(h)	BxKt
23	R—K3	P—R3
24	QR—K	R—Kt

25	P—Kt3	B—Q2
26	K—Q2	RxR
27	RxR	R—K
28	P—QB3(i)	R—Kt
29	B—B2	P—B3
30	B—Q	P—QB4
31	B—B2	R—Kt3
32	K—B	R—Kt
33	B—Q	B—B4
Drawn		

(a)   This singular move had been tried by Dr. Tartakower in several earlier tournament games (for instance, against Teichmann at Carlsbad, 1923, and against Rubinstein at Maehrisch-Ostrau, 1923) and is also recommended in his last book, "Die Hypermoderne Schachpartie." Predicated upon a few positional traps, it is not likely that it will open a new horizon for the sober and colorless Scotch opening.

(b)   This, in connection with the next move, is stronger than 9...Castles (as played by Rubinstein in the game referred to), whereupon White, after 10 B—Q2, B—Kt3, Castles on the Queen's side without having to make the weak move of P—QR4.

(c)   This is now forced, inasmuch as 11 Castles QR would be answered by 11...P—R5; 12 Kt—R, P—R6; 13 P—Kt3, B—Q5, etc., with advantage.

(d)   White clearly has no time to prepare for castling on the King's side.

(e)   So far Black has conducted the opening properly. The text-move, however, which makes possible a premature simplification, relinquishes all of his advantage. Correct would have been 12...P—B3 (not 12...B—R3; 13 Q—K, etc.); 13 PxP, QxP, or 13 P—KB4, PxP; 14 QxP, Q—B2, followed by P—Q3; or II, 13 P—QB4, B—R3; 14 Q—K4, Kt—Kt5; 15 P—B5, P—Q4; 16 Q—K3, BxB; 17 KRxB, BxBP, etc.

(f)   Now White, in consequence of the weakness of the black squares, has even some advantage.

(g)   Black at once proceeds to take measures in order to exchange or drive off the annoying hostile Knight and, incidentally, equalizes the position again.

(h)   If 22 Kt—Kt3, there could have followed 22...P—KKt3; 23 B—B, B—Q2; 24 B—R3, P—KB4, followed by R—K2, with an easy defense.

(i)   Likewise after 28 RxRch, KxR; 29 K—K3, K—K2; 30 K—Q4, K—Q3, followed by P—B4ch, the game is likely to be drawn.

NINTH ROUND

This was the day of Marshall's great opportunity, which he only partially grasped—a draw with Dr. Lasker, after a thrilling contest which went to 62 moves. The American, with the white side of a Queen's Gambit declined, had the satisfaction of outplaying the former world's champion. Unfortunately for him he missed a forced win. After that he still maintained the advantage, but Dr. Lasker barely managed to work out a draw in a stalemate position.

Bogoljubow vs. Capablanca was a Queen's Pawn game, characterized by the champion's incomparable precision. Bogoljubow's QB, developed at QKt2, was exchanged by Capablanca by means of B—QR6. The weakness on white squares thus created sufficed Capablanca to render his adversary's position more and more untenable with every move.

Nothing daunted, Dr. Tartakower came at Alekhine with another King's Gambit and headed into a prepared variation. Lacking precision on his 13th move, Alekhine permitted the institution of a strong attack, which was fearlessly pursued by Dr. Tartakower. In the end Alekhine had to resort to perpetual check to draw the game.

Reti entirely outplayed Janowski in a Reti Opening (reversed). The manner in which Reti increased pressure upon the center, leading to the control of important squares and the gain of a Pawn, was no less pleasing than the final simplification.

Yates essayed Alekhine's attack against Maroczy's French Defense, but failed to follow it up properly. The redeeming feature was the Queen ending, which Maroczy, as in his game with Marshall, handled faultlessly.

Dr. Lasker continued to hold a slight lead with 6—2, followed by Alekhine, 5½—2½; Capablanca, 5½—3½; Reti, 5—3, and Dr. Tartakower, 4½—3½. The black pieces had their best day of the tournament with 3 wins and 2 draws. Total record: White 22½; Black, 22½.

Game 41   NINTH ROUND—QUEEN'S GAMBIT DECLINED

Marshall	Dr. Lasker
White	Black
1 P—Q4	P—Q4
2 P—QB4	P—QB3
3 PxP(a)	PxP
4 Kt—QB3	Kt—KB3
5 Q—Kt3(b)	P—K3
6 B—B4	Kt—B3
7 Kt—B3	B—K2(c)
8 P—K3(d)	Kt—KR4(e)
9 B—Kt3	Castles
10 B—Q3	P—B4(f)
11 B—K5	Kt—B3
12 BxKt	RxB
13 R—QB	B—Q3
14 Kt—QR4(g)	Q—R4ch
15 Kt—B3(h)	R—Kt(i)
16 Castles	P—QR3(j)
17 Kt—QR4	B—Q2
18 Kt—B5	Q—B2(k)

32 P—QR4(w)	P—KR4
33 R—Kt2(x)	P—R5
34 Kt—Q3(y)	Q—QR2
35 P—Kt3	R—Kt2
36 Kt—K5	PxP
37 PxP	Q—Kt3
38 P—R5(z)	QxRP
39 KtxP	Q—Kt3
40 Kt—K5	R—QB2(aa)
41 RxR	QxR
42 P—KKt4	PxP
43 KtxP(bb)	RxP(cc)
44 QxP(dd)	RxBch
45 KxR	B—Kt4ch(ee)
46 R—K2(ff)	BxRch
47 QxB	Q—B2ch
48 Q—B2	K—Kt2(gg)
49 Kt—K3	B—B5(hh)
50 K—K2(ii)	Q—B2
51 Q—Kt2ch	K—B

After 18...Q—B2

After 51...K—B

19 Kt—K5(l)	B—K
20 P—B4(m)	Q—K2
21 P—QR3(n)	R—R3(o)
22 R—KB2	P—KKt4
23 P—Kt3	K—R(p)
24 Q—Q(q)	PxP
25 KtxKt(r)	PxKt(s)
26 KPxP	Q—KKt2(t)
27 BxRP	B—R4
28 Q—Q2	R—Kt
29 B—K2	B—K(u)
30 Q—K3	R—B3(v)
31 B—B	Q—K2

52 KtxP(jj)	Q—B7ch
53 K—B3	B—Q7(kk)
54 Q—B(ll)	QxPch
55 K—K2ch(mm)	K—K
56 Q—B5(nn)	Q—B5ch
57 KxB(oo)	QxPch
58 K—K2	Q—B5ch
59 K—B2	Q—B4ch
60 K—Kt2	Q—Q3
61 K—B3	K—Q(pp)
62 K—K4	Q—K3ch
Drawn	

(a) The simplest and perhaps also the best, as White thereby retains the initiative for a time. Usually this exchange is made after the moves, 3 Kt—KB3, Kt—KB3. Marshall, however, proves by this game that the variation selected by him possesses its definite advantages.

(b) Thereby he prevents the development of Black's QB, which, for instance, could have been played without hesitation after 5 Kt—KB3 (5...B—B4; 6 Q—Kt3, Q—Kt3; 7 KtxQP, KtxKt; 8 QxKt, P—K3; 9 Q—Kt3, QxQ; 10 PxQ, B—B7; 11 Kt—Q2, B—Kt5).

(c) With 7...B—Q3; 8 B—Kt3, Black would merely have restricted his Queen to the defense of the Bishop, inasmuch as the exchange on Kt3 would not have been desirable on account of the opening of the KK file.

(d) 8 P—KR3 also came into consideration in order to retain the Bishop. Thereupon, however, Black could have answered 8...B—Q3 even much better than on the previous move.

(e) Probably the best defense, for Black, in return for the break at K5 which he must logically concede to his opponent, receives compensation in his two Bishops, which hold out prospects for a King's side attack. The fact that White later on obtains a telling advantage is to be ascribed to further tactical omissions on the part of Black.

(f) Thereby threatening Kt—B3—K5. White, therefore, is right in removing this objectionable Knight at once.

(g) A crafty move. Black was just on the point of favorably completing his development (after 14 Castles, for instance) by playing his QB by way of Q2—K over to KR4 and finally to initiate a possible King's side attack. By means of the threat to post the Knight on B5, White deflects his opponent's Queen to R4, whereupon the move of B—Q2 would no longer do on account of QxKtP. To be sure, Black, with 15...Q—Q, could bring about the same position again, but White rightly presumed that, after his seeming loss of time, his opponent would not be satisfied with an immediate draw.

(h) After 15 K—K2, then 15...Kt—Kt5 could have forced the exchange of the Bishop on Q3, as 16 B—Kt would have been met by 16...P—QKt3; 17 P—QR3, B—R3ch; 18 K—Q, B—QB5, etc.

(i) Black actually overestimates his position and is placed at a clear disadvantage in consequence (and not at all because of his earlier maneuvers of Kt—R4 and P—B4, censured by some critics). Aside from 15...Q—Q, which, as before, would again confound White's intention of playing for a win, 15...Q—Kt5, whereby the pressure on QKt2 is likewise remitted, would also have had to be seriously considered.

(j) As Black with his last move deprived the Bishop of the square, QKt, there is now the threat of 17 Kt—Kt5, followed by the exchange, or occupation of the square, K5.

(k) A lamentable necessity, as 18...B—K would be met by 19 KtxKtP, Q—B2; 20 KtxB!, RxQ; 21 KtxB, followed by KtxRch and PxR.

(l) With the occupation of this key square White obtains by far the superior position. It is plain that Black cannot capture twice on K5 because of the subsequent loss of the exchange, for instance: 19...KtxKt; 20 PxKt, BxP; 21 P—B4!, followed by Kt—K4, etc.

(m) He could have obtained an advantage in material by means of 20 KtxKP, RxKt; 21 QxQP, Q—K2; 22 BxBP, Kt—Q; 23 BxRch, etc. In that case, however, Black would have retained good defensive weapons in his two Bishops. The simple text-move is more enduring.

(n) Should Black now remain passive, White withdraws his Queen from Kt3, plays P—QKt4 and quietly prepares for the break with P—QKt5, which would hold out an easy game with pressure on QKt7.

(o) The wing attack hereby initiated is condemned to failure from the start on account of White's powerful position in the center. However, Black hardly had any choice.

(p) Likewise after 23...PxP; 24 KtPxP, K—R; 25 R—Kt2, etc., White would have had the best of it. But there was no reason to allow him time further to improve his position through preparation for the eventual KPxP.

(q) Preparing also for P—QKt4 and thereby forcing the opponent to resort to further dynamic measures.

(r) Had Black effected the capture on B4 at his 23d move, this excursion clearly would not have been possible on account of the peril to the Queen after KtPxKt.

(s) More in order would surely have been 25...BxKt; 26 KPxP, B—K, etc. However, the idea to put the Rook to work at once on the Knight file had its points. Only he should not have surrendered the QRP on his next move.

(t)   The decisive mistake, inasmuch as Black now loses a Pawn without any compensation. 26...P—R4 could still have led to a bitter struggle, but now, on the other hand, White ought to win hands down.

(u)   The threat of 30 RxP bound up with this move can be parried without any difficulty and was certainly not worth the loss of a Pawn.

(v)   The KP was not yet threatened by the Knight on account of the reply (after KtxP) of Q—K2, etc. With the next move of the Bishop, however, White forces additional protection.

(w)   Black has really no more defense against the advance of this Pawn.

(x)   In a clearly won position White now goes astray and in the end permits himself to be taken unawares. As a matter of course, P—R5, followed by P—R6, either on this move or the next, was indicated, since Black had at his disposal no threats against the King's wing even partly serious in character.

(y)   Artificial. Yet despite his inaccurate play, White's superiority should be made to yield results.

(z)   As the Pawn as such can now be made use of only with difficulty, it is now utilized to force the opening of a new file, after which it is not possible for Black to prevent an exchange of Rooks favorable to his opponent.

(aa)   After 40...QKt2, White would play simply 41 R—Kt and then push on with the passed Pawn. After the ensuing exchange, he obtains a quickly decisive attack on the other side.

(bb)   This move, so generally criticized, is as a matter of fact the quickest road to victory. After 43 RxP, Black would have been able to defend himself somewhat longer by means of 43...R—R3; 44 Q—Kt3, B—B2!; 45 R—Kt7, BxKt; 46 BPxB, Q—K2, etc.

(cc)   After 43...R—Kt3, then 47 P—B5! would have been decisive.

(dd)   An oversight which allows the win to slip through his fingers. 44 B—Q3!, threatening 45 Q—R3ch, would have won at once, for instance: 44...B—R4; 45 Kt—R6, R—B; 46 Q—Kt5, and Black would have had no defense against 47 Q—Kt8ch.

(ee)   It is just this check which manifestly must have escaped Marshall's attention, and he seems to have considered only 45...Q—B8ch; 46 Q—K, B—Kt4ch; 47 K—B2, Q—B5ch; 48 K—Kt, QxPch; 49 K—R, whereby he could have won easily, for instance: 49...Q—Kt2 (or 49...Q—K5; 50 QxQ, PxQ; 51 Kt—B6, followed by mate); 50 Kt—K5!, BxKt; 51 RxQ, BxR; 52 O—R4ch, followed by Q—Q8ch and QxP.

(ff)   The only chance. 46 K—B2, Q—B7ch; 47 K—B3, Q—Q8ch, etc., would have been even less agreeable.

(gg)   Wrong would have been 48...QxQch; 49 KxQ, because the black QP could not have been saved thereafter.

(hh)   This again brings about a lost position for Black. By means of the elegant move of 49...B—R6, suggested by Ed Lasker (50 QxQch, KxQ; 51 KtxP, B—Kt7, etc.), he could, on the contrary, have forced a draw.

(ii)   After this there is no longer any satisfactory way in which to meet 51 Q—Kt2ch.

(jj)   Over-refinement that is incomprehensible. After 52 QxQP, BxKt; 53 KxB, etc., Black would soon have had to resign, inasmuch as the couple of checks still at his disposal would have been quite useless.

(kk)   The only move, but quite sufficient.

(ll)   Likewise 54 Q—B2, Q—Q6ch; 55 K—Kt2ch, K—K, etc., would not have sufficed any more.

(mm)   Or 55 K—K4ch, K—K; 56 Q—B6, Q—Kt8ch; 57 K—K5, Q—Ktch; 58 K—B5, Q—Bch; 59 K—K4, Q—Q!, 60 Q—Kt7, Q—Q3, etc., with an adequate defense.

(nn)   Even the winning of a piece by 56 Kt—B6ch, K—K2; 57 KxB, it is interesting to note, would not anymore have sufficed for a win, for instance: 57...Q—Kt7ch; 58 K—K3, Q—B6ch; 59 K—K4, Q—B7ch; 60 K—K5, Q—B2ch; 61 K—B5, Q—B7ch; 62 K—Kt5 (or 62 Kt—K4, Q—Bch, etc.), Q—Q7ch and QxP. After the text-move White also loses his Pawn.

(oo)   Or 57 K—Q, Q—QB8ch, followed by Q—B5ch, etc.

(pp)   Which prepares the ensuing stalemate position.

Game 42 NINTH ROUND—QUEEN'S PAWN OPENING

Bogoljubow   Capablanca   After 23 P—QR4

White   Black

	White	Black
1	P—Q4	Kt—KB3
2	Kt—KB3	P—Q4
3	P—K3	P—K3(a)
4	B—Q3	P—QB4
5	P—QKt3	Kt—B3
6	Castles	B—Q3
7	B—Kt2	Castles
8	QKt—Q2(b)	Q—K2(c)
9	Kt—K5	PxP
10	PxP	B—R6
11	BxB	QxB(d)
12	QKt—B3	B—Q2
13	KtxKt	BxKt
14	Q—Q2(e)	QR—B
15	P—QB3(f)	P—QR3(g)
16	Kt—K5	B—Kt4
17	P—B3(h)	BxB
18	KtxB	R—B2(i)
19	QR—B	KR—B
20	R—B2	Kt—K
21	KR—B	Kt—Q3
22	Kt—K5(j)	Q—R4
23	P—QR4(k)	Q—Kt3(l)
24	Kt—Q3	QxKtP
25	Kt—B5	Q—Kt3
26	R—Kt2	Q—R2
27	Q—K	P—QKt3
28	Kt—Q3	R—B5
29	P—R5(m)	PxP
30	Kt—B5	Kt—Kt4
31	R—K2(n)	KtxQP
32	PxKt	R(B)xKt
	Resigns	

(a) As a rule, 3...P—B4 is played at once; the text-move, however, is not in the least questionable since White, by locking in his QB, has foregone the immediate likelihood of more energetic methods of play.

(b) It has been known for years that Black has nothing to fear from the following double threat. Neither 8 Kt—K5 (see the game, Maroczy vs. Bogoljubow), nor 8 P—QR3 are strong enough to give White an advantage.

(c) Threatening thereby P—K4, as well as PxP, followed by B—R6, etc. In both cases Black obtains a lasting initiative.

(d) Black now has a well defined outlook along the open QB file and in the weakness of the black squares on the Queen's side of his opponent. Nevertheless, the game at this stage was still absolutely defensible, if White had played consistently thereafter to dislodge the black Queen from her hampering post by threats of exchange. Instead, he flirts so long with the square, K5, that Black actually works up a menacing pressure.

(e) Here, for instance, 14 Q—B, Q—Kt5; 15 Q—Q2, Q—Kt3 (or Q3); 16 Kt—K5, was much to be preferred.

(f) To what purpose? 15 Kt—K5 could very well have been played at once.

(g) Excellent! After the exchange of the Bishop, now practically unavoidable for White, the Knight will gain new and important squares for attack.

(h) After 17 BxB, PxB, etc., the opening of the QR file would have conduced to the benefit of Black.

(i) Now a regular siege of QB3 begins.

(j) There is nothing to be gained for the Knight at K5. 22 Kt—B5! (P—QKt3 or P—K4; 23 Kt—R4, etc.) would have added to the difficulty of his opponent's reaping the benefit of his positional advantage.

(k) A fresh weakness, after which there is probably no defense. There was still time, however, to try out the maneuver of Kt—Q3—B5—R4 to bolster up the Queen's side.

(l) This is decisive. White must give up a Pawn, for, after 24 R—Kt2, Kt—B4 (threatening KtxQP); 25 R(Kt2)—Kt, P—B3; 26 Kt—Kt4 (or Kt—Q3, RxP), P—K4;

and, after 24 P—QKt4, P—QR4; 25 P—Kt5, Kt—B5; 26 KtxKt, RxKt; 27 R—R, P—K4, etc.

(m)   Or 29 R—R2, Q—B2; 30 R—R3, Kt—B4, threatening KtxQP.

(n)   Making possible a pretty finale. After other moves, Black, of course, would also win easily through his Pawn superiority.

Game 43   NINTH ROUND—KING'S GAMBIT

Tartakower	Alekhine
White	Black
1 P—K4	P—K4
2 P—KB4	PxP
3 B—K2	Kt—K2(a)
4 P—Q4(b)	P—Q4
5 PxP(c)	KtxP
6 Kt—KB3	B—Kt5ch(d)
7 P—B3	B—K2
8 Castles	Castles
9 P—B4	Kt—K6(e)
10 BxKt	PxB
11 Q—Q3	B—B3
12 Kt—B3(f)	Kt—B3(g)
13 Kt—Q5	B—Kt5(h)
14 KtxBch	QxKt
15 P—Q5	BxKt(i)
16 RxB(j)	QxP(k)

20 RxKt	Q—R8ch
21 R—Kt	Q—B3(o)
22 P—B5	KR—Q(p)
23 QR—K	Q—KKt3(q)
24 Q—Q4	Q—KB3
25 R—K5	K—B
26 R—KB	Q—KKt3
27 P—R4(r)	R—Q2(s)
28 P—R5	Q—KR3
29 Q—K4(t)	P—KB3
30 P—Kt4	QR—Q(u)
31 P—B6	R—B2(v)
32 R—K6	Q—Kt4

After 32 R—K6

After 16 RxB

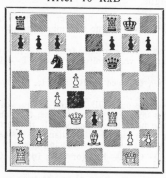

17 QR—Kt	QxP
18 RxKP(l)	Kt—Q5(m)
19 RxP	KtxBch(n)

33 QxP(w)	QxPch
34 K—B2	Q—B5ch
35 K—K2	Q—B5ch(x)
36 K—B2(y)	Q—B5ch
37 K—K2	Q—B5ch
38 K—K	Q—B8ch
39 K—K2	Q—B5ch
Drawn	

(a)   A new experiment which is satisfactory insofar as it yields Black at least an even position.

(b)   In reply to 4 Kt—QB3, there could follow 4...P—Q4; 5 PxP, KtxP; 6 KtxKt (if 6 B—B3, KtxKt, followed by B—Q3); QxKt; 7 B—B3, Q—Q3; 8 Kt—K2, P—KKt4; 9 P—Q4, B—Kt2, whereby Black would retain the gambit pawn.

(c)   After 5 P—K5, Kt—Kt3, etc., White would have been obliged to put forth still greater efforts in order to recover the Pawn.

(d)   In order not to have to reckon with the eventuality of Kt—B3 (in advance of P—B4) after White's next move which is partly forced.

(e)   After the enforced exchange, the KP should still have had a tenacious existence and the disappearance of the White QB diminishes greatly White's possibilities for an attack.

(f)   Not 12 QxP, on account of P—QB4!, etc.

(g)   Threaten ng also 13...Kt—Kt5.

(h)   This, however, is inaccurately played and permits the opponent to bring about a simplification favorable to him. Correct would have been first 13...R—K! and only after 14 QR—Q (in reply to 14 KtxBch, QxKt; 15 P—Q5, could follow Kt—Kt5, etc.), B—Kt3. And then both 15 KtxBch, QxKt; 16 Kt—K5, KtxKt; 17 PxKt, BxB, followed by QxP, as well as 15 Kt—Kt5, BxKt; 16 BxB, KtxQP!; 17 QxKt, P—K7; 18 BxP, RxB, etc., would have been favorable for Black, thereby also clearly justifying the defense of 3...Kt—K2.

(i)   15...Kt—Kt5; 16 Q—B3, etc., would clearly not have been any better.

(j)   Not 16 BxB, on account of 16...Kt—Q5, etc. After the text-move, however, White appears even to get an advantage, for instance: 16...Kt—K4; 17 RxQ, KtxQ; 18 R—B3, Kt—Kt5 (KtxQKtP?; 19 P—QR4!, etc.); 19 P—QR3, Kt—B7; 20 QR—QB, Kt—Q5; 21 RxKP, KtxBch; 22 RxKt, and the superior.ty of the pawns on the Queen's side would cause Black much trouble in the Rook ending.

(k)   This drawing combination in its many variations had to be calculated deeply and exactly.

(l)   Herewith White evades all the complications arising from 19 PxKt, but wrongly so, as he should now remain without sufficient compensation for the two pawns he is minus. After 18 PxKt, QR—Q, the following variations could have occurred: I. 19 PxP, RxQ: 20 BxR (or 20 P—Kt8(Q), QxB, etc.), P—K7! (in order to meet 21 P—Kt8 (Q) with P—K8 (Q)ch, etc.); 21 R—K3, Q—Q7!, etc., with advantage for Black. II. 19 Q—Kt3, QxB (threatening R—Q7, etc.); 20 RxKP, Q—Kt5; 21 PxP, R—Q7; 22 R—KKt3, Q—Q5ch; 23 K—R, R—QKt; 24 P—KR3, P—KR4. III. 19 Q—K4!, QR—K! (after 19...QxB; 20 RxKP, R—Q8ch; 21 RxR, QxRch; 22 R—K, followed by PxP, etc., White would have the advantage and 19...R—K is out of the question because of 20 PxP!); 20 Q—Q3 (if now 20 PxP, then 20...RxQ; 21 P—Kt8 (Q), QxB, etc.), R—Q, etc. and draws.

(m)   Herewith Black again gives away his winning chances. After the simple 18... Kt—R4, this temporary unfavorable position of the Knight on the edge would in no way have compensated Wh.te for the loss of two pawns, for instance: 19 R—K, QR—K; 20 B—B, RxR; 21 RxR, Q—Kt7!; 22 P—B5, Q—Kt5!; 23 Q—QB3, QxQ; 24 RxQ, R—Q; 25 P—Q6, PxP; 26 PxP, K—B, etc.

(n)   After 19...P—B4, the pawn on Q5 and especially the position of the Rook on the seventh row would have gained considerably in importance.

(o)   Even after 21...Q—R4; 22 Q—Q4, the move of P—QB5 could not long have been prevented.

(p)   After this move, Black exposes himself to a very dangerous attack. The correct thing for him was at once to play his trump, 22...P—QR4, for instance: 23 R—KB, Q—Kt3; 24 QxQ, PxQ!, etc., with an easy draw.

(q)   Now, after 23...P—QR4, there would have followed 24 P—Q6!, PxP; 25 PxP, threatening P—Q7, etc., with powerful pressure. The ensuing Queen maneuver has for its purpose making possible the important defensive move of K—B.

(r)   A strong continuation of the attack which almost decides the game in favor of White.

(s)   The only move which saves the situation. Wrong, for instance, would have been 27...R—K, on account of 28 R—Kt5, Q—R3; 29 Q—KB4, R—K2; 30 P—Q6, PxP; 31 PxP, R—Q2; 32 Q—B5!, QR—Q; 33 R—R5, Q—K6ch!; 34 K—R, P—Kt3!; 35 Q—B6, K—Kt; 36 R—K5, etc., with a winning position.

(t)   Probably the continuation which offers the best chances inasmuch as it forces the weakening P—KB3 through the threat of a triple attack on the King's file. After 29 Q—KKt4 (suggested as a winning line by some critics) Black could have saved himself more easily, for instance: I.—29...QR—Q; 30 KR—K, P—KB3; 31 P—B6. PxR!; 32 PxR, Q—Kt3ch! 33 K—R, Q—KB3, etc., or II.—29...KR—Q; 30 Q—K2,KR—K!; 31 R(KB)—K, RxR; 32 QxR, Q—KB3!, etc.

(u)   The same move, of course, would also have been played in reply to 30 P—Q6.

(v)   Again the only reply (31...R—Q3?; 32 R—K7, RxQP; 33 Q—K6, followed by mate.

(w)　Herewith White declares himself as satisfied with a draw. As a matter of fact, the attempt to keep on playing for a win would have been unsuccessful, for instance: 33 R—K, K—Kt; 34 R—K8ch, RxR; 35 QxRch, R—B; 36 Q—K6ch, R—B2 (K—R could also have been played). 37 P—Q6, Q—B4ch; 38 K—B, PxP; 39 R—QKt, P—KR3! and Black would have a perpetual check in case White should capture the Rook.

(x)　After 35...Q—R3; 36 QxQ, PxQ, White with an additional Pawn sacrifice would have obtained winning chances; 36 P—Q6!, RxP; 37 RxR, PxR; 38 R—QB, R—QB2; 39 K—K3, K—K2; 40 K—Q4, K—K3; 41 R—Kch, followed by 42 K—Q5, etc.

(y)　Neither could the draw have been avoided through 36 K—K3, for, after 36...Q—B4ch!, the King dare not go to KB4, on account of 37...P—Kt4ch, etc.

Game 44　　NINTH ROUND—RETI'S OPENING (DEFENSE)

Janowski.	Reti.
White.	Black.
1 P—Q4	Kt—KB3
2 Kt—KB3	P—KKt3
3 P—KR3(a)	B—Kt2
4 B—KB4	P—QKt3
5 P—K3	P—B4
6 P—B4(b)	PxP
7 PxP	Castles
8 Kt—B3(c)	P—Q4
9 B—K2	B—Kt2(d)
10 P—QKt3	Kt—K5
11 QR—B(e)	KtxKt
12 RxKt	PxP
13 PxP	Kt—B3
14 R—Q3(f)	Kt—R4
15 P—B5(g)	Q—Q4
16 Castles(h)	QxRP
17 R—K(i)	Q—Q4
18 B—KB	B—QR3
19 R—B3	BxB
20 KxB	Kt—B3
21 B—K3	KR—Q
22 Q—B(j)	P—QKt4
23 R—Q	P—Kt5
24 R—B2	P—QR4
25 Kt—Kt	P—R5
26 Kt—K2	P—Kt6
27 R(B2)—Q2	P—R6
28 Kt—B4	P—Kt7
29 Q—B3	Q—B4
30 Kt—Q3	BxP

31 BxB	RxB
32 K—Kt	RxKt(k)

After 32 K—Kt

33 RxR	QxR
34 QxQ	P—R7
35 K—R2(l)	P—R8(Q)
36 R—QKt	R—Kt
37 P—KR4	Q—R5
38 P—Kt3	Q—Q5
39 Q—B2	Q—B3
40 K—Kt2	P—R4
41 K—Kt	Kt—Q5
42 Q—Q	Q—B4
43 K—Kt2	QxP
44 Q—Q2	Q—Q4ch
Resigns	

(a)　This move is superfluous just here and in its place 3 B—B4 at once might be substituted.

(b)　Better would have been 6 P—B3, followed by B—Q3 (B4), which would have brought about a struggle between two systems (Reti's and the London method). The advantages and disadvantages on both sides were sufficiently illustrated in New York in the games, Dr. Lasker vs. Alekhine, Reti vs. Alekhine and Reti vs. Dr. Lasker. The inadequacy of the text-move is shown most convincingly by Reti in the present game.

(c)　Of greater importance than the development of the Knight was the necessity of insuring the safety of the King by means of B—K2, followed by castling. Having neglected to castle, White gets into trouble with his QP, which eventually leads to loss of material.

(d)   Here should have followed either 10 Castles or else a double exchange on Q5, followed by castling with a passable game. White's next somewhat superficial move merely creates an additional and serious weakness.

(e)   Or 11 KtxP, BxKt; 12 PxB, Kt—B6; 13 Q—B2, KtxB; 14 QxB, QxP; 15 Castles, Kt—B3, etc., with a clear preponderance in position.

(f)   After 14 B—K3, the reply of 14...P—K4 (15 P—Q5, P—K5, etc.) would have been powerful.

(g)   After 15 R—Q2, Black, by means of further developing moves (R—B, followed by B—QR3) could have easily attacked the BP. After the text-move, he obtains another advantage—the important square, Q4.

(h)   Likewise after 16 PxP, PxP; 17 R—Q2, Kt—B5, he could not have avoided loss of material in the long run. Castling, after all, held out for him his best chances.

(i)   Here, however, must be played 17 Kt—K5 in order to prevent Black's next move. After 17...KR—Q; 18 R—Q2, Q—K3; 19 R—K, Black would have found it by no means easy to realize his advantage. After the text-move, on the other hand, White gets nothing in return for the pawn.

(j)   The last opportunity is lost to create at least slight technical difficulties for the adversary by an exchange on Kt6. The forceful advance of the two passed pawns now wins with ease.

(k)   The game, of course, is won by any continuation, but this pretty combination, forcing the winning of a piece, decides the issue most quickly.

(l)   The sole possibility to avert greater loss of material.

Game 45		NINTH ROUND—FRENCH DEFENSE	
Yates	Maroczy		After 21...Kt—B3
White	Black		
1 P—K4	P—K3		
2 P—Q4	P—Q4		
3 Kt—QB3	Kt—KB3		
4 B—KKt5	B—K2		
5 P—K5	KKt—Q2		
6 P—KR4	P—KB3(a)		
7 PxP(b)	KtxP		
8 B—Q3	P—B4		
9 PxP	Kt—B3		
10 Kt—R3	Q—R4		
11 B—Q2	QxBP		
12 Kt—B4(c)	Castles(d)		
13 Q—K2(e)	Kt—Q5		
14 Q—B	B—Q3(f)		
15 Castles	Kt—Kt5		
16 Kt—R3	KtxBP(g)		
17 KtxKt	RxKt		
18 Q—K(h)	B—Q2		
19 K—Kt	R—B3(i)		
20 B—Kt5	R—B2		
21 P—R5(j)	Kt—B3		31 R—Q(m)	Q—B5
22 P—R6(k)	P—KKt3(l)		32 Q—R3	Kt—K4
23 B—K3	Q—R4		33 B—Kt5	B—B
24 Q—R4	Q—Q		34 P—R3	P—R3
25 B—Kt5	B—K2		35 B—K2	B—Q2
26 BxB	QxB		36 R—KB(n)	Q—Kt4
27 Q—Kt3	Q—B3		37 RxRch	KxR
28 KR—KB	Q—K4		38 Q—R2(o)	K—K2
29 Q—Kt4	RxR		39 Q—Kt	QxRP
30 RxR	R—KB		40 Q—Kt6	B—B3
			41 Q—B7ch	Kt—Q2(p)
			42 BxP	Q—R8ch
			43 K—R2	QxP
			44 BxP	BxB
			45 QxB(q)	Q—Kt5(r)
			46 P—R4	Q—B5ch

After 45 QxB

47	K—Kt	P—R4(s)
48	Q—R8	Kt—B4
49	Q—R7ch(t)	K—B3
50	Q—Kt8	K—B4

51	Q—B8ch	K—Kt5
52	Q—B6	P—Kt4
53	Kt—Q(u)	Q—B5
54	Q—B3	KtxP
55	Q—B6	K—B4(v)
56	Q—K8	P—R5
57	P—Kt3	Q—Q7
58	Q—B7ch	K—K4
59	Q—Kt7ch	K—B5
60	Q—B6ch	K—Kt6
61	Q—K5ch	K—B6
62	Q—B6ch	K—Kt7(w)
63	PxKt	QxKtch
64	K—Kt2	Q—Kt5
65	P—R5	P—R6
66	Q—B3(x)	Q—K7
67	P—R6	Q—Kt4ch
68	K—B	QxP
69	Q—Q2ch	K—B6
	Resigns(y)	

(a) The vitality of this defense against the attack of 6 P—KR4, introduced by the writer at Manheim in 1914, depends entirely upon the correctness of the Bishop sacrifice, 7 B—Q3 (!?), which would then be poss.ble. Unfortunately, White in the game under consideration avoids the complications resulting therefrom and selects a colorless line of play which brings about a clear positional disadvantage for him.

(b) After 7 B—Q3, PxB; 8 Q—R5ch, K—B (not P—Kt3; 9 BxPch, PxB; 10 QxRch, Kt—B; 11 PxP, BxKtP; 12 R—R7! and Black is wholly paralyzed); 9 R—R3, PxP!; 10 R—B3ch, Kt—B3; 11 Kt—R3!, Q—K (or K—Kt; 12 PxKt, BxKBP; 13 Kt—Kt5!, etc.); 12 QxP(R4); K—Kt; 14 PxKt, BxKBP; 15 RxB!, PxR; 16 QxKBP, etc., White would have an attack which should assure him at least a draw. In any event this was the only logical continuation, for, after the text-move, it is decidedly easy for Black.

(c) A spasmodic attempt to make more difficult the terrible P—K4 which is successful insofar as it induces the opponent to give new direction to his thoughts.

(d) In reply to 12...P—K4, White would have had half an excuse in 13 Kt—R5. Now, however, it threatens.

(e) In order, after 13...P—K4 (?), to answer with 14 KtxQP and, after the exchange, to win the Queen by means of B—B4.

(f) With this Black plays to win a pawn, which, however, is all too little, considering his powerful position, and suddenly allows the opponent counter-chances. Correct would have been 14...P—QKt4! (threatening both P—Kt5 as well as P—K4, etc.), for instance: I. 15 KtxKtP, KtxKt; 16 BxKt, Kt—K5; II. 15 Kt—K2, P—K4!; 16 KtxKt, PxKt; 17 Kt—Q, Kt—K5; in both cases with a decisive positional advantage.

(g) The point of the course initiated with the 14th move. White, however, now has an opportunity in a position rich in combinations to fish in troubled waters.

(h) Of course not 18 QxR, on account of 18...Kt—Kt6ch. Now, however, 19 Kt—R4 is threatened.

(i) However dangerous it seemed to take the KKtP, it could have been played unhesitatingly, for instance: 19 RxKtP (threatening Kt—B6); 20 B—K3, P—K4!; 21 Q—B, R—Kt5, and now 22 KtxQP cannot be played on account of 22...QR—KB. However, had Black resolved to adopt a strictly passive defense, it is not quite apparent why he wanted to induce B—Kt5 and did not at once play 19...R—B2.

(j) Very promising also would have been 21 B—K3, for instance: 21...P—K4; 22 Kt—K2, Q—B2; 23 KtxKt, PxKt; 24 BxQP, QR—K; 25 Q—B3, etc. The text-move, however, which holds in reserve all threats, seems to be still stronger.

(k) White cuts off his own attack! With 22 B—Kt6! he would have forced his opponent, in order to avoid greater evil, to sacrifice the exchange. (The best way would have been through 22...Kt—K4; 23 BxRch, KtxR; 24 B—K3, Q—B2, etc., with some chances of a draw. For in reply to 22...R—B (after 22...PxB; 23 PxP, threatening R—R8ch etc., Black clearly would have lost at once) there would have followed 23 P—R6!; I.

23...PxB; 24 PxP, KxP (A); 25 Q—R4, K—B2 (R—KR; 26 B—B6ch); 26 Q—R7ch, K—K; 27 QxPch, R—B2; 28 R—R8ch, B—B; 29 KtxQP!, QxKt (or PxKt; 30 QR—Kch, Kt—K2; 31 RxBch, followed by mate in three moves); 30 RxQ, PxR; 31 Q—R5! (threatening RxBch, followed by mate), Kt—K2; 32 B—R6 and wins (A) 24... R—B4; 25 Q—R4, K—B2; 26 P—KKt4!, R—B7 (or RxB; 27 QxR, etc.); 27 QR—KB, and wins.   II. 23...Q—B7; 24 PxP, KxP; 25 RxRPch!, KxP; 26 Q—R!, KxB; 27 Q—R6ch, K—B4; 28 P—Kt4ch, KxP; 29 R—Kt7ch, followed by mate in two moves. III. 23...PxP; 24 RxP, PxP; 25 RxPch, K—B2; 26 R—Bch, K—Kt2 (K—K; 27 RxQP); 27 Q—R4, RxR (R—KR; 28 B—R6ch); 28 BxRch, K—B2; 29 R—KB and wins.

(l)   Now, however, Black has no more file opening to fear and, after simplification on the KB line, must eventually win with his pawn plus.

(m)   Even after the exchange of Rooks, which in any event could not long be prevented, White's position would have been hopeless.

(n)   As a matter of fact, there is not a move left that is even half way satisfactory. After the exchange, however, the KR pawn becomes untenable.

(o)   In order to bring the Queen over to the other s.de by way of Kt square, inasmuch as there is nothing to be found against Kt—B7.

(p)   There was no necessity for Black to sacrifice his Queen wing. After 41... K—B3; 42 Q—Q8ch, K—Kt2; 43 Q—K7ch, Kt—B2; 44 QxKP, Q—R8ch; 45 K—R2, QxKtP, White might just as well have resigned.

(q)   Now the advance of the QRP threatens to become very disagreeable. Maroczy in the subsequent part of the game, however, understands how to combine attack and defense most cleverly and finally turns his superiority successfully into victory.

(r)   Preventing the check of the Queen on QKt4 and preparing thereby the unhampered advance of the KRP.

(s)   Threatening to reach R8 with mate.

(t)   The subsequent Queen maneuvers merely forward the opponent's plans. Certainly more chances would have been offered by 49 P—R5, P—R5; 50 Q—KR8, etc.

(u)   Here, too, 53 P—R5 should have been preferred, inasmuch as the last hope disappears with the loss of this Pawn.

(v)   In order to reply to 56 P—Kt3 with 56...Q—Q7.

(w)   If now 62...K—K7 (?), then 63 Q—B2ch, KxKt; 64 Q—B8ch, Q—K8; 65 Q—Q3ch, etc., with perpetual check.

(x)   Or 66 P—R6, P—R7; 67 P—R7, P—R8 (Q); 68 P—R8 (Q), Q—Kt5ch, followed by mate on the next move.

(y)   If now 70 QxKtP, then 70...Q—R8ch; 71 K—Q2, Q—Q5ch, followed by Q—K6ch, winning.

TENTH ROUND

With the competitors nearing the half-way mark, the games in the tenth round were most stubbornly contested, but Dr. Lasker, who won, drew away slightly from his nearest rivals. Capablanca, with a Pawn to the good, allowed Marshall to get away from him, and Alekhine was fortunate in not dropping a point to Ed. Lasker.

Reti's uncertainty in the handling of a French defense was admirably taken advantage of by Dr. Lasker, notwithstanding the fact that his opponent had two Bishops. Dr. Lasker's final attack was pleasing and conclusive.

Capablanca had all the best of a Reti Opening (reversed), emerging in the middle game with the advantage of two Bishops. In the difficult ending the world's champion was a Pawn ahead, so that Marshall deserves great credit for the fine uphill fight which earned him a draw.

The game between Ed. Lasker and Alekhine was a Ruy Lopez, in which the great Russian master went astray in the opening! Lasker played aggressively and obtained the superior game, but then relaxed. Alekhine was enabled to consolidate his position, with the better chance in the ending. Both players were extended in meeting the exigencies of the occasion and in making a draw.

Bogoljubow was the only other victor, at the expense of Yates, in this round. Playing the white side of a Ruy Lopez, Yates once more essayed his somewhat illogical advance of the center Pawns. Bogoljubow, at his best, soon won a Pawn and obtained the better position in the bargain, which sufficed for a win after 33 moves.

In the game, Janowski vs. Dr. Tartakower, the latter handled his side of a Queen's Gambit in excellent style, so much so that he entered upon the middle game with the exchange to the good and a free QBP to boot. Misjudging the position, he castled on the Queen's side, where Janowski, playing vigorously, kept him very busy. Dr. Tartakower found a drawing line in a very precarious position.

After ten rounds, the standing of the leaders was as follows: Dr. Lasker, 7-2; Alekhine, 6-3; Capablanca, 6-4; Reti and Dr. Tartakower, each 5-4. The score between White and Black remained even.

Game 46   TENTH ROUND—FRENCH DEFENSE

Dr. Lasker	Reti	After 23...KR—B
White	Black	

1	P—K4	P—K3
2	P—Q4	P—Q4
3	Kt—QB3	Kt—KB3
4	B—Kt5	B—Kt5
5	Kt—K2	PxP
6	P—QR3	B—K2
7	BxKt	PxB(a)
8	KtxP	P—KB4(b)
9	QKt—B3	B—Q2(c)
10	Q—Q2	B—Q3(d)
11	Castles	Q—K2(e)
12	Kt—Kt3(f)	Q—R5
13	Q—K	Kt—B3(g)
14	KtxP	Q—B5ch
15	Kt—K3	KtxP
16	P—KKt3	Q—K4
17	B—Kt2	Kt—B3(h)
18	P—B4	Q—Kt2
19	Kt—Kt5(i)	CastlesKR(j)
20	KtxB	PxKt
21	RxP	KR—Q
22	Q—Q2	B—K
23	R—Q	KR—B

24	P—B5(k)	P—K4
25	P—B6	Q—B
26	Kt—B5	K—R
27	Q—Kt5	R—B2(l)
28	BxKt	RxB(m)
29	R—Q8	KR—B
30	Q—Kt7ch	QxQ
31	PxQch	K—Kt
32	Kt—K7ch	Resigns

(a)   Better than 7...BxB (compare the game, Bogoljubow vs. Reti, fourth round). Black, however, treats the subsequent part of the opening in a style not dictated by the best position judgment.

(b)   This move, which weakens the pawn formation, should only be made in case of dire necessity. Correct would have been 8...P—QKt3, whereby Black would have obtained a satisfactory game (compare Bogoljubow vs. Alekhine, 17th round).

(c)   Herewith Black unnecessarily increases the difficulty of developing his Queen's side, for, if now a piece, B or Kt, should play to QB3, the QP always threatens to advance with a tempo.   9...P—QKt3 was still indicated.

(d)   After 10...B—QB3; 11 Castles QR, there would be the threat of 12P—Q5, etc.

(e)   Another loss of a tempo.   A better method of defense would have been to strengthen the center with P—QB3 and to forego castling, for instance: 11...P—QB3; 12 Kt—Kt3 (otherwise Kt—R3—B2, etc.), Q—R5; 13 Q—K, K—Q, followed by P—QR4, Kt—R3, etc.   Possibly in the course of time an attack on the Queen's Wing might have developed therefrom.

(f)   Threatening 13 KtxP, PxKt; 14 R—K, B—K3; 15 P—Q5.

(g)   Allowing the opponent an additional open file which, because of the unsafe position of the King, should have been avoided at all costs.   Better would have been 13...Q—B5ch; 14 K—Kt, Kt—B3, etc.

(h)   Likewise 17...B—B3 would not have been quite sufficient, for instance: 18 P—B4, Q—Kt2 (or Q—B3; 19 BxBch, KtxB; 20 Kt—K4, Q—K2; 21 Q—B3, Castles QR; 22 KR—K); 19 BxBch, KtxB; 20 Kt—B5, Q—B; 21 KtxBch, PxKt; 22 Kt—Kt5, Castles; 23 Q—B3, winning a pawn.

(i)   Not 19 Kt—B5, on account of 19...BxPch, etc.   The text move forces the win of a pawn (19...Q—B; 20 Kt—Q5! etc.).

(j)   With 19...Castles QR, Black could have offered longer resistance.

(k)   The introduction to a final attack, which leads to the goal in a few moves.

(l)   Losing a Rook, but the position, of course, has long been hopeless.   A game played by Reti without energy.

(m)   Also after 28...BxKt, would follow 29 R—Q8, etc.

Game 47   TENTH ROUND—RETI'S OPENING (for Black)

	Marshall White	Capablanca Black
1	P—Q4	Kt—KB3
2	Kt—KB3	P—KKt3
3	P—K3(a)	B—Kt2
4	QKt—Q2	P—QKt3
5	B—B4(b)	Castles
6	Q—K2	P—B4(c)
7	P—B3	B—Kt2
8	Castles	P—Q4(d)
9	B—Q3	Kt—K5
10	BxKt(e)	PxB
11	Kt—Kt5	P—K4
12	Kt(Kt5)xKP	KPxP
13	KPxP	B—QR3(f)

After 13 KPxP

14	P—QB4	QxP
15	R—Kt	Kt—B3
16	P—QKt3	QR—Q
17	B—Kt2	Q—Q6
18	QxQ	RxQ
19	Kt—KB3	BxB
20	RxB	P—B4
21	Kt(K4)—Kt5	R—K(g)
22	Kt—R3(h)	B—Kt2
23	Kt—B4	R—Q3
24	Kt—Q5	Kt—K2(i)
25	Kt—B7(j)	KR—Q
26	R—K2	QR—Q2
27	Kt—K6	BxKt
28	PxB	R—Q7
29	KR—K	RxR
30	RxR	R—Q2(k)
31	Kt—Q8	K—B
32	Kt—K6ch	K—B2

33	Kt—Kt5ch	K—Kt2
34	Kt—K6ch	K—B3
35	K—Kt2(l)	P—KR3
36	P—KR4 (m)	K—B2
37	Kt—B4	R—Q8
38	R—K3(n)	R—Q5
39	Kt—Q3(o)	RxP
40	Kt—K5ch	K—B(p)
41	Kt—Q7ch	K—K
42	Kt—K5	K—Q
43	Kt—B7ch	K—Q2
44	Kt—K5ch	K—B2
45	Kt—B7	Kt—B3(q)
46	R—K6(r)	R—Q5
47	RxKKtP	R—Q7
48	P—B4(s)	RxRP
49	R—Kt7	Kt—Q5
50	KtxPch	K—B3
51	Kt—B7	K—Q2(t)

After 51 Kt—B7

52	Kt—K5ch	K—K3
53	R—Kt6ch	K—K2
54	R—Kt7ch	K—B
55	R—QKt7	KtxP(u)
56	R—B7ch	K—K
57	RxP	Kt—Q7(v)
58	R—R5	R—B7
59	R—R8ch(w)	K—K2
60	P—B5(x)	Kt—K5
61	K—B3	Kt—Q3
62	R—R7ch	K—B3
63	Kt—Kt4ch	KxP
64	Kt—K3ch	K—Kt3
65	RxP	R—B6
66	R—R6(y)	Drawn

(a) This voluntary locking up of the QB is the source of all subsequent difficulties. Better here would be 3 B—B4 or P—B4, of course, with an entirely different plan of development.

(b) Merely giving the opponent a "tempo" in connection with the subsequent P—Q4. Better, therefore, would have been 5 B—Q3.

(c) By means of this move Black gains the balance in the center, a feature characteristic of Reti's system.

(d) The same procedure (with the colors reversed and minus the "tempo") was adopted successfully by Reti against Bogoljubow in a later round. Black obtains thereby a clear advantage.

(e) White (after so few moves!) has hardly any choice in his cramped position. Were Black to remain passive, the continuation for him would be Kt—Q2, followed by P—K4.

(f) A somewhat artificial idea which deprives Black of the most of his superiority in position. Likewise 13...R—K would have yielded little after 14 Q—B3, etc.; but with the simple 13 ...PxP (whereupon PxP was not feasible, on account of 14...B—QR3 and Q—Q4), Black could have maintained a clear advantage in position. After the text-move, this is changed into a small end-game superiority, which eventually turns out to be insufficient.

(g) Black has reached the goal for which he strove with his 13th move; he occupies the open files and the prospects for action on the part of the white Knights are very slight. Marshall, however, defends himself very cleverly from now on.

(h) 22 P—R3, followed by P—KKt4, was threatening.

(i) To be considered also was 24...Kt—K4; 25 KtxKt, BxKt, leaving White merely a choice between two unfavorable Rook endings: 26 KtxP, BxBP; 27 PxB, PxKt, etc.; or 26 Kt—B3, BxKt; 27 PxKt, R—Q6; 28 K—Kt2, P—B5, followed by 29...P—KKt4, etc. But the text-move also leads to a serious deterioration of White's pawn position.

(j) The best at his disposal.

(k) Now Black threatens to reinforce his position by means of Kt—B3, etc., which White prevents in surprising fashion. The subsequent ending is very instructive.

(l) Now the effectiveness of Black's move, Kt—B3, is somewhat diminished, because the White Knight, after Kt—B4, would threaten to occupy Q5 with the gain of a "tempo." Evidently this was the idea underlying the move of Kt—Q8.

(m) In order to rid himself of the annoying doubled pawns after 36... P—KKt4; 37 PxPch, PxP; 38 P—KB4, P—Kt5; 39 Kt—Kt5, followed by P—B3, etc.

(n) White is practically forced to make this pawn sacrifice, which offers some counterplay, on account of the threatened entrance of the black Knight. If, for instance, 38 K—Kt3, then 38...Kt—B3; 39 R—K6, Kt—Q5; 40 RxKKtP, Kt—K7ch and wins.

(o) Not 39 K—Kt3, on account of 39...P—KKt4, etc.

(p) In consequence of the transfer of the King to the Queen's side, which he now contemplates, Capablanca deprives himself of his last opportunity to win. If victory were attainable at all, it would have been possible only through 40...K—Kt2 and, if 41 Kt—Q3 (Kt—Q7, Kt—Kt, followed by R—Q5, etc.) then 41...K—B3; 42 P—B4, P—KKt4, etc. After the removal of the King, the white Rook finds a bit of welcome booty on the King's wing.

(q) There was still time, by means of K—Q2—Q—K—B—B2—Kt2, to continue along the line indicated above.

(r) By this means the balance of material is restored.

(s) Marshall actually appears willing to play for a win; otherwise he might have achieved an easy draw through the simple 48 KtxP, for instance: 48...Kt—Q5 (or RxP; 49 KtxP, Kt—Q5; 50 KtxKt, PxKt; 51 R—Kt5 and R—Q5) 49 R—Kt7ch, K—Kt; 50 Kt—B7, RxP; 51 Kt—O6, KtxKtP; 52 R—Kt7ch, K—R1; 53 R—Kt7, P—R4; 54 R—Kt8ch, K—R2; 55 R—Kt7ch, K—R3; 56 R—Kt8, etc.

(t) Neat would have been 51...Kt—K3; 52 Kt—K5ch, K—Q3; 53 R—Q7 mate. If 51...KtxP, then White forces a draw immediately by means of 52 Kt—O8ch, K—Q3; 53 R—KB7 (threatening perpetual check), for, after 53...P—Kt4; 54 Kt—Kt7ch, K—B3; 55 Kt—Q8ch, K—Kt3 (?), the black Rook would be won after 56 R—Kt7ch, K—R3; 57 PxPch, etc.

(u) Clearly there is no other way in which to strengthen his position. Now, however, White's KBP takes an important part in the discussion, thereby bringing to naught the adversary's chances on the opposite wing.

(v) Likewise, if 57...P—R4; 58 R—R5, threatening P—B5—B6, etc.

(w) Still better would have been 59 P—B5 at once.

(x) This, too, accomplishes it, for, if now 60...KtxP; 61 Kt—Kt4, Kt—Q3; 62 R—-R7ch, K—B (or K—K; 63 Kt—B6ch, etc.); 63 Kt—R6!, followed by P—B6, with a sure draw.

(y) The simplest, for, if 66...KtxP; 67 K—K2, and Black cannot save his KtP.

Game 48   TENTH ROUND—RUY LOPEZ

Ed. Lasker	Alekhine
White	Black
1 P—K4	P—K4
2 Kt—KB3	Kt—QB3
3 B—Kt5	P—QR3
4 B—R4	Kt—B3
5 Castles	B—B4(a)
6 P—Q3(b)	Q—K2(c)
7 Kt—B3(d)	Kt—Q5
8 KtxKt	BxKt
9 Kt—K2(e)	B—R2
10 Kt—Kt3	P—KKt3(f)
11 B—R6(g)	P—QKt4
12 B—Kt3	P—Q3
13 P—KR3(h)	B—K3
14 Q—B3	Kt—Q2(i)

After 29 R—KB

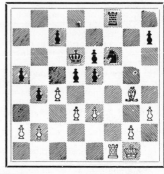

After 14...Kt—Q2

34 R—Q	Kt—B6
35 RxPch	KxP
36 K—B	R—B2(aa)
37 K—K	K—K4
38 R—Q8(bb)	R—QB2

After 38...R—QB2

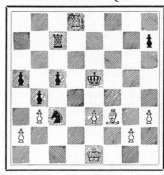

15 Kt—B5(j)	PxKt
16 PxP	P—Q4(k)
17 PxB	PxP
18 B—K3(l)	R—KB
19 Q—R5ch(m)	Q—B2
20 QxQch	RxQ
21 P—QB3	K—K2(n)
22 QR—K	P—QR4
23 B—Q	K—Q3
24 B—R5(o)	R—B3
25 B—Kt4	BxB(p)
26 PxB	P—Kt5(q)
27 P—B4(r)	QR—KB(s)
28 RxR	KtxR
29 R—KB	P—K5(t)
30 PxQP	PxP(Q6)(u)
31 PxP(v)	P—B4
32 P—QKt3(w)	P—Q7(x)
33 B—B3(y)	Kt—K5(z)

39 R—K8ch(cc)	K—B3
40 R—B8ch	K—K4(dd)
41 R—K8ch	K—B3
42 R—B8ch	K—Kt2(ee)
43 R—QR8	P—R5
44 PxP	KtxP(R7)
45 P—R5	P—B5(ff)
46 P—R6	P—B6
47 B—Q(gg)	Kt—B8(hh)
48 P—R7	K—R3
49 P—Kt4(ii)	R—KKt2(jj)
50 P—R4(kk)	P—Kt6
51 R—QB8	RxRP
52 RxP	P—Kt7
53 R—B6ch(ll)	K—Kt2

54 R—QKt6(mm) R—QR8   57 R—Kt7ch   K—Kt
55 R—Kt7ch   K—Kt   58 R—Kt8ch   K—Kt2
56 R—Kt8ch(nn) K—Kt2   Drawn

(a) This defense, which was recommended by the Danish master, J. Moeller, at the beginning of the century, has been closely examined during the last few years by the player of the Black pieces and repeatedly made use of, not without success.

(b) This tame reply cannot be regarded either as a refutation of 5...B—B4 or even as an attempt at it. The following lines of play, which lead to a game difficult to handle on both sides, deserve a further practical examination: I.—6 KtxKP, KtxKt; 7 P—Q4, KtxKP!; 8 Q—K2 (or R—K), B—K2; 9 QxKt (or RxKt), Kt—Kt3, followed by Castles, etc. II.—6 P—B3, B—R2!; 7 P—Q4, KtxP; 8 Q—K2, P—B4; 9 PxP, Castles, etc.

(c) As a matter of course the only correct continuation here is 6...P—QKt4; 7 B—Kt3, P—Q3, which promises Black fair equalization. The move of the Queen really should not have been considered at all, because of the possibility of the development of the White QKt. Now White obtains a superior game for some time to come.

(d) Threatening 8 B—Kt5 as well as Kt—Q5, KtxKt; 9 PxKt, etc. Black's answer, therefore, is almost forced.

(e) This maneuver with the Knight, which forces a considerable weakening of the Black King's side, looks very promising and in fact retains the advantage. But even the simpler 9 K—R, P—QKt4; 10 B—Kt3, P—Q3; 11 P—KB4, etc., would have been unpleasant enough for Black.

(f) At any rate more passable than 10...P—QKt4; 11 Kt—B5, Q—B; 12 B—Kt3, P—Q3; 13 Q—B3, etc.

(g) Not only preventing castling, but also P—KR3 (or P—KR4), and threatening Q—B3, followed by B—Kt5 (Kt7). There is only one defense against it.

(h) Otherwise 13...Kt—Kt5.

(i) Just at the right time! It almost seems as though Black had overcome the worst; White's next move, however, revives the attack.

(j) This pretty exchange combination, which Black could not very well prevent—should result, if properly continued, in a clear positional advantage for White.

(k) The only move which holds the position. Quite without prospect would have been 16...P—K5; 17 QxKP, P—Q4; 18 BxP, Kt—B3; 19 B—B6ch, K—Q; 20 Q—B3, etc.; and also 16...Castles QR; 17 Q—R8ch, B—Kt; 18 QxP mate was hardly worth striving for.

(l) Until now White had played quite excellently, but here he lets down noticeably. Correct would have been 18 P—QB4!, for instance: 18...P—B3; 19 PxQP, PxP; 20 QR—B, Q—B2 (Black had nothing better: if 20... Q—R5, for instance, the sacrifice of the Bishop on Q5 is too strong); 21 QxQch, KxQ; 22 R—B7, K—K2; 23 KR—QB (B—Kt7, B—Kt3), KR—KKt; 24 B—Q2!, and Black could then, to be sure, defend himself with difficulty and stress (24...B—Kt3), but White's advantage all the same would be evident. After the unnecessary retreat of the Bishop, on the other hand, he little by little is placed at a disadvantage.

(m) White cannot very well avoid the exchange of Queens, for otherwise Black, with 19...Q—KB2, followed by R—KKt, etc., would obtain good counter play on the open lines.

(n) It would have been a mistake here (and also subsequently) to play 21...P—B4, inasmuch as White, with 22 P—QB4!, would have blocked the hostile Bishop and, after 22...KtPxP; 23 PxP, P—Q5; 24 B—Q2, followed by B—B2, would have gained the advantage through the co-operation of his Bishops in spite of Black's passed pawns.

(o) Likewise 24 B—Kt4 at once would have changed the situation but little, for, after 24...Kt—B3; 25 B—B3, BxB; 26 PxB, P—B4 (27 P—KKt4, QR—KKt), Black would have stood very well.

(p) Now the time has arrived for the exchange, for Black cannot strengthen his position otherwise.

(q) Herewith is prepared the subsequent complicated pawn sacrifice. Another more promising plan would have been the blocking of the doubled pawn with 26...P—B4 in order, after 27 P—K4!, to continue with P—Q5. After 28 PxQP, RxRch; 29 RxR, KPxP, Black would have obtained the advantage through possession of the square, K4, and through the penetration of his King after 28 RxR, KtxR; 29 PxQP, KtxB; 30 PxBPch, KxP; 31 PxKt, K—Q5. Otherwise, however, he would have threatened eventually to establish a passed pawn on the extreme Queen's wing after PxP; PxP, P—Kt5. But the selected continuation likewise was cause for uneasiness.

(r) Otherwise Black, through the opening and command of the QKt file, would get the advantage.

(s) Threatening a double exchange of Rooks, followed by Kt—B4—R5.

(t) The point of Black's counter-play, by which a Pawn is sacrificed in order to obtain a clear superiority on the Queen's wing. The attempt to win, to be sure, was without great risk, but finally comes to naught in consequence of White's exact defense.

(u) Even after 30 ...PxQP; 31 P—Q4, P—B4; 32 PxPch, KxP; 33 R—Bch, K—Kt3; 34 B—K2, etc., the ending would have remained drawn.

(v) Much better than 31 BxKP, P—Q7!; 32 KR—Q, Kt—K5; 33 B—Kt4, KxP; 34 B—B3, K—K4; 35 BxKt, KxB; 36 RxQP, P—B4, and Black, in spite of his being a Pawn down for the time being, has the whip hand.

(w) Wrong would have been 32 B—B5, on account of 32 ...P—B5; 33 P—Kt3, P—Q7; 34 PxP, Kt—K5, and wins. Now, however, comes a threat.

(x) The sacrifice of the exchange by 32 ...KtxB; 33 RxR, K—K2, would have been incorrect on account of 34 R—B7ch!, KxP; 35 R—B, etc.

(y) The saving move. After 34 R—Q, KtxB; 35 RxPch, KxP; 36 PxKt, P—R5!, etc., White, in consequence of his isolated Pawns and cut-off King, would be decidedly at a disadvantage.

(z) Also the immediate 33 KxP would not have sufficed for a win, for instance: 34 R—Q, R—Q; 35 K—B2, P—R5; 36 K—K2, P—R6; 37 RxP, RxRch; 38 KxR, P—B5; 39 K—B2!, P—B6; 40 P—Kt4, K—K4; 41 K—Q3, etc. The strong position of the Pawn on B6 assures Black a draw, but no more.

(aa) Unnecessary artistry. Black saw that the opponent after 36 ...P—R5; 37 PxP, KtxP; 38 K—K2!, Kt—B6ch; 39 K—Q3, R—Qch; 40 K—B2, RxRch; 41 KxR, KtxP; 42 K—Q3, etc., would have had an easy draw and, therefore, did not search any more after winning chances that did not exist.

(bb) Threatening, among other things, 39 R—QB8, etc.

(cc) In reply to the immediate 39 R—QR8 Black, after 39 ...P—R5; 40 PxP, KtxP (R2); 41 P—R5, P—Kt6!; 42 P—R6, P—Kt7; 43 R—K8ch, K—Q3; 44 R—QKt8, Kt—Kt5; 45 B—K4, R—K2, etc., would have actually attained winning chances. The same would apply if the King were posted on K3 or Q3. For that reason White pursues the King until Black is either satisfied with a draw or chooses the unhappy square, Kt2, as actually happens.

(dd) Black is still struggling against the temptation. In reply to 40 ...K—K2, there would of course follow 41 R—KR8.

(ee) Now White really gets a chance. As already stated, Black should have been content with a draw.

(ff) The difference is now apparent. Should Black continue with 45 ...P—Kt6, then, after 46 P—R6, P—Kt7; 47 R—QKt8, Kt—Kt5; 48 B—K4, the move of 48 ...R—K2 would have been met convincingly by 49 R—Kt7. Black, however, should have selected that variation, inasmuch as after 48 ...KtxRP (instead of 48 ...R—K2); 49 RxP, Kt—Kt5, etc., White's winning chances would have been rather slim. As played, however, the situation becomes much more serious.

(gg) The only defense, but sufficient. Wrong, of course, would have been 47 P—R7, P—B7; 48 R—Kt8ch, KxR; 49 P—R8 (Q)ch, K—Kt2, and wins.

(hh) Other moves would not have been any better, for instance: 47 ...R—B4; 48 P—R7, R—QR4; 49 B—Kt3, Kt—B8; 50 R—Kt8ch, K—B3; 51 P—R8 (Q), RxQ; 52 RxR, KtxB; 53 K—Q, Kt—Q7; 54 K—B2, etc.; or 47 ...P—B7; 48 BxBP, RxB; 49 P—R7, and the Knight prevents the Rook from reaching the saving QR file.

(ii) The only correct move. He would have been trapped, on the contrary, had he played 49 B—B2, P—Kt6; 50 K—Q, on account of 50 ...R—KB2!, etc.

(jj) A sad necessity in view of the threat of 50 P—Kt5ch, etc. Insufficient would have been here (or on the next move) the interesting attempt at rescue through 49 ...R—KB2 (threatening perpetual check), on account of 50 B—B2! (not 50 P—Kt5ch, KxP; 51 R—K8ch, K—R3, etc.), P—Kt6; 51 P—Kt5ch, K—R4; 52 P—Kt6, PxB; 53 PxR, Kt—Q6ch; 54 K—K2, P—B8 (Q); 55 P—B8 (Q), Q—Q7ch; 56 K—B3, Q—B7ch; 57 K—K4 and wins.

(kk) Again threatening 51 P—Kt5ch, etc., and, therefore, forcing Black to surrender one of his valuable passed Pawns.

(ll) This check gives Black a draw at once. With 53 B—B2! White would still have had winning chances, for instance: 53 ...K—Kt2; 54 P—Kt5, P—R3; 55 P—Kt6, P—R4; 56 B—Kt, R—Q2; 57 K—B2, and White must endeavor to advance with his King, without permitting the hostile Knight to escape from his prison. The ending might still have been highly interesting. Now it is all over.

(mm) Or 54 B—B2, R—R8; 55 K—Q2, Kt—Kt6ch, etc., winning a piece.

(nn) White clearly must be satisfied with a draw, as otherwise he could not save the piece.

Game 49   TENTH ROUND—RUY LOPEZ

	Yates White	Bogoljubow Black	After 16...B—R4

	Yates White	Bogoljubow Black
1	P—K4	P—K4
2	Kt—KB3	Kt—QB3
3	B—Kt5	P—QR3
4	B—R4	Kt—B3
5	Castles	B—K2
6	R—K	P—QKt4
7	B—Kt3	P—Q3
8	P—QB3	Castles
9	P—Q4	B—Kt5
10	B—K3	PxP(a)
11	PxP	Kt—QR4
12	B—B2	Kt—B5
13	B—B(b)	P—QB4
14	P—QKt3	Kt—QR4
15	QKt—Q2(c)	Kt—B3
16	P—KR3	B—R4
17	P—K5(d)	Kt—Q4(e)
18	B—Kt2(f)	KtxP
19	PxP	B—B3(g)
20	B—K4(h)	QxP
21	Q—Kt	B—Kt3
22	KtxKt	BxKt
23	QBxB	PxB
24	Q—Q3(i)	Kt—Kt5
25	Q—KB3	QR—B
26	P—QR3	R—B6
27	Q—K2(j)	P—Q6
28	Q—Kt4	Kt—B7
29	BxB	RPxB
30	Kt—K4	Q—QB3
31	KtxR	QxKt(k)
32	Q—Q	P—Q7
33	R—KB	KtxR(l)
34	Resigns	

(a) See the game, Yates-Ed. Lasker, for this whole system of defense.

(b) In the XXth round Yates tried 13 QKt—Q2 against Capablanca, which is not any better.

(c) Up to here the game is identical with the Capablanca-Bogoljubow game (London, 1922), except for a minor, though noteworthy difference in the order of the moves. There Capablanca played 15 B—Kt2 in this position with the continuation 15...Kt—B3; 16 P—Q5, Kt—Kt5; 17 Kt—Q2, KtxB; 18 QxB, and Black is clearly quite free. The text move is not a whit stronger since at the best it means a return to the above variation, and if a different line is adopted even less pleasant consequences can follow.

(d) Not sufficiently convinced by his game with Eduard Lasker, Mr. Yates again attempts in a similar position this advance, which is contrary to the canons of position judgment, and soon drifts into a lost position. The lesser evil was even now 17 P—Q5 and, after 17...Kt—Q5, continue with B—Kt2.

(e) Now, although winning of the Queen is not threatened (because of the reply BxPch), the win of a Pawn is imminent either after 18 PxQP, B—B3! (what would have perhaps led to the same position as in the actual course of the game by a transposition of moves) or, after PxBP, PxKP!, would have left Black with an overwhelming game.

(f) This, however, loses a Pawn without the slightest compensation.

(g) Considerably stronger than the immediate recapture of the Pawn, which in any event would have sufficed for the purpose.

(h) Parries at least the threat of KtxKt ch, etc.

(i) It is naturally a matter of indifference as to what White now plays, the Pawn plus and the better position assures an easy win for the second player.

(j) 27 Q—Q would have prolonged the agony somewhat.

(k) A neat double-fork!

(l) Now, after 34 QxKt, QxQ; 35 RxQ, the move, 35...R—B, wins immediately.

Game 50   TENTH ROUND—QUEEN'S GAMBIT DECLINED

	Janowski	Tartakower				
	White	Black				
1	P—Q4	Kt—KB3				
2	Kt—KB3	P—Q4				
3	P—QB4	P—K3				
4	Kt—B3	P—B3				
5	B—Kt5(a)	P—KR3(b)				
6	B—R4(c)	PxP				
7	P—K3(d)	P—QKt4				
8	B—K2	QKt—Q2				
9	P—QR4	Q—Kt3				
10	Castles	B—Kt5				
11	Q—B2	B—Kt2				
12	P—QKt3(e)	PxKtP				
13	QxP	BxKt				
14	QxB	P—Kt5				
15	Q—Kt2	P—QR4(f)				
16	Kt—K5	KtxKt				
17	PxKt	Kt—Q4				
18	KR—B(g)	Q—B2				
19	P—K4	Kt—B6				
20	RxKt	PxR				
21	QxP	P—Kt4(h)				

22	B—Kt3	CastlesQR
23	R—Kt(i)	P—QB4(j)
24	R—Kt5	K—Kt
25	P—B3	R—Q5
26	RxBP(k)	Q—Q2
27	B—B2	RxRP
28	RxP	RxR
29	QxR	Q—B2(l)
30	Q—Kt6	Q—B8ch
31	K—B2	K—B(m)
32	B—QB5	P—KKt5(n)

After 32 B—QB5

33	B—Q6	PxP
34	Q—R7(o)	PxB(p)
35	Q—Kt8ch	K—Q2
36	QxBch	K—Q
37	Q—Kt8ch	K—Q2
38	Q—R7ch	K—Q
39	Q—R5ch	K—B
40	Q—R6ch	K—Q2
41	Q—Kt7ch	K—Q
42	Q—Kt6ch	K—Q2
43	Q—R7ch	K—Q
44	Q—Kt6ch	K—Q2
45	Q—Kt7ch	Drawn

After 21 QxP

(a)   This allows Black, if White, as in this instance, intends to keep this Bishop, to accept the gambit subsequently and maintain the extra Pawn, because of which the game is very lively and complicated from the start.

(b)   In reply to 5...PxP at once, advantage would be derived from 6 P—K4, P—QKt4; 7 P—K5, P—KR3; 8 B—R4, P—Kt4; 9 KtxKKtP, etc. (Bogoljubow vs. H. Wolf, Carlsbad, 1923.)

(c)   More solid by all means is 6 BxKt. With the move in the text White plays a real gambit.

(d)   This, on the contrary, is too tame. By means of 7 P—K4, P—KKt4; 8 B—Kt3, P—QKt4; 9 Q—B2, White would have loosened the adversary's King's side at least and thereby justified his own sacrifice somewhat. Now Black obtains a comfortable development.

(e)   Hereupon Black obtains a protected passed Pawn without any attack by White being noticeable.   Anyway, better chances lay in 11 Kt—K5 (12 Castles, 13 Kt—K4, etc.).

(f)   Black, by mere matter of fact developing moves, has attained a "won" position, which need not be wondered at after White's seventh move.   However, the game has yet in store several unexpected incidents.

(g)   Prepares for the ensuing desperate sacrifice.   The position of the Knight on B3, in conjunction with the two passed Pawns, would otherwise have become speedily unbearable.

(h)   Unbelievable, but true!   Black, in this position, wants to castle on the Queen's side, whereas the ordinary procedure would have forecasted a sure and easy victory. For instance, 21...Castles, KR; 22 Q—KKt3 (or 22 P—B4, P—QB4; or 22 Q—B5, B— R3; 23 BxB, RxB; 24 B—K7, R—K; 25 B—Q6, Q—Kt3, etc.), K—R2; 23 P—B4, P—QB4; 24 B—B3, P—B5; and this Pawn would Queen composedly, as there are no serious threats at the disposal of White.   After the overbold castling, on the Queen's side, White obtains a dangerous attack, from which Black ultimately escapes laboriously and painfully by perpetual check.

(i)   It was important to exclude the black Queen from Kt3.

(j)   In the event of other moves, there would follow P—B3, followed by B—B2 and Kt6.

(k)   If 26 B—B2, then follows simply 26...KR—Q (27 RxBP, R—Q8ch; 28 B—B, B—R3).

(l)   After the exchange of Rooks, the chief peril to Black is removed.   The text-move forces the entrance of the Queen into White's game, whereby is made possible a saving counter-attack.

(m)   Or at once 31...P—Kt5; 32 B—B5, etc., equivalent to a transposition of moves.

(n)   The only possibility of meeting the threat of 33 B—Q6, followed by Q—R7. Now the game resolves itself into a forced draw.

(o)   If 34 BxP, R—Kt (the same move also, of course, after 34 PxP); 35 Q—R7, Q—Q7ch, with a drawn game.

(p)   There is no choice.

ELEVENTH ROUND

The half-way mark was reached with the five games of the eleventh round, not one of which was finished in less than fifty moves. Dr. Lasker, with 7½—2½, had the satisfaction of leading by a full point at this stage of the contest, Alekhine being second. Capablanca was 1½ points behind the leader, a difference which persisted until the end of the tournament, notwithstanding the champion's individual triumph over Dr. Lasker. Reti was bracketed with Capablanca, while, one point below, four others were on equal terms. These were Bogoljubow, Maroczy, Marshall and Dr. Tartakower.

Dr. Lasker, in a Ruy Lopez, could make no impression upon Yates and a drawing position was soon reached. The former chose to play on, but eventually gave up the task of trying for a win.

Adopting Reti's opening, as the Russian desires this debut—a refinement of Zukertort's—to be known, Alekhine obtained a shade the better of the argument with Bogoljubow, but lacked in precision. Thereupon, Bogoljubow by plucky play improved his prospects considerably. In the very difficult ending, with Bishops on squares of different colors, however, Bogoljubow missed his way and the game was drawn.

Ed. Lasker was outplayed by Marshall in a Three Knights Game, the latter obtaining a winning attack by forceful methods. Unnecessarily "brilliant" at the critical stage, Marshall permitted his alert adversary to slip from the toils. In the end a so-called "Swindle" enabled Marshall to recoup and to win the game.

The longest game in this round was between Reti and Dr. Tartakower. It was started as a Zukertort, but transposed into a Sicilian Defense, in which Dr. Tartakower characteristically refused to follow precedent by utilizing the open QB file. Instead he played for the advance of his KB Pawn and complications. The method Reti adopted to gain a Pawn and the better position as well is well worth close study. The ending was also faultlessly conducted.

Maroczy vs. Janowski was a Two Knights Defense well handled by the French representative, who made a very good strategical sacrifice of a piece for two Pawns and a pressure which should have endured. Maroczy defended doggedly and Janowski, unable to work out a winning combination, committed a serious blunder which cost him the game.

The white pieces scored two of the games, drew two and lost one, which made the record for the first half of the tournament: White, 28; Black, 27.

Although Dame Fortune smiled upon him in his game with Marshall, Dr. Lasker had played consistently and with his old-time assurance and poise up to this point. Alekhine, notwithstanding his loss to Dr. Lasker, had also given a good account of himself. His game with Reti was a particularly fine effort. Capablanca, after a poor start, had got his bearings. With the white pieces, Reti produced some masterpieces, his game with Janowski also being especially pleasing. Marshall was surely but slowly finding himself. Dr. Tartakower, after scoring 2½ points in the first three rounds, only doubled his score in the next eight. Bogoljubow, after six rounds, had 3½ to his credit, but Janowski's classical victory over him started his reverses. Maroczy's play was marked by a steady, persevering grind.

Game 51 ELEVENTH ROUND—RUY LOPEZ

Dr. Lasker.	Yates.
White.	Black.
1 P—K4	P—K4
2 Kt—KB3	Kt—QB3
3 B—Kt5	P—QR3
4 B—R4	Kt—B3
5 Castles	B—K2
6 R—K	P—Q3
7 BxKtch(a)	PxB
8 P—Q4	PxP(b)
9 KtxP	B—Q2
10 Kt—QB3	Castles
11 B—Kt5	P—R3(c)
12 B—R4	R—K
13 Q—Q3	Kt—R2
14 BxB	QxB
15 R—K3(d)	Kt—B(e)
16 QKt—K2	Q—B3(f)
17 Q—B3	P—B4
18 Kt—B3	QxQ
19 KtxQ	QR—Kt
20 P—QKt3	P—KB3
21 Kt—K	B—B3
22 R—Q	Kt—K3
23 P—B3(g)	K—B2
24 K—B2	Kt—Q5
25 Kt—K2	KtxKt
26 RxKt(h)	R—K2
27 R(K2)—Q2	QR—K
28 Kt—Q3	R—QKt
29 Kt—Kt2	B—Kt4
30 R—KR	QR—K
31 Kt—Q	B—B3
32 Kt—K3	R—QKt
33 P—KR4	R(K2)—K
34 K—K2	R—Kt5

35 K—Q	R(Kt5)—Kt
36 K—B	R—K3
37 R—Kt	P—Kt3
38 P—KKt4	R—KR
39 R—R2	QR—K
40 K—Q2	R—KR
41 P—R3	R—QKt
42 K—B3	KR—K
43 P—Kt5	BPxP
44 PxP	P—KR4(i)
45 R—R4	K—Kt2
46 K—Q2	R—KB
47 K—K2	QR—K
48 Kt—B	B—Kt4ch
49 P—B4	B—B3
50 Kt—Q2	P—R4
51 P—R4	R—K2
52 K—K3	R(B)—K
53 R—B4	R—B2
54 R—R4	R(B2)—K2
55 R—B4	Drawn

After 55 R—B4

(a) With this move White obtains a similar position to that in the Steinitz Defence—only with this difference: The Black QRP stands on QR3 instead of on QR2, where it is admittedly more exposed. On the other hand, the White Queen is prevented from going to QR6 and the White Knight from establishing itself on QKt5 (after P—QB4 for Black). This difference, however, is more or less unimportant in weighing the chances of either side.

(b) In case Black attempts to hold the center in accordance with the principles of Tschigorin by 8...Kt—Q2, then White can play his Queen's Knight via Q2 to B4 with the three-fold threat: Pressure on K5, diversion toward QR5 and, finally, the eventual maneuver to KB5 via K3. The text-move is simpler and less hazardous, as the experience of the last years shows.

(c) The well-known maneuver to assure the interaction of all the fighting forces through the exchange of the KB, which comes into action with difficulty.

(d) Perhaps in order to play Q—B4 eventually, a move that would be bad now because of P—Q4. Black acts rightly, however, in not worrying much about this eventuality.

(e) Because, after 16 Q—B4, P—QB4; 17 Kt—Q5, Q—Q, etc., White would be forced to withdraw without accomplishing anything.

(f) This immediate threat (17...P—QB4) shows most clearly that Black has overcome the difficulties of the opening. White, therefore, prepares for an exchange of Queens and an end-game which in any case he can only hope to win through a lack of elementary precaution on the part of his opponent.

(g) Or Kt—KB3, Kt—Kt4, etc. White cannot well prevent the coming exchange of his Knight.

(h) The Bishop now guards all entrances by the hostile Knight. A draw might here have been agreed upon. The following attempt to win on the part of White leads only to the setting up of a passed Pawn on the extreme King's wing, which in any case does not alter matters because of the blocked position. The rest of the game is dull and easy to understand.

(i) In case one side is better off, it is certainly not White.

Game 52   ELEVENTH ROUND—RETI'S OPENING

	Alekhine	Bogoljubow			
	White	Black	23	P—B4(l)	Kt—B2
1	Kt—KB3	Kt—KB3	24	KR—K	QR—K
2	P—QB4	P—K3	25	RxR(m)	QxR
3	P—KKt3	P—Q4	26	B—QB	Kt—Q3
4	B—Kt2	QKt—Q2	27	B—Q2	Q—KB2(n)
5	P—QKt3	B—Q3	28	Q—Q3	Q—Kt3
6	Castles	Castles	29	QxQ(o)	PxQ
7	B—Kt2	P—B3	30	K—B2	B—R3
8	P—Q3(a)	R—K	31	B—KB3	K—B2
9	QKt—Q2	P—QR4(b)	32	P—QKt4(p)	BPxP
10	P—QR3	R—Kt(c)	33	PxP	P—R5
11	Q—B2	Q—K2	34	R—QB(q)	B—B5(r)
12	P—Q4(d)	P—QKt3	35	P—Kt5(s)	Kt—K5ch
			36	BxKt	RxB(t)
			37	B—K3	BxQP
			38	BxP(u)	R—Kt5(v)

After 12...P—QKt3

After 38 BxP

13	Kt—K5(e)	B—Kt2
14	P—K4(f)	BxKt
15	PxB	Kt—Kt5(g)
16	Kt—KB3	P—QB4(h)
17	KPxP	PxP
18	P—R3	KKtxKP
19	KtxKt	KtxKt
20	PxP(i)	Q—Q3
21	Q—B3(j)	P—B3
22	QR—Q(k)	R—K2

39	R—B7ch	K—Kt(w)
40	R—B5	B—B5
41	B—R5	R—Kt7ch
42	K—K3	BxP
43	B—B3	R—Kt6
44	K—Q2(x)	B—Q2
45	P—Kt4	R—Kt2(y)
46	R—QR5	K—B2

47	P—Kt5(z)	R—Kt3	
48	P—R4	R—Q3ch	
49	K—K3	R—K3ch	
50	K—Q3	R—Q3ch	
51	K—K3	B—B4(aa)	
52	R—R7ch	K—K3	
53	B—Q4	B—B7	
54	R—QB7(bb)	B—Kt8	
55	R—Kt7	B—B4	
56	RxP	PxP	
57	RPxP	K—Q4	
58	R—QR7	R—K3ch	
59	B—K5	B—B7	
60	R—Q7ch	K—B4(cc)	
61	R—B7ch	Drawn	

(a) The identical error in position judgment as in the game Reti vs. Yates (6tn round). Correct would have been P—Q4 in order to prevent once for all the unlimbering move of P—K4. The fact that White in this game gets an advantage anyhow must be attributed to the circumstance that Black does not avail himself of the possibility of obtaining an unimpeded development of his Queen's side.

(b) As a rule his advance is strong only if White is unable to reply with P—QR3, as, for instance, if in the present position the moves, Q—K2 and QR—QB, had been made (compare the games Reti vs. Alekhine, 8th round, and Reti vs. Dr. Lasker, 16th round.) Even so there is not much harm done so long as Black makes up his mind to play P—K4 on one of his next two moves and does not wait until his opponent after all decides to play P—Q4.

(c) A mysterious move the object of which is not apparent in the course of the game. If by chance P—QKt4 was intended, that move would not do on account of the reply of Kt—Q4.

(d) Better late than never. White prepares for an open game at a moment when his opponent's development is still incomplete and should obtain a clear advantage by this procedure.

(e) But this inaccurate sequence of moves is utilized by Bogoljubow in fine style to bring about equalization. Correct would have been first of all 13 P—K4 (in order to force the exchange on that square), and if thereupon 13...PxKP, then 14 Kt—K5!, B—QKt2; 15 KtxKP, BxKt; 16 PxB, KtxKt; 17 BxKt, Kt—KB (or P—KKt3, orP—KR3); 18 P—QKt4!, with important positional advantage, as Black clearly dared not play 18... PxP; 19 PxP, QxP, on account of 20 B—R3, etc. Therefore, it would have been best for Black to answer 13 P—K4 with KtxP; but even in that case White's advantage would show plainly after 14 KtxKt, PxKt; 15 Kt—K5, etc.

(f) Seemingly in order but insufficient. After 14 KtxKt, QxKt; 15 P—K4, etc., White's position would still have been preferable.

(g) By this shift (instead of 15...KtxKP, which would have led to one of the variations above) Black suddenly obtains a counter-initiative, which forces his opponent into an unwelcome simplification.

(h) Threatening P—Q5, etc.

(i) In spite of his two Bishops, White by no means has any advantage, as his pawn on both sides is somewhat weakened and the passed QP, which is easily stopped is likely to be weak in the ensuing ending. Hence, White, lacking the resolution to seek more than equalization, gradually gets the worst of it.

(j) Threatening 21 P—B4, thereby forcing the counter-move.

(k) Loss of time, as Black clearly could not take the pawn on account of the ensuing pin. 22 KR—K at once, followed by doubling of the Rooks on the K file, would have been in order.

(l) This dislodging of the Knight, through which the King's position is weakened further, should merely have been threatened and actually executed only in case of utmost necessity. 23 KR—K, followed by R—K3, etc., was still to be preferred.

(m) This exchange was not exactly necessary, but White was already uncomfortable. After 25 K—B2, for instance, Black could have answered advantageously with 25...Q—Q2 followed by Kt—Q3, etc.

(n) With correct appraisement of the position Black seeks to make good his advantage in the ending. Alluring would have been 27...Kt—K5, for if 28 BxKt, QxB; 29 R—K, then 29...QxQP!; 30 RxRch, K—B2; 31 Q—B4 (if 31 R—K2, then mate in three moves), KxR; 32 QxQ, BxQ, etc., with a winning ending in spite of the Bishops on squares of different colors. White, however, would have answered 27...Kt—K5 with 28 Q—Q3, whereupon a decisive turn in favor of Black would not have been manifest. The intent of the text-move is clearer and more convincing.

(o) White clearly cannot avoid the exchange of Queens.

(p) The weakness of his pawn position induces White to adopt this violent measure which in the end is frustrated by a simplifying maneuver on the part of Black. By this time, however, it was difficult to defend the position, as the exchange of Rooks by means of 32 R—K, RxR; 33 KxR, was as good as forbidden on account of 33...B—Q6, followed by Kt—Kt4. After other moves, however, Black could have safely played for the capture of the weakling on Q4, to which White, with the text-move, hoped to g.ve a new lease of life.

(q) 31 P—Kt5 right away would have been met v:ctoriously by Black with 31... BxP; 32 B—QKt4, Kt—K5ch; 33 K—Kt2, Kt—B4!; 34 BxKt, PxB; 35 R(Q)—Kt, B—Q2; 36 R—Kt7, K—K2, etc. With the text-move White seeks to bring about the exchange of Rooks, because after 34...R—QB; 35 RxR, BxR; 36 P—Kt4, etc., he could just about hold h.s own in the end-game.

(r) Threatening to secure the Queen's side with P—Kt4, after which the passed QR pawn would have led to a decision.

(s) Under these circumstances this counter-thrust, which had been planned with 32 P—Kt4, offers the only chance. After 35...BxP, White would have obtained a counter-attack w.th 36 B—Kt4, R—QB; 37 R—K!, R—Q; 38 R—K6, etc.

(t) Notwithstanding the Bishops on squares of different colors, the QR pawn should now bring about the decision and mainly because its advance to R7 cannot very well be prevented.

(u) Or 38 R—QR, R—Kt5; 39 BxP, RxP; 40 B—Q4, R—Kt5, etc., with a winning pos:tion.

(v) In this manner Black wins a pawn, but at the same time surrenders a well-earned victory. After 38...P—R6, White would not have had an adequate defense, for instance: I. 39 B—B5, P—R7; 40 B—R3, R—B5; 41 R—R or KR—B6, etc. II. 39 R—B7ch, K—Kt; 40 R—R7, P—R7; 41 B—B5, R—B5, etc. It is obvious that White's Kt pawn would have been of no consequence in this variat.on and that Black in any event could have removed if later on in case of need. After the text-move the game with correct defense, is no longer to be won.

(w) After 39...K—K3 would follow 40 B—B5 and Black would not have dared capture the QKt pawn on account of 41 R—K7ch, K—B4; 42 P—Kt4ch, KxP; 43 B—K3 mate.

(x) White has surrendered the pawn under the most favorable conditions, inasmuch as now 44...P—R6 would lead to nothing after 45 R—B8ch, K—B2; 46 R—R8, B—B5; 47 R—R4 (not 47 K—B2, P—R7; 48 RxP, RxBch, etc.), B—K3; 48 P—Kt4, etc.

(y) If 45...K—B2 at once, then of course, 46 R—B7, followed by P—Kt5, etc.

(z) In order to force the hostile Pawn to a white square, whereupon the draw would be assured.

(aa) A last attempt.

(bb) In order to force the Bishop to B4 before capturing the KtP so as to deprive the Black King of that square.

(cc) After 60...K—B5, Black might even have lost, for instance: 61 R—B7ch, K—Kt6; 62 R—B3ch, K—Kt7; 63 R—B6ch, RxBch; 64 PxR, P—R6; 65 R—R6, P—R7; 66 P—K6, P—R8 (Q); 67 RxQ, KxR; 68 K—B4, K—Kt7; 69 K—K5, K—B6; 70 K—B6, K—Q5; 71 P—K7, B—R4; 72 KxP, K—K4; 73 K—B7, K—B4; 74 P—Kt6, and wins. Now, however, White forces the exchange of Rooks.

Game 53 ELEVENTH ROUND—THREE KNIGHTS OPENING

	Ed. Lasker White	Marshall Black
1	P—K4	P—K4
2	Kt—KB3	Kt—KB3
3	Kt—B3	B—Kt5
4	B—B4(a)	Castles
5	Castles	Kt—B3
6	Kt—Q5(b)	KtxKt
7	BxKt	P—Q3
8	P—B3	B—R4(c)
9	P—Q3	B—KKt5
10	P—KR3	B—Q2(d)
11	B—Kt5	Q—K
12	Kt—R4(e)	K—R
13	K—R	P—B3
14	B—K3	Kt—K2
15	BxKtP(f)	R—QKt
16	B—QR6	RxP
17	Q—B	R—QKt
18	P—Kt4(g)	P—KB4(h)

After 18 P—Kt4

19	P—B3(i)	PxKtP
20	BPxP(j)	P—Q4(k)
21	Q—R3	B—Kt3
22	B—KKt5(l)	P—B4
23	P—Q4(m)	RxRch
24	BxR(n)	KPxP
25	BPxP	QPxP
26	PxP	B—B2
27	B—Kt2(o)	Kt—B4(p)
28	B—B4	BxB
29	KtxKt	BxKt
30	PxB	B—B2(q)
31	Q—K3	Q—K4
32	Q—Kt	P—K6(r)
33	R—K	P—K7(s)

After 27 B—Kt2

34	B—B3(t)	R—Kt7(u)
35	Q—Kt2	P—KR3(v)
36	P—KB6(w)	QxKBP(x)
37	BxP	Q—QB6(y)
38	R—KB	QxP(z)
39	Q—R8ch	R—Kt
40	Q—Kt2	Q—QB7
41	B—Q	Q—B6
42	B—Kt3	R—K
43	B—B2	B—Q3
44	B—Kt3	Q—B(aa)
45	R—KKt	R—K2(bb)
46	R—Q(cc)	R—K6(dd)

After 46 R—Q

47	RxB	RxPch
48	K—Kt	Q—B8ch
49	B—Q	Q—K6ch
50	K—B	Q—B5ch
51	K—Kt(ee)	R—KKt6
52	R—Q8ch	K—R2

53 B—B2ch	P—Kt3	56 QxRch	KxQ
54 BxPch(ff)	K—Kt2	57 R—Kt2ch	K—B4
55 R—Q2	RxB	Resigns	

(a) After this Black has no difficulty in equalizing the game. The surest way in which to retain the advantage of the opening is by means of 4 KtxP in order then to force the exchange of the Bishop on Kt5 through the retreat of the Knight to Q3.

(b) White gets absolutely nothing from the exchange brought about herewith. The most plausible would have been 6 P—Q3, as the continuation of 6...BxKt; 7 KtPxB, P—Q4; 8 PxP, KtxP, would favor White somewhat after 9 Q—K!, R—K; 10 Kt—KKt5, B—B4; 11 R—Kt (threatening R—Kt5). Black clearly cannot play 11... Kt—QR4, on account of 12 BxKt, QxB; 13 P—QB4, Q—B4; 14 R—Kt5, etc.

(c) Herewith Marshall offers a pawn in order, after 9 BxKt, PxB; 10 Q—R4, B—Kt3; 11 QxP, B—Kt5, etc., to obtain a strong initiative.

(d) After 10...B—R4, then could have followed without question 11 P—KKt4, B—KKt3; 12 B—Kt5, followed by Kt—R4, etc.

(e) Because of his fruitless effort to make something out of nothing White at last obtains an enduring disadvantage. He might have equalized by means of 12 Kt—Q2— B4, followed by the exchange of the Knight for Black's KB, which would have permitted him at the proper moment to remain with Bishops on squares of opposite colors. That, of course, would not have been interesting chess, but it is only then permissible to play for a win in case the game has been soundly developed.

(f) White perceives that there is no hope for him in a direct attack and therefore attempts to bring about complications on the other side. After 15 B—Kt3, Black could have gained some advantage through P—KKt4, followed by establishing the Knight on B5, as well as through 15...P—KB4; 16 P—KB4, KPxP; 17 BxP, PxP; 18 PxP, B—Kt3, etc.

(g) The white pieces do not co-operate and White must take extraordinary measures in order not to succumb to an immediate counter-attack. The text-move, which is directed against P—KB4, but above all against the threat of 18...Q—R4; 19 Kt—B3, BxRP, is elegantly met by Marshall.

(h) A surprising counter-stroke, which is made possible by the exposed position of the Bishop at R6. After 19 KPxP, would follow 19...KtxP!; 20 PxKt (or 20 KtxKt, BxKt; 21 PxB, Q—B3ch, etc.), Q—R4; 21 B—Kt5 (or 21 Kt—Kt2, QxPch; 22 K—Kt, RxP, etc.), BxKBP!; 22 K—R2, P—R3; 23 KtxB, RxKt; 24 B—K3, R—B6, with a winning position.

(i) This is about the best defense.

(j) Here, however, 20 RPxP would have been wiser for defensive purposes. White's position is becoming worse and worse.

(k) Marshall conducts this part of the game with great energy. 21...B—B3, etc., is now threatened.

(l) After 22 BxB, RxB, the threat would have been R—KR3.

(m) The opening of the position in the center when the King's side is unprotected should lead to a catastrophe, but even with a less forceful continuation, White would have difficulty in holding the square, K4, for instance: 23 RxRch, QxR; 24 K—Kt2, B—B3; 25 R—KB, Q—K; 26 R—K, Kt—Kt3; 27 Kt—B5, Q—Q2, threatening P—B5, etc.

(n) It is comprehensible that White should utilize the first opportunity to bring back for the defense the Bishop so long inactive. Even after 24 RxR, and the exchange of the center pawns, the opening of the diagonals would have gained a decisive advantage for Black.

(o) This should lead to immediate loss, but even after 27 R—Q, B—B3, etc., White's position would have been quite helpless.

(p) This artificiality is punished at once. After the simple 27...Kt—Q4 (Kt—Kt3 also suffices), White, in view of the threat of Q—K4, might have cheerfully resigned, for instance: 28 Q—B, Q—K4; 29 K—Kt, R—KB, etc. After the text-move, on the contrary, the winning process becomes very difficult, the more so as White now defends himself capitally.

(q) Always the threat of Q—K4 looks to be dreadfully dangerous, but White has just one defense.

(r) It soon becomes apparent that this pawn, so far advanced, cannot be held, but likewise after 32...QxKBP. White would have had excellent drawing chances, for instance: 33 R—KB, Q—Kt3; 34 R—K, R—K; 35 Q—K3, etc.

(s) If 33...R—K, then 34 P—B6, etc.

(t) The saving move.

(u)   Or 34...QxKBP; 35 B—Kt4! (not 35 Q—Kt2, on account of R—Kt8), Q—Q5ch; 36 Q—Kt2, QxP; 37 QxKP, etc., with a position similar to the one in the actual game.

(v)   If 35...B—R4, White saves himself through 36 P—KB6!, PxP (or QxBP; 37 BxKP!); 37 R—Kt4, Q—KKt4; 38 QxKP, etc.

(w)   With this move White gets rid of the dangerous KP.

(x)   Of course not 36...PxP; 37 R—KKt, etc.

(y)   If 37...RxP, White forces exchange of Queens through 38 Q—R8ch, for, after 38...B—Q, then would follow 39 R—Q.

(z)   Thereby Black has at least maintained his material superiority, but, because of the Bishops on squares of opposite colors, his chances of winning have become highly problematical.

(aa)   Black, who can no longer count upon a regular win, now plays for small traps. The text-move threatens 45...R—K6, which can be defended in the simplest way by 45 Q—Kt4.

(bb)   Now 46 Q—Kt4 would have been a mistake on account of 46...Q—B3ch; 47 Q—Kt2, R—K7!, etc., but 46 Q—B3, as well as 46 B—Q5, would have sufficed for the defense.

(cc)   Forgetting the opponent's only threat.

(dd)   A winning combination, fairly simple to be sure, but exactly calculated.

(ee)   Or 51 K—K, R—K6; 52 B—K2, QxR, etc.

(ff)   If 54 R—Q7ch, K—R! (after K—Kt?; 55 B—Kt3ch, etc., the game would have been drawn); 55 R—Q8ch, K—Kt2, and wins.

Game 54   ELEVENTH ROUND—SICILIAN DEFENSE
(By Transposition of Moves)

Reti	Tartakower	After 20...BxP
White	Black	

Reti White	Tartakower Black
1 Kt—KB3	P—KKt3
2 P—K4(a)	P—QB4(b)
3 P—Q4(c)	PxP
4 KtxP	Kt—KB3
5 QKt—B3(d)	P—Q3
6 B—K2	B—Kt2
7 Castles	Kt—B3
8 B—K3(e)	Castles
9 Kt—Kt3(f)	B—K3(g)
10 P—B4	Q—B(h)
11 P—KR3	Kt—K
12 Q—Q2	P—B4(i)
13 PxP	PxP
14 QR—K	K—R
15 Kt—Q4	B—Kt
16 P—KKt4(j)	KtxKt
17 BxKt	P—K4
18 B—K3	PxKtP
19 BxKtP	B—K3(k)
20 P—B5(l)	BxP(m)
21 RxB(n)	RxR
22 Q—Q3	P—K5(o)
23 KtxP	P—KR4(p)
24 Kt—Kt3	PxB
25 KtxR(q)	Q—K3
26 R—K2	B—K4(r)
27 B—Q4(s)	Kt—B3
28 PxP	R—KKt

29 BxB	PxB
30 R—R2ch	Kt—R2
31 Kt—K3(t)	R—Kt2
32 Q—Q8ch	R—Kt
33 Q—Q3	R—Kt2
34 Q—K4	K—Kt(u)
35 R—Q2	Kt—B3
36 R—Q8ch	K—B2
37 QxPch	K—Kt3
38 Q—B3(v)	K—Kt4
39 R—Q2	P—K5
40 Q—Kt3	R—Q2
41 RxR	KtxR
42 Q—B2	Kt—B4
43 Q—B5ch	QxQ

44 PxQ	Kt—R5		
45 P—Kt3	Kt—B6		
46 P—R4	P—R4		
47 K—B2	Kt—R7		
48 K—K2	K—B3		
49 K—Q2	Kt—Kt5		
50 K—B3	K—K4		
51 P—B6(w)	KxP		
52 K—Q4	K—K3		
53 KxP	K—Q3		
54 K—Q4	Kt—B3ch		
55 K—B4	Kt—R2		
56 P—B3	K—B3		
57 K—Q4	K—Kt3		
58 Kt—B4ch	K—R3		

After 37...K—Kt3

59 K—Q5	Kt—B		
60 K—K6(x)	Kt—Kt3		
61 KtxKt	KxKt		
62 K—Q6	K—R3		
63 K—B6	K—R2		
64 K—Kt5	K—Kt2		
65 KxP	K—R2		
66 P—Kt4	K—Kt2		
67 P—Kt5	K—R2		
68 P—Kt6ch	K—Kt2		
69 K—Kt5	K—Kt		
70 K—R6	K—R		
71 P—Kt7ch	K—Kt		
72 P—B4	K—B2		
73 K—R7	K—B3		
74 P—Kt8(Q)	Resigns		

(a) The simplest reply to 1...P—KKt3, inasmuch as White thereby switches to a favorable variation of the Sicilian defense.

(b) Manifestly the only move to prevent the construction of a Pawn center hard to assail (after 3 P—Q4).

(c) Thereby White permits himself to be drawn into the so-called "dragon variation," which gives Black an acceptable game. In order would have been 3 P—QB4! (in order to continue with 4 P—Q4 after 3...Kt—QB3 as well as after 3...B—KKt2) whereby the danger of pressure upon the QB file, which as a rule constitutes Black's best chance, would be immediately eliminated.

(d) After 5 B—Q3, Black could very well have played 5...Kt—B3; 6 B—K3, P—Q4, etc. Thus it is seen that White by means of his third move deprived himself of his most favorable deployment.

(e) More cautious would have been first 8 P—KR3, for now Black could have brought about a simplification favorable to him by means of 8...Kt—Kt5. However, he omits to utilize this opportunity—perhaps in the hope of being able to obtain still more in a complicated game.

(f) After other moves (as, for instance, 9 P—KR3) Black could have evened up with Dr. Meitner's maneuver of 9...P—Q4; 10 PxP, Kt—QKt5!, etc. But neither does White accomplish much with the text-move.

(g) Black clears the deck for counter-action against the King's side. Positionally more accurate, however, appears to be 9...B—Q2, with the subsequent R—B and eventually Kt—QR4, in order to make use of the advantage of the open QB file, which, strangely enough, does not manifest itself in this game. Moreover, the Bishop on K3, as shortly will appear, is somewhat exposed.

(h) And here 10...Kt—QR4 still came under consideration. Black's entire structure makes an artificial impression.

(i) The logical outcome of the last moves by Black, for White was already threatening to become dangerous with 13 P—KKt4. But the opening of new lines is favorable to White for the simple reason that he is better developed.

(j) Reti plays determinedly for the attack in full accord with the existing conditions as, after other moves (16 B—B3, for instance), Black would have seized the initiative through 16...P—K4; 17 KtxKt, PxKt, etc. Now, however, he is forced to exchange the Knight without strengthening his center thereby.

(k) The complications invited hereby turn out in favor of White. After 19 Q—B5; 20 R—Q! (20 B—K2, Q—B, followed by B—K3, etc.), the positional superiority of White would still have been meagre.

(l) Simple, but correctly calculated.

(m) The lesser evil would have been 20...B—Q2, although White would then also have stood much better after 21 Kt—Q5, etc.

(n) After this obvious maneuver, Black, in order to avoid material disadvantage, is forced to compromise his King's position seriously.

(o) So that, after 23 QxP, he may save himself through 23...R—K4, etc.

(p) Clearly again the only move.

(q) Threatening to win at once with 26 B—Q4, etc.

(r) Or 26...PxP; 27 B—Q4, Q—Kt3ch; 28 K—R, Kt—B3; 29 QxPch, Q—R2; 30 QxQch, KxQ; 31 R—K7 and wins.

(s) Thereupon Black no longer has time to save his KtP, on account of the threat of KtxQP!.

(t) White now possesses a healthy Pawn plus, besides his lasting attack, and in consequence must win without difficulty.

(u) Somewhat better would have been at once 34...R—Q2, for now the entrance of the white Rook forces additional gain of material.

(v) Apparently White falls into the trap of his opponent, for, after 38...KtxP, he could not retake either with the Queen or the Knight (39 QxKtch, K—R2; or 39 KtxKt, Q—Kt3ch, winning the Rook). In reality, however, he would have won immediately by means of 39 R—Q6!, QxR; 40 QxKtch, followed by QxRch and Kt—B5ch. One can hardly believe that the "fight" could have lasted 36 moves longer.

(w) The simplest.

(x) Reti amused himself by constructing a little "Zugzwang" problem (60...Kt—R2; 61 K—Q7, etc.). The last ten moves present an instructive conflict between the King and three Pawns against His lone Majesty.

Game 55   ELEVENTH ROUND—TWO KNIGHTS DEFENSE

Maroczy	Janowski		
White	Black.		

After 13 P—KKt4

	Maroczy White	Janowski Black.
1	P—K4	P—K4
2	Kt—KB3	Kt—QB3
3	B—B4	Kt—B3
4	P—Q3(a)	B—B4
5	Kt—B3	P—Q3
6	Castles(b)	B—Kt3(c)
7	Kt—QR4(d)	B—Kt5
8	B—QKt5(e)	Castles
9	BxKt	PxB
10	P—KR3(f)	B—KR4
11	KtxB	RPxKt
12	Q—K2(g)	P—R3(h)
13	P—KKt4(i)	KtxKtP(j)
14	PxKt	BxP
15	Q—K3	P—KB4
16	PxP	RxP
17	Kt—R2	B—R4
18	Q—Kt3	Q—B3
19	P—KB3	QR—KB
20	B—K3(k)	K—R2(l)
21	R—B2	Q—K3(m)
22	P—Kt3	QR—B3
23	K—R	B—K(n)
24	R—KKt	P—KKt4
25	P—Q4(o)	P—B4
26	PxKP	PxP
27	R—K	B—B3
28	K—Kt	P—R4(p)
29	P—QB4	B—Kt2
30	Q—R3	K—Kt3
31	R—KKt2	Q—K2
32	R—Q(q)	R—Q3
33	R(Kt2)--Q2	Q—B3(r)
34	RxR	PxR
35	Q—Kt2	K—R2
36	Q—R3	K—Kt3

37	Q—Kt2(s)	K—Kt2(t)
38	R—KB	K—Kt3
39	Q—QB2	K—Kt2
40	Q—K2	Q—K3
41	B—Q2	K—Kt3
42	B—B3(u)	R—B5
43	Q—Q2	R—B3
44	R—Q	BxP(v)
45	KtxB	кxKt
46	QxP	K—B4
47	BxP	P—R5
48	QxQch	KxQ
49	B—B7	P—Kt5
50	BxP	P—Kt6
51	BxP	R—B6
52	B—Kt4	R—B7
53	R—Q2	R—B8ch

After 44 R—Q

54	K—Kt2	K—B4
55	B—K7	Resigns

(a)   The most solid method by which, however, White straightway yields every advantage of the move.

(b)   The usual move is 6 B—K3, whereupon 6...B—Kt3 is about the best reply.

(c)   A good move for position which has the advantage of committing Black as little as possible and in consequence sett.ng the adversary a difficult choice.

(d)   This merely leads eventually to the opening of the QR file for Black and to the strengthening of his pawn position.   A thoroughly good continuation, however, is not eas ly to be found, as castling on the King's side would be premature.   Black, for instance, could have answered 7 P—KR3 with P—KR3, followed by P—KKt4, etc., and, after 7 B—KKt5, there would have followed P—KR3.

(e)   White perceives that his position is no longer satisfactory and seeks to ease his game through exchanges.   In reality there is little future for his Bishop in this position.

(f)   Now, after Black has castled, this move is much more in order.

(g)   In preparation for the next attempt at freedom, which, if made at once, would be quite mistaken; for instance: 12 P—KKt4, KtxKKtP; 13 PxKt, BxP; 14 Q—K2, P—KB4, etc., with a winning position.

(h)   In order to prevent B—Kt5, which, for instance, would have been poss.ble after 12...Q—Q2, being at the same time wholly conscious of the correctness of the subsequent sacrifice.

(ι)   There was no good reason for this headlong procedure.   After 13 Q—K3, Black would have had only a minimum advantage (the open QR file and a more compact pawn position).   After the sacrifice, on the contrary, White can only hope for a draw after a troublesome defense.

(j)   A well-considered positional sacrifice, which is to be esteemed h gher than a combination leading to a forced win.   For the Knight Black, for the present, gets two pawns, but in add.tion a lasting pressure which holds promise of the capture of a third.

(k)   After the last forced moves, White is beginning to feel uncomfortable and, although he could now protect the BP with 20 K—Kt2, he prefers to offer it as an atoning sacrifice.

(1)   Quite correct!   After 20...BxP; 21 KtxB, RxKt; 22 RxR, QxR; 23 QxQ, RxQ; 24 B—B2, the ending would be favorable to White, inasmuch as he would have had a chance to establish a passed pawn on the QR file, for instance: 24...P—QB4; 25 P—QR4, K—B2; 26 P—B3!, RxQP (or R—B5; 27 B—K, etc.); 27 P—Kt4.   The text-move maintains the pressure.

(m)   Now of course, 21...BxP would not do on account of the reply of 22 QR—KB; but 21...P—QB4, in order to prevent P—Q4 and at the same time prepare to bring over the Bishop to B3, seems to be more exact.

(n) 23...P—B4 at once was to have been preferred here (24 QR—KKt, P—KKt4; 25 P—B3, Q—Q4, etc.).

(o) Naturally, White seeks to open files for his Rooks.

(p) This weakening of the King's position could have had serious consequences. White, however, fails to profit from the favorable opportunity.

(q) Correct would have been K—R, in order to be able to double the Rook on the KKt file or, after P—Kt5, to sacrifice the Knight with a decisive attack. After the text move, Black could have easily held the draw.

(r) Forcing a favorable exchange.

(s) White can see no way to win and clearly is satisfied with a draw.

(t) Neither is Black able to figure it out, but changes his moves only to be able to play on.

(u) This new position of the Bishop really is no more effective than the former.

(v) Suicidal. After 44...Q—R6; 45 Q—Kt2, Q—B4, etc., there would have been in sight no continuation holding out victory for White. Now, of course, the game is lost.

TWELFTH ROUND

This round, the opening of the second stage of the struggle, was a repetition of the fourth, with the colors reversed. Dr. Lasker added to his score and maintained his one-point lead, but only after a narrow escape from defeat at the hands of Janowski. The former world's champion drifted into trouble after an ill-timed advance of his KR Pawn early in the game. Thereafter he sought safety in exchanges, but Janowski retained his two Bishops and gradually improved his game. At last it became apparent that a Pawn must be won in order to drive home the advantage, but Janowski, quite characteristically, hesitated to part with a Bishop. Then he went completely astray and Dr. Lasker, quick to seize an opportunity and turn it cleverly to account, turned a "lost game" into victory. It was the second defeat of Janowski by Dr. Lasker.

Alekhine vs. Capablanca was a Queen's Gambit declined of very short duration—18 moves to be exact—and it ended in a draw, as had their first encounter. At his fourth turn, Capablanca deployed his QB at KB4, only to withdraw that piece to its original square, two moves later. Seemingly, there was a real loss of time in this maneuver, but Alekhine could find no way in which to profit from it.

Reti, with his own opening, produced an artistic little gem at the expense of Bogoljubow, which turned out to be the winner of the first brilliancy prize. It was by no means so spectacular as the Marshall-Bogoljubow game, winner of the second prize, which more nearly met the requirements of the popular conception of "brilliancy." Against Reti the loser was not guilty of any serious error. He was battling with a "system" (Reti's). His adversary's method simply was his undoing and the triumph, combined with the problem-like finish, which lent additional charm to the game, earned for Reti the laurel wreath. All in all it was an epochal game and a capital example of hyper-modern play. Incidentally, Reti squared accounts with Bogoljubow.

Dr. Tartakower paid Alekhine the compliment of adopting his defense in his game against Maroczy, who did not attempt to hold the Pawn at K5 with P—KB4, but played the more conservative PxP instead. From this he obtained just a shade the better of it, but hardly enough to constitute a refutation of the defense. Exchanges followed in due course and then a peaceful conclusion, as in their first encounter.

Ed. Lasker made no headway at all against the so-called Indian defense to his Queen's Pawn opening and almost from the start had a poor game. In the ending, to be sure, a drawing chance did offer itself, but this he missed. Thereupon Yates wound it up in vigorous fashion. It was the British player's second success against the same opponent.

At the close of this round, Dr. Lasker had a score of 8½—2½, with other leading scores as follows: Alekhine and Reti, each 7—4; Capablanca, 6½—4½; Maroczy and Dr. Tartakower, each 5½—5½; Marshall, who had a bye, 5—5. Once more the white pieces won two games, drew two and lost one. Score: White, 31; Black, 29.

Game 56 TWELFTH ROUND—RUY LOPEZ

Dr. Lasker Janowski
White Black

1 P—K4	P—K4
2 Kt—KB3	Kt—QB3
3 B—Kt5	P—QR3
4 B—R4	Kt—B3
5 Castles	P—Q3
6 R—K(a)	B—Kt5(b)
7 P—B3	B—K2
8 P—KR3(c)	B—R4
9 P—Q3	Q—Q2(d)

After 9 P—Q3

10 BxQKt	QxB
11 B—KKt5	B—Kt3(e)
12 QKt—Q2	P—KR3
13 BxKt(f)	BxB
14 Kt—KB	Castles KR
15 Kt—K3(g)	QR—K
16 Q—Kt3	B—Q
17 Q—Q5(h)	QxQ
18 KtxQ	P—KB4
19 Kt—Q2	B—B2(i)
20 Kt—K3	P—B5(j)
21 Kt(K3)—B4	B—B3
22 P—QR4(k)	R—Q
23 Kt—R5	R—QKt
24 Kt—KB3	P—KKt4
25 Kt—R2	P—R4
26 Kt—B4	B—K3
27 P—KB3(l)	KR—Q
28 R—K2	K—B2
29 P—R5	R—KKt
30 R—R4	QR—Q(m)
31 R—Kt4	B—B
32 P—QKt3	R—R(n)

33 Kt—Kt2(o)	P—Q4(p)
34 PxP(q)	RxP
35 R—B4	P—B3
36 P—QKt4(r)	B—B4
37 R—Q2	R(R)—Q(s)
38 K—B2	R—Kt4(t)

After 38 K—B2

39 K—K2	R(Kt4)—Q4(u)
40 K—Q(v)	K—K3(w)
41 K—B2	B—K2(x)
42 Kt—B	P—B4(y)
43 PxP	BxP
44 R—R4	R(Q)—Q2
45 R—Q	B—QR2(z)
46 R—R3	P—Kt5
47 RPxP	PxP
48 P—B4	R(Q4)—Q3
49 Kt—Q2(aa)	B—K6(bb)
50 R—KR	PxP
51 PxP	R—Kt2
52 R—R2	B—Kt8(cc)
53 R—K2	R—Kt6(dd)
54 Kt—Q	R—Q2
55 R—Kt3	R(Q2)—Kt2
56 Kt—B3(ee)	B—K6(ff)
57 Kt—Q5	R—Kt7(gg)
58 RxB(hh)	PxR
59 R—Kt6ch	K—Q2(ii)
60 KtxP	K—B2(jj)
61 KtxB	R—R2
62 Kt—Q6	R(R2)—R7
63 Kt—K4	R—R8
64 K—B3	R—B8ch
65 K—Kt4	R—Q8
66 Kt—Kt3	RxP

67	RxPch	K—B
68	R—KB7	R—QKt7
69	Kt—B5	R—Q3
70	R—B5	R—K7
71	Kt—K4	R—Q6
72	RxP	R—QKt7
73	Kt—B5	RxP
74	R—K8ch	K—B2
75	R—K6	R—QB7
76	KtxPch	K—Kt2
77	Kt(R6)—B5ch	K—R2
78	R—K7ch	K—R
79	Kt—R4	R—KR7(kk)
80	Kt(Kt3)—B5	K—Kt
81	R—Kt7ch(ll)	K—B
82	P—R6	Resigns

After 57 . . . R—Kt7

(a)   The protection of the KP, after P—Q3 by Black, is really no longer necessary. 6 P—B3 may very well be played at once, in order to retire the Bishop immediately to B2 after P—QKt4. If thereupon, however, 6...KtxKP, then 7 P—Q4 and White at the very least will recover the pawn with considerable superiority in development.

(b)   This premature development of the Bishop can only succeed, as in this game, against inexact play. Otherwise, however, 6...P—QKt4, followed by Kt—QR4, seems to be the logical continuation after Black's previous move.

(c)   A mistake in the opening with serious consequences. In case White should wish to play P—Q3 (which here is actually the best), then the move of P—KR3 should follow only after the transfer of the Queen's Knight to KKt3 (by way of Q2 and KB) and after duly waiting for Black to castle. The difference between the two methods of play at once becomes apparent.

(d)   A fine move which gives Black at once a clear advantage. His idea is to make possible an immediate pawn attack against the King's wing (for instance: 10 QKt—Q2, P—KKt4!, etc.; or 10 B—K3, P—KR3, etc.), in addition to preparing to castle on the Queen's side. Dr. Lasker at once recognizes the full meaning of the danger and, by means of several exchanges, seeks to counteract the pending threat of a King's side attack.

(e)   This move does no harm, to be sure, but why not at once 11...P—KR3, which manifestly would have forced the exchange on KB6?

(f)   In reply to 13 B—R4, Black could have played 13...B—R2, followed by KKt4, etc.

(g)   White has no squares for his Knights immune against attack and consequently no proper cooperation. The Black Bishops, on the other hand, have a splendid future, as the opening of every line will be helpful to them.

(h)   After this second mistake, White gets a strategetically lost game. Inasmuch as Black did not yet threaten anything, White, instead of the aimless exchange of Queens, could have made the attempt to obtain some counter-play on the Queen's side, for instance: 17 P—QR4, K—R; 18 P—R5, P—KB4 (otherwise R—R4); 19 PxP, BxP; 20 KtxB, RxKt; 21 Q—R4, etc., with a tenable ending. After the text-move, Black can play·P—KB4 without being obliged to exchange the Bishop—and thereby hangs the fate of the game.

(i)   Preventing the maneuver of PxP, followed by Kt—K4, etc.

(j)   Black realizes quite correctly that the opponent, because of his cramped position, will not be in a position in the long run to defend himself successfully against the two strategetical breaches by means of P—Q4 and P—KKt4 at the same time. Janowski's play to the point where he obtains a winning position (38th move) is throughout clear and convincing.

(k)   This is done merely for the purpose of occupying the opponent's attention for a while with the protection of the QKtP. Another indication of the helplessness of White's position!

(l)   Now the Knight on R2 is prevented for a long time from co-operating in the center, as he must prevent P—Kt5 under all circumstances.

(m)   In order to transfer the protection of QKt2 to the Bishop.

(n)   Threatening to double on the KR file, followed by P—KKt5, in case the opponent should remain wholly passive.

(o)   With the intention of Kt—Q—KB2.

(p)   At the right moment!

(q)   Otherwise Black, after PxP, PxP, would win by occupying the Q file, and, after PxP, BPxP, by means of P—KKt5, etc.

(r)   It would have been risky to imprison the Rook in this manner—if in this position forsooth there was aught of danger for White at all.

(s)   Thereupon White should have lost a Pawn without the slightest compensation.

(t)   The beginning of over-refinements which, to be sure, do not relinquish the win for a long time, but make it always more difficult until finally, in consequence of an oversight by Black, the situation suddenly changes in favor of White.   Right would have been 38...BxQP; 39 KtxB, RxKt; 40 RxR, RxR; 41 K—K2, P—K5; 42 RxP, RxP, and Black has a pawn plus besides the superior position.

(u)   Black is aware of the fact that he would have threatened nothing with 39... B—K3, for, after BxR?, PxB, his Rook would also have been lost.

(v)   White has nothing better than to try out Fate in this manner or rather his opponent—whether or not the latter with a winning position would capture the QP. After 40 Kt—B, then 40...P—KKt5 would have won easily.

(w)   Of course, 40 BxQP would have been possible also here, for instance: 41 KtxB, RxKt; 42 RxR, RxRch; 43 K—B2, P—K5!, and White would not dare to play 44 Kt—B, on account of 44...PxBP!; 45 KxR, PxP, and wins.

(x)   Black's position is so strong that this move, together with the following, should force a win.

(y)   Threatening 43...PxP; 44 PxP, R—Kt4; 45 K—Kt3, R—Q5!, etc.

(z)   More enduring than 45...B—K2 (intending B—Q), whereupon White would still have been able to defend himself with 46 P—B4, R—Q5 (or R—B4; 47 Kt—Q2); 47 Kt—R2.

(aa)   For the first time in the game, one of the Knights obtains some prospects.

(bb)   Why not 49...B—Q5; 50 Kt—K4, BxKt; 51 KxB, BxKt; 52 PxB, R—KR2, with a Rook ending giving promise of victory.   Moreover, the immediate 49...R—KR2 also had its advantages.

(cc)   With this and the next move Black pursues a phantom, but in any event the game is now to be won only with difficulty.   In reply to 52...R—Kt6, for instance, White would play 53 R—QKt3 and, if 53...R—Q2, then 54 Kt—R4, etc., with several winning chances.

(dd)   The loss of yet another tempo.   Much better chances lay in 53...R—Q, followed by R—KKt, in order thereupon to take possession of the seventh row.

(ee)   Now at last White is saved.

(ff)   If 56...R—Kt7, then 57 RxP!, etc.

(gg)   57...BxKt; 58 RxB, RxKBP (?) would not do on account of 53 R—Kt6ch, winning a piece.

(hh)   This combination long prepared should eventually yield White a Pawn which, however, would hardly have sufficed for a win.   But Black was clearly demoralized by the unexpected turn of events and leaves a whole piece en prise.

(ii)   Not 59...K—B2; 60 KtxKP, R—K7; 61 KtxB, R(Kt2)—Kt7; 62 Kt—Q6ch, followed by Kt—K4, winning.

(jj)   A perfectly unintelligible move which makes further resistance impossible. After 60...R—K7!; 61 RxKtPch, K—B3; 62 RxR, RxKt; 63 Kt—K4, RxKBP, etc., this game, so full of vicissitudes, would have been drawn.

(kk)   Black is still playing for a stalemate trap: 80 Kt—Kt6ch, K—Kt; 81 P—R6 (?), RxKtch; 82 KxR, R—Kt7ch, etc.

(ll)   Not 81 Kt—Kt6 (?), R—Kt7ch; 82 K—R4, R—R6ch; 83 KxR, R—Kt6ch, etc., with a draw.

Game 57   TWELFTH ROUND—QUEEN'S GAMBIT DECLINED

Alekhine	Capablanca
White	Black
1 P—Q4	P—Q4
2 P—QB4	P—QB3
3 Kt—QB3	Kt—KB3(a)
4 P—K3	B—B4(b)
5 PxP	PxP(c)
6 Q—Kt3(d)	B—B
7 Kt—B3	P—K3
8 B—Q3(e)	Kt—B3
9 Castles	B—Q2(f)
10 B—Q2(g)	Q—Kt3
11 Q—Q(h)	B—Q3
12 R—B(i)	Castles KR
13 Kt—QR4	Q—Q
14 Kt—B5	BxKt
15 RxB(j)	Kt—K5
16 BxKt(k)	PxB

After 7...P—K3

17 Kt—K5(l)	KtxKt
18 PxKt	Drawn

(a)   After 3...P—K4, White obtains slightly the better game through 4 BPxP, BPxP; 5 Kt—B3, P—K5; 6 Kt—K5, Kt—QB3 (P—B3; 7 Q—R4ch, K—K2; 8 Q—Kt3— Dr. Bernstein vs. Marshall, Ostend, 1906); 7 B—B4, followed by P—K3, etc.

(b)   Just in this situation the development of the Bishop is uncalled for. Black would do best to switch over to the new Rubinstein variation by means of 4...P—K3; 5 Kt—B3, QKt—Q2; 6 B—Q3, PxP, etc.

(c)   After 5...KtxP, White develops favorably by 6 B—B4, P—K3; 7 KKt—K2 (Rubinstein vs. Bogoljubow, Hastings, 1922).

(d)   After this Black has no means of easily guarding his KtP and he must reconcile himself to the following retreat of the Bishop, which yields the opponent a long start in development.

(e)   White should have utilized his extra "tempi" in order to build up a pressure by means of 8 Kt—K5, followed by P—B4. The contemplated P—K4 is fully parried by Black's fine ninth move.

(f)   Capablanca finds the only move which promises equalization. Insufficient would have been I.—9...Q—Kt3; 10 QxQ, PxQ; 11 Kt—QKt5; II.—9...B—K2; 10 Kt—K5, followed by P—B4, etc.; III.—9...B—Q3; 10 P—K4, PxP; 11 KtxP, KtxKt; 12 BxKt, Castles; 13 P—Q5 (or R—Q; the sacrifice of the Bishop on R7, on the other hand, would have been incorrect here, and likewise the winning of a Pawn by 13 Q—B2, P—KR3; 14 BxKt, PxB; 15 QxP, R—Kt, would have been of doubtful value), PxP; 14 QxP, etc.

(g)   If now I.—10 Kt—K5, KtxKt; 11 PxKt, Kt—Kt5; 12 P—B4, B—B4; II.— 10 P—K4, Kt—QKt5; 11 B—Kt, PxP; 12 KtxP, B—B3; 13 KtxKtch, PxKt.

(h)   Likewise an exchange of Queens would surely not have been of advantage to White.

(i)   The Pawn sacrifice through 12 P—K4, KtxQP; 13 PxP (or 13 KtxKt, QxKt; 14 B—K3, Q—Kt5) would have led, after the simple 13 Castles, to equalization at the most.

(j)   After 15 PxB, Black, by means of 15...P—K4, obtains a strong counter offensive in the center, which would certainly make up for White's extra Pawn on the Queen's side.

(k)   Or 16 R—B2, KtxB; 17 QxKt, Q—Kt3.

(l)   Of course not 17 Kt—Kt5, P—QKt3, etc.

Game 58   TWELFTH ROUND—RETI'S OPENING

Reti	Bogoljubow		
White	Black	12 P—B3(f)	PxP
		13 BxP(g)	Q—B2(h)
1 Kt—KB3	Kt—KB3	14 KtxKt	BxKt
2 P—B4	P—K3(a)	15 P—K4	P—K4(i)
3 P—KKt3	P—Q4	16 P—B5	B—KB
4 B—Kt2	B—Q3	17 Q—B2(j)	PxQP(k)
5 Castles	Castles	18 PxP	QR—Q(l)
6 P—Kt3	R—K	19 B—R5(m)	R—K4
7 B—Kt2	QKt—Q2	20 BxP	RxKBP(n)
8 P—Q4(b)	P—B3	21 RxR	BxR
9 QKt—Q2(c)	Kt—K5(d)	22 QxB	RxB
10 KtxKt	PxKt	23 R—KB	R—Q(o)
11 Kt—K5	P—KB4(e)	24 B—B7ch	K—R
		25 B—K8(p)	Resigns

After 18...QR—Q

After 25 B—K8

(a) As to the merit of this system of defense, compare the game Reti vs. Yates in the sixth round.

(b) To our way of thinking, this is the clear positional refutation of 2...P—K3, which, by the way, was first played by Capablanca (as Black) against Marshall and is based upon the simple circumstance that Black cannot find a method for the effective development of his QB.

(c) In the game referred to Capablanca, in a wholly analogous position, played Kt—K5 and likewise obtained an advantage thereby. Of course, Reti's quieter developing move is also quite good.

(d) If the liberating move of 9...P—K4, recommended by Rubinstein and others, is really the best here—and this appears to be the case—then it furnishes the most striking proof that Black's entire arrangement of his game was faulty. For the simple continuation of 10 BPxP, BPxP; 11 PxP, KtxP; 12 KtxKt, BxKt; 13 BxB, RxB; 14 Kt—B4, R—K; 15 Kt—K3, B—B3; 16 Q—Q4, would have given White a direct attack against the isolated QP, without permitting the opponent any chances whatsoever. Moreover, the move selected by Bogoljubow leads eventually to a double exchange of Knights, without removing the principal disadvantage of his position.

(e) Obviously forced.

(f) The proper strategy. After Black has weakened his position in the center, White forthwith must aim to change the closed game into an open one in order to make as much as possible out of that weakness.

(g) Not 13 PxP, because the KP must be utilized as a battering-ram.

(h) Also after 13...KtxKt; 14 PxKt, B—B4ch; 15 K—Kt2, B—Q2 (after the exchange of Queens, this Bishop could not get out at all); 16 P—K4, White would have retained a decisive advantage in position.

(i) Otherwise would follow 16 P—K5, to be followed by a break by means of P—Q5 or P—KKt4. After the text-move, however, Black appears to have surmounted the greater part of his early difficulty and it calls for exceptionally fine play on the part of White in order to make the hidden advantages of his position count so rapidly and convincingly.

(j) Attacking simultaneously both of Black's center pawns.

(k) Black's sphere of action is circumscribed; for instance, 17...BPxP clearly would not do on account of the two-fold threat against KR7 and K5, after 18 BxP.

(1) After 18... R—K4; 19 Q—B4ch, K—R; 20 P—B6, among other lines, would be very strong.

(m) The initial move in an exactly calculated, decisive maneuver, the end of which will worthily crown White's model play.

(n) If 20...R—Q4; 21 Q—B4, K—R; 22 B—Kt4, with a pawn plus and a superior position.

(o) Or 20...Q—K2; 24 B—B7ch, K—R; 25 B—Q5, Q—B3; 26 Q—B8, etc. Black is left without any defense.

(p) A sparkling conclusion! Black resigned, for, after 25...BxPch, he loses at least the Bishop. Rightfully, this game was awarded the first brilliancy prize.

Game 59   TWELFTH ROUND—ALEKHINE'S DEFENSE

Maroczy	Tartakower
White	Black

After 12...P—KR3

	Maroczy White	Tartakower Black
1	P—K4	Kt—KB3
2	P—K5	Kt—Q4
3	P—QB4	Kt—Kt3
4	P—Q4	P—Q3
5	PxP(a)	KPxP(b)
6	Kt—QB3	B—B4
7	B—K2	B—K2
8	B—K3	QKt—Q2
9	Kt—B3	Castles
10	P—QKt3(c)	Kt—B3
11	Castles	R—K
12	P—KR3	P—KR3
13	B—Q3(d)	Q—Q2
14	R—K	QR—Q
15	Q—B2(e)	BxB
16	QxB	Kt—R2
17	R—K2	B—B3
18	QR—K	R—K2
19	P—Q5	QR—K
20	B—Q4	RxR
21	RxR	RxR
22	QxR	P—R3(f)
23	BxKt	BxKt
24	Q—K3	B—B3
25	B—Q4	Q—K2
26	QxQ	BxQ
27	K—B	B—B3
28	K—K2	K—B
29	K—Q3	K—K2
	Drawn	

(a) This, while it yields quite a good game similar to a variation of the Petroff Defense, can in no way be considered as a refutation of Black's first move. That, if possible, could be found only in connection with 5 P—KB4.

(b) 5...BPxP would have caused greater difficulties in development and, moreover, the insufficiently protected King's side of Black would have been exposed to a possible attack.

(c) Probably played in order to be able to meet a subsequent P—Q4 with P—QB5, without being obliged to reckon with the entry of the black Knight at B5. White commands a somewhat more extended range of action, but there is not much in it for him after all.

(d)   Here, and even a little later, White's only' slight chance was in the advance of his QRP, whereby he would have utilized the uncomfortable position of Black's Knight on Kt3.   Inasmuch as he does not avail himself of it, Black without effort is enabled to bring about liquidation on the K file.

(e)   15 P—QR4, etc., still was to be seriously considered.

(f)   In order to give White every opportunity to exchange still another piece. Both players are animated by the same noble thought of peace.

Game 60   TWELFTH ROUND—QP OPENING (INDIAN DEFENSE)

Ed. Lasker	Yates
White	Black

After 22 BxB

	Ed. Lasker	Yates
1	P—Q4	Kt—KB3
2	Kt—KB3	P—KKt3
3	P—B3(a)	B—Kt2
4	Q—B2	Castles
5	P—K4	Kt—B3
6	B—Q3(b)	P—Q3
7	QKt—Q2(c)	Kt—Q2(d)
8	Kt—B4	P—K4
9	B—Kt5	Q—K
10	P—Q5(e)	Kt—K2
11	CastlesQR	Kt—QB4
12	P—KR4	P—KB4
13	PxP	KtxBch
14	QxKt	BxP
15	Q—K2(f)	P—QR4(g)
16	Kt—K3	B—Q2
17	P—R5	Kt—B4
18	PxP	QxP
19	KtxKt	BxKt(h)
20	Q—Q2	Q—B2(i)
21	B—R6(j)	B—Kt3
22	BxB(k)	Q—B4(l)
23	Q—Q3	KxB(m)
24	QxQ	RxQ
25	R—Q2	QR—KB
26	R—R4	P—R3
27	R—QB4	R(B)—B2
28	P—QKt4(n)	PxP
29	PxP	R—B5
30	RxR	RxR
31	P—R3	K—B3
32	K—Kt2	P—R4
33	Kt—K(o)	R—Q5(p)
34	RxR	PxR
35	P—Kt3	K—K4
36	K—Kt3	KxP
37	Kt—Kt2	B—B2
38	P—B3	P—B4
39	P—Kt5	K—K4ch
40	K—B2	B—Q4
41	Kt—K	P—B5
42	P—Kt6(q)	B—B3
43	K—Q2	K—Q4
44	Kt—B2	P—B6ch
45	K—B	K—B5
46	P—B4	P—Q6
47	Kt—K3ch	K—Kt6
48	Kt—B	B—K5
49	Kt—Q2ch	PxKtch
50	KxP	KxP
	Resigns	

(e)   A strategical blunder of serious consequences.   Without obtaining the least the center with both Pawns after the principles of the "good old school."   The present game illustrates in an instructive manner how unsuitable this procedure is here.

(b)   A more desirable place for this Bishop is certainly B4.

(c)   And now the development of the QB to Kt5 would have been preferable.

(d)   Better than immediately 7...P—K4; 8 PxP, PxP; 9 Kt—B4, etc.

(e)   A strategical blunder of serious consequences.   Without obtaining the least chance on the Queen's side, White allows his opponent to establish a permanent offensive in the semi-center.   The attempts of the first player in his subsequent play to obtain an attack on the King merely lead to the opening of new avenues for the black pieces and thereby facilitate the opponent's transition into a winning ending. By far the smaller evil would have 10 PxP, KKtxP; 11 QKtxKt, KtxKt; 12 KtxKt, QxKt; 13 B—K3, etc., after which the game would have been only slightly in favor of Black.

(f) The situation is more clarified. Besides the open line, Black has obtained a no less important advantage in the exposed hostile QP, which in this phase of the game cannot very well be defended by a neighboring Pawn, because this would mean further compromising of the white King's position.

(g) This move, however, turns out to be a loss of time, as Black soon convinces himself that he is able to gain a decisive positional advantage by means of a simple exchange and without the strain of a direct attack. Simplier, therefore, would have been 15..P—KR3 in order to force the Bishop to exchange or retreat, the more so as, for instance, after 16 B—K3, the reply of 16...B—Kt5 would have been very strong.

(h) All these exchanges were merely favorable to Black. The player of the white pieces, however, cannot be blamed for this because his position from the move of 10 P—Q5 (?) has been "sick unto death," as it were.

(i) 21 Kt—R4 was threatening.

(j) The exchange of one of the hostile Bishops holds out but little consolation, inasmuch as the remaining one is the more dangerous because of the weakness of the white squares.

(k) Likewise after 22 Q—Kt5, Black, by means of 22...BxB, followed by 23...Q—B5ch, etc., would force an ending similar to the one in the actual game.

(l) The decesive turn. Having forced the exchange of Queens, Black, on account of his pressure upon the KB file and the weakness of Q4, should have had technically an easy game since all he really needed was to strive merely after additonal exchanges.

(m) Much simplier and more convincing would have been 23...QxQ; 24 RxQ, BxR; 25 BxR, RxB. After the text-move, White still retains a small chance to draw.

(n) Suicide, because the QP is isolated thereby and must soon fall. At all events 28 Kt—R4 was called for, after 28...RxP as well as after 28...R—B5, White could still have defended his inferior position. In the subsequent ending, on the contrary, there is no longer a fighting chance.

(o) Otherwise would follow P—R5—R6.

(p) The simplest method of capturing the weakling.

(q) White, of course, could have resigned with grace long before this.

THIRTEENTH ROUND

Decisive results were the order of the day and Dr. Lasker, Capablanca, Marshall, Reti and Ed. Lasker all improved their standing to the extent of a full point apiece. Alekhine experienced his second setback—the first since the defeat by Dr. Lasker.

One of his best efforts in the tournament was Dr. Lasker's game with Bogoljubow, which the latter defended with a Sicilian. Bogoljubow made a slight slip in the opening, but this was enough for Dr. Lasker, who pressed his positional advantage home in faultless style. It required 61 moves in which to complete the task, the final Rook and Pawn ending being very instructive. The result was the same as in the eighth round.

Maroczy, who has always been a most formidable opponent of Capablanca's and who drew the first game with him, was this time doomed to suffer defeat, as he met the champion at his best. The Hungarian chose the Ruy Lopez for his debut and, instead of P—Q4, played the less aggressive P—Q3. Capablanca was not long in seizing the initiative, taking admirable advantage of the infinitesimal weakness in White's game. This he followed up with a pleasing combination and a forceful series of moves, entirely destroying the King's side position of his opponent.

Hoist with his own petard, Reti, opposed to Alekhine, had to deal with a reversed form of the opening which the Russian has named after him. Reti employed the London method of proceeding against his system and the masters emerged into the middle game with fairly even chances. Here, however, Alekhine based his play upon a strategical plan (the advance of his K side Pawns), which, as ably demonstrated by Reti, simply would not work. This game, with an ending which called for exact handling, was an illuminating example of the winner at his best. It left Alekhine and Reti on even terms insofar as their personal encounters were concerned.

Marshall's Queen's Gambit was accepted by Janowski, who played the opening well, but subsequently missed several good continuations. For this he paid the penalty when Marshall pitched in and by forceful tactics gained the upper hand, winning two minor pieces for a Rook. His play in the ending left little to be desired.

With the black side of a Queen's Gambit Declined, Dr. Tartakower obtained a satisfactory game against Ed. Lasker, but then indulged in some unnecessary moves with his Queen. This loss of time was cleverly turned to account by Lasker, who wound up the game with a clear gain of a piece.

At the end of the day's play, following Dr. Lasker ($9\frac{1}{2}$—$2\frac{1}{2}$), Reti had the supreme satisfaction of holding second place with 8—4, which score, however, was destined to remain unchanged for the next three days. Capablanca, $7\frac{1}{2}$—$4\frac{1}{2}$, also passed Alekhine, 7—5. Marshall had 6—5. These were the eventual prize-winners. The stock of the white pieces took a jump upward to the tune of 4—1, which made the record: White, 35; Black, 30.

Game 61 THIRTEENTH ROUND—SICILIAN DEFENSE

Dr. Lasker	Bogoljubow	After 20 B—B3
White	Black	

1 P—K4	P—QB4	
2 Kt—KB3	P—K3	
3 P—Q4(a)	PxP	
4 KtxP	Kt—KB3	
5 B—Q3(b)	Kt—B3	
6 KtxKt(c)	KtPxKt(d)	
7 Castles	B—K2(e)	
8 P—K5	Kt—Q4	
9 Q—Kt4	P—Kt3(f)	
10 Kt—Q2	P—KB4(g)	
11 Q—B3	Kt—Kt5(h)	
12 Kt—B4	B—R3(i)	

After 12...B—R3

13 B—Q2(j)	KtxBP(k)
14 QR—Q	Castles
15 Kt—Q6(l)	Kt—Q5
16 Q—K3	BxB
17 QxB	BxKt(m)
18 PxB	P—K4
19 KR—K	Q—B3
20 B—B3(n)	QR—K
21 P—B4	Q—R5(o)
22 Q—B4ch	Kt—K3
23 BxP	K—B2(p)
24 Q—K3(q)	Q—Q
25 R—QKt3	Q—R4(r)
26 R—Kt7	Q—B4ch
27 R—Q4(s)	R—Q
28 P—QKt4	QxQ
29 RxQ	P—Kt4

30 RxRP	KtxP(t)
31 BxKt	PxB
32 RxQBP	R—KKt(u)
33 K—B2	R—Kt(3)
34 P—Kt5	K—K3
35 R—B2	KR—Kt
36 K—B3(v)	R—QR
37 R—K2ch	KxP
38 R—Q2ch	K—B4
39 KRxP	KxP
40 RxR	RxR
41 RxP	R—R6ch(w)
42 KxP	RxP
43 R—Kt7	R—B7ch
44 K—K5	P—B5
45 K—K4	K—B4(x)
46 P—R4	K—Q3
47 P—R5	R—B8(y)
48 R—Kt4	R—KR8(z)
49 R—Kt5	R—R5
50 K—B5	K—K2
51 K—Kt6	K—B
52 R—R5	R—R7
53 R—R2	P—B6
54 R—R8ch	K—K2
55 PxP	R—Kt7ch
56 K—B5	R—KR7
57 R—R7ch	K—K
58 K—Kt6	R—Kt7ch
59 K—B6	R—KB7
60 R—R8ch	K—Q2
61 R—R3(aa)	Resigns

(a) Against Dr. Tartakower in an earlier round Dr. Lasker played the less enduring 3 Kt—QB3.

(b)   More usual here is first 5 Kt—QB3, B—Kt5 and then 6 B—Q3 in order to be able to reply to 6...Kt—B3, with KtxKt, KtPxKt; 8 P—K5, Kt—Q4; 9 Q—Kt4!

(c)   And now 6 B—K3 seems to hold out better prospects, because Black, after the text-move, could have obtained an even game by 6...QPxKt; 7 Càstles, P—K4 (8 P—KB4?, B—B4ch; 9 K—R, Kt—Kt5; 10 Q—K, Q—Q5, etc.).

(d)   Black evidently and laudably is striving for more, but on the very next move commits a fatal blunder.

(e)   Correct would have been 7...P—Q4 and, only after 8 Q—K2 (or 8 P—K5, Kt—Q2, with splendid chances in the center), then 8...B—K2, etc.   For now the black QP remains backward permanently and besides the black squares of the second player become perforce weak.

(f)   Clearly forced.

(g)   This, of course, removes every vestige of danger from the King's side, but the future of Black's QP on the other hand becomes still more hopeless.   With the text-move, however, Black follows out a definite tactical idea.

(h)   He desires, for instance, either to secure for himself the two Bishops or else to capture a pawn as compensation for his own unfavorable pawn position.

(i)   Threatening 13...BxKt, followed by KtxBP, as well as 13...KtxBP right away. White, by means of Q—K2, could have parried both with a good game, but chooses a much more vigorous continuation.

(j)   An interesting pawn sacrifice which has for its purpose, by the most rapid mobilization of all available fighting forces and by displacement of the black Knight, the utilization of the weaknesses in the hostile center.

(k)   Black is justified in accepting the sacrifice because he has a right to assume that he may be able later on and at the proper moment to relieve his position by return- ing the pawn.   It is highly instructive to observe how Dr. Lasker sets about thwarting this intention.

(l)   This introduces a new turn which reveals the real reason for the sacrifice.   It is not the backward QP, which Black will now make safe through the blocking of the file, but the uncertain position of the Knight which must become instrumental in the attainment of a decisive advantage.

(m)   All of Black's moves are compulsory.   After 17...P—B4, for instance, White, by means of 18 B—R6, BxKt; 19 PxB, R—B2; 20 P—QKt4, etc., would win back his pawn with a splendid game.

(n)   Now is seen the result of the attack carried out exemplarily and by unpreten- tious means.   Against the threats of 21 P—B4 and 21 Q—B4ch, Black no longer has a fully sufficient defense and, despite the return of his surplus material, cannot avoid serious positional disadvantage.   After 20...QxP, for instance, White obtains a win- ning ending after 21 Q—B4ch, Q—Q4 (forced, for if I. 21...Q—K3; 22 RxKt; II. if 21...K any; 22 RxP!; III. if 23... R—B2; 22 P—B4, etc., with a winning position.; 22 QxQch, PxQ; 23 RxP, Kt any; 24 KRxP, followed by RxP, etc.

(o)   Or 21...Q—B2; 22 RxP, RxR(?); 23 QxKt and wins.

(p)   This, of course, is not altogether comprehensible.   Preferable certainly would have been 23...Q—Q at once.

(q)   Threatening 25 R—KR3.

(r)   The entrance of the Rook at Kt7 had to be prevented at any cost.   With 25... Q—R! Black could have offered a still longer and stubborn resistance.

(s)   This fine parry had evidently been overlooked by Black at his 25th move. After 27 QxQ, KtxQ; 28 RxRP, R—QR; 29 RxR, RxR, followed by K—K3, etc., he would indeed have had excellent chances for a draw.

(t)   He should at least have saved his QBP with 30...K—Kt3, inasmuch as the ultimate tussle against the two connected passed pawns is utterly hopeless for him.

(u)   This maneuver with the Rook is fruitless, but really it scarcely matters what Black may play now.

(v)   The struggle is hereby prolonged unnecessarily.   Simpler would have been 36 P—QR4, R—QR; 37 RxR, RxR; 38 R—B4, KxP; 39 K—B3, etc., with an easily won game.   Of course this also accomplishes it.

(w)   A bit of finesse.   After 41...RxP; 42 R—KKt7, R—R5; 43 R—Kt5, etc., Black would have had to resign immediately.   Now, however, he retains his last Pawn for a spell.

(x)   In reply to 45...P—B6, he would win by means of 46 PxP, RxRP; 47 R— QB7, etc.

(y)   And if now 47...P—B6, then the best would be 48 P—Kt4!, R—B8; 49 K—K3, etc.

(z)   Here, however—if indeed he cared to play still longer—he should have decided upon 48...P—B6; 49 PxP, K—K3, etc., because when Pawns are separated it is sometimes very difficult to achieve victory. Now, on the contrary, after the successful participation of White's King, Black has not even the trace of a chance left.

(aa)   After 61...R—KR7, White would now win with 62 R—R5, K—K; 63 P—B4, R—R5; 64 R—B5, etc.

Game 62   THIRTEENTH ROUND—RUY LOPEZ

	Maroczy	Capablanca			
	White	Black			
1	P—K4	P—K4	26 KR—K	Q—K3(h)
2	Kt—KB3	Kt—QB3	27 B—K3	R—Q6
3	B—Kt5	P—QR3	28 Kt—Q2	Kt—K2
4	B—R4	Kt—B3	29 P—B3	Kt—R4
5	Castles	B—K2	30 Kt—B	P—B4
6	R—K	P—QKt4	31 B—B2(i)	Q—KKt3(j)
7	B—Kt3	Castles	32 K—R2(k)	Q—Kt4(l)
8	P—B3	P—Q3	33 B—K3	Kt—B5(m)
9	P—KR3	Kt—QR4	34 Kt—Kt3(n)	RxB(o)
10	B—B2	P—B4		
11	P—Q3(a)	Kt—B3		
12	QKt—Q2	P—Q4		
13	Kt—B	PxP(b)		
14	PxP	B—K3		
15	B—Q2(c)	R—R2		
16	Kt—Kt5(d)	B—B5		
17	Kt—K3	B—Q6		
18	BxB	QxB		
19	Kt—B5	P—R3(e)		
20	R—K3	Q—Q		
21	Kt—B3	R—Q2		
22	Q—B2	P—B5		

After 34 Kt—Kt3

After 22...P—B5

23	KtxBch(f)	QxKt	35	RxR	KtxKtP
24	P—QR4(g)	KR—Q	36	R—K2	Kt—B5
25	PxP	PxP	37	R—Q2(p)	R—KB(q)
			38	Kt—R(r)	Q—R4
			39	Kt—B2	Kt(K2)—Kt3(s)
			40	Q—Q	Kt—R5
			41	R—Q8	KtxPch
			42	K—R	Kt—Q6(t)
			43	RxKt	PxR
			44	QxP	P—B5(u)
			45	Q—Q(v)	R—B3
			46	R—R8ch	K—R2
			47	Q—Q8	Kt—Kt4(w)
			48	Q—Kt8ch	K—Kt3
			49	Q—K8ch	Kt—B2
			50	Q—QB8	Q—B6ch
			51	K—Kt	Q—Kt6ch(x)
			52	K—B	P—B6

53 Q—Kt4ch	QxQ	56 Kt—Q3	KxP
54 PxQ	K—Kt4(y)	57 KtxPch	K—Kt6
55 R—R5	Kt—Q3	Resigns.	

(a) If White desired to adopt this backward mode of play, he need not have played P—KR3, which should be a preparation for P—Q4. After the text move, Black gains the initiative without trouble.

(b) Inasmuch as an attack on the King can be prepared by White only with difficulty (for instance: 14 P—KKt4, P—KR4, etc.), Black without much ado could play 13...P—Q5 in order to obtain a counter pressure in the center as well as on the other wing. After the dissolution of the center, White has really nothing more to fear.

(c) There seemed to be no reason to avoid the exchange of Queens, inasmuch as the chances for a direct attack are very slim on account of Black's superior development. After 15 QxQ, KRxQ; 16 B—Kt5, followed by Kt—K3, White could have drawn without difficulty.

(d) Yielding the square, Q3, in order, after the exchange of Bishops, to gain KB5 for his Knight. Not a bad idea—had he later on only made a proper use of that square.

(e) Neither could Black have obtained any advantage from 19...R—Q2; 20 B—K3, etc.

(f) With this exchange, lacking motive, White annuls all the advantages he had gained with his strategy up to this time, and, in consequence, the drawbacks of his position (Black's pressure upon the Q file, enhanced through the vulnerability of Q3) become always more perceptible. Instead, he might have played at once 23 P—QR4; for instance: 23...B—B4; 24 R—K2, Q—Kt3; 25 BxRP, PxB; 26 Q—B, etc.; or 24... R—Q6; 25 PxP, PxP; 26 R—R6, etc.—in any case with much more counter play than after the text move.

(g) The attempt to bring the second Knight via R4 to B5 could have been easily frustrated, not, to be sure, with 24...P—KKt3, which would have given White an attack (25 R—Kt3, K—R2; 26 BxRP, KxB; 27 Q—Bch, K—R2; 28 Kt—B5, PxKt; 29 Q—Kt5, Kt—Kt5; 30 QxPch, K—R3; 31 QxKt, and wins), but by means of 24...Q—Q; 25 R—K2, Kt—K2, etc.

(h) In order to transfer the QKt to the King's wing—in itself a good idea, which, however, is tactically not quite possible, as White is permitted to take a strong defensive position. Correct would have been 26...R—Q6; 27 B—K3, Q—Q3; 28 R—K2 (28 R—R6, KtxP; 29 BxRP, Kt—B4, etc.), Kt—K2; 29 Kt—Q2, Kt—R4, and White cannot play P—B3, which in the actual game made a successful defense possible for him.

(i) Now the process of development is happily ended and the principal danger—the unsettled condition of the minor pieces—is past.

(j) Threatening 32...Kt—B5, etc.

(k) In order to neutralize the threat with 33 B—Kt3.

(l) To make room for the Knight at K2, but White again has a telling defense.

(m) Perhaps the most practical continuation offering the best chances, because a number of traps are laid thereby. After 33...P—B5; 34 B—B2, etc., Black would have had no further chances for attack.

(n) After the hitherto careful defense, this mistake is truly astonishing, inasmuch as the strength of the sacrifice of the exchange was quite evident. 34 P—KKt3 would likewise have been unsatisfactory, on account of 34...Q—R4; 35 PxKt, PxBP; 36 BxP, QxBP; 37 B—Kt3 or K3, P—B5, etc.; but with the simple 34 BxKt, QxBch; 35 K—R (of course not 35 K—Kt, R—Q7; 36 KtxR, RxKt; 37 Q—B, Q—Kt4; 38 P—KKt4, Q—B5, and wins), Kt—Kt3; 36 Q—B2, etc., White would have secured a perfectly safe position so that Black, in order not to be placed at a disadvantage, would have been obliged to give attention to the defense of his weak Queen's side.

(o) An obvious sacrifice, which ought to have ended the game in a few moves.

(p) These moves of White were clearly forced.

(q) A bit of artificiality which does not seem at all like Capablanca. After the simple 37...RxRch; 38 QxR, Q—R5, White would soon have had to resign; for instance: (I) 39 Q—KB2 (if Q—K, QxPch; 40 K—Kt, Kt—Q6, etc.), KtxRP; 40 Q—K, Kt—B5ch; 41 K—Kt, Kt—Q6 and wins. (II) 39 Kt—KB, QxRPch; 40 K—Kt, QxBP (threatening Kt—K7ch, etc.); 41 R—K, PxP, and the four Pawns in return for the exchange would have made further struggle by White quite useless.

(r) Neither does White, however, adopt the strongest continuation. With 38 Q—Q (in order to be able to answer Q—R5 with Q—KB), he would have prepared a difficult problem for the adversary, which could not have been solved either by 38... Kt (K2)—Kt3 or by 38...R—B3, but, on the other hand, he could have strengthened the attack decisively only through the none too obvious 38...P—KR4 (in order, after

P—R5, to limit the Knight to the protection of KKt3, thereby making more difficult co-operation between White's pieces). The move selected makes Black's work considerably easier.

(s) Of course much stronger than 39...QxBP; 40 R—KKt, followed by Q—Q, etc.

(t) Forcing White to return the exchange, inasmuch as 43 RxRch, KxR; 44 K—Kt2 would fail through 44...Q—Kt4ch; 45 KxKt, Q—B5ch; 46 K—Kt2, QxKtch; 47 K—R, Q—Kt6, etc.

(u) Now Black possesses a strong Pawn plus, which can also be utilized for the purposes of attack.

(v) This pin is now White's only chance, slight though it be. 45 QxP would lose in a few moves after 45...R—Q, followed by R—Q7.

(w) In this way White's attempt at an attack is repelled in the simplest way and Black has the pleasant choice of deciding the struggle either in the middle game or the ending.

(x) Herewith he selects the second alternative and wrongly so, for 51...Q—K6, threatening Q—K8ch, followed by P—B6ch, would have forced the adversary to resign at once (52 Q—Kt4ch, K—R2, and wins). Of course, it can be done this way, too.

(y) The entrance of the King is decisive.

Game 63   THIRTEENTH ROUND—RETI'S OPENING (FOR BLACK)

Reti.	Alekhine.
White.	Black.

After 19 KR—Q

	Reti.	Alekhine.
1	Kt—KB3	P—KKt3
2	P—Q4(a)	Kt—KB3
3	B—B4(b)	B—Kt2
4	P—KR3	P—B4
5	P—K3	P—Kt3(c)
6	QKt—Q2	B—Kt2
7	B—Q3(d)	Castles
8	Castles	P—Q3
9	P—B3	QKt—Q2
10	Q—K2	R—B(e)
11	P—QR4	R—K
12	B—QR6(f)	Q—B2
13	P—R5	BPxP(g)
14	KPxP	P—K4(h)
15	QPxP	QPxP
16	B—K3	Kt—Q4
17	PxP	PxP
18	BxB	QxB
19	KR—Q(i)	P—K5(j)
20	Kt—Q4	P—B4(k)
21	Kt—Kt5	P—B5(l)
22	Kt—Q6	Q—B3
23	KtxKR	RxKt(m)
24	Q—B4(n)	Kt—K4
25	QxQ	KtxQ
26	Kt—B4(o)	KtxP
27	PxKt	PxB
28	KtxKP	BxP(p)
29	QR—B	Kt—Q5
30	K—B	Kt—Kt4
31	R—Q5	Resigns

(a) White does not utilize the opportunity of turning the game into a Sicilian defense by means of 2 P—K4, a chance not favorable for Black after his first move.

(b) Reti combats his own system, and with the continuation which, so far as we know, was first used in the London Tournament of 1922 (Alekhine vs. Euwe and Capablanca vs. Reti) and which indeed seems to be the best antidote.

(c) In reply to 5...Q—Kt3, White could have answered 6 Kt—B3! with advantage.

(d) In this variation the Bishop stands better at B4. For that reason the move 7 P—B3, which must be made anyway, could have been substituted here, to be followed by B—B4.

(e) 10...R—K at once would also have been pretty good. Black, however, estimated quite correctly that the opponent's coming flank attack would be quite harmless and so prepared himself for the eventual P—K4.

(f)   The proper handling of the position consisted in the advance of the King's Pawn (see the game, Reti vs. Dr. Lasker). After the exchange of Bishops, Black really has no further difficulties and finally loses the game only on account of overestimating his own pos.tion, which misled him into ill-considered violence.

(g)   With 13...BxB; 14 QxB, P—QKt4!; 15 QxP, R—Kt, followed by RxP, an effortless equalization could have been effected together with a probably general exchange on the QKt file. Instead Black plays for the alluring advance of the King's pawn, which has for its purpose the establishment of a pawn center (K4 and KB4). It becomes apparent, however, that this maneuver, even though it incurs no risk, supplies White, owing to the weakening of Q3 and the open QR file, with compensating counterchances. Hence simply 13...BxB was to have been preferred after all.

(h)   Now 14...BxB; 15 QxB, P—QKt4 would not have sufficed, on account of 16 QxKtP, R—Kt; 17 Q—B4, etc.

(i)   This fine move, with which White makes the most of Black's weakness at Q3 and the exposed position of the hostile Knight, had been underrated by Black in his calculations. Instead of now bending his efforts in the direction of persistent equalization, Black, disillusioned, commits two consecutive blunders which change his position from one st.ll defensible to a perfectly hopeless one.

(j)   Hallucination! As a matter of course the Knight had to be kept away from QKt5. After 19...Kt—B4, in order to reply to 20 Q—Kt5 with 20...Kt—B2, and to 20 Kt—B4 with 20...QR—Q, Black would have had absolutely nothing to fear.

(k)   Suicide! The game could still have been saved by 20...KtxB; 21 PxKt (or 21 QxKt, Kt—B4), BxKt; 22 KPxB, P—B4, etc., although even in that case White would have had the better prospects. After the text-move, which loses an all important tempo, the game becomes hopeless.

(l)   In case the QP is protected, the entrance of the second Knight at B4 and, if necessary, R—R7, would force material gain anyway.

(m)   In reply to 23...PxB, White would win by means of 24 KtxB PxKt (or A); 25 QxBP, QKt—B3 (or KKt—B3; 26 R—R7, R—Q; 27 Q—R6, etc.); 26 R—R7, R—B2; 27 RxR, KtxR; 28 Q—Q8ch, KxKt; 29 Q—K7ch, K—R3; 30 R—Q6, etc. (A) 24... PxPch; 25 QxP (the simplest), P—K6; 26 Q—B3, PxKt; 27 RxP, QKt—B3; 28 R—R7, etc.

(n)   White now winds up cleverly, leaving the opponent not the slightest chance.

(o)   In this variation also the importance of placing the Rook on Q square plainly comes to light.

(p)   This shortens the agony, which, however, would not have lasted very long after 28...P—QKt4; 29 Kt—Q5, etc.

Game 64   THIRTEENTH ROUND—QUEEN'S GAMBIT

Marshall	Janowski
White	Black
1 P—Q4	P—Q4
2 P—QB4	PxP
3 Kt—QB3(a)	P—K4
4 P—K3(b)	PxP
5 PxP	Kt—QB3
6 Kt—KB3	Kt—B3(c)
7 BxP(d)	B—Q3
8 Castles	Castles
9 B—KKt5	B—KKt5
10 Kt—Q5(e)	B—K2(f)
11 KtxBch	QxKt
12 B—Q5	KR—Q
13 R—K	Q—Q3
14 BxQKt	PxB(g)
15 P—KR3	B—R4(h)
16 R—QB	QR—Kt(i)
17 P—KKt4	B—Kt3

After 17...B—Kt2

18 Kt—K5(j)	P—QB4
19 PxP	Q—R3(k)
20 Q—B3(l)	RxP

21 Kt—B6	B—K5(m)	38 R—Q4	K—R
22 Kt—K7ch	K—R	39 R—Q7	P—R5
23 RxB	KtxR	40 Kt—K7(q)	RxKt
24 QxKt	R—K7	41 RxR	P—R6
25 B—K3	RxRP	42 B—R6	P—R7
26 Kt—B6	R—KKt	43 B—Kt7ch	K—R2
27 Q—Q5(n)	R—K5	44 BxPch	K—Kt3
28 Kt—K5	P—R3	45 B—B3	R—QKt
29 QxP	Q—KB3(o)	46 RxP	R—Kt6
30 QxQ	PxQ	47 R—Kt7ch	K—R3
31 Kt—B7ch	K—R2	48 P—Kt5ch	K—R4
32 KtxP	R—Q	49 B—B6	R—R6
33 Kt—B5	P—R4	50 P—B7	P—R8(Q)ch
34 P—B6	R—K5	51 BxQ	RxBch
35 R—B5	R—K4	52 K—Kt2	R—QB8
36 R—B4	R—K3(p)	53 P—B4	R—B6
37 B—B4	R—QB	54 K—B2	Resigns

(a)   The right move here is 3 Kt—KB3, in order to prevent P—K4. After the text-move, Black obtains equality without trouble.

(b)   Or 4 PxP, QxQch; 5 KtxQ, Kt—QB3; 6 P—K4, KtxP; 7 B—B4, B—Q3; 8 BxKt, BxB; 9 BxP, with an equal game.

(c)   After 6...B—KKt5, there follows 7 BxP, as Black cannot win the center Pawn, because his square, KB2, lacks protection.

(d)   Of no benefit to White would be the complications ensuing from 7 P—Q5. For instance, 7...Kt—QR4; 8 Q—R4ch, P—B3; 9 P—QKt4, PxP; 10 PxP, P—QKt4; 11 QxKt, QxQ; 12 RxQ, B—QKt5. Now, however, he threatens to displace the Knight, and Black, therefore, prepares for this eventuality with his next move, providing for that piece the square, K4.

(e)   The following line of play is practically the only one possible to prevent White getting a poor game because of his isolated pawn.

(f)   It is clear that 10...BxKt; 11 QxB, KtxP; 12 KtxKtch, etc., would lead to nothing agreeable.

(g)   Simpler would have been 14...QxB; 15 Kt—K5, Q—Q4; 16 KtxB (or 16 P—B3, B—K3), QxB; 17 KtxKtch, QxKt; 18 Q—Kt3, with an easy draw.

(h)   Here, too, 15...BxKt; 16 QxB, QxP; 17 QxP, QxP; 18 QxP, Q—Kt3, would have caused mutual blood-letting and a peaceful conclusion. Black begins gradually to go astray.

(i)   An odd misplay of critical consequence, instead of which should have been played 16...R—K (17 RxRch, RxR; 18 P—KKt4, B—Kt3; 19 Kt—K5, B—K5, etc.). This game furnishes a fine example of how a good position can be completely spoiled through a pair of seemingly plausible moves.

(j)   Winning at least a pawn, with a far superior position. Black's three pieces are posted so disadvantageously that he would have every reason to be glad if he could prevent the loss of the exchange through KtxQBP or Kt—B4. Nevertheless, the continued exact play of Marshall soon makes Black's position untenable.

(k)   To be sure, the alternative of 19...QxQ; 20 QRxQ, R—K would hardly be relished, but at least it would have made possible a more stubborn resistance than the text-move, after which White forces the win of two pieces for a Rook.

(l)   Again threatening to win the exchange.

(m)   Bitter necessity; for, after any moves of the Rook, 22 BxKt, PxB; 23 QxP would be immediately decisive.

(n)   Threatening 28 Kt—Kt4, as well as Kt—K5, etc.

(o)   Otherwise he would succumb to the attack very soon. However, the ensuing end-game is also quite hopeless.

(p)   Likewise, after 36...R—QR, the Rook would force its way, via Q4, to the seventh row with decisive results.

(q)   Threatening 41 Kt—Kt6ch, followed by B—R6 and mate.

Game 65   THIRTEENTH ROUND—QUEEN'S GAMBIT DECLINED

Ed. Lasker	Tartakower	After 16 R—Q
White	Black	

1 P—Q4	Kt—KB3		
2 P—QB4	P—K3		
3 Kt—KB3	P—Q4		
4 Kt—B3	P—B3		
5 P—K3	QKt—Q2		
6 B—Q3	PxP(a)		
7 BxBP	P—QKt4		
8 B—Q3	P—QR3		
9 Castles(b)	P—B4		
10 P—QR4	P—Kt5		
11 Kt—K4	B—Kt2		
12 KtxKtch	KtxKt		
13 Q—K2(c)	PxP(d)	26 P—Kt4	Q—Kt3(m)
14 KtxP	Q—Q4	27 BxB	PxB
15 P—B3	B—Q3	28 Kt—B6	KR—QB
16 R—Q(e)	Castles	29 B—K3(n)	P—K4
17 B—B4(f)	Q—QB4(g)	30 Q—Q2	Q—B3
18 B—Q2	Q—B2	31 K—Kt2(o)	B—B4
19 P—KKt3	Q—R4(h)	32 QxKt	BxB
20 P—K4	KR—Q	33 Kt—K7ch	QxKt
21 Kt—Kt3	Q—R4	34 RxRch	RxR
22 QR—B(i)	Kt—Q2	35 QxRch	Q—B
23 Q—B2(j)	B—B3(k)	36 R—Q8	Resigns
24 Kt—Q4	BxRP(l)		
25 P—Kt3	B—Kt4		

(a) This move in conjunction with the immediate development of the QB at Kt2 was first employed, and successfully, by Rubinstein in the tournament at Meran, January, 1924. After 6...B—Q3, White, as is well known, obtains the advantage through 7 P—K4.

(b) The merit of Rubinstein's innovation consists chiefly in the fact that White, for the moment, cannot very well play 9 P—K4, on account of 9...P—B4 (10 P—K5, PxP; 11 PxKt, PxKt, etc.).

(c) Up to here the moves are a repetition of the game, Spielmann vs. Gruenfeld, at Meran, where White at this point made the feeble move of 12 P—QKt3 and soon thereafter found himself at a disadvantage. The text-move, however, is not satisfactory, either. The best, probably, would be 13 R—K, in order to be able to parry Q—Q4 with P—K4. If then 13...Kt—K5; 14 P—R5, etc. The whole line of play deserves to be thoroughly investigated. Possibly, it is destined to create a new era in the defense of the Queen's gambit.

(d) This, however, is not the best, as White is enabled thereby to remove at once the pressure upon KKt2. More consistent is 13...Q—Q4, whereupon White seems to have nothing better than 14 R—Q, PxP; 15 B—B4 (after 15 PxP, B—K2, no adequate compensation for the isolated pawn would be in evidence), Q—KR4; 16 KtxP (16 RxP, B—B4; 17 B—Kt5ch, K—B), QxQ; 17 BxQ, leading to some sort of equalization.

(e) Here 16 Kt—Kt3 came under consideration. For instance, 16...Castles (or 16...QR—B; 17 BxP, BxB; 18 QxB, Castles; 19 Kt—Q4); 17 P—K4, Q—KR4; 18 P—KKt4, Q—K4; 19 B—K3, threatening P—KB4. The preparatory move selected is perhaps even more aggressive.

(f) Now White neglects the opportunity to turn to his advantage the opponent's premature 13th move. By 17 Kt—Kt3, Q—KR4 (17...Q—K4; 18 P—KB4, or 17... QxKt; 18 B—B4, etc.); 18 BxPch, Kt or QxB; 19 RxB, he could have won a pawn. The couple of threats at Black's disposal, on account of the temporary exposure of the Rook at Q6, could easily have been met. Now Black can readily extricate himself.

(g)   With 17...Q—KR4 (and likewise on the next move), a weakening pawn move could be provoked, since the natural protection, by means of 18 P—KKt3, would not be feasible, on account of 18...P—K4. After 18 P—KR3 or 18 P—KKt4, he could have countered with 18...Q—K4 and, after 18 P—KB4, with 18...Q—QB4, with a game full of fine prospects. The next moves by Black, directly challenging a consolidation of his opponent's game, are hardly comprehensible.

(h)   Better would have been 19...KR—Q and, only after 20 QR—B, Q—R4, etc.

(i)   The White position unquestionably has been improved with the last moves, which is not to be wondered at, since Black meanwhile has been content to let his Queen run about aimlessly. Here, however, White should have played first 22 B—K3 in order to prevent Kt—Q2, by means of which Black gets drawing chances.

(j)   Nothing better remained for him, because Black threatened 23...Kt—K4, with the eventual sacrificial combination on Kt4 or B3. Now, simply, 24 B—K2 should be in order.

(k)   Correct would have been 23...Kt—B4; 24 KtxKt (24 Kt—R5, KtxKP), BxKt; 25 B—K3, BxB; 26 QxB, Q—R4, etc. The text-move is convincingly refuted by White.

(l)   By far the lesser evil would have been 24...B—Kt2.

(m)   If 26...Q—R6, then White would win by 27 KtxB, followed by 28 B—KB.

(n)   Winning a piece.

(o)   Naturally, he did not need to go in for 31 QxB, QxP, etc.

FOURTEENTH ROUND

This was the day of days and most fortunate did they rate themselves who, unaware of the pairings, repaired to the scene of action only to find that the number of the round in which Dr. Lasker was to play Capablanca for the second time, had come out of the hat.

They had met first on the second day of the tournament, when a draw had been recorded. Since then much had happened. The champion had lost his only game to Reti and the ex-champion remained still undefeated! To win or even draw this game would mean much to Dr. Lasker and not alone for what was immediately at stake.

The scene was almost a repetition of a similar one in St. Petersburg, ten years before. Then it was Capablanca who was showing the way and at the time had not tasted the bitters of defeat. Now the tables were turned and it was the veteran who held the inside of the track with a clear lead of two points over his rival. It was truly a notable occasion at which it was well worth being present. The game produced by these grand-masters was worthy of it.

It was Capablanca's turn to have the white pieces and, by a transposition of moves, a Queen's Pawn opening was developed. Dr. Lasker, with Kt—KR4, maneuvered so that he was left with two Bishops, and, timing his moves with great precision, was able to parry all of Capablanca's threats. The latter, unable to break through, lost a move with his Queen. Dr. Lasker, however, would not make a passive move and this seemed to be exactly what Capablanca wanted, for he immediately seized the opportunity to sacrifice his Knight for three Pawns.

Black was left with a game very difficult of defense so that Dr. Lasker, with best play, could hope for no more than a draw. Soon thereafter, he went astray in offering an exchange of Queens, which the champion effected in such a way as to bring about a winning ending. This Capablanca, with classical precision, brought to a successful conclusion. For the champion it was a moment of genuine triumph, which he had richly earned.

Is Dr. Lasker beginning to feel the strain? Has he been favored by the "breaks"? Is he due to collapse or can he maintain the headlong pace being set by the champion, now clearly in his stride? These questions and others of like tenor are being asked on all sides. The tension is now very great and excitement runs high. It has about reached its climax. And it does seem as though some one must break under the cruel pressure. Will it be a repetition of St. Petersburg? Or will it be—can it be still more sensational? One can only hold his breath and await coming events!

Alekhine's great interest in the game described above and which, under the circumstances, was altogether comprehensible, was directly responsible for his failure to win from Maroczy and thereby make full amends for his loss of the day before. It was a Queen's Gambit declined, in which the Russian outplayed the Hungarian. In his anxiety, however, not to miss anything of the Capablanca-Dr. Lasker game which had reached its critical stage, Alekhine thought to make a few inconsequential moves before adjournment. Two of these were enough for the watchful Maroczy, who, with a forceful Pawn sacrifice, brought about a perpetual check. An "alibi"? Ask Alekhine!

Marshall was in for another defeat this day and Dr. Tartakower took it upon himself to inflict it. Nevertheless, it marked a turning point for the United States champion, who was not to lose again until the final round. It was another Reti opening in which Marshall unnecessarily submitted to a poor Pawn position. Dr. Tartakower, in business-like fashion, proceeded to increase his positional advantage until ultimately he was a clear Pawn to the good. Marshall fought hard in a Rook and Pawn ending, but Dr. Tartakower was not to be denied.

Ed. Lasker adopted an inferior defense to the Ruy Lopez played by Bogoljubow, who, thanks to his enterprise, soon obtained the upper hand. He also outplayed his opponent in the complications which the latter sought to create. Thereupon, like many another before him, he relaxed. Lasker then had an opportunity, by sacrificing a Pawn, of forcing a position wherein, although two Pawns down, his Bishop would have had excellent drawing chances. This he missed and Bogoljubow scored the game.

Yates, who had drawn with Janowski in the second round, did even better in their return encounter, which he won after a hard struggle lasting 81 moves. His Indian defense, however, was not at all successful, for Janowski gave him all sorts of trouble and outplayed the Briton up to the 44th move. At this stage Janowski missed a comparatively easy win, about four moves deep, and his play thereafter suffered to such an extent that he first permitted Yates to escape from the toils and later actually to win a drawn ending. Sic transit gloria mundi!

The leading scores: Dr. Lasker, 9½—3½; Capablanca, 8½—4½; Reti, 8—4; Alekhine, 7½—5½; Dr. Tartakower, 6½—6½.

White took this round by 3½—1½, making the record: White, 38½; Black, 31½.

Game 66   FOURTEENTH ROUND—QUEEN'S PAWN OPENING.

Capablanca	Dr. Lasker
White	Black
1 P—Q4	Kt—KB3
2 P—QB4	P—B3
3 Kt—QB3	P—Q4
4 PxP(a)	PxP
5 Kt—B3	Kt—B3
6 B—B4(b)	P—K3
7 P—K3	B—K2(c)
8 B—Q3	Castles
9 Castles	Kt—KR4(d)
10 B—K5(e)	P—B4(f)
11 R—B	Kt—B3
12 BxKt(g)	PxB(h)
13 Kt—KR4(i)	K—R
14 P—B4	KR—Kt
15 R—B3	B—Q2
16 R—R3	B—K(j)
17 P—R3(k)	R—Kt2(l)
18 R—Kt3(m)	RxR
19 PxR(n)	R—B
20 K—B2	Kt—R4
21 Q—B3(o)	Kt—B5
22 Q—K2	Kt—Q3
23 R—KR	Kt—K5ch(p)

After 28...R—B3

33 Q—R7ch	K—B
34 R—R6	B—Kt(z)
35 Q—B5ch	K—Kt2
36 RxR	PxR
37 K—Kt3	Q—K3(aa)

After 37 K—Kt3

After 23 R—KR

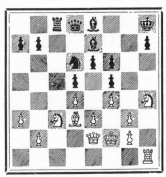

24 BxKt	BPxB(q)
25 Q—Kt4(r)	P—B4(s)
26 KtxBP(t)	PxKt
27 QxP	P—KR4
28 P—KKt4	R—B3(u)
29 P—Kt5(v)	K—Kt(w)
30 KtxQP(x)	B—B2
31 KtxBch	QxKt
32 P—KKt4	PxP(y)

38 KxP(bb)	QxQch
39 KxQ	B—Q4
40 P—Kt4	P—R3
41 K—Kt4(cc)	B—B5
42 P—B5	B—Kt6
43 K—B4	B—B7
44 K—K5	K—B2
45 P—R4	K—Kt2
46 P—Q5	BxP(dd)
47 P—Q6	P—B4
48 PxP	B—B3
49 K—K6	P—R4
50 P—B6ch	Resigns

(a) Marshall's method of conducting this variation of the Queen's gambit. After 4 P—K3 (Alekhine vs. Capablanca, 12th round) Black's best course would be to dispense with the immediate development of his QB and to switch into the line of play: 4...P—K3; 5 Kt—B3, QKt—Q2, followed by PxP, etc.

(b) Here, however, there comes into consideration first of all 6 Q—Kt3 (Kt—QR4; 7 Q—B2)—analogous to the game between Marshall and Dr. Lasker—for, after the text-move, Black could avoid quite readily the blocking of his QB: 6...B—B4; 7 Q—Kt3, Kt—QR4; 8 Q—Kt5ch, B—Q2; 9 Q—Q3, Q—Kt3, etc.

(c) Unquestionably holding out better prospects than 7...B—Q3; 8 B—Kt3, etc. If, however, White would forestall the exchange of his Bishop for the Knight with 8 P—KR3, then only would 8...B—Q3 be worthy of consideration.

(d) The logical consequence of the chosen system of development which leads to a middle game very difficult to be handled by both sides. Although White will retain the initiative a long while, nevertheless the entire line of play is neither disadvantageous nor devoid of chances for Black and cannot be deemed in any way the cause of his defeat.

(e) After 10 B—Kt3, there would not have been any need for Black to move his KBP, but he could have gone ahead, after the exchange on Kt3, to develop his Queen side.

(f) Herewith a full tempo is thrown away. After 10...P—B3!, White would have had nothing better than 11 B—Kt3, P—B4; 12 B—K5, etc., because 11 Kt—Kt5 would not have sufficed on account of 11 Q—K, for instance: 12 KtxRP (12 BxPch, K—R; 13 Q—Kt, P—B4), PxB; 13 KtxR, BxKt; 14 Kt—Kt5, Q—B2, and it would not be possible for White to obtain any compensation for the material sacrificed.

(g) It is clear that the admission of the Knight at K4 is not acceptable to White.

(h) Best; after 12...BxB (RxB; 13 Kt—K5), White could have played Kt—QR4—B5, etc., with advantage. Now, however, in order to prevent an offensive formation on the part of the opponent on the King's side (K—R, R—KKt, followed by Q—K—R4, etc.), he is obliged to take the initiative himself, whereby Black is given the necessary time to complete his development.

(i) Threatening P—KKt4.

(j) The encroachment of the Queen on R5 must be prevented. Unfavorable to this end, however, would have been 16...Q—KB (17 Q—R5, B—K), inasmuch as White, by means of the sacrifice of a piece with 17 KtxQP!, PxKt; 18 KtxP, BxKt; 19 BxB. R—Kt2; 20 Q—Kt3!, etc., would have obtained excellent chances of victory owing to the weakness of the adversary's white squares.

(k) A subtle positional move, which above all secures the square, B2, for the Queen. If, for instance, I. 17...Q—Q2; 18 Q—B2!, with the powerful threat of KtxBP, etc.; or II. 17...R—QB; 18 Q—B2, B—Q2; 19 K—R, followed by R—KKt, Q—K2 and P—KKt4; or 19 R—B, followed by QR—B3—Kt3, etc., with good prospects for an attack.

(l) An excellent defensive move. Aside from 18 Q—B2, Black had to bear in mind also the possibility of Kt—R4—B5, which, for instance, could have been played advantageously after 17...B—B2.

(m) If now 18 Q—B2, then 18...B—B2 (19 BxP, PxB; 20 KtxBP, B—Kt3). Therefore, White decides upon an exchange of Rooks which probably increases his offensive possibilities but, at the same time, cedes a counter-initiative to his opponent, who thereby will be able to effect a correctly timed regrouping operation for defensive purposes.

(n) White now has before him a clearly indicated procedure: K—B2, a clearance move with the Queen and then R—KR, followed by opening of the diagonals for the Bishops through P—KKt4, which could not be done at once on account of PxP, followed by P—B4. The transfer of the Knight to Q3, however, insures for Black an adequate defense.

(o) Plainly a loss of time. Yet even with the more exact 21 Q—K2, Kt—B5; 22 R—KR, Kt—Q3, White could have achieved but little, for instance: I. 23 P—KKt4, Kt—K5ch; 24 BxKt, BPxB; 25 P—B5, B—B2; 26 Kt—Kt6ch, K—Kt2; 27 Kt—B4, Q—Q2, etc. II. 23 KtxQP, PxKt; 24 KtxP, Kt—K5ch; 25 BxKt, PxB; 26 Q—Kt4, B—K, etc.

(p) Black has succeeded in fully consolidating his position. As has just been remarked, there was nothing he had to be afraid of, even with White on the move. It was only necessary for him now to see to it that he could bring his Knight to K5, after first waiting for P—KKt4. For this end the move 23...Q—Q2, or 23...R—B2 would have sufficed, since there were no effective preparatory moves ready at hand for White.

In fact, it would have been difficult then to predict the outcome of the game. The premature text-move permits White to make a perfectly sound sacrifice promising a lasting initiative and a safe draw.

(q) After 24...QPxB; 25 P—KKt4, PxP, White would have had the choice between the sacrifice, 26 QxP, P—B4; 27 KtxBP, etc., and the possibly more energetic 26 P—B5.

(r) Compelling thereby the following sacrificial line of play. Inferior would have been 25 P—B5, PxP; 26 KtxBP, B—B, etc.

(s) There was nothing else left, as, for instance, 25...R—B3 would no longer suffice on account of 26 P—B5, PxP; 27 QxP, etc.

(t) White obtains three Pawns in return for the Knight, and a permanent offensive against the exposed hostile King. The correctness of the sacrifice for that reason is unquestionable.

(u) The Rook is posted here most effectively for the defense.

(v) Better chances of victory were offered by the immediate 29 KtxQP, because 29...B—R5ch would involve no danger for White, for instance: 30 P—Kt3! (not 30 K—Kt B—Kt6!), R—B7ch (or A); 31 K—Kt, R—B8ch; 32 K—Kt2, R—B7ch; 33 K—R3, PxPch; 34 KxP!, B—Q2; 35 RxBch, QxRch (K—Kt; 36 Kt—B6ch, followed by QxB, or 35...K—Kt2; 36 R—R7ch, etc.); 36 PxQ, BxQch; 37 KxB, with a winning ending, for instance: 37...RxP; 38 K—K6!, K—Kt2; 39 P—B5, K—B; 40 P—R5, R—QR7 (or R—KR7; 41 Kt—B4); 41 P—B6, RxP; 42 P—R6, R—R3ch; 43 K—B5, K—Kt; 44 Kt—K7ch, etc., A. 30...B—Kt3; 31 Q—K5ch, B—B3; 32 KtxB, QxKt; 33 QxQch, RxQ; 34 PxP, B—B4; 35 R—R4, followed by P—KKt4.

(w) Herewith Black unnecessarily gives his opponent the benefit of a choice. More accurate would have been 29...R—Q3!; 30 P—KKt4, K—Kt; 31 PxP, Q—Q2; 32 QxQ (Q—K5, Q—Kt5; 33 QxB, R—K3; 34 Q—Q8, Q—B6ch), BxQ, and the two Bishops would have been quite able to withstand the pressure of the passed Pawns.

(x) With 30 P—KKt4, R—Q3!, etc., White could have switched into the foregoing variation, but he prefers to be rid of one of his opponent's Bishops.

(y) Again Dr. Lasker selects a somewhat difficult continuation. It is indeed doubtful if, after the plausible 32...B—Kt3; 33 Q—Q5ch, B—B2; 34 Q—K5, QxQ; 35 QPxQ, PxP; 36 P—B5, R—B4; 37 K—Kt3, RxP; 38 KxP, etc., although White would have obtained thereby only two Pawns for his piece—he would have commanded quite such easy drawing chances as in the actual game, for in that case the weakness of his KP, as well as the entrance of the Rook to the seventh row, would have caused him fresh troubles. A simpler drawing variation would have been 32...R—B7ch; 33 K—Kt3 (after 35 K—B, Q—B2, Black would actually obtain a mating attack), R—K7; 34 P—Kt6, P—R5ch!; 35 RxP, RxPch; 36 K—Kt2, R—K7ch; 37 K—B, R—K8ch, and White could not have escaped perpetual check.

(z) Black might have safely taken this Rook, for instance: 34...RxR; 35 QxRch, K—Kt; 36 P—Kt6, B—Kt6 (only not B—K3, on account of 37 P—Kt7!, etc.); 37 P—B5, Q—QB2! and, after 38 P—B6, he would again have had perpetual check; 38... Q—B7ch; 39 K—Kt3, Q—B2ch; 40 K—B2 (and 40 KxP would actually have brought on a catastrophe after 40...B—K3ch), Q—B7ch, etc.

(aa) Hereupon Black gets a hopelessly lost ending. The move is the more astonishing, as in this position Black was not being menaced (at the worst, 38 P—Kt4); after 38 QxKtP, the powerful rejoinder of 38...P—B4! was always at his disposal. There were different ways, therefore, in which to wind up with a draw, for instance: 38...B—Q4; 39 QxKtP, Q—Kt2 (40 P—Kt4, Q—R3); and, after the entrance of the Black Queen, White could not have avoided perpetual check. The simplest, however, would have been 38...B—B2! (threatening 39...Q—K3, whereupon 40 KxP could not have been played on account of B—R4ch); 39 QxKtP, P—B4!, for instance: 40 P—B5 (40 Q—Q, Q—Q3), Q—Q3ch; 41 Q—B4, QxQch; 42 KxQ, PxP; 43 KxP (or 43 PxP, B—Q4, and the White King is tied to the KP for ever after), PxP; 44 KxP, B—Kt6!, followed by P—R4—R5.

(bb) It may almost be assumed that Dr. Lasker for the moment had forgotten the possibility of this capture. Now the exchange of Queens, under circumstances very unfavorable to him, can no longer be avoided, inasmuch as his Queen dared not abandon the protection of the square, KB3, on account of a mate in two moves.

(cc) The maneuver which decides.

(dd) Also, after 46...PxP; 47 KxP, BxP; 48 KxP, etc., the three connected passed Pawns would have won quite easily.

Game 67   FOURTEENTH ROUND—QUEEN'S GAMBIT DECLINED

Alekhine.	Maroczy.
White.	Black.
1 P—Q4	Kt—KB3
2 P—QB4	P—K3
3 Kt—KB3	P—Q4
4 Kt—B3	B—K2(a)
5 B—Kt5	Castles
6 P—K3	Kt—K5(b)
7 BxB	QxB
8 Q—B2(c)	KtxKt
9 QxKt	P—QB4(d)
10 PxQP	BPxP
11 KtxP	PxP
12 B—K2	Kt—Q2
13 Castles	Kt—B3
14 QR—B	B—K3(e)
15 Q—R5	KR—B
16 RxRch	BxR
17 R—B	B—Q2
18 P—QR3(f)	P—KKt3
19 P—R3(g)	R—QB(h)
20 RxRch	BxR
21 QxRP	Q—B2(i)
22 B—B(j)	B—Q2
23 Kt—K2	B—Kt4
24 Kt—B3	BxB
25 KxB	Kt—K5(k)
26 Q—Q4	KtxKt
27 QxKt	Q—R7(l)
28 P—B3(m)	Q—R8ch
28 K—B2	Q—Q8
30 Q—B8ch(n)	K—Kt2
31 QxP(o)	Q—Q7ch
32 K—Kt3	P—Q5(p)

33 PxP(q)   Q—Kt4ch

Drawn

After 19 P—R3

After 27...Q—R7

(a)   Better here, it seems, would have been 4...P—B3; 5 P—K3, PxP, etc. (see the game, Ed. Lasker vs. Dr. Tartakower, 12th round). The orthodox defense, introduced by the text-move, has been going out of fashion steadily of late.

(b)   The present game illustrates most convincingly the inferiority of this variation, which anyway makes an unfavorable impression at the first glance, as Black, instead of developing, moves again with the same piece in order later to exchange it without deriving any benefit.

(c)   At Carlsbad, 1923, the player of the white pieces, with less exactness, played 8 Q—Kt3 against the same opponent, whereupon Black was not forced to capture the QKt, inasmuch as he also had at his disposal the reply of 8...P—QB3. Now, however, he has no choice.

(d)   With other moves as well Black's development would remain backward. But now he gets an isolated Pawn, which is so much the weaker because White obtains a lasting pressure upon the only open file.

(e)   As is easily to be seen, Black has an absolutely prescribed marching route.

(f)   It would have been premature, either here or on the next move, to play R—B7, on account of Q—Q, Q—B5, R—B!, etc.

(g)   Threatening 20 B—B3, Q—Q3; 21 Q—B7!, etc., which at this stage could have been parried by R—B!

(h) Black has been wholly outplayed and, therefore, tries this Pawn sacrifice to be able, perhaps, to fish yet a while in troubled waters. In quite similar fashion Maroczy, in London, 1922, was successful against the player of the White pieces in saving a game that was strategically lost.

(i) Threatening thereby 22...Q—B8ch and QxKtP, as well as 22...Kt—K5, followed by Q—B8ch and Q—K8 or Kt—Q7, etc.

(j) An interesting defensive maneuver: the Bishop relinquishes the square, K2, to the Knight, which for his part clears the square, Q4, for the Queen. After 22...Q—B8, would now follow 23 Q—Kt6, Kt—K5; 24 Q—Q8ch, K—Kt2; 25 QxP, Kt—Q7, 26 Q—QKt5, etc., with decisive advantage.

(k) There is nothing more left for Black than to enter upon a Queen ending, wherein, however, he will not only be at a material disadvantage, but positionally so as well.

(l) Desperation!

(m) This move and subsequent omissions are the result of a punishable carelessness. In the knowledge that the game was quite easily to be won, White in his haste before adjournment thought to make a few inconsequential moves in order to be able to watch the sensational game between Capablanca and Dr. Lasker which just then had arrived at its critical stage. After the self-evident 28 Q—B8ch, K—Kt2; 29 QxP, Q—R8ch; 30 K—K2, QxKtP; 31 P—QR4, Black, of course, would have to resign very soon.

(n) To be sure, this does not spoil anything, but the right way to win would have been 30 Q—Q4!, Q—B7ch; 31 K—Kt3 (threatening 32 QxQP, etc.), Q—Kt6; 32 P—QR4, etc.

(o) Whereupon the game does actually end in a draw. 31 Q—B3ch and Q—Q4 should have been played.

(p) This simple move was overlooked by White.

(q) Otherwise this Pawn, after P—Q6 or PxP, would go on to Queen.

Game 68   FOURTEENTH ROUND—RETI'S OPENING

Dr. Tartakower.	Marshall.
White.	Black.
1 Kt—KB3	Kt—KB3
2 P—QB4	P—KKt3(a)
3 P—QKt3	B—Kt2
4 B—Kt2	Castles
5 P—Kt3	P—B4
6 B—Kt2	Kt—QB3
7 Castles	P—K3(b)
8 P—Q4	PxP
9 KtxP	P—Q4
10 PxP	PxP(c)
11 Kt—Q2	R—K
12 QKt—B3	B—Kt5(d)
13 KtxKt	PxKt
14 Kt—K5	B—Q2
15 KtxB	KtxKt
16 BxB	KxB
17 R—B	Q—B3
18 P—K3(e)	QR—Q
19 R—B2(f)	R—K3
20 Q—Q2(g)	R—Q3(h)
21 R—Q(i)	Kt—K4
22 Q—Q4	QR—Q2

23 KR—QB   K—Kt(j)

After 23..K—Kt

24 P—B4(k)	Kt—Kt5
25 QxQch	RxQ
26 B—R3	P—KR4
27 RxP	RxR
28 RxR	P—Q5
29 BxKt	PxB
30 K—B2(l)	PxPch

31 KxP(m)	R—K2ch	47 P—QR4	K—Q2
32 K—Q3	R—Q2ch	48 R—B6	K—Q
33 K—B2	K—Kt2	49 R—B6	K—K
34 P—Kt4	R—K2	50 R—Q6	R—K7(p)
35 K—Kt3	R—K7	51 K—R6	RxP
36 R—B2	R—K6ch	52 KxP	R—R7
37 K—B4	R—QR6	53 R—Q4	R—R6
38 P—Kt5	R—R5ch	54 P—Kt6	RxP
39 K—Kt3	R—K5	55 P—Kt7	R—Kt6
40 R—B7(n)	R—K6ch	56 P—Kt8(Q)	RxQ
41 K—Kt4	R—K5ch	57 KxR	P—B4
42 K—Kt3(o)	R—K6ch	58 P—R5	P—Kt4
43 R—B3	R—K8	59 P—R6	P—Kt6
44 R—B2	K—B3	60 P—R7	PxP
45 K—Kt4	K—K3	61 P—R8(Q)	Resigns
46 K—R5	R—K5		

(a)   This fianchetto formation generally produces symmetrical positions, in which the first player's tempo is apt to be of greater importance. Probably the safest would be 2...P—QB3, followed by P—Q4 and B—B4, which, through a transposition of moves, might have led to the opening in the game between Reti and Dr. Lasker.

(b)   An idea not in accordance with good position play, showing plainly that Marshall has not as yet sufficiently penetrated the depth of the modern method of treating the openings, which every master must know nowadays in order to be able, like Dr. Lasker, for instance, to combat it successfully. Instead of completing his development with 7...P—Q3 (not 7...P—Q4; 8 PxP, KtxP; 9 BxB, KxB; 10 P—Q4, etc.); 8 P—Q4, B—Kt5, etc., he plays for the isolation of the QP, which is here the more unfavorable since, after an open game has been attained, only the disadvantage of fianchettoing his KB (weakening of the black squares) will remain and with its exchange the hoped for advantages will disappear.

(c)   After 10...KtxQP; 11 KtxQKt, etc., Black would have a fatal weakness on his QB3.

(d)   White utilizes this insufficiently thought out move to afflict his opponent by well known methods with a backward Pawn, which, after the subsequent simplification, becomes truly weak. The lesser evil here would have been 12...Q—Kt3 (intending Kt—K5), with a wholly defensible game.

(e)   The superiority of White's position is now manifest.

(f)   19 Q—Q2 at once would also have been quite good.

(g)   Plainly with the object of Q—R5. It is strange that Black does not seem to pay any attention to this threat and that White, despite his neglect, never executes it.

(h)   Inasmuch as this as well as other defensive moves (for instance: 20...Kt—K4; 21 Q—Q4, etc., similar to the actual game) would not have sufficed, a counter attack—wholly in accord with Marshall's style—should have been undertaken, beginning with 20...P—KR4. Had White in that case replied with P—KR4, Black in the subsequent development would at least have gained the square, K—Kt5, for his Knight. If not, the opening of the KR file would have reminded White of the necessity of being careful.

(i)   Unnecessary! 21 Q—R5 could quite properly have been played, inasmuch as both the defense of 21...R—QR, after 22 KR—QB, P—B4; 23 P—K4!, R—R3; 24 Q—Q2, as well as the counter attack of 21...P—B4, after 22 QxRP, P—Q5; 23 PxP, PxP; 24 R—Q, would have resulted favorably for White. Moreover, 21 KR—QB would also have been better, since the Rook in any event must come to QB two moves later.

(j)   The decisive blunder, instead of which 23...R—B2, protecting everything for the time being, should have been played. White, of course, would then have had the superior game.

(k)   Thereby White wins the weakling on QB6 and then brings about a readily won Rook ending.

(l)   Winning an important tempo.

(m)   A Pawn plus on the Queen's side easily turned to account, the better position of his Rook, the preferable King's position—more than this surely no one could expect!

(n)   Most energetic, but the simplest would have been P—R4—R5, etc.

(o) Now, however, White unnecessarily sounds a retreat and thereby prolongs the game for a dozen moves. The variation, 43 K—R5, R—K7; 44 P—QR4, RxP; 45 K—R6, R—QR7; 46 P—R5, R—R6; 47 R—B2, RxP; 48 KxP, R—KB6; 49 P—Kt6, etc., surely would have been sufficiently convincing.

(p) He might still have tried 50...R—B5 and, after 51 R—Q2, R—K5, whereupon White would have won in the end, although not without difficulty, by means of 52 R—R2. R—K3; 53 K—Kt4, followed by P—R5. After the text-move, the game ends abruptly

Game 69   FOURTEENTH ROUND—RUY LOPEZ

Bogoljubow	Ed. Lasker	29 BxQ	RxQ
White	Black	30 BxPch	K—Kt2
1 P—K4	P—K4	31 B—Kt3	R—B2(p)
2 Kt—KB3	Kt—QB3	32 B—KB4	QR—QB
3 B—Kt5	Q—B3(a)	33 B—K6(q)	R—K2
4 Kt—B3(b)	KKt—K2(c)	34 BxR	BxB
5 P—Q3	Kt—Q5(d)	35 R—QB	B—Kt2
6 KtxKt	PxKt	36 R—B7(r)	K—B2(s)
7 Kt—K2	P—B3		
8 B—R4	P—Q4		
9 Castles	P—KKt3(e)		

After 36 R—B7

10 P—QKt4(f)	Q—Q3
11 P—QR3(g)	B—Kt2
12 B—Kt2	P—QKt4
13 B—Kt3	P—QB4
14 PxBP	QxP
15 R—B(h)	Castles
16 P—QB3	PxP
17 KtxP	P—Q5(i)
18 Kt—Q5	Q—Q3
19 P—B4(j)	KtxKt
20 BxKt	R—Kt
21 R—B6	Q—Q
22 Q—Kt3(k)	B—Kt2
23 R—B5	Q—Q3(l)
24 Q—B2	KR—B
25 R—B	B—B(m)

37 RxRch	KxR
38 B—Q2	K—K3
39 K—B2	K—Q3
40 K—K3	K—B4
41 B—R5	B—B
42 B—Q8	B—Q2
43 B—R5	P—Kt4
44 B—B3	P—KR4(t)
45 B—Q4ch	K—Q3
46 BxP	P—R5
47 B—Q4	K—K3
48 B—B3	K—B2
49 P—Q4	K—Kt3
50 P—Q5	B—B
51 B—R5	B—Q2
52 B—Q8	P—R6
53 PxP	BxP
54 K—Q4	B—Q2
55 P—K5	K—B4
56 P—K6	B—K
57 BxP	Resigns

After 25 R—B

26 BxP	QxP(n)
27 R—B	BxR
28 BxB	Q—K6ch(o)

(a)   A defense that is rightly rarely played, as Black makes his own development more d.fficult because of the early exposing of his Queen.

(b)   Threatening Kt—Q5 already.

(c)   An interesting line but favorable to White would have resulted from 4... Kt—Q5, for instance: 5 KtxKt, PxKt; 6 Kt—Q5, Q—Kt4 (or Q—Q; 7 Kt—B4!) 7 KtxPch, K—Q; 8 KtxR, QxB; 9 P—Q3, P—Kt3; 10 B—B4, P—Q3; 11 P—QR4, Q—B3; 12 Q—R5, P—Kt3; 13 Q—QKt5, Q—Kt2; 14 P—R5, etc., with a strong attack. The text-move makes the development of the KB very difficult.

(d)   More in the spirit of the continuation chosen was P—KR3 with the fianchetto-ing of the Bishop later. Black now embarks upon an unfavorable variation of the in-ferior Bird's Opening.

(e)   Else the King's side pieces can hardly be developed.

(f)   With this move White centers his attack on the Pawn at Q5 and holds his advantage with an iron hand. Black also always finds the only moves to hold his com-promised position. But his defense is not sufficient to attain equality.

(g)   This protecting move forces Black to compromise his position still further in order to hold his exposed Pawn.

(h)   Simple and conclusive. The consequent unavoidable opening of the QB file promises White further advantages. Black would hardly care to bet on his chances now. (Freely translated).

(i)   At least 17...PxP; 18 Kt—Q5!, Q—Q3; 19 BxB,! KxB; 20 PxP was not better.

(j)   Threatening P—K5.

(k)   As so often happens, one weak move is enough to lose the advantage gained by faultless play. Correct would have been 22 Q—B2, B—Kt2; 23 R—B5, BxB; 24 RxB, Q—Kt3; 25 P—K5, QR—B; 26 Q—KB2; Or 23...Q—Kt3, 24 BxB, QxB; 25 P—K5, KR—B; 26 KR—QB, etc.

(l)   This reply makes all the difference RxP is not poss.ble on account of BxB; and, as the KB Pawn is attacked, White must lose a valuable tempo.

(m)   Black is eventually outplayed during the following maneuvers. Instead there was a chance here to save the game. 25...RxR; 26 QxR, QxP!; 27 BxB (or 27 R—KB, Q—K6ch; 28 K—R; BxB; 29 QxB, QxQP; 30 Q (or R)xKBP, K—R, etc.) 27 ...B—K4! and White cannot avoid the draw; for instance: 28 Q—B2 (or 28 P—KKt3, Q—K6ch, etc.), QxRPch; 29 K—B, Q—R8ch; 30 K—B2, Q—R5ch; 31 K—K2, Q—R4ch!, etc.

(n)   With this move Black wins the exchange, but only for a short time.

(o)   If 28...Q—K4, White wins easily by 29 P—Q4!, Q—R4(Kt4); 30 BxPch, K—Kt2; 31 P—Q5! But the following ending is also hopeless for Black.

(p)   Obviously forced, because of the terrible threat of 32 R—B7ch.

(q)   A bit fanciful, but sufficient. Simpler would have been 33 B—K5ch, K—R3; 34 BxR, RxB; 35 R—B7; then if 35...R—B6; 36 B—K6!, with a winning position.

(r)   But this plausible move is a mistake which gives the opponent a chance to obtain a difficult draw. 36 K—B2 was now necessary, whereupon the united passed pawns would have won without difficulty.

(s)   Black fails to seize the lucky opportunity. After 36...RxR; 37 BxR, P—Kt5!, a draw would result despite the two pawns minus; for instance: 38 PxP, B—R3; 39 P—Q4, B—Q6; 40 P—K5, B—B5; 41 K—B2, P—QR3; 42 K—K3, B—Q4; 43 P—Kt3, K—B2; 44 K—B4, P—R3; 45 B—Q6, K—K3; 46 B—B8, P—KR4; 47 B—Kt5, B—K5, etc. After the move in the text, no real fighting chances are left.

(t)   Or 44...P—QR3; 45 B—B6, P—KKt5; 46 B—K7ch, K—B3; 47 P—Q4, to be followed by P—Q5, etc.

Game 70   FOURTEENTH ROUND—IRREGULAR DEFENSE (INDIAN)

Janowski	Yates
White	Black
1 P—Q4	Kt—KB3
2 Kt—KB3	P—KKt3
3 B—B4	B—Kt2
4 P—KR3(a)	Castles(b)
5 P—K3	P—Q3
6 B—B4	Kt—B3(c)
7 Castles	Kt—Q2(d(
8 Kt—B3	P—KR3(e)
9 Q—Q2	P—K4
10 B—Kt3	K—R2
11 QR—Q	Kt—Kt3(f)
12 B—K2	Q—K2
13 KR—K(g)	B—Q2
14 B—Q3	QR—K(h)
15 PxP	PxP
16 P—K4	Kt—Kt5(i)
17 B—B	R—Q
18 Q—B	P—KB3(j)

36 R—Q7	BxB
37 QxBch	Q—Kt3
38 Q—B3	K—R
39 R—K4	QR—K(o)
40 R—KKt4	Q—Kt8ch
41 K—R2	R—K3(p)
42 Q—Q5	Q—B4
43 RxP	P—R4

After 43...P—R4

44 R—KR4(q)	B—R3
45 Q—B3(r)	QxQ
46 PxQ	R—Q3
47 RxP	R—Q7ch
48 K—R	RxB
49 RxBch	K—Kt
50 R—Q7(s)	R(Q7)—KKt7
51 R—Q	K—Kt2
52 R—KR4(t)	R—QB7
53 R—KKt	RxRch
54 KxR	RxP
55 R—R4	R—B4(u)
56 K—B2	P—B4

After 18 Q—B

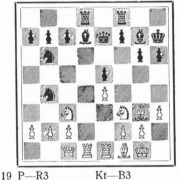

19 P—R3	Kt—B3
20 Kt—Q5(k)	KtxKt
21 PxKt	Kt—Kt
22 P—B4	P—Kt3
23 B—Q3	B—K
24 Q—B2	Kt—Q2
25 P—Kt4	P—QR4
26 Kt—Q4	R—B
27 Kt—K6	R—KKt
28 P—B5	PxBP
29 PxBP	B—B2
30 P—B6(l)	Kt—B
31 P—B4(m)	KtxKt
32 PxKt	QxP
33 P—B5	Q—K
34 B—K4	PxP(n)
35 BxPch	B—Kt3

After 69...K—B3

57 K—Kt3(v)	K—B3	70 R—K8(bb)	RxP
58 P—B4(w)	P—K5	71 P—R4	R—B6
59 K—R4	K—K3	72 K—R4	R—R6
60 R—Q4(x)	R—Kt4(y)	73 R—QR8	K—K4
61 R—R4	K—Q4	74 K—Kt5	R—Kt6ch
62 K—Kt3	R—B4	75 K—R5	P—K6
63 K—B2	K—K3	76 P—R5	K—B5
64 K—Kt3	R—B6ch	77 P—R6	R—Kt8
65 K—R4	R—B6(z)	78 P—R7	R—QR8
66 K—Kt5(aa)	RxKRP	79 K—Kt6	R—R3ch
67 RxP	R—Kt6ch	80 K—R5	P—K7
68 K—R5	R—Kt5	81 R—K8	K—B6
69 R—K5ch	K—B3	Resigns	

(a) This is not absolutely necessary, and substituted for it could be 4 P—K3 or 4 QKt—Q2, inasmuch as 4...Kt—R4 is not really a threat, on account of 5 B—Kt5, etc.

(b) Black, however, does not utilize the tardy method of development on the part of the opponent and proceeds undisturbed along "Indian" lines, instead of 4...P—B4! If then 5 P—B3 (or 5 P—K3, Q—Kt3), 5...PxP; 6 PxP, P—Kt3, followed by B—Kt2, with good prospects (compare Dr. Lasker vs. Alekhine, 18th round).

(c) Again, more to be recommended was a transition into Reti's system for the second player through 6...P—B4; 7 P—B3 (7 PxP, Q—R4ch), P—Kt3, followed by B—Kt2. The formation planned by Black in the center is not sound for the reason that the square, Q4, is weak.

(d) If his object is to play P—K4, he could do it to the best advantage right now: 7...P—K4; 8 PxP, Kt—KR4; 9 B—R2 (or 9 B—KKt5, Q—K; 10 P—KKt4 KtxP; 11 KtxKt, QxKt, etc.), KtxP; 10 KtxKt, BxKt, etc. Consequently, White's best would be 8 B—R2, but in that case Black, in contrast to the effective continuation selected, would have gained at least an important "tempo."

(e) For now he is obliged to make this preparatory move, because after 8...P—K4; 9 B—KKt5, Q—K; 10 Kt—Q5, his Queen would be in difficulties.

(f) In this game also is demonstrated the truth of the long established principle that QKt3 is not a desirable post for the Knights.

(g) Move by move, White is strengthening his position, without lessening the pressure. If 13...P—K5, White would break the center with 14 Kt—R2 and P—B3, thereby gaining an advantage.

(h) If 14...P—B4; 15 PxP, PxP; 16 P—K4, P—B5; 17 B—R2, followed by Kt—Q5 (likewise if 16...B—K3), with advantage. Better would have been 14...QR—Q, as will presently appear.

(i) In order to prevent, with toil and distress, the entrenchment of the Knight at Q5, which constitutes the light-motif of this strategy on the part of White.

(j) This is almost equivalent to capitulation without a fight. Unquestionably necessary was 18...P—QB3, inasmuch as the possible weakening of the pawns on the Queen's side, after 19 P—R3, Kt—R3; 20 BxKt, would have been much less serious than the surrender of the square, Q4; moreover, it is doubtful whether White (and Janowski of all people!) would have decided to part with his KB in such a manner.

(k) The attack thus initiated carries on automatically.

(l) Convinced that the game can be easily won, White plays somewhat carelessly. Immediately decisive would have been 30 P—B4, BxKt; 31 BxPch, K—R; 32 PxB, QxPch; 33 QxQ, KtxQ; 34 P—K7, etc. Of course, even after the text-move, Black's position is still lost.

(m) A good alternative would have been 31 KtxB, RxKt; 32 P—B4, etc.

(n) Again the only reply.

(o) Evidently 39...P—B4 would not do on account of 40 RxKP, etc.

(p) White threatened 42 KRxB, followed by QxP, etc.

(q) After 44 R(Kt4)xB, RxR; 45 RxR, KxR; 46 Q—Q7ch, K—Kt3; 47 P—B7, Black without more ado might have resigned. White, however, has such a superiority that he could still win even after this striking omission.

(r) The correct procedure would have been 45 RxP, QxR; 46 QxR, Q—Kt4 or Kt3 (RxB obviously leads to nothing), 47 Q—Kt4, etc. Now there is a draw in sight for Black.

(s) Black could have forced an immediate draw by perpetual check after 50 RxP, R(Q7)—KKt7.

(t) Or 52 R—QB, KxR; 53 P—B7, R—Kt, etc.

(u) And now we have reached a situation which, if handled with ordinary care, should not be lost by either party. At his next turn it was possible for White, by means of 56 P—B4, to force further simplification.

(v) Somewhat better would have been 57 K—K3, for, after 57...K—B3; 58 P—B4, Black could not well have played 58...P—K5, on account of 59 K—Q4, etc. This sort of thing, however, is bound to happen.

(w) A dreadful move, which allows the adversary a supported passed pawn and at the same time endangers his own KB pawn. A draw was still to be had through 58 K—B2; if then 58...K—Kt4; 59 P—B4ch, PxP; 60 K—B3, R—B6ch; 61 K—Kt2, R—Kt6ch; 62 K—R2, etc.

(x) Of course not 60 K—Kt5, on account of 60...P—K6, etc.

(y) The win which Black attains at his 65th move might now be his through 60... R—B6; 61 R—R4, R—B6, etc.

(z) A correctly calculated winning combination, the point of which will stand out more clearly after Black's 69th move.

(aa) The connected passed pawns would have likewise decided the issue in favor of Black after 66 RxP, RxBPch; 67 K moves, R—B8, etc.

(bb) For the first time now evidently White realizes that, after the intended 70 RxP, he would lose his Rook through 70...R—Kt (or Kt8). But it is too late—much too late.

FIFTEENTH ROUND

Those who came to see Dr. Lasker in action were disappointed, as it was his turn for a bye, this being a repetition of the first round—in pairings if not in results. Capablanca made the most of his rival's absence by equaling his total of wins, but, inasmuch as he had played one game more and lost that, he still remained in second place. Alekhine also kept up the pace, and Marshall asserted himself by wresting a game from Reti. The other winners were Bogoljubow and Maroczy. Not a draw was scored.

A Reti opening chosen by Capablanca was well defended by Janowski, who obtained a promising game. However, the latter weakened his King's side by playing P—KR3 unnecessarily so that, later on, when he was compelled to play P—KB3, his white squares were naturally none too strong. With unerring accuracy Capablanca proceeded to make the most of the disadvantage his adversary was laboring under and forced a win in most instructive fashion.

The game between Alekhine and Yates was an Indian defense in which the latter was outplayed, being obliged to part with the "exchange" at an early stage in order to obtain some freedom. Alekhine never relaxed and the game was not greatly prolonged.

Reti played his own opening against Marshall and both were seen to good advantage. When complications arose, the American worked out a line of play whereby he brought his QR over to the opposite side of the board, thereby adding greatly to the burden of the white King. Reti had a way out, but missed it and therefore Marshall, with a forceful combination, entirely destroyed his opponent's position on the King's side.

Edward Lasker held his own well with the black side of a Queen's Gambit Declined against Maroczy, but, when he committed himself to an advance on the King's side, he seriously weakened his game. Maroczy's after-play, while not faultless, was good enough finally to bring about a win.

Bogoljubow vs. Dr. Tartakower was a Dutch defense and a capital game, although its main interest was in the ending. Bogoljubow sacrificed a Pawn in order to establish his Rook on the seventh row, subsequently recovering the Pawn by means of very accurate play. He retained his advantage in position in face of an ingenious counter-attack by Dr. Tartakower, which barely failed to save the game. It was one of Bogoljubow's best efforts in the tournament.

The leading scores: Dr. Lasker, 9½—3½; Capablanca, 9½—4½; Alekhine, 8½—5½; Reti, 8—5; Marshall, 7—6; Bogoljubow and Maroczy, each 7—7.

It was another successful day for the white forces by the ratio of 4—1, bringing the totals to 42½ for White, and 32½ for Black.

Game 71   FIFTEENTH ROUND—RETI'S OPENING

Capablanca	Janowski
White	Black
1 Kt—KB3	P—Q4
2 P—KKt3	P—QB4
3 B—Kt2	Kt—QB3
4 Castles	P—K4
5 P—B4(a)	P—Q5
6 P—Q3	B—Q3
7 P—K3	KKt—K2
8 PxP(b)	BPxP
9 P—QR3	P—QR4
10 QKt—Q2	Kt—Kt3
11 R—K	Castles
12 Q—B2	R—K
13 P—Kt3(c)	P—R3(d)
14 R—Kt	B—K3
15 P—KR4(e)	R—QB(f)
16 P—B5	B—Kt(g)
17 Kt—B4(h)	P—B3
18 B—Q2	K—R
19 P—QKt4	PxP
20 PxP	Kt—R2
21 Q—B(i)	Kt—Kt4(j)
22 Kt—R2	Q—K2
23 R—R	R—B2
24 R—R5	B—Q2
25 Kt—Kt6	B—B3
26 Q—B4	Kt—R2
27 Kt—Q5	BxKt
28 QxB(k)	P—B4
29 Q—B3	Q—B3
30 P—R5	Kt—K2

31 P—Kt4(l)	P—B5
32 Q—K4	KKt—B3
33 QR—R	QR—K2
34 Q—Kt6	Q—B(m)

After 34...Q—B

35 Kt—B3(n)	R—K3
36 Kt—R4	R—B3(o)
37 B—K4	Q—Kt
38 B—Q5(p)	Kt—K2(q)
39 QxR	PxQ
40 BxQ	RxB
41 P—B3	P—B4(r)
42 BxP	KKt—B3
43 Kt—Kt6ch	K—R2(s)
44 BxKP	KtxB
45 RxKt	BxR
46 RxKt	Resigns

(a) With this move the game assumes a character of its own. Yet it is doubtful if the intended increase of efficiency for the fianchettoed Bishop compensates for the confinement of the rest of White's fighting force. Therefore, it seems more desirable first to play 5 P—Q3 and, in case 5...Kt—B3, then 6 P—B4, but if 5...P—KB4, then 6 P—K4!, somewhat similar to the game between Alekhine and Ed. Lasker, but with an additional tempo.

(b) As Capablanca himself properly pointed out after the game, this exchange is premature. 8 QKt—Q2 at once should have been played, with the positional threat of forcing the exchange of Black's KB by means of Kt—K4. If Black, in order to avoid this, had replied with 8...P—KB4, then the exchange on Q4, followed by R—K, threatening P—QB5, etc., would have offered better prospects than in the actual game. After the text move, Black remains steadily at the wheel.

(c) It is very difficult for White to establish himself promisingly on the Queen's side, for, until he is ready for P—QB5, his pawn superiority there is quite illusory. That move, moreover, could quite easily be prevented by Black.

(d) The most suitable preparation for B—K3 would be 13...P—KB3, which Black was going to play anyway. The seemingly harmless weakening of Black's King's side caused hereby will be utilized effectively by Capablanca at the right moment.

(e) The move to cause embarrassment, acquiring importance only because of the inadequate reply. Yet 15 P—QB5, B—KB; 16 P—QKt4, PxP; 17 PxP, R—R7, etc., clearly would have been premature.

(f) Just the kind of move for which White had hoped. With 15...Q—K2 and, if 16 P—R5 (or 16 Q—Kt2, P—KB3), then 16...Kt—B; 17 P—B5, KBxP; 18 KtxKP, KtxKt; 19 RxKt, B—Q3, followed by QR—B, etc., would have retained the advantage.

(g) In reply to 16...B—KB, there would have followed obviously 17 P—R5, etc.

(h) Now at last White gets into the game and in the next moves makes use of his pressure on the Queen's wing to force the exchange of one of the hostile Bishops.

(i) Threatening 22 BxP, etc.—a consequence of Black's superfluous 13th move.

(j) Parrying this threat (22 BxP?, Kt—B6; 23 R—R, P—K5!, etc.). On the whole Janowski defends himself quite well, after his mistake on the 15th move, but now there is little left to be done.

(k) All this is played very convincingly. Aside from a majority of pawns on the Queen's wing, White now has a strong pressure upon the weakened squares of the hostile position.

(l) In order to tear open again the holes which Black vainly attempted to close up with his 28th move. The momentary shutting in of White's QB is immaterial.

(m) Even after 34...QxQ; 35 PxQ, followed by the eventual B—Q5—B4 and P—Kt5, the game could not be saved in the long run. The text-move involves the following trap: 35 B—K4, Q—Kt; 36 Kt—B3, R—K3; 37 Q—B5 (or Kt—R4, Kt—K2), R—KB, etc. Capablanca, however, destroys this hope.

(n) Threatening 36 Kt—R4, against which there is no sufficient defense. The smallest evil for Black would have been to take back his last move with 35...Q—B3, but in that case also the opponent, after 26 QxQ, PxQ; 37 Kt—R4, etc., would have gradually forced his way through. As Black plays, he loses the exchange in the end.

(o) Or 36...Q—Kt; 37 B—Q5, etc.

(p) Decisive.

(q) If 38...Q—B, then of course 39 Q—K4, etc.

(r) Shortening the agony.

(s) Or 43...RxKt; 44 PxR, PxB; 45 R—K8ch, followed by 46 RxB, winning.

Game 72   FIFTEENTH ROUND—INDIAN DEFENSE (FOUR-PAWN GAME)

Alekhine	Yates	After 14 R—B
White	Black	
1 P—Q4	Kt—KB3	
2 P—QB4	P—Q3	
3 Kt—QB3	P—KKt3	
4 P—K4	B—Kt2	
5 P—B4	Castles	
6 Kt—B3(a)	Kt—B3(b)	
7 B—K2(c)	Kt—Q2(d)	
8 B—K3(e)	P—K4	
9 BPxP	PxP	
10 P—Q5	QKt—Kt	
11 P—B5(f)	P—QR4	
12 Castles	Kt—R3	
13 Kt—QR4	Q—K2	
14 R—B(g)	P—R3(h)	

15 BxKt(i)	RxB	24 KtxP(m)	B—R3
16 P—B6	PxP	25 Kt—QB4(n)	BxKt
17 PxP	Kt—Kt(j)	26 RxB	Q—K4
18 B—B5	Q—K	27 Q—B3	P—B4
19 BxR	BxB	28 KtxKt	PxKt
20 Kt—B3(k)	RxP	29 PxP	R—KB3
21 Kt—Q5(l)	R—Q3	30 Q—K4	B—B4ch
22 RxP	Kt—R3	31 K—R	RxP
23 R—B3	Kt—Kt5	32 RxR	Resigns

(a) Herewith the normal position of the "Four-Pawn" game is brought about. With regard to the moves up to this point, compare the game between Alekhine and Marshall in the seventh round.

(b) This maneuver, recommended by Amos Burn in similar situations, is not however suited to this occasion. While he may freely ignore the possibility of P—QB4, Black sooner or later will be compelled to play P—K4 and in that case, after BPxP, PxP, the move, P—Q5, could be made with an important tempo. Better replies here would be 6... QKt—Q2 or 6...P—K4.

(c) With the intention, after 7...B—Kt5, to continue with 8 P—Q5 and to turn into the continuation, favorable to White, as in the Alekhine-Marshall game.

(d) To lose so much time after a restrictive opening in order to force an advance not particularly favorable—that, of course, must have sad consequences instantly. 7... B—Kt5 and after 8 P—Q5, Kt—Kt; 9 Castles, then not at once QKt—Q2, but first BxKt, would have been more in order.

(e) In order after 8...P—K4; 9 BPxP, PxP; 10 P—Q5, to prevent the Knight from coming to Q4.

(f) Herewith the game—and that so early—is won from a strategical point of view, since only occupation of the square, QB4, would allow Black in this variation to combat successfully the opponent's superiority in the "half-center."

(g) White's last moves have not only secured the pawn on B5, but also brought several threats to bear, which taken together it will be impossible for Black, owing to his neglected development, to parry with any measure of success.

(h) Black is unable to make any attempt to free himself before he protects the square, Kt4, against the entrance of the hostile Knight In reply to 14...R—K or Q, for instance, then 15 Kt—Kt5, threatening RxP, or 16 P—Q6, followed by 17 B—QB4, would follow at once; and, in case 14...P—KB4, then 15 B—QB4, K—R; 16 PxP!, PxP; 17 Kt—Kt5 (threatening KtxRP), P—B5; 18 Q—R5, Kt—B3; 19 P—Q6, etc., with a winning attack. After the text-move, however, he loses the exchange without any compensation.

(i) White's position already is so strong that, apart from this possibility, he has at his disposal also the winning of a pawn by 15 Q—Q2, aiming at both KR6 and QR5.

(j) In order to capture at least the QBP in return for the exchange, but immediately thereafter his own BP succumbs.

(k) 20 Q—Kt3, KtxP; 21 Q—Kt5, Q—K3, etc., would have been less convincing.

(l) After which the squares, QB7 and K5, cannot be protected simultaneously.

(m) Whereby several exchanges are effected, clearing up the situation at once.

(n) Of course not 25 KtxP, on account of 25...RxKt, etc.

Game 73 FIFTEENTH ROUND—RETI'S OPENING

Reti	Marshall
White	Black

	Reti White	Marshall Black
1	KKt—B3	KKt—B3
2	P—QB4	P—Q4(a)
3	PxP(b)	KtxP
4	P—Q4(c)	B—B4(d)
5	Kt—B3(e)	P—K3
6	Q—Kt3	QKt—B3(f)
7	P—K4	KtxKt
8	PxB	Kt—Q4
9	B—QKt5(g)	B—Kt5ch
10	B—Q2	BxBch
11	KtxB	PxP
12	BxKtch	PxB
13	Castles	Castles(h)
14	Q—R4(i)	R—QKt(j)
15	Kt—Kt3(k)	R—Kt3(l)
16	QxRP	Q—Kt4
17	Q—R5	P—B4(m)
18	QxP(n)	Kt—B5(o)
19	P—Kt3	R—KR3(p)
20	QxP(q)	Kt—K7ch
21	K—Kt2	Q—Kt5
22	R—R	P—B5
23	P—B3(r)	Q—R6ch
24	K—B2	R—QB(s)
25	Q—R5	KtxKtP
26	KR—KKt(t)	QxPch
27	R—Kt2	Q—R5
28	R—QB	R—K(u)
29	Q—QKt5	Kt—K5ch
30	K—B	Q—R8ch
	Resigns	

After 19...R—KR3

After 24 K—B2

(a) It cannot be sound strategy to permit a center Pawn to disappear in this way before the opponent has committed himself to his plan of developing the opening. It would have been better to prepare for the move of P—Q4 with P—QB3.

(b) The best rejoinder which, in the shortest possible way demonstrates the deficiency of Black's second move. If 3 P—QKt3, Black with 3 P—QB3, could have steered into the best London system of defense against Reti's development.

(c) This, however, is inconsistent, inasmuch as White takes possession of only half the center and, moreover, limits his own possibilities of development without cramping the position of his opponent. He should either have selected the delaying method of 4 P—KKt3 and B—Kt2 (by which Black would have been at a disadvantage in consequence of the unsafe position of the Knight at Q4, which could easily be driven away by P—K4), or by at once taking possession of the center with 4 P—K4, Kt—KB3; 5 Kt—B3, followed by P—Q4, with advantage. After the text-move, however, he can only count upon equality at the best.

(d) After this simple rejoinder, White can play P—K4 only after great effort and Black meanwhile gains time to complete his development.

(e) Likewise in answer to the immediate 5 Q—Kt3, Black could have played Kt—QB3.

(f) Now Black obtains the initiative. It is clear that White can gain no advantage from the acceptance of the Pawn sacrifice, and not only after 7 QxKtP, QKt—Kt5, but also after 7...KKt—Kt5, etc.; and, inasmuch as after 7 B—Q2 (on account of the threat of Kt—Kt5), B—QKt5, Black would retain the advantage in development. The next move of White seems to be the best to bring about equalization.

(g) This Pawn sacrifice, on the other hand, was not necessary, nor did it open up opportunities. To be sure, 9 PxP was also not good, on account of 9...B—Kt5ch; 10 B—Q2, BxBch; 11 KtxB, Castles; 12 PxPch, RxP, etc.; but 9 QxKtP was playable at this stage. For instance, 9...QKt—Kt5 (or B—Kt5ch; 10 K—Q); 10 Q—Kt5ch, P—B3; 11 Q—R4, PxP; 12 P—QR3, Kt—Kt3; 13 Q—Kt3, Kt—Q4; 14 B—K2, etc., with a satisfactory game. Now at last Black gets an advantage.

(h) Now Black has assured himself of a small advantage, which, of course, could be turned to account only with great difficulty, if White subsequently had played with good position judgment. The position in its outstanding features has a remarkable similarity to a variation of the 3...B—B4 defense in the Ruy Lopez, which occurred, among others, in a game of the return match between Dr. Lasker and Steinitz at Moscow (compare 1 P—K4, P—K4; 2 Kt—KB3, Kt—QB3; 3 B—Kt5, B—B4; 4 P—B3, KKt—K2; 5 P—Q4, PxP; 6 PxP, B—Kt5ch; 7 B—Q2, BxBch; 8 QxB, P—Q4; 9 PxP, KtxP; 10 Bx Ktch, PxB; 11 Castles, Castles; 12 Kt—QB3). In the position before us White has the same favorable deployment on the Queen's side as above. Black, however, has a sufficient equivalent in his pawn at KB4, which eventually (but by no means certainly) might take part in an aggressive movement. The same error of judgment underlies the following moves of White. Instead of safeguarding his King's position in the simplest manner (Kt—KB3) and then planning a promising attack upon Black's Queen's side, to be defended only with difficulty, he believes, in view of Black's well-nigh illusory material advantage, that he must attack at any cost—and eventually is mated himself.

(i) An important loss of a "tempo." 14 Kt—KB3, which would have protected the entire right wing and, incidentally, the square, Q4, was absolutely a matter of course.

(j)   But Marshall likewise plunges unnecessarily into adventure, instead of making secure his advantage in material in simple fashion through 14...Kt—B5; 15 Kt—B3, Q—Q4; 16 KR—K, P—B3, etc.   The attempt to get the Rook over to the other side of the board against the weakly protected White King is ingenious, to be sure, but, with correct play, should make victory somewhat questionable.

(k)   At any rate, more consistent than the passive defensive move of 15 QR—Kt, after which White would not have threatened even to capture the QRP, because the opponent, by means of R—R, would in turn have gained the RP.

(l)   Now White must take the RP if he wants to justify his last move and Black, by a second sacrifice, obtains an attack which appears very dangerous.

(m)   The reason for the preceding maneuvers of the Rook by means of which Black is assured of at least an immediate draw.

(n)   With correct intuition, White takes the Pawn in this manner, for 18 PxP, R—Kt3!; 19 P—Kt3, P—KB5; 20 Q—Q2, P—KR4, etc., would have exposed him to an even greater danger than the continuation in the text.   Moreover, an attempt at simplification, 18 P—KB4, KtxBP; 19 Q—Q2, Kt—R6ch; 20 K—R, QxQ; 21 KtxQ, RxP; 22 Kt—B4, R—Kt5, would not have led to an entirely satisfactory result.

(o)   Now Black, because of the menace to his Knight, must adopt this somewhat less effective mode of attack.

(p)   Involving a whole series of threats, of which the most effective is 20...Q—R4; 21 P—KR4, Q—B6, etc.

(q)   This capture alone is the decisive mistake.   After 20 Q—B2, Black would have had the choice either of forcing a draw through 20...RxP; 21 KxR, Q—R4ch; 22 K—Kt, Q—B6; 23 PxKt, Q—Kt5ch, etc., or to continue with the attack, with somewhat doubtful results.   For instance, 20...Kt—R6ch; 21 K—R (if 21...P—B5; 22 Q—QB5, or 21... R—K; 22 QR—K, etc., with an easy defense).   Marshall plays the ending with great vigor.

(r)   If 23 P—KR3, P—B6ch; 24 K—B, RxP; 25 RxR, QxRch; 26 K—K, KtxQP; 27 R—B, KtxKt; 28 PxKt, Q—Kt7, with a winning position.

(s)   The winning move.   After 24...KtxKtP; 25 QxP, KtxRch; 26 RxKt, White could still have defended himself.

(t)   Or 26 PxKt, QxPch; 27 K—K2, Q—Kt7ch; 28 K—Q3, RxR; 29 RxR, QxPch, to be followed by QxR, with an easy win.

(u)   Threatening mate in two moves by 28...R—K7ch, etc.

Game 74   FIFTEENTH ROUND—QUEEN'S GAMBIT DECLINED

Maroczy	Ed. Lasker
White	Black
1 P—QB4	P—K3
2 Kt—KB3	P—Q4
3 P—Q4	Kt—KB3
4 Kt—B3	QKt—Q2
5 B—Kt5	B—Kt5
6 PxP(a)	PxP
7 P—K3	P—B3(b)
8 B—Q3	Castles
9 Castles	R—K
10 Q—B2	P—KR3(c)
11 B—R4	Kt—B
12 P—QR3	B—K2
13 P—QKt4(d)	P—KKt4(e)
14 B—Kt3	Kt—R4(f)
15 B—K5	B—K3(g)
16 P—Kt5	P—B3
17 B—Kt3	P—QB4(h)
18 PxP	KtxB
19 RPxKt	BxP
20 Kt—K2(i)	Q—K2
21 Q—Kt2	Kt—Q2

After 19...BxP

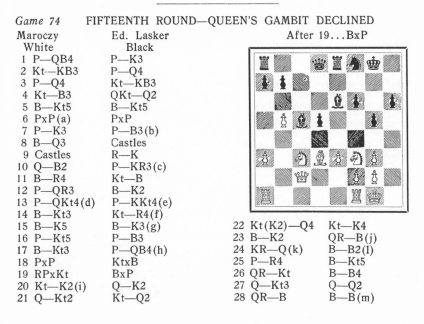

22 Kt(K2)—Q4	Kt—K4
23 B—K2	QR—B(j)
24 KR—Q(k)	B—B2(l)
25 P—R4	B—Kt5
26 QR—Kt	B—B4
27 Q—Kt3	Q—Q2
28 QR—B	B—B(m)

29	P—R5	RxR
30	RxR	R—B
31	R—B2	Kt—B5(n)
32	P—R6	PxP
33	PxP	Q—Q3
34	R—R2	Kt—K4(o)
35	Q—Q	Q—Kt3
36	R—R	R—Kt
37	Kt—B5	Q—Kt6
38	Q—KB(p)	R—Kt3(q)
39	Kt(B3)—Q4	Q—Kt7
40	Kt—Kt5	B—R4(r)
41	BxB(s)	RxKt
42	B—K2	R—Kt3
43	Q—Q(t)	Q—Kt6
44	QxQ	RxQ
45	R—Q	R—Kt7
46	K—B	Kt—B3
47	RxP	Kt—Kt5(u)
48	R—Q	K—R2
49	P—Kt4	Kt—B3
50	R—Q7ch	K—R
51	B—B3(v)	R—Kt8ch
52	K—K2	R—Kt7ch
53	K—Q	R—Kt8ch
54	K—Q2	R—Kt7ch
55	K—B3	R—Kt3
56	B—K2(w)	B—Kt5ch
57	K—B2	B—R6
58	R—Kt7(x)	B—B4
59	KtxP	Kt—K4
60	B—Q3(y)	KtxB
61	RxR	Kt—K8ch

After 55...R—Kt3

62	K—Q	BxR
63	KxKt	K—Kt2
64	Kt—B5ch	K—B2
65	K—Q2	K—K3
66	K—B3	K—Q4
67	K—Kt4	K—B3
68	Kt—K7ch	K—Q3
69	Kt—Kt8(z)	B—Q
70	K—Kt5	K—Q4
71	Kt—R6	B—Kt3
72	Kt—B5	B—Q
73	P—B3	B—Kt3
74	P—Kt3	B—Q
75	P—K4ch	K—K4
76	K—B6	B—Kt3
77	Kt—Q6	B—B7
78	Kt—B8	Resigns

(a) This move here is illogical to the extent that it unnecessarily grants an alternative to the opponent. First 6 P—K3, and only after 6...P—B4, 7 BPxP, etc., is probably the most prom sing way in which to meet the little used fifth move by Black.

(b) Black indeed utilized the opportunity to avoid the dubious variation beginning with 7...P—B4. Thereupon could have been ·played effectively 8 B—Q3, P—B5; 9 B—B2, Q—R4; 10 Castles, for instance: 10...BxKt; 11 PxB, QxBP; 12 Kt—K5, Castles; 13 KtxKt, KtxKt; 14 Q—Kt, and White, on account of the threat of B—K7—Kt4, would recover his pawn with a promising game.

(c) This move was not necessary and could have been replaced to advantage with the immediate 10...Kt—B.

(d) This interesting advance, in a similar position, was recommended by Maroczy in the Third Karlsbad Congress book. If there is indeed an advantage for White in this it is questionable, because the possible weaknesses of Black on the Queen's side would be balanced in many cases by the harmonious co-ordination of the pieces on the file opened there. In the present game White's play is crowned with complete success only because Black unnecessarily compromised his King's wing and thereby hindered the mobility of his pieces.

(e) Neither useful nor pleasant. The most plausible would have been at once 13 ...B—K3; but still better would have been 13...P—QR3 to make more difficult P—Kt5, so as to render that move possible in the course of the game only in conjunction with the opening of the new file. The hole at QKt3, as experience has shown (similar to the variation frequently adopted by Rubinstein: 1 P—Q4, P—Q4; 2 P—QB4, P—K3; 3 Kt—QB3, P—QR3, etc.), would have been negligible. In any event Black's defensive position would have been still sounder, had he not played 10...P—KR3.

(f) In order at least to rid himself of the hostile QB, but that piece was hardly worth all this effort.

(g) More in order at any rate would have been at once 15...P—B3 (16 B—Kt6?, KtxB; 17 QxKtch, Kt—Kt2; 18 B—Kt3, B—B4; 19 QxRP, K—B2), as, after the text-move, white could prevent the exchange of his Bishop by means of 16 P—R3.

(h) Thereupon the squares, Q4 and KB5, became accessible to the white pieces and White should now have had an easy game. More to the point would have been 17... KtxB; 18 RPxKt, Q—R4 (19 PxP, QR—B!; 20 B—Kt6, KR—Q, etc.).

(i) The beginning of complicated maneuvers which in the end deprive White of all his advantage. The most obvious and best plan would have been to accentuate the weakness of Black's QP just isolated. To that end 20 B—B5! at once would have been proper in order either to exchange the protecting Bishop or to force his retreat, whereby the Rooks would have been deprived of QB square, for instance; I.—20...R—QB; 21 BxB ch, RxB; 22 Q—Kt3; or II.—20...B—B2; 21 KR—Q, B—QKt3; 22 Q—Q3, etc., with an easily winning continuation. Strangely enough, White in the course of the game utterly disregards the weakness of Q5.

(j) Insufficient would have been 23...Kt—B5, on account of 24 BxKt, PxB; 25 KtxB, QxKt; 26 Q—B2, followed by Kt—Q2, winning a pawn.

(k) Again a favorable chance to simplify the game by means of 24 KtxB, QxKt; 25 KR—Q, followed by Kt—Q4, etc., is not utilized.

(l) Retention of this Bishop makes a win much harder for the opponent.

(m) Black has made the most of his opponent's incorrect play and obtained a good waiting position. The next attempt of White to win by establishing a sentinel at QR6 is subtly conceived, to be sure, but could have been parried without any difficulty.

(n) Black apparently hopes to gain an advantage, otherwise 31...RxR; 32 QxR, Kt—B5, etc., would have been simpler.

(o) Neither necessary, nor, on the other hand, harmful. In reply to 34...R—Kt, White could have replied with 35 Q—B2, Kt—R6; 36 Q—B6!, etc.

(p) In the subsequent middle-game play White should not have attained his end. A small chance still offered in 38 QxQ, RxQ; 39 KtxKt!, PxKt; 40 R—QB, B—K3; 41 P—Kt4, threatening R—B7, etc.

(q) The decisive blunder, as White now forces the exchange of the B on KB2. After 38...Q—Kt3, everything would have been protected with no win for White in sight.

(r) After 40...Kt—B3, White would gain the advantage by means of 41 Kt (B5)—Q4, B—B4; 42 KtxKt, RxKt; 43 R—B!, B—K; 44 B—B3, Q—K4; 45 Q—Q3, etc.

(s) In reply to 41 P—B3, Black could have answered with 41...Kt—B3, etc., inasmuch as the foregoing variation was no longer to be feared on account of the unprotected KP.

(t) After this the QP cannot be saved, as, after 43...R—Q, White would have won easily by means of R—Kt7, etc.

(u) Likewise after 47...R—Kt8ch; 48 R—Q, RxRch; 49 BxR, Kt—Kt5; 50 B—Kt3ch, K—R2; 51 B—B4, the ending eventually would have been lost, chiefly because of the imprisoning of the black King in the corner. With the Rooks, of course, White would have had a still easier task.

(v) As Maroczy himself correctly stated, 51 P—Kt3, etc., would have been considerably simpler.

(w) Needlessly prolonging the struggle. With the simple 56 R—QB7, B—Kt5ch!; 57 K—B2, Kt—Kt!; 58 KtxP, KtxP; 59 RxP, threatening 60 B—K4 or Q5, White would have increased his material superiority without surrendering the pressure, thereby making further resistance useless.

(x) In the face of the threat of 58...R—Kt7ch, there now remains nothing better than the exchange of Rooks.

(y) In order to rid himself of the scepter of Bishops on squares of different colors.

(z) After Kt—B8ch and KtxB (?), the pawn ending would result in a draw.

Game 75   FIFTEENTH ROUND—DUTCH DEFENSE

Bogoljubow	Tartakower
White	Black
1 P—Q4	P—KB4
2 P—KKt3	P—K3
3 B—Kt2	Kt—KB3
4 P—QB4(a)	P—Q4(b)
5 Kt—KB3	P—B3
6 Castles	B—Q3
7 Kt—B3	QKt—Q2(c)
8 Q—B2	Castles(d)
9 PxP	BPxP
10 Kt—QKt5	B—Kt
11 B—B4	BxB
12 PxB	Kt—Kt3(e)
13 Kt—B7	R—Kt
14 Kt—KKt5(f)	Q—Q3
15 Q—B5	R—Q(g)
16 QxQ	RxQ
17 Kt—Kt5	R—Q
18 P—QR4(h)	P—KR3(i)
19 Kt—KB3	B—Q2
20 Kt—K5	P—QR3
21 Kt—QB3	KR—QB(j)
22 KR—QB	BxP(k)

35 BPxKt	Kt—Kt4
36 BxKt	PxB
37 R—B7ch	K—B
38 P—Kt4(r)	R—R
39 R—B6(s)	K—B2
40 RxKtP	P—B5(t)

After 40 RxKtP

41 R—Kt7ch(u)	K—B(v)
42 PxP	R—R8ch
43 K—Kt2	R—Q8
44 RxQKtP	RxP
45 K—Kt3	P—KR4
46 R—Kt7	P—KKt3(w)
47 P—Kt5	R—Kt5
48 P—Kt6	R—Kt6ch
49 P—B3	R—Kt5
50 R—Kt8ch	K—K2(x)
51 P—Kt7	K—Q2
52 R—Kt8	RxKtP
53 R—Kt7ch(y)	K—B3
54 RxP	K—B4(z)

After 22 KR—QB

After 54 RxP

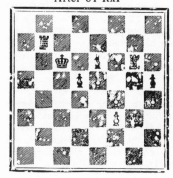

23 KtxB	RxRch
24 RxR	KtxKt
25 P—Kt3	Kt—Kt3
26 R—B7	Kt—B(1)
27 Kt—Q3	Kt—Q3(m)
28 P—K3	P—QKt3(n)
29 R—B6	Kt(B3)—K
30 B—B3(o)	K—B2
31 B—R5ch	K—K2
32 P—R4(p)	Kt—B3
33 B—K2(q)	Kt—Q2
34 Kt—K5	KtxKt

55	RxP	P—Q5
56	P—B5	R—Q2
57	K—B2	K—Q4
58	R—K8	R—QR2
59	P—B6	R—KB2
60	R—K7	R—B

61	P—B7	P—Q6
62	K—K3	K—B5
63	P—K6	R—Q
64	R—Q7	RxR
65	PxR	Resigns

(a) It is not clear why White makes possible the exchange of Black's KB. He might just as well have played 4 KKt—B3, followed by Castles, and save P—QB4 in readiness for the eventful P—Q4.

(b) This variation has been tried out repeatedly by Dr. Tartakower with intermittent success. Its sole advantage is that it renders Black's position difficult of access; its disadvantages, on the other hand (condemning the QB to passivity and weakening the black squares in a manner hardly to be remedied), are much more weighty. More alluring appears to be 4...B—Kt5ch; 5 B—Q2, BxBch; 6 QxB, Kt—B3, followed by Castles and, eventually, P—Q4 and B—Q2, etc.

(c) After 7...PxP, the Pawn is immediately regained by means of 8 Kt—Q2.

(d) But, if now 8...PxP, then 9 P—K4, PxP; 10 KtxP, KtxKt; 11 QxKt, Kt—B3; 12 Q—K2, followed by Kt—K5, etc. After the text-move, White obtains permanent pressure upon the QB file.

(e) Since castling, Black has made none but forced moves.

(f) Probably holding out better prospects than the obvious move of 14 Kt—K5, whereupon Black, with 14...B—Q2, would have threatened to win a piece. The white Queen is not posted to advantage on B2 and for that reason White endeavors to bring about an exchange in order to occupy without hindrance the square, K5.

(g) If 15...QxBP, White would win a clear Rook by means of 16 QxRch, etc.

(h) Of course not 18 KtxRP, on account of 18...B—Q2, etc.

(i) Not at once 18...B—Q2, because of 19 Kt—B7, etc.

(j) Black has extricated himself nicely and now threatens, by means of 22...Kt—B5, to assume the initiative. White's next move parries this threat, but permits further simplification which should soon dissolve the game into a draw.

(k) Because 22...Kt—B5 will not do at this stage, on account of 23 KtxB, KtxKt; 24 KtxQP, etc., Black has indeed no reason to invite additional complications through 22...R—B2; 23 P—R5, Kt—B5; 24 KtxB, RxKt; 25 Kt—R4, etc. Therefore, without perturbation he accepts the proffered Pawn, figuring that the subsequent entrance of the Rook to the seventh rank will yield White no better than a draw.

(l) The correct way of releasing the Rook from the task of guarding the KtP.

(m) Threatening 28...Kt—Kt4.

(n) Hereupon the white Rook gains the square, B6, and Black's position becomes highly critical. He would have had a simple draw by playing 28...R—QB; 29 RxR (R—K7, R—K), KtxR; 30 Kt—B5, Kt—Q3; 31 KtxKP, K—B2; 32 Kt—B7, Kt(Q3)—K5; or 32 Kt—B5, P—R4, etc.

(o) Threatening to win a Pawn with 31 B—R5.

(p) Bogoljubow handles this part of the game very cleverly. The text-move prevents P—Kt4 and prepares for the crippling of Black's King's side by means of P—R5.

(q) Threatening 34 Kt—K5, with a winning position; for instance: 33...P—R4; 34 Kt—K5, R—Kt2; 35 B—R6, etc. Consequently, the following moves of Black are forced.

(r) Necessary, for otherwise Black saves himself by advancing both QKt Pawns, thereby nullifying a double attack on the Kt and K pawns.

(s) After 39 R—Kt7, P—B5; 40 RxQKtP, K—B2, the play, except for transposition of moves, would be identical.

(t) The only move, but by no means such a poor alternative.

(u) A false alarm, yet not without profit. The best continuation, however, was immediately 41 PxP, R—R8ch; 42 K—Kt2, R—Q8; 43 RxKtP, RxQP; 44 K—Kt3, K—Kt3; 45 R—Kt7 (K—B4, P—B3!), etc., after which the Pawn would decide in the long run. Uncertain, on the other hand, would have been 41 P—R5, R—R8ch; 42 K—Kt2, PxP; 43 PxP, R—R7ch, and Black would win either the KP or KRP.

(v) As a matter of course, 41...K—Kt3 was essential. Black evidently was afraid of 42 P—R5ch, yet this very line of play, after 42...K—B4; 43 R—B7ch, K—K5; 44 RxPch, K—Q6, would have given him splendid chances, for instance: 45 R—B7, K—B5; 46 RxP, KxP; 47 R—Kt6 (or 47 R—K7, R—R3), R—K!, and the black KtP becomes very powerful. White, therefore, after 41 K—Kt3, would have done best by selecting the variation, 42 PxP, R—R8ch; 43 K—Kt2, R—Q8; 44 RxKtP, RxQP; 45 K—Kt3, after which, however, he would have had a full "tempo" less than with the move mentioned in the other variation. This circumstance would have tended to make the attainment of victory much more difficult. After the ultra-careful retreat (of the King), the not too difficult end-game is wound up by Bogoljubow in irreproachable fashion.

(w) This temporary barricade makes White's KtP harmless, because the hostile King cannot approach him from any side. White, however, exchanges that Pawn for the KP or KtP and thereupon wins with his center Pawns.

(x) Likewise inadequate would have been 50...K—Kt2; 51 P—Kt7, K—R2 (or R—Kt7; 52 P—B5, etc); 52 R—K8, RxKtP; 53 RxKP, K—Kt2 (R—Q2, 54 R—Q6); 54 R—Q6, R—Kt4; 55 P—B5, etc.

(y) The gain of a "tempo" which decides.

(z) The KP cannot be saved, for instance: 54...K—Q2; 55 P—B5! (after 55 R—Kt7ch, followed by exchange of Rooks, the pawn-ending would end in a draw), PxP; 56 P—K6ch, K—Q3 (B3); 57 P—K7ch, K—Q2; 58 R—Kt8!, P—B5ch; 59 K—R3, and wins. An instructive variation, which enhances considerably the total merit of this game (it was honored with a special prize).

SIXTEENTH ROUND

In Reti Dr. Lasker was called upon to face not alone the sole conqueror of Capablanca, but likewise one of the rivals for high honors who at the time was pressing him most closely. Reti at that stage of the play had five points in his debit column, in which respect Dr. Lasker had one and a half games the better of it. It was small wonder then that the gallery expected much of their encounter, and in this they were not disappointed.

Naturally, it was a Reti opening, since the godfather of the debut was on the white side. Dr. Lasker seemed to be very much at home, even if the singular maneuvering of the adversary behind the lines gave him occasion to arch his eyebrows. As he realized that Dr. Lasker had the position well in hand and was gradually tightening the pressure upon the center, Reti decided upon giving up the exchange in return for a Pawn. Right after that, however, he missed a chance to win a second Pawn, the capture of which would have made the outcome indeed problematical. Thereafter Dr. Lasker was at his best, made every move tell and turned the advantage of the exchange splendidly to account.

While Dr. Lasker was thus forging ahead, Marshall held Capablanca in check by drawing a Queen's Gambit Declined, in which the champion did not quite make the most of the opening. Marshall's subsequent good play saw him safely through the middle game. In an even Queen and Rook ending the United States champion went so far as to seek for a win, but Capablanca was not to be caught napping.

Alekhine vs. Ed. Lasker was a most interesting Indian Defense, in which Alekhine forced matters on the Queen's wing, the while Lasker was busy on the King's side. This time Alekhine did not find the best method of keeping up the pressure and then went astray trying to gain a definite advantage. Lasker's failure to profit thereby brought about an ending replete with possibilities. Although both disregarded risks in playing for a win, this was eventually drawn.

After bringing about an exchange of Queens which he desired in a Queen's Gambit Declined, wherein he had the white side, Bogoljubow reached an ending with Yates which held forth every promise of success. As a penalty for a lack of precision the tables were turned and the Briton energetically took hold of the situation. The latter appeared actually to have a winning position at his disposal when he committed himself to an inviting advance of his passed Pawn. The white King, however, came over to the rescue just in the nick of time. After that it was a losing fight for Yates.

Dr. Tartakower also resorted to a Reti Opening, which he treated in a somewhat novel manner, so much so that Janowski, adversely affected apparently, lost his bearings. After establishing a very strong position, Dr. Tartakower sacrificed the exchange, as a result of which he completely overran the hostile terrain, under-developed as it was.

At the close of the round, Dr. Lasker, with $10\frac{1}{2}$—$3\frac{1}{2}$, was in comfortable circumstances, his nearest neighbors being Capablanca, 10—5; Alekhine, 9—6; Reti, 8—6; Bogoljubow, 8—7; and Marshall, $7\frac{1}{2}$—$6\frac{1}{2}$.

The white pieces gained another point, with the totals at $45\frac{1}{2}$—$34\frac{1}{2}$.

Game 76   SIXTEENTH ROUND—RETI'S OPENING

White	Dr. Lasker		
Reti	Black		
1 Kt—KB3	P—Q4	23 Kt—Q4	Q—Q2
2 P—B4	P—QB3(a)	24 K—R2(o)	P—R4(p)
3 P—QKt3(b)	B—B4(c)	25 Q—R(q)	P—R5
4 P—Kt3	Kt—B3	26 KtxP(r)	PxPch
5 B—KKt2	QKt—Q2(d)	27 PxP	KtxKt
6 B—Kt2	P—K3	28 BxKt	B—B3(s)
7 Castles	B—Q3	29 BxP	R—B4
8 P—Q3	Castles	30 B—R6(t)	B—Kt3
9 QKt—Q2	P—K4(e)	31 Q—Kt7	Q—Q(u)
10 PxP	PxP	32 P—QKt4(v)	R—B2
11 R—B	Q—K2	33 Q—Kt6	R—Q2(w)
12 R—B2(f)	P—QR4(g)		
13 P—QR4	P—R3(h)		
14 Q—R	KR—K		
15 KR—B	B—R2		
16 Kt—B(i)	Kt—B4(j)		
17 RxKt(k)	BxR		
18 KtxP	QR—B		
19 Kt—K3	Q—K3		
20 P—R3(l)	B—Q3(m)		
21 RxR	RxR		

After 21...RxR

22 Kt—B3(n)   B—K2

After 33 Q—Kt6

34 QxQ	RxQ
35 P—K3	PxP
36 K—Kt2(x)	BxKt
37 PxB(y)	B—B4
38 B—Kt7	B—K3(z)
39 K—B3	B—Kt6
40 B—B6	R—Q3
41 B—Kt5	R—B3ch
42 K—K3	R—K3ch
43 K—B4(aa)	R—K7
44 B—B	R—B7
45 B—K3	B—Q4
Resigns	

(a) If, as we surmise, this should be the best reply to Reti's second move of P—B4, then at all events that move by White has the merit of maneuvering Black into a variation of the Queen's gambit hitherto not considered as fully satisfactory. (1 P—Q4, P—Q4; 2 P—QB4, P—QB3; 3 Kt—KB3, etc.).

(b) Reti, however, makes no use of this possibility, doubtless in the hope that his whole system may achieve glorious success even against the best defense. This praiseworthy aim lends the game important theoretical interest.

(c) With this move Dr. Lasker as second player applies the London system of development, which, with colors transposed, has several times stood the test against the double fianchetto. There is indeed no reason for Black to cut off the QB with P—K3, as, for instance, Yates and Bogoljubow have done in the tournament.

(d) More cautious would have been first 5...P—K3, as White might assure himself of a positional advantage, even if microscopical, by means of, 6 PxP!, PxP; 7 B—Kt2, followed by Kt—B3, etc., (compare the game, Dr. Lasker vs. Alekhine, wherein, with colors transposed, this method was adopted successfully).

(e)   Now a Pawn formation, similar to that in the game between Reti and Yates, is reached, which is the more favorable for Black since his QB has already been developed.

(f)   Reti follows out his tried plan of development but, after a few moves, is forced to play for a liberating sacrifice which at the best will yield drawing chances. Rather a dubious outcome for the "opening of the future!"

(g)   To be sure this cedes to the opponent a square, QKt5, otherwise difficult of access, but, on the other hand, weakens in return not only the corresponding square of QKt4, but also chiefly White's QKt Pawn. All in all a very good transaction.

(h)   Preparing for the retreat of the Bishop later on and strengthening thereby the eventual threat of P—K5, inasmuch as White would not then attack the Bishop with Kt—Q4.

(i)   A defensive move against the now really serious threat of P—K5—K6, etc.

(j)   By means of 16...P—K5; 17 PxP, PxP; 18 Kt—Q4, P—K6; 19 KtxP, BxR; 20 RxB, etc., the exchange could have been won, but thereupon the two united white Bishops would have acquired altogether too much power.   Black, therefore, prefers rightly to put on additional pressure.

(k)   With correct position judgment White seeks his salvation in this sacrifice by which he can dispose of one of Black's center pawns, 17 Q—R2, for instance, would have been apparently less profitable on account of 17...Kt—R3.

(l)   White gets no adequate compensation for the exchange and for the present must be content to wait.   The harmless text-move nevertheless has a distinct object which, strangely enough, is overlooked by Dr. Lasker.

(m)   A mistake which might have had unpleasant consequences and in place of which might best have been played 20...P—QKt3 in order to safeguard the Queen's wing as well as the position of the Bishop.   After 21 P—Q4, he would still have had sufficient counter-play by occupying the square, K5, and in the event of other moves a plan leading eventually to simplification could have been undertaken with 21...P—Q5; 22 Kt—B4, Kt—Q2, etc., after which his material superiority would finally have been decisive.   Now, however, something quite different should happen.

(n)   White is not aware that Dame Fortune smiles at him.   By means of the obvious 22 Kt(K5)—Kt4, KtxKt; 23 PxKt, he could have won a second pawn for the exchange and thereby have avoided anyway the danger of loss.   After 23...B—B (23... BxKtP; 24 BxQP, etc.); 24 BxP, Q—Q2; 25 KB—B3, it would have been for Black, possibly through 25...P—QKt4, to strive for a difficult draw.   After the not easily understood text-move, Black holds fast until the end.

(o)   The beginning of an artificial maneuver, the insufficiency of which is demonstrated by Dr. Lasker with marvelous clearness and precision.   Better drawing chances were offered by 24 Kt—Kt5, which, on account of the threat of B—Q4, followed by Kt—B3, etc., would have forced Black, after B—KB4—K3, to permit the exchange of that Bishop, strengthening thereby the power of the hostile pair of Bishops.

(p)   By this advance and the subsequent exchange the White King is deprived of one of his protecting pawns, a fact which will be of decisive importance in connection with the attack by the Rook later on.   It is now evident that the King was much safer on KKt and should have remained there.

(q)   Even for Reti himself this is almost too "original."   In any event this move would have been ineffective if Black had been merely content to protect his pawn simply by means of 25...R—Q.   His next move, however, is much more energetic and to the point.

(r)   The only chance.   After 26 BxP, KtxB; 27 QxKt (or 27 KtxKt, B—QB4!, etc.), QxQ; 28 KtxQ, B—QB4; 29 Kt—Kt5, B—B4, the ending could not have been held together long for White on account of the weakness of his Queen's wing.

(s)   Because of this unpleasant pin, White, notwithstanding his subsequent ingenious attempts, must perish eventually.

(t)   Threatening 31 Q—R8ch, etc.

(u)   For the success of the following maneuver the white Queen must be deprived of the possibility of gaining a tempo by means of a check on the eighth row (as, for instance, would have been the case with 31...Q—Q3).

(v)   32 P—K3 would not do on account of 32...BxKt; 33 BxB, R—B7ch; 34 K—R, Q—Q3, etc.

(w)   The point of the winding maneuver.   White, for instance, after 34 QxQch, RxQ, may not play 35 Kt—B6, as he would lose a Bishop after 35...R—Q3; 36 BxB, RxKt. For that reason he must allow his opponent a strong passed pawn which brings about a decision in a few moves.

(x) A trifle better would have been 36 B—B4, but even then Black would have won eventually after 36...R—R; 37 B—Kt5, B—B4, followed by the transfer of this Bishop to QKt6.

(y) Forced, as, after 37 BxB, Black would have won at once with 37...RxB; 38 PxR, P—Kt6; 39 B—B4, P—Kt7; 40 B—R2, BxP, etc.

(z) In order to be able to meet 39 P—R5 with 39...B—Q4ch, etc.

(aa) There is no satisfactory move left, for, if 43 K—B3, then 43...B—Q8ch, etc.; and if 43 K—Q2, then 43...R—KKt3; 44 P—Kt4, R—KR3, winning a pawn.

Game 77 SIXTEENTH ROUND—QUEEN'S GAMBIT DECLINED

	Capablanca	Marshall
	White	Black

After 25 QxP

	White	Black
1	P—Q4	P—Q4
2	Kt—KB3	P—K3
3	P—B4	Kt—KB3
4	Kt—B3	B—Kt5 (a)
5	B—Kt5	P—QB4
6	BxKt (b)	QxB
7	PxQP	KPxP
8	P—K3	Kt—B3 (c)
9	B—Kt5	Castles
10	Castles	BxKt
11	PxB	B—Kt5 (d)
12	R—Kt	QR—B
13	PxP (e)	QxP
14	QxP	KR—Q
15	Q—K4	BxKt
16	QxB	QxBP
17	BxKt	PxB
18	R—Kt7	R—KB
19	Q—B4 (f)	Q—QR4
20	P—QR4	P—QB4
21	Q—B4	R—Kt
22	R—Kt5 (g)	RxR
23	PxR	R—Kt
24	R—Q	P—KR3
25	QxP	P—R3 (h)
26	Q—R7	R—Q
27	R—KB	QxP
28	P—Kt3	Q—B3
29	R—R	R—Q3
30	P—R4	R—B3

31	Q—Kt8ch	K—R2
32	Q—Ktch	P—Kt3
33	P—R5	Q—KB6
34	PxPch	PxP
35	Q—B2	P—KR4
36	R—R4 (i)	R—B3
37	R—QB4	R—Q3 (j)
38	R—Q4	RxR
39	PxR	P—R4
40	K—B	Q—Q4
41	Q—B7ch	K—Kt
42	Q—Kt6	K—B2
43	Q—R7ch	K—B3
44	Q—Kt8	Q—R8ch
45	K—K2	Q—K5ch
46	K—B	Q—R8ch
		Drawn

(a) This method of developing the Bishop has hitherto been attempted usually after the moves 4...QKt—Q2; 5 B—Kt5. At this stage White could profitably reply with 5 Q—R4ch, Kt—B3; 6 P—K3. For, until Black manages to make the liberating move of P—K4 in this variation, White can secure a lead in his development. For instance, 6...Castles; 7 B—Q2, R—K; 8 B—Q3, B—Q2; 9 Q—B2, and Black's game would be permanently hampered by the blocking of the QBP.

(b) This game clearly demonstrates that the action against the isolated QP bears little fruit. 6 P—K3 at once was in order, as the variation, 6...Q—R4; 7 BxKt, BxKtch; 8 PxB, QxPch; 9 Kt—Q2, PxB; 10 BPxP, followed by R—B, need not be feared at all. In the event of other moves White, at a favorable moment, could always have brought about the exchange at KB6.

(c) Threatening an early simplification through several exchanges on Q4.

(d) As may be seen, Black, after his opponent's sixth move, is permitted unlabored and easy deployment of his pieces. Even now White is not able to enforce the favorable exchange on Q4, as he is obliged to speculate on the eventuality of P—B5. However, after he has decided to cut loose for himself on the 13th move, the game is rapidly dissolved into an ending which must result in a draw.

(e) Likewise without winning prospects would have been 13 BxKt, QxB; 14 Kt—K5, BxQ; 15 KtxQ, RxKt; 16 KRxB, PxP; 17 RxQP, P—QKt3, etc.

(f) Even with 19 P—Kt3, Q—R4 or R6; 20 Q—K2, followed by KR—Kt, whereby the position of the Rook on the seventh rank could be sustained a while longer, nothing could be gained in the long run through a reduction of material.

(g) Manifestly it will not do to guard by means of 22 KR—Kt, because of the ultimate mate on K.

(h) Marshall plays with great care. After 25...RxP; 26 Q—B8ch, K—R2; 27 Q—Q7, P—B3; 28 P—KR4, he might still have found himself in an uncomfortable situation. With the text-move he is enabled to seize for a while the initiative, however harmless. The game might well have been given up as a draw.

(i) After this, Black can no longer avoid the exchange of Rooks.

(j) A last hope. If 38 R—B7ch, K—R3, winning.

Game 78 SIXTEENTH ROUND—INDIAN DEFENSE (FOUR-PAWN GAME)

Alekhine	Ed. Lasker
White	Black
1 P—QB4	Kt—KB3
2 P—Q4	P—KKt3
3 Kt—QB3	B—Kt2(a)
4 P—K4	P—Q3
5 P—B4	Castles
6 Kt—B3	P—K4(b)
7 BPxP	PxP
8 P—Q5	QKt—Q2(c)
9 B—Q3(d)	Kt—B4
10 B—B2	P—QR4
11 Castles	Q—Q3(e)
12 Q—K(f)	B—Q2
13 Q—R4	QR—K(g)
14 K—R(h)	P—KR4(i)
15 P—QKt3	Kt—R2
16 P—QR3	P—B4
17 P—QKt4	Kt—R3(j)

18 P—B5(k)	Q—KB3
19 QxQ(l)	KtxQ
20 P—B6(m)	KtPxP
21 QPxP	BxP(n)
22 P—Kt5(o)	KtxKP
23 KtxKt(p)	PxKt(q)
24 PxB	PxKt
25 B—K4(r)	PxPch
26 KxP	RxR
27 KxR	K—R2(s)
28 B—K3	B—B(t)
29 R—Q(u)	BxP(v)
30 R—Q5(w)	B—Kt5(x)
31 R—Q7ch	K—R(y)
32 B—Kt5(z)	R—Bch(aa)
33 K—K2	P—QR5(bb)

After 17...Kt—R3

After 33...P—QR5

34 BxP(cc)	Kt—B4(dd)
35 R—K7	P—R6
36 RxBP(ee)	Kt—K3

37 R—R7ch	K—Kt	45 K—K2	R—B7ch
38 B—B	P—R7(ff)	46 K—K	RxP(ii)
39 R—QR7	Kt—Q5ch	47 B—K4	Kt—Q5
40 K—Q3	R—B6ch	48 BxKt	B—Kt5ch
41 K—K4(gg)	R—B8	49 K—B	RxR
42 B—Kt2	KtxP	50 B—Q5ch	K—B
43 RxP	R—B5ch	51 BxR	PxB
44 K—K3(hh)	B—B4ch	52 B—Kt(jj)	K—Kt2
		53 K—Kt2	Drawn

(a) Black, by means of 3...P—Q4, could have led up to the Gruenfeld variation, so rich in possibilities, but prefers to be led into a line of play twice adopted by the first player in this tournament (against Marshall and Yates), as he desires to try out an interesting novelty.

(b) Here it is. White cannot very well accept the offered Pawn sacrifice, for instance: 7 BPxP, QPxP; 8 KtxP (8 PxP?, QxQch; 9 KxQ, Kt—Kt5; 10 Kt—Q5, Kt—R3, etc.), P—B4!, 9 P—Q5, KtxKP, etc., with advantage for Black. For that reason he is forced to clear the position in the center and afford his opponent an opportunity thereby to face the situation at once.

(c) It was necessary to prevent the move of P—B5. In spite of the improvement, Black has not an easy time as on the one hand he is forced to watch the square, QB4, and on the other hand to consider the move of P—KB4, which is here his only counterchance. White, on the contrary, has much greater freedom of action and, moreover, can prepare an offensive in the center as well as on the King's wing.

(d) Of course not B—K3, on account of 9...Kt—Kt5, followed by P—KB4.

(e) Quite correct, as the move of 12 Kt—Kt5 would have meant no more than a cast into the water after 12...Q—K2.

(f) This Queen maneuver so timely in this position forces in the first place—because of the necessity for the moment of bringing additional protection to K2—a transfer of Black's Rook from the QR file, thereby facilitating the advance of the white Pawns on the Queen's side. Aside from this, Black, in need of freedom, would soon be forced to make the weakening move of P—KR4 in order finally to make the attempt at liberation by means of P—KB4. Because of Black's excellent, but still not quite adequate defense, the game is theoretically noteworthy.

(g) Necessary in order to be able to withdraw the Knight after B—Kt5.

(h) Unsatisfactory would have been 14 B—R6, Kt—R4!; 15 BxB, KxB, etc.; likewise after 14 B—Kt5, Black would have had a sufficient defense with 14...Kt—R4, for instance: 15 P—KKt4, Kt—B5; 16 BxKt, PxB; 17 P—K5, Q—Kt3! (not BxKP, on account of 18 Kt—Kt5), and White must lose an important tempo by K—R. For that reason the King's move is made at once, the more so as it is necessary as a preparation for the displacement of the Knight on B5 (for instance: after P—QKt3, the move, P—R3, cannot be made on account of KtxB, followed by Q—Kt3ch and QxB, etc.

(i) Clearly preparing for Kt—R2, followed by P—KB4. White, however, has just time to storm the enemy's ramparts on the other side of the board.

(j) Black continues to select the best move. 17...PxKtP; 18 PxKtP, Kt—R3; 19 B—R3, etc., as well as 17...KtxKP; 18 KtxKt, PxKt; 19 BxP, B—B4; 20 B—K3!, B—KB3; 21 Q—K, etc., would have been less efficient than the text-move.

(k) Because of this haste White surrenders all of his positional advantage and, as it frequently happens in complicated situations, it is the opponent who gets the initiative. Correct would have been first 18 R—QKt! in order, after protecting the QKtP (18...PxKtP; 19 PxKtP; KtxP?; 20 B—R3) to hold all threats in abeyance. In reply to 18 Q—KB3, he could very well have answered with 19 Q—B2 (intending later on P—Kt5 or Q—K2). In any event the game would have taken a normal course in accord with the characteristic tendency of the opening selected. The text-move, on the other hand, takes it along quite a thorny path.

(l) The exchange of Queens, which is not at all desirable for White, cannot now very well be avoided, as the QKtP hangs and 19 B—Kt5 is forbidden on account of 19...KtxB; 20 KtxKt, B—R3, etc.

(m) A psychological effect of the omission on the 18th move. Notwithstanding this White strives to gain something and in the attempt out-combines himself in most elementary fashion. The position was not any too pleasant, but not at all untenable. The best perhaps would have been 20 R—QKt, for instance: 20...PxKtP; 21 PxKtP, KtxKP; 22 BxKt, PxB; 23 KtxP, B—B4; 24 KR—K, R—Q; 25 P—Q6, PxQP; 26 PxQP, BxKt; 27 RxB, RxOP; 28 B—Kt2, etc., with drawing chances.

(n) By means of this simple counter combination, Black obtains a definite winning position.

(o) Even 22 PxBP would have been insufficient, for instance: 22...P—K5; 23 Kt—Q4, Kt—Kt5; 24 KtxB, BxKt; 25 R—QKt, RxP; 26 RxR, PxR; 27 KtxRP, P—K6, and wins.

(p) If 23 BxKt, PxB; 24 Kt—Q2, P—K6; 25 RxRch, RxR; 26 Kt—KB3, P—K5, etc.

(q) Hereupon White, notwithstanding his material inferiority and thanks to his two Bishops, obtains a fairly good game. Correct would have 23...BxP!; 24 R—K (or 24 Kt (K4)—Q2, BxR, followed by P—K5, etc), PxKt; 25 BxKP, Kt—B4; 26 B—Q5ch, K—R; 27 Kt—Kt5, P—K5; 28 QR—Kt, B—Q6, etc., with an easy win.

(r) Encouraged by the lucky accident, White overlooks the simple equalizing variation of 25 BxP, PxPch (or P—K5; 26 BxR, BxR; 27 BxRP, etc.); 26 KxP, RxR; 27 KxR, R—KBch; 28 K—K2, Kt—B4; 29 B—K3, Kt—K3; 30 BxRP, Kt—B5ch, and induces his opponent thereby to play also for a win. Consequently the game once more assumes a very lively character.

(s) In reply to 27...Kt—B4, White intended 28 B—Q5ch, K—R2; 29 B—K3, followed by R—OKt, etc.

(t) In order by all mean possible to get the Knight into play.

(u) By degrees White obtains a strong attacking position which fully balances his material losses.

(v) Black is obliged to sink his teeth into the sour apple, inasmuch as 30 R—Q5 would have been very strong against the defensive move of 29...B—Q3.

(w) The intention of this awkward move is to force the black Bishop to Kt5 before entering with the Rook at Q7, thereby depriving the Knight of a flight square. Soon, however, it becomes apparent that it would have been still better for White to leave the Bishop on R6, where he would have locked the advance of the QRP. In any event, it was difficult to figure out in advance the significance of these movements.

(x) Even after 30...B—Q3; 31 RxRP, Kt—Kt5; 32 B—Q2, White would have had a sure draw on account of the possibility of Bishops on squares of opposite colors.

(y) Serious risk of loss would have been involved in other moves, for instance: I.—31...R—K2; 32 B—Kt5 (the same reply obviously to 31...B—K2), R—Kt2; 33 B—B6, etc. II.—31...K—Kt; 32 B—Q5ch, K—R; 33 B—B7, R—KB (or R—K2; 34 B—Kt5) ; 34 B—R6, etc.

(z) Better than 32 BxKtP R—K3; 33 B—K4, P—QR5; 34 R—Q8ch, K—Kt2; 35 R—QR8, Kt—B4, etc., with an easy draw.

(aa) Mate in three moves through 33 B—B6ch was threatened.

(bb) In reply to the more tempting 33...Kt—B4, White had intended 34 BxP, Kt—K3; 35 P—R4! with some chances of a win, for instance: I.—35...Kt—B5ch; 36 BxKt, PxB; 37 RxP, P—B6ch; 38 K—B; or II.—35...KtxB; 36 PxKt and 37 B—B2, threatening 38 P—Kt6, etc. The text-move is bound up with an eventual sacrifice of the exchange.

(cc) Even with 34 B—R6 the win could not have been forced, for instance: 34...R—KKt; 35 B—Q5, P—R6!; 36 BxR, KxB; 37 B—B, P—R7; 38 B—Kt2, B—Q3, and Black in an event had nothing to fear. In reply to the text-move, on the contrary, he dare not advance his QRP, for instance: 34...P—R6; 35 B—R6!, P—R7; 36 B—Kt7ch, K—Kt; 37 BxKP, and wins.

(dd) The only salvation, after which White should have been content with the simplest drawing variation: 35 RxP, Kt—K3; 36 R—R7ch, K—Kt; 37 B—K3, R—QB!, etc. He believes, however, that he can still permit himself a desperate winning attempt and thereby drifts into dangerous situations.

(ee) A bitter pill to take, as, after 36 B—R6, Kt—R5!, and, after 36 B—QKt, Kt—K5!, etc., would have been decisive for Black.

(ff) In reply to 38...R—R, White would have saved himself by means of 39 R—QKt7!, P—R7; 40 B—B7ch, K—R; 41 B—Kt2, etc.

(gg) Likewise 41 B—K3, KtxP; 42 RxP, B—B4; 43 R—K2, etc., would have sufficed for a draw. White, however, is still hoping for a miracle (41..R—B6; 42 B—R6!, or 41...B—R6; 42 P—B7, etc.).

(hh) Simpler would have been 44 K—Q3.

(ii) Or 46...Kt—Kt5; 47 R—R5!, B—Kt3; 48 RxP, RxB; 49 RxP, and draws.

(jj) What can now sacrifice his Bishop for the QP, inasmuch as the King has settled himself in the all-important corner.

Game 79   SIXTEENTH ROUND—QUEEN'S GAMBIT DECLINED

Bogoljubow	Yates
White	Black
1 P—Q4	Kt—KB3
2 P—QB4	P—K3
3 Kt—KB3	P—Q4
4 Kt—B3	B—K2
5 B—Kt5	Castles
6 P—K3	QKt—Q2
7 R—B	P—QB3
8 Q—B2(a)	P—QR3
9 PxP(b)	KPxP
10 B—Q3	R—K
11 Castles	Kt—B
12 P—QR3(c)	Kt—Kt3
13 Kt—K5	Kt—Kt5(d)
14 BxB	QxB
15 KtxKt(Kt3)	RPxKt
16 P—KR3	Kt—R3(e)
17 Kt—K2	Q—R5
18 Q—B5	P—KKt4(f)
19 Q—Q6	P—Kt5(g)
20 P—KKt3	Q—K2(h)
21 QxQ	RxQ
22 P—KR4	B—Q2(i)
23 Kt—B4	P—KKt3
24 P—QKt4	B—B4(j)
25 P—QR4	BxB
26 KtxB	P—QR4(k)
27 P—Kt5	PxP
28 PxP	Kt—B4

34 P—Kt6	K—K3
35 R(B7)—B5	R—QR
36 R—B7(o)	RxR
37 PxR(p)	Kt—Q3(q)
38 P—KB3	P—R5
39 P—K4	P—R6
40 KtxP(r)	P—R7(s)

After 40 KtxP

41 R—R	KxKt
42 P—K5ch	K—K3
43 PxKt	K—Q2
44 K—B2(t)	P—QKt4
45 K—K	P—Kt5
46 K—Q2	KxP(u)
47 P—B8(Q)	RxQ
48 RxP	R—B3
49 R—R7	K—K3
50 R—QKt7	R—B6
51 K—K2	P—Kt6
52 P—Kt4	K—B3(v)
53 R—Kt6ch	K—B2
54 P—Kt5	K—Kt2(w)
55 P—Kt5	R—B7ch
56 K—Q3	R—KR7
57 RxKtP	RxP
58 R—Kt7ch	K—Kt
59 R—Q7	R—B5
60 K—K3	R—B4
61 P—B4	K—B
62 K—B3(x)	K—Kt
63 K—Kt4	K—B
64 R—QR7(y)	K—Kt
65 R—K7	R—KB
66 R—K5	R—Q
67 R—K6	K—B2
68 R—B6ch	K—Kt2

After 28...Kt—B4

29 Kt—K5(l)	K—Kt2
30 R—B5	P—B3
31 KtxP(Kt5)(m)	R—Q2
32 KR—QB	K—B2
33 R—B7(n)	QR—Q

69 P—B5	PxPch		80 K—B3	R—B8ch
70 KxP	R—Q2		81 K—Q2	R—KKt8
71 K—K6(z)	R—R2		82 R—K5	R—Kt6(cc)
72 K—K5	R—R8		83 R—K3(dd)	RxP
73 R—Q6	R—K8ch		84 K—Q3	R—R4
74 K—B5(aa)	R—B8ch		85 K—K4	K—Kt3
75 K—K6	K—Kt3		86 R—KB3	K—Kt2
76 RxP	R—Q8		87 P—Q5	R—R2
77 K—Q6(bb)	K—R4		88 K—K5	R—K2ch
78 K—B5	R—B8ch		89 K—Q6	R—R2
79 K—Kt4	R—Kt8ch		90 K—K6	Resigns

(a)   More enduring is 8 B—Q3 if for no other reason than that Black may without hesitation reply to the text-move with 8...P—KR3, followed by 9...P—B4.

(b)   Rated nowadays as the best continuation. In reply to 9 P—QR3, Black, by means of 9...R—K!; 10 B—Q3, PxP; 11 BxP, P—QKt4; 12 B—R2, P—B4!, etc., can obtain a wholly satisfactory game.

(c)   The idea of playing Kt—K5, if possible, only after Kt—Kt3, is quite good enough in itself, only it had to be worked out more accurately. Correct would have been 12 P—KR3 and, if 12...Kt—Kt3, then 13 Kt—K5, Kt—Q2; 14 BxB, QxB; 15 P—KB4!, followed by QR—K, etc., with a fine positional pressure. After the text-move, Black succeeds in bringing about equalization cleverly.

(d)   Eliminating the unpleasant Knight on K5.

(e)   So as to be in a position to exchange the Bishops on B4. Strangely enough, however, Black in his next moves hesitates in the execution of this plan.

(f)   Obviously good would have been 18...B—B4; 19 BxB, KtxB, followed by the doubling of the Rooks on the K file and the eventual advance of the KKt pawn, with a game rich in chances. After the premature text-move, Black no longer will be able to avoid the exchange of Queens.

(g)   If now 19...B—B4?, then 20 BxB, KtxB; 21 Q—Q7, etc.

(h)   If 20...QxP?; 21 Kt—B4.

(i)   Again putting his foot in it. In order would have been 22...B—B4; 23 Kt—B4, P—B3, followed by Kt—B4—Q3, etc., with an easy defense of the Queen's wing, where White is gradually getting an advantage.

(j)   At last! White, however, has meanwhile made considerable progress.

(k)   The isolation of the QP, after P—Kt5, etc., is hardly to be avoided. Black hopes to find a counter-chance in his QRP, but, even so, that would by no means balance his several weaknesses (Q4 and KKt5).

(l)   White has obtained a position promising victory, but now endangers his prospects through this unhappy transposition of moves. 29 R—B5! should have been played, for instance: I.—29...R—Q2; 30 Kt—K5, R—Q3; 31 KtxP(Kt5) (threatening 32 RxP), and the Knight returns into the game by way of K5; II—29...R—Q; 30 Kt—B4!, KR—Q2; 31 P—Kt6, R—Q3; 32 R—Kt, etc.—likewise with the win of a pawn, besides a safe pos.ton. Mr. Yates now makes excellent use of his opportunity, at least up to a certain point.

(m)   After 31 Kt—Q3, Black could have protected his QP comfortably with R—Q2, followed by Kt—K2. This retreat would have been superior to the capture, after which the Knight is kept permanently out of play.

(n)   With this and the following moves White loses valuable time and actually exposes himself to the danger of losing. 33 Kt—R2 should have been played in order to transfer the Knight, by way of B3—K—Q3, etc., into the center of action. In all cases, however, Black would have had excellent drawing chances.

(o)   He could not very well have done any better than to exchange his RP for the KtP by means of 36 R—R, P—R5; 37 R—Kt5, followed eventually by R—Kt4, etc., and thereafter to transfer his King and Knight as speedily as possible to the Queen's side. Now he should have lost.

(p)   If 37 RxR, then simply 37...Kt—Q3, and White will not be able to save the QKtP.

(q)   The two connected passed Pawns should now have been decisive. In the following line of play White undertakes the only possible attempt at salvation.

(r)   Clever, but insufficient.

(s)   A blunder which is an object lesson and which not only lets victory sl.p through his fingers, but also holds out new prospects to the opponent. Black needed to hold in reserve this threat to dislodge the Rook with the gain of a tempo. Thereby he would have connected anew h.s passed Pawns and brought about a winning Rook ending, for instance: 40...KxKt; 41 P—K5ch, K—K3; 42 PxKt, K—Q2; 43 K—B2, P—QKt4; 44 K—K2, P—Kt5; 45 K—Q2, P—Kt6; 46 K—B3, P—Kt7; 47 R—K, KxP; 48 K—Kt3, KxP (threatening R—K and K6ch, etc); 49 K—R2, K—Kt3; 50 P—Kt4 (R—K6ch and RxP clearly would not do, on account of R—QB—B8), K—Kt4; 51 P—R5, PxP; 52 PxP, K—Kt5; 53 P—R6, R—QB; 54 R—QKt (or 54 K—Kt, K—Kt6, etc.), R—B6; 55 P—R7, R—R6, and wins.

(t)   Now the King arrives betimes and Black can capture the hostile passed Pawns only at the expense of his own RP, after which he rema.ns at a disadvantage so far as material is concerned.

(u)   Better drawing chances would have been offered after 46...R—R6, for instance: 47 K—B, R—B6ch; 48 K—Kt2, KxP; 49 RxP, KxP; 50 R—R7ch (50 R-R6, P—Kt4!, etc.),K—Kt3; 51 R—KKt7, RxP; 52 RxPch, K—Kt4; 53 P—R5, K—B5.

(v)   After 52...K—Q3, White would win by bringing h.s King over to the King's side by way of B2 and Kt3.

(w)   As is easily to be seen, Black is confronted by a "Zugzwang."

(x)   A preparation for the subsequent P—B5.

(y)   A move to gain a tempo.

(z)   S.mpler would have been 71 K—K5, followed by R—Q6.

(aa)   Why not 74 KxP, R—KKt8; 75 P—Kt6, etc.?

(bb)   White seems to gloat over his opponent's suffering, for otherwise he doubtless would have played 77 R—Q8, KxP; 78 P—Q5, followed by P—Q6, thereby arriving at a theoretically won position.

(cc)   Or 82...RxP; 83 RxRch, KxR; 84 K—B3, K—B3; 85 K—B4, K—K3; 86 K—B5, and wins.

(dd)   The KtP could not very well have been saved. However, there was no neces-s.ty for it.

Game 80   SIXTEENTH ROUND—RETI'S OPENING

Dr. Tartakower   Janowski   After 22...P—K4
    White   Black

	Dr. Tartakower White	Janowski Black
1	Kt—KB3	P—Q4
2	P—B4	P—Q5(a)
3	P—QKt4	P—QR4(b)
4	P—Kt5	P—QB4
5	P—K3	P—KKt3
6	PxP	PxP
7	P—Q3	B—Kt2
8	P—Kt3(c)	Kt—Q2(d)
9	B—KKt2	Kt—B4
10	B—QR3	Q—Kt3(e)
11	Castles	B—B4(f)
12	Kt—R4	B—QB(g)
13	Q—K2	B—B3(h)
14	Kt—Q2	BxKt
15	PxB	Kt—K3
16	Q—K5	P—B3(i)
17	Q—Kt3	Kt—R3
18	B—K4	Kt—KB4(j)
19	BxKt	PxB
20	Q—B3	Kt—B
21	Q—R5ch	Kt—Kt3(k)
22	QR—K	P—K4
23	P—B4(l)	K—Q
24	PxP	R—KKt
25	QxRP	B—K3
26	K—R	KtxKP
27	Q—K7ch	K—B
28	B—B5	Q—Q(m)
29	QxBch	K—Kt
30	RxKt	PxR
31	QxPch	K—B
32	QxPch	Resigns

(a)   With this move, as also with 2...PxP, which Janowski tried against Reti in the last round, Black can compel a modification of his opponent's plan for development— but not at all for his own good.   It is not unimportant to stipulate that the advance of the QP on the part of White (which means a tempo plus) is to be recommended for tactical reasons, as was splendidly demonstrated by Rubinstein in his game against Spielmann (Vienna, 1922).   The opening phase of that game went as follows: 1 P—Q4, Kt—KB3; 2 Kt—KB3, P—B4; 3 P—Q5, P—QKt4; 4 P—B4, B—Kt2; 5 P—QR4, PxBP; 6 Kt—B3, P—K3; 7 P—K4, KtxKP; 8 KtxKt, PxP; 9 Kt—B3, P—Q5, whereupon White decided the game by means of the combination, 10 BxP!, PxKt; 11 BxPch, followed by Q—Kt3ch and QxB.   Inasmuch, however, as Black does not for obvious reasons command this attack after P—Q4, the prematurely advanced pawn occasions its owner nothing but anxiety without seriously impeding the adversary's development.   All in all, the fortification of the square, Q4, by means of 2...P—QB3, is the defense for Black most to be recommended.

(b)   In reply to 3...P—B4, there could have been followed 4 B—Kt2 and, in case 4...P—QR4, then 5 PxBP, Kt—QB3; 6 P—K3, P—K4; 7 KtxKP, KtxKt; 8 PxP, Kt—QB3; 9 P—Q5, etc., with a splendid game, as 9...BxP clearly would not do, on account of 10 BxP.

(c)   So far both sides have made pawn moves exclusively, but while White has acquired a sentinel on QKt5 to check his opponent's development on the Queen's side, the Black QP merely serves as an object for attack, the inconvenient defense of which will permanently hinder the normal deployment of Black's fighting forces.

(d)   Occupation of the square, QB4, has here a more esthetic than real value. Preferable first would have been 8...Kt—KR3 (not 8...Kt—KB3; 9 B—QKt2), followed by Castles, etc.

(e)   And here, too, it would have been better to bring the King to safety by means of Kt—K3, Kt—KB3, followed by Castles.

(f)   With this thoughtless move, for which 11...Kt—KR3 should invariably be substituted, Black merely gives away additional tempi.   No wonder that he shortly finds himself in a losing position.

(g)   Fine!

(h)   In an undeveloped position, to lose two more moves in order to exchange the flanchettoed Bishop and thereby create new holes—that is indeed incomprehensible!   In this game Janowski cannot be recognized.

(i)   In reply to 16...Kt—B3, would follow 17 Kt—K4, with a winnning position.

(j)   He could have held out somewhat longer with 18...Kt—Kt2, as the sacrifice with 19 BxPch, PxB; 20 QxPch, K—B, etc., would not then have been decisive.

(k)   After 21...K—Q, then, for instance, 22 Kt—Kt3, threatening B—B5, would have sufficed for a win.

(l)   Herewith White forces capitulation in a few moves.   He did not experience much trouble in this game.

(m)   What hope is there left?

SEVENTEENTH ROUND

With Capablanca resting, Dr. Lasker was given an opportunity to make up for time lost through his bye in the fifteenth round. At the expense of Yates he gained another point so that he opened up a gap of one and a half games, both in wins and losses, between himself and Capablanca. This he maintained until the end of the tournament, to accomplish which, however, it was necessary for him to score 4½ games out of the next five! Yates did not make a particularly impressive showing against Dr. Lasker's Sicilian Defense. Nevertheless, he appeared to emerge in fairly good shape, only to drift into a hopelessly lost ending.

The longest game of the round and one to try nerves of steel was that between Bogoljubow and Alekhine, who adopted the French Defense. Bogoljubow, soon after the opening, played for an unsound combination. Alekhine did not find the strongest defense, but was left with a Rook and two Bishops against two Rooks in the hands of Bogoljubow. The Pawns so blocked the center of the board that there was not sufficient scope for the Bishops. Alekhine was given a chance to play for a win, but this would have been possible only through a complicated and problematical continuation, upon which the Russian thought it wiser not to embark. After an arduous game lasting 85 moves, a draw was agreed upon.

The game between Marshall and Ed. Lasker was a Queen's Pawn Opening, in which the United States champion seemed to get a shade the better of it. Lasker's sturdy defense, however, was good enough for a draw. Two Knights were opposed by two Bishops in this game.

Dr. Tartakower, adopting the Ruy Lopez, was outplayed by Reti, who, following the disappearance of Queens from the board, obtained the better position and then enterprisingly sacrificed the exchange. Unable to find the saving clause, Dr. Tartakower succumbed in the ending.

Janowski and Maroczy discussed a very lively Queen's Gambit in which the latter outplayed his opponent. Although his play then became none too exact, he was certainly holding his own, despite the fact that Janowski was the exchange to the good. His Bishops were posted to excellent advantage. With the outcome somewhat problematical, Maroczy inadvertently overstepped the time limit and the victory went to Janowski. It was the only game of the 110 in the tournament which was forfeited in this way, and quite costly to the Hungarian.

There was no change this day in the respective positions of the six leaders; Dr. Lasker, 11½—3½; Capablanca, 10—5; Alekhine, 9½—6½; Reti, 9—6; Bogoljubow, 8½—7½; Marshall, 8—7.

Black reversed the result of the previous round and the totals were: White 47½, Black 37½.

Game 81   SEVENTEENTH ROUND—SICILIAN DEFENSE

	Yates	Dr. Lasker			
	White	Black	27	P—B4	B—B5
			28	B—B2	P—Q5
1	P—K4	P—QB4	29	P—B5(m)	Kt—Q2
2	Kt—KB3	P—K3(a)	30	PxP	BxP
3	P—Q4	PxP	31	B—KKt3(n)	Kt—B
4	KtxP	Kt—KB3	32	R—K5	R—Kt3
5	Kt—QB3	Kt—B3	33	B—KR4	B—B2
6	KtxKt(b)	KtPxKt	34	B—KKt3	B—Kt3
7	P—K5	Kt—Q4	35	R—K7(o)	R—K3
8	Kt—K4	P—KB4	36	RxR	KtxR
9	PxP,e.p.	KtxP	37	BxB	PxB(p)
10	Kt—Q6ch	BxKt	38	B—K5(q)	R—KB(r)
11	QxB	Q—R4ch(c)	39	P—QKt3	R—B8ch
12	B—Q2	Q—Q4	40	K—B2	K—B2
13	Q—R3	Q—K5ch(d)	41	B—Kt3(s)	K—K2
14	B—K3	P—QR4(e)			

After 14...P—QR4

After 41...K—K2

15	Castles(f)	Q—QKt5	42	P—QR4(t)	K—Q2
16	QxQ(g)	PxQ(h)	43	K—Q3	R—B8
17	B—QB4	P—Q4	44	R—B2	R—QKt8
18	B—Kt3	Kt—Q2(i)	45	K—B4	K—B3
19	KR—K	Castles	46	R—K2(u)	R—B8ch
20	P—KB3	R—R3(j)	47	K—Q3	R—B6ch
21	B—Q2	P—B4	48	K—Q2	K—Q2
22	P—QB4	PxP,e.p.(k)	49	P—Kt4	PxP
23	BxP	Kt—Kt3	50	K—Q	P—Kt6
24	P—QR3	B—Q2	51	P—R5	Kt—B4
25	B—K5	R—QB	52	P—R6	Kt—R5
26	R—Q2(l)	B—Kt4	53	R—K5	P—Kt7
				Resigns	

(a) Against Janowski in the fourth round Dr. Lasker somewhat more precisely played 2...Kt—QB3. After the text-move, White, by means of 3 B—K2, Kt—QB3 (Kt—KB3; 4 P—K5); 4 P—Q4, PxP; 5 KtxP, Kt—B3; 6 B—B3, etc., could avoid the blocking of his QBP by Kt—QB3.

(b) This, jointly with the next move, is an old variation which does not promise White anything out of the ordinary. 8 P—QR3 at once would have been the simplest here if perchance White did not feel disposed to venture upon the promising pawn sacrifice with 6 B—K2, B—Kt5; 7 Castles, etc.

(c) Neither could the weakness of the black squares have been eliminated by 11...Q—K2; 12 B—KB4, Kt—K5; 13 QxQch, KxQ; 14 P—KB3, followed by Castles QR, etc. However, by means of 11...Q—Kt3! (threatening QxPch) Black would have obtained a sat.sfactory game, for instance: 12 B—Q3, P—QB4; 13 B—KB4, B—Kt2; 14 Castles, R—B, etc. By means of the following Queen maneuver he seeks to obtain counter-chances through an alteration of the pawn structure, but might easily have got into trouble thereby.

(d) Likewise 13...Kt—K5; 14 B—K3 would no longer have sufficed.

(e) If 14...QxBP?; 15 B—Q3.

(f) Herewith Wh.te without resisting falls in with his opponent's designs and thereby gets a little the worst of it. Correct would have been 15 B—Q3, for instance: 15... Q—Kt5ch (or 15...QxKtP; 16 Castles QR, etc., with a strong attack hardly to be parried); 16 QxQ, PxQ; 17 B—QB5, Kt—Q4 (or R—Kt; 18 B—Q6, R—Kt3; 19 P—QR4, etc.); 18 B—K4, R—R4; 19 B—Q6, etc., with a clear advantage.

(g) 16 B—B5 would not do on account of 16...QxQ; 17 BxQ, Kt—K5!, etc.

(h) Now the open QR file becomes an important factor favorable to Black.

(i) Making possible P—QB4 and thereby removing all danger. In view of Black's menacing center, White can now merely hope to hold his own through the co-operation of his Bishops.

(j) Not yet 26...P—B4, on account of 21 RxP, etc.

(k) Certainly better than the blockade by means of 22...P—Q5, because Black will get the opportunity, at the proper moment, to establish the pawn formation in the center favorable to him.

(l) Obviously to avoid the exchange of Bishops (B—R5).

(m) White at last obtains some counter-play through the opening of this file. To be sure, Black's passed pawn is very troublesome, but, owing to the paucity of pieces and pawns, this advantage should not have been decisive.

(n) White's position has improved measurably during the last moves which probably is ascribable to the maneuver begun by Black with B—Kt4 with a loss of time. On account of the opening of the K and KB files, Black cannot very well prevent further simpl.fication.

(o) Threatening a counter-attack by means of 36 B—K5, Kt—K3; 37 B—R4, etc.

(p) A simple end-game has now come to pass, which would have been wholly tenable for White if, while threatening to split the black pawns, by P—QKt4, he had played consistently for the entrance of the King to the center.

(q) Not the best, because Black obtains thereby the KB file as a base for operations. Simpler would have been 38 B—B2 and, if 38...R—Q; 39 K—B2—Q3 and, ultimately, P—Kt4, etc.

(r) In order to reply to 39 P—Kt4 with 39...R—B4, followed by P—B5.

(s) Of no avail! 41 K—Q3 (threatening P—Kt4) would have assured him an easy draw, as, after 41...R—QKt8 (41...R—K8; 42 R—K2; or 41...R—QB8; 42 R—QB2); 42 K—B4, R—B8ch; 43 K—Q5, White would have threatened to win a piece by R—KB2 ch, etc.

(t) In spite of the time lost, 42 K—Q3 would probably still have sufficed, for instance: I. 42...R—QKt8; 43 K—B4, R—B8ch; 44 K—Q5, threatening R—K2, etc. II. 42...K—Q2; 43 P—QKt4!, K—B3; 44 PxP, KtxPch (or KxP; 45 R—K2!); 45 K—K2, etc. III 42...R—QR8; 43 P—QR4, K—Q2; 44 R—K2, R—QB8; 45 R—K5, R—B6ch; 46 K—K4, etc. After the text-move, which spoils all prospects of scattering the pawns, Black's passed pawn becomes overpowering.

(u) Th s is tantamount to resignation. After 46 P—R5!, R—R8; 47 P—Kt4, PxP; 48 KxPch, K—Q4, etc., White could have offered a longer, if eventually unsuccessful opposition. Mr. Yates has played the last part of this game much below his class.

Game 82　　SEVENTEENTH ROUND—FRENCH DEFENSE

Bogoljubow	Alekhine
White	Black
1 P—K4	P—K3
2 P—Q4	P—Q4
3 Kt—QB3	Kt—KB3
4 B—KKt5	B—QKt5
5 KKt—K2	PxP
6 P—QR3	B—K2
7 BxKt	PxB
8 KtxP	P—Kt3(a)
9 KKt—B3	P—KB4(b)
10 Kt—Kt3	B—Kt2
11 B—Kt5ch(c)	P—B3(d)
12 B—B4	Kt—Q2(e)
13 Q—K2(f)	Kt—B3
14 CastlesQR	Q—Q3
15 KR—K	Kt—Q4(g)
16 KtxKt	BPxKt
17 B—Kt5ch	K—Q(h)
18 K—Kt	P—KR4(i)
19 KtxRP	QxKRP
20 Kt—Kt3	Q—R5(j)
21 R—R	Q—B3
22 Kt—R5	Q—Kt4(k)
23 P—KB4	Q—Kt3
24 R—Q3(l)	P—R3
25 R—KKt3(m)	RxKt(n)
26 QxR(o)	QxQ(p)

After 26 QxR

27 RxQ	PxB
28 R—R7	K—Q2
29 RxP	R—KB
30 R—R7	R—K
31 R—KKt6(q)	B—B
32 P—B3	K—B2(r)
33 K—B2	B—Q2
34 R(Kt6)—Kt7	K—Q3

35 K—Q2	B—QB3
36 R—Kt6	R—KB
37 K—K3	B—B3
38 R—QR7(s)	B—Q2
39 K—B3	B—Q
40 R(Kt6)—Kt7	B—B2
41 R—R7	R—Q
42 P—KKt3	B—Kt
43 R—QKt7	B—B2(t)
44 R—R7	K—B3

After 44...K—B3

45 P—QR4(u)	PxP
46 RxP	P—Kt4(v)
47 R—QR	P—Kt5
48 K—K3	B—Kt3(w)
49 R—QR4	PxP
50 PxP	R—KKt
51 K—B2	R—QB
52 R—QR3	K—Q3
53 R—KR	R—QKt
54 R(R3)—R	B—Kt4
55 K—K3(x)	R—KKt
56 R(KR)—KKt	K—B3
57 K—Q2	B—B5(y)
58 R(R)—K	K—Q3
59 R—QR	B—B2
60 K—K3	K—B3
61 K—Q2	B—Q(z)
62 R(R)—K	R—Kt3
63 R—QR	B—K2(aa)
64 R(R)—K	B—Q3
65 K—B2	K—Q2
66 R—QR(bb)	B—B2
67 K—Q2	K—B3
68 R(R)—K	B—Q3
69 K—B2	K—B2

70	K—Q2	K—Q2
71	R—QR	K—B3
72	R(R)—K	K—B2
73	R—QR	R—Kt
74	R(R)—K	K—Q2
75	R—QR	B—B2
76	R(R)—Kt	R—QR(cc)
77	R—QR	R—R
78	R—R	R—KKt
79	R(KR)—KKt	B—Q(dd)
80	R(R)—K·	B—K2
81	R—Kt	K—B2
82	R(QKt)—K	B—Q3
83	R—QR	K—B3
84	R(R)—K	K—B2
85	R—QR	K—Q2

After 79 R(KR)—KKt

Drawn

(a) This is the correct method of handling this difficult variation which makes possible a logical development of Black's pieces, at the same time holding out hope of counter play.

(b) The same mistake occurred in the game, Dr. Lasker versus Reti. Black should simply play 8 B—Kt2 and in reply to 9 Q—B3, P—B3, followed by Kt—Q2. It was quite sufficient that the Knight should remain at K4 under the threat of being driven back; however, this threat should become a reality only in that moment when it is combined with a distinct advantage in position. Here the move is premature and should place the second player under a handicap.

(c) But White likewise lacks exactness. In order would have been 11 P—Q5! for, after 11...BxQP (if P—B5; 12 Q—Q4 or 12 B—Kt5ch, K—B; 13 Q—Q4, etc.); 12 KtxB, QxKt; 13 QxQ, PxQ; 14 KtxP, etc., White's end-game position would have been quite favorable on account of the dominating post held by the Knight. The move in the text permits the second player to consolidate his position.

(d) Not 10...Kt—Q2, on account of 12 P—Q5, etc.

(e) Black might have entered without disquietude upon the complications bound up with 12...B—B3, as for instance: 13 Q—R5 (or 13 QKt—K2, P—KR4), QxP; 14 BxP, Q—K4ch; 15 K—Q (15K—B, B—R3ch, followed by QxB, winning), Q—Q3ch; 16 Kt—Q5, Castles; 17 BxP (or 17 KtxBP, QxB; 18 Kt (Q5)—K7ch, K—R, etc.), QxKtch; 18 K—B, R—Q; 19 BxPch, K—B; 20 Kt—B5, Q—Q7ch; 21 K—Kt, Q—Kt4, and White has spent himself. Even with the move selected, however, he manages eventually to obtain an advantage.

(f) Clearly, the sacrifice of BxP would have been incorrect.

(g) After 15...Castles QR; 16 KtxP, Q—B5ch; 17 Kt—K3, RxP; 18 P—KKt3, RxRch; 19 RxR, Q—B2; 20 P—B4, threatening P—B5, etc., White would have stood somewhat better. By means of the Knight move Black assures himself of the advantage of two Bishops, of which one, however, will have limited action.

(h) The King stands much safer here than on B sq.; moreover, Black need not fear 18 Q—R5, on account of 18...Q—B5ch; 19 K—Kt, R—KB; 20 QxRP (otherwise Q—R5 by Black), QxBP, etc.

(i) Seemingly risky, but in fact the only continuation, for, if 18...Q—B5, in order to bring about the variation in question, the reply of 19 B—Q3 would be unpleasant.

(j) The only move, because of the double threat of 21 R—R and 21 KtxP.

(k) Not 22...Q—Kt3, on account of 23 Kt—B4, Q—Kt; 24 RxR, QxR; 25 KtxPch, PxKt; 26 QxP and wins.

(l) The beginning of an incorrect combination. White, however, no longer had a satisfactory position. For instance, if 24 P—KKt4 (24 B—O3, K—Q2, etc.), PxP; (24...QxP: 25 O—K5, etc., was also to be considered); 25 Q—K5 (25 P—B5, Q—Kt4), R—R2; 26 B—Q3, P—B4; 27 Kt—Kt3, R—R6!

(m) Natural, but fatal. Even after 25 B—R4, P—Kt4; 26 B—Kt3, K—Q2, etc., White would have stood poorly, inasmuch as R—KKt3 would at no time be possible.

(n) As a matter of course.

(o) Or 26 RxQ, RxRch; 27 K—R2, PxB (simplest); 27 R—Kt8ch, K—B2, with an easy win.

(p) Black overlooked in the variation, 26...QxR; 27 QxP (B7), PxB; 28 R—R7, the recourse of 28...Q—K8ch; 29 K—R2, Q—Kt5; 30 R—R8ch, K—Q2; 31 RxR, Q—B5ch, etc., whereupon White naturally would have had to give up. The exchange of Queens, on the other hand, leads to a certain draw.

(q) The position now arrived at, if carefully handled, cannot be won either by White or by Black and might very well have been abandoned here as drawn.

(r) Black desires to bring about an exchange, before the White King can approach and support his Rook. That is the simplest method of drawing.

(s) A questionable adventure, thanks to which Black actually gets another chance. The simplest way to bring the struggle to an end would have been through 38 R(R7)— R6, K—K2; 39 R—R7ch, R—B2; 40 RxRch, followed by R—Kt3, etc.

(t) Threatening 44...K—B3; 45 R—R7, B—Kt, followed by K—Kt2, etc.

(u) White has reason to be thankful that he is able in this manner to free the threatened Rook, but the Black QB at last obtains some elbow room. Clearly without aim would have been 45 P—KKt4, PxPch; 46 KxP (in order to meet 46...P—K4 with 47 RxB, followed by QPxP), because Black would then have helped himself to the BP with 46...R—KB.

(v) In combination with the following move, this holds out the only slight chance for a win.

(w) After this White forces an immediate clearance on the Queen's side. With 48...K—Kt4; 49 R—R7, K—Kt3; 50 R—QR, B—Kt4, this might have been avoided. This circumstance, however, could hardly have had a greater significance for the general run of the following end-game.

(x) Of course, the Bishop must not be permitted to reach K5.

(y) Black's only prospect of winning lies in the Pawn sacrifice, P—K4, in order to bring about co-operation between the Bishops, and all the subsequent maneuvers have in view the object of leading up to this break at a favorable moment. White is fully aware of the danger and defends himself excellently.

(z) Now the threat is 62...P—K4! For instance: (i) 63 BPxP, B—Kt4ch; 64 K—B2, B—K6; 65 R—Kt2, B—B5. (ii) 63 QPxP, B—Kt3; 64 R—Kt2, P—Q5; 65 PxP, K—Q4!, with decisive entry of the King.

(aa) If 63...P—K4, White would have had the important intervening move of 64 R—R8, which would have destroyed Black's plan.

(bb) Right at this moment White may abandon his guard over the square, K2, as for instance: 66...B—K7; 67 K—Q2, B—B6; 68 R—R7ch, K—B3 (or 68... B—B2, 69 R—Kt); 69 R(Kt)—QR, etc.

(cc) Now at least the way seems to be paved for a decisive continuation.

(dd) With the last move of his Rook, Black had led up to a favorable position for P—K4 and should now have aimed at a realization of his idea: 79...P—K4! (i) 80 QPxP, B—Kt3; 81 R—Kt2, K—B3, followed by P—Q5. (ii) 80 BPxP, B—Q; 81 R—R7ch, K—K3; 82 R—KR; B—Kt4ch; 83 K—B2, P—B5; 84 P—Kt4, P—B6; 85 R(R)—R7 (or 85 R—QKt, B—Q, followed by RxP, etc.), P—B7; 86 R(KR7)—Q7 (or 86 R(KR7)—QKt7, B—Q; or R(KR7)—QB7, B—Kt4!), R—Q; 87 R(Q7)—QKt7, B—Q6ch; 88 K—Kt3 (or Kt2), R—Q3; 89 R—KB7, R—Kt3ch, and wins. All things considered, however, this last variation could not have been worked out easily over the board. After the move in the text, the game is practically drawn, because any attempt to arrive at the favorable layout once more would involve a three-fold repetition of position.

Game 83	SEVENTEENTH ROUND—INDIAN DEFENSE		
Marshall	Ed Lasker	10 Kt—Q2(f)	B—B4(g)
White	Black	11 KtxP	P—K4
1 P—Q4	Kt—KB3	12 PxP	KtxP
2 Kt—KB3	P—KKt3	13 P—K4	B—K3
3 Kt—B3	P—Q4(a)	14 BxKt(h)	BxB
4 B—B4	B—Kt2	15 Kt—KB3	B—Kt2
5 P—K3	B—B4(b)	16 P—QB3	Q—Q3
6 P—KR3(c)	Castles	17 P—B4(i)	QR—Q
7 B—Q3	Kt—K5(d)	18 Q—K2	P—QB3(j)
8 BxKt	BxB	19 P—K5	BxP
9 Castles(e)	Kt—Q2	20 QxB	PxKt(k)

21 QxQ	RxQ
22 P—B5(l)	R—R3
23 P—QR4(m)	B—Q2
24 KR—Q(n)	RxP
25 RxR	BxR
26 R—R	B—B3
27 RxP	R—K
28 P—QKt4	R—K3(o)
29 P—Kt5(p)	BxP
30 RxP	B—R5
31 R—Kt8ch	K—Kt2
32 R—QB8	B—Q8
33 Kt—Kt5(q)	R—K8ch
34 K—R2	P—R3
35 P—B6	B—R5(r)
36 Kt—B3	R—QB8
37 R—R8	BxP
38 R—QB8	R—B5(s)
39 Kt—K5	B—Kt2
40 RxR	PxR
41 KtxQBP(t)	K—B3

After 18...P—QB3

42 P—B4	B—R3
43 Kt—K5	P—R4
44 P—Kt4	PxP
45 PxP	B—B
46 K—Kt3	P—Kt4
	Drawn

(a)   Concerning the merit of this move compare the game between Capablanca and Yates (7th round).

(b)   There is no need here for hurry in developing the Bishop, inasmuch as there is no threat of cutting him off by means of P—K3. First 5...Castles and then P—B4, as in the game referred to, would have been much more in order.

(c)   Rather mysterious chess.   Why not at once 6 B—Q3?

(d)   As a result if his premature fifth move Black has the unpleasant choice between this jump and an exchange developing his opponent: 7...BxB; 8 QxB, QKt—Q2, which, as will be seen at once, was nevertheless to be preferred.

(e)   By means of 9 KtxB, PxKt; 10 Kt—Q2, P—KB4; 11 P—QB3, followed by Q—Kt3, etc., the opening advantage could have been maintained.   After the text-move, on the contrary, Black, thanks to his two Bishops, might still have had a fair game with 9...B—B4, but instead loses a Pawn.   The handling of the opening on both sides left much to be desired.

(f)   Forcing a material advantage which Black in vain endeavors to balance through the co-operation of his strongly posted Bishops.

(g)   Still worse would have been 10...Kt—B3, on account of 11 P—KKt4!, with the threat of P—KB3, etc.

(h)   It is certainly a pity to exchange this Bishop, but, if 14 Kt—KB3, then 14...BxKt; 15 PxB, Kt—B5, recovering the Pawn.

(i)   This Pawn move on top of the previous play appears a bit artificial, but is cleverly conceived.   Yet, inasmuch as Black for the time being was threatening nothing, 17 Q—Q3, to be followed by KR—Q, would have been quite good enough.

(j)   Seemingly compelling the retreat of the Knight, whereupon the mighty force of the pair of Bishops would have made itself felt, for instance: 19 Kt—B3, Q—Q6!, or 19 Kt—K3, Q—B5, etc.   Marshall, however, had fully prepared himself for this variation and, returning the extra Pawn, now forces a favorable ending.

(k)   Of course not 20...QxQ, on account of 21 Kt—K7ch, etc.

(l)   Because of his majority of Pawns on the Queen's side and aided by the "fixed" position of his Knight on Q4, White has obtained excellent winning chances.

(m)   In conjunction with the following move, this is better than 23 P—QKt4, whereupon Black, by means of 23...P—Q5, would have obtained counter-play sooner.

(n)   By no means 24 P—QKt3, on account of 24...P—QKt3!, etc.   The exchange forced by the text-move permits the entrance of the Rook on the seventh row.

(o)   Better drawing chances were offered by 28...R—K5; 29 P—Kt5, BxP; 30 RxP, B—K; 31 R—Kt8, K—Kt2, etc.

(p) And as a matter of course White should have utilized the opportunity to advance the KtP through 29 R—R5! It soon becomes apparent that the QBP by itself does not suffice for a win.

(q) Surely an odd idea. However, likewise by 33 Kt—Q4 the win apparently is no longer to be forced, for instance: 33...R—K5; 34 Kt—Kt5, B—R5; 35 Kt—Q6 (or Kt—B3, R—K8ch; 36 K—R2, B—Q2; 37 R—Q8, P—Q5, etc.), R—K8ch; 36 K—R2, P—Q5, and, after 37 P—B6, the Pawn would be stopped by means of 37...R—QB8, etc.

(r) Black avoids complications, which might have arisen from 35...B—R4; 36 P—B7, R—QB8; 37 KtxP!

(s) Indeed the only, although fairly obvious salvation.

(t) The next five moves could very well have been dispensed with by the gentlemen.

Game 84   SEVENTEENTH ROUND—RUY LOPEZ

Tartakower	Reti
White	Black
1 P—K4	P—K4
2 Kt—KB3	Kt—QB3
3 B—Kt5	P—QR3
4 B—R4	Kt—B3
5 P—Q3(a)	P—Q3
6 P—B3(b)	B—K2
7 QKt—Q2	Castles
8 Kt—B	P—QKt4
9 B—B2	P—Q4
10 B—Q2(c)	R—K
11 Kt—Kt3	B—B
12 Castles	PxP(d)
13 PxP	B—K3(e)
14 P—Kt3(f)	B—KKt5(g)
15 Q—K2(h)	Kt—KR4(i)
16 QR—Q	Q—B3
17 P—KR3(j)	BxKt
18 QxB	QxQ
19 PxQ	Kt—B5
20 K—R2(k)	P—Kt5(l)
21 KR—K(m)	KR—Q(n)
22 Kt—K2	RxB(o)

After 22 Kt—K2

23 RxR   PxP

24 KtxP	B—Kt5
25 R—K3	Kt—Q5(p)
26 P—R3(q)	BxP

After 26..BxP

27 Kt—Q5(r)	B—B8
28 R—Q(s)	BxR
29 PxB	KtxKt
30 PxQKt	Kt—K6
31 R—QB	KtxB
32 RxKt	PxP
33 RxP	R—Q(t)
34 K—Kt3(u)	P—Q6
35 R—B	P—Q7
36 R—Q	P—Kt4
37 K—B2	K—Kt2
38 P—Kt4(v)	K—B3
39 K—K2	K—K4
40 K—K3	R—Q2
41 P—R4	PxP
42 P—B4ch	K—K3
43 K—B3	P—R6
44 K—Kt3	R—Q6ch
45 K—R2	K—B3
46 K—R	K—Kt3
47 K—R2	K—R4
Resigns	

(a) In this "slow form" (literally, "holding back") variation Black has no difficulties to obtain at least an equal game and for this reason it is very seldom played.

(b) With this move White acquires a weakness at Q3 for no reason whatsoever. This is the chief fault with this variation—analogous to the Hanham variation in the Philidor.

(c) Up to now all this has often been played before. The text-move seems slightly stronger than 10 Q—K2, after which 10...B—K3 can follow with the idea of QPxP and B—B5. Simpler, however, is 10 Kt—Kt3 immediately, as White has no need to avoid the exchange of Queens in the present position.

(d) After letting up the pressure in the center, Black has not much to expect. Better chances were offered by the mobilization of the remaining pieces (through B—K3, Q—Q3, QR—Q, etc.), in order to force White to reckon a while yet with P—Q5 and PxP.

(e) B—KKt5 immediately could have been met quite well by B—K3.

(f) With this move the square, QB3 (and, as a consequence, Q4 indirectly, too) is uselessly weakened and the range of the KB cramped. White did not need to defend himself. With P—QR4! (P—Kt5...15 P—R5!) he would have obtained a counter-initiative which would have offset the weakness at Q3. No direct danger, however, is involved for White by the text-move.

(g) Here still 15 B—K3 would have given him an easy game. For instance, 15... P—Kt5; 16 PxP, KtxKtP; 17 QxQ, QRxQ; 18 KR—QB, etc.; or 15...P—QR4; 16 B—Q3!, etc.

(h) Only after this move does Black obtain a slight advantage.

(i) Because of the pin (even after KtxKt, BxKt(R4), now or on the next move), which now becomes unpleasant.

(j) There is no reason for allowing the Knight to establish itself at B5. Better and more obvious would have been 17 KtxKt, BxKt(R4); 18 P—KR3 (18...P—Kt5; 19 B—Q3!, etc.).

(k) Or 20 BxKt, PxB; 21 Kt—K2, B—Q3, threatening Kt—K4, etc., with obvious advantage for Black.

(l) At last the punishment for 14 P—QKt3, although for the moment it does not seem so terrible. However, its consequences will soon make themselves felt.

(m) To get rid of the pressure of the Knight at B5 through KKt—K2. It would have been far simpler to exchange the Knight five moves ago!

(n) The Queen's Rook stays at its own square in order eventually to make a demonstration on the Queen's side (P—QR4).

(o) An interesting and promising sacrifice of the exchange which aims at the complete command of the Black center. However tempting it may have been, it seems as if Black has thus given up his winning chances. After the simple 22...KtxKt (not 22... Kt—Q6; 23 BxKt, RxB; 24 B—K3!, etc.); 23 RxKt, P—QR4!, White would have had a very difficult game. For instance, 24 B—K, PxP; 25 BxP, B—Kt5!; 26 RxR (26 B—Kt2 is only a transposition of moves) 26...RxR; 27 B—Kt2, B—Q7!; 28 K—Kt2, P—B3; 29 B—R3, Kt—Kt5, etc., with a winning position. Even against other White defenses Black obtains good winning chances.

(p) Now it becomes clear what Black meant by his sacrifice. White's pieces are partly pinned and partly "fixed" (Pat). Moreover, the winning of a piece, or a double winning of the exchange is threatened by 26 Kt—Kt4. Yet White has an adequate defense!

(q) Besides momentarily displacing the Black Bishop, this also aims at obtaining the square, QR2, for the Rook. On the other hand, an attempt to give back the exchange voluntarily would not have been sufficient. For instance, 26 B—Q, Kt—Kt4; 27 R—B2, KtxKt; 28 R(B2)xKt, BxR; 29 RxB, R—Q, Black still has a decisive attack, despite his reduced forces: 30 RxP (or 30 B—B2, R—Q7, etc.), 30...P—KR4; 31 B—B2, R—Q7; 32 K—Kt3 (or 32 K—Kt, KtxPch; 33 K—Kt2, KtxBP; 34 K—B, P—R5!; 35 K—K, P—R6 wins), 32...P—R5ch; 33 KxP, RxBP, and White has no adequate defense against the threat of 34 R—Kt7 and P—KKt4.

(r) This attempt to simplify fails because of a bidden point (see note to White's 28th move). Correct was 27 B—Q!! in order to answer B—B8 with R—R2. With this not only was a draw threatened by R—R, B—Q7, R—R2, etc., but also the simple continuation (after 28...QKt—K3, for example) 29 R—K, Kt—Q6; 30 R—KB. Then it would have been up to Black to find a sufficient compensation for the sacrificed exchange. In any case, after 28...P—QB3, White had nothing better than 29 R—R, for an attempt to win, beginning with 29 R—K, Kt—Q6; 30 R—KB(Kt), P—KR4, would have been hopeless for him because of his hemmed-in position. Thus, after 27 B—Q, the game would have been drawn.

(s)   White notes too late that 28 RxKt fails because of 28...PxR!; 29 R—K, P—Q!; 30 RxB, Kt—K7. But the text also leads to a hopeless end-game.

(t)   This general exchange of pieces has given Black a strong passed Pawn, whose advance forces the hostile Rook to take up a very defensive position.

(u)   Very slightly better was 34 R—B2, P—Q6; 35 R—Q2.

(v)   Or 38 K—K3, K—Kt3; 39 RxP, RxR; 40 KxR, K—R4; 41 K—B3, K—R5; 42 K—Kt4, KxP; 43 K—R5, P—KR4; 44 KxP, P—Kt5, etc. The rest of the game explains itself.

Game 85   SEVENTEENTH ROUND—QUEEN'S GAMBIT

Janowski	Maroczy	14	P—KB4	P—KR3
White	Black	15	B—R4(g)	KtxP
		16	QxKt(h)	BxB
1 P—Q4	P—Q4	17	P—B5	B—Kt4
2 Kt—KB3	Kt—KB3	18	PxP	Castles(i)
3 P—B4	P—B3	19	Kt—B3(j)	P—KB4(k)
4 Kt—B3	PxP	20	Q—B2	B—K6ch
5 B—KKt5(a)	P—QKt4	21	K—R	QR—K(l)
6 P—K3	Kt—Q4(b)	22	Kt—K5	P—B4(m)
7 B—K2	Kt—Q2	23	Kt—Q7	B—K5
8 Castles	Q—B2(c)	24	Q—Kt2	PxP
9 Q—Q2(d)	QKt—B3(e)	25	PxP	P—R3
10 Q—B2	P—K3	26	KtxR	RxKt
11 P—K4	KtxKt	27	P—QR4	R—Kt
12 PxKt	B—Kt2	28	PxP	PxP
13 Kt—Q2(f)	B—K2	29	P—K7(n)	

After 21 K—R

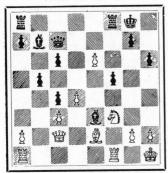

After 29 P—K7

Black having overstepped the time limit, the game was awarded to White.

(a)   This gambit is not correct. Comparatively better is 5 P—K3, P—QKt4; 6 P—QR4—a variation which of late years has been held as favorable for White and is now again playable for Black in consequence of the improvement of 6...P—Kt5 recommended by the writer at London, 1922.

(b)   The move of the Knight, although sufficient, somehow gives the impression of too much elaboration. Simpler would have been 6...B—B4 (7 BxKt, KtPxB; 8 P—K4, B—Kt3), followed by QKt—Q2, Q—Kt3, P—K3 and B—QKt5, etc.

(c)   Probably in order to be able to answer 9 P—K4 with 9...KtxKt; 10 PxKt, P—K4. Black has an easy game for the opening, inasmuch as his extra Pawn will prevent White's every attempt to build up an effective formation.

(d)   In his inferior position White indulges himself in the loss of tempi. In order would have been 9 Q—B2.

(e)   Prevent.ng at the same time P—K4 and threatening KtxKt, followed by Kt—K5, etc.

(f)   This attempt to obtain some kind of a game by the advance of the KBP is cleverly thwarted by Black.   However, a satisfactory continuation was not at the disposal of the first player.

(g)   In reply to 15 BxKt, Black would recapture with the Pawn in order to meet the eventual P—K5 with P—KB4, and P—KB5 with P—K4.   Nevertheless White had to play just so, for now he will lose a second Pawn.

(h)   The sacrifice of the exchange by 16 BxB, KtxKt; 17 B—B5, KtxR; 18 RxKt, P—QR3, followed by Castles QR, etc., would likewise have opened up no prospects.

(i)   Of course, the Knight could not be captured on account of 19 RxP, etc.

(j)   After 19 PxPch, RxP; 20 Kt—B3, P—B4, etc., Black would have had a still easier game than in the actual continuation.

(k)   Herewith the Pawn on K6 is condemned to death.   Strangely enough, however, he is later on spared by Black.

(l)   With 21...Q—K2 (Q3) the Pawn might have been taken without risk, whereupon White doubtless would soon have acknowledged the futility of further efforts.   With the text-move Black begins to play a "major combination," in the course of which his chances of winning gradually dwindle.

(m)   Even now he would have done better to play 22...RxP, although the fact that White would have recovered one of his lost Pawns through 23 RxP, RxR; 24 QxR would have rendered victory considerably more difficult.   After winning the exchange, White will find in his passed Pawn an adequate weapon with which to combat the terrible Bishops.

(n)   In this interesting position Black unfortunately overstepped the time limit. The continuation of the game might have become quite interesting.   The best move, suggested by Maroczy himself, appears to be 29...Q—B3, whereupon White would have had to play with great caution, for instance: 30 P—Q5 (30 B—R5, P—Kt3; 31 B—B3, BxB; 32 RxB, B—Kt4, etc., with almost even chances), QxP; 31 B—R5, B—Q5; 32 Q—Q2, BxR (P—B6; 33 Q—K2); 33 QxQ, BxQ; 34 P—K8 (Q), RxQ; 35 BxR, B—Kt7; 36 BxP, P—B6; 37 B—Q3, B—K5!, which would have been fatal for White.

EIGHTEENTH ROUND

Ths day's play was a repetition of the third round, in which Alekhine faced Dr. Lasker—this time with the black pieces. What Alekhine elects to call a Reti Opening "reversed" was the subject for debate. The Russian appeared to have just the shade of an advantage all the way through, but Dr. Lasker's careful play at no time permitted him to make any serious impression. A draw was the legitimate outcome.

Capablanca gained upon his rival to the extent of half a point by winning from Edward Lasker after quite an eventful contest. The world's champion resorted to a King's Fianchetto Defense, which gave him a very cramped game. Judiciously giving up a more or less useless Pawn, Capablanca, as it were, then obtained his place in the sun and thereafter gave his opponent plenty to think about. Lasker was outplayed in an instructive ending.

This also was the day on which Marshall was found to be in one of his happiest moods. The result was a grand victory over Bogoljubow that will long be remembered by those who actually witnessed it no less than those who played it over from the printed score. It earned the United States champion the second brilliancy prize. There are many, both here and abroad, who think they know a fine game when they see one, who have pronounced it as the most brilliant of the tournament. However, that's neither here nor there. The really important fact is that it yielded a full point to the American at a critical stage of the conflict and in the end helped him materially to win the fourth prize. In the opening Marshall created a weakness by inviting P—KR3 and this later formed the basis of one of his wonderful, whirlwind attacks upon the castled King. The familiar offensive operation along the diagonal, QKt to KR7, was in evidence and everything went exactly to Marshall's taste. When all was ready to catapult his forces upon the enemy, Marshall offered both of his Rooks and the Queen, winding up most appropriately with an announced mate in five moves! This great game should find a place in the next edition of "Marshall's Chess Swindles."

The game between Reti and Maroczy was a hard-fought Ruy Lopez and one of the few games in which Reti managed to hold his own with the black pieces. Where this happened, it may be mentioned en passant, he resorted to 1...P—K4, a move which he seems to regard as insufficient. The game with Maroczy was nip and tuck until the end and was drawn.

Yates fairly outplayed Dr. Tartakower, who adopted the Sicilian Defense. The British expert established a distinct superiority upon the Queen's side, whereupon Dr. Tartakower attempted a somewhat rash diversion on the other wing with P—KKt4. Yates, however, was master of the situation and finished off the game with a forced mate.

The five eventual prize winners were all clear of the field at the close of this round. Barring Bogoljubow, who entered the charmed circle in the twentieth and twenty-first rounds, none of the other contestants troubled them from then on until the end of the tournament. The scores: Dr. Lasker, 12—4; Capablanca, 11—5; Alekhine, 10—7; Reti, 9½—6½; Marshall, 9—7. It was White's round by 3—2, with the totals at 50½—39½.

Game 86   EIGHTEENTH ROUND—RETI'S OPENING (For Black)

Dr. Lasker. White.	Alekhine. Black.	After 21 P—R5

Dr. Lasker. White.	Alekhine. Black.
1 Kt—KB3	Kt—KB3
2 P—Q4	P—KKt3
3 B—B4	P—B4
4 P—B3(a)	P—QKt3
5 QKt—Q2(b)	PxP(c)
6 PxP	B—QKt2
7 P—K3	B—KKt2
8 B—Q3	Castles
9 Castles	Kt—B3(d)
10 P—KR3	P—Q3
11 Q—K2	P—QR3(e)
12 KR—Q	Q—Kt(f)
13 B—R2	Q—R2
14 P—QR3	QR—B
15 QR—B	P—QKt4(g)
16 P—QKt4(h)	Kt—Q2
17 Kt—Kt3	Kt—Kt3
18 R—B2(i)	Kt—R5
19 KR—QB	Q—R
20 P—R4(j)	Kt—R2
21 P—R5	B—K5(k)
22 Kt—K	BxB
23 KtxB	RxR
24 RxR	R—B(l)
25 PxP	RPxP
26 Kt—R5	Kt—Kt3(m)
27 Kt—K	Q—K5
28 B—Kt3	RxR(n)
29 QxR	QxQ
30 KtxQ	K—B
Drawn	

(a) Likewise P—K3 may be played with effect, for, if 4...Q—Kt3, then either the Pawn sacrifice 5 Kt—B3, or the simple 5 Q—B would be favorable for White, chiefly because the position of the Queen at Kt3 would enhance the difficulty of fianchettoing the QB, so closely interwoven with this entire system.

(b) Dr. Lasker plays the opening move in the exact sequence adopted by him (with the colors reversed) against Reti in the 14th round. As, however, the game under consideration shows, the right course is to play next 5 P—K3 and afterwards QKt—Q2.

(c) But now he must recapture with the BP, and Black, who henceforth has to reckon with an immovable pawn structure, thereupon is able to develop his QKt on the favorable square, B3 (instead of Q2 or Q7, as occurred in the other game), by means of which he obtains an even game without difficulty.

(d) The position of this Knight has a two-fold advantage—to lessen very considerably the realization of the opponent's chances both on the Queen's side (through P—QR4), as well as in the center (through P—K4). For, after P—QR4, the Knight would have been able to take immediate possession of Kt5; and, after P—K4, White would find it difficult to protect the doubly attacked QP (for instance, after 10...Kt—KR4; 11 B—K3, P—B4, etc.). And for this reason White determines to restrict his maneuvers to the open QBfile, where, however, the opponent can easily balance the position.

(e) Allowing an exchange of Bishops at this stage would bring trouble to Black on account of the weakness of his White squares.

(f) In order to strengthen the Queen's wing, as well as to bring pressure upon Q5 from QR2 and by that means to make P—K4 still more difficult. Moreover, 12... P—Kt4 would be premature here on account of the reply, 13 P—QR4.

(g) Now, however, this reply is no longer to be feared and Black, with the move in the text, discloses the intention to make as much as possible out of the somewhat unsafe pawn position on the hostile Queen's side by transferring his KKt to QKt3.

(h)   Herewith the square, QB4, for which White has no compensation in Black's corresponding square, QB4, is marked as a potential weakness. White, however, believes that he has sufficient means of defense with which to ward off the danger involved.

(i)   The exchange of both Rooks, which is hard for Black to avoid in carrying out his plan, is, of course, an important simplification and, therefore, favors White.

(j)   A harmless demonstration, which, while it does not matter, is also not profitable, because White is entirely too busy on the Queen's wing in order seriously to contemplate an attack on the King.

(k)   The exchange hereby forced rather increases Black's chances, inasmuch as he obtains access to the White squares for his Queen and Knights, but it is not sufficient, because of the diminished material, to bring about a decisive turn.

(l)   24...Q—Q4; 25 Kt—R5, etc., would have had no real object, as the pawn, following exchange of Queens on KR4, could not be held indefinitely.

(m)   Threatening 27...Kt—B5, etc.

(n)   28...Kt—B3 would be courting danger, on account of 29 P—B3, Q—Q4; 30 P—K4, etc. There is nothing more to be done with the position—the open file turned out to be a too strong leveling factor.

Game 87   EIGHTEENTH ROUND—IRREGULAR DEFENSE

Ed Lasker	Capablanca		
White	Black	18 Q—Q2	P—QR3
1 P—K4	P—KKt3(a)	19 Q—Kt4	Q—Q2(o)
2 Kt—KB3(b)	B—Kt2	20 QxKP	QxQ
3 B—B4(c)	P—QB4	21 BxQ	KR—K
4 Castles(d)	Kt—QB3	22 B—Kt4(p)	R—B7
5 P—B3	Q—Kt3	23 B—B3	B—R3(q)
6 R—K(e)	P—Q3	24 P—Kt3	B—Q2
7 B—Kt3(f)	Kt—B3	25 QR—Q(r)	B—QKt4
8 P—Q4	PxP	26 Kt—B	Kt—Kt2
9 PxP	Castles(g)	27 Kt—KR2(s)	Kt—K3
10 P—KR3(h)	Kt—KR4	28 Kt—Q3(t)	BxKt
11 B—K3	Kt—R4	29 RxB	B—B8(u)
12 Kt—B3	KtxB	30 Kt—B	Kt—Kt4
13 PxKt(i)	Q—Q	31 K—Kt2	Kt—K5
14 P—K5(j)	P—B4(k)	32 R—B3	K—B2(v)
15 B—Kt5(l)	P—Q4	33 P—KKt4	K—K3(w)
16 Q—B(m)	B—K3	34 Kt—K3	BxKt
17 Kt—K2(n)	R—B	35 R(K)xB	R—QB
		36 K—B(x)	P—QKt4

After 19 Q—Kt4

After 43...P—B5

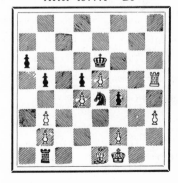

37	PxPch	PxP	
38	R—B4(y)	P—KR4(z)	
39	R—K2	R—B8ch	
40	R—K	RxRch	
41	BxR	R—B8(aa)	
42	R—R4	R—Kt8(bb)	
43	RxP	P—B5(cc)	
44	K—K2(dd)	P—B6ch	
45	KxP	RxB	
46	R—R6ch	K—B4	
47	RxP	Kt—Kt4ch	
48	K—Kt2	Kt—K3(ee)	
49	P—R4	R—K5	

50	R—Kt6	R—Kt5ch	
51	K—B	KtxP	
52	P—K6(ff)	R—K5	
53	P—R5	RxP	
54	R—Kt8	R—KR3	
55	K—K	RxP	
56	K—Q2	R—R6	
57	R—B8ch	K—K4	
58	P—Kt4	R—QKt6	
59	R—K8ch	Kt—K3	
60	P—B4ch	K—B4	
	Resigns		

(a)   From the present-day theoretical standpoint this move cannot be regarded as wholly valid, because Black commits himself to a certain position without being able to influence in any way his adversary's development in the center.

(b)   If the center must be commanded at all by two Pawns, then it must be done in the present situation and for the following reasons: 1. It has to be done at a time when White has not committed himself to a definite grouping of his pieces and consequently is able to choose the formation which is most suitable for the protection and strengthening of his Pawn position in the center. 2. This task is made the easier for him inasmuch as only P—QB4 comes into consideration for Black in reaction against the formation, Q4 and K4, because, after P—Q4, P—K5, he would be compelled sooner or later (on account of the necessity of developing the King's Knight) to close the chain of Pawns with P—K3, which would have weakened his black squares on the King's side without compensation. All this as a consequence of the untimely move of P—KKt3!

(c)   3 P—Q4 would still have been the proper move. Now Black gets the opportunity of bringing about a kind of Sicilian, wherein the development of the Bishop at QB4 is quite out of place.

(d)   With 3 P—B3 he could have made possible the move of P—Q4, but, after 4...Kt—QB3; 5 P—Q4, PxP; 6 PxP, Black, by means of 6...Q—Kt3, would get some counter-play. After the text-move, however, he will be able to prevent for a long time the capture of the center.

(e)   In order, after 6...Kt—B3, to be able to reply with 7 P—Q4. But Black is under no compulsion to develop the Knight in that manner.

(f)   For this waiting move, with which White speculates further concerning the opponent's difficulties in developing the King's side, Black had not less than four plans, which at the very least would not have brought him any decisive disadvantage: I. 7...B—Q2, in order, if White sooner or later plays P—Q4, to take possession of the QB file after PxP, PxP. II. The radical 7...P—K4, in connection with which the weakness of Q4 was to be dreaded (for instance, after P—Q3, followed by B—K3 QKt—Q2, etc.). III. 7...P—K3, followed by KKt—K2, Castles, etc IV. (Last, but not least) 7...P—KR3 (as a preparation for B—Kt5 and, if 8 P—KR3, then 8...P—KKt4!, etc. This last idea would have been perhaps the most energetic rejoinder to White's waiting policy. Black's next move, on the other hand, is an actual positional error which is probably traceable to some tactical oversight in his calculations, for otherwise it would be inexplicable in the world's champion.

(g)   Also 9...B—Kt5; 10 B—K3, BxKt; 11 PxB, etc., would have been clearly advantageous for White.

(h)   Thereby the development of Black's QB is made considerably more difficult, as, after 10...B—Q2, for instance, the reply of P—K5 would have been very strong. For that reason Capablanca in his next moves seeks to gain the advantage of two Bishops as compensation for his unfavorable development, but thereby opens the important QR file for his opponent.

(i)   Threatening, among other things, to win a Pawn by 14 P—Q5.

(j)   Very strong. The dangerous position of the King's Knight now compels Black to take extraordinary measures, the immediate result of which is the indefensibility of the KP.

(k)   After 14...PxP; 15 PxP, the QRP would be lost at once on account of the threat of 16 P—KKt4.

(l)   Threatening 15 PxQP, as well as 15 Kt—Q5, etc.

(m)   Here, however, 16 Q—Q2, followed by Kt—K2 and Q—Kt4, etc., would have been still more forcible. Nevertheless White's position is already so strong that even this loss of a tempo does not help his opponent much.

(n)   Threatening 18 Q—B5

(o)   With his usual position judgment Capablanca recognizes the fact that the immediate surrender of the weak Pawn offers him the best chances of defense. As a matter of fact Black, after 19...R—QB2; 20 KR—QB, KR—K; 21 Kt—K, followed by Kt—Q3—B5, etc., would have succumbed through virtual suffocation.

(p)   Even after 22 B—B5, B—R3!, followed by B—Q2 and Kt—Kt2—K3, etc., White would not have found it easy to make his material advantage count; but at any rate the chances of winning would then have been on his side, and therefore, as he plays, he can hope at the best only for a draw, inasmuch as the black Rook on B7 turns out to be a downright unpleasant prisoner.

(q)   Now the strength of the united Bishops shows itself to the fullest extent. White's obstructed extra Pawn, on the other hand, clearly does not here come into consideration at all.

(r)   In order to be able to transfer the Knight to Q3 by way of QB, which at this stage would have been prevented by 25...B—Kt4.

(s)   Somewhat better would have been at once 27 Kt—Q3, etc. With the text-move White probably intended to meet 27...Kt—K3 with 28 P—B4 and only later on noticed that this would have had catastrophic consequences after 28...P—Kt4, etc.

(t)   If 28 Kt—R2, then 28...P—QR4!; 28 BxP?, R—QR; 30 Kt—QKt4, RxP, threatening also 31...B—Q7.

(u)   Herewith Black assures himself of the restoration of material equality. Still more convincing, however, appears to be at once 29...Kt—Kt4, as, after 30 K—Kt2, Kt—K5; 31 R—KB3, R—QB, followed by an exchange and the recovery of the Pawn on QB3, the ending, on account of the white Pawn on the black square, would have been more easily won for Black with the Bishop against the Knight than vice versa, as in the game.

(v)   Here as well as on the previous move the capture of the KtP clearly would not have been healthy, as Wh te, after BxP; BxB, RxB, would have taken possession of the open file with R—QB, with excellent drawing chances.

(w)   Now the threat is R—QB, which makes it necessary for White to exchange his Knight. The following ending, nevertheless, is to be won by Black only with difficulty.

(x)   In order at last to get rid of the intruder through an exchange, which Black cannot very well prevent.

(y)   If at once 38 R—K2 in order, after 38...R—B8ch; 39 R—K, RxRch, to be able to recapture with the King, then Black would obtain winning chances with 40... P—Kt5!, followed by the entrance of his second Rook. Among other things, this was the point of his 36th move.

(z)   In order to weaken the effect of the counter attack by R—R4.

(aa)   Preventing 42 P—B3, on accocunt of 42...Kt—Q7ch, followed by KtxP, etc.

(bb)   The beginning of a deep ending maneuver which promises Black splendid winning chances, notwithstanding the opponent's preponderance.

(cc)   Threatening to win at once by 44...P—B6, etc.

(dd)   A deplorable mistake, because of which the instructive ending comes to an untimely end. Necessary was 44R—R6ch in order, after 44...K—B4!, to drive away the Knight from his dominating square by means of 45 P—B3. After 45...Kt—Kt6ch; 46 K—Kt2!, Black, to be sure, did not need to accept the sacrifice of the piece, which would have actually led to defeat after 46...RxB?; 47 R—B6ch, K—Kt4; 48 P—R4ch!, K—R4; 49 RxBP, Kt—B8; 50 K—B2, etc. However, he could have played much better 46...RxPch; 47 B—B2, K—Kt4!; 48 RxQRP, Kt—B4, which would have assured him the recovery of both Pawns with a superior position. Now, of course, matters are made much easier for him, as White has no compensation in his single Pawn for the piece which he loses.

(ee)   Decisive.

(ff)   Instead of this he might have quietly resigned.

Game 88   EIGHTEENTH ROUND—QUEEN'S PAWN OPENING

	Marshall	Bogoljubow
	White	Black
1	P—Q4	Kt—KB3
2	Kt—KB3	P—K3
3	B—Kt5(a)	P—Q4
4	P—K3	QKt—Q2(b)
5	P—B4	P—B3
6	PxP(c)	KPxP
7	Kt—B3	Q—R4(d)
8	B—Q3	Kt—K5
9	Q—B2(e)	KtxB(f)
10	KtxKt	P—KR3(g)
11	Kt—B3	B—K2(h)
12	Castles	Castles
13	P—QR3(i)	Q—Q(j)
14	QR—K(k)	P—QR4(l)
15	Q—K2	Kt—B3(m)
16	Kt—K5	B—Q3
17	P—B4(n)	P—B4
18	B—Kt	B—Q2
19	Q—QB2(o)	B—B3(p)

20	PxP(q)	BxP
21	K—R(r)	R—K(s)
22	P—K4	B—Q5(t)
23	KtxB	PxKt
24	P—K5	Kt—Kt5
25	Q—R7ch	K—B
26	P—KKt3(u)	Q—Kt3(v)
27	B—B5	Kt—B7ch

After 27...Kt—B7ch

28	RxKt(w)	BxR
29	Q—R8ch	K—K2
30	QxKtP(x)	K—Q
31	Q—B6ch	R—K2
32	P—K6(y)	B—Q5(z)
33	PxP	BxQ
34	P—B8(Q)ch	K—B2
35	RxRch	BxR
36	QxR(aa)	K—Q3
37	Q—R8	Q—Q(bb)
38	Q—K5ch	Resigns

After 21 K—R

With his 38th move, Marshall announced checkmate in five moves.

(a) It is better to play first P—B4, for after the text-move, Black does not need to resort to the defense of the Queen's Gambit but, as is well known, may work up most promising counter-play with 3...P—B4!; 4 P—K3, Q—Kt3; 5 Q—B, Kt—B3, etc.

(b) Even now 4...P—B4 would have its good points. Black clearly is bent upon playing the Cambridge Springs variation, even after the opponent offers him more favorable opportunities (see his seventh move).

(c) Marshall's specialty. Here, however, he might have done better to develop his Queen's Knight first and to play 7 PxQP only after 6...Q—R4 (see the game between Janowski and Bogoljubow), for after the exchange of pawns it was not at all necessary for Black to send his Queen to R4.

(d) The beginning of a series of inferior moves which gradually bring about a lost position for the second player. By means of the simple 7...B—K2 he could have obtained a worthwhile game, for instance: 8 B—Q3, Kt—K5!; 9 BxB (A), QxB; 10 BxKt, PxB; 11 Kt—Q2, Kt—B3; 12 Q—B2, B—B4; 13 Castles (13 P—B3?, PxP; 14 QxB,

QxPch; 15 K—Q, PxP, and wins). Castles; 14 P—B3,· KR—K, etc. Or A—9 B—KB4, P—KB4; 10 Kt—K5, KtxKt; 11 BxKt, Castles; 12 P—B3 (or 12 Castles, B—Q3; 13 P—B4, B—K3), KtxKt; 13 PxKt, B—Q3; 14 P—B4, BxB; 15 BPxB, Q—Kt4; 16 Q—K2 (B3), P—B5, etc.

(e)   Just a trifle better perhaps is 9 Castles, as played by Janowski against the same opponent, as for one thing Black could not very well capture twice on B3 and, on the other hand, the white Queen would be at least as effective in aiding an attack on the King from Q square as from B2. Likewise with the text-move, however, White gains an advantage.

(f)   Otherwise the previous move of the Knight would have had no meaning at all.

(g)   A wholly unnecessary weakening of the King's wing. To be sure 9...B—K2 would have been a mistake on account of 10 KtxRP!, P—KKt3; 11 BxP, PxB; 12 QxPch, K—Q; 13 Kt—Kt5!, BxKt; 14 QxBch, K—B2; 15 P—KR4, etc.; but with 9...Kt—B3; 10 Castles, B—K2 and, if 11 P—B4, then 11...B—Q2, followed eventually by P—QB4, etc., he would have obtained much better counter-chances.

(h)   Why not at least 11...B—Q3; 12 Castles, Castles, with the subsequent R—K or Q—B2, in order to prevent the posting of the Knight on K5?

(i)   A fine move with which White threatens to cause a weakness on B6 by P—QKt4 —Kt5.

(j)   Had the Bishop been developed at Q3, then 13...Q—B2 could have been played here much better, but which would not do now on account of 14 KtxP. It goes to show how Black by purposeless play has rendered the defense difficult.

(k)   However, this move by White is certainly somewhat obscure and could have been answered adequately by Black with 14...B—Q3, inasmuch as P—K4 in this position need not be feared at all. More to the point, therefore, would have been 14 Q—K2 immediately, on account of the regrouping of the pieces later carried out.

(l)   Loss of a tempo and at the same time a weakening of the position. There was no need for preventing P—QKt4, as Black could always have met that move with P—QR3, and perhaps would have been in a position to make use of the loosening of the Queen's wing in order to open a file for himself there. In this game Bogoljubow clearly found himself off form.

(m)   And even now, despite all his sins, after 15...B—Q3 (16 P—K4, PxP; 17 KtxP, Kt—B3, etc.), he could easily have prevented the worst, namely, the entrance of the Knight at K5.

(n)   White now has before him a path plainly mapped out: B—Kt, Q—B2, followed by the advance of the KKtP to drive away the KKt. For that reason Black unquestionably must undertake something in the center in order to attempt to discount this simple plan, even if indirectly.

(o)   Threatening 20 KtxQP, etc.

(p)   In the hope of partially consolidating his game after 20...PxP; 21 PxP, BxKt; 22 BPxB, Kt—K5, etc. Marshall, however, unearths a new and subtle, if not altogether perfect method of attack.

(q)   After 20 Kt—Kt4, Black, by means of 20...P—KKt3, as well as by 20... Kt—K5, could have defended himself by offering a pawn sacrifice not without prospects.

(r)   With the double threat of 22 P—K4 or 22 Kt—Kt4.

(s)   The last mistake. Necessary would have been 21...R—B, whereby the threat of 22 P—K4 would have been completely parried. After 22 Kt—Kt4. however, Black could have defended himself with 22...P—KKt3!, for instance: 23 KtxRPch (or 23 Kt—K5, B—K!), K—Kt2; 24 KtxBP, RxKt; 25 OxPch, K—B, and White, to be sure, would have quite sufficient material for his piece, but there is no decisive turn in sight. and thereafter the struggle might have gone on for a long time. The text-move is utilized by Marshall very energetically.

(t)   Good counsel is already at a premium.In reply to 22...PxP, White after 23 KtxP. PxKt; 24 KtxP, KtxKt; 25 RxKt, RxR; 26 QxR, P—Kt3; 27 P—B5!, would win at least two pawns after 27...Q—Q4. In case of other moves, continuations analogous to the one in the actual game would be decisive.

(u)   The simplest. However, 26 O—R8ch, K—K2; 27 QxKtP, R—KKt; 28 Q—R7, Kt—B7ch: 29 RxKt, BxR; 30 R—K2, threatening 31 P—K6 ,etc., also would have won eventually.

(v)   Of course it does not matter any longer what Black moves now.

(w)   An unnecessary sacrifice which merely prolongs the game somewhat. After the simple 28 K—Kt2, Kt—K5 (or QxP; 29 R—OKt, QxKt: 30 O—R8ch. followed by mate in three moves): 29 KtxKt, PxKt; 30 Q—R8ch, K—K2; 31 QxKtP, QxPch; 32 K—R, Black, because of the several threats that are not to be parried, might as well have given up.   ;

(x)   Threatening 31 Q—B6ch, K—B; 32 QxRPch, followed by mate in three moves.

(y) More compelling perhaps than 22 R—Q or 32 Q—Q6ch, K—K; 33 QxRP, which would also have sufficed.

(z) Or I.—32 ...BxR; 33 PxP; II.—32...PxP; 33 RxP, followed by 34 Q—B8ch, etc.; III.—32...Q—Q5; 33 R—K5!

(aa) Threatening Q—B8ch, K—Q3; 38 Q—Q7ch, followed by 39 Kt—R4ch, winning the Queen.

(bb) There was no remedy against 38 Q—K5ch, etc. Now White will mate in five moves: 38 Q—K5ch, K—B4; 39 Kt—R4ch, K—B5 (or 39...K—Kt4; 40 Q—K2ch, KxKt; 41 B—B2 mate); 40 Q—B3ch, K—Kt4; 41 B—Q3ch, KxKt; 42 Q—B2 mate. For this game, conducted with great animation, Marshall received the second brilliancy prize.

Game 89   EIGHTEENTH ROUND—RUY LOPEZ

Maroczy   Reti   After 23 B—B2
  White   Black

	White	Black
1	P—K4	P—K4
2	Kt—KB3	Kt—QB3
3	B—Kt5	P—QR3
4	B—R4	Kt—B3
5	Castles	B—K2
6	R—K	P—QKt4
7	B—Kt3	P—Q3
8	P—B3	Castles
9	P—KR3	Kt—QR4
10	B—B2	P—B4
11	P—Q4	Q—B2
12	QKt—Q2	B—Q2
13	Kt—B	BPxP
14	PxP	KR—B
15	B—Q3(a)	Kt—B3
16	B—K3	Q—Kt2(b)
17	Kt—Kt3	R—B2
18	R—QB	QR—QB
19	B—Kt	Kt—K(c)
20	Q—Q2	P—KKt3
21	KR—Q	P—B3
22	Kt—K2	B—B
23	B—B2(d)	Kt—R4(e)
24	Kt—Kt3	Kt—B5
25	B—Kt3	K—R
26	Q—K2	KtxB(f)
27	RxR	KKtxR
28	QxKt	Kt—K3
29	Kt—K2(g)	P—Kt5(h)
30	R—QB	RxRch
31	KtxR	Q—Kt3
32	Kt—K2	B—Kt2
33	Q—Q2(i)	Kt—B
34	Q—Q3	P—R3
35	B—B4	P—QR4
36	PxP	QPxP
37	Kt—Q2(j)	P—B4(k)
38	K—B	B—KB3
39	P—QKt3	B—KR5
40	P—Kt3	B—KB3(l)
41	Q—Q5	B—K3
42	Q—R8	Q—Q(m)
43	QxQ	BxQ
44	BxB	KtxB
45	PxP	PxP
46	Kt—B4	B—B2
47	Kt—K3	Kt—Kt2
48	P—B4(n)	PxP
49	KtxP(B4)	BxKt
50	PxB	Kt—K3(o)
51	KtxP	KtxP
52	KtxP	Kt—Q6(p)
53	Kt—B5	Kt—B8
54	Kt—Q6	KtxRP
55	Kt—B4	Kt—B8
56	KtxP	K—R2
57	Kt—B6(q)	KtxP
58	KtxP	Drawn

(a) Up to here the game is identical with the one between Dr. Lasker and Edward Lasker in the sixth round, in which at this point White played 15 R—K2. The text-move, which has for its object the possession of the QB file with the QR, seems to refute in the simplest manner Black's plan initiated with the twelfth move.

(b) Black in any event can double the Rooks in this fashion on the open file, but the future holds out desperate little mobility for all of his m.nor pieces.

(c) In order, by means of P—B3, to free the Knight from the necessity of protecting the KP and thereupon to bring about an easy exchange of Rooks.

(d) White clearly overlooks the reply of the adversary. Even 23 P—QR3 would not have been conv.ncing, on account of the reply of 23 P—QKt5!, but, after 23 Kt—K!, which would have made ready for P—KB4, as well as B—B2, the difficulties of the second player would have become still greater.

(e) Herewith Black has overcome the worst, for 24 P—QKt3 would now be of doubtful merit, on acount of 24...P—Q4! (threaten.ng B—R6). White's only chance still lay in the strong diagonal from QR2 to KKt8, but with correct play on the part of Black, this would no longer suffice for a win.

(f) This exchange, which could no longer be avoided by Black, was not yet necessary here and should better have been prepared for with B—K3 in order to increase its effectiveness.

(g) Probably with the intention of landing this Knight on Q5—something Black, however, could have permitted unhesitatingly.

(h) Thereby both Pawns on the Queen's side are weakened and the square, B4, is ceded to the opponent who forthwith makes excellent use thereof.

(i) Threatening 34 PxP, BPxP; 35 Kt—Kt5, etc.

(j) Here, however, he should have first prevented P—KB4 by mans of 37 Kt—R4 (threatening Q—Q5), K—R2; 38 P—Kt4, followed by Kt—Kt2—Q5, whereupon he would have maintained the superior game.

(k) Liberating at last the KB.

(l) Of course not 40...PxP, on account of 41 Q—Q5!, winn.ng a piece.

(m) Black clearly has nothing better, but it is just sufficient for a draw.

(n) Thereby White at last wins a Pawn, but too few pieces are then left on the board. Somewhat better w.nning chances were offered by 48 K—K—Q2, etc.

(o) This counter-attack saves the game

(p) More to the point than 52...KtxP, whereupon White, in the race of the Kings to the Queen's wing, would have been two tempi in advance.

(q) Or 58 K—K, K—R3; 59 K—Q2, KtxPch; 60 KtxKt, K—R4, and White w.ll not be able to save the KRP.

Game 90   EIGHTEENTH ROUND—SICILIAN DEFENSE

Yates	Tartakower
White	Black
1 P—K4	P—QB4
2 Kt—KB3	P—K3
3 P—Q4	PxP
4 KtxP	P—QR3
5 Kt—QB3(a)	Q—B2
6 B—Q3	Kt--QB3(b)
7 B—K3	Kt—KB3
8 Kt—Kt3(c)	P—QKt4
9 Q—K2(d)	Kt--K4(e)
10 P—KB4	KtxB
11 PxKt(f)	B—Kt2
12 Castles	B—K2
13 QR—B	Q—Q
14 P—KR3	Castles
15 Q—B2	P—Kt5(g)
16 Kt—R4	B—B3
17 Kt—Kt6	R—Kt
18 Kt—B4	P—Q4
19 Kt(B4)—R5	B—R
20 P—K5	Kt—Q2
21 Kt—B6(h)	BxKt
22 RxB	P--QR4

| 23 KR—QB | P—KKt4(i) |

After 23 KR—QB

24 Q—Kt3	K—R
25 PxP	R—Kt4(j)
26 Kt—Q4	R—B4
27 R(B6)xR	BxR
28 Kt—Kt3	B—K2
29 P--KR4	P—R5

30 Kt—Q4	B—B4	41 RxR	QxPch
31 Kt—K2(k)	BxB	42 K—Kt	QxPch
32 QxB	Q—Kt	43 K—B	Q—Q6ch
33 P—Q4	P—Kt6(l)	44 K—B2	K—Kt(o)
34 PxP	PxP	45 RxKtch	KxR
35 R—B3	Q—Kt5	46 Q—B8ch	K—K2
36 Kt—B4	R—R	47 Q—B7ch	K—K
37 K—R2(m)	Q—Kt4	48 Kt—B6ch	K—B
38 Kt—R5	Q—B8	49 Q—Q8ch	K—Kt2
39 Q—QB	Q—B7(n)	50 Q—Kt8 mate	
40 R—B8ch	Kt—B		

(a) In the Paulsen variation White should strive to reserve the best chance of P—QB4 in order to evade the pressure on the QB file. For that reason 5 B—K2 first, followed by Castles, etc., was to have been preferred.

(b) This move of the Knight does not exactly fit into the system. More promising is the development by Kt—KB3, QKt—Q2 (providing incidentally for the square, QKt3) and, after first castling, P—QKt4 (3), followed by B—Kt2, etc.

(c) Already threatening to deprive the adversary of one of his Bishops by Kt—R4—Kt6.

(d) Clearing the square (Q) for the Knight in the event of P—QR4, P—Kt5.

(e) The exchange hereby brought about is the source of all subsequent embarrassments. Certainly to be preferred would have been 9...B—K2, followed by Castles, P—Q3 and B—Kt2, etc.

(f) The QB file has become a very important factor favorable to White, in that he is ahead of the opponent in development and Black's Queen's wing shows several weaknesses. Black's two Bishops do not compensate in any way for these disadvantages. Mr. Yates, as will be seen, makes good use of his opportunities.

(g) Weakening the Queen's side still more, without obtaining any counter-play in return. Even if not exactly pleasant, at any rate more opportune would have been 15...P—Q4; 16 B—Kt6, Q—Kt; 17 B—B5!, R—K, etc.

(h) Forcing, after a long journey, the exchange of the important defensive Bishop and thereby assuring himself of the undisputed control of the QB file.

(i) Black in desperation continues in a manner which the situation fully justifies. Against the entrance of the white pieces (R—B7 or maybe R—R6, followed by Q—B2 —B6, etc.) there was as a matter of fact nothing to be done.

(j) Speculating upon the possibility of 26...P—Q5, etc., which in any event would have been easily met by 26 P—KR4.

(k) White goes quietly about his task and permits the opponent no counter-play whatever. This game, played by Dr. Tartakower far below his form, has been practically finished for sometime.

(l) Sealing the fate of a second Pawn.

(m) Of course, 37 RxP could also have been played.

(n) Sacrificing the Rook for a couple of checks, but the exchange of Queens would likewise have been equivalent to resignation.

(o) Or 44...Q—Q5ch; 45 K—Kt3, QxPch; 46 Q—B4, Q—K8ch; 47 K—R2, etc. Now White mates in six moves.

NINETEENTH ROUND

With Capablanca only one point behind and hanging on with bulldog tenacity, it was necessary for Dr. Lasker to keep on winning to maintain his advantage in position. This he succeeded in doing at the expense of his namesake, who had drawn with him in the sixth round, after giving him so much trouble. Capablanca defeated Dr. Tartakower, and Alekhine won from Janowski. Marshall, with a draw against Maroczy, came up level with Reti and raised the hopes of his friends, who were prophesying for him fourth place or better. Reti's loss to Yates was most untimely for the author of "New Ideas," upon whom the strain of the long tournament had begun to tell.

Edward Lasker had the white side of a Queen's Gambit declined, but failed to make the most of it. He allowed the exchange of Queens and was left with a doubled QB Pawn. Notwithstanding the fact that he had two Bishops, he came into an inferior ending, in which Dr. Lasker's skill asserted itself.

Dr. Tartakower had the temerity to play a King's Gambit against Capablanca. It was most unwise, even though a notable precedent was set by Charousek in his defeat of Dr. Lasker in the last round at Nuremberg. There is nothing quite so toothsome to the present world's champion as a gambit Pawn. In the minds of many the result was a foregone conclusion as soon as Dr. Tartakower advanced his KBP, and yet the game was worth while as still another illustration of the champion's forceful style. There was hardly a move made by the loser that can be seriously censured, unless it be 2 P—KB4. It was still another proof, albeit hardly needed, that no living player can give Capablanca the odds of such a gambit.

Alekhine, on the black side of a Reti opening (reversed), had to deal with an interesting sacrifice of a Knight on the part of Janowski in the middle game, which was good for at least a draw. Janowski played to win, but underrated the danger of the Russian's two connected passed Pawns on the Queen's side. These resulted in his downfall, so that Alekhine kept step with the leaders.

Marshall, who lost to Maroczy in the sixth round, did his best to square accounts with the Hungarian. The latter adopted the Indian Defense. The American invited complications in the opening. Maroczy found a good defense and soon had the white forces retreating, without, however, taking toll from his opponent's slightly inferior position. Equalization thereupon ensued. Oddly enough, this state of affairs was repeated in the ending. Then a draw was agreed upon.

Yates vs. Reti was a very pretty effort on the part of the Briton against a Caro-Kann Defense. Reti injudiciously allowed the exchange of his QB on KKt3, naturally recapturing with the KRP. Thereby his castled King was placed in grave danger. Of this he seemed to be quite unconscious until Yates, with a neat Knight maneuver, threatened to win the Queen for two pieces, or worse. Thereupon he saw the light and resigned.

The scores of the leaders: Dr. Lasker, 13—4; Capablanca, 12—5; Alekhine, 11—7; Marshall and Reti, each 9½—7½. The black pieces took the round by 3½—1½. Totals: White, 52; Black, 43.

Game 91   NINETEENTH ROUND—QUEEN'S GAMBIT DECLINED

Ed. Lasker	Dr. Lasker		
White	Black		
1 P—Q4	Kt—KB3	18 PxP	PxP
2 P—QB4	P—K3	19 KR—Q	B—R3
3 QKt—B3	P—Q4	20 BxB(g)	RxB
4 Kt—B3	QKt—Q2	21 P—QR4	KR—R
5 B—Kt5	P—B3	22 K—B	P—KB4(h)
6 P—K3	Q—R4	23 QR—Kt(i)	KR—R2
7 Kt—Q2	B—Kt5	24 P—Kt4(j)	PxP
8 Q—B2	Kt—K5(a)	25 R—Kt4	Kt—B3
9 KKtxKt	PxKt	26 B—Kt8	R—R
10 B—B4(b)	Castles	27 R—Q8ch	K—B2
11 B—K2	P—K4	28 B—B7	RxP(k)
12 PxP(c)	KtxP	29 R(Q8)xR	RxR(R1)
13 Castles	BxKt	30 RxKtP(l)	Kt—Q4
14 QxB(d)	QxQ	31 R—Kt7(m)	K—K3
15 PxQ	R—K(e)	32 P—QB4	Kt—K2
16 P—B5	Kt—Q2(f)	33 R—Kt4(n)	R—R8ch
		34 K—K2	R—R7ch
		35 K—K	Kt—B4
		36 R—Kt6	K—Q2
		37 B—K5	R—R5
		38 P—B5	K—K3
		39 B—Q6	K—Q4
		40 R—Kt7	P—R4
		41 B—B8	P—Kt3
		42 R—Q7ch	K—B5
		43 R—Q	R—R6
		44 R—Q8	Kt—R5
		45 B—Kt7	Kt—B6ch
		46 K—K2	R—R7ch
		47 K—B	R—Q7
		48 RxR(o)	KtxRch
		49 K—Kt2	KxP
		50 P—R3	PxPch
		51 KxP	P—Kt4
		Resigns	

After 16 P—B5

17 B—Q6   P—QKt3

(a) This is the older continuation. Bogoljubow's variation runs as follows: 8...Castles; 9 B—K2 (9 BxKt, followed by 10 B—Q3, promises no advantage for White), P—K4; 10 PxKP, Kt—K5; 11 KKtxKt, PxKt; 12 Castles, BxKt; 13 PxB, P—B3!; 14 B—R4 (14 B—B4, KtxP; 15 Q—K4?, B—KB4!, played between Gruenfeld and Bogoljubow at Maehrisch-Ostrau, 1923), QxKP!; 15 B—Kt3, Q—K2; 16 KR—Q, KR—K, followed by Q—KB2, with a wholly satisfactory game.

(b) The theoretical move is 10 B—R4 in order to be able to Castle simply after 10...Castles; 11 B—K2, P—K4. The difference between the two methods of play becomes manifest at once.

(c) After 12 B—Kt3, P—KB4, Black would be threatening the win of a piece, thereby practically forcing 13 PxKP. After the text-move, however, he runs into a favorable line of the Bogoljubow variation.

(d) Likewise after 14 PxB, B—B4, etc. Black's game would have been preferable.

(e) Now White has no adequate compensation for the doubled Pawns and should have limited his activity to occupying the open files (16 KR—Q, B—B4; 17 QR—Kt, P—QKt3; 18 P—KR3), whereupon his game might have just held together. His next move affords Black the opportunity of opening for himself new lines and thereby obtaining the upper hand.

(f) Not at once 16...P—QKt3, on account of 17 BxKt, RxB; 18 PxP, PxP; 19 KR—Kt, etc., with a probable draw. The subsequent utilization of the QR file simultaneously with the stifling of White's counter-action on the Q file is clear and convincing.

(g) It would have been somewhat better to permit the King to participate at once with 20 K—B, etc.

(h) Of course not 22...RxP; 23 RxR, RxR; 24 B—B7, etc.

(i) Threatening 24 B—B7.

(j) White attempts to switch the play by sheer force into another channel, inasmuch as in a simpler continuation (24 R—Kt4, K—B2, etc.) his QRP could not have been held. The following development, on the other hand, apart from the Pawn plus, results in a far superior position for Black.

(k) Not 28...Kt—Q4; 29 RxKP (KtxB); 30 R—Q7ch).

(l) If 30 BxP, then 30...Kt—Q4, followed by R—QKt, etc., would win.

(m) If 31 RxP?, R—QB, etc.

(n) White attempts to maintain the Pawn on B4. It cannot be long, however, before he must yield the square, Q5, to the black King. The following ending is easily comprehended.

(o) Or 48 R—Q6, KxP, and White, on account of the threatened mate, would have to exchange the Rooks.

Game 92   NINETEENTH ROUND—KING'S GAMBIT

Tartakower	Capablanca		After 9 BxKt
White	Black		

	White	Black			
1	P—K4	P—K4			
2	P—KB4	PxP			
3	B—K2	P—Q4			
4	PxP	Kt—KB3			
5	P—B4	P—B3			
6	P—Q4 (a)	B—Kt5ch (b)			
7	K—B (c)	PxP			
8	BxP (d)	PxP (e)			
9	BxKt (f)	Kt—Q4 (g)			
10	K—B2 (h)	RxB			
11	BxP	Castles			
12	Kt—KB3 (i)	Kt—B3			
13	Kt—B3 (j)	P—QKt4 (k)	23	K—B (o)	P—B4
14	B—Q3	Kt—Kt5ch	24	B—B6	R—B3
15	K—Kt	B—Kt2 (l)	25	P—Q5	R—Q (p)
16	B—B5	BxKt	26	R—Q	RxB
17	PxB	Kt—K6 (m)	27	PxR	RxQ
18	BxPch	K—R	28	RxR	Kt—K3 (q)
19	Q—Q3	BxKt	29	R—Q6	Q—B5ch
20	PxB	Kt—Q4 (n)	30	K—Kt2	Q—K7ch
21	B—K4	Kt—B5		Resigns	
22	Q—Q2	Q—R5			

(a) Concerning these opening moves compare the game between Dr. Tartakower and Bogoljubow in the first round.

(b) This, Capablanca's novelty, strengthens very considerably Black's entire system of development.

(c) There is nothing better for White than to abandon castling, for instance: 7 Kt—B3, Kt—K5, or 7 B—Q2, Kt—K5!; 8 BxB?, Q—R5ch; 9 P—Kt3, PxP, and wins.

(d) This simplifying of the position is altogether in favor of Black, who is better developed, and in consequence can soon make it unpleasant for the enemy's uncastled King. More in the spirit of gambit play would have been the more complicated 8 P—B5 and, if 8...P—KKt4, then 9 Kt—KB3, P—KR3; 10 P—KR4, Kt—K5?; 11 PxKKtP!, Kt—Kt6ch; 12 K—B2, KtxRch; 13 QxKt, etc., with full positional compensation for the exchange sacrificed.

(e)   This natural move is bound up with a bit of finesse, however.

(f)   Of which finesse the opponent, who plainly thinks that the world's champion has simply left a piece to be taken, takes no notice whatever. 9 BxBP at once would have been by far the lesser evil.

(g)   Coming to the rescue of the Bishop threatened by 10 Q—R4ch, and thereby assuring himself of the far superior game.

(h)   If 10 B—B4, then 10...Q—B3!, again threatening 12...Kt—K6ch, etc.

(i)   Thereupon the black Knight becomes quite disagreeable and White can no longer obtain a normal development for his King's side. Somewhat better for that reason would have been 12 BxKt, QxB, 13 QKt—B3, followed by Kt—B3 and the development of the KR, but Black would still have had the advantage.

(j)   The conciliatory sacrifice hereby offered could just as well have been accepted by Black, for instance: 13...BxKt; 14 PxB, Kt—K5ch; 15 K—Kt, KtxP; 16 Q—Kt3, Kt—K5; 17 R—K, Kt—Q3, etc. He hopes, however, to get more out of the position by means of the following energetic counter-stroke.

(k)   With the idea, in reply to 14 KtxP, of penetrating decisively with the Rook to QKt7, after 14...P—QR3; 15 Kt—B3, BxKt; 16 PxB, Kt—Kt5ch; 17 K—Kt.

(l)   This development of the Bishop, by means of which the QP is threatened, was one of the consequences of Black's thirteenth move.

(m)   The pawn sacrifice, which compels further loss of time on the part of the adversary, constitutes the only logical continuation of Black's attack.

(n)   Again the best. The inviting 20...Kt4ch; 21 K—B2, KR—K would have been by no means convincing, on account of 22 B—K4.

(o)   In order to be able to play Q—KB2; but it does not come to this.

(p)   Decisive. Because of the threat of 26...RxB, White has no defense, as the Queen dare not move on account of 26 Q—R6ch, etc.

(q)   Simpler than 28...Q—R6ch, which at any rate would have sufficed, for instance: 29 K—B2 (29 K—Kt or K—K, QxBP), Q—Kt7ch; 30 K—K3, QxR; 31 R—Q8ch (31 KxKt, Q—QB8!, etc.), K—R2; 32 P—B7, Q—B8ch; 33 K—B2, Q—B7ch; 34 K—Kt3, Q—Kt7ch; 35 KxKt, QxRPch, and wins.

Game 93   NINETEENTH ROUND—RETI'S OPENING (FOR BLACK)

Janowski	Alekhine
White	Black

After 17...QR—Q

	Janowski (White)	Alekhine (Black)
1	P—Q4	Kt—KB3
2	Kt—KB3	P—B4(a)
3	P—K3	P—KKt3(b)
4	B—Q3	P—Kt3
5	Castles	B—QKt2
6	P—B4(c)	PxP
7	PxP	B—Kt2
8	Kt—B3	P—Q4(d)
9	B—Kt5	PxP(e)
10	BxP	Castles
11	R—K(f)	Kt—B3
12	P—QR3(g)	R—B(h)
13	Q—Q3	Q—B2
14	B—R2(i)	P—K3
15	P—R3(j)	Kt—K2
16	QR—B	Q—Kt
17	Kt—K5(k)	QR—Q
18	KtxBP(l)	RxKt(m)
19	BxP	R—KB
20	P—Q5(n)	QKtxP(o)
21	KtxKt	BxKt
22	BxB(p)	KtxB
23	QxKt	BxP(q)
24	R—B2(r)	BxP
25	B—R6	R—Q
26	Q—K6(s)	B—B4
27	QR—K2(t)	Q—B2
28	Q—Kt3	Q—Q2
29	K—R(u)	B—B
30	R—Q2	Q—B
31	KR—Q	RxR
32	BxR	P—QKt4(v)
33	R—QB(w)	Q—Q2

34 B—B4	P—QR4		43 R—KB	P—R6(y)
35 B—K5(x)	P—R5		44 K—R2(z)	Q—Q6
36 Q—R2	P—Kt5		45 R—K	B—Kt5
37 Q—B4	Q—Q7		46 R—KR	B—Q7
38 P—B4	P—Kt6		47 Q—K6(aa)	Q—B4
39 R—QKt	Q—Kt5		48 Q—Kt3	BxPch
40 Q—K6	Q—K5		49 BxB	QxBch
41 R—Q	P—Kt7		50 K—Kt	K—Kt2
42 Q—R2	Q—B7		Resigns	

(a) If this move can be refuted positionally, it would only be by 3 P—Q5 and, if 3...P—QKt4, then 4 P—B4, B—Kt2; 5 P—QR4!, etc. As White plays in the present game, Black could obtain equality in the first moves of the opening.

(b) As will be seen later, the intention of Black is to bring about the Rubinstein variation (even with a tempo less), but it is impracticable and this tact lends the game a certain theoretical interest. Correct would have been 3...P—Q4 in order to lead into a well-known variation of the Queen's Pawn game not unfavorable to Black.

(c) Threatening by means of P—Q5 to cut off Black's QB which has just been developed and then to undertake a promising Pawn maneuver in the center. For that reason Black must exchange the Pawns.

(d) This move was also made by Reti against the same opponent (ninth round) in a similar position and soon thereafter he gained the advantage. The similarity, however, was merely superficial because in the aforementioned game White, instead of B—Q3 and Castles, had used two moves for the purpose of developing his QB with less effect (P—KR3 and B—B4). For that reason it would have been in order in this game for Black first to play 8...Castles, in order to keep the opponent in doubt as long as possible concerning the future Pawn structure in the center.

(e) The first result of his premature last move. 9...Castles; 10 R—K! (not 10 BxKt, PxKt!; 11 PxP, BxP; 12 KtxB, QxKt; 13 R—K, P—B4, etc.) would merely have been a transposition of moves, as Black anyhow would have had to play 10...PxP.

(f) Now Black can no longer occupy the square, Q4, and the threat of the probable advance of the QP interferes considerably with his plan of development.

(g) It was indeed important to make sure of the diagonal, QR2 to KKt8, for the Bishop.

(h) Here or on the next move P—K3 would not do, on account of the disagreeable pin after P—Q5, PxP, KtxP, etc.

(i) White falls in with his opponent's plan (command of Q5), as he hopes to gain an advantage thereby. Against 14 P—Q5 Black could have defended himself fully by means of 14...KR—Q.

(j) By means of this waiting move White clearly intends to encourage a further development of his opponent's plan to free himself, in order then to be able to proceed with the attack on the square, KB7. It will be seen, however, that Black's resources are just sufficient to parry this attack without danger.

(k) Threatening 18 BxKt, followed by Kt—Q7

(l) This interesting sacrifice, to be sure, is not incorrect, but should only yield a draw. In the event of other moves, however, Black by occupying the square, Q4, would have nipped in the bud all further attempts to attack White would have done better by substituting the developing move of 15 QR—B for the somewhat artificial 15 P—KR3.

(m) Of course not 18...KxKt; 19 BxPch, K—K; 20 Kt—Kt5, with a winning position.

(n) Inadequate would have been 20 Kt—Kt5, on account of 20...Kt(K2)—Q4, as well as 20 Q—B4, on account of 20...Kt—B4, etc. Now, however, Black frees himself completely by means of the following counter sacrifice.

(o) Otherwise the advancing Pawn would have become too troublesome

(p) In the event of 22 BxKt, 22...B(Q4)xB; 23 BxB, B—B4 would win a piece.

(q) Hereby material equality is restored and Black has nothing more to fear.

(r) There is not sufficient warrant for this new sacrifice. Correct would have been 24 B—K7!, BxR; 25 BxR, QxB; 26 RxB, Q—K2! (the simplest), with a draw as the most likely outcome. After the text-move, Black would have had good winning chances with his passed pawn, notwithstanding the pinning position, however difficult it may be to avoid.

(s) Threatening among other things to draw by 27 B—Kt5, R—KB; 28 B—R6, etc., which is prevented by Black's next move.

(t) With the intention of 28 Q—QB6, followed by R—K8ch.

(u) Threatening 30 R—Q2, Q—B; 31 RxRch, QxR; 32 Q—Kt5, which for the present is frustrated by BxPch.

(v) Notwithstanding the advantageous exchange of Rooks, it is still d fficult to make the material superiority count, as the white Queen cannot be challenged on the diagonal, QR2 to KKt8, and in addition the Rook threatens to force an entrance. For that reason Black decides to offer an exchange of Pawns in order to expose the hostile King somewhat and then to rid h.mself of the unpleasant pin by means of a possible counter-attack.

(w) White should have taken the pawn in any case. After 33 QP, RxP; 34 Q—Q5ch, R—B2; 35 R—KB, Q—Kt2; 36 Q—B4, B—Kt2, etc., a win for Black, if not impossible, in any event would have been quite difficult. Now, on the contrary, the tables are quickly turned, as the passed Pawns at last obtain mobility.

(x) In reply to 35 R—B7 would follow 35...P—R5!; 36 Q—R2, Q—Q8ch; 37 K—R2, Q—Kt6, and wins.

(y) 43...Q—B8; 44 R—Kt, B—B4 would have been immediately decisive.

(z) In order to be able to answer 44...Q—B8 with 45 R—R.

(aa) Threatening perpetual check.

Game 94   NINETEENTH ROUND—QUEEN'S PAWN OPENING

Marshall	Maroczy
White	Black
1 P—Q4	Kt—KB3
2 Kt—KB3	P—KKt3
3 B—B4	B—Kt2
4 Kt—B3(a)	P—Q3
5 P—K4	QKt—Q2(b)
6 B—B4(c)	P—B4(d)
7 P—K5(e)	Kt—R4
8 Kt—Kt5(f)	Castles(g)
9 Q—B3	PxKP(h)
10 BxP	KtxB
11 PxKt	P—K3(i)
12 Q—K3	Q—Q5(j)

17 CastlesQR(l)	KR—Q
18 B—Kt5(m)	P—QR3
19 BxB	RxB
20 P—QB3	QR—Q
21 Kt—QKt3	K—B
22 RxR	RxR
23 R—Q	K—K2
24 Kt—B5(n)	R—B2
25 P—QKt4(o)	P—QR4
26 R—QR3	Kt—B3
27 Kt—Q4	PxP
28 RPxP	P—Kt3(p)

After 12 Q—K3

13 QxQ	PxQ
14 Kt—K2	BxP
15 Kt—KB3	B—Kt2
16 KKtxP	B—Q2(k)

After 28 RPxP

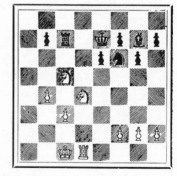

29 Kt—Kt5	R—B3
30 Kt—R7	R—B2
31 Kt—Kt5	R—B3
32 Kt—R7	R—B2
33 Kt—Kt5	Drawn

(a) In this variation there is no reason for obstructing the BP with the Knight. The logical formation of the pawns in order to render the fianchetto Bishop inert is QB3, Q4 and K3.

(b) In order as quickly as possible to undertake a counter action in the center by means of P—QB4. Otherwise 5....Castles would also have been safe.

(c) Threatening the well-known sacrificial combination beginning with BxPch, followed by Kt—Kt5ch, Kt—K6 and KtxBP. With correct counter play, however, this continuation by White is harmless.

(d) But this is a case of playing with fire. Castling is quite good enough, as for instance: 6...Castles. (I) 7 Q—Q2, P—B4; 8 PxP, QKtxP; 9 P—K5, KKt—K5, etc. (II) 7 P—K5, Kt—R4; 8 B—KKt3, PxP; 9 BxP, KtxB; 10 KtxKt, P—QB4, etc.; both lines of play being safe for Black.

(e) Fascinating, but hasty. Simply, 7 PxP, QKtxP (or Q—R4; 8 PxP, KtxP; 9 Castles); 8 P—K5, Kt—R4; 9 B—K3 would have assured positional advantage without complications for White.

(f) The consequence of the last move. Downright disadvantageous for White would be 8 BxPch, KxB; 9 P—K6ch, K—Kt (not KxP; 10 Kt—K5ch, followed by mate in a few moves); 10 PxKt, BxP.

(g) Surely the safest. Acceptance of the sacrificed piece would have led to "swindle" positions, with Marshall entirely in his element. However, imminent danger for Black there would have been none, for instance: 8...KtxB; 9 BxPch (KtxBP, Q—R4, etc., leads clearly nowhere), K—B; 10 Q—B3 (if 10 Kt—Q5, PxKP; 11 KtxKt, Q—R4ch), PxKP; 11 PxQP, BxP; 12 P—KKt3, P—KR3, or 11 BxP, Kt—B3, etc. Even if White by hook or crook should regain his piece, Black meanwhile would effect undisturbed coordination of his forces. But the subsequent evolution also secures for him a superior position.

(h) Not 9...BPxP; 10 KtxBP, RxKt; 11 BxRch, KxB; 12 P—K6ch, KxP; 13 Q—Q5ch, K—B3; 14 B—Kt5 mate.

(i) Protecting KB2 and attacking the Knight.

(j) Just retribution for a premature attack. White is compelled to exchange Queens and to regroup his fighting material speedily to avoid loss. Order! Counter-order! Disorder!

(k) This plausible move suffices to annul all of Black's positional advantages. Necessary was 16...P—QR3 in order once for all to keep White's piece from QKt5, with the additional menace of posting the Bishop on the splendid diagonal, QR to KR8, for instance: 17 Castles QR, P—QKt4; 18 B—Kt3, B—Kt2, and White will have difficulties with his KKt pawn, inasmuch as 19 P—KB3 is not good on account of P—K4. If, however, 17 P—QR4, B—Q2 (threatening P—QKt4); 18 Castles, QR—B, etc.

(l) Threatening, by means of Kt—B5, to exchange one of the Black Bishops.

(m) After the exchange hereby forced, White should have nothing more to fear.

(n) Following the exchange of Rooks, the game, of course, would be an easy draw. The text-move introduces a forced maneuver, which, by correct counter-play, might have had perilous consequences for White.

(o) Very risky. He would have done better, without false pride, to recall his last move with 25 Kt—QKt3.

(p) Black contents himself with a draw at the very moment when, through 28...Kt—Q4, he could have won at least a Pawn, thus: 29 K—Kt2 (or K—B2), P—QKt3; (I) 30 Kt—Kt5, R—B; 31 Kt—R7, R—QR; 32 Kt—B6ch, K—Q3. (II) 30 QKt—R4, KtxRP; 31 PxKt, R—B5.

Game 95 NINETEENTH ROUND—CARO-KANN DEFENSE

Yates	Reti
White	Black
1 P—K4	P—QB3
2 P—Q4	P—Q4
3 Kt—QB3	PxP
4 KtxP	B—B4(a)
5 Kt—Kt3	B—Kt3
6 Kt—B3(b)	Kt—Q2
7 P—B3(c)	KKt—B3
8 B—QB4	P—K3
9 Q—K2	B—K2
10 Castles	Castles
11 R—K	Kt—Q4(d)
12 B—Kt3	P—QR4(e)
13 P—QR3	Q—B2
14 P—B4	Kt—B5
15 BxKt	QxB
16 QR—Q	B—B3
17 B—B2	KR—Q(f)
18 BxB	RPxB
19 Kt—K4	Kt—Kt3(g)

20 P—QKt3	B—K2
21 R—Q3(h)	BxP(i)
22 Kt—K5(j)	Q—R5(k)
23 R—R3	Q—K2
24 Kt—Kt5(l)	Resigns

After 24 Kt—Kt5

(a) Interesting here is Niemzowitsch's move of 4...Kt—Q2 with the idea of later developing the QB on Kt2 after Kt—B3, P—K4, B—K2, Castles, and finally P—QB4. However, the old method, by means of which a quick co-operation of the Rooks is made possible, also has much in its favor.

(b) The formerly so popular "attacking" move, 6 P—KR4, which is suitable only for a Kt attack and weakens the King's position without compensation, has been discarded little by little and rightly so.

(c) A lost tempo. If White did not wish to exchange Bishops by 7 B—Q3, for which as a matter of fact there is still time, he could have played at once without hesitation B—QB4, followed by Castles and Q—K2.

(d) This running about with the same piece profits little. If Black desired to parry the move of BxKP, which is only an apparent threat (PxB; QxPch, R—B2; Kt—Kt5, B—B, etc., with a good game), he could have done so most simply with 11...R—K preparing besides for P—QB4.

(e) This flank thrust likewise is uncalled for. 12...Q—B2; 13 P—QR3, B—B3, etc., would have saved an important tempo.

(f) Black clearly did not recognize that this doubling, which makes immobile the Pawn formation on the King's wing, compromises considerably the position of the castled King. After 17...BxB; 18 QxB, Q—B2, he would still have had a fairly defensible position, notwithstanding the great loss of time.

(g) After 19...Kt—B, there could have followed 20 R—Q3, followed by KR—Q, threatening R—QKt3 and P—B5, etc. White has handy objects of attack on both wings.

(h) A sound Pawn sacrifice which Black should not accept.

(i) To remove all protective pieces from the King's side of the board is astonishing thoughtlessness. With 21...Kt—Q2 there would have been still some prospect of saving the game, although White even then would have had much the better of it after 22 P—QR4, followed by KR—Q, etc.

(j) Decisive would have been 22 KKt—Kt5!, for instance: I. 22...P—KB4; 23 Kt—B6ch, etc. II. 22...R—Q2; 23 P—Kt3, Q—B4 (or Q—B2; 24 Q—Kt4); 24 R—KB3, Q—Kt5; 25 Q—K3, threatening R—B4, etc. III. 22...B—K2 (in order, after 23 R—KB3, to sacrifice the Queen for the Rook and Knight); 23 P—Kt3!, Q—B2; 24 Q—Kt4, BxKt; 25 KtxB, Kt—Q2; 26 R—KB3!, Kt—KB3; 27 Q—R4 (threatening 28 RxKt!, PxR; 29 Q—R7ch, K—B; 30 KtxKPch, etc.), Q—K2; 28 P—Q5! (not 28 P—KKt4, RxP), BPxP; 29 P—KKt4!, and wins. After the actual blunder, Black could have saved himself in quite simple fashion.

(k) Losing at once. As a matter of course, 22...RxP; 23 RxR, QxKt; 24 KR—Q, B—K2, with two Pawns in return for the exchange and excellent drawing chances. Now there ensues a pretty finale.

(l) If black captures this Knight, then he would lose the Queen after 25 R—R8ch, KxR; 26 KtxPch, with a hopeless position. Otherwise, however, KtxP would have been decisive, or Q—Kt4 which, incidentally, apart from the elegant text-move, would also have won.

TWENTIETH ROUND

The ultimate victor of the tournament goes serenely on his way, increasing his total point by point, thereby taking good care that no rival may trouble him by too close proximity. Maroczy, after a game not lacking in exceptional opportunities for the Hungarian, falls victim to Dr. Lasker's remarkable staying powers. In addition to that, the leader is helped materially through a great effort on the part of Yates, who draws with Capablanca. Alekhine, too, is held to a draw, but he is quite content inasmuch as it is Marshall who is his opponent. Reti's slump continues and endangers the prospects of his being a prize-winner, while Bogoljubow advances to a tie with him.

Maroczy had the black side of an enterprising, if somewhat indifferently conducted French defense. Dr. Lasker gave up a Pawn to avoid the beaten path, thereby obtaining a strong attack. Maroczy's defense was splendid and no headway could be made against it. Thereupon, Dr. Lasker captured a Pawn with his Queen, which probably was an oversight on his part for it should have incurred the loss of the game in a few moves. At this critical stage, however, Maroczy's customary precision failed him and shortly thereafter went entirely astray. This paved the way for Dr. Lasker to bring about an easily won ending.

The game between Yates and Capablanca was a Ruy Lopez in which Yates again experimented with the somewhat injudicious advance of the center Pawn. Capablanca, after driving his KR well out of the game and establishing a superiority, somehow went wrong, at any rate sufficiently to enable the Englishman to draw with a vigorous line of play ending with perpetual check.

The most spectacular game of the round was that between Marshall and Alekhine, which was a hard-fought encounter resulting from a Queen's Gambit Declined in which Marshall handled the white pieces. Such daring complications as these rivals ventured upon are rarely witnessed in serious play between masters with high stakes depending upon the outcome, and the "gallery" was in high glee. Suffice it to say for this brief description that Black's QKtP traveled all the way down to White's KB2! This involved a combination fifteen moves deep to force a draw by perpetual check!

Edward Lasker vs. Reti was another Ruy Lopez and unquestionably Lasker's best and most vigorously conducted game in the tournament. His break of the center with P—KB4 will be found very artistic leading to a better game for White in all variations. It showed the hand of the master.

Janowski played White in a Queen's Gambit Declined against Bogoljubow, who moved K—B in order to avoid a well-known attacking formation. Thereafter he brought about a judicious exchange of major pieces and an even ending was reached. Janowski, however, played to win and brought about his own downfall.

With two rounds remaining to be contested, Dr. Lasker, 14—4, had a clear lead of 1½ points over Capablanca, 12½—5½. Under the circumstances, therefore, it was not surprising that the victory was being generally conceded to him. The other leading scores: Alekhine, 11½—7½; Marshall, 10—8: Bogoljubow and Reti, each 9½—8½. White's score for the day was 3—2 and for the twenty rounds, 55—45.

Game 96   TWENTIETH ROUND—FRENCH DEFENSE

Dr. Lasker	Maroczy		
White	Black		
1 P—K4	P—K3	25 Q—Kt4	Kt—Kt2(p)
2 P—Q4	P—Q4	26 KR—R	KR—B
3 Kt—QB3	B—Kt5(a)	27 P—R4	Kt—R5(q)
4 P—K5	P—QB4(b)	28 B—Q3	P—Kt4
5 P—QR3	PxP(c)	29 QR—R2	R—R
6 PxB	PxKt	30 K—Kt2(r)	QR—QB(s)
7 PxP	Q—B2	31 R—KR	Q—B2(t)
8 Kt—B3(d)	Kt—K2(e)	32 Kt—Q4	Q—Q2(u)
9 B—Q3	Kt—Kt3	33 KtxKtch	KPxKt
10 Castles	Kt—Q3(f)	34 Q—Q4	Q—K3
11 R—K(g)	QxBP(h)	35 QxRP(v)	P—Q5(w)
12 B—Q2	Q—B2	36 R(R2)—R	QxP(x)
13 Q—K2	Castles		
14 Q—K3(i)	Kt—Kt3		
15 Q—Kt5	Kt—QB5		
16 B—B3(j)	P—KR3(k)		
17 Q—Kt4	Kt—K8		
18 Q—R5	B—Q2		
19 P—Kt4(l)	B—Kt4(m)		
20 P—Kt5	P—KKt3		
21 QxP	Kt—Kt3(n)		

After 21 QxP

After 36 R(R2)—R

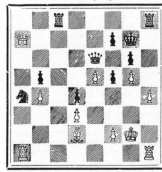

37 QR—K	Q—Q4ch
38 K—Kt3(y)	KR—K
39 P—R5	PxP
40 RxR	RxR
41 RxP	Kt—B6(z)
42 Q—Kt6	Kt—K7ch
43 K—R2	Q—K3(aa)
44 QxKtP	Q—Q3ch
45 K—Kt2	Kt—B5ch(bb)
46 BxKt	QxB
47 QxR	Q—Kt5ch

22 R—R3	BxB
23 PxB	Kt—B4
24 Q—B3	Q—K2(o)

48 K—B	QxR
49 Q—K5ch	K—Kt
50 QxBP	Resigns

(a) Quite a good move, which gives promise of excellent drawing chances to the second player after the customary exchange of pawns, thanks to the symmetrical pawn formation and notwithstanding the development of the KB which is not exactly favorable for this variation. White's subsequent attempt to avoid this line of play, which eventually results in disadvantage for him, lends the game a theoretical value.

(b) The attempt to break through on the other wing by means of 4...P—KB3 also came into consideration here, for instance: 5 Q—Kt4, Q—K2; 6 P—B4, Kt—KR3; 7 Q—R3, Kt—B4; 8 Kt—B3, P—B4, etc. With the text-move and the subsequent play to win a pawn Black exposes himself to an attack on the King which is not without danger.

(c) Not 5...B—R4; 6 P—QKt4!, PxKtP; 7 Kt—Kt5, etc., with advantage.

(d) Likewise after 8 Q—Q4, Kt—K2, the pawn could not have been easily defended, for instance: 9 Kt—B3, Kt—B4; 10 Q—Q3, Kt—B3; 11 B—KB4, P—B3, etc.

(e) Black rightly prefers to finish his development first, inasmuch as even a later protection of the pawn would exclude every prospect for an attack on the part of White. The game, even after the first few moves, has assumed a very distinct character.

(f) Quite out of place, of course, would have been 10...KtxP; 11 B—KB4, KtxKtch; 12 QxKt, Q—K2; 13 Q—Kt3!, followed by QxKtP, etc.

(g) The pawn could still have been saved by 11 BxKt, followed by Q—Q4. White, however, clearly hopes for more from this position.

(h) The KP could not even now be taken on account of 12 KtxKt, followed by 13 B—KB4, P—B3; 14 BxKt and Q—R5ch, etc. The winning of the seemingly harmless QBP, however, is of importance insofar as Black in order to repel the hostile attack, can preferably make a possible counter-sacrifice.

(i) Winning a tempo by threatening the QRP in order to bring the Queen over to the scene of action.

(j) Probably played to prevent either P—B3 or B4. Black, however, makes use of the awkward position of this Bishop for the purpose of a fine defensive maneuver. More promising, therefore, appears to be 16 B—QB, threatening Q—R5, followed by Kt—Kt5, P—KR3, Kt—KB3 and, finally, the sacrifice of the Bishop on KR6. If Black, however, thereupon plays 16...P—B3, then, after 17 PxP, RxKBP; 18 Q—R5!, he would have had to reckon at once with a number of threats (B—KKt5, Kt—Kt5), and his pawn position in the center would have remained permanently weak.

(k) Because White cannot well reply with 17 Q—R, on account of 17...Kt—B5.

(l) White has scarcely any other continuation for his attack. Black, however, has just time to save himself by returning the pawn and exchanging the hostile KB.

(m) In order, after 20 Kt—Q4, to be able to defend himself with 20...B—K; 21 P—KKt5, KtxKP!; 22 PxRP, P—B4; 23 Q—Kt5, Kt—Kt3, etc. Black's game hangs upon a thread, but it holds.

(n) The point of the ingenious defense. It is no longer possible for White to bring his Rook over to KR3, for instance: 22 R—K3, BxB!; 23 Kt—Q4, Kt—B4; 24 KtxKt, BxKt, followed by Kt—QB5 or P—KB3, etc. After the following exchange of Knights, the Knight on KB4 hinders any further attempt at attack and Black, because of White's loose pawn position, must gain the advantage.

(o) Up to here Maroczy's play has been exemplary, but from now on he begins to lose time and thereby permits his opponent to consolidate his position again. The logical continuation would have been 24...Kt—R5!, for instance: 25 R—QB, P—Kt4; 26 B—Q2, Q—Kt3; 27 R—R2, KR—B; 28 R—B2, Q—Kt2; 29 Q—Kt4, RxR; 30 RxR, R—QB; 31 RxRch, QxR 32 Kt—Q4, KtxKt; 33 QxKt, Q—B7; 34 B—K3, Kt—B6, and White dare not take the QRP on account of 35...Q—Q8ch; 36 K—Kt2, Q—Kt5ch; 37 K—B, O—B6!, rate that Black ought to have made use of the OB file for a basis of operation. He hits rate that Black ought to have made use of the QB file for a basis of operation. He has upon this idea, however, only much later on.

(p) Also loss of a tempo.

(q) Even now this move is still the best.

(r) White lets the opportunity slip to exchange the troublesome Knight on KB4 by means of 30 Kt—Q4, for 30...KtxKP; 31 KtxQKtP, etc., would clearly not have been worth while for Black to strive for. After the text-move, Black could have obtained for himself new possibilities for attack.

(s) For example, he should have played here 30...O—Q2, and, if 31 R—R, P—Q5, etc., which would have cramped the adversary considerably. The latter now succeeds in avoiding the chief danger.

(t) Hoping against hope to prevent Kt—Q4. 31...Q—Q2 at once would have saved an important tempo.

(u) A sorry necessity, for if 32...QxP?, then 33 Kt—B3!, followed by B—B4—K5ch, winning the exchange.

(v) A mistake which has important consequences. After 35 R—QB, RxR; 36 BxR, R—QB; 37 B—Q2, followed by the transfer of the King to Q square and QR—OB2, White would have had some advantage mainly because of the possibility of his King breaking through by way of Q4 in the ending. Nevertheless the game in all probability would have ended in a draw.

(w) As a matter of course!

(x) As an offset to his opponent's mistake, Black makes three errors in succession and in consequence loses the game, which could have been quite easily decided through a mating attack by means of 36...R—B7. for instance: I.—37 OR—Q. Q—Q4ch; 38 P—KB3 (or 38 K—Kt3, RxB; 39 P—K6, P—B5ch!, etc.). QxP: 39 K—B (39 KR—K, RxBch), Kt—B6: 40 R—K O—O4. etc. 11.—37 B—B4. O—O4ch: 38 K—Kt3. Kt—B6; 39 KR—K, RxRP!; 440 KxR. O—B: 41 R—KKt, Q—R4ch; 42 K—Kt3, Q—Kt5ch; 43 K—R2, Q—R5ch and 44...RxBP mate.

(y) Threatening B—B44 and B—K5ch.

(z) In order would have been 41...P—B5ch; 42 K—R4! (if KxP, R—K7 and wins; or 42 BxP, R—K8, etc.), Q—R8ch; 43 K—Kt4, Q—Kt7ch (Q—Q8ch is useless, as White always threatens R—R7ch!, etc.); 44 K—B5, Q—Q4ch; 45 K—Kt4, R—K7; 46 Q—Kt8!, and Black would have to content himself with a draw. It is remarkable that there is no more to be gained from this position.

(aa) The third and decisive error. He should have led up to a drawing ending by means of 43...R—K3; 44 Q—Kt8, Q—Q3ch; 45 QxQ, RxQ; 46 K—Kt2, R—QR3; 47 K—B3, Kt—B6, etc. The sacrifice of a Pawn was not warranted.

(bb) The game is no longer to be saved even with other moves, inasmuch as there was no compensation in sight for White's passed pawn.

Game 97   TWENTIETH ROUND—RUY LOPEZ

Yates	Capablanca
White	Black

1 P—K4	P—K4
2 Kt—KB3	Kt—QB3
3 B—Kt5	P—QR3
4 B—R4	Kt—B3
5 Castles	B—K2
6 R—K	P—QKt4
7 B—Kt3	P—Q3
8 P—B3	Castles
9 P—Q4	B—Kt5
10 B—K3	PxP
11 PxP	Kt—QR4
12 B—B2	Kt—B5
13 QKt—Q2(a)	KtxB(b)
14 RxKt(c)	P—B4
15 Q—K	Kt—Q2
16 P—KR3	B—R4
17 PxP(d)	KtxP(e)
18 R—Q(f)	R—B
19 P—K5(g)	B—Kt4(h)
20 R—B3	P—Kt5
21 R—B4	P—Q4(i)

22 RxP	Q—K2(j)

After 22 RxP

23 KtxB(k)	BxR(l)
24 BxPch	K—R
25 R—KR4(m)	QxKt
26 P—B4	Q—K2
27 B—B2ch	K—Kt
28 B—R7ch	K—R(n)
	Drawn

(a) For this line of play compare the games of Yates-Ed. Lasker and Yates-Bogoljubow. The text move is a new line only favorable to White if Black accepts the Pawn sacrifice.

(b) Soundly and well played. White's position in the center is weakened through the exchange of the QB. Moreover, the R at K3 is exposed. Not so good would have been 13...KtxKtP, e. g., 14 Q—Kt, Kt—B5 (or 14...BxKt; 15 KtxB); 15 P—K5, and Black eventually must give up the KRP or three minor pieces for the queen and two Pawns by 15...Kt—R6; 16 PxKt, KtxQ; 17 PxB, QxP; 18 RxKt, etc., which was after all a two-edged undertaking. Besides, after 13...KtxKtP, White had the promising continuation 14 Q—B, Kt—R5; 15 BxKt, PxB; 16 Q—B2, B—Q2 (or Q—Q2); 17 P—Q5, with a strong pressure. In short, the Pawn sacrifice would have paid dividends.

(c) The best way to remove the pin.

(d) Here again there is practically no choice. Consideration is due to 17 R—B, after which Black could strengthen his position with 17...R—B, wthout removing the pressure.

(e) After the plausible 17...PxP, White would have obtained a counter-attack with P—K5. The text not only makes such a plan more difficult for White to execute in the center, but also opens the Bishop file for future operations.

(f) Pinning one's own pieces is certainly not good. But P—K5 immediately would also lead to Black's advantage; e. g. 18...P—Q4; 19 Kt—Q4, B—Kt4; 20 R—QB3,

Q—Kt3, and as in this game the Rook would be in danger. Relatively best was still 18 R—B.

(g) This should lead to an immediate loss, but White is already without a plausible continuation, e. g., after 19 B—Kt, Kt—R5; 20 R—Kt3, P—KB3, with the threat, B—B2.

(h) The opening maneuver of the winning line of play. After 20 R—K2 (which was the best), Black obtains a winning end game through 20... BxQKt; 21 QxB, BxKt; 22 PxB, PxP; 23 QxQ, KRxQ; 24 RxRch, RxR; 25 RxP, Kt—K3 (26 B—B5, Kt—B5; 27 R—K4, P—Kt4; 28 P—KR4, P—KR3, etc).

(i) Through this fine Pawn sacrifice, which forces the Rook into a blind alley, Black obtains an evident winning position.

(j) With this move Capabalanca makes the win more difficult. Up to the present he has conducted the game in his very best style. 22...B—K2 would have been decisive. (On the other hand, less forceful would have been the knotty complications arising from 22...P—QR4; 23 R—Kt5,etc.) The double threat was 23...Kt—Q6 and 23...Kt—K3. Then the following defences for White would have been worthy of consideration: (I) 23 P—KKt4, Kt—K3; 24 R—Kt7, RxB; 25 PxB, B—B4, with a winning attack; e. g., 26 Kt—K4 (A) PxKt; 27 RxQ, RxR; 28 QxP, RxBP, etc.; or (A) 26 R—B, RxR; 27 QxR, Q—B, and the threat 28 BxPch wins a Rook; (II) 23 Kt—B4, BxKt; 24 PxB, Kt—Q6; 25 BxKt, BxR; 26 QxB, Q—Kt4ch, followed by PxKt winning.

(k) Undoubtedly the only chance.

(l) Here still Black could make an attempt to win the game without risks through 23...QxKt; e. g., 24 P—KKt4, B—Kt3 (not 24...Kt—K3; 25 B—B5, etc.); 25 BxB, BPxB! (better than QxB; 26 Q—K3, etc.); 26 Q—K3! (as good as forced, since, after other moves, the blocking of the King side would be too strong. On 26 Kt—Kt3 follows, for instance, 26...Kt—K5, whereupon the sacrifice of the exchange would be insufficient. 27 RxKt, PxR; 28 QxP, because of 28...P—KR4, threatening R—KB5, etc.) 26...Kt—K3 (26...QxQ, followed by Kt—Q6, naturally comes in for consideration); 27 QxQ, KtxQ; 28 K—Kt2 (or R—Kt3), R—QB7, and Black clearly stands better in this ending, despite his Pawn minus. Now White forces an immediate draw.

(m) The point of the sacrifice of the exchange. 25 P—B4 immediately would be insufficient; e. g., 25...P—Kt3; 26 Q—R4 (or 26 QxB, Kt—K3), 26...B—R4; 27 P—Kt4, Kt—K3; 28 PxB, KtxKt; 29 PxKt, QxKP; 30 PxP, Q—K6ch, and wins.

(n) If 29 P—B5 (threatens P—B6, etc.), the simplest continuation is 30...Kt—Q6; 31 Q—Kt3, KtxKP, and White is still forced to give perpetual check.

Game 98   TWENTIETH ROUND—RUY LOPEZ

Ed. Lasker	Reti	After 20...Q—Kt2
White	Black	

	White	Black
1	P—K4	P—K4
2	Kt—KB3	Kt—QB3
3	B—Kt5	P—QR3
4	B—R4	Kt—B3
5	Castles	B—K2
6	R—K	P—QKt4
7	B—Kt3	P—Q3
8	P—B3	Castles
9	P—KR3	Kt—QR4
10	B—B2	P—B4
11	P—Q4	Q—B2
12	QKt—Q2	Kt—Q2(a)
13	P—Q5(b)	P—B4(c)
14	PxP	Kt—Kt3
15	Kt—K4(d)	BxP
16	QKt—Kt5(e)	Q—Q2(f)
17	P—KKt4(g)	BxB
18	QxB	P—Kt3
19	Q—K4(h)	BxKt(i)
20	KtxB	Q—QKt2(j)
21	P—KB4(k)	QxP(l)
22	PxP	QR—K(m)
23	QxQch	KtxQ
24	P—K6(n)	R—B3
25	R—Q	Kt—B2
26	RxP	P—R3(o)
27	Kt—K4	KRxP(p)
28	Kt—B6ch	RxKt

29 RxR	K—Kt2	33 PxP	KtxP
30 R—Q6	R—K2	34 R—Kt	Kt—R4
31 P—Kt3	P—B5	35 RxRP	KtxR
32 B—R3	PxP	36 BxR(q)	Resigns

(a) An interesting departure from 12...BPxP, followed by B—Q2 and KR—QB, etc., which was twice tried in this tournament. The Knight must be brought over to the Queen's side, in order to support an eventual counter-attack. At the same time the Pawn formation on the King's side must be kept intact as long as possible—a precaution that Black does not observe.

(b) With the obvious intention of playing for a King's side attack, which is nevertheless not easy to work out. Therefore, Black should not trouble himself about his opponent's intentions, but should play for an advance upon the Queen's side; e. g., 13...Kt—Kt3; 14 Kt—B, Kt—Kt2, followed by P—QR4 and P—QKt5, etc. (with the preliminary P—QB5). The game loses all further theoretical interest through his next move, which is contrary to good position judgment.

(c) Opens powerful lines for his opponent, thus giving him chances in the center as well as on the King's side—all this without compensation. Any hope to make capital out of the apparent isolation of the P at Q5 soon proves futile. The method by which White utilizes his advantages is noteworthy.

(d) Another equally advantageous line of play for White was 15 P—KKt4; e. g., 15...B—Kt2 (15...KtxP?; 16 Kt—Kt3!, B—Kt2 (or A); 17 KtxKt, QxKt; 18 B—K4; (A) 16...Kt—KB3; 17 KtxKt, QxKt; 18 P—Kt5, with decisive advantage); 16 Kt—K4, KtxP; 17 Kt(B3)—Kt5, BxKt; 18 KtxB, Kt—KB5; 19 BxKt, PxB; 20 Kt—K6, Q—B3; 21 B—K4, P—Q4; 22 B—B3, etc. But the text-move is also sufficient to defeat the strategy of his opponent.

(e) Forces the exchange of Bishops and causes a weakness at Black's K3.

(f) 16...Q—Kt2 would not have prevented Black from having the worst of it; e. g., 17 BxB, RxB; 18 Q—Q3, P—Kt3, and Black will suffer in the future because his Knights are out of play and because of the weakness of his King's position.

(g) Prevents the Queen from going to B4 and thus forces P—Kt3.

(h) By this move the P at Q5 is definitely made safe, as it can always be protected again by R—Q. It soon becomes apparent, however, that White need not bother himself defending it, but can successfully break through the enemy center.

(i) Otherwise, after Kt—K6, the other Knight threatens to go to Kt5.

(j) In the hope of exerting a counter-pressure on the KB file (after R—Q, R—B3). But something quite different takes place.

(k) Energetic play, accurately calculated! No matter how Black plays, he will be at a lasting disadvantage.

(l) Or (1) 21...PxP; 22 BxP, QR—K (22...KtxP; 23 BxP); 23 QxR!, RxQ; 24 RxRch, K—Kt2; 25 BxP, KtxP; 26 R—KB, etc., with a winning attack. (II) 21... QR—K; 22 P—B5!, QxP; (A) 23 PxP, QxQ; 24 KtxQ, PxP (24...QR—Q; 25 B—Kt5); 25 KtxQP, QR—Q; 26 Kt—K4, etc., with a very superior end-game. (A) 22...PxP; 23 PxP, QxP; 24 Q—KKt4, K—R; 25 KtxRP!, KxKt (25...KR—Kt; 26 Kt—Kt5); 26 Q—Kt6ch, K—R; 27 Q—R6ch, K—Kt; 28 K—R2, K—B2; 29 B—Kt5 wins. The move chosen should have permitted the most drawn out resistance.

(m) After this the KP becomes very strong. Other moves were less satisfactory; e. g., (I) 22...QxQ; 23 KtxQ, PxP; 24 KtxBP, QR—K; 25 Kt—K4, etc.; (II) 22...PxP; 23 QxQch KtxQ; 24 RxP, Kt—KB5; 25 BxKt, RxB; 26 Kt—K6, R—K; 27 QR—K, Kt—B5; 28 KR—K2, and White now wins the QBP.

(n) Threatening among other things, Kt—B7, with the double menace of KtxP and B—R6.

(o) An oversight which costs the exchange. With 26...R—K2 Black could have made a stubborn resistance, despite his Pawn minus. Now it is all over.

(p) Or 27...R—B6; 28 K—Kt2, etc.

(q) The QKtP is now also lost (36...Kt—B3; 37 B—Q6, etc.).

Game 99   TWENTIETH ROUND—QUEEN'S GAMBIT DECLINED

Marshall	Alekhine
White	Black
1 P—Q4	Kt—KB3
2 Kt—KB3	P—K3
3 P—B4	P—Q4
4 Kt—B3	P—B3
5 PxP(a)	KPxP
6 B—Kt5	B—K2
7 P—K3	B—KB4(b)
8 B—Q3	BxB
9 QxB	QKt—Q2(c)
10 Castles	Castles
11 Q—B5(d)	Kt—K5(e)
12 BxB	QxB
13 KtxKt	PxKt
14 Kt—Q2	Kt—B3
15 QR—B(f)	KR—K
16 R—B5	Kt—Q4

17 KR—B	QR—Q
18 P—QKt4(g)	P—QR3
19 P—QR3	R—Q3
20 P—KKt3(h)	P—KR3(i)
21 Kt—Kt(j)	P—KKt3
22 Q—R3	Q—Kt4(k)
23 Kt—B3(l)	P—Kt3(m)
24 KtxKt(n)	PxR(o)
25 Kt—B7	PxQP(p)
26 KtxR	PxP (q)

After 26...PxP

27 KtxR(r)	PxPch
28 KxP	Q—Q7ch
29 K—Kt	Q—K6ch(s)
30 K—Kt2	Q—B6ch
31 K—Kt	Q—K6ch
32 K—Kt2	Q—B6ch
	Drawn

After 22...Q—Kt4

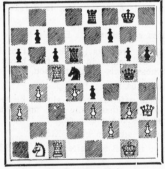

(a) This exchange is not justified before Black has played QKt—Q2, because the QB can thereupon be developed at once. Perhaps, after all, the best may be B—Kt5, so that, in case of 5...P—KR3, he could continue with 6 BxKt, QxB; 7 P—K3, in order to obtain a speedy development, while foregoing possession of both Bishops.

(b) This solves the chief problem of the defense and Black can await the future with confidence.

(c) To prevent Kt—K5, which, however, need not be feared before White has castled. Castling at once, therefore, was to have been considered. For instance, 9... Castles; (I) 10 Kt—K5, QKt—Q2: 11 P—KB4, Kt—K; 12 BxB, QxB. (II) 10 Castles, Kt—K5; 11 BxB (11 B—B4, P—KB4), QxB; 12 Kt—Q2, KtxKKt; 13 QxKt, QKt—Q2, with an easier game than after the actual play.

(d) A clever thought. After the following exchange, which seemingly frees Black's game, White obtains a definite chance for the ending on the Queen's side. This Black must neutralize by counter action in the center and on the King's side during the middle game. In accomplishing it the presence of the White Queen on B5 is very disconcerting. In order to dispossess that piece ultimately, Black will be compelled to pay the price, that is, to block several of his own important lines of offense.

(e) Accordingly, the preparatory move of 11...R—K would have been of greater weight. Because of the continuation selected, it will be without doubt Black's task to seek equalization, notwithstanding his control of several strong points.

(f) This partly open file guarantees White a permanent, indirect pressure upon the entire position of his opponent.

(g) A typical Marshall sortie. Instead of preparing quietly with 18 P—QR3, which would have led to a reversal of moves, he sets his opponent a little, albeit time-taking problem. Black, before declining the Grecian gift, had to assure himself that the main line of play would not turn out disadvantageously for him in the end. For instance, 18 ...KtxKtP; 19 R—K5, Q—B3; 20 QxQ; PxQ; 21 RxRch, RxR; 22 R—Kt, KtxP: 23 RxP, P—QR4; 24 R—R7, R—Kt; 25 RxP, R—Kt7; 26 Kt—B, Kt—B8; 27 P—Kt4, Kt—Q6; 28 R—KB5, etc.

(h) Hereby White forestalls a possible attack, after his Queen has been driven off, by means of P—KB4 and B5 and, in addition, prepares for the transfer of his Queen to the Queen's side by way of R3.

(i) It was surely disagreeable to deprive the Rook of the control of R3, and yet there appeared to be no other way of preparing for R—B3 (which would not do now on account of 21 QxP, QxQ; 22 KtxQ, RxKt; 23 RxKt). On the other hand 20...P—KKt3; 21 Q—R3, P—KB4, at that stage, would have permitted occupation of K5 by the White Knight.

(j) With the obvious intention of exchanging his Knight, thereby making possible P—QR4 and P—Kt5. Black, however, finds an adequate reply.

(k) Threatening 23...P—KB4, followed by P—B5, or, according to circumstances, sacrifice of the Knight on K6. Black's counter offensive begins to crystallize.

(l) Herewith terminates the jockeying for position and a keen, tactical struggle commences, leading in a few moves to a forced draw. The ensuing combinations had to be calculated most accurately by both players.

(m) Planned, of course, with the previous move. The Knight Pawn is now about to undertake a forced march clear to KB7.

(n) Not 24 R—B4, KtxKP, etc. The sacrifice of the exchange, on the other hand, seems to usher in a decided turn in favor of White.

(o) After 24...PxKt; 25 R—B6, Black's end-game would collapse.

(p) The introduction of the counter combination. After 25...R—K2, White would have had several methods of winning. One of these was 26 Q—B8ch, K—R2; 27 KtPxP, R—B3 (RxP; 28 R—Kt, etc.); 28 R—Kt, Q—B4; 29 QxQ, RxQ; 30 KtxP, R—R2; 31 R—Kt6, with a decisive advantage.

(q) Entirely wrong would be 26...R—Q on account of 27 Q—Kt4, Q—K2; 28 QxKP, etc. With 26...R—K3, however, only a draw could be obtained. For instance, 27 R—B5, Q—K2 (not P—KB4; 28 Kt—B7, R—K2; 29 RxQBP, PxP; 30 Q—B, etc.); 28 QxP, QxKt; 29 PxP, P—K6; 30 PxP, RxP; 31 R—K5, RxR; 32 PxR, QxP; 33 Q—B. The text-move is more forceful.

(r) White selects the shorter line of play. A final trap might have been set by him with 28 P—B4, PxP, e. p.; 29 KtxR, P—K7 (seemingly deadly); 30 Q—B8ch, K moves; 31 Q—R8ch, followed by KtxBPch and wins. Black, therefore would have played 29...P—B7ch, thereby assuring himself a draw. For instance, 30 K—B, P—K7ch! (I) 31 KxKP, QxR; 32 Q—B, Q—Kt7ch; 33 K—K3, Q—B6ch, and White cannot save the Knight. (II) 31 KxBP, QxR; 32 Q—B8ch, K—R2; 33 KxP, Q—B7ch; 34 K—K3, Q—B6ch; 35 K—K4, Q—B7ch; 36 K—Q4, Q—B7ch, and White cannot escape perpetual check without losing his Knight. This was the most difficult variation which had to be figured out beforehand, after White's 21st move.

(s) Of course not 29...QxRch; 30 Q—B, threatening QxPch, etc.

Game 100   TWENTIETH ROUND—QUEEN'S GAMBIT DECLINED

Janowski	Bogoljubow	7 PxP(a)	KPxP
White	Black	8 B—Q3	Kt—K5
1 P—Q4	P—Q4	9 Castles(b)	KtxB
2 Kt—KB3	Kt—KB3	10 KtxKt	B—K2
3 P—B4	P—K3	11 P—B4(c)	Kt—B3
4 Kt—B3	QKt—Q2	12 Q—K	Q—Kt3
5 B—Kt5	P—B3	13 R—Kt	B—Q2
6 P—K3	Q—R4	14 Kt—B3	K—B(d)

After 14 Kt—B3

15 Kt—K5	B—K
16 P—QKt4	P—QR3(e)
17 Kt—R4(f)	Q—R2
18 Kt—B5	P—KR4
19 P—QR4(g)	R—R3
20 P—R5	R—Q
21 P—Kt3	Q—Kt
22 R—Kt2	B—Q2(h)
23 K—Kt2	B—B(i)
24 P—R3	Q—B2
25 R—KR(j)	R—K
26 K—Kt	B—Q3
27 R—Kt2	Q—K2
28 Q—K2(k)	Kt—Q2

After 28 Q—K2

29 P—Kt4	KtxKt(K5)
30 BPxKt	BxKt
31 KtPxB	PxP
32 PxP	RxRch
33 KxR	Q—R5ch
34 K—Kt	K—K2
35 Q—KB2(l)	QxQch

36 KxQ	P—KKt3(m)
37 K—Kt3	R—R
38 R—Kt	R—R3
39 R—KB	B—Q2
40 B—K2	R—R
41 B—B3	B—B
42 B—Kt2(h)	B—K3
43 R—QKt	B—B
44 R—Kt6(o)	R—Q
45 B—B3	R—R
46 R—Kt2	P—B3(p)
47 PxPch	KxP
48 R—KB2	K—Kt4
49 R—QKt2	R—K
50 R—K2	R—K2
51 R—K(q)	R—K
52 P—K4	R—K2(r)

After 52...R—K2

53 P—K5(s)	B—K3
54 K—B2(t)	R—R2
55 R—QKt	K—B5
56 R—Kt3(u)	R—R7ch
57 B—Kt2	BxP
58 K—Kt (v)	R—R2
59 K—B2	P—KKt4
60 R—QB3	R—KB2(w)
61 R—QKt3	R—R2
62 R—QB3	R—KB2
63 R—K3	R—K2
64 R—QKt3	R—Kt2
65 R—K3	R—QB2
66 R—QKt3	R—Q2
67 R—K3	R—QB2
68 R—QKt3	R—Kt2
69 R—K3	R—Q2
70 R—QKt3	R—K2
71 R—K3	R—KB2

72 R—QKt3	R—QB2		78 R—R	RxR
73 R—K3	R—R2		79 BxR	B—B4
74 R—QKt3	B—Q8		80 B—Kt2	B—K3
75 R—Q3	B—R4		81 B—R(y)	P—Kt6ch
76 R—K3(x)	P—Kt5		82 K—K2	B—R6
77 R—K	B—Kt3		Resigns	

(a) Probably the soundest reply to Black's Queen's move. If now 7...KtxP; 8 Q—Kt3, B—Kt5; 9 R—B, Black will be unable to increase his pressure upon B6.

(b) Marshall, against the same opponent, first played Q—B2, which, however, is unnecessary, as Black can hardly afford to accept the Pawn preferred by castling; for instance: 9...KtxKt; 10 PxKt, QxP; 11 P—K4, PxP; 12 R—K, P—KB4; 13 R—QB, Q—R6; 14 Kt—R4, Kt—B3; 15 BxKt, PxB; 16 Q—R5ch, K—Q; 17 B—B4, etc.

(c) After 11 Q—R5, BxKt; 12 QxB, Castles, Black could easily have defended himself. The text-move prepares for the posting of the Knight on K5.

(d) At all events an interesting defense. White had already formed his forces for stereotyped attack in the event of Black's castling, for instance: 14...Castles; 15 Kt—K5, followed by Q—R4 and P—KKt4. Black for that reason dispenses with co-operation between his Rooks and so renders it difficult for his opponent to obtain a definite objective for attack. The second player, to be sure, commits himself to lasting pacifity, which is not to everyone's taste. He is enabled, however, to reach an actual drawing position.

(e) After 16...BxP, there simply follows 17 P—QR3, BxKt; 18 QxB, Q—B2; 19 Q—Kt4ch and QxP.

(f) So far, Janowski had maneuvered excellently. Here, however (or even at his next turn), he should have anticipated, by means of P—KKt4, the move of P—KR4, which makes more difficult the formation of an attack. The move of the Knight could have been made later just as well. Furthermore, he gives his opponent too much time, allowing the latter eventually to bring about simplifying exchanges.

(g) The binding of the square, QKt7, positionally considered, is certainly quite good, but it was of greater importance to prepare to break through on the King's side by means of P—Kt3 and P—KR3, for there alone can a decision come.

(h) The beginning of a well-calculated defensive maneuver. While White exerts himself to bring about P—KKt4, a double exchange on K5 and QB5 should be prepared for, whereupon Black will retain only the QB necessary for the defense of QKt2. This, however, can take place without danger only in the event that Black is able to force an exchange of Queens through a timely occupation of the KR file. This difficult problem is solved by Bogoljubow with mathematical exactness.

(i) Manifestly disadvantageous to Black would have been 23...Q—B; 24 KKtxB, KtxKt; 25 B—B5, BxKt; 26 KtPxB.

(j) Or 25 B—K2, B—Q3, etc.

(k) Precisely at the moment when White has completed his preparations for the intended P—KKt4, Black compels the simplification outlined above which leads to a draw in a few moves.

(l) If otherwise, then, of course, 35...R—KR, etc.

(m) After B—B5, White would have obtained winning chances in the Rook ending. Now, on the other hand, the game is assuredly drawn. Janowski, however, loses it because, as in his game with Yates, he demolishes his position with his own hand.

(n) Or 42 R—KR, RxR: 43 BxR, P—B3; 44 PxPch, KxP; 45 P—K4, B—K3; 46 PxP (P—K5ch, K—Kt4), BxP; 47 BxB, PxB; 48 K—R4, K—B2; 49 K—Kt5, K—Kt2, drawing.

(o) For what reason?

(p) A harmless attempt to bring about a new turn. Black risks nothing whatever thereby.

(q) If White intended to play P—K4, he could have done so more simply now. Obviously, the game might have been drawn immediately with R—K—K2—K, etc., because Black could not very well occupy the KR file with his Rook, on account of P—K4.

(r) A draw could be forced by 52...PxP: 53 RxP, RxR; 54 BxR, BxP; 55 BxKtP, KxB; 56 KxB, K—B3; 57 K—B4, K—K4; 58 K—K3, K—Q2; 59 K—B5, K—B2; 60 K—K6, K—B, followed by K—Q—B or K—B2—B, etc. Black, however, wants to wait awhile to see if the opponent will force this line by means of 53 R—K2, or allow himself to be misled into a truly elementary positional error.

(s) This loses, as the black Rook threatens to break through to B4. It takes quite a while, however, before Black discovers the correct method of winning.

(t) Or 54 R—KR, R—KB2—B5, etc.

(u) Of course, it was no longer possible, to save the KKtP.

(v) Or 58 RxP, B—R6, etc.

(w) Starting a tedious series of Rook moves, obviously to gain time, the chief difficulty being for Black to avoid a three-fold repetition of position, with the same player to move. Otherwise, the correct play was 60...B—R4, which eventually happens on the 75th move.

(x) If 76 R—R3, Black wins by means of 76...P—Kt5; 77 R—R4, B—Kt3; 78 RxR, BxR; 79 P—K6, B—Kt3; 80 P—K7, B—R4; (I) 81 B—R, P—Kt6ch, followed by K—K6.

(II) B—B, K—K5.   (III) 81 K—K2, K—Kt6, etc.

(y) Again White is in the throes of the "Zugzwang.

TWENTY-FIRST ROUND

This is the day of the great decision. Although not officially crowned with the laurel wreath, Dr. Emanuel Lasker, before the round was over, made sure of the first prize by winning from Dr. Tartakower. Before the adjournment, the German master had played so well that, when recess was taken, he had the advantage and even then the game was conceded to him. It required the finishing touch, which so few can administer in quite his finished style, to place the game to his credit after a brief period of play in the evening.

No sooner had Dr. Tartakower resigned and those nearest the board, who had been intently watching every move and gesture of the combatants in this fateful game, become aware of what had happened, then hearty and vigorous applause broke forth among the many assembled spectators—a rare occurrence indeed at chess meetings, except on unusual occasions such as this. For the time being the signs requesting silence were ignored and play at the other boards was temporarily suspended until committee members could restore order.

Stepping out from the enclosure, the hero of the New York tournament was quickly surrounded by enthusiastic friends and well-wishers. Dr. Lasker was smiling happily and, gradually edging his way through the crush, returned with a will the handshakes that were tendered him in congratulation. At last he reached the hall and his progress to the door of the press room, his immediate destination, was one of triumph. Arrived there among the scribes, he shook hands all round.

The roar of the applause had preceded Dr. Lasker and the news of his success by that time was on its way to the four corners of the earth. His first thought then was of home and he wrote out a brief message to Mrs. Lasker in Berlin. This and another to Holland were intrusted to the writer for dispatch downtown. Thereupon, after chatting briefly, he resigned himself to his personal friends and disappeared below.

So far as he was concerned, the competition was at an end. The hard work and the worry were past. History, as made in St. Petersburg, had repeated itself. Lasker again was King! Once more the chess world, expressed in terms of tournament play, lay at his feet.

Dr. Tartakower, with the white pieces, selected 1 P—QB4, which has come to be known as the English opening, although referred to by Alekhine as a transposed Sicilian. After pushing P—Q5, he advanced P—KB4, expecting to obtain the upper hand on the King's side. Dr. Lasker's play was accuracy personified. His exploitation of the adversary's strategical misconception of position, culminating in the clear gain of the exchange, and the after-play to realize on his material advantage, will be found worthy of very close study.

Capablanca, too, after squaring accounts with Reti in a well-fought game, knew positively then that the second prize was his and that his score could no longer be equaled. As the unquestioned champion of the world, as demonstrated by his match play, neither he nor his friends exactly relished the idea of his being ranked below even so great an artist as Dr. Lasker—possibly his only peer today. However, he enjoyed the satisfaction of feeling that the play of no other contestant had been throughout quite as flawless as his.

Capablanca's game with Reti was a French defense, adopted by the latter, who certainly held his own in the opening and middle game. In the ending, which at first sight appeared to be an easy draw, he lacked precision. The champion's method of extracting a win from a position in which many would have seen no hope, was a genuine revelation.

It was an idle day for Alekhine, and Marshall made the most of it by creeping up to within half a point of him. The American had to deal with Yates, who had the white pieces and obtained just a shade the better of it with a Ruy Lopez. Then the Britisher seemed to hesitate and Marshall, quick to take the cue, consolidated his position. The initiative thereby gained and some clever maneuvering enabled him to score the game. The possibility of finishing third was still open to him.

Bogoljubow vs. Maroczy was a Queen's Gambit declined, with White castling on the Queen's side. The venture was not successful and thereupon he attempted a diversion on the opposite wing. The moves of Maroczy were timed to a nicety and he was ever ready with the most effective reply. Finally, he emerged in the ending with a clear Rook to the good and the game was his.

Janowski, white, outplayed by Edward Lasker in a Queen's Pawn opening, gave up his Queen for two minor pieces and improved his game until a position was reached where it seemed that White must win. From then on the play became somewhat erratic and eventually the game was drawn after a series of odd vicissitudes.

Although the two chief prizes had been safely allotted and the fourth at least assured to Marshall, there was still much to happen before everything could be settled and the excitement allowed to abate. Alekhine was in third place and feeling fairly safe, as Marshall for his last pairing had Dr. Lasker with whom to reckon. Reti, Bogoljubow and Maroczy were pressing each other close for the honor of fifth place. None of the others could any more be a prize winner.

The following were the totals of the seven leaders: Dr. Lasker, 15—4; Capablanca, $13\frac{1}{2}$—$5\frac{1}{2}$; Alekhine, $11\frac{1}{2}$—$7\frac{1}{2}$; Marshall, 11—8; Reti and Bogoljubow each $9\frac{1}{2}$—$9\frac{1}{2}$; Maroczy, 9—10. It had been a poor day for the white pieces, which could show only $1\frac{1}{2}$ points. The totals: White, $56\frac{1}{2}$; Black, $48\frac{1}{2}$.

Game 101   ENGLISH OPENING (SICILIAN FOR WHITE)

	Dr. Tartakower	Dr. Lasker			
	White	Black		25 R—Kt4	B—R4(l)
1	P—QB4	P—K4		26 Kt—B5	BxR
2	P—QR3(a)	Kt—KB3		27 KtxB	Q—K
3	P—K3	B—K2		28 B—B3	Kt—K4
4	Q—B2(b)	Castles		29 KtxKt	QxKt
5	Kt—QB3	P—Q3(c)		30 KtxRP	BxKt
6	Kt—KB3	R—K		31 QxB(m)	P—KB4(n)
7	B—K2	B—B		32 PxP	RxP
8	Castles	Kt—B3(d)		33 R—K(o)	QxKtP
9	P—Q4	B—Kt5		34 B—Kt4	Q—Q5ch
10	P—Q5(e)	Kt—K2		35 K—R2	QR—KB
11	P—R3	B—Q2		36 Q—K7	Q—B5ch
12	Kt—KR2	Q—B		37 K—R	R—K4
13	P—K4	Kt—Kt3		38 RxR(p)	PxR
				39 QxBP	P—K5(q)
				40 Q—K7	Q—B3(r)

After 13...Kt—Kt3

After 40 Q—K7

14 P—B4(f)	PxP				
15 BxP	KtxB				
16 RxKt	B—K2(g)		41 QxKtP	Q—R8ch
17 QR—KB	R—B		42 K—R2	Q—K4ch
18 Q—Q3	B—K		43 K—Kt	R—Kt
19 Q—Kt3	Q—Q		44 Q—Q7	R—Kt8ch
20 Kt—Q	Kt—Q2		45 K—B2	P—K6ch
21 Kt—K3(h)	B—Kt4		46 K—K2	R—Kt7ch
22 R—Kt4(i)	P—KB3(j)		47 K—K	Q—B6ch
23 Q—B2	P—KR4		48 K—B	Q—B8ch(s)
24 R—Kt3	P—R5(k)		Resigns	

(a)   The introductory move to Paulsen's system of defense.

(b)   The posting of the Queen here has a definite purpose only after the opponent's QP has moved two squares. Instead, there could have been played quite as well 4 Kt—QB3 (P—Q4; 5 PxP, KtxP; 6 Q—Kt3, etc.).

(c)   This conservative method of building up the game has the advantage of destroying White's hopes of placing pressure upon the QB file (as, for instance, would be the case with the natural continuation of P—Q4, PxP, etc.). Its disadvantage, on the other hand, consists in the permanent restriction of the KB. At any rate it would lead to a game thoroughly difficult for both sides to handle.

(d)   Premature here would have been 8...P—K5; 9 Kt—Kt5, B—B4; 10 P—B3, PxP; 11 QxB, PxB; 12 KtxKP, etc.

(e) Maintenance of pressure by R—Q could now be fully met with by Black with
10...P—K5. The blocking text-move has its points since it promises White an easy
initiative on the Queen's side.

(f) A positional misconception. On the principle, "Let sleeping dogs lie," he
should have left the King's side undisturbed and advanced on the opposite side with
15 P—Kt4. To be sure the breach with P—B5 tactically would not have been easily
carried out; nevertheless, it would have been a plan more in accord with the position
which might have been prepared without risk. If, however, Black had thereupon played
his trump card, Kt—B5, in order to assure himself of the two Bishops then, after BxKt,
PxB; Kt—B3, followed by R—K, B—B, etc., he would have been confronted with the
triple task: first and second, to reckon with the possibilities bound up with P—QB5 and
P—K5, and, third, to guard the BP. With the text-move White permits himself to be
buried with a temporary extension of his range but in return surrenders to his adversary permanent advantages, such as the control of the black squares and the weakness
on K4. In the play that follows Black uses these advantages in classical fashion to
obtain a win.

(g) The beginning of a deeply calculated, typically Lasker-like regrouping
maneuver, by means of which every vestige of danger is removed from the King's side.

(h) White underrates the import of the counter-move. With 21 Kt—B3 or 21
P—KR4 the material inferiority could have been avoided, but the positional disadvantage
was not to be evaded after 21...B—B3, etc.

(i) After 22 R—B5 would follow 22... B—R5, followed by Kt—K4 or P—KKt3,
and, after 22 R—B3, then Kt—K4, etc. With the text-move, White hopes to be able to
sacrifice the exchange advantageously The opponent, however, accepts, but in a manner
which does not leave White any serious counter-change.

(j) Threatening 23...P—KR4.

(k) And not 24...B—R5; 25 RxKtPch, etc., with excellent prospects.

(l) Herewith is decided the fate of the game.

(m) During the leveling process, Black was obliged to give up a Pawn, but the
position was simplified to such an extent that the capitalization of his material preponderance no longer offered any real difficulty. The possibility of the Bishop getting into the
fight alone needs to be watched.

(n) This opening of the file constitutes the shortest road to victory.

(o) Likewise 33 Q—B2, QR—K, etc., would yield in the long run a hopeless
struggle.

(p) Herewith he rests his last hope upon the Pawn about to become passed. After
38 B—K6ch, K—R2; 39 R—KKt, Black would win by means of 39...Q—B7; 40 QxBP,
R—K8, etc.

(q) After 39...Q—K6, White would still have the reply of 40 K—R2.

(r) The death blow, for Black easily wins the end-game after 41 QxKP, Q—B8ch;
42 K—R2, Q—B5ch; 43 QxQ, RxQ, for instance: 44 P—B5, R—B; 45 P—B6 (P—Q6,
K—B). PxP; 46 PxP. RxP; 47 P—QR4, K—B; 48 K—Kt3, R—B5; 49 B—Q (or 49 B—Q7,
P—R3!, etc.) R—Q5; 50 B—B2, P—R3!; 51 K—B3, R—Q7; 52 B—K4, R—R7;
53 B—B6, K—K2; 54 P—Kt3, K—Q3; 55 B—K8, R—R6ch; 56 K—B4, R—Kt6, threatening R—Kt, followed by R—Kt5ch, etc. It is clear that White's QRP was not to be
saved even in other continuations. Therefore, White prefers to make an end of it
quickly.

(s) Followed by mate on the next move.

Game 102   TWENTY-FIRST ROUND—FRENCH DEFENSE.

Capablanca	Reti	8 P—B4	P—QB4
White	Black	9 Kt—B3	Kt—QB3(a)
1 P—K4	P—K3	10 PxP	KtxBP
2 P—Q4	P—Q4	11 B—Q3	P—B3
3 Kt—QB3	Kt—KB3	12 PxP	QxP
4 B—Kt5	B—K2	13 P—KKt3	B—Q2(b)
5 P—K5	KKt—Q2	14 Castles, KR	KtxB
6 BxB	QxB	15 PxKt	B—K(c)
7 Q—Q2	Castles	16 KR—K	B—Kt3

After 13 P—KKt3   After 26...P—KR3

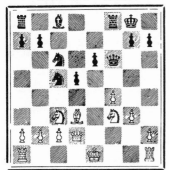   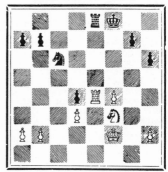

17	Kt—QKt5(d)	P—K4(e)
18	Kt—B3(f)	P—Q5(g)
19	Kt—K4	BxKt
20	RxB	PxP
21	RxBP	Q—Q3
22	R—K	RxR
23	QxR	QxQ(h)
24	PxQ	K—B(i)
25	R—K4	R—K(j)
26	K—B2	P—KR3(k)

27	Kt—K5(l)	KtxKt(m)
28	PxKt	K—B2
29	K—B3	R—Q(n)
30	R—Kt4	P—KKt4
31	P—KR4	K—Kt3
32	PxP	PxP
33	K—K4	K—R4
34	R—Kt	K—R5
35	P—K6	P—Kt5
36	P—K7(o)	Resigns

(a) So far everything in accordance with the old style. Now, however, White, in place of the tested variation introduced by Rubinstein (against Loewenfisch, Karlsbad, 1911), P—KKt3, followed by B—R3, etc., tries out something new which turns out to be less effective.

(b) Thereby Black allows a favorable tactical opportunity to escape. At once 13...KtxBch should have been played; if then 14 PxKt, P—K4!; 15 Castles (15 KtxQP, Q—B2, followed by PxBP), B—R6; 16 KR—K or B2, QR—K!, and if White should capture the Queen's Pawn, Black would always find compensation therefor in the KBP and thereby obtain a good game. If, however, White, after 13...KtxBch, recaptures with the Queen then Black, after B—Q2—K—Kt3, followed by QR—B, would have a fully compensating counter-pressure for the weak King's Pawn. After the inexact text-move, on the other hand, White must remain permanently at the helm.

(c) Now, having lost a tempo, 15...P—K4 would place Black at a disadvantage after 16 QR—K!; and thus the weakling on K6 remains (or, more correctly speaking, must remain) permanently fixed.

(d) Probably an oversight, for there was no reason to grant Black the opportunity to get rid of his principal weakness, the more so as White, with 17 Kt—K5, would have had good prospects after the exchange to assure for the remaining Knight a permanent post on K5 or Q4. And, as Black would have had no real counter-play, victory in the long run could hardly have escaped the world's champion.

(e) Forcing a dissolution with probably an easily drawn ending.

(f) 17 KtxKP? would lead to the loss of a piece after 17...KtxKt, followed by Q—Kt3ch.

(g) Beginning useless finessing. 18...PxP!; 19 KtxP, Q—Q3 (Q); 20 KtxBP, BxQP!, etc., would have deprived White of every hope of winning. But that's the way things go.

(h) Simpler would have been 23...Q—Q4; 24 Q—K4!, R—Q (not 24 QxRP?, on account of 25 Kt—Kt5, P—KKt3; 26 Q—R4, P—KR4; 27 Q—K4 and wins), inasmuch as the KBP can be used by White as support for the Knight.

(i) The Rook opposition prepared thereby turns out to be aimless. In order would have been 24...R—Q; 25 K—B2, P—KR3! (as preparation for R—Q4, which at this point would have been met by 26 Kt—Kt5), and if 26 Kt—K5, then 26...KtxKt; 27 PxKt, K—B2; 28 K—B3, K—K3, threatening R—Q4, etc.

(j) 25...R—Q (26 Kt—Kt5, K—Kt!) was always still more effective.

(k) Also 26...RxR; 27 PxR, Kt—Kt5; 28 KtxP, KtxQ6ch (KtxRP; 29 Kt—B2, etc.); 29 K—K3, KtxKtP; 30 Kt—K6ch, K—Kt!; 31 K—Q4!, etc., would have been more than questionable for Black. After the text-move, Capablanca forces the win in an elegant manner.

(l) Threatening to bring about a winning Pawn ending with 28 KtxKt, RxR; 29 PxR, PxKt; 30 P—Kt4!, K—K2; 31 K—K2, K—Q3; 32 K—Q3, P—B4; 33 PxPch, KxP; 34 P—B5!, etc.

(m) The alternative 27...R—Q; 28 KtxKt, PxKt; 29 R—K5, followed by K—B3—K4, etc., would likewise have been hopeless.

(n) Now becomes apparent the importance of the tempo loss at 25...R—K?, as a result of which Black now perishes.

(o) An energetic finish. If 36...R—K, White would obtain an easily won ending by means of 37 K—B5!, RxP; 38 RxPch, K—R4; 39 RxP, R—K7; 40 R—QKt4, etc.

Game 103　　　　TWENTY-FIRST ROUND—RUY LOPEZ

Yates	Marshall	After 22...P—QR4
White	Black	

	White	Black
1	P—K4	P—K4
2	Kt—KB3	Kt—QB3
3	B—Kt5	P—QR3
4	B—R4	Kt—B3
5	Castles	B—K2
6	R—K	P—QKt4
7	B—Kt3	Castles
8	P—Q3(a)	P—Q3
9	P—B3	B—K3(b)
10	BxB(c)	PxB
11	P—QR4(d)	P—Kt5(e)
12	Q—K2(f)	Kt—KR4(g)
13	P—Q4	KtPxP
14	KtPxP	PxP
15	KtxP	KtxKt
16	PxKt	Kt—B5
17	BxKt	RxB
18	Kt—Q2	Q—Q2(h)
19	Kt—B(i)	R—B2(j)
20	KR—QB	QR—KB(k)
21	P—B3	P—Q4
22	P—K5(l)	P—QR4(m)
23	Kt—Kt3(n)	B—Kt5(o)
24	R—R2	R—B(p)
25	K—R(q)	P—B4
26	PxP	RxP
27	QR—B2	RxR
28	QxR	R—B5
29	R—Q(r)	Q—K(s)
30	Kt—K2	R—B5
31	Q—Kt3	Q—R4
32	Q—Kt2	Q—B4(t)
33	Q—R	B—B4
34	R—QB	Q—Q6
35	Kt—Kt3(u)	B—Q5
36	Q—Kt	QxQ
37	RxQ	BxP
38	R—K	RxP(v)
39	K—Kt	R—R8
40	RxR	BxR
41	Kt—B	B—Kt7
	Resigns	

(a) The suggestion worked. White is afraid that Marshall will make his incorrect Pawn sacrifice of P—Q4, after 8 P—B3. Therefore, he chooses the slow variation.

(b) With this move Black engages sooner or later, unless his opponent himself does not exchange, to open the QR file through BxB, and this without any compensation. Better is the old continuation 9...Kt—QR4, P—B4, etc. (see, for instance, the game, Maroczy-Capablanca, in the 13th round).

(c) This exchange is not directly disadvantageous, but it falls in line with the plan of Black, in that it opens the KB file as a basis of operations for a counter-attack. A more lasting attack was 10 QKt—Q2, as Maroczy played against Yates in the last round.

(d) Threatens to win a Pawn by exchanges on Kt5 and R8, followed by Q—Kt3.

(e)   Far better than leaving White in possession of the R file by 11...R—Kt. White cannot now well afford to play for the win of a Pawn because of his backward development, for instance: 12 Q—Kt3, Q—Q2; 13 PxP, KR—Kt; 14 B—Q2, KtxKtP; 15 BxKt, P—B4; 16 Kt—Kt5, RxB; 17 QxPch, QxQ; 18 KtxQ, RxKtP, to Black's advantage.

(f)   Preparing for P—Q4 at once would have been unsuccessful, as Black would have had the counter P—Q4, after 12...PxBP; 13 PxP, PxP (or 14 KtxQP, KtxKt; 15 PxKt).

(g)   As a result it would have been better for Black to hold this counter in reserve in case his opponent carried out his purpose—this in the simplest way by 12... Q—Q2 (13 P—Q4, PxBP; 14 PxBP, PxP; 15 PxP, P—Q4!; 16 PxP, PxP; 17 Q—K6ch, QxQ; 18 RxQ, B—Q3, etc. After the move in the text which completes White's development through several exchanges, Black remains at a slight disadvantage because of his weakened pawn position.

(h)   If now 18...P—Q4, then 19 PxP, QxP; 20 Kt—B3, B—B3; 21 QR—Q to White's advantage.

(i)   A defensive move too many. Simple and good was 19 Q—B4, for after 19... QR—KB (P—Q4; 20 PxP, PxP; 21 RxB, etc.), either 20 QxRP, RxBP; 21 Kt—B3, R—B7 (or QKt7); 22 R—K2, etc.; or even the simple 20 R—K2 was good.

(j)   A good positional move that paves the way, among other things for P—Q4.

(k)   Black utilizes every opportunity for a counter-attack. 21 QxRP, RxP, would now be hazardous for White, because of the unfortunate withdrawal of the Kt—B. In this case Black would be threatening to bring his Queen over to the King side with decisive effect either through P—K4 or O—K. White must therefore resolve on the following weakening of his position which, however, does not appear so dangerous immediately but does turn out to be fatal.

(l)   Still the best; if 22 PxP, QxP; 23 QxRP, then B—B3; 24 R—Q, BxPch; 25 K—R, RxP, with a decisive attack. A genuine Marshall swindle!

(m)   But now he must mix water with his wine and give his opponent an easy opportunity to gain the initiative.

(n)   An unintelligible move. Surely it was obvious that White should unconditionally prevent the move P—B4, which removes the most evident weakness of Black. This objective could be obtained without trouble through 23 Q—R6, for instance: I. 23... B—Kt5; 24 R—B6, R—B5; 25 R—Q and, though White does not threaten RxKP immediately (because of B—B6), he is threatening Kt—K2 against which a defense would be very difficult.

II 23...R—B5; 24 Q—R7, B—Q; 25 Kt—Kt3 and Black again with difficulty can defend all his weak spots (QR4, QB2, K3). After the very weak text-move, the scene changes with amazing rapidity.

(o)   Prevents first an expedition of the white Queen because of the answer B—Q7, the first consequence of the above move of White!

(p)   Threatens P—B4 for which there is no remedy.

(q)   The ending, too, resulting from 25 Q—Kt5, QxQ; 26 PxQ, R—Kt, could not be saved for long by White.

(r)   After 29 Q—B8ch, QxQ; 30 RxQch, B—B the Pawn at R4 is immediately lost.

(s)   The opening maneuver for a decisive break through by the Queen. Marshall plays the final phase very energetically and correctly.

(t)   Black now commands the whole board.

(u)   This unlucky and greatly sinning Kt, as a punishment, can find no rest until the end.

(v)   A good harvest.

Game 104   TWENTY-FIRST ROUND—QUEEN'S GAMBIT DECLINED

Bogoljubow White	Maroczy Black		
		9 P—B5(h)	B—B2
		10 Kt—B4(i)	Kt—Q2
1 P—Q4	P—Q4	11 B—Q2	Kt—B3
2 P—QB4	P—QB3	12 P—B3(j)	Castles
3 Kt—KB3(a)	Kt—KB3	13 Castles	P—QKt3(k)
4 P—K3(b)	P—K3	14 Kt—K5	KtPxP
5 Kt—Q2(c)	Kt—K5(d)	15 B—B4(l)	Q—K(m)
6 KtxKt(e)	PxKt	16 P—Kt4(n)	KBPxP
7 Kt—Q2	P—KB4	17 PxKtP	P—QR4
8 Q—Kt3(f)	B—Q3(g)	18 P—Kt5(o)	BxKt

19	PxKt(p)	BxBP	
20	PxP	Q—R4(q)	
21	Q—B2(r)	K—R	
22	B—Kt3(s)	B—R3(t)	

After 22 B—Kt3

23	QxP	B—K7
24	B—B2	B—B6
25	QxKP	B—Q4

26	Q—Q6	QR—Q
27	Q—Kt3	BxR(u)
28	RxB	RxB
29	KxR	Q—Q4ch
30	K—K2	QxR
31	Q—R3	P—R3
32	Q—B5	Q—Kt7ch
33	K—Q	Q—Q4ch(v)
34	QxQ	PxQ
35	B—B5	BxP
36	B—K6	P—Kt4
37	K—B2	R—B7ch
38	K—Q3	RxP
39	BxP	K—Kt2
40	K—B4	B—K4
41	K—Kt5	R—K7
42	KxP	RxKP
43	P—R4	B—Q5
44	K—Kt5	P—Kt5
45	P—R5	R—QB6
46	B—B4	P—Kt6
47	P—B6	P—Kt7
48	P—B7	RxB
	Resigns	

(a) In our opinion, 3 Kt—QB3 first is better.

(b) White cannot obtain any advantage with this move, because Black, besides the continuation selected by him, has also at his disposal the plausible development of 4... B—B4. Probably the best after all would be 4 PxP, by means of which White would retain, for a while at least, the initiative belonging to the first player.

(c) Evidently to forestall the Meran variation (5 Kt—B3, Kt—Q2; 6 B—Q3, PxP, etc.)

(d) Quite a good idea. Now White, at the best, could attain a mutual stonewall formation, after which his minute lead in development would mean nothing, on account of the blockaded position, for instance: 6 B—Q3, P—KB4; 7 Kt—K5, Q—R5; 8 Castles, Kt—Q2; 9 P—B4 (after 9 P—B3, Black would have the choice between I.—9...KtxQKt; 10 BxKt, PxP; 11 P—KKt3, Q—R3; 12 BxP, B—Q3; 13 P—B4, P—KKt4, and II.— 9...KtxKKt; 10 QPxKt, Kt—B4; 11 B—K2, followed by Castles), B—Q3, to be followed by Castles, etc.

(e) The subsequent course of this game proved that the KP exerts a cramping influence over White's game and that a later elimination of it is not going to improve matters for the first player. Therefore, 6 B—Q3 would have been preferable.

(f) Through castling on the Queen's side, for which he is preparing with this move, White soon drifts into an undesirable position. More passable, at any rate, would have been 8 P—B3, B—Q3; 9 P—KKt3, PxP (Q—Kt4; 10 Q—K2); 10 KtxP, Kt—Q2; 11 B—Q3 (in order to play 12 P—K4 in reply to Castles), Kt—B3; 12 Castles, Castles; 13 Q—B2, P—B4, followed by P—QKt3, etc.

(g) Another plan of mobilization, likewise auguring well, could be led up to through 8...P—B4. However, the text-move is all-sufficient to demonstrate the inferiority of White's position.

(h) Relinquishing the square, Q5, without compensation, yet there was hardly another method of developing the pieces.

(i) An error of position judgment with serious consequences. Under all circumstances he should have made as difficult as possible the development of Black's Knight through 10 B—B4, in order to make an attempt, in reply to 10...Q—K2 or B3, to break Black's center by means of P—B3, followed by Q—B2, even at the cost of the exchange.

(j) Much too late, for White merely burdens himself thereby and not his opponent. 12 B—K2, followed by Castles, however perilous it might appear, would have yielded better prospects for defense.

(k)   Forcing a decisive opening of the file, as ,White, unable to resort to serious counter-play, is restricted to harmless, tactical sorties.

(l)   Or 15 KtxP, Q—K; 16 Kt—K5 (16 B—Kt5, B—Q2), R—Kt, with an easy mating attack.

(m)   Not to mention the ominous menace of his position, Black has also gained material plus.   The win, therefore, is merely a question of time.

(n)   Without prospect, as anything else, for that matter.

(o)   Somewhat better would have been 18 Q—B2.

(p)   If 19 PxB, Kt—Q4; 20 Q—B2, Q—Kt3.

(q)   Maroczy plays this game with much energy and does not allow his opponent a moment in which to breathe.

(r)   Or I.—21 BxPch, K—R; 22 BxB, QxPch; 23 Q—B2, QxQch (BxPch; 24 K—Kt!); 24 KxQ, KRxB.   II.—21 Q—Kt6, B—Q2; 22 BxP, KR—Kt; 23 RxB, RxQ; 24 BxR, Q—B6; 25 R—K, B—Kt4; 26 BxPch, K—R.   After the text-move, his progress downhill is by so much accelerated.

(s)   Likewise 22 QxP, QxBP; 23 K—Kt, R—QKt, etc., would not have led to anything.

(t)   The zigzag maneuver of the Bishop hereby begun, by means of which White's poor Queen is chased about heartlessly, forces the win of additional material.

(u)   Much simpler than 27...B—K4; 28 P—K4, BxQ; 29 RPxB, and Black would have had to content himself with only winning the exchange.

(v)   Black enters the ending with "only" a Rook plus.   The rest, of course, requires no comment.

Game 105   TWENTY-FIRST ROUND—QUEEN'S PAWN OPENING

Janowski	Ed. Lasker	16 QxRch(i)	KtxQ
White	Black	17 PxKt	Kt—Q3
1 P—Q4	P—Q4	18 R—B	Kt—B5(j)
2 B—B4(a)	Kt—KB3	19 BxKt	PxB
3 P—K3(b)	P—K3(b)	20 QKt—Q2	P—QKt4
4 B—Q3	P—B4	21 R—R5	P—B3
5 P—QB3	Q—Kt3	22 P—Kt5	K—Q(k)
6 Q—B2	QKt—Q2(c)	23 QR—KR	B—K
7 Kt—Q2	B—Q3	24 RxP	RxR
8 BxB(d)	QxB	25 RxR(l)	PxR
9 P—KB4	Kt—Kt5(e)	26 KtxP	K—B(m)
10 Kt—B	PxP	27 R—R8	K—Kt2
11 BPxP	Q—Kt5ch	28 QKt—K4(n)	K—Kt3
12 K—K2(f)	Kt—Kt3	29 Kt—B5(o)	B—B3(p)
13 P—QR3	Q—K2	30 KKtxP	B—Q4(q)
14 Kt—B3(g)	B—Q2	31 Kt—Kt5	K—R4
15 P—R3	R—QB(h)	32 P—K4	B—B3

After 15...R—QB

After 35...B—Kt4

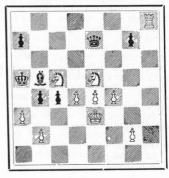

33	K—K3	B—K(r)	
34	Kt—B3	P—Kt5(s)	
35	Kt—K5	B—Kt4(t)	
36	P—R4(u)	BxP	
37	KtxPch	K—Kt4	
38	Kt—K5	K—R4	
39	R—QKt8(v)	B—Kt4	
40	P—KKt3(w)	P—Kt4	
41	Kt—B3	PxPch	
42	PxP	Q—R2	
43	P—B5(x)	Q—R8	
44	Kt—Kt3ch	K—R5	
45	Kt(Kt3)—Q2	Q—R3ch	
46	K—B2	B—Q6	
47	R—Kt8	Q—B5(y)	
48	R—KR8(z)	P—Kt6	
49	R—R4	Q—B2	
50	P—B6	B—B5	
51	R—R5(aa)	B—K3	
52	R—K5(bb)	Q—KB2(cc)	

After 52...Q—KB2

53 RxB(dd)   QxR

54	P—K5	K—Kt5	
55	K—K3	P—R4	
56	K—B4	P—R5	
57	Kt—Kt5	Q—Q2	
58	P—B7	Q—K2(ee)	
59	P—Q5	P—R6	
60	PxPch	K—B6(ff)	
61	P—Q6	Q—B	
62	Kt(Kt5)— K4ch(gg)	K—Q6	
63	P—K6	Q—R3ch	
64	K—B5	P—Kt7	
65	P—Q7	Q—B	
66	P—R4(hh)	Q—QR	
67	P—K7	Q—Q4ch	
68	K—B6	Q—Q5ch	

After 68...Q—Q5ch

69	K—K6(ii)	P—Kt8(Q)	
70	KtxQ(jj)	QxKtch	
71	K—B6(kk)	Q—R5ch(ll)	

Drawn

(a)   This yields White no prospect of any advantage before Black has locked in his QB with P—K3. A capital example of how Black must develop himself in this line of play is furnished by the game between Maroczy and Capablanca in the ninth round.

(b)   Analogous to the play in the game referred to, 3...P—B4; 4 P—B3, Q—Kt3, etc., would be better here. After the text-move, White's development is rounded out.

(c)   More to the point would have been 6...Kt—B3, followed by B—Q2, in order to occupy the QB file with the Rook as quickly as possible; but even this line of play would leave White some advantage, for instance: 7 Kt—KB3, B—Q2; 8 Castles, R—B; 9 PxP!, BxP; 10 QKt—Q2, B—K2; 11 P—QR3, followed eventually by P—K4, etc.

(d)   The subsequent stonewall formation contemplated hereby has no substance, as the outcome clearly shows. More in the spirit of the variation would have been the simple developing continuation of 8 Kt—KB3, as the exchange on B4 would have assured White the unchallenged command of the squares in the center and Black would later on have been embarrassed as to how to make his QB fully effective.

(e)   Forcing the next defensive move, after which the co-operation between the White Rooks is rendered considerably more difficult.

(f)   The alternative of 12 Q—B3, QxQch, etc., would have resulted in lasting weakness for White on B3.

(g)   The immediate 14 P—KR3 could have been met effectively with 14...Q—R5; 15 P—KKt3, Q—R4, etc.

(h)   Black obviously failed to take seriously into account the following interesting scheme of his opponent, for otherwise he would first have played 15...Kt—B3 and then in good time have taken possession of the QB file with a clear positional advantage. Now the game follows a new course.

(i)   In view of the by no means enviable position of White, this unexpected sacrifice of the Queen is undoubtedly his best chance. To be sure, he obtains only a Rook and Knight for the Queen for the time being, but the open KR file and the impossibility for Black to make quick use of his Rook render the game very complicated and double-edged.

(j)   Thereby Black obtains a majority of Pawns on the Queen's side and eliminates the undesirable white Bishop. Less good would have been 18...Kt—K5 on account of 19 Kt—K5!, threatening R—B7, etc.

(k)   The beginning of an inconsequential and time-robbing King maneuver which could have been replaced to better advantage by 22...B—B3 and, in case 23 QR—KR, then simply 23...BxKtch; 24 KtxB (or 24 PxB, PxP, followed by P—Kt3) P—Kt5, etc. In the further course of the game it will only be with great difficulty that he will be enabled to exchange his unfortunate Bishop for one of the Knights.

(1)   The atoning sacrifice has in no way improved Black's position, for he now faces the unpleasant alternative of yielding either the square, K5, to the Knight or the seventh row to the Rook. The former evil, which he actually selects, is perhaps the more endurable.

(m)   27 RxP, etc., was threatened.

(n)   Threatening 29 RxB.

(o)   An oversight which, however, is not taken advantage of by Black. Correct would have been 29 Kt—KB3, B—B3; 30 Kt—B5, BxKtch; 31 KxB, etc., with fair prospects.

(p)   The deciding error. With the obvious 29...P—K4! Black not only would have avoided every danger of loss, after the exchange of Pawns in the center, but would have gained the upper hand because of the unsafe position of White's King. Now White should win quite easily.

(q)   Why not at least 30...BxP? In any event, it could not have led to anything worse.

(r)   Thereby the Rook is kept from the Queen's side only for a short time, as the Knights must dominate the whole board and Black, for the want of moves, be compelled to expose himself anew.

(s)   By means of 34..K—Kt3 he could have held out anyhow a little longer.

(t)   If 35...P—B6; 36 PxP!, PxRP, White would win by means of 37 RxB!, QxR; 38 Kt—B4ch, K—Kt4; 39 Kt—Q6ch, etc.

(u)   Immediately decisive would have been 36 R—QKt8 (threatening mate in two), P—Kt6 (or PxP; 37 KtxPch, BxKt; 38 P—Kt4 mate); 37 P—R4!, P—R3; 38 PxB, with mate in short order. Of course, the text-move suffices for a win.

(v)   Inasmuch as mate can no longer be forced, 39 P—KKt3 and, after 39...P—Kt4; 40 P—B5, P—Kt5; 41 Kt—K6, etc., would have been more forceful. Likewise on his 41st move White could have played more energetically with P—B5. At this point there are several roads which lead to the goal.

(w)   Threatening now 41 R—Kt7, etc.

(x)   Simpler would have been 43 R—Kt7.

(y)   Thanks to White's inexact play, Black has obtained some kind of counter-play, but in turn loses valuable time. Here, for instance, 47 P—R4 would have saved an important tempo.

(z)   Indirectly protecting the KP.

(aa)   Why not simply 51 KtxB QxKt; 52 R—B4, Q—B2; 53 P—K5, etc.?

(bb)　After the foregoing omission, the sacrifice of the exchange planned hereby is certainly the surest road to victory.

(cc)　Or 52...B—Kt5; 53 K—Kt3, etc., with an easy win.

(dd)　Now the passed pawns, supported by the Knights, soon become overwhelming. Black's only small chance centers in the QRP which the opponent for his part so proudly spurned and which also—but of course "per nefas"—in the end saves the day. Without doubt this is the oddest game of the tournament!

(ee)　Or 58...QxQPch; 59 Kt(Q2)—K4, Q—Q; 60 Kt—K6, Q—R5ch; 61 K—B5, and the King would have been able easily to escape the checks.

(ff)　Black does all that is humanly possible; it should have been all in vain, however.

(gg)　In any event more interesting would have been 52 Kt(Q2)—K4ch, K—B7; 63 P—K6, P—Kt7; 64 P—K7, Q—R3; 65 P—B8 (Q), Q—R5ch; 66 K—B5, P—Kt8 (Q); 67 P—K8 (Q), etc., which would have led to a "fight" with two Queens, two Knights and two Pawns against two Queens.

(hh)　With the intention of advancing this Pawn to R7 and then playing K—Kt6, followed by P—R8 (Q) and P—K7. Black, therefore, makes a desperate sortie

(ii)　After this the game is really drawn. Correct would have been 69 K—Kt6!, P queens (or Q—Kt8ch; 75 Kt—Kt5); 70 P—Q8 (Q), etc.

(jj)　If now 70 P—Q8 (Q), then 70...Q—R7ch!; 71 K—B5, QxPch, and White would not have been able to avoid perpetual check.

(kk)　There is no safety for the King on the Queen's side, for, if he finally reaches Q8, he would be mated by Q—QKt.

(ll)　If now 72 K—Kt7, then 72...QxP; 73 P—Q8 (Q), QxQ; 74 P—B8 (Q), Q—Q2ch and QxP, etc.

TWENTY-SECOND ROUND

For the twenty-second and last round of the tournament there was left the pairing which had done duty for the ninth, in which Marshall had made it so very interesting for Dr. Lasker. This time the colors are reversed and Dr. Lasker, serene in the knowledge that the first prize and the homage of the chess world are already his, has the white pieces and elects to play the Ruy Lopez. Presently, the "exchange variation" makes its appearance on the board, and one is strongly reminded of St. Petersburg and the havoc it wrought there early in 1914.

At first it seemed to indicate that the ex-champion would be content with a draw, but a draw did not suffice for Marshall if he would attain third place. He boldly sacrificed a Pawn and that straightway put Dr. Lasker on '.is mettle. A gambit, especially in Ruy Lopez form, cannot safely be ventured upon when he sits at the other side of the board. And so it turned out.

Marshall tried in vain to advance at the Doctor's expense and, after his somewhat short-lived attack had been repulsed, he succumbed to the deadly accuracy of the tournament victor. For that reason Marshall had to be content with fourth place, an honor, however, which was most gratifying to his friends and brought him the heartiest congratulations from all sides.

Meanwhile Capablanca, quite safe from pursuit as second prize winner, had his hands full with Bogoljubow, who likewise had much to gain, could he but win his last game. The fight he made was a splendid one. He chose the French defense with his own improvement, which has served to revive interest in the defense considerably. A slight advantage came to him early and this persisted throughout the middle game.

There were times when Capablanca seemed to be laboring a bit heavily and friends would shake their heads dubiously, but no one was quite able to place his hand upon any fatally weak spot in the champion's armor. It has remained for Alekhine to point out just where Bogoljubow missed the grand opportunity that was beckoning him on to duplicate the feat of Reti in the fifth round. That would have meant a tie for fifth prize, let alone the greater satisfaction in lowering the colors of Cuba's famous son. But it was not to be. At the first sign that the pressure was lessening Capablanca asserted himself and the tables were turned in the ending after a hard fight of 65 moves.

Alekhine, keeping a close watch upon the game between Dr. Lasker and Marshall, played, it may safely be assumed, "to the score." So long as Marshall was not winning or merely drew, the Russian's half-point lead sufficed. The latter played the Ruy Lopez against Dr. Tartakower, who gave no indication of weakening in the face of the very slight positional advantage of his alert opponent. Alekhine had two Bishops for the ending, but even this did not serve to avert the inevitable yet welcome draw. And so Alekhine remained undisputed third with a score that would have made him the winner of the tournament, barring the presence of Dr. Lasker and Capablanca!

Reti, for his last game with Janowski, again resorted to his own opening, once, because of the first move, accredited to the lamented Zukertort. His superior technique in development yielded him a good harvest in the form of the "exchange." Although Janowski succeeded in obtaining strong posts for his pieces, the ingenuity of Reti prevailed and he at last gained the coveted point he had vainly worked for in the three preceding rounds and which he needed to clinch his title to fifth prize.

Had Reti wavered at this most critical stage, Maroczy assuredly would have been upon him, for the Hungarian was at his best in the game with Yates, who, on the black side of a Ruy Lopez, was completely outplayed. The clever manipulation of his Knights coupled with perfect timing of his moves gave him full control of the board and a well earned point. Owing to Reti's last-minute effort, however, Maroczy was left in sixth place.

The final scores: Dr. Lasker, 16—4; Capablanca, 14½—5½; Alekhine, 12—8; Marshall, 11—9; Reti, 10½—9½; Maroczy, 10—10; Bogoljubow, 9½—10½; Dr. Tartakower, 8—12; Yates, 7—13; Ed. Lasker, 6½—13½; Janowski, 5—15.

Except for the sixth round, this last day brought the worst rout of the tournament for the sable forces, who were defeated to the tune of 4½—½. At the finish the record read: White, 61; Black, 49.

And thus the play ended. There was not a single tie for any of the eleven places. Each competitor had carved out for himself his own niche in this Caissa's Hall of Fame.

Game 106   TWENTY-SECOND ROUND—RUY LOPEZ

	Dr. Lasker. White.	Marshall Black.

After 17...P—KKt4

	White.	Black.
1	P—K4	P—K4
2	Kt—KB3	Kt—QB3
3	B—Kt5	P—QR3
4	BxKt	QPxB
5	P—Q4	B—KKt5 (a)
6	PxP	QxQch
7	KxQ	Castles ch
8	K—K (b)	B—QB4
9	P—KR3	B—R4
10	B—B4	P—B4 (c)
11	QKt—Q2	Kt—K2
12	B—Kt5 (d)	BxKt
13	PxB	KR—K
14	R—Q (e)	PxP
15	PxP (f)	P—R3
16	B—R4	B—Q5
17	Kt—B4	P—KKt4 (g)
18	P—QB3 (h)	Kt—Kt3
19	PxB (i)	KtxB
20	K—K2	R—Q2
21	P—B3	Kt—Kt3 (j)
22	Kt—K3 (k)	P—B4
23	PxP	Kt—B5ch
24	K—B2	RxR
25	RxR	RxP (l)
26	Kt—Q5	KtxPch (m)
27	K—Kt3	P—Kt5 (n)
28	Kt—B6	P—KR4
29	P—B4 (o)	RxBP

30	R—K (p)	R—QKt4
31	P—K5	K—Q
32	KtxRP	K—K2
33	P—B5	Kt—Kt4 (q)
34	KxP	Kt —R2
35	Kt—B4	RxKtP
36	Kt—Q5ch	K—Q2
37	P—K6ch	K—Q3
38	P—K7	KxKt
39	R—K6 (r)	R—Kt7ch
40	K—B4	R—Kt
41	P—K8 (Q)	RxQ
42	RxR	P—B4
43	R—Q8ch	K—B3
44	R—KR8 (s)	Resigns

(a) This peculiar gambit prepares difficulties for Black for the reason that he is later forced so to play, with more or less success, in order to recover the pawn sacrificed. Much simpler and better is the old variation of 5...PxP; 6 QxP, QxQ; 7 **KtxQ**, B—Q2, followed by Castles QR, etc., with at least an even game.

(b) If 8 K—K2, Black, by means of 8...P—B3, can either compel the opening of the lines in the center or recover the Pawn at once.

(c) An interesting move which prepares for Black a way to a most promising continuation. If 11 PxP, BxKt; 12 PxB, Kt—K2, and, after the disappearance of the KBP, Black would still retain pressure upon the KB file.

(d) Threatening 13 Kt—Kt3, as well as 13 PxP, thereby forcing the exchange of Black's troublesome QB.

(e) Not 14 PxP, on account of R—Q4, etc.

(f) If 15 KtxP, B—Q5, for which White has evidently prepared the showy move of Kt—B4.

(g) If 17...P—QKt4, then 18 P—B3, etc.

(h) Herewith the situation is cleared at last, for the exchange which follows strengthens the position for White in the center quite decisively, and even the fact that Black, in the progress of the game, succeeds finally in regaining the gambit pawn cannot any more alter the result of the game.

(i) Simpler than 19 BxKtP, BxPch, etc.

(j) If 21...KR—Q; 22 P—Q5, PxP; 23 P—K6, etc.

(k) White could also prevent the subsequent clearing of the center through 22 P—QKt4, but this was not essential, inasmuch as he remains with a clear advantage.

(l) He might have offered a somewhat longer resistance with 25...KtxPch; 26 K—Kt3, Kt—B5; 27 Kt—Q5, Kt—Kt3, etc.

(m) Now the Knight is imprisoned and White obtains two connected passed Pawns, but even after the retreat of the Knight White could win easily by means of 27 P—Kt4, etc.

(n) Black had relied upon this reply to let him out of his difficulties (28 KxP, Kt—Kt4, etc.). The rejoinder, however, destroys all his hopes.

(o) The following variation would have been also sufficiently convincing: 29 PxP, Kt—Kt4 (if PxP; 30 KtxP); 30 PxP, KtxPch; 31 KtxKt, RxKt; 32 R—KR, etc.

(p) Not 30 P—K5 at once, on account of 30...P—R5ch; 31 KxRP, KtxBP; 33 P—K6, R—K4, etc.

(q) Otherwise the further advance of the passed pawns would decide matters.

(r) Now Black is obliged to sacrifice his Rook for the passed Pawn and further resistance is, of course, without prospect.

(s) Winning the Knight (44...Kt—B3; 45 R—R6, etc.).

Game 107 TWENTY-SECOND ROUND—FRENCH DEFENSE.

Capablanca	Bogoljubow
White	Black
1 P—Q4	P—K3
2 P—K4	P—-Q4
3 Kt—QB3	Kt—KB3
4 B—KKt5	B—Kt5
5 PxP	QxP
6 BxKt	PxB(a)
7 Q—Q2	Q—QR4(b)
8 KKt—K2 (c)	Kt—Q2
9 Kt—B(d)	Kt—Kt3
10 Kt—Kt3	Q—KKt4
11 P—QR3(e)	QxQch
12 KxQ(f)	B—K2(g)
13 B—Kt5ch(h)	P—B3
14 B—Q3	B—Q2
15 Kt—B5	Castles QR
16 KtxB	RxKt
17 Kt—K2	P—QB4(i)
18 PxP	BxP

After 18...BxP

19 K—K(j)	P—B4
20 R—KKt	P—KR4(k)

21 P—KKt3	Kt—Q4(l)
22 B—Kt5	QR—Q(m)
23 R—Q	P—R3
24 B—B4	Kt—B3
25 RxRch	RxR
26 Kt—B4(n)	Kt—K5
27 R—Kt2	P—R5
28 B—Q3(o)	PxP
29 RPxP	R—R
30 P—KKt4(p)	R—R8ch(q)

After 30 P—KKt4

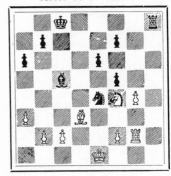

31 K—K2	R—R5(r)
32 BxKt	PxB
33 P—KB3(s)	P—K6(t)
34 Kt—Q3	B—Q5
35 P—B3	B—Kt3(u)
38 Kt—K5	R—R8
37 Kt—B4(v)	B—R2
38 KtxP	P—Kt4
39 P—Kt5(w)	K—Q2
40 Kt—B(x)	K—Q3
41 P—QR4(y)	PxP
42 R—Kt4	P—R6

43	PxP	P—R4	
44	R—KB4	B—B4	
45	Kt—Q2	K—K2	
46	R—QR4	R—KKt8	
47	Kt—K4(z)	B—Kt3	
48	R—B4	K—Q2	
49	Kt—B6ch	K—Q	
50	Kt—Kt4(aa)	R—Kt7ch	
51	K—Q3	R—Kt6	
52	K—K4	R—Kt8	
53	R—B6	B—B2	
54	R—R6(bb)	K—Q2	
55	R—R8	R—QR8	
56	Kt—B6ch	K—B3(cc)	
57	R—KB8	R—K8ch	
58	K—Q3	B—B5	
59	Kt—K4	K—Kt4(dd)	
60	RxP	P—K4	
61	P—Kt6	R—K6ch	
62	K—B2	R—K7ch	
63	K—Q	R—KKt7	
64	P—Kt7	K—B5	
65	Kt—B6	Resigns	

(a) Better than exchanging the Kt for B first (see the game between Capablanca and Alekhine in the fourth round), as hitherto played for the most part, probably under the influence of the unfavorable course for Black of the eleventh match game between Dr. Lasker and Dr. Tarrasch in Munich, 1908. The two black Bishops here constitute a weapon not to be underrated and White must still exert himself before he succeeds in disposing of one of them.

(b) This and not 7..BxKt?, as occurred in the game referred to, is the logical continuation.

(c) Clearly with the intention of freeing himself as quickly as possible and, in the event of an exchange on QB3, to avoid doubling of the Pawns. This idea, however, is not carried out consistently in the following moves.

(d) Instead of this time wasting maneuver with the Knight, 9 P—QR3 was to have been preferred, for instance: 9...Kt—Kt3; 10 R—Q (of course not 10 Castles QR, BxP; followed by Kt—B5), B—K2; 11 Kt—Kt3 and White, by means of a move with the Queen's Knight, would have been able to force an exchange of Queens with a more favorable development than in the actual game.

(e) If White did not wish to be drawn into a complicated middle game after 11 P—B4, then 11 QxQ, PxQ; 12 Castles, BxKt; 13 PxB, with about even chances, would have been preferable. After the continuation selected, he drifts into inferiority in consequence of his unsafe King's position.

(f) Even after 12 KtxQ, BxKt; 13 PxB, B—Q2, followed by K—K2 and eventually P—QB4, Black would have had distinctly the better of it.

(g) Of course not 12...BxKtch; 13 KxB, Kt—R5ch; 14 K—Kt4!, KtxKtP?; 15 R—Kt, P—R4ch; 16 KtxP, P—Kt3; 17 B—Kt5ch, followed by Kt—B6, wnning.

(h) In order for the time being to block the escape of the black QB to QB3 and to be able to exchange him. But it all takes time—much time.

(i) With the removal of White's center Pawns Black obtains a lasting initiative.

(j) This sorry retreat, by which White leaves his KR imprisoned for a long time, is almost forced, for, after 19 KR—B, Black by means of maneuvers close at hand would have been able to increase his positional advantage, for instance: 19...Kt—B5ch; 20 K—B3, Kt—K4 (also threatening Kt—Kt5); 21 P—R3, R—B2; 22 K—Kt3, KtxB; 23 PxKt, KR—Q; 24 QR—Q, R—Q3, etc. Now, on the other hand, Black's Knight is at least not able to reach favorable squares as quickly.

(k) Preventing the eventual effort at liberation by 21 P—KKt4.

(l) This, however, is premature, as it facilitates an exchange for the opponent. More in order would have been first 21...P—R3!, in order to meet 22 QR—Q with the doubling of the Rooks (threatening Kt—R5, etc.). In the event of other rejoinders there would have come into consideration for Black either B—Q3—K4, followed by Kt—R5, or Kt—Q4—KB3—K5, etc. Capablanca at once takes advantage of the opportunity offered with the text-move.

(m) On account of 23 P—QKt4, followed by P—QB4—B5, etc., the Rook cannot very well move to Q3.

(n) The threat was 26...Kt—Kt5; 27 R—Kt2, Kt—K4, etc., which here could have been parried by 28 B—K2.

(o) The immediate 28 P—KKt4 would have been a mistake on account of 28... BxBPch; 29 RxB, KtxR; 30 KxKt, R—Q5 and wins.

(p) White might well have overcome the worst, but the text-move at the least is questionable. In order would have been 30 K—K2, followed by P—KKt4 or eventually P—KB3, etc., with a game of open possibilities.

(q)   Herewith Black deprives himself of his last winning chance.   Correct would
have been 30...BxPch; 31 RxB (or 31 K—K2, B—Q5; 32 PxP, PxP, etc.),
KtxR; 32 KxKt, PxP, and White would not have been able to win the KtP, for instance:
33 K—Kt3, R—KKt; 34 Kt—R5 (or 34 B—K2, K—Q; 35 K—R4, P—K4; 36 Kt—Kt2,
P—KB4; 37 Kt—K3, P—Kt6, etc.), K—Q! (not P—B4; 35 Kt—B4!, and the Pawn on
K3, strangely enough, could not have been saved, inasmuch as the Knight would still
capture it in the event of its being protected by the King as well as by the Rook!); 35
Kt—B6, R—Kt4, whereupon 36 K—B4 (R4) could not have been played on account of
36 P—Kt6!, and the three connected passed Pawns would have finally won.   Moreover,
30...R—R5 would have been preferable to the useless check.

(r)   Now 31...KtxP could have been simply answered by 32 PxP, etc.

(s)   Disposing at once of the troublesome Pawn, after which the game should have
ended in a draw.

(t)   No fault is to be found with this somewhat complicated move, inasmuch as
it leads to a forced drawing variation and Black could not achieve anything even with
33...PxPch; 34 KxP, followed by Kt—Q3.

(u)   This, however, is a mistake which permits White to gain a tempo by means of
a subsequent attack on the Bishop.   He should have played 35...B—R2!, 36 Kt—K5,
R—R8 37 Kt—B4, R—QKt8, and White, after 38 K—Q3 (38 KtxP, RxPch; 39 K—Q3,
R—Kt6!), R—Q8ch; 39 K—K2, R—Kt8, must be satisfied with a draw inasmuch as
there would follow after 39 K—K4, P—Kt4!, and after 39 K—B2, R—KB8, etc.   The
following ending is conducted by Capablanca with classical accuracy until the victory
is gained.

(v)   Of course not 37 KtxP, R—QKt8; 38 K—Q3, R—Q8ch; 39 K—B2, R—KB8,
etc.

(w)   Settling the weakness at KB7.   The following complicated maneuvers, which
finally lead up to the capture of that Pawn, are quite instructive.

(x)   The Knight is to be finally played over to K4.   Inadequate, however, for that
purpose would have been 40 Kt—Kt4, and indeed because of 40...R—QKt8; 41 K—Q3,
R—Q8ch; 42 K—K4, R—K8ch; 43 K—B4?, B—Ktch, etc.

(y)   Gaining new objects for attack on the Queen's side, no matter how Black
may play.

(z)   More promising than 47 RxP, RxP; 48 Kt—K4, R—Kt7ch; 49 K—Q3, B—Kt8,
etc.

(aa)   Threatening (after 50...R—QR8, for instance) a double attack against the
KBP by means of Kt—K5 and R—KB4.   The subsequent Rook moves on the part of
Black were designed to prevent White's Rook getting to KB4.

(bb)   The Rook's range of action has been appreciably increased in the last moves
and in the long run he cannot be prevented from reaching his goal, KB8.

(cc)   If 56...K—K2, then would follow 57 P—QB4!, RxP; 58 P—B5, winning.

(dd)   Or 59...R—K6ch; 60 K—B4, RxBP; 61 RxP, P—K4; 62 P—Kt6, R—KB8; 63
P—Kt7 R—KKt8; 64 Kt—B6, and wins.

Game 108   TWENTY-SECOND ROUND—THREE KNIGHTS OPENING

Alekhine	Dr. Tartakower
White	Black

16 KR—K

	White	Black
1	P—K4	P—K4
2	Kt—KB3	Kt—QB3
3	Kt—B3	B—QKt5
4	Kt—Q5	B—K2(a)
5	P—Q4(b)	PxP(c)
6	KtxP(d)	KtxKt
7	QxKt	Kt—B3
8	KtxB(e)	QxKt
9	B—Q3	P—QB4(f)
10	Q—K3(g)	P—Q4
11	PxP	KtxP
12	QxQch	KxQ
13	B—Kt5ch	P—B3

is explainable only through the circumstance that the retreat of B—K2 had beed consid-

14 B—Q2(h)	B—K3	24 P—QB4	Kt—B2
15 CastlesQR	K—B2	25 P—R5	P—B4
16 KR—K	QR—Q(i)	26 B—KB3	K—Q2
17 R—K2	P—KKt3	27 B—B4	B—B2
18 QR—K	KR—K	28 PxP	PxP
19 P—KR4	B—Kt5(j)	29 K—Q2	Kt—K3
20 RxR	RxR	30 B—K5(l)	Kt—Q
21 RxR	KxR	31 K—K3	Kt—B3
22 B—K4	B—K3	32 BxKtch(m)	KxB
23 P—QKt3(k)	P—Kt3		Drawn

(a) The correct move here should probably be 4...Kt—B3. The move in the text is somewhat disadvantageous to Black.

(b) This natural move has been, strange to say, rarely played heretofore, and this is explainable only through the circumstance that the retreat of B—K2 had been considered fully adequate. Black is now compelled either to abandon the center at once or to follow a cramped defense in the Ruy Lopez with two "tempi" less. He selects the first, and rightly so.

(c) Much more promising than 5...P—Q3. For instance, 6 B—QKt5 (threatening to win a pawn) PxP; 7 KtxP, B—Q2; 8 Castles, Kt—B3; 9 R—K, Castles; 10 BxKt, PxB; 11 KtxBch, QxKt; 12 B—Kt5, P—KR3; 13 B—R4, Q—K4, and White, by means of 14 B—KKt3 (instead of Kt—KB3) could maintain his advantage (see Borowski vs. Alekhine, London, 1922).

(d) Of course, 6 B—KB4 would have forced the rejoinder, P—Q3, but would not have been so effective, because the square, KB4, is not the proper place for the Bishop in this variation. For instance, 6...P—Q3; 7 B—QKt5, Kt—B3; 8 KtxQP, B—Q2; 9 Castles, Castles, etc. After the text move, White threatened 7 Kt—QKt5 as well as 7 Kt—KB5.

(e) Herewith White, in an otherwise even position, assures himself of the advantage of two Bishops.

(f) An interesting move, which partly maintains the equality of position. After 9...P—Q4, White would have obtained the better ending with 10 B—KKt5, PxP; 11 BxKt, PxB; 12 QxKP, etc.

(g) If 10 Q—R4, Black could have played 10...P—B5; 11 QxQBP, P—Q4, etc.

(h) Thanks to his two Bishops and the weak points in the center of the hostile camp, White has still the better of it and he manages as the game goes on even to increase his advantage. However, it does not lead to a forced win.

(i) A mistake would have been to play 16...Kt—Kt5, because of 17 BxKt, PxB; 18 R—K4; P—QR4; 19 QR—K, QR—K; 20 RxB, RxR; 21 B—B4, R—K; 22 P—KKt4, P—KKt3; 23 P—KB4, P—B4; 34 P—Kt5, P—Kt4; 25 B—Q5, and Black has now only the move, R—K2, of which White can take advantage in order to prepare a winning pawn ending. For instance, P—QR3 (not K—Q2, because of R—Q), PxP; PxP, to be followed by K—Kt2—B3—Q4, winning.

(j) Simpler probably would have been 19...B—Q2, in order, after the exchange of Rooks, to bring the Bishop to B3 for the defense of his Queen's wing.

(k) In reply to 23 P—QB4, Black could play unhesitatingly 23...Kt—Kt5. For instance, 24 P—QR3, Kt—B3; 25 BxKt, PxB; 26 P—QKt3, K—K2; 26 B—K3, K—Q3; 28 K—Q2, P—QR3, and the end-game remains drawn, notwithstanding Black's poor pawn position.

(l) It would have been clearly useless, by means of 30 B—Kt8, to force the answer, P—QR4.

(m) In order to continue playing for a win, after 32 K—B4, Kt—Kt5!, White, with 33 K—Kt5, would have been compelled to make a pawn sacrifice, which would have been doubtful to say the least. But, inasmuch as the accompanying penetration of the King (33...KtxRP; 34 K—B6, B—K, etc.), did not promise any tangible advantage, the leader of the White forces at once makes him an offer to end it peacefully.

Game 109   TWENTY-SECOND ROUND—RETI'S OPENING

Reti	Janowski	After 28...P—KR4
White	Black	

	Reti (White)	Janowski (Black)
1	Kt—KB3	P—Q4
2	P—B4	PxP(a)
3	Kt—R3(b)	Kt—KB3
4	KtxP	P—K3(c)
5	P—KKt3	QKt—Q2
6	B—Kt2	Kt—Kt3
7	Castles(d)	KtxKt
8	Q—R4ch	P—B3(e)
9	QxKt	B—K2
10	P—Kt3	Castles
11	B—Kt2	Kt—Q4
12	P—Q4	P—KB4(f)
13	Kt—K5	B—B3
14	P—K4	BxKt
15	PxB	PxP
16	BxP	B—Q2
17	Q—Q3(g)	P—KR3(h)
18	B—R3(i)	R—K
19	B—R7ch	K—R
20	B—Kt6	P—Kt3(j)
21	P—B4	Q—B(k)
22	BxR	QxB
23	R—B2	P—Kt3(m)
24	P—R4	P—B4(n)
25	P—R5(o)	K—Kt2
26	QxPch(p)	QxQ
27	PxQ	KxP
28	R—K	P—KR4(q)

29	P—B5ch(r)	PxP
30	P—K6	B—B3
31	P—K7	Kt—B2
32	R—Q2	K—B2
33	R—Q8	Kt—K
34	B—B	P—R4
35	RxR	BxR
36	B—Kt5	B—Q4
37	K—B2	Kt—Kt2
38	B—B4	Kt—K3(s)
39	P—K8(Q)ch	KxQ
40	R—K5	BxP
41	PxB	K—Q2
42	R—Q5ch	K—K2
43	B—K3	Resigns

(a) This attempt to "refute" the move of 2 P—B4 is quite as inadequate as 2... P—Q5, which Janowski played against Dr. Tartakower, because White in due order develops his pieces and then has the safe assurance later on in the game of occupying the center with his Pawns in the proper manner and at a time most opportune for him.

(b) Better than 3 P—K3 for, after the disappearance of the black QP, the fianchettoing of the KB is done as a matter of course.

(c) There was as yet no good reason to imprison the QB. Black, for instance, could even now execute the maneuver of QKt—Q2—Kt3 in order subsequently to develop the Bishop at KB4 or Kt5.

(d) With this thoughtless move White risks his entire opening advantage. Correct would have been 7 P—QKt3!, in order, among other things, to be able to answer B—Q2 with KKt—K5. In that case Black would have had to worry for some time concerning the development of his QB.

(e) Quite incomprehensible, where it was possible simply through 8... B—Q2; 9 QxKt, B—B3, etc., to develop the Bishop and to obtain thereby a valid game. Because of this blunder alone Black deserves to lose the game and from here on White permits no further trifling.

(f) A heroic decision! Black, to be sure, thereby secures the position of his Knight on Q4, but at a very high price. With 12...P—KB3; 13 P—K4, Kt—B2, the game perhaps could have been better held together.

(g) Forcing a further deterioration in Black's position.

(h) This, however, is the greatest evil, because the exchange is thereupon lost by force without compensation. 17...P—KKt3 would not have been exactly pleasant, but in that case an absolute win for White would not be apparent, inasmuch as the sacrifice of the Bishop on KKt6 would not then have been decisive.

(i) The black Rook is now imprisoned by the two Bishops.

(j) To curtail, if possible, the action of the white QB by means of P—QB4. However, White does not permit it.

(k) 21...P—B4 would have been met with 22 BxR, followed by 23 P—B5.

(l) In order not to have to reckon any more with the threat of B—Kt4, after a possible P—B4.

(m) A better chance for counter-play than this attempt at plugging, which merely offers the opponent opportunity for new attacks, would have been 23...Q—R4, followed by the transfer of the Bishop to KKt3 by way of K square. The commanding position of the Knight on Q4 would then have made it quite difficult for Black to win.

(n) After 24...P—KR4, White, after K—R2, followed by R—KKt, would have opened up important lines by means of P—KKt4, etc.

(o) Reti plays this part of the game with great decision and energy.

(p) After 26 PxP, Black would still have been able to reply with 26...Kt—K2.

(q) The ensuing break could not have been staved off for long. After 28...K—B4, for instance, White would have first played 29 R—R2, R—R; 30 K—B2, followed by QR—KR. etc.

(r) The decisive finale.

(s) Hereupon White wins a piece, but likewise after 38...Kt—K; 39 R—Q, B—K3; 40 R—Q8, KxP; 41 R—QKt8, etc., the game could not have been saved.

Game 110   TWENTY-SECOND ROUND—RUY LOPEZ

Maroczy	Yates	After 14...P—Kt3
White	Black	

White	Black
1 P—K4	P—K4
2 Kt—KB3	Kt—QB3
3 B—Kt5	P—QR3
4 B—R4	Kt—B3
5 Castles	B—K2
6 R—K	P—QKt4
7 B—Kt3	P—Q3
8 P—B3	Castles
9 P—Q3	B—K3(a)
10 QKt—Q2(b)	Kt—KR4(c)
11 P—Q4	BxB
12 PxB	Kt—B5(d)
13 Kt—B	Q—B(e)
14 Kt—Kt3	P—Kt3(f)
15 P—Q5(g)	Kt—Q
16 BxKt	PxB
17 Kt—K2	P—Kt4
18 Kt(B3)—Q4	R—K
19 Kt—B5	B—B
20 Kt(K2)—Q4	P—KB3(h)
21 P—Kt3	PxP
22 RPxP	P—B4(i)
23 Kt—B3	Kt—B2
24 Kt—R2	R—R2
25 Q—R5	B—Kt2
26 Kt—Kt4	Q—Q2
27 K—Kt2(j)	Kt—K4
28 KtxQP	R—Q
29 KtxKt	PxKt
30 Kt—B5	B—B3
31 R—R	R—KB
32 Q—Kt4(k)	K—R
33 R—R6	P—R4
34 Kt—K3	Q—K(l)
35 QR—R	KR—B2
36 Q—B5	Q—KB
37 Kt—Kt4	B—Q(m)
38 RxPch	Resigns

(a) Mr. Yates chooses this same unusual variation which he had to meet when playing Marshall in the previous round. In this case, however, simple moves show it to be unsatisfactory.

(b) Not 10 P—Q4 immediately, because of 10...PxP; 11 PxQP, P—Q4, etc. After 10...Kt—QR4, White obtains a superior position through 11 BxB, PxB; 12 P—QKt4, Kt—Kt2; 13 P—QR4 (the same after 12...Kt—B3), because of the displacement of the black QKt.

(c)   This maneuver with the Knight is useless and paves the way for the loss of the game.   The logical sequence of the previous moves was 10...Q—Q2, with QR—Kt to follow, in order on the one hand to attempt the advance of the QP and on the other hand to be able to answer P—Q4 with PxP and PxP with P—Q4.

(d)   Consistent, but suicidal.   After all, the consequences of 12...PxP were less to be feared, e. g.: (I) PxP, P—Q4; 14 PxP (or 14 P—K5, Kt—B5), QxP; 15 Kt—K4! (15 Kt—K5?, KtxQP!; 16 QxKt, Kt—B7, etc.), B—Kt5; 16 Kt—QB3, BxKt; 17 PxB, Kt—KB3; (II) 13 KtxQP, KtxKt! 14 PxKt, Kt—B3, and White is in a strong position, but just the same cannot follow up successfully the weakness at Black's QB2 through P—Q5 because of 15...P—QB3; 16 PxP, Q—B2; 17 Q—B2, KR—B, etc.   In both cases he has to reckon with P—QB4 and P—Q4.

(e)   Further futile subtleties.   The lesser evil on this—or still on the next move— was to bring the Knight back to Kt3.   In any case he has made three moves to go from a better square to a worse one.

(f)   As events show Black's KB4 square cannot be protected from White any longer. Maroczy shows up the mistaken strategy of his opponent in a classical manner.

(g)   The winning move.   After the coming exchange, the exposed position of P at B5 will force the surrender of the Black KB4 square (through P—KKt4) and later on in the game enable White to open the KR file, which will further an irresistible King's side attack.   The rest of the game is easy to understand and plays itself.

(h)   21 Q—R5 was threatened.

(i)   Creating a new weakness at Q3.   But Black is beyond the stage of good or bad moves.

(j)   The annihilating threat of R—R now forces the win of a Pawn.

(k)   Threatening 33 RxQRP and Kt—R6ch.

(l)   Or 34...QxQ, 35 KtxQ, B—Kt2; 36 R—K6, etc., with an easy win.

(m)   White announced mate in three by 38 RxPch, K—Kt; 39 Q—Kt6ch, any; 40 R—R8 mate.

The Significance of the New York Tournament in the Light of the Theory of the Openings.

OPEN GAMES—Ruy Lopez

(Translated by H. Ransom Bigelow)

Of the 19 Ruys played in the New York Tournament more than half of them were devoted to the theme 1 P—K4, P—K4; 2 Kt—KB3, Kt—QB3; 3 B—Kt5, P—QR3; 4 B—R4, Kt—B3; 5 Castles, B—K2. In our opinion, the reason why this close variation enjoyed such a popularity is simply because it is fashionable—just as, for instance, the variation 5...KtxKP was played most of the time in the St. Petersburg Tournament of 1914. In any case, this fashion has at least given the solution to one of the problems of this variation. Namely, it was not very clear until lately whether White could calmly allow the advance of the Queen's Pawn two squares after the moves 6 R—K1, P—QKt4; 7 B—Kt3, P—Q3; 8 P—QB3, Castles without troubling himself about the pin through 8...B—KKt5. This question was again brought to the fore in the game Capablanca-Bogoljubow (London, 1922). In this game the second player successfully tried out the interesting idea of 8...PxP, giving up the center in order to free his Queen's Knight from the need to protect the King's Pawn and then, after Kt—QR4 and P—QB4, quickly to force his opponent to declare his intentions. Equality was obtained without any trouble. The game played between Dr. Lasker and Bogoljubow in the following year (Mahrisch-Ostrau, 1923) showed, however, that the tactical execution of this plan was still insufficient and that White, after the moves 9 P—Q4, PxP (?); 10 PxP, B—KKt5 should play the much stronger 11 Kt—QB3! rather than 11 B—K3 (as played by Capablanca).

Thereupon the variation contemplated by Black (11...Kt—QR4; 12 B—B2, P—QB4) proved to be downright unfavorable because of 13 PxBP, PxBP; 14 P—K5, etc. Bogoljubow realized for the first time in his game against Yates in New York that his idea was sound when carried out correctly. He thus played 9...B—KKt5 and after 10 B—K3 (if 10 P—Q5, Kt—QR4 to be followed by P—QB3, etc., Black obtains as you know, the initiative because of the open QB file); 10...PxOP! 11 PxP, Kt—QR4; 12 B—B2, Kt—QB5.

White

This position was reached in the New York Tournament in the games Yates-Bogoljubow, Yates-Ed. Lasker and Yates-Capablanca. In the first two White tried the withdrawal move B—B1 previously played by Capablanca against Bogoljubow. But after 13...P—QB4; 14 P—QKt3; 14...Kt—QR4 (Bogoljubow) or Kt—Kt3 (Ed. Lasker) he obtained at least no advantage.

Still less favorable for White was the line adopted by Yates against Capablanca which allowed the exchange of the Queen's Bishop, as after 13 Kt—Q2, KtxB! 14 RxKt, P—QB4, etc., his badly protected position in the center soon brought him into difficulties. Thus the Bogoljubow move 10...PxQP! proved to give a more lasting attack and therefore it is better for White to prepare for P—Q4 with 9 P—KR3.

The chances for both sides in the position reached after this "Preventative" move were in anv case only partly cleared up in New York. In two games (Dr. Lasker-Ed. Lasker and Maroczy-Reti) Black tried to bring about a counter-attack on the open file after 9...Kt—QR4; 10 B—B2, P—QB4; 11 P—Q4, Q—B2; 12 Kt—Q2 with 12...B—Q2; 13 Kt—KB1; 13...PxP; 14 PxP, KR—QB1.

It turned out, however, that White obtained a lasting positional advantage both after the somewhat elaborate 15 R—K2 (Dr. Lasker) as also after the simple 15 B—Q3 (Maroczy) as a result of the almost irremovable obstacle of lack of freedom of movement of the opposing pieces.

The game between Ed. Lasker-Reti was also worthless for the theory of this variation. Here Black after 12... KKt—Q2 indicated his intention to initiate a counter-attack on the Queen's side through bringing over this Knight. After 13 P—Q5, however, he let himself in for the quite illogical push in the center of P—KB4, which brought him immediately into a disadvantageous position.

The "Holding-Back" variation 9 P—Q3 was also played in three of the games. Once (Maroczy-Capablanca) this variation took a more or less unpromising aspect as White played P—KR3, which is only necessary to provide for the eventuality of P—Q4. As a result he presented Black with an extra move for his further development. Actually, Black was soon able to play P—Q4 with which he at least obtained equality.

In two other games (Yates-Marshall and Maroczy-Yates), the insufficiency of the reply 9...B—K3 (to 9 P—Q3) was clearly demonstrated. This is a move which only compromises Black. Both after the somewhat "two-edged" move 10 BxB (Yates) as also—and still better—the move appropriate to the position 10 Kt—Q2 (Maroczy) White obtained an advantage without undue exertion.

Finally, Yates against Dr. Lasker played (after 5...B—K2; 6 R—K1) 6...P—Q3 instead of the usual P—QKt4. After this, obviously, the first player has the opportunity to force a kind of a Steinitz defense with 7 BxKt, to be followed with 8 P—Q4 (with the P at QR3 instead of at QR2). This gives Black at the best only drawing chances. In any case Black, thanks to the somewhat unenergetic play in the opening on the part of his opponent in this game had no real difficulties to overcome before he obtained equality.

A quite different picture is shown in the two Ruy Lopezs defended by Janowski, with 5...P—Q3, played by Rubinstein. Both of his opponents (Dr. Lasker and Yates) then played 6 R—K1 (a more enduring advantage is obtained through 7 P—QB3), which allowed the second player to drive away the attacking Bishop through 6...P—QKt4; 7 B—Kt3, Kt—R4; 8 P—Q4, KtxB; 9 RPxKt, B—Kt2 (Yates-Janowski). Through this maneuver he obtains anyway as compensation for his weakened Pawn position

two Bishops. 6...B—KKt5 occurred in the game Dr. Lasker-Janowski, which was of less consequence. This would have remained without effect if White had quietly proceeded with his development after 7 P—QB3, B—K2, with 8 P—Q3, and then Kt—Q2 and Kt—B1, Kt—Kt3 instead of giving his opponent eventually a point of attack through 8 P—KR3. After 8 P—KR3? 8...B—R4; 9 P—Q3, Q—Q2,

Black

White

he was soon in great embarrassment on account of his threatened attack beginning with P—KKt4, etc. A very instructive mistake in the opening!

Other variations were played only once and therefore provide but little material for theoretical analysis. For instance, in the game Ed. Lasker-Alekhine, the importance of the until now never disproved defense 5...B—QB4 (after 5 Castles) completely lost its significance because of the weak move 6 ——; Q—K2? after 6 P—Q3 (instead of the natural 6...P—QKt4; 7 B—Kt3, P—Q3). For the time the Dr. Tartakower-Reti game showed that after 5 P—Q3 (instead of 5 Castles) Black could obtain equality easily provided the counter-move P—Q4 were properly timed.

The "fantastic" 3...Q—B3 move by Ed Lasker was disproved by Bogoljubow over the board by 4 Kt—QB3. The improvement introduced by Dr. Lasker against Marshall (8 K—K1 instead of K—K2) in the Gambit Defense to Exchange Variation of the Ruy (for years considered unsatisfactory), made it easier for him to make more of his material superiority.

The remaining three Ruys were somewhat more significant.

1. Capablanca proved in his game against Dr Lasker that Black after 1 P—K4, P—K4; 2 Kt—KB3, Kt—QB3; 3

B—Kt5, Kt—B3; 4 Castles, P—Q3; 5 P—Q4, B—Q2; 6 Kt—B3, can quite well play 6...PxP, in order to avoid the variation 6...B—K2; 7 BxKt to be followed by Q—Q3, or perhaps even 7 PxP, etc. without on that account having to fear the immediate fianchetto development after 7 KtxP; B—K2 of 8 P—QKt3 and B—Kt2.

2. As second player against Bogoljubow, Dr. Lasker was able in a most subtle (raffinierter) manner to give the game the character of a variation of the Scotch which is favorable to Black(after the in itself harmless move of 4 P—Q4). He then could have taken the initiative himself had he chosen the energetic 8...P—Q4 instead of the "holding-back" move, 8...P—Q3. This game thus proved that the move 4 P—Q4 assures the first player no pronounced advantage.

3. Finally Yates induced his opponent Alekhine, who had chosen the Berlin variation (3...P—QR3 and 4...P—Q3), to attempt the fianchetto development of his Bishop by a temporary letting up of the fight in the center, in order then to show so much the more vigorously that Black will still have to combat against enduring difficulties as a result of the timed exchange at K5 as a result of the weakness of the square QB4.

1 P—K4, P—K4; 2 Kt—KB3 Kt—QB3; 3 B—Kt5, P—QR3; 4 B—R4, P—Q3; 5 Castles P—KKt3; 6 P—B3, B—Kt2; 7 P—Q4, B—Q2; 8 B—KKt5, KKt—K2; 9 PxP, PxP; 10 Q—Q3, P—KR3; 11 B—K3 B—Kt5; 12 Q—K2,

Black

White

Castles; 13 B—B5. (Instead White played the weak QKt—Q2).

KING'S GAMBIT.

In the four games in which this opening was adopted, Dr. Tartakower tried to repopularize the seldom employed move

B—K2. Despite his success over the board (2½ out of 4 points), this prehistoric "innovation" can in no way be considered as valid. In the first place, the most logical line was not chosen in any of these games (3...P—KB4; 4 PxP, Q—R5ch, etc.), in which Black opens the KB file for an attack upon the uncastled white King. Secondly, even in two of the variations adopted by Black, White had to contend against considerable difficulties.

1. Dr. Tartakower-Alekhine. 3...Kt—K2; 4 P—Q4, P—Q4; 5 PxP, KtxP; 6 Kt—KB3, B—Kt5ch; 7 P—B3, B—K2; 8 Castles, Castles; 9 P—B4, Kt—K6; 10 BxKt, PxB; 11 Q—Q3, B—B3; 12 Kt—B3, Kt—B3; 13 Kt—Q5 and now 13...R—K (instead 13...B—Kt5 was played).

Black

White

White will have difficulty in winning back the Gambit Pawn and still have a free game.

Black

White

2., Dr. Tartakower-Capablanca. 3...
P—Q4; 4 PxP, Kt—KB3; 5 P—B4,
P—B3; 6 P—Q4, B—Kt5ch! (Diagram
V) (instead of Bogoljubow's move 6...
PxP). White is obliged to forego
castling or to give up the Pawn at KB4
(after 7 B—Q2, Kt—K5!). The only
move disadvantageous for Black in this
variation is the indifferent 3...Kt—QB3
(Yates), which leaves a free hand to the
opponent.

THREE KNIGHTS.

In two games (against Maroczy and
Ed. Lasker) Marshall, as second player,
obtained a good game along one of the
lines greatly favored by Pillsbury: 1
P—K4, P—K4; 2 Kt—KB3 (or Kt—Q,
B3), Kt—KB3; 3 Kt—QB3 (or Kt—
KB3), B—Kt5. This result, however, is
in our opinion rather unimportant
theoretically as both the Maroczy move 4
P—Q3 `and the Lasker move 4 B—B4
could very well have been changed for
the simple 4 KtxP!. Then, obviously,
Black must exchange his Bishop for the
Kt at QB3 in order to win back the Pawn
and thus must leave his opponent with
two Bishops, which is no small advantage, particularly in the open game.
What is perhaps of still more importance whether in the Petroff after 1
P—K4, P—K4; 2 Kt—KB3, Kt—KB3;
whether 3 KtxP or P—Q4 is the stronger.

It is yet a more interesting problem to
know how White can assure himself an
advantage, even though it is very slight,
in case Black (after 1 P—K4, P—K4; 2
Kt—KB3, Kt—QB3) avoids the Four Knights Game with 3 B—QKt5.
After 4 Kt—Q5, B—R4; 5 B—B4 (to be
followed by Castles) the black Bishop
will be out of the game for a long time.
The few games played along these lines
(Leonhardt-Dr. Tarrasch, Hamburg, 1910,
and Alekhine-E. Cohn, Karlsbad, 1911)
augur well for the first player. After
4...Kt—KB3; 5 KtxB; 5...KtxKt; 6
P—B3, Kt—QB3; 7 P—Q3, P—Q4; 8
Q—B2 (to be followed by B—K2 and
Castles), White can also look the future
in the face with full confidence, thanks to
his two Bishops and a strong position in
the center.

There is also the withdrawal move
B—K2. This is the one usually adopted.
The following occurred in the game be-
tween Alekhine and Dr. Tartakower:
5 P—Q4, PxP; 6 KtxP, KtxKt; 7 QxKt,
Kt—B3; 8 KtxB, QxKt; 9 B—Q3, P—B4;
10 Q—K3, P—Q4; 11 PxP, KtxP; 12
QxQch, KxQ; 13 B—Kt5ch, P—B3; 14

Black

White

B—Q2 (Diagram 6). Now White has
obtained excellent chances for the End
Game.

It is naturally a question whether the
advantage thus obtained is sufficient to
assure a win. But it is certainly a variation not to be sought after by Black.

SCOTCH GAME

It fell to the lot of Ed. Lasker in the
only game played with this antiquated
opening to prove the harmlessness of
the mobilization plan successfully car-
ried out by Dr. Tartakower at Mahrisch
Ostrau. After the moves 1 P—K4,
P—K4; 2 Kt—KB3, Kt—QB3; 3
P—Q4, PxP; 4 KtxP, Kt—B3; 5
KtxKt, KtPxKt; 6 QKt—Q2, B—B4; 7
P—K5, Q—K2; 8 Q—K2, Kt—Q4; 9
Kt—Kt3, he played 9...B—Kt3! (in-
stead of the Rubinstein move 9...

Black

White

Castles?); 10 B—Q2, P—QR4. Thus
the answer 11 P—QR4 is as good as

forced. This leaves the square QKt5 free for the Black Knght (in case P—QB4 be played). As a result Black obtains an easy game.

TWO KNIGHTS DEFENSE (TURNING INTO THE GIUOCO PIANO)

The game between Maroczy and Janowski confirmed the long known fact that after the symmetrical position reached on the fifth move (1 P—K4, P—K4; 2 Kt—KB3, Kt—QB3; 3 B—B4, Kt—KB3; 4 P—Q3, B—B4; 5 Kt—QB3, P—Q3), it is still somewhat premature for White to castle because of the uncomfortable pin which follows through B—KKt5. In this instance it will be up to White to strive for eventual equality through exchanges.

PHILIDOR'S DEFENSE (HANHAM VARIATION).

The player of the White pieces in the game between Ed. Lasker and Bogoljubow obtained no advantage against this defense (which is rightly condemned by theory, for in it Black needlessly and without obtaining any compensation whatever hems himself in and besides makes a potential weakness for himself at Q3). The reason was because he developed his Bishop at KKt5—a move contrary to positional development in this instance. Through it this square is taken away from the Kt (at KB3) for purely tactical threats—and Black obtains an opportunity through a later Knight move to force an exchange which frees his game or forces the withdrawal of the Bishop with the ensuing loss of time.

It is unfortunate that one of the weightiest problems of the Open Game—the Four Knights—was on the whole not touched upon.

CLOSE GAMES—(AFTER 1 P—K4).

THE FRENCH DEFENSE—McCUTCHEON VARIATION.

Five games were devoted to this much disputed defense. Undoubtedly, they have contributed considerably to a further clearing up of the problem as the result of two of the lines adopted. The H. Wolf move 5 Kt—K2 (Dusseldorf, 1908) caused a slight surprise, as it confirmed the real strength of this long known move, which has been under suspicion mainly because of its extraordinary unnaturalness. Although Bogoljubow had employed it successfully again in Pistyan in 1922 against Dr. Tarrasch, this victory was rightly attributed to his superior handling of the Middle Game, which at the beginning did not look favorable to him. As a result, the opening part of the game was given little consideration.

In the 4th Round of the New York Tournament the game between Bogoljubow and Reti ran 1 P—K4, P—K3; 2 P—Q4, P—Q4; 3 Kt—QB3, Kt—KB3; 4 B—Kt5, B—Kt5; 5 Kt—K2 and then the most natural continuation 5...PxP; 6 P—QR3, B—K2; 7 BxKt, BxB; 8 KtxP. Now Black already finds himself embarrassed as to how to get rid of the commanding position occupied by the White Queen's Pawn in the center without loss of time. 8...P—QB4 is prevented for a long time and after the obvious 8... P—K4 White simply plays 9 Q—Q3! with the possible continuaton 9...PxP (Kt—B3; 10 P—Q5); 10 KtxBch, QxKt 11 QxP, QxQ; 12 KtxQ.

Black

White

Thereupon a free development on the Black Queen side is prevented through the central position occupied by the White Knight, which can only be driven away through the weakening advance of the Queen's Bishop Pawn. Therefore the positions can in no way be considered as equal. This consideration caused Reti to plan an elaborate and time-losing maneuver (beginning with 8... B—Q2). (If 8...P—QKt3; 9 P—Kt3, with B—Kt2 to follow would be very strong.) This brought him into a still more disadvantageous position after White's Q—Q3 and Castles.

Bogoljubow thus obtained a winning position without any unusual effort. After he had recognized the insufficiency of 7...BxB, Reti tried out the better plan of 7...PxB against Dr. Lasker.

The idea is to drive away the Knight by P—KB4 at the proper time (i. e., after the pieces have been developed whenever possible). After 8 KtxKP he was induced to make this weakening move immediately, and consequently collapsed surprisingly quickly.

Comparatively better would therefore, seem to be...P—QKt3 (Bogoljubow-Alekhine) in order to continue with 9... B—Kt2, 10 Q—B3, P—QB3! (to be followed with Kt—Q2, etc.) if White plays 9 Kt(K2)—B3! In this case Black at least has prospects of a bearable game. It is understood, however, that this continuation cannot be considered as an attempt to disprove the validity of the move 5 Kt—K2. The latter has thus proved to be an enduring, valid theoretical acquisition.

Capablanca, in two games (against Alekhine and Bogolbubow) chose the old move 5 PxQP. Different lines were adopted by both of his opponents. While Alekhine, following the line of Tarrasch-Alekhine, St. Petersburg, 1914, deprived himself of his two Bishops with 5... QxP; 6 BxKt, BxKtch without obtaining any compensation and also strengthened his opponent's chain of Pawns in the center, Bogoljubow played much more logically 6...PxB; 7 Q—Q2: Q—R4! and obtained in this way at least an equal game. Thus, something was accomplished in New York as far as deciding the merits of this line of play.

The Classical Defence 5...B—K2, was adopted in two games (Capablanca-Reti and Yates-Maroczy).. In the first White after 6 P—K5; KKt—Q2, tried the old 7 BxB, QxB; 8 Q—Q2, which also gives an enduring pressure. But after 8... Castles; 9 P—KB4, P—QB4; 10 Kt—KB3, Kt—QB3, he attempted 10 PxQBP which at this time furthers the development of his opponent (instead of the usual P—KKt3 and B—R3) in order to assure the square Q3 for his Bishop.

It turned out, however, that Black, through exchanging this Bishop at the right time, either obtains freedom in the center through P—K4 or a pressure on the QB file, which will be sufficient to equalize matters. The above innovation will scarcely find any imitators.

The line chosen by Yates against Maroczy with 7 P—KR4 (aiming for an attack) was more or less of no importance theoretically, as White after 7...P—KB3! did not permit himself to embark upon the promising sacrificial line 8 B—Q3, which is in the spirit of this variation. He chose instead to put himself in a clearly inferior position rather than take this "risk" with 8 PxP.

The defence 3...B—Kt5 was chosen only once (Dr. Lasker-Maroczy). Theoretically, however, this was a very important game.

Previously, several games of Niemzowitsch (as second player) had shown clearly enough that White is not in a position to obtain an advantage in the opening, even though it be small, after 4 PxQP, 4...PxP.

Dr. Lasker tried against Maroczy the "two-edged" line of play 4 P—K5? and after 4...P—QB4; 5 P—QR3, BPxP; 6 RPxB, PxKt; 7 KtPxP, Q—B2! was al-

Black

Black

ready faced by the unpleasant alternative of either devoting himself entirely to the defence of the threatened point (which would permit his opponent to equalize matters easily) or to set out to force a decision in the Middle Game through the sacrifice of a Pawn. He decided for the attack, which broke down finally thanks to the fine and deeply thought-out defence of Maroczy. Even if White on his 16th move (see notes to this game) had played the stronger B—B1 instead of B—B3, his pressure would only have compensated for his loss of the Pawn. Thus this game does not offer very rosy prospects for the move 4 P—K5 promises a brilliant future.

ALEKHINE'S OPENING

Three games were played with this modern opening (Maroczy—perhaps because of his sad experiences with it—opposes himself obstinately to naming it so, and characterizes it as an anonymous "King's Pawn Game.") It must be admitted that none of these resulted in solving the problem as to whether or not the opening is fundamentally correct. Let one examine, e. g.:

(a) The game Maroczy vs. Dr. Lasker. 1 P—K4; Kt—KB3; 2 Kt—QB3, P—Q4 (simple and good is P—K4); 3 P—K5 (better is 3 PxP), KKt—Q2; 4 P—Q4, P—K3 (more energetic is 4...P—QB4), etc.

(b) Maroczy vs. Dr. Tartakower. 1
P—K4, Kt—KB3; 2 P—K5, Kt—Q4; 3
P—QB4, Kt—Kt3; 4 P—Q4, P—Q3; 5
PxP (refrains from hemming in the opponent and allows a free development of
his pieces); 5...KPxP; 6 Kt—QB3,
B—B4; 7 B—K2, B—K2; 8 B—K3,
QKt—Q2; 9 Kt—KB3; Castles. It is
really astonishing how seldom, up to
now, the only logical move 5 P—KB4 has
been attempted in serious practice!

(c) Maroczy vs. Alekhine. 1 P—K4,
Kt—KB3; 2 P—Q3 (after this move
Black can turn the game into a favorable
variation of the Sicilian through 2...
P—QB4. The following interesting com-
plication is by no means forced for him:
2...P—K4!?; 3 P—KB4, Kt—QB3;
4 Kt—KB3, P—Q4; 5 PxQP, KtxP; 6
PxKP, B—KKt5; 7 B—K2, BxKt; 8
BxB, Q—R5ch. Now White could have
obtained an equal game easily through 9
P—KKt3, Q—Q5; 10 Q—K2, as Black

Black

White

after the following P—QB3 must simply
content himself with winning back the
Pawn he sacrificed.

SICILIAN OPENING

Of the six Sicilians, two played by Dr.
Tartakower took the form of his favorite
Paulsen variation (against Dr. Lasker
and Yates). After the moves 1 P—K4,
P—QB4; 2 Kt—KB3, P—K3; 3 Kt—QB3,
P—QR3; 4 P—Q4, PxP; 5 KtxP, Q—B2
(SEE DIAGRAM)
he chose the here somewhat indifferent
move 6 B—K2. Then after 6...B—QKt5!;
7 Castles, Kt—KB3 (actually these moves
were inverted by Black); 8 B—B3!, Kt—
QB3! he was faced with the unpleasant
choice either to exchange his King's
Bishop after Kt—K4 or to concede his
opponent a free hand in his development
through 9 KtxKt, PxKt.

Black

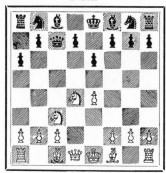

White

Yates played a much better variation.
6 B—Q3!, Kt—QB3; 7 B—K3, Kt—KB3;
8 Kt—Kt3. This leads to a very promising game for the first player on account
of his better development. In any case,
his task was obviously made easier
through the following unfortunate
maneuver of the Knight on the part of
Black: Kt—K4 and KtxBch.

Three games were played with the
more usual variation (without Q—QB2).
These, however, did not change previous
theories held concerning the value of the
individual variations.

1. Dr. Lasker vs. Bogoljubow. 1 P—
K4, P—QB4; 2 Kt—KB3, P—K3; 3
P—Q4, PxP; 4 KtxP, Kt—KB3; 5 B—Q3
(is rightly considered less strong than
5 Kt—QB3, B—QKt5; 6 B—Q3); 5...
Kt—QB3; 6 KtxKt (if 6 B—K3 then 6...
P—Q4) 6... KtPxKt (6...QPxKt is
sufficient to obtain equality).

7 Castles, B—K2? (P—Q4 is here
necessary); 8 P—K5, etc., with advantage
to White. This has all happened before!

2. Yates vs. Dr. Lasker. After the
same four opening moves, White
played 5 Kt—QB3 and turned the
game into a channel which has been
analyzed thoroughly and in detail for
years after 5...Kt—QB3; 6 KtxKt and
P—K5 (the "grandfather's" move, 6
KKt—Kt5, B—QKt5; 7 P—QR3 leads
only to equality. Therefore, in our
opinion, 6 P—QR3 is more advisable).

This variation is very favorable owing
to the weakness in Black's game, but yet
on account of them having been analyzed
in detail for many years already it is
less enduring. There followed 6 KtPxKt;
7 P—K5, Kt—Q4; 8 Kt—K4, P—KB4
(the theoretical move is 8 Q—QB2!); 9
PxPe.p., KtxP; 10 Kt—Q6ch, BxKt; 11

QxKt., and even now Black could obtain a free game with 10...Q—Kt3! (instead of Q—R4ch, and Q—Q4, etc.).

3. In the game between Janowski and Dr. Lasker, the defense system favored by the Dutch players, with Dr. Euwe as their leader, was employed successfully. (1 P—K4, P—QB4; 2 Kt—KB3, Kt—QB3; 3 P—Q4, PxP; 4 KtxP, Kt—KB3; 5 Kt—QB3, P—Q3; 6 B—K2, P—K3;

Black

White

7 Castles, B—K2, etc. In this position it appears to be best for White, after he has removed his King away from the diagonal Kt1—R7, to play P—KB4 immediately in order to place his King's Bishop on B3. (Similar to the game Maroczy vs. Euwe in Scheveningen in 1923.)

Hereupon any counter-attack on the Queen is made considerably more difficult for Black. The "slow pressure game" attempted by Janowski proved eventually to be less forceful as Black, after his development was finished, soon found an opportunity to use the open QB file for a counter attack. Up to now the last word concerning this difficult advance has not yet been said.

4. Once Black, in the game between Dr. Tartakower vs. Reti, tried the classical variation (1 P—K4, P—QB4; 2 Kt—KB3, Kt—QB3; 3 P—Q4, PxP; 4 KtxP, Kt—B3; 5 Kt—QB3, P—Q3; 6 B—K2, P—KKt3; 7 Castles, B—Kt2, etc.) which, as is known, promises him sufficient counterattacking prospects. This took place only because White, after the moves 1 Kt—KB3, P—KKt3; 2 P—K4, P—QB4, neglected the opportunity to forestall a possible pressure on the part of his opponent upon the QB file through 3 P—QB4! (followed by P—Q4, etc.) which

Black

White

would thus invalidate the leading idea of the move 1...P—KKt3.

THE SICILIAN OPENING PLAYED BY FIRST PLAYER

Black gave the game between Dr. Tartakower and Dr. Lasker greater theoretical interest for the theory (future) of the middle game than of the opening because of his deeply thought out defensive maneuvers. This was due to the fact that in the first moves White also adopted a purely passive defense of development (a la Paulsen) after the holding back variation of his opponent of B—K2 and P—Q3, etc. Obviously he thus renounced any immediate opportunity to profit by the advantage of the first move.

1 P—K4, P—KKt3(?)

Capablanca took the liberty once of playing this Joke Opening. He was favored by the fates, as his opponent, Ed. Lasker, voluntarily renounced taking possession of the center through P—Q4 and only made this move later (even then per nefas). Naturally, this experiment has no claim to any theoretical significance.

CARO-KANN DEFENSE

The game between Yates and Reti is worthy of note only insofar as White (1) very prudently refrained from making the move of 6 P—KR4, which was formerly so liked (after 1 P—K4, P—QB3; 2 P—Q4, P—Q4; 3 Kt—QB3, PxP; 4 KtxP, B—B4; 5 Kt—Kt3, B—Kt3) and (2) with a correct insight into the merits of the position, recognized that Black's Queen's Bishop (whose development in this variation is the only thing Black has to boast about) is really ineffective on KKt6 and as a result White does not need to hurry to exchange off the Bishops through B—Q3, but can play much more strongly B—QB4. Through his following loss of time (P—QB3) the theoretical significance of this conclusion is left open so that further games must be played with this variation to determine the chances for both sides.

QUEEN'S GAMBIT, QUEEN'S PAWN AND DUTCH DEFENSE

The Queen's Gambit Acccepted was played twice, once in the game between Bogoljubow and Janowski and once in the game Marshall vs. Janowski. The first is interesting because of the fact that Black in the normal variation 1 P—Q4, P—Q4; 2 Kt—KB3, Kt—KB3; 3 P—QB4, PxP; 4 P—K3, P—K3; 5 BxP, P—QB4; 6 Kt—QB3, Kt—QB3; 7 Castles, B—K2; 8 Q—K2!, Castles; 9 KR—Q!, Q—B2; 10 P—QR3! refrained from developing his Bishop at QKt2—a maneuver which has already often proved itself to be insufficient after 10...P—QR3; 11 PxP, BxP; 12 P—QKt4, B—K2; 13 B—Kt2 in order to follow in the footsteps of Steinitz with B—Q2 and eventually B—K1 and thus to take up a workable defensive position with this Bishop. The continuation, however, shows that White's game is still to be preferred despite this improvement. There followed namely, 13...B—Q2; 14 QR—B1, QR—B1; 15 B—Q3, KR—Q1. In this position

Black

White

tion White has two very promising plans: 1—King's side attack, beginning with 16 Kt—KKt5; or 2—To bring the pressure against the Queen's side through Kt—QR4 and Kt—B5. In both cases Black would be condemned to submit to a difficult defense. However, the result of this game, which White eventually lost, has nothing to do with the way the opening was played.

That Black, after 1 P—Q4, P—Q4; 2 P—QB4, PxP; 3 Kt—QB3(?) (Marshall vs. Janowski), obtains equality easily through 3...P—K4! was a feat long known and in need of no further confirmation. In this game also the result of the game was the fault of the loser and not of the opening.

QUEEN'S GAMBIT DECLINED

(1) No less than fourteen games were played along the lines of the Normal Variation of the Orthodox Defense, viz., after the moves 1 P—Q4, Kt—KB3; 2 P—QB4, P—K3; 3 Kt—KB3, P—Q4; 4 Kt—QB3, although this position can be reached through an entirely different sequence of moves.

First, we must point out the failure of the few attempts to treat this defense in the most orthodox manner (B—K2, followed by Castles or Kt—Q2 immediately).

(a) In the game between Janowski and Capablanca a difficult problem faced the second player through the interesting innovation 10 P—KR4!? after the further moves 4 ——, B—K2; 5 B—Kt5, Castles; 6 P—K3, QKt—Q2; 7 R—B, P—B3; 8 B—Q3, PxP; 9 BxP, Kt—Q4; 10 P—KR4.

Black

White

He solved it with 10...P—KB3, but not quite satisfactorily because of the ensuing weakness at K3. 10...P—KR3, after which White would have a target for an attack with his Pawns, or also 10...QKt—KB3 (White now threatens 11 Kt—K5, Q—B3 and P—K4) should not lead to any satisfactory result. Therefore, it appears that after 10...KtxKt the most bearable defensive system would be a prompt mobilization of the Queen's side through P—QKt3 and B—Kt2. Perhaps then the "seamy side" of White's impertinent tenth move (weakening of the right wing) would have made itself felt later. In any case Janowski's innovation is worthy of further investigation.

(b) In the game between Bogoljubow and Yates, which was identical up to the seventh move, White with Rubinstein's move 8 Q—B2 (instead of 8 B—Q3) after 8...P—QR3; 9 PxP, PxP; 10 B—Q3, R—K1; 11 Castles, Kt—KB1) obtained an obviously overwhelming position. He might have strengthened it still further with 12 P—KR3! (Gruenfeld vs. J. Bernstein, Karlsbad, 1923), to be followed by Kt—K5.

However, before one pronounces judgment against this method of handling the opening, it must first be determined: (1) Whether Black, after 8 Q—B2 has anything better than 8...P—QR3 (and, as is known, 8...Kt—K5 is played in this position—Gruenfeld—H. Wolf, Mahrisch-Ostrau, 1923).

(2) Whether after 9 BPxP, BPxP; 10 B—Q3, P—KR3, followed eventually by P—QKt4, etc., White disposes of sufficient means to profit by the temporary weakness of the opponent in the QB file. Perhaps these questions will be answered over the board in the next tournament.

(c) The attempt to free the Black position through 9...P—QB4 gave clearly an inferior game (Alekhine vs. Maroczy) in the following variation, which is not very favorable to Black, viz., 4...B—K2; 5 B—KKt5, Castles; 6 P—K3, Kt—K5; 7 BxB, QxB; 8 Q—B2!, KtxKt; 9 QxKt. There followed simply 10 BPxQP, BPxP; 11 KtxQP, PxP; 12 B—K2 and

Black

White

Black must eventually collapse by degrees as the result of the backward development of his pieces and the practical difficulty of further developing his weakness at Q4 taken in connection with the pressure of his opponent on the QB file. In practice White obtains very quickly an obviously winning position.

In five games the move 4...Kt—Q2 was played. The objective of this is to make an immediate sally after 5 B—Kt5 and to attempt to profit by the absence of the White QB from its own wing through 5...B—QKt5 (or 5...P—QB3); 6 P—K3, Q—R4 (Cambridge Springs Variation).

The line of play followed in the opening completely confirms the conclusions of Dr. Tarrasch in his excellent book "The Defense to the Queen's Gambit."

It can now be considered as proved.

(I) That after 5 B—Kt5, P—QB3; 6 P—K3, Q—QR4, the move 7 Kt—Q2 (thought to be for a long time the only saving move) promises on the whole no advantage for the White forces because of Bogoljubow's innovation 7...B—Kt5; 8 Q—B2, Castles; 9 B—K2, P—K4!; 10 PxP, Kt—K5, etc. (a similar variation occurred in the game between Ed. Lasker and Dr. Lasker after 7...Kt—K5—in any case as a result of a mistake in the opening by the first player).

(II) As a consequence White must play 7 PxP! (the game between Capablanca and Ed. Lasker is a telling proof of the harmlessness of 6 BxKt) 7...PxP; 8 B—Q3, Kt—K5; 9 Castles! (Janowski-Bogoljubow; Marshall's move 9 Q—B2 is also good). Thus the premature Black attack is repulsed without loss of time and as a result the second player is at a lasting disadvantage because of his backward development.

5...B—Kt5 in conjunction with P—QB4 also does not promise well for Black. Thereupon White does best to hold back and play 6 P—K3 (more exact than 6 PxP, as played in the game between Maroczy and Ed. Lasker) and only to declare his intentions in the center after 6...P—QB4; 7 PxQP, KPxP; 8 B—Q3! and, If 8...P—B5; 9 B—B2, Q—R4; 10 Castles; BxKt; 11 PxB, QxP; 12 Q—Kt!

Black

White

with a promising attack (12...Castles; 13 P—K4!, etc.). All this goes to prove that White need not fear a possible action of the queen's side by his opponent and as a result the immediate 5 PxQP, as played in the game Alekhine-Dr. Lasker, is to say the least ill-timed.

Even less to be recommended is the development of the B—QKt5 on the fourth move, as played in the game between Capablanca and Marshall. The reason is that White can then play 5 Q—R4ch! and force the reply 5...Kt—B3, thus making it much more difficult for Black to open his lines in the center which are of such great importance to him. Strange to say the World's Champion made no use of this possibility in the above game.

In our opinion of much more importance and of more value to the defense are the variations connected with 4...P—QB3 which aim eventually at the subsequent capture of the Gambit Pawn, particularly all the more so as their significance was brought to the fore through an improvement by Rubinstein at Meran in 1924 in one of the important variations. It was held until recently as proved that White in the position here

Black

White

reached had only to play 5 P—K3 in order to force the break through with P—K4 a few moves later and that through the great freedom of movement which he would thus obtain he would have a real advantage (viz. 5...Kt—Q2 6 B—Q3, B—Q3(?) 7 P—K4, etc.)

Rubinstein, however, proved in his game with Gruenfeld at Meran that Black could obtain a promising game through causing a diversion on the Queen's side instead of aping the moves of his opponent on the 6th move (6 B—Q3,

B—Q3) by playing 6...QPxP! 7 BxP, P—QKt4; 8 B—Q3, P—QR3. White can now in no way prevent the move P—QB4 which completes this system of defense. We are of the opinion that it would be premature to express a final judgment on the exact worth of this line of play. In any case the practical outcome until now has shown that Black can thus obtain at least a good equal game, provided he does not attempt too much.

Secondly, which is of great importance from the practical point of view, he can obtain a much more promising game than in most of the defense systems of the Queen's Gambit. In the only game which was played with this variation in New York, viz., between Ed. Lasker and Dr. Tartakower, Black took the initiative after the plausible continuation, 9 Castles, P—QB4; 10 P—QR4, P—QKt4; 11 Kt—K4, B—Kt2; 12 KtxKtch, KtxKt; 13 Q—K2 with 13...Q—Q4.

Black

White

In two other cases White avoided this variation (in the games between Janowski and Dr. Tartakower and Marshall and Alekhine). Once 4...P—QB3 was answered by 5 B—Kt5 (Janowski) and after 5...P—KR3 the daring 6 B—R4 was played (6...PxP, to be followed by P—Kt4, holding the Gambit Pawn). In the other instance, the immediate drawish (Lit: "equalizing") 5 PxP, PxP; 6 B—Kt5, B—K2; 7 P—K3, B—B4! was to be preferred As this last variation clearly offers Black no difficulties, 5 B—Kt5 is much worthier of consideration. Consequently, two questions arise:

(1) After 5...P—KR3; 6 B—R4, PxP; 7 P—K4 (Janowski's move 7 P—K3 proved insufficient). 7...P—KKt4; 8 B—Kt3, P—QKt4, etc., does White obtain a more than sufficient compensation in position for the pawn sacrificed?

(2) If this is not the case, can he reckon on a definite advantage after 6 BxKt, QxB; 7 P—K3 because of his somewhat better development?

In our opinion, the future of the Defense system beginning with 4...P—QB3 hangs upon the correct answer to these questions.

THE 2...P—QB3 DEFENSE

After 1 P—Q4, P—Q4; 2 P—QB4, P—QB3, three continuations must be considered by White.

(a) The simple and yet sound line employed by Marshall, 3 PxP, PxP, etc., in order to try and profit by the advantage of the first move in the again symmetrical pawn position which results from this exchange.

(b) The move, 3 Kt—QB3, the idea of which is to force the hemming in of the Black QB after 3...Kt—KB3 through 4 P—K3, (without resorting to an exchange of Pawns in the center). In this instance, White must be resigned to submit to the interesting move of Winawer, 3...P—K4, which, in our opinion, is not quite sufficient. Even if Black answers 4 P—K3 with 4...P—K3, White's best plan is to go in for the Meran variation.

(c) The variation very much favored until recently, 3 Kt—KB3, Kt—KB3; 4 Kt—QB3 (White gains nothing by 4 P—K3, B—B4, etc.) appears to exert a dubious pressure according to the latest investigations.

Black has now no less than four lines of play, none of which should bring him to any disadvantage:

I 4...QPxP; 5 P—K3, P—QKt4, followed by P—QKt5! after which White must strive against having to win back the Gambit Pawn with any loss of time.

II 4...B—B4; 5 BPxP, KtxP; 6 Q—Kt3, Q—Kt3, etc., which enables Black to complete his development without effort.

III 4...P—K3, thus bringing the line of play into the Orthodox Defense system with 4...P—QB3.

IV Breyer's move of 4...Kt—K5, with a probable "Double Stonewall" formation after 5 P—K3, which is perhaps the least promising continuation but one not yet disproved.

The variation mentioned under (a) was played in the game between Marshall and Dr. Lasker and also in the one between Capablanca and Dr. Lasker, where there was an unessential inversion of the moves. Whereas Marshall through playing Q—Kt3 at the opportune time as good as forced the hemming in of the QB through P—K3, Dr Lasker voluntarily allowed this to happen in his game

with Capablanca in order to try out for the second time the interesting maneuver Kt—KR4 and P—KB4. Despite the fact that the annotators with one voice blame the thus forced withdrawal (removal) of the Bishop at KB4 (where it is always unpleasant to Black), we are inclined to believe that this was correct. In practice White in the game Marshall vs. Dr. Lasker found nothing better than the maneuver 14 Kt—QR4, Q—R4ch; 15 Kt—QB3! etc., already on the fourteenth (!) move, a result which promises well for the strength of the Black defense.

Even in the game between Capablanca and Dr. Lasker Black, despite his loss of time on the tenth move, was nevertheless in a satisfactory position in the middle game, only to permit later, and unnecessarily, a very promising sacrifice by White. But Marshall's method of play has the great advantage of preventing any early "flattening" of the game and it is therefore most probable that the practice of the next tournaments will cause it to be adopted as the most promising line.

The game Alekhine-Capablanca shows clearly that Black after 3 Kt—QB3, Kt—KB3; 4 P—K3 cannot very well permit himself to play 4...B—B4 because of 5 PxQP, PxP (or 5...KtxP; 6 B—QB4 followed by Kt—K2) 6 Q—Kt3! etc., as after 6...B—B1; 7 Kt—KB3, P—K3, White establishes his knight at K5 and obtains a much superior game thanks to his better development. As a result he must content himself with the discreet 4...P—K3, which appears to be quite playable after the discovery at Meram.

After 3 Kt—KB3, Kt—KB3; 4 Kt—QB3, the subsequent capture of the pawn was attempted (4...PxP). However, this was met by the obviously incorrect Pawn sacrifice 5 B—KKt5 (?). Thereupon Black obtained a winning position after a few moves.

Finally, the tame 4 P—K3 (Bogoljubow-Maroczy) was also once employed with a somewhat elaborate handling of the opening on both sides. It was not favorable to the first player.

QUEEN'S PAWN OPENING.

I The development of the Bishop to KB4 together with the advance of the QBP one square to QB3 was played three times (Bogoljubow vs. Marshall, Capablanca vs. Maroczy and Janowski vs. Lasker).

As a result of the opening moves it seems

(a) That this system of development can only be successful if Black hems in his QB through a premature P—K3 (Bogoljubow vs. Marshall). Otherwise—

similar to some of the variations arising after the 2...P—QB3 Defense to the Queen's Gambit—he is able to play B—KB4, which promises him a free development of his forces and thus, upon very plausible moves (Capablanca vs. Maroczy), soon seizes the initiative.

(b) Even in this case Black need not be at a disadvantage, provided he aims at exchanging the White Bishop at KB4 (after B—Q3) only when this exchange is not interlocked with the surrender of the squares K4 and Q5 (viz., if, for instance, after BxB, PxB, BPxP, the QBP must retake immediately, or after the ensuing exchange of the Kt at Q5). This game between Bogoljubow and Marshall (and also the one between Saemisch and Kostitsch, Toplitz-Schoenau, 1922) is a shining example of the difficulties with which the second player must contend if he does not recognize this intention of his opponent in time and does not attempt to thwart it.

2. The "Hemming-in-move," 3 P—K3, in connection with the ensuing fianchettoing of the QB and the eventual occupation of the square K5 (Maroczy vs. Bogoljubow and Bogoljubow vs. Capablanca) will in our opinion, quickly go totally out of fashion. In practice White is soon faced by a dilemma after 1 P—Q4, P—Q4; 2 Kt—KB3, Kt—KB3; 3 P—K3, P—K3; 4 B—Q3, P—QB4; 5 P—QKt3, QKt—B3; 6 Castles, B—Q3; 7 B—Kt2, Castles as

Black

White

to how he is to carry through his intended plan in its full entirety.

(1) After 8 QKt—Q2, 8...Q—K2! follows. Already White must decide to play 9 Kt—K5 because of the threat 9... P—K4, whereby he is pledged to exchanging his Queen's Bishop and the consequent weakening of his Black squares after 9...PxP, B—R6.

(2) After 8 Kt—K5 (Maroczy vs. Bogoljubow), the best continuation is 8...Q—QB2! (more convincing than Bogoljubow's move 8...QKt—K2), 9 P—KB4, BPxQP; 10 KPxQP, Kt—QKt5, to be followed by exchanging off the White B and a further easy defense.

(3) Finally, after the preventative move 8 P—QR3, Black simply plays 8... Q—B2, followed by P—K4, and White's mobilization plan is again totally upset. set.

THE DUTCH DEFENSE

All three games played with this antiquated and, in our opinion, fundamentally unsound defense (because of the insecure Pawn Skeleton, the constant breakthrough threats with P—K4 or P—Q5 and, in the event of P—Q4, the hole at K5!) took an unsatisfactory form for the second player and it was only with great care that he was able to rescue one of them through a draw! And this despite the in no way energetic handling of the opening on White's part.

In two games (Marshall vs. Dr. Tartakower and Capablanca vs. Dr. Tartakower) White played 4 B—KKt5 (and P—K3, Kt—KB3, B—Q3, etc.), through which the command of the square K4 was left to the second player for at least for a while. On the other hand, the opening position arising in the game between Bogoljubow vs. Dr. Tartakower was somewhat more interesting, viz.:

1 P—Q4, P—KB4; 2 P—KKt3, P—K3; 3 B—Kt2, Kt—KB3; 4 P—QB4 (more exact is 4 Kt—KB3, Castles) 4...P—Q4; 5 Kt—KB3, P—QB3; 6 Castles, B—Q3. Now not 7 QKt—Q2 (as, for instance, in the game Dr. Tarrasch-Mieses, Toplitz-Schoenau, 1922), but much more energetically; 7 Kt—QB3! QKt—Q2; 8 Q—B2!, Castles; 9 PxP, PxP; 10 Kt—QKt5, B—Kt1; 11 B—KB4, BxB; 12 PxB, after

Black

White

which the advantage of White is clear. Despite the fact that the tactical skill of Dr. Tartakower enabled him to eventually equalize matters, the Dutch Stonewall defense can be considered even less satisfactory than ever.

MODERN OPENINGS—THE INDIAN DEFENSE.

After 1 P—Q4, Kt—KB3, two moves which often lead to identical positions are worthy of major consideration on the part of White, namely, 2 P—QB4 and 2 Kt—KB3.

Despite that both of these undoubtedly have their own objectives, it seems to us that the first named is far more logical and opportune in order to utilize the advantage of the first move wherever possible. In practice White, after his second move, has to reckon with the following mobilization plans on the part of his opponent in order to carry on the struggle in the opening for the center.

(1) A subsequent P—Q4, through which Black comes back into the variations of the Queen's Gambit. In this eventuality Kt—KB3 in the first moves is not always necessary, viz., after Black defends with P—QB3 (see above). It is often more important that White should immediately force the imprisoning move P—K3 through timely pressure on the square Q5 (Kt—QB3 and Q—QKt3).

(2) The development 2...P—K3, followed by P—QKt3 and B—QKt2, which right after 2 P—QB4 can be fought successfully with Kt—QB3, Q—B2 (or Q—Kt3 after B—QKt5) to be followed eventually with P—K4.

(3) Gruenfeld's method 2...P—KKt3, followed eventually by P—Q4, the carrying out of which can obviously be made more difficult after 2 P—QB4 through a timely (and after 2 Kt—KB3 impossible to carry out) pressure on Q5 through 3 P—KKt3! and B—KKt2, and then only Kt—QB3. Thereupon Black, provided he still wishes to carry through his plan, is forced to decide upon P—QB3, which obviously is in flagrant contradiction with the leading opening idea of the discoverer (attacking the White center through P—QB4). But even apart from this, White's move Kt—KB3 is by no means indispensable even in the main variation of the Gruenfeld opening: 1 P—Q4, Kt—KB3; 2 P—QB4, P—KKt3; 3 Kt—QB3, P—Q4; 4 BPxKt, B—Kt2. For instance, Kt—K2 can be played advantageously after the KB has been developed.

(4) Finally, in the Indian Defense proper (2...P—KKt3, followed by P—Q3, or—though incorrect—inverting the moves, as it was often played in New York) White quite groundlessly prevented himself from taking advantage of the possibility of what is in our opinion a very strong advance of the KBP through 2 Kt—KB3 (Indian Four Pawns Game).

The circumstance that White, after 2 P—QB4, gives his opponent opportunity to play the Budapest Defense, can in no way be held against this move, as the practice of the masters during the last few years has shown very conclusively that White can obtain a strong initiative at least along these lines. The move 2 Kt—KB3 thus has a meaning of its own only in the case when White decides in advance to give battle to the Indian formation through the system 3 B—KB4, to be followed by P—K3, P—QB3, etc., which is not disadvantageous, but allows Black to build up a very secure defensive system (Reti's System for Black; see further on). In any case it offers him more opportunities to counter attack than an opening plan aiming at an unobstructed control of the central squares.

Strongly Indian Defenses, viz., with the idea preferably neither to go in for the Gruenfeld Defense nor for the Reti system, were played by the second player eleven times in New York. In their totality they gave a fairly clear picture of the chances for both sides in this opening.

The following system proved favorable to White; 1 P—Q4, Kt—KB3; 2 P—QB4, P—KKt3; 3 Kt—QB3, B—Kt2 (offering more chances is 3...P—Q4); 4 P—K4, P—Q3; 5 P—KB4 (or 6 Kt—KB3, see (2), Castles; 6 Kt—KB3 (Alekhine vs. Marshall, Alekhine vs. Yates and Alekhine vs. Janowski). In this position Black must absolutely carry through the "clearing up" advance, P—K4, before the Pawn formation of his opponent becomes overpowering upon the completion of his development, as 6...P—QB4 would be disadvantageous for him because of the simple 7 QPxBP, QPxBP; 8 QxQ (to be followed by P—K5, Kt—Q5, etc.). To this end time-losing preparatory moves were tried unsuccessfully (Kt—K1, KKt—Q2, QKt—Q2, Kt—QB3, B—KKt5).

Black discovered for the first time in the game between Alekhine and Ed. Lasker that 6...P—K4 can be played immediately! In practice White must decide upon the maneuver appropriate to the position 7 BPxKP, QPxKP; 8 P—Q5, as the acceptance of the Pawn sacrifice would lead him into a disadvantageous position. (See the notes to this game.) Even in the following position Black is still,

Black

White

in our opinion, somewhat at a disadvantage despite the saving in time, as he cannot opportunely begin at the right time on the only possible counter-attack, beginning with P—KB4, because he is faced with the necessity of now making the square QB4 safe against the advance of the QBP. Anyhow it would be interesting to determine further in practice the more exact consequences of Ed. Lasker's innovation, as the only game played with this variation provides insufficient material to allow of a verdict.

(2) The move 5 Kt—KB3, approved among others by Gruenfeld, occurred through an inversion of moves in the game between Marshall and Reti. It is also advantageous to White. However, he must play 6 B—K2! after 5 Castles,

Black

White

rather than 6 B—Q3 (as Marshall played) on account of the weakness at the square Q4 after 6...B—KKt5. Nor must he play 6 P—KR3 (as occurred in

the games between Saemisch and Reti, Toplitz and Schonau, 1922, and Gruenfeld and Reti, Vienna, 1923) because of 6... P—QB4. Thus he weakens the effect of Black's B—KKt5 and lessens the power of the counter-move 6...P—QB4 (7 PxBP, Q—QR4; 8 BPxQP, KtxKP; 9 PxP, KR—K, 10 Castles, etc). It is. however, questionable whether even in this eventuality, after 6...P—K4!; 7 P—Q5 (7 PxKP, PxKP, QxQ, KRxQ; 9 KtxKP, KtxKP, etc), QKt—Q2 and QB4, etc., he obtains more than in the position shown in Diagram 21.

(3) The already referred to fianchettoing of the King's Bishop pointing also against the Gruenfeld variation (Alekhine-Reti), which leads to a vastly superior position for White after the moves 1 P—Q4, Kt—KB3; 2 P—QB4, P—KKt3; 3 P—KKt3, B—Kt2; 4 B—Kt2, Castles; 5 Kt—QB3, P—Q3 (more bearable is, according to Gruenfeld P—QB3 and P—Q4). 6 Kt—KB3, QKt—B3 (Burn, Yates), 7 P—Q5!, Kt—QKt, Castles. Both 8...

Black

White

P—K4; 9 KPxKP! (Alekhine vs. Sir George Thomas, Karlsbad, 1923), as well as the development of the B at KKt5 attempted by Reti in the referred to game (9 P—KR3, BxKt; 10 PxB!) lead to no satisfactory results. Even the securing of the Black Kt on the square QB4 (after P—QR4), as recommended by Maroczy, would give White the necessary time to carry out a successful pawn attack on the Queen's side after the completion of his development.

As you see, White has at least three ways at his disposal to meet the Indian system successfully. Less to be recommended, on the other hand, are the following mobilization plans also attempted in New York: (4) Kt—QB3 (or 3 B—KB4 in connection with this move) before P—QB4, whereupon Black does best after P—Q3 to aim at a speedy P—QB4, as in this eventuality the White QP cannot be protected by his neighbor on the left, and thus the "trading" freedom in the center of the first player is considerably lessened. (Marshall vs. Maroczy, and Er. Lasker vs. Maroczy). Less powerful, on the other hand, after Kt—QB3 is the answer P—Q4, through which the square, K5, is surrendered needlessly to White, which appears to be aimless, particularly after the development of the B at KB4. In practice Black reached a disadvantageous position in both the games handled in this fashion (Capablanca vs. Yates, and Marshall vs. Ed. Lasker).

The inadequacy of the attempt to popularize the Pawn formation of P—QB3, P—Q4 and P—K4 (so warmly recommended by the gifted and paradoxical American theoretician, Mr. Young) also against the Indian system was clearly demonstrated by Mr. Yates in his games against Marshall and Ed. Lasker. The stratagem is simple, as White does nothing to prevent P—K4 after suitable preparation. Thus Black forces either (a) an exchange on K4, whereupon White remains at a disadvantage through the weakened Queen's file (Square Q3), or (b) forces the advance of the Pawn to Q5 (Ed. Lasker), whereupon Black obtains a good counter attack quickly on the KB file through P—KB4; or, finally (c), permitting the exchange at Q4 (Marshall), whereby White is somewhat at a disadvantage, owing to his hanging central Pawns.

(6) A proof that Black must not under all circumstances direct his efforts towards playing P—K4 but, in case his opponent tries to make this advance more difficult through 3 B—B4, can divert the game much quicker into the Reti system with P—QB4 (see further on) was demonstrated in the game between Janowski and Yates. Here the first player, through fine opening strategy, was able to discover the "Achilles Heel" (i. e., weak spot) in Black's structure (the square Q4) at the opportune time with deadly effect.

Finally, Capablanca played against Janowski a "white" Indian Opening, viz.: 1 Kt—KB3, P—Q4; 2 P—KKt3, P—QB4; 3 B—Kt2, Kt—QB3; 4 Castles (in case the Gruenfeld variation is playable for Black, it could be forced here already through P—Q4!), P—K4; 5 P—QB4 (thus White allows himself to be hemmed in without compensation and in practice had to contend with considerable difficulties. It would have been interesting

to investigate how far the advantage of the move could improve his chance in this not very pleasing position, after 5 P—Q3, P—KB4 or Kt—KB3 (see this variation above with the colors changed around), P—Q5, and White can only hope for an eventual equalization after the opening of the King's file through P—K3.

B. THE RETI SYSTEM

I. In the normal position of the Reti Opening (viz., after 1 Kt—KB3, P—Q4; 2 P—QB4, Black has to decide whether to postpone to a later and more favor-

Black

White

able moment the struggle of the Pawns in and around the center, as the second move of his opponent has clearly made manifest his intentions there (P—Q3 or P—Q4) (a) whether possibly he dares facilitate it appreciably by 2...PxBP or 2...Kt—KB3, whereby he allows his central Pawn to disappear; (b) whether he will anticipate him with 2...P—Q5; or (c) while he is protecting his QP with one of its neighbors, whether he should direct his attention to making the plan of his opponent, wherever possible, harmless. These three continuations were treated in a sufficient number of games in New York to determine clearly their respective worth.

(1) The unsatisfactory results of the premature exchange of the black QP were illustrated in the game between Reti and Janowski and partly through the game between Reti and Marshall. In the first game there occurred 2...PxBP; 3 Kt—QR3 (much better than the time-losing maneuver of Q—R4ch and QxP), Kt—KB3; 4 KtxBP, and White already, after so few moves, has obtained the undisputed command with his pieces of the square K5, an advantage which he will later make secure through fianchetto-

ing his QB, as this maneuver cannot be prevented. If one takes into account the ensuing slight inaccuracies on both sides (7 Castles?, 8...P—QB3), one gets the impression from the way this game ran that Black was already beaten in the opening phase of the fight over the center and, as a result of the impossibility to provide himself at the right time with secure supports, finally collapsed.

The game between Reti and Marshall is of use insofar as it shows that White could have assured himself an obvious advantage in the opening after the moves 1 Kt—KB3, P—Q4; 2 P—QB4, Kt—KB3 (actually these moves were played by Black in the reverse order); 3 PxP, KtxP, by playing, instead of 4 P—Q4?, 4 P—K4 (quite apart from the very forceful fianchettoing of his KB at this time), Kt—KB3; 5 Kt—QB3, P—QB4!; 6 P—Q4, PxP; 7 QxP, QxQ; 8 KtxQ (8... P—K4; 9 Kt—QKt5, Kt—QR3; 10 B—K3). These two examples are sufficient, in our opinion, to express the conviction that giving up the Pawn center in so early a phase of the game brings no compensation to the second player.

(2) Even the in itself commendable attempt to give the game its own character through 2...P—Q5 turned out to be favorable in New York for the first player, despite the fact that the line was recommended by no less an expert in the opening than the great Rubinstein. In the game played along these lines between Dr. Tartakower and Janowski there followed 3 P—QKt4!, P—QR4; 4 P—Kt5!, P—QB4; 5 P—K3, P—KKt3 (obviously the most plausible way to make use of the KB); 6 PxP, PxP; 7 P—Q3, B—Kt2; 8 P—KKt3. White will obviously be able to bear almost irremovable pressure on

the diagonal KR—QR8, whereas a counter-attack in the center (beginning with P—K4) on the part of Black is a thing of the distant future as a result of his poor development. Actually White won this game with surprising obviousness (at least in part thanks to the tempi presented to him by his opponent shortly afterwards through B—KB4 and B—QB).

(3) The system calling for the strengthening of the Pawn center was tried several times in New York and brought out the following chief phases:

(a) Black hems in his Bishop through P—K3, but yet is able later, per nefas, to play P—K4 and thus obtain a free game. Thus ran the type game between Reti and Yates: 1 Kt—KB3, P—Q4; 2 P—QB4, P—K3; 3 P—KKt3, Kt—KB3; 4 B—Kt2, B—Q3; 5 P—Kt3, Castles; 6 Castles, R—K; 7 B—Kt2, QKt—Q2; 8 P—Q3?, P—QB3; 9 QKt—Q2, P—K4!; 10 PxP, PxP; 11 R—B, Kt—B; 12 R—B2.

Black

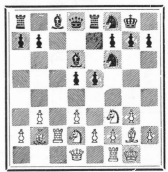

White

After the above moves, a position was reached which every unbiased chess player will consider at least very satisfactory for Black. After 12...B—B4; 13 Q—R, Kt—Q2; 14 KR—QB, P—KR3 (to be followed by B—KR2), White has already to parry the threat of P—K5 (similar to the game between Reti and Dr. Lasker) so that there can be no talk of the initiative being taken by him. But even later Black would be able to obtain a good equal game if he had recognized in time the significance of the opponent's threat of P—Q4.

In the game between Alekhine and Bogoljubow, in which White also refrained from moving his QP forward two squares, Black, through the opportune playing of P—K4, could also have obtained a similar position. Only through over-

Black

White

looking this opportunity did he get a disadvantageous position. Of less theoretical importance, on the other hand, is the game between Reti and Ed. Lasker in which the time-losing maneuvers of Black's Knight could have been shown to be totally wrong both tactically (through a Pawn sacrifice on the 6th move) as also strategically (as was actually the case).

(b) The hemming in of the QB finds its own punishment, as White can effectually hinder it from freeing itself through P—Q4! Reti, in his game with Bogoljubow, discovered the correct handling of this line. After the first seven moves of the game Reti-Yates had been repeated, White played 8 P—Q4!, following the

Black

White

footsteps of Capablanca (as Black) in his game with Marshall. Now Black is seriously hindered in his opportunities for development, as he has no outlook in the near future for open lines with which to ease his game. Further his blocked in QB prevents the co-operation of his Rooks for a long time. Against this White has well-founded hopes to force further gain of ground later through P—K4 and then to undertake a decisive action both on the King's wing and particularly in the center. As a result of this confirmation the "stocks and shares" of the Reti Opening soared, until his game with Dr. Lasker. The latter's handling of the opening cleared up the situation further, viz.:

(c) Black combines the strengthening of his Pawn center with the development of his QB and thus avoids all difficulties. Actually Black, as he chose a development system which is known to be sound for the first player since the time of the London Tournament of 1922, came to a position similar to the one shown in Diagram 26 (Reti-Yates) and brought it about in one move less. After 1 Kt—KB3, P—Q4; 2 P—B4, P—QB3; 3 P—QKt3, B—B4; 4 P—KKt3, Kt—KB3; 5 B—Kt2, QKt—Q2; 6 B—Kt2, P—K3; 7 Castles, B—Q3, 8 P—Q3, Castles; 9 QKt—Q2, P—K4; 10 PxP, PxP; 11 R—B, Q—K2; 12 R—B2. There is this difference in his favor that he did not have to execute the time-losing maneuver of his Knight, Kt—KB and Kt—Q2 or KKt3, in order to develop his QB (as did Yates)! Through the further course of this game the at first appearance seemingly paradoxical defense of White against a hostile advance in the center (P—K4) was, in our opinion, finally condemned. In this game within a few moves White carried out a partially forced sacrifice of the exchange and eventually also lost the game after a number of happenings which are unimportant when considered as a whole. If, however, White, as Dr. Tartakower, among others, has recommended in his very significant monograph, "The Opening of the Future," plays P—Q4, instead of P—Q3 on his eighth move, Black, after 8 ...Castles, obtains several very signifi-

Black

White

cant objectives (compared with the position reached in Diagram 28, Reti vs. Bogojubow) through the development of his Bishop to KB4, viz.:

(1) Unhampered co-operation of his Rooks;

(2) Renders more difficult P—K4, and

(3) Above all makes difficult the development of the white Queen.

In brief we are obliged to consider this position as satisfactory for Black until further developments occur. If latter researches confirm the correctness of this opinion, White will come around to reverting to a variation of the Queen's Gambit Declined after 2...P—QB3!, with P—Q4 (in any case with the move Kt—KB3, which is not to be dispensed with in this eventuality). For upon a final judgment regarding this defense, the "Czech Defense"?, according to Dr. Tarrasch, would then depend the fate of the proper worth of Reti's move, 2 P—QB4.

Of the other possible development plans, after 1 Kt—KB3, it appears that 1...Kt—KB3; 2 P—QB4, P—QB4 (Reti vs. Maroczy) are the best. This method of handling the opening is correct insofar as it keeps the positions symmetrical for a long time and thus promises Black good drawing chances, provided White does not soon decide to embark upon the always somewhat "two-edged" move of P—Q4. From a purely theoretical standpoint it fails, as Black thus does not attempt even once to solve his chief task in the opening, viz., annuling the advantage of the first move and only postpones the attempt indefinitely.

Besides the above, two games were also played with the "Indian" move 2... P—KKt3, after 1 Kt—KB3; 2 P—QB4 (Reti vs. Capablanca and Dr. Tartakower vs. Marshall). White answers best with 3 P—Q4, B—Kt2; 4 P—KKt3! and thus turns the game into a variation of the Indian Defense (see above) or eventually into the Gruenfeld Defense. The moves, 3 P—QKt3 (Dr. Tartakower) or 3 P—QKt4 (Reti), lead generally to the double fianchettoing of the Bishops on both sides with more or less equal prospects for both The fact that Black finally lost both of the above games had little to do with these first opening moves.

C. RETI'S SYSTEM FOR BLACK.

Even though Reti's move in connection with the following double fianchetto was played less often as a method of attack in New York than once seemed likely, it was shown that a similar system for defensive purposes was much more in the spirit of the thing, viz., with the leading thought to maintain equality in the opening phase of the game. As an illustration in looking back this way is the above referred to game between Marshall and Capablanca, in which White early hemmed in his Bishop and was at a clear disadvantage after but a few moves. 1 P—Q4, Kt—KB3; 2 Kt—KB3, P—KKt3; 3 P—K3, B—Kt2; 4 QKt—Q2, P—QKt3; 5 B—B4, Castles; 6 Q—K2, P—QB4; 7 P—QB3, B—Kt2; 8 Castles, P—Q4; 9 B—Q3, Kt—K5.

Black

Therefore, White would do much better to develop the B on KB4 before playing P—K3. The game between Reti and Alekhine, after 1 Kt—KB3, P—KKt3; 2 P—Q4, Kt—KB3 (Inverting these moves is correct for Black); 3 B—KB4, B—Kt2; 4 P—KR3, P—QB4; 5 P—K3, P—QKt3; 6 QKt—Q2, B—Kt2; 7 B—Q3, Castles; 8 Castles, reached a similar position to the one reached in the game between Reti and Dr. Lasker, with the colors reversed. Black would now have done best to continue with 8...P—Q4!, instead of 8... P—Q3, which would have promised him

Black

Black

good chances for an equal game (in our opinion no longer so). After 8...P—Q3, Reti might have obtained an advantage at least through Dr. Lasker's continuation of P—K4, which he could have played here with a tempo to the good.

The games between Dr. Lasker and Alekhine and Janowski and Marshall illustrate the various consequences of exchanging in the center (QBPxQP) during an early stage in the Reti Defense System Whereas Marshall carried out this exchange at a time when White could recapture with the KP and could thus obtain a light pressure on the King's file, Alekhine exchanged only—

(1) Because the opponent's QP, as a result of a tactical inaccuracy on the part of the enemy, was not yet protected by the KP and consequently the QBP had to retake:

(2) He could then develop advantageously his QKt at QB3 (instead of the more usual Kt—Q2), through which P—K4, on the part of White, was obviously made more difficult. He thus obtained a good game which goes to prove that White answers P—QB4 best with an immediate P—K3.

The games between Janowski and Reti and Janowski and Alekhine show in an instructive manner in what instances Black can pay for the isolation of his opponent's QP in the Reti System (through PxQBP) if White chooses the aggressive stationing of his Pawns through P—Q4 and P—QB4, instead of fortifying the center with P—QB3. In the first-named game the attempt was crowned with success, but it failed in the second instance. The difference between these several results lies in the fact that in the game between Janowski and Reti there was played before P—QB4 a move which was necessary in this position, B—KB4, and then again P—KR3, which gave Black the necessary time to strengthen his square Q4. After 1 P—Q4, Kt—KB3; 2 Kt—KB3, P—KKt3; 3 P—KR3, B—Kt2; 4 B—KB4, P—QKt3; 5 P—K3, P—QB4; 6 P—QB4, PxQP; 7 PxQP, Castles; 8 Kt—QB3, P—Q4; 9 B—K2, B—QKt2, Black obviously has overcome his difficulties in the opening, as he would have

been able also to develop himself unhampered even had not 10 P—QKt3? followed in that position A quite different treatment was given the game between Janowski and Alekhine where, after 1 P—Q4, Kt—KB3; 2 Kt—KB3, P—QB4 (this has been proven to be premature when played before White plays B—KB4); 3 P—K3, P—KKt3 (Naturally 3...P—Q4 is good here, too; this same position could also have been reached after 1 P—Q4, Kt—KB3; 2 Kt—KB3, P—KKt3; 3 P—K3, P—QB4, and thus the later moves are not uninteresting), White first brought his King into safety with 4 B—Q3, P—QKt3; 5 Castles. Then, after 5...B—QKt2, he undertook an action in the center with 6 P—QB4!, which is very powerful here (it threatens P—Q5; in the game between Marshall and Capablanca White blocked the square QB4 by occupying it with his KB). After the further moves 6...PxQP; 7 PxQP, B—KKt2; 8 Kt—QB3, P—Q4; 9 B—KKt5, Black already had to decide to

Black

White

give up the square Q4 on account of the threat KR—K, to be followed by BPxQP, and was thus placed at a lasting disadvantage.

ECCENTRICITIES

As such we can point out—

(1) The shutting in of the QB in the game referred to between Alekhine and Janowski, which as a result of this extraordinary strategy was already lost for Black after eight to ten moves.

(2) The quite uncalled for systematic weakening of the White squares (after P—QKt3, P—Q3?, P—K4, and again P—KR3 and P—KKt4?) played by Black in the game between Ed. Lasker and

Black

White

Janowski, which also gave the opponent an easy game to win;

(3) Finally, the "Orang-Outang" move of 1 P—QKt4 (Dr. Tartakower vs. Maroczy) which provides Black with no difficulties in development and only makes more difficult the future fight for the center as a result of a premature defense on the Queen's side.

As a result of this review of the opening phases of individual games, one can see that, although the New York tournament brought into prominence but few tactical innovations (few variations) yet, in looking back into chess history and the evolution of opinions concerning the handling of the opening, it marks a very significant stage in this evolution.

ALEXANDER ALEKHINE.

THE RAPID TRANSIT TOURNAMENT

Seven of the eleven international experts who participated in the masters' tournament, got into action on March 11 at the rooms of the Manhattan Chess Club where a rapid transit tourney was arranged for their benefit. A field of eighteen, divided into three sections of six each, started out in the preliminaries. Among them were Capablanca, Maroczy, Dr. Tartakower, Reti, Bogoljubow, Yates and Edward Lasker. The rest were for the most part members of the Manhattan Chess Club.

The latter showed up very well in the encounters with the masters; in fact, of the six that qualified for the final round in which the prizes were decided three were club members. These were Morris A. Schapiro of Columbia University, who made a clean sweep of five wins in his section; Oscar Tenner and Leonard B. Meyer.

Capablanca, as expected, emerged the winner with a total of 8—2. He lost one game in the preliminaries to Samuel Katz, secretary of the club, and drew two games in the finals with Maroczy and Tenner. Schapiro did not do so well in the later games, winning only two out of the five. Nevertheless, he tied for second and third prizes with Tenner, who, like him, finished with 7—3. Tenner had the satisfaction of defeating both Maroczy and Dr. Tartakower, besides drawing with champion Capablanca.

Geza Maroczy received the fourth prize with a score of 6½—3½. Dr. Tartakower, 5—5, was placed fifth and Meyer, 4—6, sixth. Rudolph Smirka, N. Y. State Champion, tied with Tenner in Section 3, but lost in the playoff, which gave Tenner the place in the finals.

Capablanca was still suffering from a heavy cold. Dr. Lasker, his predecessor, did not play, preferring to rest and save his strength for the more important games of the international tournament.

The full score of the play in the finals for the prizes follows:

PLAYERS	Capablanca.	Schapiro...	Tenner.....	Maroczy....	Tartakower.	Meyer......	First Round	Total Won.
Capablanca	...	1	½	½	1	1	4	8
Schapiro	0	...	0	0	1	1	5	7
Tenner	½	1	...	1	1	0	3½	7
Maroczy	½	1	0	...	0	1	4	6½
Tartakower	0	0	0	1	...	1	3	5
Meyer	0	0	1	0	0	...	3	4
First Round	1	0	1½	1	2	2	...	
Total Lost	2	3	3	3½	5	6		...

THE PROBLEM SOLVING COMPETITION

Seven of the experts engaged in the New York International Chess Tournament at the Hotel Alamac, together with eighteen amateurs, took part in the problem solving contest arranged for their benefit by the Good Companion Chess Problem Club and conducted by Frank Janet of Mount Vernon, the vice president for New York State on April 1. Although they competed in two separate classes, one for the masters, for whom four liberal cash prizes had been provided, and the other for the amateurs, who had to be content with medals and books, the same twelve problems, ten in two moves and two in three moves, were given to all to solve.

The amateurs had all the better of the test of skill in unraveling the puzzles direct from the diagrams, without setting up the pieces on boards. Three of them handed in the right solutions for the entire dozen, although at various intervals, while the best any of the masters could do was to get eleven of the solutions. The latter tried for time records, and in that way slipped up.

Isaac Kashdan of the College of the City of New York and a member of the Rice-Progressive Chess Club, 18 years of age, carried off the gold medal by handing in solutions of the problems in 1 hour and 5 minutes. Kashdan is also the champion of the Hungarian Chess Club.

John F. Barry, president of the Boston Chess Club, and Alfred Schroeder of the Manhattan Chess Club divided the second and third prizes in the amateur class, having solved all the problems in 1 hour and 45 minutes. A silver medal was awarded to each.

Samuel Rzeschewski came to the competition, expecting to enter the masters' class, having once played in an important tournament here. He was placed among the amateurs and won the fourth prize by solving eleven of the problems in 1 hour and 28 minutes. He received one of five books presented by Alain C. White, president of the Good Companion Club. The other prize winners among the amateurs were the following: Fifth, Samuel Seplowin, 10 problems, (all two-movers) in 55 minutes; sixth, Leonard B. Meyer, 10 in 1 hour and 25 minutes; seventh, Arthur S. Meyer, 10 in 2 hours; eighth, Alexander Kevitz, 9 in 1 hour and 49 minutes.

Richard Reti of Czechoslovakia carried off the honors in the masters' class with a record of 11 problems in 1 hour and 23 minutes. Next came Geza Maroczy of Hungary and Dr. S. Tartakower of Austria, both of whom solved 10 in 2 hours. The fourth prize went to Alexander Alekhine of Russia, who made the quick time of 1 hour and 1 minute, but had correct answers for only 9 problems. The prizes in this section amounted to $150, divided into four prizes, thus: $60, $40, $30 and $20. Marshall, Edward Lasker and Yates also tried their luck, but fell just outside the limit of the winners.

ALEKHINE'S RECORD BLINDFOLD PERFORMANCE

On April 27, in the Japanese Room of the Alamac Hotel, Alexander Alekhine established a new world's record for blindfold play in an exhibition wherein he was opposed by 26 players of more than the average skill. The remarkable seance lasted from 2 P. M. to 2 A. M., with a brief intermission for dinner. Alekhine wound up the performance with a score of 16 wins, 5 drawn games and 5 losses. M. Peckar, I. Kashdan, A. S. Pinkus, M. B. Downs and J. Salzman were the winners, and Erling Tholfsen, J. C. Myers, J. H. Friedman, Lloyd Garrison and Max Kleiman drew their games. Geza Maroczy and Norbert L. Lederer acted as tellers.

Alekhine divided his opponents into four groups, playing P—K4 on the first eight boards, P—Q4 on Boards 9 to 13, P—K4 on Boards 14 to 21 and P—Q4 on Boards 22 to 26. This made a total of 16 King's Pawn and 10 Queen's Pawn openings. The King's Pawn openings divided themselves into eight different forms of development, including four Vienna games, three Ruy Lopez, three Sicilian defenses, two Center Gambits, one Philidor defense, one French defense, one King's Gambit declined and one irregular defense.

The organizations represented among the players were the Manhattan Chess Club, Marshall Chess Club, I. L. Rice Progressive Chess Club, Stuyvesant Chess Club, Chess Club International, Brooklyn Chess Club, Columbia University, City College, New York University and the Interborough High School Chess League.

SUBSCRIBERS TO THE TOURNAMENT FUND

The following is the list of subscribers referred to in the Treasurer's Report on Page XII:

Harry Latz	$1300.00	Dr. I. Grushlaw	25.00
Herbert R. Limburg	500.00	Dr. A. J. Rongy	25.00
Arthur S. Meyer	250.00	W. H. Failing	25.00
Julius Finn	250.00	R. W. Randall	25.00
Felix E. Kahn	250.00	H. Thompson	25.00
Mischa Elman	200.00	J. M. Schatzkin	25.00
A. H. Loeb	200.00	A. C. Cass	25.00
Leonard B. Meyer	125.00	P. C. Maas	25.00
H. R. Ickelheimer	100.00	J. W. Barnhart	25.00
Harold M. Phillips	100.00	F. Rose	25.00
J. Malsman	100.00	P. Stevens Jr.	25.00
J. Schwarz	100.00	S. A. Fox	25.00
Herman Behr	100.00	A. Landau	25.00
J. Rosenzweig	100.00	Rudolph Raubitschek	25.00
Edwin Dimock	100.00	Bradley Martin	25.00
Alrick H. Man	100.00	A. Schroeder	25.00
John W. Griggs	100.00	A. W. Paull	25.00
E. L. Torsch	75.00	R. Stutz	25.00
Francis H. French	75.00	H. Goldvogel	25.00
Abb Landis	60.00	L. Goldvogel	25.00
A. Lamport	50.00	Charles C. Nichols	25.00
G. J. Frickman	50.00	J. M. Schulte	25.00
J. Helburn	50.00	Udo M. Reingeh	25.00
E. S. Maddock	50.00	N. W. Banks	25.00
Dr. E. Moschkowitz	50.00	O. I. Wormser	25.00
Dr. Louis Cohn	50.00	A. A. Spadone	25.00
George J. Beihoff	50.00	H. Shapiro	25.00
Walter P. Shipley	50.00	F. F. Russell	25.00
G. E. Northrup	50.00	S. C. Lamport	25.00
Robert Raubitschek	50.00	Boston Chess Club	39.00
W. M. Vance	50.00	S. J. Tankos	25.00
R. Beinecke	50.00	H. R. Bigelow	25.00
M. Barish	50.00	R. W. Ferguson	25.00
N. Y. Staatz Zeitung	50.00	Ed. Friedman	25.00
R. G. Wahrburg	50.00	S. W. Howland	25.00
Moses Jaffe	50.00	Toscha Seidl	25.00
W. J. Rosston	50.00	H. B. Weil	25.00
M. Steinberg	50.00	O. Campbell	25.00
City Club, Chicago	50.00	L. Schofield	25.00
Hamilton Club	50.00	Friend of L. B. Meyer	20.00
L. W. Schwarz	25.00	Friend of H. Taylor	25.00
F. N. Sard	25.00	L. Rosen	25.00
S. Siegman	25.00	J. Radin	25.00
W. M. Russell	25.00	B. B. Hoffman	25.00
H. Helms	25.00	J. Eisner	25.00
C. Van der Voort	25.00	Providence Chess Club	25.00
J. Glucksman	25.00	M. L. Schiff	25.00
F. Gross	25.00	Rodney Berg	25.00
E. Hymes	25.00	Meyer London	25.00
E. L. Gluck	25.00	Otis W. Field	25.00
A. Kahn	25.00	Ed. Mandell	25.00
Howard S. Hoit	25.00	S. Mendel	35.00
M. Wild	25.00	Dr. B. W. Kirchner	25.00
H. I. Ladd	25.00	J. F. Magee Jr.	25.00
L. Zeckendorf	25.00	P. G. Fredericks	25.00

LIST OF SUBSCRIBERS—Continued

Dr. G. C. Dohme	25.00	A. D. Denis Jr	10.00
H. M. Gorham	25.00	E. T. Gundlach	10.00
Dr. R. W. Mathes	35.00	F. Henschell	10.00
C. S. Howell	25.00	Dan Levy	10.00
E. B. Edwards	25.00	E. Millard	10.00
Addison Brown	25.00	D. H. Adler	10.00
John F. Barry	25.00	L. J. Rosenwald	10.00
City Club, Boston	25.00	William Rosenwald	10.00
Christian Union, Boston	25.00	Meyer Levy	10.00
L. W. Stephens	25.00	M. L. Rippe	10.00
H. Davidson	25.00	Walter C. Louchheim	10.00
F. Gross	25.00	Prof. D. Melamet	10.00
J. J. Bunting	25.00	Jacob H. Rhoads	10.00
A. H. Beckman	25.00	Alex Siegel	10.00
David Rosenbaum	25.00	F. A. Lidbury	10.00
M. D. Hago	25.00		
J. C. Stokes	25.00	Hartwig Perez	10.00
F. W. Doerr	25.00	Sidney Crystal	10.00
S. W. Addleman	25.00	Hyman S. Crystal	10.00
S. D. Friedman	25.00	Miss Crystal	10.00
Empire City C. C.	25.00	W. H. Beers	10.00
Maurice Wertheim	25.00	A. B. Hodges	10.00
Leo Levy	20.00	Paul Schwarz	10.00
Z. L. Hoover	20.00	F. P. Hier	10.00
Arthur Hess	20.00	Stouin	10.00
Ed. Cahn	15.00	B. Forsberg	10.00
H. L. Lurie	15.00	M. Cherry	10.00
J. Cunningham	12.00	A. Horowitz	10.00
H. Atlas	10.00	F. W. Rothschild	10.00
J. L. Emerson	10.00	E. J. Becker	10.00
G. Carpenter	10.00	Bernhard Cline	10.00
H. G. Cunningham	10.00	F. W. C. Crane	10.00
M. A. Schapiro	10.00	R. London	10.00
H. L. Lurie	10.00	L. B. London	10.00
H. Rosenfeld	10.00	H. London	10.00
F. M. Teed	10.00	Dr. H. E. Leede	8.00
Charles Spicehandler	10.00	Dr. A. Freundlich	5.00
H. Cassel	10.00	P. J. Wortman	5.00
Dr. H. Spitzer	10.00	F. W. Barker	5.00
L. M. Fishel	10.00	Mrs. N. Nixdorff	5.00
G. Apfelbaum	10.00	A. Tozer	5.00
H. H. Koehler	10.00	J. A. Lec	5.00
H. Zirn	10.00	J. Szold	5.00
H. Lowenthal	10.00	K. Hall	5.00
A. A. Link	10.00	Dr. E. Sokal	5.00
S. Landon	10.00	R. W. Lovejoy	5.00
S. G. Hammel	10.00	H. T. D. Colladay	5.00
W. Apfelbaum	10.00	I. Rosenbaum	5.00
B. Gelles	10.00	C. C. Morris	5.00
W. H. Lyons	10.00	Dr. L. G. Miller	5.00
O. M. Bostwick	10.00	E. W. Lovejoy	5.00
J. Bernstein	10.00	A. Cartier	5.00
Dr. H. Siff	10.00	C. M. Hamblen	3.00
H. de Fries	10.00	Pot	1.00
A. Cohen	10.00	D. A. Wahrburg	1.00
I. Witkin	10.00	A. T. Rex	1.00
J. W. Carroll	10.00	X.	1.00
E. E. Shearns	10.00	Y.	1.00
H. Eckstein	10.00	Daily	1.00

A CATALOGUE OF SELECTED DOVER BOOKS
IN ALL FIELDS OF INTEREST

A CATALOGUE OF SELECTED DOVER BOOKS
IN ALL FIELDS OF INTEREST

AMERICA'S OLD MASTERS, James T. Flexner. Four men emerged unexpectedly from provincial 18th century America to leadership in European art: Benjamin West, J. S. Copley, C. R. Peale, Gilbert Stuart. Brilliant coverage of lives and contributions. Revised, 1967 edition. 69 plates. 365pp. of text.

21806-6 Paperbound $3.00

FIRST FLOWERS OF OUR WILDERNESS: AMERICAN PAINTING, THE COLONIAL PERIOD, James T. Flexner. Painters, and regional painting traditions from earliest Colonial times up to the emergence of Copley, West and Peale Sr., Foster, Gustavus Hesselius, Feke, John Smibert and many anonymous painters in the primitive manner. Engaging presentation, with 162 illustrations. xxii + 368pp.

22180-6 Paperbound $3.50

THE LIGHT OF DISTANT SKIES: AMERICAN PAINTING, 1760-1835, James T. Flexner. The great generation of early American painters goes to Europe to learn and to teach: West, Copley, Gilbert Stuart and others. Allston, Trumbull, Morse; also contemporary American painters—primitives, derivatives, academics—who remained in America. 102 illustrations. xiii + 306pp. 22179-2 Paperbound $3.00

A HISTORY OF THE RISE AND PROGRESS OF THE ARTS OF DESIGN IN THE UNITED STATES, William Dunlap. Much the richest mine of information on early American painters, sculptors, architects, engravers, miniaturists, etc. The only source of information for scores of artists, the major primary source for many others. Unabridged reprint of rare original 1834 edition, with new introduction by James T. Flexner, and 394 new illustrations. Edited by Rita Weiss. 6⅝ x 9⅝.

21695-0, 21696-9, 21697-7 Three volumes, Paperbound $13.50

EPOCHS OF CHINESE AND JAPANESE ART, Ernest F. Fenollosa. From primitive Chinese art to the 20th century, thorough history, explanation of every important art period and form, including Japanese woodcuts; main stress on China and Japan, but Tibet, Korea also included. Still unexcelled for its detailed, rich coverage of cultural background, aesthetic elements, diffusion studies, particularly of the historical period. 2nd, 1913 edition. 242 illustrations. lii + 439pp. of text.

20364-6, 20365-4 Two volumes, Paperbound $6.00

THE GENTLE ART OF MAKING ENEMIES, James A. M. Whistler. Greatest wit of his day deflates Oscar Wilde, Ruskin, Swinburne; strikes back at inane critics, exhibitions, art journalism; aesthetics of impressionist revolution in most striking form. Highly readable classic by great painter. Reproduction of edition designed by Whistler. Introduction by Alfred Werner. xxxvi + 334pp.

21875-9 Paperbound $2.50

HOW TO KNOW THE WILD FLOWERS, Mrs. William Starr Dana. This is the classical book of American wildflowers (of the Eastern and Central United States), used by hundreds of thousands. Covers over 500 species, arranged in extremely easy to use color and season groups. Full descriptions, much plant lore. This Dover edition is the fullest ever compiled, with tables of nomenclature changes. 174 full-page plates by M. Satterlee. xii + 418pp.   20332-8 Paperbound $2.75

OUR PLANT FRIENDS AND FOES, William Atherton DuPuy. History, economic importance, essential botanical information and peculiarities of 25 common forms of plant life are provided in this book in an entertaining and charming style. Covers food plants (potatoes, apples, beans, wheat, almonds, bananas, etc.), flowers (lily, tulip, etc.), trees (pine, oak, elm, etc.), weeds, poisonous mushrooms and vines, gourds, citrus fruits, cotton, the cactus family, and much more. 108 illustrations. xiv + 290pp.   22272-1 Paperbound $2.50

HOW TO KNOW THE FERNS, Frances T. Parsons. Classic survey of Eastern and Central ferns, arranged according to clear, simple identification key. Excellent introduction to greatly neglected nature area. 57 illustrations and 42 plates. xvi + 215pp.   20740-4 Paperbound $2.00

MANUAL OF THE TREES OF NORTH AMERICA, Charles S. Sargent. America's foremost dendrologist provides the definitive coverage of North American trees and tree-like shrubs. 717 species fully described and illustrated: exact distribution, down to township; full botanical description; economic importance; description of subspecies and races; habitat, growth data; similar material. Necessary to every serious student of tree-life. Nomenclature revised to present. Over 100 locating keys. 783 illustrations. lii + 934pp. 20277-1, 20278-X Two volumes, Paperbound $6.00

OUR NORTHERN SHRUBS, Harriet L. Keeler. Fine non-technical reference work identifying more than 225 important shrubs of Eastern and Central United States and Canada. Full text covering botanical description, habitat, plant lore, is paralleled with 205 full-page photographs of flowering or fruiting plants. Nomenclature revised by Edward G. Voss. One of few works concerned with shrubs. 205 plates, 35 drawings. xxviii + 521pp.   21989-5 Paperbound $3.75

THE MUSHROOM HANDBOOK, Louis C. C. Krieger. Still the best popular handbook: full descriptions of 259 species, cross references to another 200. Extremely thorough text enables you to identify, know all about any mushroom you are likely to meet in eastern and central U. S. A.: habitat, luminescence, poisonous qualities, use, folklore, etc. 32 color plates show over 50 mushrooms, also 126 other illustrations. Finding keys. vii + 560pp.   21861-9 Paperbound $3.95

HANDBOOK OF BIRDS OF EASTERN NORTH AMERICA, Frank M. Chapman. Still much the best single-volume guide to the birds of Eastern and Central United States. Very full coverage of 675 species, with descriptions, life habits, distribution, similar data. All descriptions keyed to two-page color chart. With this single volume the average birdwatcher needs no other books. 1931 revised edition. 195 illustrations. xxxvi + 581pp.   21489-3 Paperbound $4.50

POEMS OF ANNE BRADSTREET, edited with an introduction by Robert Hutchinson. A new selection of poems by America's first poet and perhaps the first significant woman poet in the English language. 48 poems display her development in works of considerable variety—love poems, domestic poems, religious meditations, formal elegies, "quaternions," etc. Notes, bibliography. viii + 222pp.

22160-1 Paperbound $2.00

THREE GOTHIC NOVELS: THE CASTLE OF OTRANTO BY HORACE WALPOLE; VATHEK BY WILLIAM BECKFORD; THE VAMPYRE BY JOHN POLIDORI, WITH FRAGMENT OF A NOVEL BY LORD BYRON, edited by E. F. Bleiler. The first Gothic novel, by Walpole; the finest Oriental tale in English, by Beckford; powerful Romantic supernatural story in versions by Polidori and Byron. All extremely important in history of literature; all still exciting, packed with supernatural thrills, ghosts, haunted castles, magic, etc. xl + 291pp.

21232-7 Paperbound $2.00

THE BEST TALES OF HOFFMANN, E. T. A. Hoffmann. 10 of Hoffmann's most important stories, in modern re-editings of standard translations: Nutcracker and the King of Mice, Signor Formica, Automata, The Sandman, Rath Krespel, The Golden Flowerpot, Master Martin the Cooper, The Mines of Falun, The King's Betrothed, A New Year's Eve Adventure. 7 illustrations by Hoffmann. Edited by E. F. Bleiler. xxxix + 419pp. 21793-0 Paperbound $2.50

GHOST AND HORROR STORIES OF AMBROSE BIERCE, Ambrose Bierce. 23 strikingly modern stories of the horrors latent in the human mind: The Eyes of the Panther, The Damned Thing, An Occurrence at Owl Creek Bridge, An Inhabitant of Carcosa, etc., plus the dream-essay, Visions of the Night. Edited by E. F. Bleiler. xxii + 199pp. 20767-6 Paperbound $1.50

BEST GHOST STORIES OF J. S. LEFANU, J. Sheridan LeFanu. Finest stories by Victorian master often considered greatest supernatural writer of all. Carmilla, Green Tea, The Haunted Baronet, The Familiar, and 12 others. Most never before available in the U. S. A. Edited by E. F. Bleiler. 8 illustrations from Victorian publications. xvii + 467pp. 20415-4 Paperbound $3.00

THE TIME STREAM, THE GREATEST ADVENTURE, AND THE PURPLE SAPPHIRE—THREE SCIENCE FICTION NOVELS, John Taine (Eric Temple Bell). Great American mathematician was also foremost science fiction novelist of the 1920's. *The Time Stream*, one of all-time classics, uses concepts of circular time; *The Greatest Adventure*, incredibly ancient biological experiments from Antarctica threaten to escape; The *Purple Sapphire*, superscience, lost races in Central Tibet, survivors of the Great Race. 4 illustrations by Frank R. Paul. v + 532pp.

21180-0 Paperbound $3.00

SEVEN SCIENCE FICTION NOVELS, H. G. Wells. The standard collection of the great novels. Complete, unabridged. *First Men in the Moon, Island of Dr. Moreau, War of the Worlds, Food of the Gods, Invisible Man, Time Machine, In the Days of the Comet*. Not only science fiction fans, but every educated person owes it to himself to read these novels. 1015pp. 20264-X Clothbound $5.00

East O' the Sun and West O' the Moon, George W. Dasent. Considered the best of all translations of these Norwegian folk tales, this collection has been enjoyed by generations of children (and folklorists too). Includes True and Untrue, Why the Sea is Salt, East O' the Sun and West O' the Moon, Why the Bear is Stumpy-Tailed, Boots and the Troll, The Cock and the Hen, Rich Peter the Pedlar, and 52 more. The only edition with all 59 tales. 77 illustrations by Erik Werenskiold and Theodor Kittelsen. xv + 418pp.   22521-6 Paperbound $3.00

Goops and How to be Them, Gelett Burgess. Classic of tongue-in-cheek humor, masquerading as etiquette book. 87 verses, twice as many cartoons, show mischievous Goops as they demonstrate to children virtues of table manners, neatness, courtesy, etc. Favorite for generations. viii + 88pp. 6½ x 9¼.
                    22233-0 Paperbound $1.25

Alice's Adventures Under Ground, Lewis Carroll. The first version, quite different from the final *Alice in Wonderland,* printed out by Carroll himself with his own illustrations. Complete facsimile of the "million dollar" manuscript Carroll gave to Alice Liddell in 1864. Introduction by Martin Gardner. viii + 96pp. Title and dedication pages in color.   21482-6 Paperbound $1.25

The Brownies, Their Book, Palmer Cox. Small as mice, cunning as foxes, exuberant and full of mischief, the Brownies go to the zoo, toy shop, seashore, circus, etc., in 24 verse adventures and 266 illustrations. Long a favorite, since their first appearance in St. Nicholas Magazine. xi + 144pp. 6⅝ x 9¼.
                    21265-3 Paperbound $1.75

Songs of Childhood, Walter De La Mare. Published (under the pseudonym Walter Ramal) when De La Mare was only 29, this charming collection has long been a favorite children's book. A facsimile of the first edition in paper, the 47 poems capture the simplicity of the nursery rhyme and the ballad, including such lyrics as I Met Eve, Tartary, The Silver Penny. vii + 106pp.   21972-0 Paperbound $1.25

The Complete Nonsense of Edward Lear, Edward Lear. The finest 19th-century humorist-cartoonist in full: all nonsense limericks, zany alphabets, Owl and Pussycat, songs, nonsense botany, and more than 500 illustrations by Lear himself. Edited by Holbrook Jackson. xxix + 287pp.   (USO) 20167-8 Paperbound $2.00

Billy Whiskers: The Autobiography of a Goat, Frances Trego Montgomery. A favorite of children since the early 20th century, here are the escapades of that rambunctious, irresistible and mischievous goat—Billy Whiskers. Much in the spirit of *Peck's Bad Boy,* this is a book that children never tire of reading or hearing. All the original familiar illustrations by W. H. Fry are included: 6 color plates, 18 black and white drawings. 159pp.   22345-0 Paperbound $2.00

Mother Goose Melodies. Faithful republication of the fabulously rare Munroe and Francis "copyright 1833" Boston edition—the most important Mother Goose collection, usually referred to as the "original." Familiar rhymes plus many rare ones, with wonderful old woodcut illustrations. Edited by E. F. Bleiler. 128pp. 4½ x 6⅜.   22577-1 Paperbound $1.25

AMERICAN FOOD AND GAME FISHES, David S. Jordan and Barton W. Evermann. Definitive source of information, detailed and accurate enough to enable the sportsman and nature lover to identify conclusively some 1,000 species and sub-species of North American fish, sought for food or sport. Coverage of range, physiology, habits, life history, food value. Best methods of capture, interest to the angler, advice on bait, fly-fishing, etc. 338 drawings and photographs. 1 + 574pp. 6⅝ x 9⅜.

22383-1 Paperbound $4.50

THE FROG BOOK, Mary C. Dickerson. Complete with extensive finding keys, over 300 photographs, and an introduction to the general biology of frogs and toads, this is the classic non-technical study of Northeastern and Central species. 58 species; 290 photographs and 16 color plates. xvii + 253pp.

21973-9 Paperbound $4.00

THE MOTH BOOK: A GUIDE TO THE MOTHS OF NORTH AMERICA, William J. Holland. Classical study, eagerly sought after and used for the past 60 years. Clear identification manual to more than 2,000 different moths, largest manual in existence. General information about moths, capturing, mounting, classifying, etc., followed by species by species descriptions. 263 illustrations plus 48 color plates show almost every species, full size. 1968 edition, preface, nomenclature changes by A. E. Brower. xxiv + 479pp. of text. 6½ x 9¼.

21948-8 Paperbound $5.00

THE SEA-BEACH AT EBB-TIDE, Augusta Foote Arnold. Interested amateur can identify hundreds of marine plants and animals on coasts of North America; marine algae; seaweeds; squids; hermit crabs; horse shoe crabs; shrimps; corals; sea anemones; etc. Species descriptions cover: structure; food; reproductive cycle; size; shape; color; habitat; etc. Over 600 drawings. 85 plates. xii + 490pp.

21949-6 Paperbound $3.50

COMMON BIRD SONGS, Donald J. Borror. 33⅓ 12-inch record presents songs of 60 important birds of the eastern United States. A thorough, serious record which provides several examples for each bird, showing different types of song, individual variations, etc. Inestimable identification aid for birdwatcher. 32-page booklet gives text about birds and songs, with illustration for each bird.

21829-5 Record, book, album. Monaural. $2.75

FADS AND FALLACIES IN THE NAME OF SCIENCE, Martin Gardner. Fair, witty appraisal of cranks and quacks of science: Atlantis, Lemuria, hollow earth, flat earth, Velikovsky, orgone energy, Dianetics, flying saucers, Bridey Murphy, food fads, medical fads, perpetual motion, etc. Formerly "In the Name of Science." x + 363pp.

20394-8 Paperbound $2.00

HOAXES, Curtis D. MacDougall. Exhaustive, unbelievably rich account of great hoaxes: Locke's moon hoax, Shakespearean forgeries, sea serpents, Loch Ness monster, Cardiff giant, John Wilkes Booth's mummy, Disumbrationist school of art, dozens more; also journalism, psychology of hoaxing. 54 illustrations. xi + 338pp.

20465-0 Paperbound $2.75

A HISTORY OF COSTUME, Carl Köhler. Definitive history, based on surviving pieces of clothing primarily, and paintings, statues, etc. secondarily. Highly readable text, supplemented by 594 illustrations of costumes of the ancient Mediterranean peoples, Greece and Rome, the Teutonic prehistoric period; costumes of the Middle Ages, Renaissance, Baroque, 18th and 19th centuries. Clear, measured patterns are provided for many clothing articles. Approach is practical throughout. Enlarged by Emma von Sichart. 464pp. 21030-8 Paperbound $3.50

ORIENTAL RUGS, ANTIQUE AND MODERN, Walter A. Hawley. A complete and authoritative treatise on the Oriental rug—where they are made, by whom and how, designs and symbols, characteristics in detail of the six major groups, how to distinguish them and how to buy them. Detailed technical data is provided on periods, weaves, warps, wefts, textures, sides, ends and knots, although no technical background is required for an understanding. 11 color plates, 80 halftones, 4 maps. vi + 320pp. 6⅛ x 9⅛. 22366-3 Paperbound $5.00

TEN BOOKS ON ARCHITECTURE, Vitruvius. By any standards the most important book on architecture ever written. Early Roman discussion of aesthetics of building, construction methods, orders, sites, and every other aspect of architecture has inspired, instructed architecture for about 2,000 years. Stands behind Palladio, Michelangelo, Bramante, Wren, countless others. Definitive Morris H. Morgan translation. 68 illustrations. xii + 331pp. 20645-9 Paperbound $2.50

THE FOUR BOOKS OF ARCHITECTURE, Andrea Palladio. Translated into every major Western European language in the two centuries following its publication in 1570, this has been one of the most influential books in the history of architecture. Complete reprint of the 1738 Isaac Ware edition. New introduction by Adolf Placzek, Columbia Univ. 216 plates. xxii + 110pp. of text. 9½ x 12¾. 21308-0 Clothbound $10.00

STICKS AND STONES: A STUDY OF AMERICAN ARCHITECTURE AND CIVILIZATION, Lewis Mumford. One of the great classics of American cultural history. American architecture from the medieval-inspired earliest forms to the early 20th century; evolution of structure and style, and reciprocal influences on environment. 21 photographic illustrations. 238pp. 20202-X Paperbound $2.00

THE AMERICAN BUILDER'S COMPANION, Asher Benjamin. The most widely used early 19th century architectural style and source book, for colonial up into Greek Revival periods. Extensive development of geometry of carpentering, construction of sashes, frames, doors, stairs; plans and elevations of domestic and other buildings. Hundreds of thousands of houses were built according to this book, now invaluable to historians, architects, restorers, etc. 1827 edition. 59 plates. 114pp. 7⅞ x 10¾. 22236-5 Paperbound $3.00

DUTCH HOUSES IN THE HUDSON VALLEY BEFORE 1776, Helen Wilkinson Reynolds. The standard survey of the Dutch colonial house and outbuildings, with constructional features, decoration, and local history associated with individual homesteads. Introduction by Franklin D. Roosevelt. Map. 150 illustrations. 469pp. 6⅝ x 9¼. 21469-9 Paperbound $4.00

PLANETS, STARS AND GALAXIES: DESCRIPTIVE ASTRONOMY FOR BEGINNERS, A. E. Fanning. Comprehensive introductory survey of astronomy: the sun, solar system, stars, galaxies, universe, cosmology; up-to-date, including quasars, radio stars, etc. Preface by Prof. Donald Menzel. 24pp. of photographs. 189pp. 5¼ x 8¼.
21680-2 Paperbound $1.50

TEACH YOURSELF CALCULUS, P. Abbott. With a good background in algebra and trig, you can teach yourself calculus with this book. Simple, straightforward introduction to functions of all kinds, integration, differentiation, series, etc. "Students who are beginning to study calculus method will derive great help from this book." Faraday House Journal. 308pp. 20683-1 Clothbound $2.00

TEACH YOURSELF TRIGONOMETRY, P. Abbott. Geometrical foundations, indices and logarithms, ratios, angles, circular measure, etc. are presented in this sound, easy-to-use text. Excellent for the beginner or as a brush up, this text carries the student through the solution of triangles. 204pp. 20682-3 Clothbound $2.00

TEACH YOURSELF ANATOMY, David LeVay. Accurate, inclusive, profusely illustrated account of structure, skeleton, abdomen, muscles, nervous system, glands, brain, reproductive organs, evolution. "Quite the best and most readable account,' Medical Officer. 12 color plates. 164 figures. 311pp. 4¾ x 7.
21651-9 Clothbound $2.50

TEACH YOURSELF PHYSIOLOGY, David LeVay. Anatomical, biochemical bases; digestive, nervous, endocrine systems; metabolism; respiration; muscle; excretion; temperature control; reproduction. "Good elementary exposition," The Lancet. 6 color plates. 44 illustrations. 208pp. 4¼ x 7. 21658-6 Clothbound $2.50

THE FRIENDLY STARS, Martha Evans Martin. Classic has taught naked-eye observation of stars, planets to hundreds of thousands, still not surpassed for charm, lucidity, adequacy. Completely updated by Professor Donald H. Menzel, Harvard Observatory. 25 illustrations. 16 x 30 chart. x + 147pp. 21099-5 Paperbound $1.25

MUSIC OF THE SPHERES: THE MATERIAL UNIVERSE FROM ATOM TO QUASAR, SIMPLY EXPLAINED, Guy Murchie. Extremely broad, brilliantly written popular account begins with the solar system and reaches to dividing line between matter and nonmatter; latest understandings presented with exceptional clarity. Volume One: Planets, stars, galaxies, cosmology, geology, celestial mechanics, latest astronomical discoveries; Volume Two: Matter, atoms, waves, radiation, relativity, chemical action, heat, nuclear energy, quantum theory, music, light, color, probability, antimatter, antigravity, and similar topics. 319 figures. 1967 (second) edition. Total of xx + 644pp. 21809-0, 21810-4 Two volumes, Paperbound $5.00

OLD-TIME SCHOOLS AND SCHOOL BOOKS, Clifton Johnson. Illustrations and rhymes from early primers, abundant quotations from early textbooks, many anecdotes of school life enliven this study of elementary schools from Puritans to middle 19th century. Introduction by Carl Withers. 234 illustrations. xxxiii + 381pp.
21031-6 Paperbound $2.50

ADVENTURES OF AN AFRICAN SLAVER, Theodore Canot. Edited by Brantz Mayer. A detailed portrayal of slavery and the slave trade, 1820-1840. Canot, an established trader along the African coast, describes the slave economy of the African kingdoms, the treatment of captured negroes, the extensive journeys in the interior to gather slaves, slave revolts and their suppression, harems, bribes, and much more. Full and unabridged republication of 1854 edition. Introduction by Malcom Cowley. 16 illustrations. xvii + 448pp. 22456-2 Paperbound $3.50

MY BONDAGE AND MY FREEDOM, Frederick Douglass. Born and brought up in slavery, Douglass witnessed its horrors and experienced its cruelties, but went on to become one of the most outspoken forces in the American anti-slavery movement. Considered the best of his autobiographies, this book graphically describes the in-human treatment of slaves, its effects on slave owners and slave families, and how Douglass's determination led him to a new life. Unaltered reprint of 1st (1855) edition. xxxii + 464pp. 22457-0 Paperbound $2.50

THE INDIANS' BOOK, recorded and edited by Natalie Curtis. Lore, music, narratives, dozens of drawings by Indians themselves from an authoritative and important survey of native culture among Plains, Southwestern, Lake and Pueblo Indians. Standard work in popular ethnomusicology. 149 songs in full notation. 23 draw-ings, 23 photos. xxxi + 584pp. $6\frac{5}{8}$ x $9\frac{3}{8}$. 21939-9 Paperbound $4.50

DICTIONARY OF AMERICAN PORTRAITS, edited by Hayward and Blanche Cirker. 4024 portraits of 4000 most important Americans, colonial days to 1905 (with a few important categories, like Presidents, to present). Pioneers, explorers, colonial figures, U. S. officials, politicians, writers, military and naval men, scientists, inven-tors, manufacturers, jurists, actors, historians, educators, notorious figures, Indian chiefs, etc. All authentic contemporary likenesses. The only work of its kind in existence; supplements all biographical sources for libraries. Indispensable to any-one working with American history. 8,000-item classified index, finding lists, other aids. xiv + 756pp. $9\frac{1}{4}$ x $12\frac{3}{4}$. 21823-6 Clothbound $30.00

TRITTON'S GUIDE TO BETTER WINE AND BEER MAKING FOR BEGINNERS, S. M. Tritton. All you need to know to make family-sized quantities of over 100 types of grape, fruit, herb and vegetable wines; as well as beers, mead, cider, etc. Com-plete recipes, advice as to equipment, procedures such as fermenting, bottling, and storing wines. Recipes given in British, U. S., and metric measures. Accompanying booklet lists sources in U. S. A. where ingredients may be bought, and additional information. 11 illustrations. 157pp. $5\frac{5}{8}$ x $8\frac{1}{8}$.
(USO) 22090-7 Clothbound $3.50

GARDENING WITH HERBS FOR FLAVOR AND FRAGRANCE, Helen M. Fox. How to grow herbs in your own garden, how to use them in your cooking (over 55 recipes included), legends and myths associated with each species, uses in medicine, per-fumes, etc.—these are elements of one of the few books written especially for Amer-ican herb fanciers. Guides you step-by-step from soil preparation to harvesting and storage for each type of herb. 12 drawings by Louise Mansfield. xiv + 334pp. 22540-2 Paperbound $2.50

THE ARCHITECTURE OF COUNTRY HOUSES, Andrew J. Downing. Together with Vaux's *Villas and Cottages* this is the basic book for Hudson River Gothic architecture of the middle Victorian period. Full, sound discussions of general aspects of housing, architecture, style, decoration, furnishing, together with scores of detailed house plans, illustrations of specific buildings, accompanied by full text. Perhaps the most influential single American architectural book. 1850 edition. Introduction by J. Stewart Johnson. 321 figures, 34 architectural designs. xvi + 560pp.

22003-6 Paperbound $4.00

LOST EXAMPLES OF COLONIAL ARCHITECTURE, John Mead Howells. Full-page photographs of buildings that have disappeared or been so alteɪed as to be denatured, including many designed by major early American architects. 245 plates. xvii + 248pp. 7⅞ x 10¾. 21143-6 Paperbound $3.00

DOMESTIC ARCHITECTURE OF THE AMERICAN COLONIES AND OF THE EARLY REPUBLIC, Fiske Kimball. Foremost architect and restorer of Williamsburg and Monticello covers nearly 200 homes between 1620-1825. Architectural details, construction, style features, special fixtures, floor plans, etc. Generally considered finest work in its area. 219 illustrations of houses, doorways, windows, capital mantels. xx + 314pp. 7⅞ x 10¾. 21743-4 Paperbound $3.50

EARLY AMERICAN ROOMS: 1650-1858, edited by Russell Hawes Kettell. Tour of 12 rooms, each representative of a different era in American history and each furnished, decorated, designed and occupied in the style of the era. 72 plans and elevations, 8-page color section, etc., show fabrics, wall papers, arrangements, etc. Full descriptive text. xvii + 200pp. of text. 8⅜ x 11¼.

21633-0 Paperbound $5.00

THE FITZWILLIAM VIRGINAL BOOK, edited by J. Fuller Maitland and W. B. Squire. Full modern printing of famous early 17th-century ms. volume of 300 works by Morley, Byrd, Bull, Gibbons, etc. For piano or other modern keyboard instrument; easy to read format. xxxvi + 938pp. 8⅜ x 11.

21068-5, 21069-3 Two volumes, Paperbound $8.00

HARPSICHORD MUSIC, Johann Sebastian Bach. Bach Gesellschaft edition. A rich selection of Bach's masterpieces for the harpsichord: the six English Suites, six French Suites, the six Partitas (Clavierübung part I), the Goldberg Variations (Clavierübung part IV), the fifteen Two-Part Inventions and the fifteen Three-Part Sinfonias. Clearly reproduced on large sheets with ample margins; eminently playable. vi + 312pp. 8⅛ x 11. 22360-4 Paperbound $5.00

THE MUSIC OF BACH: AN INTRODUCTION, Charles Sanford Terry. A fine, nontechnical introduction to Bach's music, both instrumental and vocal. Covers organ music, chamber music, passion music, other types. Analyzes themes, developments, innovations. x + 114pp. 21075-8 Paperbound $1.25

BEETHOVEN AND HIS NINE SYMPHONIES, Sir George Grove. Noted British musicologist provides best history, analysis, commentary on symphonies. Very thorough, rigorously accurate; necessary to both advanced student and amateur music lover. 436 musical passages. vii + 407 pp. 20334-4 Paperbound $2.25

JIM WHITEWOLF: THE LIFE OF A KIOWA APACHE INDIAN, Charles S. Brant, editor. Spans transition between native life and acculturation period, 1880 on. Kiowa culture, personal life pattern, religion and the supernatural, the Ghost Dance, breakdown in the White Man's world, similar material. 1 map. xii + 144pp.
22015-X Paperbound $1.75

THE NATIVE TRIBES OF CENTRAL AUSTRALIA, Baldwin Spencer and F. J. Gillen. Basic book in anthropology, devoted to full coverage of the Arunta and Warramunga tribes; the source for knowledge about kinship systems, material and social culture, religion, etc. Still unsurpassed. 121 photographs, 89 drawings. xviii + 669pp.
21775-2 Paperbound $5.00

MALAY MAGIC, Walter W. Skeat. Classic (1900); still the definitive work on the folklore and popular religion of the Malay peninsula. Describes marriage rites, birth spirits and ceremonies, medicine, dances, games, war and weapons, etc. Extensive quotes from original sources, many magic charms translated into English. 35 illustrations. Preface by Charles Otto Blagden. xxiv + 685pp.
21760-4 Paperbound $4.00

HEAVENS ON EARTH: UTOPIAN COMMUNITIES IN AMERICA, 1680-1880, Mark Holloway. The finest nontechnical account of American utopias, from the early Woman in the Wilderness, Ephrata, Rappites to the enormous mid 19th-century efflorescence; Shakers, New Harmony, Equity Stores, Fourier's Phalanxes, Oneida, Amana, Fruitlands, etc. "Entertaining and very instructive." *Times Literary Supplement*. 15 illustrations. 246pp.
21593-8 Paperbound $2.00

LONDON LABOUR AND THE LONDON POOR, Henry Mayhew. Earliest (c. 1850) sociological study in English, describing myriad subcultures of London poor. Particularly remarkable for the thousands of pages of direct testimony taken from the lips of London prostitutes, thieves, beggars, street sellers, chimney-sweepers, street-musicians, "mudlarks," "pure-finders," rag-gatherers, "running-patterers," dock laborers, cab-men, and hundreds of others, quoted directly in this massive work. An extraordinarily vital picture of London emerges. 110 illustrations. Total of lxxvi + 1951pp. 6⅝ x 10.
21934-8, 21935-6, 21936-4, 21937-2 Four volumes, Paperbound $14.00

HISTORY OF THE LATER ROMAN EMPIRE, J. B. Bury. Eloquent, detailed reconstruction of Western and Byzantine Roman Empire by a major historian, from the death of Theodosius I (395 A.D.) to the death of Justinian (565). Extensive quotations from contemporary sources; full coverage of important Roman and foreign figures of the time. xxxiv + 965pp. 21829-5 Record, book, album. Monaural. $3.50

AN INTELLECTUAL AND CULTURAL HISTORY OF THE WESTERN WORLD, Harry Elmer Barnes. Monumental study, tracing the development of the accomplishments that make up human culture. Every aspect of man's achievement surveyed from its origins in the Paleolithic to the present day (1964); social structures, ideas, economic systems, art, literature, technology, mathematics, the sciences, medicine, religion, jurisprudence, etc. Evaluations of the contributions of scores of great men. 1964 edition, revised and edited by scholars in the many fields represented. Total of xxix + 1381pp. 21275-0, 21276-9, 21277-7 Three volumes, Paperbound $7.75

ALPHABETS AND ORNAMENTS, Ernst Lehner. Well-known pictorial source for decorative alphabets, script examples, cartouches, frames, decorative title pages, calligraphic initials, borders, similar material. 14th to 19th century, mostly European. Useful in almost any graphic arts designing, varied styles. 750 illustrations. 256pp. 7 x 10. 21905-4 Paperbound $4.00

PAINTING: A CREATIVE APPROACH, Norman Colquhoun. For the beginner simple guide provides an instructive approach to painting: major stumbling blocks for beginner; overcoming them, technical points; paints and pigments; oil painting; watercolor and other media and color. New section on "plastic" paints. Glossary. Formerly Paint Your Own Pictures. 221pp. 22000-1 Paperbound $1.75

THE ENJOYMENT AND USE OF COLOR, Walter Sargent. Explanation of the relations between colors themselves and between colors in nature and art, including hundreds of little-known facts about color values, intensities, effects of high and low illumination, complementary colors. Many practical hints for painters, references to great masters. 7 color plates, 29 illustrations. x + 274pp. 20944-X Paperbound $2.75

THE NOTEBOOKS OF LEONARDO DA VINCI, compiled and edited by Jean Paul Richter. 1566 extracts from original manuscripts reveal the full range of Leonardo's versatile genius: all his writings on painting, sculpture, architecture, anatomy, astronomy, geography, topography, physiology, mining, music, etc., in both Italian and English, with 186 plates of manuscript pages and more than 500 additional drawings. Includes studies for the Last Supper, the lost Sforza monument, and other works. Total of xlvii + 866pp. 7⅞ x 10¾. 22572-0, 22573-9 Two volumes, Paperbound $10.00

MONTGOMERY WARD CATALOGUE OF 1895. Tea gowns, yards of flannel and pillow-case lace, stereoscopes, books of gospel hymns, the New Improved Singer Sewing Machine, side saddles, milk skimmers, straight-edged razors, high-button shoes, spittoons, and on and on . . . listing some 25,000 items, practically all illustrated. Essential to the shoppers of the 1890's, it is our truest record of the spirit of the period. Unaltered reprint of Issue No. 57, Spring and Summer 1895. Introduction by Boris Emmet. Innumerable illustrations. xiii + 624pp. 8½ x 11⅝. 22377-9 Paperbound $6.95

THE CRYSTAL PALACE EXHIBITION ILLUSTRATED CATALOGUE (LONDON, 1851). One of the wonders of the modern world—the Crystal Palace Exhibition in which all the nations of the civilized world exhibited their achievements in the arts and sciences—presented in an equally important illustrated catalogue. More than 1700 items pictured with accompanying text—ceramics, textiles, cast-iron work, carpets, pianos, sleds, razors, wall-papers, billiard tables, beehives, silverware and hundreds of other artifacts—represent the focal point of Victorian culture in the Western World. Probably the largest collection of Victorian decorative art ever assembled—indispensable for antiquarians and designers. Unabridged republication of the Art-Journal Catalogue of the Great Exhibition of 1851, with all terminal essays. New introduction by John Gloag, F.S.A. xxxiv + 426pp. 9 x 12. 22503-8 Paperbound $4.50

VISUAL ILLUSIONS: THEIR CAUSES, CHARACTERISTICS, AND APPLICATIONS, Matthew Luckiesh. Thorough description and discussion of optical illusion, geometric and perspective, particularly; size and shape distortions, illusions of color, of motion; natural illusions; use of illusion in art and magic, industry, etc. Most useful today with op art, also for classical art. Scores of effects illustrated. Introduction by William H. Ittleson. 100 illustrations. xxi + 252pp.

21530-X Paperbound $2.00

A HANDBOOK OF ANATOMY FOR ART STUDENTS, Arthur Thomson. Thorough, virtually exhaustive coverage of skeletal structure, musculature, etc. Full text, supplemented by anatomical diagrams and drawings and by photographs of undraped figures. Unique in its comparison of male and female forms, pointing out differences of contour, texture, form. 211 figures, 40 drawings, 86 photographs. xx + 459pp. 5⅜ x 8⅜.

21163-0 Paperbound $3.50

150 MASTERPIECES OF DRAWING, Selected by Anthony Toney. Full page reproductions of drawings from the early 16th to the end of the 18th century, all beautifully reproduced: Rembrandt, Michelangelo, Dürer, Fragonard, Urs, Graf, Wouwerman, many others. First-rate browsing book, model book for artists. xviii + 150pp. 8⅜ x 11¼.

21032-4 Paperbound $2.50

THE LATER WORK OF AUBREY BEARDSLEY, Aubrey Beardsley. Exotic, erotic, ironic masterpieces in full maturity: Comedy Ballet, Venus and Tannhauser, Pierrot, Lysistrata, Rape of the Lock, Savoy material, Ali Baba, Volpone, etc. This material revolutionized the art world, and is still powerful, fresh, brilliant. With *The Early Work*, all Beardsley's finest work. 174 plates, 2 in color. xiv + 176pp. 8⅛ x 11.

21817-1 Paperbound $3.00

DRAWINGS OF REMBRANDT, Rembrandt van Rijn. Complete reproduction of fabulously rare edition by Lippmann and Hofstede de Groot, completely reedited, updated, improved by Prof. Seymour Slive, Fogg Museum. Portraits, Biblical sketches, landscapes, Oriental types, nudes, episodes from classical mythology—All Rembrandt's fertile genius. Also selection of drawings by his pupils and followers. "Stunning volumes," *Saturday Review*. 550 illustrations. lxxviii + 552pp. 9⅛ x 12¼.

21485-0, 21486-9 Two volumes, Paperbound $7.00

THE DISASTERS OF WAR, Francisco Goya. One of the masterpieces of Western civilization—83 etchings that record Goya's shattering, bitter reaction to the Napoleonic war that swept through Spain after the insurrection of 1808 and to war in general. Reprint of the first edition, with three additional plates from Boston's Museum of Fine Arts. All plates facsimile size. Introduction by Philip Hofer, Fogg Museum. v + 97pp. 9⅜ x 8¼.

21872-4 Paperbound $2.00

GRAPHIC WORKS OF ODILON REDON. Largest collection of Redon's graphic works ever assembled: 172 lithographs, 28 etchings and engravings, 9 drawings. These include some of his most famous works. All the plates from *Odilon Redon: oeuvre graphique complet*, plus additional plates. New introduction and caption translations by Alfred Werner. 209 illustrations. xxvii + 209pp. 9⅛ x 12¼.

21966-8 Paperbound $4.00

INCIDENTS OF TRAVEL IN YUCATAN, John L. Stephens. Classic (1843) exploration of jungles of Yucatan, looking for evidences of Maya civilization. Stephens found many ruins; comments on travel adventures, Mexican and Indian culture. 127 striking illustrations by F. Catherwood. Total of 669 pp.
20926-1, 20927-X Two volumes, Paperbound $5.00

INCIDENTS OF TRAVEL IN CENTRAL AMERICA, CHIAPAS, AND YUCATAN, John L. Stephens. An exciting travel journal and an important classic of archeology. Narrative relates his almost single-handed discovery of the Mayan culture, and exploration of the ruined cities of Copan, Palenque, Utatlan and others; the monuments they dug from the earth, the temples buried in the jungle, the customs of poverty-stricken Indians living a stone's throw from the ruined palaces. 115 drawings by F. Catherwood. Portrait of Stephens. xii + 812pp.
22404-X, 22405-8 Two volumes, Paperbound $6.00

A NEW VOYAGE ROUND THE WORLD, William Dampier. Late 17-century naturalist joined the pirates of the Spanish Main to gather information; remarkably vivid account of buccaneers, pirates; detailed, accurate account of botany, zoology, ethnography of lands visited. Probably the most important early English voyage, enormous implications for British exploration, trade, colonial policy. Also most interesting reading. Argonaut edition, introduction by Sir Albert Gray. New introduction by Percy Adams. 6 plates, 7 illustrations. xlvii + 376pp. 6½ x 9¼.
21900-3 Paperbound $3.00

INTERNATIONAL AIRLINE PHRASE BOOK IN SIX LANGUAGES, Joseph W. Bátor. Important phrases and sentences in English paralleled with French, German, Portuguese, Italian, Spanish equivalents, covering all possible airport-travel situations; created for airline personnel as well as tourist by Language Chief, Pan American Airlines. xiv + 204pp.
22017-6 Paperbound $2.00

STAGE COACH AND TAVERN DAYS, Alice Morse Earle. Detailed, lively account of the early days of taverns; their uses and importance in the social, political and military life; furnishings and decorations; locations; food and drink; tavern signs, etc. Second half covers every aspect of early travel; the roads, coaches, drivers, etc. Nostalgic, charming, packed with fascinating material. 157 illustrations, mostly photographs. xiv + 449pp.
22518-6 Paperbound $4.00

NORSE DISCOVERIES AND EXPLORATIONS IN NORTH AMERICA, Hjalmar R. Holand. The perplexing Kensington Stone, found in Minnesota at the end of the 19th century. Is it a record of a Scandinavian expedition to North America in the 14th century? Or is it one of the most successful hoaxes in history. A scientific detective investigation. Formerly *Westward from Vinland.* 31 photographs, 17 figures. x + 354pp.
22014-1 Paperbound $2.75

A BOOK OF OLD MAPS, compiled and edited by Emerson D. Fite and Archibald Freeman. 74 old maps offer an unusual survey of the discovery, settlement and growth of America down to the close of the Revolutionary war: maps showing Norse settlements in Greenland, the explorations of Columbus, Verrazano, Cabot, Champlain, Joliet, Drake, Hudson, etc., campaigns of Revolutionary war battles, and much more. Each map is accompanied by a brief historical essay. xvi + 299pp. 11 x 13¾.
22084-2 Paperbound $6.00

DESIGN BY ACCIDENT; A BOOK OF "ACCIDENTAL EFFECTS" FOR ARTISTS AND DESIGNERS, James F. O'Brien. Create your own unique, striking, imaginative effects by "controlled accident" interaction of materials: paints and lacquers, oil and water based paints, splatter, crackling materials, shatter, similar items. Everything you do will be different; first book on this limitless art, so useful to both fine artist and commercial artist. Full instructions. 192 plates showing "accidents," 8 in color. viii + 215pp. 8⅜ x 11¼. 21942-9 Paperbound $3.50

THE BOOK OF SIGNS, Rudolf Koch. Famed German type designer draws 493 beautiful symbols: religious, mystical, alchemical, imperial, property marks, runes, etc. Remarkable fusion of traditional and modern. Good for suggestions of timelessness, smartness, modernity. Text. vi + 104pp. 6⅛ x 9¼. 20162-7 Paperbound $1.25

HISTORY OF INDIAN AND INDONESIAN ART, Ananda K. Coomaraswamy. An unabridged republication of one of the finest books by a great scholar in Eastern art. Rich in descriptive material, history, social backgrounds; Sunga reliefs, Rajput paintings, Gupta temples, Burmese frescoes, textiles, jewelry, sculpture, etc. 400 photos. viii + 423pp. 6⅜ x 9¾. 21436-2 Paperbound $4.00

PRIMITIVE ART, Franz Boas. America's foremost anthropologist surveys textiles, ceramics, woodcarving, basketry, metalwork, etc.; patterns, technology, creation of symbols, style origins. All areas of world, but very full on Northwest Coast Indians. More than 350 illustrations of baskets, boxes, totem poles, weapons, etc. 378 pp. 20025-6 Paperbound $3.00

THE GENTLEMAN AND CABINET MAKER'S DIRECTOR, Thomas Chippendale. Full reprint (third edition, 1762) of most influential furniture book of all time, by master cabinetmaker. 200 plates, illustrating chairs, sofas, mirrors, tables, cabinets, plus 24 photographs of surviving pieces. Biographical introduction by N. Bienenstock. vi + 249pp. 9⅞ x 12¾. 21601-2 Paperbound $4.00

AMERICAN ANTIQUE FURNITURE, Edgar G. Miller, Jr. The basic coverage of all American furniture before 1840. Individual chapters cover type of furniture—clocks, tables, sideboards, etc.—chronologically, with inexhaustible wealth of data. More than 2100 photographs, all identified, commented on. Essential to all early American collectors. Introduction by H. E. Keyes. vi + 1106pp. 7⅞ x 10¾. 21599-7, 21600-4 Two volumes, Paperbound $11.00

PENNSYLVANIA DUTCH AMERICAN FOLK ART, Henry J. Kauffman. 279 photos, 28 drawings of tulipware, Fraktur script, painted tinware, toys, flowered furniture, quilts, samplers, hex signs, house interiors, etc. Full descriptive text. Excellent for tourist, rewarding for designer, collector. Map. 146pp. 7⅞ x 10¾. 21205-X Paperbound $2.50

EARLY NEW ENGLAND GRAVESTONE RUBBINGS, Edmund V. Gillon, Jr. 43 photographs, 226 carefully reproduced rubbings show heavily symbolic, sometimes macabre early gravestones, up to early 19th century. Remarkable early American primitive art, occasionally strikingly beautiful; always powerful. Text. xxvi + 207pp. 8⅜ x 11¼. 21380-3 Paperbound $3.50

FUNDAMENTAL FORMULAS OF PHYSICS, edited by Donald H. Menzel. Most useful reference and study work, ranges from simplest to most highly sophisticated operations. Individual chapters, with full texts explaining formulae, prepared by leading authorities cover basic mathematical formulas, statistics, nomograms, physical constants, classical mechanics, special theory of relativity, general theory of relativity, hydrodynamics and aerodynamics, boundary value problems in mathematical physics, heat and thermodynamics, statistical mechanics, kinetic theory of gases, viscosity, thermal conduction, electromagnetism, electronics, acoustics, geometrical optics, physical optics, electron optics, molecular spectra, atomic spectra, quantum mechanics, nuclear theory, cosmic rays and high energy phenomena, particle accelerators, solid state, magnetism, etc. Special chapters also cover physical chemistry, astrophysics, celestian mechanics, meteorology, and biophysics. Indispensable part of library of every scientist. Total of xli + 787pp.
60595-7, 60596-5 Two volumes, Paperbound $5.00

INTRODUCTION TO EXPERIMENTAL PHYSICS, William B. Fretter. Detailed coverage of techniques and equipment: measurements, vacuum tubes, pulse circuits, rectifiers, oscillators, magnet design, particle counters, nuclear emulsions, cloud chambers, accelerators, spectroscopy, magnetic resonance, x-ray diffraction, low temperature, etc. One of few books to cover laboratory hazards, design of exploratory experiments, measurements. 298 figures. xii + 349pp.
(EUK) 61890-0 Paperbound $2.50

CONCEPTS AND METHODS OF THEORETICAL PHYSICS, Robert Bruce Lindsay. Introduction to methods of theoretical physics, emphasizing development of physical concepts and analysis of methods. Part I proceeds from single particle to collections of particles to statistical method. Part II covers application of field concept to material and non-material media. Numerous exercises and examples. 76 illustrations. x + 515pp.
62354-8 Paperbound $4.00

AN ELEMENTARY TREATISE ON THEORETICAL MECHANICS, Sir James Jeans. Great scientific expositor in remarkably clear presentation of basic classical material: rest, motion, forces acting on particle, statics, motion of particle under variable force, motion of rigid bodies, coordinates, etc. Emphasizes explanation of fundamental physical principles rather than mathematics or applications. Hundreds of problems worked in text. 156 figures. x + 364pp. 61839-0 Paperbound $2.50

THEORETICAL MECHANICS: AN INTRODUCTION TO MATHEMATICAL PHYSICS, Joseph S. Ames and Francis D. Murnaghan. Mathematically rigorous introduction to vector and tensor methods, dynamics, harmonic vibrations, gyroscopic theory, principle of least constraint, Lorentz-Einstein transformation. 159 problems; many fully-worked examples. 39 figures. ix + 462pp. 60461-6 Paperbound $3.00

THE PRINCIPLE OF RELATIVITY, Albert Einstein, Hendrick A. Lorentz, Hermann Minkowski and Hermann Weyl. Eleven original papers on the special and general theory of relativity, all unabridged. Seven papers by Einstein, two by Lorentz, one each by Minkowski and Weyl. "A thrill to read again the original papers by these giants," *School Science and Mathematics*. Translated by W. Perret and G. B. Jeffery. Notes by A. Sommerfeld. 7 diagrams. viii + 216pp.
60081-5 Paperbound $2.00

THE PHILOSOPHY OF THE UPANISHADS, Paul Deussen. Clear, detailed statement of upanishadic system of thought, generally considered among best available. History of these works, full exposition of system emergent from them, parallel concepts in the West. Translated by A. S. Geden. xiv + 429pp.

21616-0 Paperbound $3.00

LANGUAGE, TRUTH AND LOGIC, Alfred J. Ayer. Famous, remarkably clear introduction to the Vienna and Cambridge schools of Logical Positivism; function of philosophy, elimination of metaphysical thought, nature of analysis, similar topics. "Wish I had written it myself," Bertrand Russell. 2nd, 1946 edition. 160pp.

20010-8 Paperbound $1.35

THE GUIDE FOR THE PERPLEXED, Moses Maimonides. Great classic of medieval Judaism, major attempt to reconcile revealed religion (Pentateuch, commentaries) and Aristotelian philosophy. Enormously important in all Western thought. Unabridged Friedländer translation. 50-page introduction. lix + 414pp.

(USO) 20351-4 Paperbound $2.50

OCCULT AND SUPERNATURAL PHENOMENA, D. H. Rawcliffe. Full, serious study of the most persistent delusions of mankind: crystal gazing, mediumistic trance, stigmata, lycanthropy, fire walking, dowsing, telepathy, ghosts, ESP, etc., and their relation to common forms of abnormal psychology. Formerly *Illusions and Delusions of the Supernatural and the Occult.* iii + 551pp. 20503-7 Paperbound $3.50

THE EGYPTIAN BOOK OF THE DEAD: THE PAPYRUS OF ANI, E. A. Wallis Budge. Full hieroglyphic text, interlinear transliteration of sounds, word for word translation, then smooth, connected translation; Theban recension. Basic work in Ancient Egyptian civilization; now even more significant than ever for historical importance, dilation of consciousness, etc. clvi + 377pp. 6½ x 9¼.

21866-X Paperbound $3.95

PSYCHOLOGY OF MUSIC, Carl E. Seashore. Basic, thorough survey of everything known about psychology of music up to 1940's; essential reading for psychologists, musicologists. Physical acoustics; auditory apparatus; relationship of physical sound to perceived sound; role of the mind in sorting, altering, suppressing, creating sound sensations; musical learning, testing for ability, absolute pitch, other topics. Records of Caruso, Menuhin analyzed. 88 figures. xix + 408pp.

21851-1 Paperbound $2.75

THE I CHING (THE BOOK OF CHANGES), translated by James Legge. Complete translated text plus appendices by Confucius, of perhaps the most penetrating divination book ever compiled. Indispensable to all study of early Oriental civilizations. 3 plates. xxiii + 448pp. 21062-6 Paperbound $3.00

THE UPANISHADS, translated by Max Müller. Twelve classical upanishads: Chandogya, Kena, Aitareya, Kaushitaki, Isa, Katha, Mundaka, Taittiriyaka, Brhadaranyaka, Svetasvatara, Prasna, Maitriyana. 160-page introduction, analysis by Prof. Müller. Total of 826pp. 20398-0, 20399-9 Two volumes, Paperbound $5.00

AGAINST THE GRAIN (A REBOURS), Joris K. Huysmans. Filled with weird images, evidences of a bizarre imagination, exotic experiments with hallucinatory drugs, rich tastes and smells and the diversions of its sybarite hero Duc Jean des Esseintes, this classic novel pushed 19th-century literary decadence to its limits. Full unabridged edition. Do not confuse this with abridged editions generally sold. Introduction by Havelock Ellis. xlix + 206pp. 22190-3 Paperbound $2.00

VARIORUM SHAKESPEARE: HAMLET. Edited by Horace H. Furness; a landmark of American scholarship. Exhaustive footnotes and appendices treat all doubtful words and phrases, as well as suggested critical emendations throughout the play's history. First volume contains editor's own text, collated with all Quartos and Folios. Second volume contains full first Quarto, translations of Shakespeare's sources (Belleforest, and Saxo Grammaticus), Der Bestrafte Brudermord, and many essays on critical and historical points of interest by major authorities of past and present. Includes details of staging and costuming over the years. By far the best edition available for serious students of Shakespeare. Total of xx + 905pp. 21004-9, 21005-7, 2 volumes, Paperbound $7.00

A LIFE OF WILLIAM SHAKESPEARE, Sir Sidney Lee. This is the standard life of Shakespeare, summarizing everything known about Shakespeare and his plays. Incredibly rich in material, broad in coverage, clear and judicious, it has served thousands as the best introduction to Shakespeare. 1931 edition. 9 plates. xxix + 792pp. (USO) 21967-4 Paperbound $3.75

MASTERS OF THE DRAMA, John Gassner. Most comprehensive history of the drama in print, covering every tradition from Greeks to modern Europe and America, including India, Far East, etc. Covers more than 800 dramatists, 2000 plays, with biographical material, plot summaries, theatre history, criticism, etc. "Best of its kind in English," New Republic. 77 illustrations. xxii + 890pp. 20100-7 Clothbound $8.50

THE EVOLUTION OF THE ENGLISH LANGUAGE, George McKnight. The growth of English, from the 14th century to the present. Unusual, non-technical account presents basic information in very interesting form: sound shifts, change in grammar and syntax, vocabulary growth, similar topics. Abundantly illustrated with quotations. Formerly Modern English in the Making. xii + 590pp. 21932-1 Paperbound $3.50

AN ETYMOLOGICAL DICTIONARY OF MODERN ENGLISH, Ernest Weekley. Fullest, richest work of its sort, by foremost British lexicographer. Detailed word histories, including many colloquial and archaic words; extensive quotations. Do not confuse this with the Concise Etymological Dictionary, which is much abridged. Total of xxvii + 830pp. 6½ x 9¼. 21873-2, 21874-0 Two volumes, Paperbound $6.00

FLATLAND: A ROMANCE OF MANY DIMENSIONS, E. A. Abbott. Classic of science-fiction explores ramifications of life in a two-dimensional world, and what happens when a three-dimensional being intrudes. Amusing reading, but also useful as introduction to thought about hyperspace. Introduction by Banesh Hoffmann. 16 illustrations. xx + 103pp. 20001-9 Paperbound $1.00

THE PRINCIPLES OF PSYCHOLOGY, William James. The famous long course, complete and unabridged. Stream of thought, time perception, memory, experimental methods—these are only some of the concerns of a work that was years ahead of its time and still valid, interesting, useful. 94 figures. Total of xviii + 1391pp.
20381-6, 20382-4 Two volumes, Paperbound $8.00

THE STRANGE STORY OF THE QUANTUM, Banesh Hoffmann. Non-mathematical but thorough explanation of work of Planck, Einstein, Bohr, Pauli, de Broglie, Schrödinger, Heisenberg, Dirac, Feynman, etc. No technical background needed. "Of books attempting such an account, this is the best," Henry Margenau, Yale. 40-page "Postscript 1959." xii + 285pp. 20518-5 Paperbound $2.00

THE RISE OF THE NEW PHYSICS, A. d'Abro. Most thorough explanation in print of central core of mathematical physics, both classical and modern; from Newton to Dirac and Heisenberg. Both history and exposition; philosophy of science, causality, explanations of higher mathematics, analytical mechanics, electromagnetism, thermodynamics, phase rule, special and general relativity, matrices. No higher mathematics needed to follow exposition, though treatment is elementary to intermediate in level. Recommended to serious student who wishes verbal understanding. 97 illustrations. xvii + 982pp. 20003-5, 20004-3 Two volumes, Paperbound $6.00

GREAT IDEAS OF OPERATIONS RESEARCH, Jagjit Singh. Easily followed non-technical explanation of mathematical tools, aims, results: statistics, linear programming, game theory, queueing theory, Monte Carlo simulation, etc. Uses only elementary mathematics. Many case studies, several analyzed in detail. Clarity, breadth make this excellent for specialist in another field who wishes background. 41 figures. x + 228pp. 21886-4 Paperbound $2.50

GREAT IDEAS OF MODERN MATHEMATICS: THEIR NATURE AND USE, Jagjit Singh. Internationally famous expositor, winner of Unesco's Kalinga Award for science popularization explains verbally such topics as differential equations, matrices, groups, sets, transformations, mathematical logic and other important modern mathematics, as well as use in physics, astrophysics, and similar fields. Superb exposition for layman, scientist in other areas. viii + 312pp.
20587-8 Paperbound $2.50

GREAT IDEAS IN INFORMATION THEORY, LANGUAGE AND CYBERNETICS, Jagjit Singh. The analog and digital computers, how they work, how they are like and unlike the human brain, the men who developed them, their future applications, computer terminology. An essential book for today, even for readers with little math. Some mathematical demonstrations included for more advanced readers. 118 figures. Tables. ix + 338pp. 21694-2 Paperbound $2.50

CHANCE, LUCK AND STATISTICS, Horace C. Levinson. Non-mathematical presentation of fundamentals of probability theory and science of statistics and their applications. Games of chance, betting odds, misuse of statistics, normal and skew distributions, birth rates, stock speculation, insurance. Enlarged edition. Formerly "The Science of Chance." xiii + 357pp. 21007-3 Paperbound $2.50

JOHANN SEBASTIAN BACH, Philipp Spitta. One of the great classics of musicology, this definitive analysis of Bach's music (and life) has never been surpassed. Lucid, nontechnical analyses of hundreds of pieces (30 pages devoted to St. Matthew Passion, 26 to B Minor Mass). Also includes major analysis of 18th-century music. 450 musical examples. 40-page musical supplement. Total of xx + 1799pp.
(EUK) 22278-0, 22279-9 Two volumes, Clothbound $15.00

MOZART AND HIS PIANO CONCERTOS, Cuthbert Girdlestone. The only full-length study of an important area of Mozart's creativity. Provides detailed analyses of all 23 concertos, traces inspirational sources. 417 musical examples. Second edition. 509pp. (USO) 21271-8 Paperbound $3.50

THE PERFECT WAGNERITE: A COMMENTARY ON THE NIBLUNG'S RING, George Bernard Shaw. Brilliant and still relevant criticism in remarkable essays on Wagner's Ring cycle, Shaw's ideas on political and social ideology behind the plots, role of Leitmotifs, vocal requisites, etc. Prefaces. xxi + 136pp.
21707-8 Paperbound $1.50

DON GIOVANNI, W. A. Mozart. Complete libretto, modern English translation; biographies of composer and librettist; accounts of early performances and critical reaction. Lavishly illustrated. All the material you need to understand and appreciate this great work. Dover Opera Guide and Libretto Series; translated and introduced by Ellen Bleiler. 92 illustrations. 209pp.
21134-7 Paperbound $1.50

HIGH FIDELITY SYSTEMS: A LAYMAN'S GUIDE, Roy F. Allison. All the basic information you need for setting up your own audio system: high fidelity and stereo record players, tape records, F.M. Connections, adjusting tone arm, cartridge, checking needle alignment, positioning speakers, phasing speakers, adjusting hums, trouble-shooting, maintenance, and similar topics. Enlarged 1965 edition. More than 50 charts, diagrams, photos. iv + 91pp. 21514-8 Paperbound $1.25

REPRODUCTION OF SOUND, Edgar Villchur. Thorough coverage for laymen of high fidelity systems, reproducing systems in general, needles, amplifiers, preamps, loudspeakers, feedback, explaining physical background. "A rare talent for making technicalities vividly comprehensible," R. Darrell, *High Fidelity*. 69 figures. iv + 92pp. 21515-6 Paperbound $1.25

HEAR ME TALKIN' TO YA: THE STORY OF JAZZ AS TOLD BY THE MEN WHO MADE IT, Nat Shapiro and Nat Hentoff. Louis Armstrong, Fats Waller, Jo Jones, Clarence Williams, Billy Holiday, Duke Ellington, Jelly Roll Morton and dozens of other jazz greats tell how it was in Chicago's South Side, New Orleans, depression Harlem and the modern West Coast as jazz was born and grew. xvi + 429pp.
21726-4 Paperbound $2.50

FABLES OF AESOP, translated by Sir Roger L'Estrange. A reproduction of the very rare 1931 Paris edition; a selection of the most interesting fables, together with 50 imaginative drawings by Alexander Calder. v + 128pp. 6½x9¼.
21780-9 Paperbound $1.50

LAST AND FIRST MEN AND STAR MAKER, TWO SCIENCE FICTION NOVELS, Olaf Stapledon. Greatest future histories in science fiction. In the first, human intelligence is the "hero," through strange paths of evolution, interplanetary invasions, incredible technologies, near extinctions and reemergences. Star Maker describes the quest of a band of star rovers for intelligence itself, through time and space: weird inhuman civilizations, crustacean minds, symbiotic worlds, etc. Complete, unabridged. v + 438pp.   21962-3 Paperbound $2.50

THREE PROPHETIC NOVELS, H. G. WELLS. Stages of a consistently planned future for mankind. *When the Sleeper Wakes,* and *A Story of the Days to Come,* anticipate *Brave New World* and *1984,* in the 21st Century; *The Time Machine,* only complete version in print, shows farther future and the end of mankind. All show Wells's greatest gifts as storyteller and novelist. Edited by E. F. Bleiler. x + 335pp.   (USO) 20605-X Paperbound $2.25

THE DEVIL'S DICTIONARY, Ambrose Bierce. America's own Oscar Wilde— Ambrose Bierce—offers his barbed iconoclastic wisdom in over 1,000 definitions hailed by H. L. Mencken as "some of the most gorgeous witticisms in the English language." 145pp.   20487-1 Paperbound $1.25

MAX AND MORITZ, Wilhelm Busch. Great children's classic, father of comic strip, of two bad boys, Max and Moritz. Also Ker and Plunk (Plisch und Plumm), Cat and Mouse, Deceitful Henry, Ice-Peter, The Boy and the Pipe, and five other pieces. Original German, with English translation. Edited by H. Arthur Klein; translations by various hands and H. Arthur Klein. vi + 216pp.
20181-3 Paperbound $2.00

PIGS IS PIGS AND OTHER FAVORITES, Ellis Parker Butler. The title story is one of the best humor short stories, as Mike Flannery obfuscates biology and English. Also included, That Pup of Murchison's, The Great American Pie Company, and Perkins of Portland. 14 illustrations. v + 109pp.   21532-6 Paperbound $1.00

THE PETERKIN PAPERS, Lucretia P. Hale. It takes genius to be as stupidly mad as the Peterkins, as they decide to become wise, celebrate the "Fourth," keep a cow, and otherwise strain the resources of the Lady from Philadelphia. Basic book of American humor. 153 illustrations. 219pp.   20794-3 Paperbound $1.50

PERRAULT'S FAIRY TALES, translated by A. E. Johnson and S. R. Littlewood, with 34 full-page illustrations by Gustave Doré. All the original Perrault stories— Cinderella, Sleeping Beauty, Bluebeard, Little Red Riding Hood, Puss in Boots, Tom Thumb, etc.—with their witty verse morals and the magnificent illustrations of Doré. One of the five or six great books of European fairy tales. viii + 117pp. 8⅛ x 11.   22311-6 Paperbound $2.00

OLD HUNGARIAN FAIRY TALES, Baroness Orczy. Favorites translated and adapted by author of the *Scarlet Pimpernel.* Eight fairy tales include "The Suitors of Princess Fire-Fly," "The Twin Hunchbacks," "Mr. Cuttlefish's Love Story," and "The Enchanted Cat." This little volume of magic and adventure will captivate children as it has for generations. 90 drawings by Montagu Barstow. 96pp.
(USO) 22293-4 Paperbound $1.95

"ESSENTIAL GRAMMAR" SERIES

All you really need to know about modern, colloquial grammar. Many educational shortcuts help you learn faster, understand better. Detailed cognate lists teach you to recognize similarities between English and foreign words and roots—make learning vocabulary easy and interesting. Excellent for independent study or as a supplement to record courses.

ESSENTIAL FRENCH GRAMMAR, Seymour Resnick. 2500-item cognate list. 159pp.
(EBE) 20419-7 Paperbound $1.25

ESSENTIAL GERMAN GRAMMAR, Guy Stern and Everett F. Bleiler. Unusual shortcuts on noun declension, word order, compound verbs. 124pp.
(EBE) 20422-7 Paperbound $1.25

ESSENTIAL ITALIAN GRAMMAR, Olga Ragusa. 111pp.
(EBE) 20779-X Paperbound $1.25

ESSENTIAL JAPANESE GRAMMAR, Everett F. Bleiler. In Romaji transcription; no characters needed. Japanese grammar is regular and simple. 156pp.
21027-8 Paperbound $1.25

ESSENTIAL PORTUGUESE GRAMMAR, Alexander da R. Prista. vi + 114pp.
21650-0 Paperbound $1.35

ESSENTIAL SPANISH GRAMMAR, Seymour Resnick. 2500 word cognate list. 115pp.
(EBE) 20780-3 Paperbound $1.25

ESSENTIAL ENGLISH GRAMMAR, Philip Gucker. Combines best features of modern, functional and traditional approaches. For refresher, class use, home study. x + 177pp.
21649-7 Paperbound $1.25

A PHRASE AND SENTENCE DICTIONARY OF SPOKEN SPANISH. Prepared for U. S. War Department by U. S. linguists. As above, unit is idiom, phrase or sentence rather than word. English-Spanish and Spanish-English sections contain modern equivalents of over 18,000 sentences. Introduction and appendix as above. iv + 513pp.
20495-2 Paperbound $2.75

A PHRASE AND SENTENCE DICTIONARY OF SPOKEN RUSSIAN. Dictionary prepared for U. S. War Department by U. S. linguists. Basic unit is not the word, but the idiom, phrase or sentence. English-Russian and Russian-English sections contain modern equivalents for over 30,000 phrases. Grammatical introduction covers phonetics, writing, syntax. Appendix of word lists for food, numbers, geographical names, etc. vi + 573 pp. 6⅛ x 9¼.
20496-0 Paperbound $4.00

CONVERSATIONAL CHINESE FOR BEGINNERS, Morris Swadesh. Phonetic system, beginner's course in Pai Hua Mandarin Chinese covering most important, most useful speech patterns. Emphasis on modern colloquial usage. Formerly *Chinese in Your Pocket.* xvi + 158pp.
21123-1 Paperbound $1.75

THE PSYCHOLOGY OF INVENTION IN THE MATHEMATICAL FIELD, Jacques Hadamard. Important French mathematician examines psychological origin of ideas, role of the unconscious, importance of visualization, etc. Based on own experiences and reports by Dalton, Pascal, Descartes, Einstein, Poincaré, Helmholtz, etc. xiii + 145pp. 20107-4 Paperbound $1.50

INTRODUCTION TO CHEMICAL PHYSICS, John C. Slater. A work intended to bridge the gap between chemistry and physics. Text divided into three parts: Thermodynamics, Statistical Mechanics, and Kinetic Theory; Gases, Liquids and Solids; and Atoms, Molecules and the Structure of Matter, which form the basis of the approach. Level is advanced undergraduate to graduate, but theoretical physics held to minimum. 40 tables, 118 figures. xiv + 522pp. 62562-1 Paperbound $4.00

POLAR MOLECULES, Pieter Debye. Explains some of the Nobel Laureate's most important theories on dielectrics, including fundamental electrostatic field relations, polarization and molecular structure, measurements of polarity, constitution of simple polar molecules, anomalous dispersion for radio frequencies, electrical saturation effects, connections with quantum theory, energy levels and wave mechanics, rotating molecules. 33 figures. 172pp. 60064-5 Paperbound $2.00

THE CONTINUUM AND OTHER TYPES OF SERIAL ORDER, Edward V. Huntington. Highly respected systematic account of modern theory of the continuum as a type of serial order. Based on the Dedekind-Cantor ordinal theory. Mathematics held to an elementary level. vii + 82pp. 60130-7 Paperbound $1.00

CONTRIBUTIONS TO THE FOUNDING OF THE THEORY OF TRANSFINITE NUMBERS, Georg Cantor. The famous articles of 1895-1897 which founded a new branch of mathematics, translated with 82-page introduction by P. Jourdain. Not only a great classic but still one of the best introductions for the student. ix + 211pp. 60045-9 Paperbound $2.00

ESSAYS ON THE THEORY OF NUMBERS, Richard Dedekind. Two classic essays, on the theory of irrationals, giving an arithmetic and rigorous foundation; and on transfinite numbers and properties of natural numbers. Translated by W. W. Beman. iii + 115pp. 21010-3 Paperbound $1.50

GEOMETRY OF FOUR DIMENSIONS, H. P. Manning. Part verbal, part mathematical development of fourth dimensional geometry. Historical introduction. Detailed treatment is by synthetic method, approaching subject through Euclidean geometry. No knowledge of higher mathematics necessary. 76 figures. ix + 348pp. 60182-X Paperbound $3.00

AN INTRODUCTION TO THE GEOMETRY OF N DIMENSIONS, Duncan M. Y. Sommerville. The only work in English devoted to higher-dimensional geometry. Both metric and projective properties of n-dimensional geometry are covered. Covers fundamental ideas of incidence, parallelism, perpendicularity, angles between linear space, enumerative geometry, analytical geometry, polytopes, analysis situs, hyperspacial figures. 60 diagrams. xvii + 196pp. 60494-2 Paperbound $1.50

THE RED FAIRY BOOK, Andrew Lang. Lang's color fairy books have long been children's favorites. This volume includes Rapunzel, Jack and the Bean-stalk and 35 other stories, familiar and unfamiliar. 4 plates, 93 illustrations x + 367pp.
21673-X Paperbound $2.50

THE BLUE FAIRY BOOK, Andrew Lang. Lang's tales come from all countries and all times. Here are 37 tales from Grimm, the Arabian Nights, Greek Mythology, and other fascinating sources. 8 plates, 130 illustrations. xi + 390pp.
21437-0 Paperbound $2.50

HOUSEHOLD STORIES BY THE BROTHERS GRIMM. Classic English-language edition of the well-known tales — Rumpelstiltskin, Snow White, Hansel and Gretel, The Twelve Brothers, Faithful John, Rapunzel, Tom Thumb (52 stories in all). Translated into simple, straightforward English by Lucy Crane. Ornamented with headpieces, vignettes, elaborate decorative initials and a dozen full-page illustrations by Walter Crane. x + 269pp.
21080-4 Paperbound $2.50

THE MERRY ADVENTURES OF ROBIN HOOD, Howard Pyle. The finest modern versions of the traditional ballads and tales about the great English outlaw. Howard Pyle's complete prose version, with every word, every illustration of the first edition. Do not confuse this facsimile of the original (1883) with modern editions that change text or illustrations. 23 plates plus many page decorations. xxii + 296pp.
22043-5 Paperbound $2.50

THE STORY OF KING ARTHUR AND HIS KNIGHTS, Howard Pyle. The finest children's version of the life of King Arthur; brilliantly retold by Pyle, with 48 of his most imaginative illustrations. xviii + 313pp. 6⅛ x 9¼.
21445-1 Paperbound $2.50

THE WONDERFUL WIZARD OF OZ, L. Frank Baum. America's finest children's book in facsimile of first edition with all Denslow illustrations in full color. The edition a child should have. Introduction by Martin Gardner. 23 color plates, scores of drawings. iv + 267pp.
20691-2 Paperbound $2.25

THE MARVELOUS LAND OF OZ, L. Frank Baum. The second Oz book, every bit as imaginative as the Wizard. The hero is a boy named Tip, but the Scarecrow and the Tin Woodman are back, as is the Oz magic. 16 color plates, 120 drawings by John R. Neill. 287pp.
20692-0 Paperbound $2.50

THE MAGICAL MONARCH OF MO, L. Frank Baum. Remarkable adventures in a land even stranger than Oz. The best of Baum's books not in the Oz series. 15 color plates and dozens of drawings by Frank Verbeck. xviii + 237pp.
21892-9 Paperbound $2.00

THE BAD CHILD'S BOOK OF BEASTS, MORE BEASTS FOR WORSE CHILDREN, A MORAL ALPHABET, Hilaire Belloc. Three complete humor classics in one volume. Be kind to the frog, and do not call him names . . . and 28 other whimsical animals. Familiar favorites and some not so well known. Illustrated by Basil Blackwell. 156pp.
(USO) 20749-8 Paperbound $1.25

MICROSCOPY FOR CHEMISTS, Harold F. Schaeffer. Thorough text; operation of microscope, optics, photomicrographs, hot stage, polarized light, chemical procedures for organic and inorganic reactions. 32 specific experiments cover specific analyses: industrial, metals, other important subjects. 136 figures. 264pp.
61682-7 Paperbound $2.50

THE ELECTRONIC THEORY OF ACIDS AND BASES, by William F. Luder and Saverio Zuffanti. Full, newly revised (1961) presentation of a still controversial theory. Historical background, atomic orbitals and valence, electrophilic and electrodotic reagents, acidic and basic radicals, titrations, displacement, acid catalysis, etc., are discussed. xi + 165pp.
60201-X Paperbound $2.00

OPTICKS, Sir Isaac Newton. A survey of 18th-century knowledge on all aspects of light as well as a description of Newton's experiments with spectroscopy, colors, lenses, reflection, refraction, theory of waves, etc. in language the layman can follow. Foreword by Albert Einstein. Introduction by Sir Edmund Whittaker. Preface by I. Bernard Cohen. cxxvi + 406pp.
60205-2 Paperbound $3.50

LIGHT: PRINCIPLES AND EXPERIMENTS, George S. Monk. Thorough coverage, for student with background in physics and math, of physical and geometric optics. Also includes 23 experiments on optical systems, instruments, etc. "Probably the best intermediate text on optics in the English language," *Physics Forum*. 275 figures. xi + 489pp.
60341-5 Paperbound $3.50

PIEZOELECTRICITY: AN INTRODUCTION TO THE THEORY AND APPLICATIONS OF ELECTROMECHANICAL PHENOMENA IN CRYSTALS, Walter G. Cady. Revised 1963 edition of most complete, most systematic coverage of field. Fundamental theory of crystal electricity, concepts of piezoelectricity, including comparisons of various current theories; resonators; oscillators; properties, etc., of Rochelle salt; ferroelectric crystals; applications; pyroelectricity, similar topics. "A great work," *Nature*. Many illustrations. Total of xxx + 840pp.
61094-2, 61095-0 Two volumes, Paperbound $6.00

PHYSICAL OPTICS, Robert W. Wood. A classic in the field, this is a valuable source for students of physical optics and excellent background material for a study of electromagnetic theory. Partial contents: nature and rectilinear propagation of light, reflection from plane and curved surfaces, refraction, absorption and dispersion, origin of spectra, interference, diffraction, polarization, Raman effect, optical properties of metals, resonance radiation and fluorescence of atoms, magneto-optics, electro-optics, thermal radiation. 462 diagrams, 17 plates. xvi + 846pp.
61808-0 Paperbound $4.25

MIRRORS, PRISMS AND LENSES: A TEXTBOOK OF GEOMETRICAL OPTICS, James P. C. Southall. Introductory-level account of modern optical instrument theory, covering unusually wide range: lights and shadows, reflection of light and plane mirrors, refraction, astigmatic lenses, compound systems, aperture and field of optical system, the eye, dispersion and achromatism, rays of finite slope, the microscope, much more. Strong emphasis on earlier, elementary portions of field, utilizing simplest mathematics wherever possible. Problems. 329 figures. xxiv + 806pp.
61234-1 Paperbound $3.75

MATHEMATICAL FOUNDATIONS OF STATISTICAL MECHANICS, A. I. Khinchin. Introduction to modern statistical mechanics: phase space, ergodic problems, theory of probability, central limit theorem, ideal monatomic gas, foundation of thermodynamics, dispersion and distribution of sum functions. Provides mathematically rigorous treatment and excellent analytical tools. Translated by George Gamow. viii + 179pp. 60147-1 Paperbound $2.00

INTRODUCTION TO PHYSICAL STATISTICS, Robert B. Lindsay. Elementary probability theory, laws of thermodynamics, classical Maxwell-Boltzmann statistics, classical statistical mechanics, quantum mechanics, other areas of physics that can be studied statistically. Full coverage of methods; basic background theory. ix + 306pp. 61882-X Paperbound $2.75

DIALOGUES CONCERNING TWO NEW SCIENCES, Galileo Galilei. Written near the end of Galileo's life and encompassing 30 years of experiment and thought, these dialogues deal with geometric demonstrations of fracture of solid bodies, cohesion, leverage, speed of light and sound, pendulums, falling bodies, accelerated motion, etc. Translated by Henry Crew and Alfonso de Salvio. Introduction by Antonio Favaro. xxiii + 300pp. 60099-8 Paperbound $2.25

FOUNDATIONS OF SCIENCE: THE PHILOSOPHY OF THEORY AND EXPERIMENT, Norman R. Campbell. Fundamental concepts of science examined on middle level: acceptance of propositions and axioms, presuppositions of scientific thought, scientific law, multiplication of probabilities, nature of experiment, application of mathematics, measurement, numerical laws and theories, error, etc. Stress on physics, but holds for other sciences. "Unreservedly recommended," *Nature* (England). Formerly *Physics: The Elements*. ix + 565pp. 60372-5 Paperbound $4.00

THE PHASE RULE AND ITS APPLICATIONS, Alexander Findlay, A. N. Campbell and N. O. Smith. Findlay's well-known classic, updated (1951). Full standard text and thorough reference, particularly useful for graduate students. Covers chemical phenomena of one, two, three, four and multiple component systems. "Should rank as the standard work in English on the subject," *Nature*. 236 figures. xii + 494pp. 60091-2 Paperbound $3.50

THERMODYNAMICS, Enrico Fermi. A classic of modern science. Clear, organized treatment of systems, first and second laws, entropy, thermodynamic potentials, gaseous reactions, dilute solutions, entropy constant. No math beyond calculus is needed, but readers are assumed to be familiar with fundamentals of thermometry, calorimetry. 22 illustrations. 25 problems. x + 160pp. 60361-X Paperbound $2.00

TREATISE ON THERMODYNAMICS, Max Planck. Classic, still recognized as one of the best introductions to thermodynamics. Based on Planck's original papers, it presents a concise and logical view of the entire field, building physical and chemical laws from basic empirical facts. Planck considers fundamental definitions, first and second principles of thermodynamics, and applications to special states of equilibrium. Numerous worked examples. Translated by Alexander Ogg. 5 figures. xiv + 297pp. 60219-2 Paperbound $2.50

MATHEMATICAL PUZZLES FOR BEGINNERS AND ENTHUSIASTS, Geoffrey Mott-Smith. 189 puzzles from easy to difficult—involving arithmetic, logic, algebra, properties of digits, probability, etc.—for enjoyment and mental stimulus. Explanation of mathematical principles behind the puzzles. 135 illustrations. viii + 248pp.
20198-8 Paperbound $1.75

PAPER FOLDING FOR BEGINNERS, William D. Murray and Francis J. Rigney. Easiest book on the market, clearest instructions on making interesting, beautiful origami. Sail boats, cups, roosters, frogs that move legs, bonbon boxes, standing birds, etc. 40 projects; more than 275 diagrams and photographs. 94pp.
20713-7 Paperbound $1.00

TRICKS AND GAMES ON THE POOL TABLE, Fred Herrmann. 79 tricks and games— some solitaires, some for two or more players, some competitive games—to entertain you between formal games. Mystifying shots and throws, unusual caroms, tricks involving such props as cork, coins, a hat, etc. Formerly *Fun on the Pool Table*. 77 figures. 95pp.
21814-7 Paperbound $1.00

HAND SHADOWS TO BE THROWN UPON THE WALL: A SERIES OF NOVEL AND AMUSING FIGURES FORMED BY THE HAND, Henry Bursill. Delightful picturebook from great-grandfather's day shows how to make 18 different hand shadows: a bird that flies, duck that quacks, dog that wags his tail, camel, goose, deer, boy, turtle, etc. Only book of its sort. vi + 33pp. 6½ x 9¼.
21779-5 Paperbound $1.00

WHITTLING AND WOODCARVING, E. J. Tangerman. 18th printing of best book on market. "If you can cut a potato you can carve" toys and puzzles, chains, chessmen, caricatures, masks, frames, woodcut blocks, surface patterns, much more. Information on tools, woods, techniques. Also goes into serious wood sculpture from Middle Ages to present, East and West. 464 photos, figures. x + 293pp.
20965-2 Paperbound $2.00

HISTORY OF PHILOSOPHY, Julián Marias. Possibly the clearest, most easily followed, best planned, most useful one-volume history of philosophy on the market; neither skimpy nor overfull. Full details on system of every major philosopher and dozens of less important thinkers from pre-Socratics up to Existentialism and later. Strong on many European figures usually omitted. Has gone through dozens of editions in Europe. 1966 edition, translated by Stanley Appelbaum and Clarence Strowbridge. xviii + 505pp.
21739-6 Paperbound $3.00

YOGA: A SCIENTIFIC EVALUATION, Kovoor T. Behanan. Scientific but non-technical study of physiological results of yoga exercises; done under auspices of Yale U. Relations to Indian thought, to psychoanalysis, etc. 16 photos. xxiii + 270pp.
20505-3 Paperbound $2.50

Prices subject to change without notice.
Available at your book dealer or write for free catalogue to Dept. GI, Dover Publications, Inc., 180 Varick St., N. Y., N. Y. 10014. Dover publishes more than 150 books each year on science, elementary and advanced mathematics, biology, music, art, literary history, social sciences and other areas.